GOD'S MARCH TO THE
NEW JERUSALEM

By
Shirley J. Vaughn, D. Min.

Freddie Alan
May the Lord bless
you as you read this
book. In Yeshua's name!
Shirley Vaughn

TABLE OF CONTENTS

ACKNOWLEDGMENTS

I wish to thank God for helping and guiding me in completing this paper which was an extensive work over a period of many years. When the time was right, He led me to M-K Ferguson who took on the responsibility of typing and setting up this doctorate on the computer. Without her help, I would not have been able to complete this tremendous task.

THE MARCH TO JERUSALEM, GOD'S DWELLING PLACE

"The March to Jerusalem, God"s Dwelling Place" is the topic of my thesis. It will trace God"s presence or Shekinah glory from the beginning of the Creation of the angelic hosts down through time to the period of the New Jerusalem.

Such areas of study will include the following:

• The Creation of mankind and his fall. Tracing through the line of Seth to the time of Messiah. God's destruction of mankind by the flood a thousand years later and the saving of Noah's family and a remnant of all God's creatures. Tracing the line of Messiah through the line of Shem. The importance of Abraham, Jacob (also known as Israel) and his sons.

Joseph, one of Jacob's sons, brings the children of Israel into Egypt for their preservation where they stay for over four hundred years. After that time, Moses becomes the chosen instrument of God to take the children of Israel out of Egypt and out of the cruel grasp of the Pharaoh Ramses.

From Egypt, Moses takes the children of Israel into the wilderness on their journey to their Promised Land. While they are in the wilderness, Moses gives the people their laws of conduct and worship, as well as the plans for the tent-like tabernacle which he received from God.

My thesis will explain how Joshua, who was a young man, was chosen in place of Moses to take the people into the Promised Land. My thesis will cover how several generations later the children of Israel desired a king to rule them and that David was God's choice. David desired to build God a house where He could live; however, God said no. His son Solomon would do the job. So David collected the materials and pattern needed for the work and Solomon built the temple.

After many years the nation's people and its kings were rebellious and worshiped other gods, so the Shekinah glory left the temple and Jerusalem. Then Jerusalem and the temple were later destroyed and the people were taken into exile.

In time, several prophets prophesied of the return to Jerusalem. Under the direction of King Cyrus, the Jews who wished could return to Jerusalem and rebuild the temple. A remnant returned to build the temple. Twenty years later under another king, the walls of Jerusalem were rebuilt. It was during the inter-testimental period that Antiochus Epiphanies tried to force the Greek culture on the Israelites. They rebelled with the help of the leadership of the Maccabeus family.

The temple, which was desecrated by Antiochus Epiphanies, was cleansed and restored.

Years later, prior to, during and after the time of Messiah, King Herod rebuilt and expanded the temple. God's presence was not there, but it was revealed in the presence of Yeshua. After Yeshua's death and Resurrection, God's presence was revealed in the Church that was born at Pentecost and is still revealed in the believers today.

From 70 AD, Jerusalem was without a temple for two thousand years. Israel is now restored as a nation. Preparations are now being made for a future temple which will be built during the tribulation.

After the desecration of the tribulation temple, Yeshua will return and establish a new temple and will rule the world with an iron rule. After his thousand-year reign, Yeshua will judge Satan and his angels, as well as rebellious mankind, and put them in hell.

The New Jerusalem will become the new home of believers of all ages with God as well as the obedient angelic host.

The materials to be used in this thesis will be many and varied. I will use a chronological Bible and reference books on the Bible and biblical topics. Historical materials, current books on prophecy, newspapers, prayer letters with news items, videos, as well as Christian magazine articles will be included as sources to help show God's workings throughout the ages.

ABSTRACT

The purpose of this thesis is to show how God, from the beginning, wanted a creature who would love and obey Him willingly. It also shows the journey of God through time and space to accomplish His desire.

The resources used in this paper are many and varied. The Bible, in various versions, was researched. The Reese Chronological Bible was used for most of the chronological dating in this research paper.

Other resources which were relevant were magazine articles, newspaper articles, religious newsletters and prayer letters. There were also quotes from religious television programs and DVD's. Additional reference materials used include commentaries, as well as other religious and end-time books related to the thesis topics.

The result of the findings of this thesis can be traced over a period of many years. I pursued my education to finish my B.A. in home economics, and then I met my husband in the church I was attending in southern California. Had I not met him, I would have gone on to Bible school and seminary for a biblical degree.

After being married a few years, I was growing in the Lord and I attended a Bible school at a local church and received my B.A. After this, I went to Friends University International Church to receive my master's in Old Testament studies. I grew in knowledge of the Lord and saw God's moving in history to accomplish His purpose of getting people of His own through His Son, Yeshua. When the time came to do the thesis, about thirteen years ago, the Lord gave me a burden to write on the topic of tracing God's march through time to the New Jerusalem. I realized that the Lord wanted me to do this thesis, but I knew it was too large for me to do on my own. I knew I would need help with the typing and gathering of material. So I asked the Lord to help me to accomplish this before His return to rapture His saints. I know the time is very short as I see so many of the prophecies being fulfilled in the last few years and even in the last few months.

During the years while I waited to find the person to help me with the typing, I was gathering a great deal of the material that has to do with end times, establishment of Israel and the third temple, and the rise of the European Union, as well as other end-time prophecies.

This study also shows that God—through Messiah, Yeshua—is and will accomplish what He sets out to do, regardless of what obstacles Satan or mankind throws at Him over the eons of time. God proves that the bigger the obstacle the more exciting it is to see how He overcomes that which is humanly impossible. His children can rejoice now and in the New Jerusalem that God will take care of them while they are on Earth and through eternity.

PART I

OLD TESTAMENT HISTORY

CHAPTER ONE

In the Beginning

A. First Creation

In the beginning God, the Creator, had a dream. He wanted a creature who would love Him and do His will from his heart and not by force. His first experience was when He created the angelic host. They had the freedom to either do His will or not. For eons there was peace in heaven. One day Lucifer, who was the most beautiful and powerful angel, became very proud and conceited and decided to be like God. He wanted to be obeyed and worshiped like the Creator God. A revolt started in heaven. Lucifer became the ring leader and one third of the angelic host followed him. So Lucifer and his angels were kicked out of their heavenly home.

> *12 How art thou fallen from heaven, O Lucifer, son of the morning! how art thou cut down to the ground, which didst weaken the nations! 13 For thou hast said in thine heart, I will ascend into heaven, I will exalt my throne above the stars of God: I will sit also upon the mount of the congregation, in the sides of the north: 14 I will ascend above the heights of the clouds; I will be like the most High. 15 Yet thou shalt be brought down to hell, to the sides of the pit. 16 They that see thee shall narrowly look upon thee, and consider thee, saying, Is this the man that made the earth to tremble, that did shake kingdoms; 17 That made the world as a wilderness, and destroyed the cities thereof; that opened not the house of his prisoners? 18 All the kings of the nations, even all of them, lie in glory, every one in his own house.1*
>
> (Isaiah 14:12-18, KJV)

Satan's Lie

> *The devil......was a murderer from the beginning, and does not stand in the truth, because there is no truth in him. When he speaks a lie, he speaks from his own resources, for he is a liar; and the father of it.*
>
> (John 8:44, NKJ)

---

[1] The Holy Bible: King James Version. Oak Harbor: Logos Research Systems, Inc., 1995.

According to the Bible, however, Satan is a real personal being, but not with a fleshly body. He is a spirit being; and, like other spirit beings (John 3:8), he can come and go as the wind, he is invisible, yet very powerful. As Lucifer (Isa 14:12), and as represented by the king of Tyre (Ezek. 28:12), he was perfect until he sinned (v. 15). Other angels, of lower rank, sinned also; and Satan, having superior powers, became their ruler or prince, and as such is called "the prince of devils" (Matt. 12:24-27).

We know that Satan and his angels are not in some far off fiery abyss, torturing millions of the human family, for nothing of the kind is taught in the Bible. Instead, the Scriptures show that at the time of the Flood, Satan (who had been cast down from heaven-Luke 10:18) together with his host of evil spirit beings, are imprisoned in Tartarus, in restraints under darkness in the earth's atmosphere; "unto the judgment of the great day" (2 Pet. 2:4; Jude 6). They are not at liberty to go about, without restraint, throughout the universe any longer (compare Job 1:7). Satan is therefore, "the prince of the power of the air" (Eph. 2:2), and has associated with him in this sphere, the other wicked angels. They are evil and oppose everything that is of God and righteousness, and especially oppose and persecute those of humanity who renounce the works of the devil, the flesh and the world, and seek to walk in Jesus' footsteps.[2]

B. Second Creation

Time passed. The Lord God was lonely for a special creature with whom to have fellowship. One day after spending time in recreating the earth (by separating the land from water, and the light from the darkness), He created all of its living creatures that would inhabit land and seas and He created His special creature—man, and called him Adam. He placed him in Eden, a beautiful garden, to cultivate and rule over the animals there. God would come each day in the cool of the day and fellowship with Adam in the Garden of Eden. Adam enjoyed God's presence and he loved Him. God only had one thing that He commanded Adam to do. He said, "You may eat of any tree of the Garden except the Tree of Good and Evil. In the day that you do, you will surely die." Adam obeyed God.

Adam kept busy in the Garden and time passed quickly with the work he did, as well as the wonderful fellowship he had with his Creator. One day, after Adam had given names to all of the creatures, he realized he was lonesome. All the creatures had a mate. He needed a mate, but there was none for him. God, knowing that Adam needed a helpmate, put Adam to sleep. While Adam slept, God took one of Adam's ribs and built Adam a beautiful helper to be Adam's wife.

God woke Adam. Adam opened his eyes and saw the gift God had given him. He was so excited, and he said, "Wow! She is beautiful! She shall be called woman because she is bone of my bone and flesh of my flesh; therefore I shall call her name Eve."

Adam and Eve were very happy together—they were naked but not ashamed. Daily they were together pruning the trees and eating the delicious fruit from the trees. They also enjoyed time with God in the cool of the day. Adam spent time telling Eve about what had happened and about the commandment God had given him before she was created, not to eat of the Tree of Good and Evil, but any other tree would be acceptable. Adam and Eve were very happy as they fellowshipped with each other, as well as with God each day. They also spent time with God's creatures, talking with

---

[2] "Satan''s Lie." The Bible Standard. #101. Chester Springs: The Bible Standard Ministries. Page 8.

them and loving them. Everything was perfect except for one jealous, critical creature, Lucifer, who was now going to try to mess up God's special Creation.

One day when Eve was alone, Satan had entered into the body of a beautiful serpent. He purposed to mess up God's Creation by approaching Eve, Adam's wife, as a beautiful serpent. The serpent thought: "How can I get man to disobey God and follow me? I know if I get near that special tree that is off limits to man and get them to eat of that tree, then they will be mine and God will lose this round of the battle between God and me."

Eve was walking in the garden by herself. She was eating fruit. Her thoughts were far away, thinking about her happy life in the Garden. Then she heard a voice saying, "Eve! Eve! Did God say you can eat of every tree in the Garden?"

Eve answered, "We can eat of every tree of the Garden except the Tree of Good and Evil. We cannot eat it or touch it or we will surely die."

The serpent said, "God was fooling you. You will not die if you eat it. You will be like God, knowing good and evil. Look, that fruit is beautiful; you can tell it is very ripe and sweet to the taste." When Eve looked and saw the fruit was beautiful and ripe, she took one in her hand and took a bite.

About this time Adam approached Eve and said, "What have you done? You know you have disobeyed God. You are going to die."

Eve said "I have not died. Look, this fruit is delicious and now we will be like God knowing good and evil."

Adam thought, "What am I going to do? I don't want to lose my wife but I don't want to disobey God." He felt he was being pulled in two directions.

Eve said, "Adam, eat, it is delicious." Adam obeyed his wife and ate of the fruit of the tree. Suddenly a veil went over their minds. They lost God's presence and realized they were naked and separated from God. They were scared.

They both had died spiritually; their bodies started the process of decay and they began to die.

They knew they needed to cover themselves because of their nakedness. They both made aprons of fig leaves to cover themselves. Late that afternoon, God was walking through the Garden and cried out to His special Creation, man, "Adam and Eve—where are you. I miss you."

Adam and Eve hid themselves. "What shall we do? I hear God walking the Garden. Quick, hide, so He won't know what we have done."

"Adam, Eve—where are you?" As God came closer, they became more afraid. Finally

God came near and said, "Why are you hiding yourselves?"

Adam said, "We were naked so we hid ourselves."

God asked, "Who told you that you were naked? Did you eat of the tree I told you not to eat from?"

Adam said, "The woman You gave to me, she tempted me."

Eve answered God and said, "The serpent tricked me and said I would be as wise as You, God, knowing good and evil."

God said to Adam, "Since you disobeyed Me, by the sweat of your brow you shall till the earth. It will produce thorns and thistles with the herbs which you grow."

God said to Eve, "You shall have sorrow in conception and pain in childbirth. Your husband will rule over you."

God turned to the serpent and said, "You shall be cursed above all creatures and on your belly you shall crawl all the days of your life."

Then God turned to Eve and Adam and said, "The woman's seed shall crush the serpent's head (Satan's) and he shall crush the heel of the seed of the woman (causing the promised one, who will be the Messiah, to die for the sins of mankind).

This promise set in motion God's journey to Messiah's death in Jerusalem and later the culmination of Messiah's rule, then the march to the heavenly New Jerusalem, began (ref. Genesis 1:1-3:24).

After Adam and Eve fell because of disobeying God, God covered both Adam and Eve with the skin of a lamb. He was showing them that it was the death of a future Lamb, the Messiah, the Lamb of God, who would cover their sins of disobeying God.

God then sent them out of the Garden to till the ground outside of Eden. Then the Lord God had cherubim with flaming swords guard the garden to keep mankind out (ref. Genesis 1-3).

C. The great deceiver and his deception

The Greatest of all Lies

The first lie—Satan's monstrous lie—was told in the Garden of Eden to Mother Eve, the first woman. The serpent was manipulated by Satan as his agent. Satan, himself, was originally the only rebel against God. His associates, the fallen angels who sinned, were not with him in his rebellion until some time afterward. Satan by mental domination caused the serpent to move about under his direction, not audibly speaking but rather by movement and action. Therefore, we are inclined to believe that the serpent did not speak to Eve audibly, but by its actions. As we know, "Actions speak louder than words."

God had told our first parents that they could eat of the fruit of all the trees of the garden except those in its center. He had forbidden them to eat of the tree of the knowledge of good and evil (Gen. 2:9, 16, 17), without telling them the reason why. The fruit of the trees that they were forbidden to eat were just as wholesome as that of the other trees of the Garden. They were not poisonous or contaminated in any way. It was simply a test of their obedience, their loyalty to God. He had told Adam that disobedience, disloyalty, in this matter would result in death—"you shall surely die" (Gen. 2:17; 3:3). It is impossible for an intelligent person, either a human being or a spirit being, to live eternally in God's universe, who is disobedient to Him.

> *The wages of sin is death; but the gift of God is eternal life through Jesus Christ our Lord.*
>
> (Rom. 6:23)

The serpent, by eating of the forbidden fruit without dying, seemed to Eve to support Satan's lie. Because, instead of dying, the serpent thrived by its eating of that which was prohibited. We know that in some manner through the use of the serpent, Satan declared his monstrous lie, "You will not surely die" (Gen. 3:4), to Mother Eve; and he told her also that God evidently was trying to keep her and her husband in ignorance, blindness, darkness, and that it was time for them to awake, to assert their rights, and to make it better for themselves by eating of the forbidden fruit. "For God knows that in the day you eat of it, then your eyes shall be opened, and you shall be as gods, knowing good and evil" (v. 5).

In this way, by the instrumentality of the serpent, Satan "beguiled Eve through his subtlety," impressing upon her mind "that the tree was good for food, and that it was pleasant to the eyes, and a tree desirable to make one wise" (2 Cor. 11:3; Gen. 3:6). Eve, thinking that she was bettering matters for herself and her husband, took of the fruit and ate. She also gave to her husband with her, and he ate. "Adam was not deceived, but the woman being deceived fell into transgression" (1 Tim. 2:14)-they both were in the transgression against God's command; Eve was deceived, but Adam was not deceived—he sinned willfully. He knew better; but when he found that his dear wife had disobeyed God and had eaten of the forbidden fruit, and had come under the sentence or curse of death, he evidently was overwhelmed at the thought of losing his wife, whom he loved so dearly; he evidently realized (as God had said-Gen. 2:18) that it was not good that man should be alone, without an helpmate for him, and became so discouraged that he determined to die with his wife, loving her so much that he would rather die with her than to live without her. Therefore, he manifested that he loved the creature more than he loved the Creator (Rom. 1:25).

Satan's object in telling his monstrous lie is very clear. Other Scriptures show us that as Lucifer he already had been saying in his heart that he would like to have a higher position than others and higher powers than those which God had given to him; in his overleaping ambition he even purposed to be "like the most High" (Isa. 14:13, 14). He desired to be a sovereign, so that he might work out his own plans. He evidently had no thought of supplanting the Almighty, but had the pride to suppose that he could manage affairs better than God could, and that if only he had a small section of the universe under his control, he would demonstrate his great abilities and overshadow the Almighty.

When man was created, Satan's opportunity for exercising his ambition seemed to have come. Man possessed a power that the angels did not have—he could propagate his own kind, and was commissioned to fill the earth, and to bring it all to Edenic perfection. Satan saw what appeared to be his chance. He evidently thought that by putting the first pair into subjection and making them his subjects, and alienating them from the Almighty, he would control a race, and would eventually be the spiritual prince, or ruler, of earth and its inhabitants. It was in order to carry out this program that Satan deceived Mother Eve by telling her his monstrous lie, and by it he succeeded in bringing our first parents under his control.

Another Deception

When Lucifer (*light-bearer*—Isa. 14:12; Ezek. 28:12-19) thus became Satan (*adversary)* and told his monstrous lie, he became the "murderer from the beginning"—he murdered the human race, though this was not his intention. When he perceived that his subjects were perishing under the Divine sentence of death, and that they were progressively becoming weaker, mentally, morally and physically, he thought to circumvent the Divine penalty by introducing fresh vigor, renewed life, into the human family. He did this by seducing some of the angels. Originally the angels apparently had the power of materialization—of taking human form or any other form that they might choose. Satan, in carrying out his program, caused some of them to deflect from their loyalty to God and to their own nature, by inducing them to materialize and live as human beings and, by taking human wives, to propagate offspring.

According to the Bible account this must have progressed for a long time, perhaps centuries. In Gen. 6:2 we read that "the sons of God saw the daughters of men that they were fair; and they took them wives of all which they chose." The children born to them were "giants" physically, and "men of renown" intellectually (v. 4). The virility of the angels, grafted upon the human stock, produced a race that was superior in some respects, but in other respects very inferior. Begotten and born in opposition to the Divine authority and will, and by their rebellious nature, these giants were very inferior morally—they were degraded, brutish, and devilish.

Soon the earth was filled with violence (v. 5). The imperfect and impaired race of Adam, was enslaved mentally, morally and physically, and rapidly became contaminated. Noah and his family, however, were not corrupted; they were of pure Adamic stock and loyal to God— Noah was "perfect in his generations" (v. 9). Then came the Deluge, which God had determined, and had withheld until that time. In it God swept away both the progeny of the angels and the impaired, contaminated Adamic stock that remained. None of those who received their life-principle from the materialized angels were of Adamic stock. None of them, therefore, has any share in the redemptive work of Jesus, which was only for Adam and his race; hence none of them will have any part in the awakening of the dead and the "restitution of all things" (Acts 3:19-21), which God has promised shall be accomplished by the glorious Messiah during His Thousand-year Kingdom reign. They merely perished—were blotted out in the Deluge, as natural brute beasts. They were an illegitimate generation not authorized or provided for by God.

Thwarted, Satan Tries Again

"The angels which kept not their first estate, but left their own habitation" and married wives of the human family and begat children, were restrained, cast down into the earth's atmosphere as a prison, no longer being permitted to go about throughout the universe (Jude 6). They—and likewise Satan—were no longer allowed to materialize in human form.

Therefore Satan's plan for an empire of his own failed. But, still rebellious in spirit, he took up a new line of battle against God. In furthering it he would be content to use humanity as his tools, even though they were imperfect and dying. They would be his slaves and he would embitter them against God.

Satan realized that the secret of his power with mankind must be in his deception of them. If the human race knew that they were being led captive into sin at the will of Satan and his fallen host, they would rebel against him. In order to hold humanity as long as possible as his slaves, he realized that he must seduce them by fostering ignorance and superstition. He must alienate them from God. Accordingly, he determined to make them think of God as a terrible being, One unworthy of their love and confidence, One ready to fiendishly torture them forever, One whom they might dread, that they could not love and worship in spirit and in truth.

As a basis for this great scheme of human ensnarement and obsession Satan used his original monstrous lie, "You will not surely die." For now well over 4,000 years he has sought by every means in his power to instill that lie into the minds of humanity in every land and to keep it there.

Satan has caused mankind in general to be deceived into believing that each one of Adam's race has something inside of him, which he called the immortal soul; claiming that it lives on and is indestructible, that God Himself cannot destroy it, and that it is sure to continue to live on after the body, as an external shell, is cast off in death. He has deceived them also into believing that good people go to heaven when they die, and bad people to a place of eternal torture, and has twisted the Bible hell into meaning a place of torture. Thus he has blasphemed God's character in order to perpetuate the deception of his original lie. He has his demon host to co-operate with him in making light appear darkness and darkness appear light, to deceive mankind and to keep them in subjection (Isa. 5:20).

How thoroughly he has succeeded in this scheme the whole world is witness. Despite the fact that man's five senses tell him that the dead are dead, not *living*, in torment or otherwise, the masses of mankind, blinded by Satan, believe to the contrary—that the dead are more alive than before they died. Despite the consistency of God's Word, "You will surely die," and the inconsistency of Satan's lie, "You will not surely die," practically the whole world is enslaved by Satan's lie, though more and more thinking people are repudiating it.

In Rev. 14:8; 17:2; 18:3, the condition of the whole world in the Gospel Age is pictured as one of being drunk with the wine of such false doctrine and consequent infidelity to God. The apostle said, "The god of this age has blinded the minds of unbelievers, so that they cannot see the light of the gospel of the glory of Christ" (2 Cor. 4:4).3

Satan, the Father of Lies

Jesus showed conclusively that Satan is an evil being, and not simply an evil principle, when he declared in the words of our text that Satan "was a murderer from the beginning, and abode not in the truth, because there is no truth in him" (John 8:44). Surely an evil principle was never in the Truth! Neither was it ever a murderer. Furthermore, He said that when Satan "speaks a lie, he speaks from his own resources for he is a liar, and the father of it." This corroborates the thought that never, until Satan started the course of sin, were there any lies. All of God's dealings with the angels and their dealings with one another had been along the lines of simplicity, truth, righteousness, purity, holiness, etc.

However, when Satan determined to exalt himself as the god of earth, he found an occasion in which a lie would serve his evil purpose, and so he used his original monstrous lie to alienate our first parents from the Almighty. He assured Mother Eve that disobedience would not bring the death penalty, as God had declared.4

---

3 "Satan's Lie." The Bible Standard. #101. Chester Springs: The Bible Standard Ministries. Page 8-10.

4 Ibid. Page 12.

CHAPTER TWO

Enoch to Noah

A. Enoch — fifty-eighth generation to Yeshua - 3363 BC

Enoch was the seventh generation from Adam. Enoch was in the line of Seth. Seth was the son born to Adam and Eve after the murder of Abel by his brother Cain.

Enoch was three hundred years old when God's presence was revealed to him.

It was the birth of Methuselah that caused Enoch to seek and know God personally. During the next sixty-five years, he walked and talked with God. He also prophesied to the sinfulness of his generation and saw into the future—the Lord's coming to judge the world and the people for their sins. This can be seen in Jude 14-16 and Enoch 1:9, the Inter- Testament Book. One day while God and Enoch were walking together, God invited Enoch to go home with Him. He went and could not be found on Earth (ref. Genesis 5:22-24).

2988 BC

> *14 And Enoch also, the seventh from Adam, prophesied of these, saying, Behold, the Lord cometh with ten thousands of his saints, 15 To execute judgment upon all, and to convince all that are ungodly among them of all their ungodly deeds which they have ungodly committed, and of all their hard speeches which ungodly sinners have spoken against him. 16 These are murmurers, complainers, walking after their own lusts; and their mouth speaketh great swelling words, having men's persons in admiration because of advantage5*
>
> (Jude 14-16, KJV) (Enoch 1:9 — inter-testament book)

B. Noah — fifty-fifth generation to Yeshua — 2919 BC - birth

Lamech was in the line of Seth. When he was 182 years old, he had a son and called his name Noah. The name Noah means rest. After the birth of his son, he said, "This son shall comfort us concerning our work and toil of our hands because of the ground which the Lord hath cursed." God's presence and guidance can be seen in the life of Noah.

---

5 The Holy Bible: King James Version. Oak Harbor: Logos Research Systems, Inc., 1995.

1. Background of the flood

As time passed since Creation, the sons of God (angelic beings) saw the daughters of men were beautiful and married them and produced giants which were hybrid humans; they were very strong. The human race became polluted and corrupt. The wickedness of man was great and the Lord regretted that He had made man.

And God said, "I will destroy both man and beast, as well as every creeping thing, as well as the fowls of the air, because all flesh is corrupted and full of violence. I will give mankind 120 years. Then I will destroy them." (2439 BC — 2319 BC)

Noah found grace in the eyes of the Lord. He was a just man and his pedigree was pure. Noah walked with God. Noah begat three sons (Shem, Ham and Japheth) when he was five hundred years old. And God said to Noah, "I will destroy all flesh."

2. God's command to build the ark and gather the creatures to be saved

Then God told Noah to make an ark (large box). Hebrew: *Tebâh 8392 — a floating box.*

You shall make many rooms and shall use pitch (or bitumen) to cover and seal the ark inside and out. The size of the ark will be three hundred cubits (four hundred and fifty feet) by eighty-seven cubits (one hundred thirty and one-half feet) and the height of it thirty cubits (forty-five feet) tall.

A window eighteen inches from the roof should be all around the top of the ark. A door shall be put in the side of the ark. There are to be three levels in the ark to hold all the animals and food. After the ark is built, I will bring a flood of waters to destroy all flesh under heaven that is on the earth they shall die.

But, I shall establish my covenant with you and you shall come into the ark with your sons, your wife and your sons' wives with you. Of every living thing, two of every kind you should bring into the ark to keep them alive, they shall be a male and a female. Whether it be flesh, fowls, cattle, every creeping thing, to keep them alive. Bring into the ark seven pairs of males and females that are of the clean beast—those that are not clean just one male and his female. Of the clean birds of the air by seven pairs male and female to keep their kinds alive on the earth. You will also need to provide all the food that is to be eaten for your family as well as all the creatures.

One hundred twenty years later, after the ark was built and supplied with food, the Lord said to Noah, "Come, you and your household, into the ark. In seven days it will rain for forty days and forty nights. Every living thing shall be destroyed off the earth."

Then Noah did according to all that God commanded him. 2319 BC.

3. Loading the ark

Noah did according to what the Lord commanded. Noah went into the ark with his family. The clean and unclean beasts went into the ark, as well as the fowls and every creeping thing. They all came into the ark two by two, the male with his female, as God had commanded Noah. Noah was six hundred years old when he went into the ark.

4. Time spent in the ark

The flood — 2319 BC

After seven days the waters of the flood were on the earth and heavy rains fell and the underground rivers and springs broke through. For a period of forty days, the waters increased greatly upon the earth; it covered all the high hills and mountains. The waters were fifteen cubits (twenty-two and a half feet) higher than the highest mountain.

All living things were destroyed. Only Noah and all that were with him in the ark were alive. The waters receded on the face of the earth 150 days.

On the eighth month—on the 224th day since the flood began, the tops of the mountains were seen.

On the 264th day Noah opened the window and released a raven but it flew back and forth until the waters dried off the earth because it lived off the carcasses that floated on the water.

On the 271st day, a dove was released. She returned because there was no place to rest her feet.

On the 278th day, the dove was again released. She returned with a freshly plucked olive leaf; therefore, Noah knew the water had receded from the earth.

On the 285th day, the dove was released but did not return to Noah; on the 316th day, the water had dried up from the earth.

Noah removed the covering from the ark and saw that the surface of the ground was dry. On the 370th day, God told Noah to come out of the ark—"you and your wife and sons and their wives and bring out every kind of living creature you have so they can multiply on the earth and be fruitful and increase in number upon it."

So Noah and all who were with him, as well as the animals and all living creatures, as well as birds, left the ark, one kind after another.

Timeline of time spent in the ark:

2nd MO May (ER) 2nd MO 17th day the flood began Gen. 7:11	3rd MO. June (Zivan)	4th MO July (Tammuz)	5th MO Aug (AB)	6th MO Sept (Elul)	7th MO Oct (Pishri) 7th MO 17th day the ark rested Gen. 8:4	8th MO Nov (Bul)	9th Mo Dec (Chisleu)	10th MO Jan (Tebeth) 10th MO 1st day mountains are seen Gen. 8:5	11th MO Feb (Sabat) after 40 days the raven, dove, and olive leaf Gen. 8:6-11	12 MO Mar (Adar)	1st MO Apr (ABIB) 601st yr. 1st mo 1st day Noah removes the cover Gen 8:13	2nd MO May (ER) 2nd MO 27th day the ark is vacated Gen. 8:14-17
		Gen. 7:24; 8:3					The waters decrease continually Gen: 8:5					

Graph of Floor Information — on page 14 — The Chronology of the Bible

5. Noah gives thanks. God's promise.

Noah then offered a sacrifice to God to show his heartfelt thankfulness.

God promised, "I will never again curse the ground because of man even though his heart is evil from childhood and never again will I destroy all living creatures as I have done."

> *22 While the earth remains, seedtime and harvest, cold and heat, summer and winter, day and night, shall not cease.6*

(Genesis 8:22, RSV)

Then God blessed Noah and his sons, saying to them, "Be fruitful and multiply and fill the earth." Man's diet was changed from being strictly vegetarian to adding meat to their diet. God said, "Everything that moves is food for you just as the green herbs. But you shall not eat the flesh with the blood in it. The only commandment I give you is the law of life."

> *5 For your own lifeblood, too, I will demand an accounting: from every animal I will demand it, and from man in regard to his fellow man I will demand an accounting for human life. 6 If anyone sheds the blood of man, by man shall his blood be shed; For in the image of God has man been made. 7 Be fertile, then, and multiply; abound on earth and subdue it7*

(Genesis 9:5-7, NABWRNT)

---

[6] The Holy Bible: The Revised Standard Version. Oak Harbor: Logos Research Systems, Inc., 1971.

[7] Confraternity of Christian Doctrine. Board of Trustees. The New American Bible : Translated from the original languages with critical use of all the ancient sources and the revised New Testament. Confraternity of Christian Doctrine, 1996, c1986.

Then God said, "I have established my covenant with you and every living thing with the sign of the rainbow in the clouds. When I see the rainbow in the clouds, I will remember the everlasting covenant between Myself and all living creatures and will never again completely destroy them with a flood."

After the flood, Noah lived 350 years — a total of 950 years — and he died.

1869 BC (ref. Genesis 6-9:1-27).

CHAPTER THREE

Age of the Patriarchs

1967 — 1606 BC

A. The line of Shem

It was after the fall of Babel that the sons of Noah: Shem, Ham, and Japheth had many descendants that multiplied and filled the earth. The descendants of Ham through Canaan lived and settled the land of Canaan—also known as Palestine...later as Israel. They would be in conflict with the descendants of Shem, principally those of the Hebrew nation. That conflict is bearing out the prophetic nature of Noah's curse on Canaan and continues until today.

The curse on Ham's descendants was a result of the sin of Ham against his father Noah.

> *24 When Noah awoke from his wine and knew what his youngest son had done to him, 25 he said, "Cursed be Canaan; lowest of slaves shall he be to his brothers." 26 He also said, "Blessed by the LORD my God be Shem; and let Canaan be his slave. 27 May God make space for Japheth, and let him live in the tents of Shem; and let Canaan be his slave."8*

> (Genesis 9:24-27, (NRSV)

2317

Shem was one hundred years old and begat Arphaxad two years after the flood. (He is fifty-three generations to Christ)

It is through the line of Arphaxad, eight generations later, that Abraham was called by God's divine grace. He was the father of the Hebrew nation. God chose him as the man through whom He would bless all of mankind.

Terah, who was of the line of Shem, was born 2097 BC to Nahor. He was the forty-sixth generation to Messiah. He lived seventy years and became father to Abram, Nahor and Haren. Terah moved his family from Ur to Haraan and settled there in time. Terah died April 1892 BC at 205 years old.

---

8 The Holy Bible : New Revised Standard Version. Nashville: Thomas Nelson, 1996, c1989.

B. Abram (Abraham)

1. Called to leave Ur.

Abram was born 1967 BC. He is forty-fifth generation to Yeshua. Abram means "high father." Later he became known as Abraham, which means "father of a multitude." The Lord said to Abram, "Get out of your country and from your kindred and from your father's house and go to the land I will show you." Abram obeyed God and left Ur. However he took Terah, his father and Lot, his nephew with him. God made a promise to Abram.

> *2 I will make of you a great nation, and I will bless you, and make your name great,*
> *so that you will be a blessing. 3 I will bless those who bless you, and the one who*
> *curses you I will curse; and in you all the families of the earth shall be blessed.9*
>
> (Genesis 12:2-3, NRSV)

2. Abram and Lot go their separate ways

Abram left Haran and went to Canaan. He took with him his nephew Lot, Haran's son, his wife Sarai —his half sister—and all his servants and possessions.
Abram was seventy years old when he departed out of Haran, went south and came to Canaan.

1891 BC
Abram and Lot had many flocks, herds and tents. The land was not able to support them both. In order to keep peace between the herdsmen of Lot and Abram, Abram gave Lot a choice of which land he wanted to go with his flocks and herds. Lot chose the plain of Jordan near Sodom which was like a lush garden. The men of Sodom were wicked. It was there that Lot chose to dwell. After Lot left Abram, the Lord said unto him.

> *13 The people of this area were unusually wicked and sinned greatly against the*
> *Lord. 14 After Lot was gone, the Lord said to Abram, "Look as far as you can see*
> *in every direction. 15 I am going to give all this land to you and your offspring as*
> *a permanent possession. 16 And I am going to give you so many descendants that,*
> *like dust, they cannot be counted! 17 Take a walk in every direction and explore the*
> *new possessions I am giving you."10*
>
> (Genesis 13:13-17, NLT)

Abram then went to Mamre and built an altar to the Lord and worshipped Him.

3. Abram rescues Lot

After a period of time, when Abram heard that Lot was taken captive by Kedorlaomer and the Dead Sea kings with him, he armed his trained servants born in his household to pursue them

---

[9] The Holy Bible : New Revised Standard Version. Nashville: Thomas Nelson, 1996, c1989.

[10] Holy Bible: New Living Translation. Wheaton: Tyndale House, 1997.

into Hobar and north into Damascus. Abram and his 318 servants brought back all the goods and people taken from Sodom: his nephew Lot, and his goods, as well as his servants.

The King of Sodom met Abram after the defeat of Kedorlaomer and the Dead Sea kings and said to Abram, "Give me the people and you take all the goods of Sodom."

Abram replied, "I will not take anything from you least you say I have made Abram rich. Only give the young men food and a portion for the men with me."

4. Melchizedek blesses Abram

After this incident, Melchizedek King of Salem brought bread and wine to Abram because he was the priest of the Most High God. He then blessed Abram:

> *18 And Mel-chizedek king of Salem brought out bread and wine; he was priest of God Most High. 19 And he blessed him and said, "Blessed be Abram by God Most High, maker of heaven and earth; 20 and blessed be God Most High, who has delivered your enemies into your hand!" And Abram gave him a tenth of everything.11*
>
> (Genesis 14:18-20, RSV)

5. Abram and Sarai desire a son

After the passing of time, Abram became concerned that he and Sarai had no children.

After about ten years since God renewed his promise that Abram would have children, Sarai realized maybe the promise of children was to Abram and not Sarai. So she approached Abram and said, "Since the Lord has kept me from having children, I employ you take my Egyptian handmaiden, Hagar, to wife that I may obtain children by her." And Abram did as she said. This was the custom in that day. If a wife could not have children, her servant would have her children for her mistress.

6. Hagar's son, Ishmael, is born

Abram then made Hagar, the Egyptian, his wife. When she became pregnant, she despised Sarai and put on airs. Sarai was beside herself so she went to Abram and said, "You are responsible for the wrong I am suffering. I gave my servant to your arms and she knows she is pregnant and she despises me. May the Lord judge between you and me."

Abram replied, "Do whatever you think is best." So Sarai mistreated Hagar and she fled from Sarai. An angel found Hagar near a well and encouraged her to return to Sarai with these words:

> *11 And the angel of the LORD said to her, "Behold, you are with child, and shall bear a son; you shall call his name Ishmael; because the LORD has given heed to your affliction. 12 He shall be a wild ass of a man, his hand against every man and every man's hand against him; and he shall dwell over against all his kinsmen." 13*

---

[11] The Holy Bible: The Revised Standard Version. Oak Harbor: Logos Research Systems, Inc., 1971.

*So she called the name of the LORD who spoke to her, "Thou art a God of seeing";
for she said, "Have I really seen God and remained alive after seeing him?" 12*

(Genesis 16:11-13, RSV)

And Hagar called the Lord the "One who sees." She returned home and bore Abram a son, called Ishmael; He was born to Abram when he was eighty-six years old.

1 When Abram was ninety-nine years old the LORD appeared to Abram, and said to him, "I am God Almighty; walk before me, and be blameless. 2 And I will make my covenant between me and you, and will multiply you exceedingly." 3 Then Abram fell on his face; and God said to him, 4 "Behold, my covenant is with you, and you shall be the father of a multitude of nations. 5 No longer shall your name be Abram, but your name shall be Abraham; for I have made you the father of a multitude of nations. 6 I will make you exceedingly fruitful; and I will make nations of you, and kings shall come forth from you. 7 And I will establish my covenant between me and you and your descendants after you throughout their generations for an everlasting covenant, to be God to you and to your descendants after you. 8 And I will give to you, and to your descendants after you, the land of your sojournings, all the land of Canaan, for an everlasting possession; and I will be their God." 9 And God said to Abraham, "As for you, you shall keep my covenant, you and your descendants after you throughout their generations. 10 This is my covenant, which you shall keep, between me and you and your descendants after you: Every male among you shall be circumcised. 11 You shall be circumcised in the flesh of your foreskins, and it shall be a sign of the covenant between me and you. 12 He that is eight days old among you shall be circumcised; every male throughout your generations, whether born in your house, or bought with your money from any foreigner who is not of your offspring, 13 both he that is born in your house and he that is bought with your money, shall be circumcised. So shall my covenant be in your flesh an everlasting covenant. 14 Any uncircumcised male who is not circumcised in the flesh of his foreskin shall be cut off from his people; he has broken my covenant." 15 And God said to Abraham, "As for Sarai your wife, you shall not call her name Sarai, but Sarah shall be her name. 16 I will bless her, and moreover I will give you a son by her; I will bless her, and she shall be a mother of nations; kings of peoples shall come from her." 17 Then Abraham fell on his face and laughed, and said to himself, "Shall a child be born to a man who is a hundred years old? Shall Sarah, who is ninety years old, bear a child?" 18 And Abraham said to God, "O that Ishmael might live in thy sight!" 19 God said, "No, but Sarah your wife shall bear you a son, and you shall call his name Isaac. I will establish my covenant with him as an everlasting covenant for his descendants after him. 20 As for Ishmael, I have heard you; behold, I will bless him and take him fruitful and multiply him exceedingly; he shall be the father of twelve princes, and I will make him a great nation. 21 But I

---

[12] Ibid.

will establish my covenant with Isaac, whom Sarah shall bear to you at this season next year." 13

(Genesis 17:1-21, RSV)

C. Isaac—forty-fourth generation to Yeshua 1867 BC

The Lord visited Sarah who was ninety years old. He caused her to conceive and give Abraham a son in his old age as God had promised. At one hundred years of age, Abraham became father to Isaac (1867 BC).

When Isaac was weaned at about three years of age, a great feast was put on. Ishmael was mocking Isaac. Sarah became angry and demanded that Abraham remove Hagar and her son, Ishmael from the camp. She also made it clear that Ishmael would not be heir with Isaac.

1. Isaac made heir

This grieved Abraham, but God said unto Abraham, "I will make Ishmael into a nation. Let them go." It is through Isaac that the promise is given. God's divine presence and direction was shown in whom He chose for the line a Messiah for mankind would come through. God's plan was marching through time.

1864 BC

Hagar and Ishmael (who was seventeen) were cast out. They wandered in the wilderness of Beersheba where they ran out of water. God showed Hagar where there was water. Ishmael lived in the desert of Paron and later married an Egyptian wife who bore him twelve sons.

Because Ishmael was the son of Abraham's convenience and choice instead of the son of God's choice, Isaac, there has been constant conflict between the sons of Ishmael and Isaac for centuries and even continues unto this day.

2. God's test

When Isaac was thirty-three years old (1834 BC), God tested Abraham and said, "Take your only son, Isaac, whom you love and go to the region of Moriah. Sacrifice him as a burnt offering on the mountain I will show you."

God was testing Abraham to see if he loved his son more than God. Abraham obeyed.

3So Abraham rose early in the morning, saddled his ass, and took two of his young men with him, and his son Isaac; and he cut the wood for the burnt offering, and arose and went to the place of which God had told him. 4On the third day Abraham lifted up his eyes and saw the place afar off. 5Then Abraham said to his young men, "Stay here with the ass; I and the lad will go yonder and worship, and come again to you." 6And Abraham took the wood of the burnt offering, and laid it on Isaac his son; and he took in his hand the fire and the knife. So they went both of them together. 7And Isaac said to his father Abraham, "My father!" And he said, "Here

---

[13] Ibid.

am I, my son." He said, "Behold, the fire and the wood; but where is the lamb for a burnt offering?" 8Abraham said, "God will provide himself the lamb for a burnt offering, my son." So they went both of them together. 9When they came to the place of which God had told him, Abraham built an altar there, and laid the wood in order, and bound Isaac his son, and laid him on the altar, upon the wood. 10Then Abraham put forth his hand, and took the knife to slay his son. 11But the angel of the LORD called to him from heaven, and said, "Abraham, Abraham!" And he said, "Here am I." 12He said, "Do not lay your hand on the lad or do anything to him; for now I know that you fear God, seeing you have not withheld your son, your only son, from me." 13And Abraham lifted up his eyes and looked, and behold, behind him was a ram, caught in a thicket by his horns; and Abraham went and took the ram, and offered it up as a burnt offering instead of his son. 14So Abraham called the name of that place The LORD will provide; as it is said to this day, "On the mount of the LORD it shall be provided." 15And the angel of the LORD called to Abraham a second time from heaven, 16 and said, "By myself I have sworn, says the LORD, because you have done this, and have not withheld your son, your only son, 17I will indeed bless you, and I will multiply your descendants as the stars of heaven and as the sand which is on the seashore. And your descendants shall possess the gate of their enemies, 18and by your descendants shall all the nations of the earth bless themselves, because you have obeyed my voice." 19So Abraham returned to his young men, and they arose and went together to Beer-sheba; and Abraham dwelt at Beer-sheba.14

(Genesis 22:3-19, RSV)

Sarah was 127 years old when she passed away (1830 BC). Abraham mourned and wept over his loss. Then he purchased the cave of Machpelah near Mamre in Canaan with its field and paid four hundred pieces of silver. This became a permanent burial place for Abraham and his descendants. It was here that Abraham buried his wife, Sarah.

3. A bride for Isaac

After a period of time, Abraham heard news about his brother Nahor's family. He learned that Milcah, Nahor's wife had eight sons. One son, named Bethuel, begat Rebekah, his daughter, and Laban, his son (ref. Genesis 11:29 - 23:20).

1827 BC
As Abraham became older, he was concerned with preserving the lineage of his son, Isaac.

Abraham approached his servant, who was in charge of his household, to go back to the land of his forefathers to get a wife from among his kinsmen. Whatever the servant did, he was not to take his son back but to the land of Ur, but he was to bring back Isaac's bride from among his kinsfolk. The servant arrived at a well in the Mesopotamian region where his brother, Nahor's family, lived. There he prayed that God would lead him to the woman of His choice. She would also be willing to water the camels and be God's choice for Isaac.

---

[14] The Holy Bible: The Revised Standard Version. Oak Harbor: Logos Research Systems, Inc., 1971.

Then a young virgin, Rebekah, approached the well and offered to water the ten camels and give the servant a drink. After she finished watering the camels, the servant found out she was a daughter of Bethuel, and her family would be able to offer shelter and food for the servant and the camels. The servant rejoiced and thanked God for His guidance.

He gave Rebekah gold jewelry to wear. Rebekah ran home and told the family of the visitor who had arrived from Abraham's home. Laban, Rebekah's brother, ran to the well and brought the servant and the other men with him as well as the camels to his home.

After the camels were provided for, the servant told Bethuel and his family of his errand and said, "Sarah, Abraham's wife, bore him a son, Isaac, in his old age. All that he has will be given to him. He is a wealthy man. Abraham made me promise to get a wife from his kinsfolk, not of the daughters of the Canaanites. Then he told of his prayer and encounter with Rebekah to show how God had led him to her. "May I now take Rebekah to Isaac to be his bride?"

Betheul and Laban answered, "Take her and go, but allow her to stay ten more days with us."

The servant replied, "Please don't hinder me; please let me go right away to my master." So they called Rebekah and asked her if she would go with this man and she answered, "I am ready to go." So Rebekah and her nurse and her damsels went with the servant and his men and returned to Canaan. Rebekah was blessed by her family.

> *60 They blessed her with this blessing as she parted: "Our sister, may you become the mother of many millions! May your descendants overcome all their enemies." 15*
>
> (Genesis 24:60, NLT)

When the caravan arrived at the well, Lahairoi, Isaac was mediating and saw the caravan of camels. He came toward them.

Rebekah asked who the man was that was coming toward them. She was told it was his master; so she covered herself with a veil. Isaac brought her into his mother Sarah's tent and Rebekah became his wife. He loved her and was comforted after his mother's death. Isaac was forty years old when he married Rebekah.

D. Jacob and Esau

1. Birth of twins

1807 BC — birth of Esau (*red*) and Jacob (*supplanter*) (forty-three generations to Yeshua) Twenty years passed and Rebekah was unable to have children. So Isaac prayed to the Lord that she would conceive. God heard his prayer and she became the mother of twins.

While she carried them, the twins were jostling in her womb. She inquired of the Lord to find out what was happening to her. The Lord said to her:

---

[15] Holy Bible: New Living Translation. Wheaton: Tyndale House, 1997.

23 and he answered her: "Two nations are in your womb, two peoples are quarreling while still within you; But one shall surpass the other, and the older shall serve the younger." 16

(Genesis 25:23, NABWRNT)

When the time had come for her to give birth to twins, the first one came out red and hairy, so his name was called Esau which means red. Then his brother came out with his hand grasping Esau's heel, so he was named Jacob which means supplanter. Isaac was sixty years old when Rebekah gave birth to them.

Esau and Jacob grew up. Esau became a skillful hunter and loved the open country. Jacob was a quiet man and stayed among the tents. Isaac loved wild game so he favored Esau, while Jacob was Rebekah's favorite.

2. Jacob steals Esau's blessings

One day Esau came from the fields famished so he willingly gave his birthright (of God's blessing and double portion of the inheritance) to Jacob for a dish of lentils and bread because he was concerned for his physical needs and did not appreciate his first-born privileges. Later Jacob, with Rebekah's help, deceived Isaac into giving the special blessing to him instead of Esau (ref. Genesis 27:1-26).

The blessing Isaac gave Jacob was: (1737 BC)

27 So he came near and kissed him; and he smelled the smell of his garments, and blessed him, and said, "See, the smell of my son is as the smell of a field which the LORD has blessed! 28 May God give you of the dew of heaven, and of the fatness of the earth, and plenty of grain and wine. 29 Let peoples serve you, and nations bow down to you. Be lord over your brothers, and may your mother's sons bow down to you. Cursed be every one who curses you, and blessed be every one who blesses you!" 17

(Genesis 27:27-29, RSV)

Afterwards, Esau came to be blessed by his father and brought him his favorite food. Isaac was scared when he realized he had been deceived and another received the blessing he intended for Esau (ref. Genesis 27:30-36).

Esau begged for a blessing and the blessing he received from Isaac caused him to hate his brother, Jacob because of the unfavorable blessing he received. He also threatened to kill his brother.

37 And Isaac answered and said unto Esau, Behold, I have made him thy lord, and all his brethren have I given to him for servants; and with corn and wine have I

---

[16] Confraternity of Christian Doctrine. Board of Trustees. The New American Bible : Translated from the original languages with critical use of all the ancient sources and the revised New Testament. Confraternity of Christian Doctrine, 1996, c1986.

[17] The Holy Bible: The Revised Standard Version. Oak Harbor: Logos Research Systems, Inc., 1971.

sustained him: and what shall I do now unto thee, my son? 38 And Esau said unto his father, Hast thou but one blessing, my father? bless me, even me also, O my father. And Esau lifted up his voice, and wept. 39 And Isaac his father answered and said unto him, Behold, thy dwelling shall be the fatness of the earth, and of the dew of heaven from above; 40 And by thy sword shalt thou live, and shalt serve thy brother; and it shall come to pass when thou shalt have the dominion, that thou shalt break his yoke from off thy neck. 41 And Esau hated Jacob because of the blessing wherewith his father blessed him: and Esau said in his heart, The days of mourning for my father are at hand; then will I slay my brother Jacob.18

(Genesis 27:37-41, KJV)

3. Jacob goes to the school of hard knocks

Rebekah, when she heard of Esau's intent to kill Jacob, called her son, Jacob. Isaac and Rebekah encouraged Jacob to go to Haran and stay with her brother, Laban. To seek a wife among his relatives, Jacob went from Beersheba toward Haran. Then he came to Bethel and made a pillow of rocks and fell asleep. Jacob dreamed there was a ladder that reached to heaven and the angels of God went up and down the ladder. Then the Lord stood above and said:

13 And behold, the LORD stood above it and said, "I am the LORD, the God of Abraham your father and the God of Isaac; the land on which you lie I will give to you and to your descendants; 14 and your descendants shall be like the dust of the earth, and you shall spread abroad to the west and to the east and to the north and to the south; and by you and your descendants shall all the families of the earth bless themselves. 15 Behold, I am with you and will keep you wherever you go, and will bring you back to this land; for I will not leave you until I have done that of which I have spoken to you."19

(Genesis 28:13-15, RSV)

Jacob awoke and said, "Surely the Lord is in this place and I did not know it. This is the gate of heaven."

And, the next morning, Jacob took the stone he had for his pillow and set it up for a pillar and poured oil upon the top of it. He called the place Bethel.

Jacob made a vow, "If God is with me and gives me bread to eat and clothes to wear, and if I come again to my father's house in peace, then the Lord shall be my God. I will give Him a tenth of whatever He gives me."

---

[18] The Holy Bible: King James Version. Oak Harbor: Logos Research Systems, Inc., 1995.

[19] The Holy Bible: The Revised Standard Version. Oak Harbor: Logos Research Systems, Inc., 1971.

a. Jacob works for his wives

1736 BC
Jacob hurried on his journey and finally arrived at Paddan-Aram.

> *2He saw in the distance three flocks of sheep lying in an open field beside a well, waiting to be watered. But a heavy stone covered the mouth of the well. 3It was the custom there to wait for all the flocks to arrive before removing the stone. After watering them, the stone would be rolled back over the mouth of the well. 4Jacob went over to the shepherds and asked them, "Where do you live?" "At Haran," they said. 5"Do you know a man there named Laban, the grandson of Nahor?" "Yes, we do," they replied. 6"How is he?" Jacob asked. "He's well and prosperous. Look, here comes his daughter Rachel with the sheep." 7"Why don't you water the flocks so they can get back to grazing?" Jacob asked. "They'll be hungry if you stop so early in the day." 8"We don't roll away the stone and begin the watering until all the flocks and shepherds are here," they replied. 9As this conversation was going on, Rachel arrived with her father's sheep, for she was a shepherd. 10And because she was his cousin, the daughter of his mother's brother, and because the sheep were his uncle's, Jacob went over to the well and rolled away the stone and watered his uncle's flock. 11Then Jacob kissed Rachel, and tears came to his eyes. 12He explained that he was her cousin on her father's side, her aunt Rebekah's son. So Rachel quickly ran and told her father, Laban. 13As soon as Laban heard about Jacob's arrival, he rushed out to meet him and greeted him warmly. Laban then brought him home, and Jacob told him his story.[20]*

(Genesis 29:2-13, NLT)

After Jacob stayed with Laban for about a month, Laban said, "I cannot let you work for me for nothing. What will your wages be?" Jacob thought a moment and said he would work seven years in exchange for the right to marry his beautiful younger daughter Rachel, whom he loved. Laban agreed.

When the seven years were up, Jacob said to Laban, "Now give to me my wife so I can marry her." March, 1724 BC (ref. Genesis 29:20-31).

Laban prepared a great wedding feast. After the feast, when it was dark, Laban gave Leah, his older daughter, to Jacob as his wife instead of Rachael. (Zilpah was given to Leah as her maid.) When it was morning, he realized the woman with him was Leah and not his beloved Rachel. He was angry. He went to Laban and asked why he had tricked him when he gave him Leah instead of Rachel. Laban made it clear that the first born daughter had to marry before the younger daughter. He then told him, "Wait a week and I will give you Rachel, also—provided you promise to work for another seven years. At the end of a week, Laban gave Rachel to Jacob. (Rachael was given a servant girl named Bilhah to be her maid.)

1724 — 1700 BC during the years that followed, twelve sons were born to Jacob. The sons of Leah

---

[20] Holy Bible: New Living Translation. Wheaton: Tyndale House, 1997.

December 1723 BC — First, Reuben 7205 *Reuwben (see a son)*
November 1722 BC — Second, Simeon 8095 *Shemown (hearing)*
October 1721 BC — Third, Levi 3878 *Leviy (attached)*

When Rachael saw she couldn't have children, she was upset; so she gave Bilhah her maid as wife to Jacob so Rachael could have children by Bilhah.

Bilhah conceived and bore Jacob a son so Rachael called his name Dan. The sons of Bilhah
December 1721 BC — First, Dan 1835 *Dan (Judge)*
July 1719 BC — Second, Naphtali 5321 *Naphtali (my wrestling or struggle)*

Leah's sons continued
August 1720 BC — Fourth, Judah 3063 *Yehuwdah (to celebrate or praise)*

After Leah saw she was not able to have anymore children, she gave Zilpah her maid to be Jacob's wife.

Zilpah's son
August 1719 BC — First, Gad 1410 *Gad (good fortune)*

For the price of Reuben's mandrake, Leah was able to spend a night with Jacob and God heard her cry and she bore Jacob a son.

Leah's sons continued
September 1719 BC — Fifth, Issachar 3485 *Issachar (reward)*

Zilpah's son
May 1718 BC - Second, Âshêr 836 *Asher (happy)*

Leah's sons continued
October 1718 BC — Sixth, Zebulun 2074 *Zebulun (honor)*

Leah's daughter
March 1716 BC- First, Dinah 1783 *Dêynâh (justice)*
Rachel's sons
July 1717 BC — First, Joseph 3130 *Yôwcêph (may he add)*
1700 BC — Second, Benjamin *(son of my right hand)*
Rachael died after Benjamin's birth.

After the birth of Joseph, Jacob asked permission to leave to his own country. He would take his wives and children for "I have completed my service."
Laban replied, "Please stay. I can tell I have become wealthy under your care. What will your wages be if you stay with me?"

b. Jacob works for cattle to support his family

Jacob

1710 BC

At the time when Jacob was planning to leave his uncle Laban he was concerned for the welfare of his wives and children, so he asked Laban to please let him leave. Laban said, "I know that I have been blessed because of you." And he said, "Why don't you stay with me and I will give you wages." He asked, "What would you want for your wages?"

Jacob said, "I need to be able to feed my family. I have nothing to support them with." So Laban asked, "What would you want?"

Jacob answered, "I would like to take from among the flocks all the speckled, spotted sheep and the brown lambs and the spotted and speckled among the goats. They will be my wages." In other words, he offered to take the off breeds and leave Laban with the purebreds. So he took his cattle three days journey from Laban so that there would be no mix up between his cattle and Laban's. Jacob took care of the cattle that were Laban's while his sons took care of Jacob's own cattle.

When it was time for the sheep to breed, Jacob took the sheep to the watering trough. He piled green poplar, hazel and chestnut the branches by the watering trough that he had cut strips into so that the healthy flock would have striped, speckled and spotted sheep. As a result, Jacob's sheep, although not perfect in appearance, were healthier and stronger than Laban's. So, eventually, as a result, Laban's sons became very angry with Jacob. They accused Jacob of taking away all that was their father's and leaving them with nothing.

c. God's call to Jacob to return to Canaan and Jacob's escape

> *2 And Jacob saw the countenance of Laban, and indeed it was not favorable toward him as before. 3 Then the LORD said to Jacob, "Return to the land of your fathers and to your family, and I will be with you."21*

(Genesis 31:2-3, NKJV)

So Jacob called for Rachel and Leah, in fear of Laban in the field. There he told them that God had asked Jacob to return to Canaan. Jacob worked hard for Laban, even though Laban had changed his wages ten times in his twenty years of service. Poor Jacob, he was perplexed and frustrated, not knowing where to turn, so God intervened. So Jacob explained to Rachel and Leah that God was blessing him to the extent that Laban and his sons became very jealous of him. In fact, they hated him. So Jacob told the reason he actually wanted to leave.

> *11 Then the Angel of God spoke to me in a dream, saying, 'Jacob.' And I said, 'Here I am.' 12 And He said, 'Lift your eyes now and see, all the rams which leap on the flocks are streaked, speckled, and gray-spotted; for I have seen all that Laban is doing to you. 13 I am the God of Bethel, where you anointed the pillar and where*

---

[21] The Holy Bible: The New King James Version. Nashville: Thomas Nelson, 1996, c1982.

you made a vow to Me. Now arise, get out of this land, and return to the land of your family.'22

(Genesis 31:11-13, NKJV)

God wanted him to leave Paddan-aram because there was at that time eleven boys growing up and they were beginning to learn some of the ways that they shouldn't be learning and God wanted to get Jacob and his boys away from a place of idolatry as he took Abram out of the house of idolatry in the land of Ur.

Rachel and Leah thought, as daughters of their father they should receive some inheritance. These two women told Jacob whatever he wants to do, they stand with him; apparently they thought their father had robbed them also. Then Jacob rose up and sent his sons and his wives upon camels and he carried away all his cattle and his goods that he had gotten while Laban was shearing his sheep. Rachel had stolen the images that were in her father's house. It is interesting to note that there is kind of a correlation between Jacob rising and leaving his brother in a post haste situation to go to Harran and now he is leaving his uncle in the same haste and oblivious to the fact that Rachel has stolen the images that were her father's. So Jacob left, when Laban was shearing his sheep, and there was a couple of days' journey between them. Jacob fled with all that he had and he rose up and passed over the river and set his face towards Mount Gilead. Jacob was three days journey ahead of Laban when Laban realized that his son-in-law and his family was gone. He had to be traveling fast to catch up with them. He had intended to kill him but God intervened and God said to Laban, "You be very careful what you say and do." So when Laban overtook Jacob, he pitched his tent in the mount and his brothers pitched their tent in the mount of Gilead. Now listen to Uncle Laban. He is a clever rascal by the way. He has been coming down breathing fire and brimstone wanting to recover all the possessions and take back his daughters and their children which Jacob had taken (ref: Genesis 31:14-25).

> *26 And Laban said to Jacob, What hast thou done, that thou hast stolen away unawares to me, and carried away my daughters, as captives taken with the sword? 27 Wherefore didst thou flee away secretly, and steal away from me; and didst not tell me, that I might have sent thee away with mirth, and with songs, with tabret, and with harp?23*

(Genesis 31:26-27, KJV)

That is just a poor excuse for what he really intended to do and when he says his sons he means his grandsons. Laban let him know he did not mean good by him but that God had prevented him from doing bad. Now he was talking about stolen gods. Actually Jacob did not know that Rachel had stolen the gods (ref. Genesis 31:28-31).

When he answered Laban, he answered by saying:

---

[22] Ibid.

[23] The Holy Bible: King James Version. Oak Harbor: Logos Research Systems, Inc., 1995.

32 With whomsoever thou findest thy gods, let him not live: before our brethren discern thou what is thine with me, and take it to thee. For Jacob knew not that Rachel had stolen them.24

(Genesis 31:32, KJV)

Laban went from tent to tent first of all to the maid servants and then to Leah's and then to Rachel's. But Rachel said I cannot rise up because of the custom of women meaning that she was having her period and she couldn't get up because it was not comfortable for her so she was sitting on the camel furniture where the idols were hidden. Rachel taking the terophim from her father is more serious than we imagine. The possession of those idols compromised the leadership of the family which meant Jacob was going to inherit everything old Laban had. That is the reason Laban was riled up over it. He surely did not want Jacob to get his estate and he felt that Jacob had gotten too much already. So Jacob got little confidence now and they could not locate the images. So Jacob is sure that they are not anywhere around so he wants to rebuke his father-in-law who came after him.25

Jacob asked, "What is my trespass? What is my sin that you have so pursued me so violently?" Jacob's voice was raising in pitch. Jacob had passed, of course, the college of hard knocks and now he was getting his degree. "These twenty years the ewes and goats have not cast their young and the rams of thy flock have I not eaten." He did eat most of those he had to pay for those so he did not have any insurance if a lamb was killed or stolen by wild animals—Jacob had to pay for that. Believe me this Laban was a hard task master so that I have been in the house twenty years. "I served fourteen years for your two daughters and six years for my cattle and you changed my wages ten times. I know if you had had your choice you would have sent me empty away and so God saw my affliction and the labor of my hand and rebuked you last night." Then Laban answered, "These daughters are my daughters, these children are my children, these cattle are my cattle and all you see is mine. What shall I do this day unto my children or unto their children which they have born; therefore, come unto me and let us make a covenant—I and thee and let it be a witness between the two of us."

Jacob set up a stone for a pillar and gathered stones and a contract was made. And Laban said, "This is a witness between you and me and the place was called Galeed. And the Lord watch between you and me and when we are absent from each other."

The words of this contract have been used by young people and groups as a benediction; I don't think I'd use this because two rascals who are going to quit stealing from each other and work on somebody else. The Lord watch between me and thee is really saying may the Lord keep his eye on you so you won't steal from me anymore. This is exactly what the men were saying. After this they separated and the pile of stones remained at Mizpah at the boundary line between Jacob and Laban each promising not to cross over to the other side (ref. Genesis 31:33-35).26

---

[24] Ibid.

[25] McGee, J. Vernon, Thru the Bible with J. Vernon McGee. Vol. 1 (Gen-Deu.). Pasadena: Thru the Bible Radio, c 1981. Page 128.

[26] Ibid. Page 129.

4. Jacob's plan to meet with Esau

Jacob went on his way. So Jacob sent messengers before him to Esau, his brother, in Edom to let him know he was coming; he just was hoping that everything would be safe between them. After he divided his family and troops in different divisions, he said to his servant, "Go to Esau, my brother; say to him: 'My lord Esau, all of the things you see before you are from your servant Jacob.'" This was not the way Jacob had spoken before. He had been manipulating for the birth-rights, stolen the blessings and he had been a rascal. Now his talk is different. Guess he learned a few things from his uncle Laban. "My lord Esau, thy servant Jacob." This message absolutely frightened poor Jacob because he did not know what to do.

The messengers returned to Jacob saying, "We have gone to thy brother Esau, He is coming to meet you with four hundred men." This message frightened poor Jacob because he did not know what it meant. He did not tell his intentions to the servants at all. I suppose Jacob was puzzled rather thoroughly. "Do you detect any note of animosity, bitterness or hatred toward me?" I suppose that was to one of the servants.

"No, he seemed to be glad to get the information you were coming to meet him."

So Jacob was afraid. He said, "If Esau came to one company and smote them, then the other company would escape." So Jacob divided his family and company of animals into three groups. Then he appealed to God in his distress. Jacob said, "O God of my father Abraham, and God of my father Isaac, the Lord who answered, 'Return to your country and to your kindred, and I will deal well with you.' I am not worthy of the least of all the mercies of Your truth which You have showed me Your servant; but with my staff I passed over this Jordan and now I have become two bands."

Jacob was scared after he pleaded to God and he divided his stock up. First he gave a very rich gift in the forefront for his brother, Esau, as a peace offering because he was not sure if his brother was approaching him with the idea of revenge or what. So he divides his troop up and then he says, "When the first group goes up, my brother Esau will say, 'Whose are these?' You are to say, 'They are for you my lord.' And the next group goes on, and the third will follow and will say 'behold thy servant Jacob is behind us.' For," he said, "I will appease him with the present that goes before me and afterward I will see his face; and perhaps he will accept me." Esau was met by one drove after another. This was the plan that Jacob was working on. So on went the present (ref. Genesis 32:1-23).

The women went on ahead and Jacob stayed behind and he spent the night wrestling with an angel until the break of day. As he wrestled, the angel touched the hollow of his thigh and the hollow of Jacob's thigh was out of joint causing him to limp. Since that time, the Jews have not been able to eat the hollow of the thigh of the sheep. So then the angel said after he wrestled Jacob all night long until the break of day, "Let me go, for the day breaks."

"I will not let you go unless you bless me." Jacob answered. Jacob was not wrestling, he was just holding on. He found out he was not going to go anywhere with God struggling and resisting.

God asked, "What is your name?" He answered, "Jacob."

"Your name shall not be called Jacob, but Israel. You are a prince and have power with God." He is not Jacob anymore, one who is an usurper and trickster, but shall be called Israel. Now the new nature in Israel will be manifested in the life of this man. God had to cripple Jacob in order to get him; but He got him. But the man Jacob refused to give up during the fight, which is typical of him, but he found out he could not overcome the Lord. But Jacob would not surrender. God pinned Jacob's shoulders because he would not yield his will to God's (ref. Genesis 32:24-32; 35:10).

5. Jacob meets Esau

In the distance, Esau approached and came to the many bands of animals and peoples. First of all he saw the band of animals and then he saw the children of Leah and Rachel and the two hand-maidens. Jacob approached him and Esau said, "Who are all these?"

He said, "They are mine, lord. They are my family, my wives, my sons and my daughter." He also said, "The animals that you saw in front are for you."

Esau said, "No my brother, I don't need those. I have plenty already."

"Please take them." So he insisted that Esau take his gift. And he said, "All that I ask is that you allow me to pass through the land that I might take my family back to Canaan," and his brother agreed (ref. Genesis 33:1-16).

1700 BC
6. Jacob returns to Bethel

They came to Ephrath where Rachel was about to give birth, and she came into hard labor and the midwife said, "Fear not; for you shall have a son also." After he was delivered, she called his name Beioni but his father called him Benjamin. Rachel died and was buried on the way to Ephrath, which is Bethlehem. And Jacob set up a pillar upon her grave; that is where the pillar of Rachel's grave is unto this day.

1699 BC
E. Joseph's dream and journey to Egypt

Joseph was the oldest son of Rachel, Jacob's favorite wife. He was next to the youngest in the family of Jacob except for Benjamin who had just been born when Joseph was seventeen years of age. Joseph was a shepherd like the rest of his brethren, and was to feed the flocks and herds of Jacob (Israel). Israel loved Joseph more than all his children because he was the son of his old age as well as the son of his favorite wife, Rachael. He made Joseph a coat of many colors. His brethren became jealous because he got this special treatment. The final straw was when Joseph dreamed a dream and was telling his brethren and his parents that the dream showed that he was going to be a ruler over them. They were very angry. One day his brothers went to feed their flock in Shechem and his father, Israel, said to Joseph,

"Would you please go find out what your brothers are doing?"

He answered, "I will do that for you father." So he went and found that the brothers had left Shechem.

Joseph was wandering around the fields trying to locate them when a gentleman who saw him wandering around said to him, "Who are you seeking?"

Joseph replied, "I am looking for my brothers." He told Joseph he heard they were going to Dothan; so Joseph followed after his brothers to Dothan.

When the brothers saw Joseph coming toward them in a distance, they said, "Behold this dreamer cometh. Now let us cast him in a pit and say that some evil beast devoured him and we shall see what becomes of his dreams."

Reuben heard it and he delivered him out of their hands; and said, "Let us not kill him." And Reuben said unto them, "I will shed no blood, but cast him into the pit that is in the wilderness and lay no hand on him; that he might rid him out of their hands." He was planning on retrieving him from them after their anger cooled. So, when they got a hold of Joseph, they took off his coat of many colors and put him into the pit that had no water in it. They sat down to eat and listened to him crying, but ignored his cry. They noticed a company of Ishmaelites coming from Gilead with their camels bearing spices and balm and myrrh to carry them to Egypt.

So the brothers said, "Why should we slay our brother? Why don't we just make a profit and sell him? Let us sell him to the Ishmaelites as a slave." So they took Joseph out of the pit and sold him for twenty pieces of silver; so Joseph went to Egypt.

When Reuben returned and saw that Joseph was not in the pit, he was upset. He rent his clothes. The brothers took Joseph's coat, killed a kid of the goats, dipped the coat in the blood and took the coat of many colors to their father and said, "We have found this. Do you know whether or not it is your son's coat?"

And Israel answered, "It is my son's coat. Some evil beast devoured him. Joseph is with no doubt rent in pieces." So Israel was deceived by his own sons. All his sons and his daughters rose up to comfort him but he refused to be comforted; and he said, "I will go down into the grave unto my son mourning." Thus, his father wept for him for an extended time (ref. Genesis 37:2-35).

Meantime in Egypt from 1699 to 1690 BC he (Joseph) prospered. He was purchased by Potiphar and he worked as his steward on the Potiphar family estate.

F. Judah
Judah born 1726 BC — forty-second generation to Messiah

About 1695 BC, Judah took a wife for Er, his firstborn son, and her name was Tamar. Er was wicked in the sight of the Lord so the Lord slew him in 1694 BC. Then Judah said to Onan, his second son, "Go in to your brother's wife and marry her and raise up seed to thy brother." Onan knew that the child should not be his so he spilt his seed on the ground which the Lord did not appreciate. So God slew him too. Then Judah said to Tamar, "Stay in the house of your parents until Shelah, his third son, is grown and he can marry you then." But in the back of his mind he was probably thinking that Shelah would probably die like the rest of them so he wouldn't even let her marry him either (ref. Genesis 39:2-11).

In 1692 BC, in the process of time, the daughter of Shuah, Judah's wife, died; and Judah was comforted, and went to the sheepshearers in Timnath; he and his friend Hirah the Adullamite. And it was told Tamar, saying; "Behold your father-in-law is going to Timnath to shear his sheep." So she put off her widow's garment and covered herself in a veil and sat in the open field. She saw that Shelah was grown and she was not given to him for a wife. And Judah saw her and he thought she was a harlot because she covered her face.

So he went into her and said, "What price will I give you?"

She answered, "Your signet ring, your bracelets and your staff and that is mine until you come with the kid of the flock as you have promised." So she arose and went away and put on her garments of her widowhood. So Judah came back with the kid and looked for the woman but did not find her. Three months later, Tamar was beginning to show that she was pregnant. So when Judah heard that his daughter-in-law was pregnant, he was going to burn her by fire. He asked, "Who is the father of this child?" And she brought forth the signet ring, the bracelets and the staff. When he saw them, he said, "You have been more righteous than me." Reason being she was righteous because he had promised her Shelah for her husband but he had reneged and God had wanted her to be the mother in the messianic line.

> *25 When she was brought forth, she sent to her father in law, saying, By the man, whose these are, am I with child: and she said, Discern, I pray thee, whose are these, the signet, and bracelets, and staff. 26 And Judah acknowledged them, and said, She hath been more righteous than I; because that I gave her not to Shelah my son. And he knew her again no more.27*

(Genesis 38:25-26, KJV)

So as a result of this conception in 1692 BC, two boys were produced. One was Pharez and the other Zerah (ref. Genesis 38:12-26). Pharez was in the line of Messiah. He was born in 1692 BC (ref. Genesis 38:27-30; 1 Chronicles 2:43). God is marching through time.

G. Joseph in Egypt

1. As a steward

Meanwhile, back in Egypt in 1690 BC, it came to pass that while Joseph was working in Potiphar's house his wife was very attracted to Joseph. She said, "Lie with me."

He answered, "No. It is not permitted that I should lie with my master's wife. I have control of anything in this house but you are one thing I have no right to touch, so the answer is no; besides God would not appreciate it. It would be a sin against God." Day by day she spoke to Joseph trying to get him to change his mind but he kept saying no.

One day, however, she caught him in the house by himself and she caught him by his garment and said, "Lie with me." There were no men in the house at this time so he just fled and left the garment behind him which was his outer coat. So she screamed and took the garment with her and showed it to her husband and said, "The Hebrew servant whom you gave me took advantage of me and I lifted my voice and cried and he left his garment with me and fled out." So his master heard the words of his wife which she spoke. He was angry with Joseph and took him and put Joseph in prison where the king's prisoners were bound (ref. Genesis 39:7-20).

2. In prison

While he was in prison in 1688 BC, it came to pass that a butler and a baker had offended the Pharaoh of Egypt. He was very wroth with his officers and they were put in prison. Each one of them had a dream and Joseph interpreted them. The butler dreamt that he was squeezing grapes into the Pharaoh's cup, so Joseph told him that it meant that he was going to be restored to service in three days. Meantime, the baker said, "I had a dream also and I had three baskets of baked goods but the birds were eating it."

Joseph said, "I'm sorry, but in three days you are going to be killed." So, the baker died as prophesied and the butler lived. Joseph said to the butler, "Be sure to remember me to the king to

---

[27] The Holy Bible: King James Version. Oak Harbor: Logos Research Systems, Inc., 1995.

let him know that I was put into jail wrongfully. Please tell him." However, the butler forgot (ref. Genesis 46:1-23).

In 1687 BC, Isaac was 180 years old and he died and was buried by Esau and Jacob (ref. Genesis 35:28-29).

Meanwhile, back in Egypt, two years later, Joseph was still in prison but he was still working as an assistant to the warden of the prison. In the meantime, Pharaoh had a terrible dream. He dreamt that he saw seven fat cattle and the next thing he saw was seven skinny ones coming up from the river that ate them up. Then he had another dream where he saw seven ears of corn that were beautiful and wonderful, and then next seven ears blasted with the east wind sprung up after them. And the seven skinny ears devoured the big ones. So Pharaoh woke up scared and wondered what in the world was going on. So he called his magicians and wise men to tell him what the dream meant but none of them could interpret it. Finally the butler said, "I do remember my faults this day: Pharaoh was wroth with his servants and put me in the captain of the guard's house both me and the chief baker. And we both dreamed dreams and a young man that was in the prison told us our interpretation. And this man was a young Hebrew; a servant to the captain of the guard. We told him and he interpreted to us our dreams; to each man according to his dream he did interpret. And it came to pass the interpretation he gave was I was restored unto my office, and the baker was hung."

3. Joseph interprets Pharaoh's dreams and becomes second ruler of Egypt.

So Pharaoh sent for Joseph. Joseph shaved himself and changed his clothes so he would look presentable to the Pharaoh. The Pharaoh said to Joseph, "I had a dream." He described his dream to Joseph.

Joseph answered, "It is not me who will give you the interpretation, but God shall give Pharaoh an answer for the interpretation." So Joseph said to Pharaoh, "The dream of Pharaoh is one: God has showed Pharaoh what He is about to do. Seven good cows are seven good years and seven ears are seven good years. The seven thin and ill favored cattle that came up are seven years of famine. The same is also true as is shown by the ears of corn. The dream is doubled to show that the thing is established by God and it will come to pass shortly." Then Joseph suggested that Pharaoh look out for a man discreet and wise and set him over the land of Egypt. "Let Pharaoh do this and let him appoint officers over the land, and take up a fifth part of the land of Egypt in the seven plenteous years. And let them gather all the food of those good years that come and lay up the food under the hand of Pharaoh, and let them keep food in the cities. And the food shall be in store for the land against seven years of famine, which shall be in the land of Egypt and the land shall perish not through the famine."

And the thing was very pleasing to Pharaoh and his servants. So Pharaoh said to his servants, "Can we find such a one as this one, a man in whom the Spirit of God is?" And Pharaoh said to Joseph, "Forasmuch as God has showed you all this, there is none so wise as you. You shall be over my house according to your word, so shall be my people and only in the throne will I be greater than you." So Joseph was put in second command. And Pharaoh said unto Joseph, "See I have set you over all the land of Egypt." He took his ring from his hand and put it upon Joseph's hand and dressed him in clothes of fine linen and put a gold chain about his neck; and so he also made him second ruler of the kingdom. Pharaoh called Joseph's name Zaphnathpaaneah and then he gave unto him a wife called Asenath, the daughter of Potipherah, priest of On. So Joseph had a wife and a family and a position over all the land of Egypt. For seven years, from 1686 — 1679 BC, Joseph took care of the land in the years of plenty, and during this time two sons were born; one was Manasseh and the other was Ephraim. Manasseh was born in 1685 BC and Ephraim 1683 BC. Manasseh means *God has made me forget all my toil and all my father's house*. Ephraim means *he has caused me to be fruitful in the land of my affliction* (ref. Genesis 41:1-53).

4. Famine in Egypt and in Canaan

a. Jacob tells his sons to go to Egypt to get food

After the seven years of plenty, 1679 — 1672 BC, there came seven years of famine. During that period of time, Joseph's family began to be without food. This was about 1678 BC—about a year into the famine. So Jacob heard that there was food in Egypt. He said to his sons, "Why are you looking at one another? I have heard there is food in Egypt. Go down and buy so that we may live and not die."

So Joseph's ten brothers went down to buy food in Egypt; but Benjamin, Joseph's youngest brother, was not sent with his brothers because his father was afraid that mischief would fall to him like it did to his brother, Joseph. They did not realize that Joseph was governor over the land; he sold food to all the people of the land. So Joseph's brothers came and bowed themselves down before him. And when Joseph saw his brothers, it reminded him of his dream where he was to rule over them. So he said to them through an interpreter, "You have come to spy out the land."

They answered, "No, we have come to buy food. We are servants and are sons of one man. There were originally twelve sons; one is no longer and the youngest one is at home with the father."

And so Joseph said to them, "You are spies. If you are not, you will have to leave one of your brothers here and I will keep him in prison." Simeon was chosen. "When you come back again you must bring your youngest brother."

So their food sacks were filled with food and they returned back to their father. When the time came that they ran out of food again their father said, "Go—get food from Egypt."

And they answered, "Well, if we are going to buy food, we have to take our youngest brother with us."

The father was afraid for his son, "There is already one son that is gone, one son is in Egypt in prison and now you want me to give up my youngest son Benjamin? I am afraid that I cannot do that."

The famine was sore in the land. Finally Judah said to him, "The man that was in Egypt protested saying, 'You will not see my face—except you bring your brother with you.'" So he convinced his father by saying, "In the event that something happens to the lad then you can kill my two little boys."

When Joseph saw his brothers he said to the servants in the Egyptian language, "Prepare my house for them and invite these men to my house." He said this because he wanted to talk to them in the privacy of his own home. But Joseph's brothers were panicky. They could not imagine him inviting them to his home for any good purpose. He had dealt with them so harshly before and now he was inviting them to lunch? So they came to the house.

They talked to the steward of Joseph's house. "Sir we came down just to buy food and every man found extra money in his sack when we went back. We are returning the money."

The steward answered, "Well, we have your money. God just gave you treasures in your sack."

Jacob told his sons to take a present to the ruler and they bowed down to the earth to him. The boyhood dreams of Joseph became fulfilled; then he asked, "How is the old man? Is he still alive?"

And they answered "Your servants' father is in good health. He is alive."

And Joseph raised up his eyes and saw his brother Benjamin, his mother's son and said, "Is this the younger brother of whom you spoke?" And he said, "God be gracious to you, my son." And Joseph looked at his brother Benjamin, his mother's son. The others were his half brothers but this brother was his full brother. What a dramatic moment; Joseph could not contain his emotions so he departed from the room and cried for his brothers and entered the chamber and wept there. He washed his face, and went out and refrained himself and said, "Sit down and we will have lunch." Had the brothers not been so scared, they would have realized that Joseph was sitting by himself, the Egyptians were sitting by themselves and they were sitting at a table by themselves. The odd thing was that they were arranged according to their birth order and they wondered how in the world he knew that.

So after the meal they had a great time and then Joseph commanded the servants to fill the men's sacks with food, as much as they could carry, and to put every man's money back in his sack. "But, put my cup, the silver one, in the sack of the youngest, and his food money" and they did according to the word of Joseph as spoken. Then Joseph sent them away. The brothers, thinking everything was alright, had no idea that the cup was in the sack of Benjamin, but the steward of the house came after them with specific instructions to accuse them of taking the cup that belonged to Joseph. He was given the instruction that whoever had the cup would have to become the servant of Joseph.

So they went from bag to bag from the oldest to the youngest and finally they found the cup in Benjamin's bag. So the sons of Israel rent their clothes and went back to Joseph's place and said, "We didn't know that Benjamin had the cup and we are very sorry." And so Judah offered to take the place of Benjamin and serve for the rest of his life and pleaded that Benjamin go home to his father. Joseph had wanted to test them in regard to the love for their brother when it was said that Benjamin was the guilty thief. Now he said, "Just leave Benjamin here and he can be my slave; he is the guilty one—the rest of you can go home."

But Judah said, "Oh my lord let the servant, I pray you, speak a word in your lord's ear and not thy anger burn against thy servant for you are as Pharaoh." You see the position was Joseph was occupying in Egypt. Then Judah recounted the feelings of his father about losing Joseph and also his feeling toward his son Benjamin. So Judah said, "Please let me be a servant in place of Benjamin and let me send the lad home." So when it turned out that the brothers passed the test, that their loyalty wasn't as distorted as it was towards him, he revealed his true identity.

So he stood before them and cried and said, "Let every man go from me except the men that are at this table." And he wept aloud and the Egyptians in the house of the Pharaoh heard it and they were pleased when they found out that his brothers had come. He told them, "Be neither grieved nor angry with yourselves that you sold me here; for God has sent me before you to preserve your lives. For these two years that the famine has been in the land there are yet five more years that there will not be harvest or planting. So God sent me before you to preserve you as a prosperity on the earth, as a savior to deliver you. So it is not you that sent me here but God. He has made me a father to Pharaoh and the lord of all the house and as a ruler throughout the land of Egypt" (ref. Genesis 45:6-8). Then Joseph said, "Go to my father and tell him that you can go to Egypt to live and I will send off carts and provisions so that you can make the journey and you can dwell in the land of Goshen, you and your children and your children's children, your flocks and your herds that you have, and there will be nourishment for you for another five years through the famine for you and all your household. Behold it was so wonderful just seeing my brother Benjamin so I am just thankful for that. Go ahead, return to my father and tell him exactly what has happened." So Joseph kissed all of his brothers and wept over them and his brothers talked with him (ref. Genesis 41:54-57; 42-45:15).

b. Israel and his family move to Egypt

The good news was heard in Pharaoh's house saying "Joseph's brothers have come"; and it pleased Pharaoh well, and his servants. And so Pharaoh said to Joseph, "Say unto your brothers, 'laden up your beasts and go into the land of Canaan and take your father and your households, come to me and I will give you the goods of the land of Egypt and you shall eat of the fat of the land. Now you are to take wagons out of the land of Egypt for your little ones and your wives and bring your father and come.'" So you see even Pharaoh was pleased. He ordered wagons to be sent. He said, "You don't need anything extra. We will help furnish everything you need." So that was wonderful.

When the men returned to Israel and said that Joseph was alive, Israel did not believe at first until he saw the carts and everything for the journey (ref. Genesis 45:16-28; 46:1-7, 28). So he took advantage of it and filled up his family in the carts and took them and his wives and their children, as well as their grandchildren. There were sixty-six males who came with Israel. Joseph and his sons and his grandsons made seventy-five males in *Egypt.

Joseph was already down in Egypt. In all, Jacob had seventy direct descendants.28
(Exodus 1:5, NLT)

So Joseph made ready to meet his father. He took a chariot and met Israel. And when Joseph saw his father, he fell on his neck and embraced him and wept there. Oh, what a marvelous meeting this was! And Joseph said to his brethren and to his father, "I will go up, and show Pharaoh, and say unto him, 'my brethren, and my father's house, which were in the land of Canaan, are come unto me. These men are shepherds, for their trade has been to feed cattle; and they have brought their flocks and their herds and all that they have.' So when it comes to pass, when Pharaoh shall call you, and shall say, 'What is your occupation?' You shall say, 'your servants have been working with cattle from our youth even until now, and also our fathers: that we may dwell in the land of Goshen for every shepherd is an abomination unto the Egyptians.'" Then Joseph presented his father and brothers unto Pharaoh and they told him that they were shepherds so Pharaoh said that he would like to have someone take care of his cattle and sheep. So they went to Goshen and took

---

[28] Holy Bible: New Living Translation. Wheaton: Tyndale House, 1997.* Referring to Exodus 1:5......says the Dead Sea Scrolls and Greek versions read seventy-five. This is according to the NLT, Second Edition. Carrol Stream: Tyndale House©1996.

care of Pharaoh's cattle as well as their own. Israel blessed Pharaoh (ref. Genesis 46:29-34; 47:1-12).

The land of Goshen is a land of Ramses; it is here, later on, that the pyramids were built in this area. So Joseph nourishes his father and his brothers with food according to their families.

1676 BC
c. Egyptians barter for food

In Egypt there was not enough food and so the famine was very severe. All the land of Egypt and the land of Canaan were faint for the reason of famine. Many people came from Canaan to get food. And when money failed in Egypt and in the land of Canaan, all the Egyptians came to Joseph and said, "Give us bread, for why should we die in thy presence for the money has failed?

And Joseph said, "In exchange for your cattle, I will give you food if money has failed." So they brought their cattle to Joseph and Joseph gave them bread in exchange for horses and flocks and cattle, for herds and donkeys and he fed them with bread for all their cattle for that year (ref. Genesis 47:13-17).

1675 BC
When that year ended, they came to him a second year and said to him, "We have no money to spend. There is nothing left in the sight of my lord. Shall we die before your eyes, we and our family? Buy us our land for food and our land will be servants to our lord, and give us our seed that we may live and not die."

So Joseph bought all the land of Egypt for Pharaoh; for the Egyptians sold every man his field because of the famine except for the land of the priests who already had an allowance (ref. Genesis 47:18-21). As for the people, he removed them to the cities from one end of the border of Egypt to the other end. There was great migration to the urban areas (1675 BC). This was where the grain was stored. And you remember that Joseph had chosen three centers throughout Egypt at the very beginning. He was now bringing the people where they would be the closest to the supply of food. So it came to pass that Joseph said to the people,

"Behold I have bought you this day and your land for Pharaoh. This is the seed for you; you shall sow the land. It shall come to pass in the increase that you shall give one fifth part unto the Pharaoh, and four parts shall be yours for the seed of the field and for your food and for your household and food for your little ones." Joseph had known that the famine was going to end in the next year and he could tell the people to sow their grain. "And thou shall save your lives and find grace in the sight of my Lord and we are to be Pharaoh's servants." So Joseph made a law over the land of Egypt unto this day that Pharaoh should have one fifth part except the land of the priests only, which did not belong to the Pharaoh (ref. Genesis 47:22-26).

5. Jacob (Israel) blesses his sons and prepares for death

Jacob lived in the land of Egypt for seventeen years so he was 147 years old. At the time Israel was close to dying, he called his son Joseph and said to him, "Bury me not in Egypt but in the field of Machpelah, in Canaan where my fathers have been buried." Joseph said he would. You can see that this was a request in the evidence of the faith of Jacob and the covenant that God made with his fathers. We need to know that he knew that in time his family would be back and return to Canaan even though they would stay in Egypt for a period of time.

In time, Joseph went with his two sons Manasseh and Ephraim to see his father. Jacob said to Joseph, "God Almighty appeared unto me at Luz in the land of Canaan, and blessed me, and He said, 'Behold I will make you fruitful and multiply and I will make you a great multitude of people and give this land of Canaan to you and your seed and it will be for an everlasting possession.' And now your sons, Manasseh and Ephraim, which are born unto you in Egypt before I came to Egypt are mine, as Reuben and Simeon are mine. And the issue that begets after them are yours and shall be called after the name of their brethren." In other words, they should also be among the twelve tribes. Now Israel's eyes were dim for age and he could not see. So he blessed Ephraim and Manasseh but he blessed the younger over the older and Joseph was not pleased. But Israel said, "I know that he is not the eldest, but the younger shall rule over the older one."

It is interesting to know that he chose to bless the younger over the older one, but this principal happens many times, like in the choice of King David who was the youngest of his family. God chose him? This strikes a great spiritual truth. God's choice must be based on a new birth; it does not depend on birth order. We say that the oldest boy has the responsibility of the family; well the oldest boy is not always whom God chooses. Israel blessed Joseph with a double blessing since God was first in his life (ref. Genesis 48:1-22). Then Jacob called all his sons and gathered them together to give them a last blessing and he blessed each son according to what they had done in life and what the Lord had promised they would do in the future. But to Judah he gave the promise that Messiah would come through him. And to Joseph and his sons, he passed on the double portion. Judah was going to be a lion. The scepter would not depart from Judah, nor a lawgiver from between his feet, until Shiloh (which is Messiah) would come and to him would be the gathering of the people.

He also spoke about Messiah coming on the foal in his prophecy. So after he blessed the boys, he passed away (1660 BC) and he was buried in the field of Machpelah which is in Mamre in the land of Canaan. It took the Egyptians forty days to embalm Jacob and they spent seventy days in mourning. After he was embalmed and they spent seventy days in mourning, Joseph requested of Pharaoh that he could go and bury his father and so he went to bury his father and they took the Egyptians with him and it was quite a big congregation that went to Canaan. And when the Canaanites saw the mourning of Jacob they thought that he must have been a great leader, so they were amazed (ref. Genesis 49:1-33; 50:1-14). After the burial of Israel, Joseph's brothers were afraid. They thought that Joseph was going to take revenge on them now that their father was gone. So Joseph, sensing their fear, said, "What you thought evil against me, God has meant for good and to save many people's lives. It was all in God's plan so don't take it upon yourselves to worry that I will get even with you."

6. Joseph's last days

So Joseph dwelt in Egypt, he and his father's house, and lived 110 years. Joseph saw Ephraim's children and the third generation of children of Machir, the son of Manasseh, were brought unto Joseph's knee. Joseph had great, great grandchildren and Joseph said to his brethren, "After I die the Lord will visit you and bring you out of this land which He swore to Abraham, Isaac and Jacob." So Joseph took an oath to the children of Israel: "God will surely visit you, and you shall carry my bones from here." So Joseph, being 110 years old, was embalmed and put in a coffin in Egypt (ref. Genesis 50:15-26).

So Joseph died as well as all his brethren and all that generation (ref. Exodus 1:6). These are the generations of Manasseh and Ephraim.

> *The sons of Manasseh, born to his Aramean concubine, were Asriel and Makir. Makir was the father of Gilead. 15 Makir found wives for Huppim and Shuppim. Makir's sister was named Maacah. One of his descendants was Zelophehad, who had only daughters. 16 Makir's wife, Maacah, gave birth to a son whom she named Peresh. His brother's name was Sheresh. The sons of Peresh were Ulam and Rakem. 17 The son of Ulam was Bedan. All these were considered Gileadites, descendants of Makir son of Manasseh. 18 Makir's sister Hammoleketh gave birth to Ishhod, Abiezer, and Mahlah. 19 The sons of Shemida were Ahian, Shechem, Likhi, and Aniam. Descendants of Ephraim 20 The descendants of Ephraim were Shuthelah, Bered, Tahath, Eleadah, Tahath.29*

(1 Chronicles 7:14-20, NLT)

---

[29] Holy Bible: New Living Translation. Wheaton: Tyndale House, 1997.

CHAPTER FOUR

The Exodus from Egypt

215-year sojourn in Egypt 1677 BC — 1462 BC

A. Moses
1. Birth — from rags to riches

After the death of Joseph, the Hebrew people multiplied and a new Pharaoh arose out of Egypt. He was determined to exterminate the male babies who were born to the children of Israel. Among these people who had a male baby after the decree was given were Amram and Jochebed who were Levites. A son was born to them March 6, 1543 BC. They hid him for three months. Jochebed realized she could no longer hide the child so she made a reed basket that she sealed with pitch and put her son in it. She had her daughter Miriam take him to the river Nile to see what would become of him (ref. Exodus 1:8-21; 2:1-4; Numbers 26:59; Exodus 6:20).

Miriam followed the basket as it floated down the river. Then the Pharaoh's daughter who was bathing in the river saw the basket among the reeds and asked one of her attendants to see what was in it. They pulled the basket over and looked inside and saw the child. The princess was quite excited and she said it must be one of the Hebrew children. She decided to take him for her own son. Miriam asked if she would like a nurse for the child. She said,

"Yes." (Jochebed, his mother, took care of him as a small child. He learned the ways of the Hebrews from her.) The princess then offered to pay for the care of the child until he was old enough to be trained at the palace. He was called Moses because he was drawn out of the water (ref. Exodus 2:5-10).

2. Moses' burden for the Hebrews

When Moses was forty years old, he was well-trained in Egyptian culture, mathematics, science and other subjects. He was now in training as a leader of the people. He happened to see an Egyptian mistreating a Hebrew so Moses took action and killed the Egyptian.

The next day Moses saw two Hebrews struggling with each other so he tried to keep them from harming each other. Their response was, "Are you going to kill us like you did the Egyptian?" Moses was shocked. He thought, "This must be well known." So he feared for his life and fled to Midian—1502 BC.

3. Moses meets God

In Midian he met Jethro, who was a priest of Midian, and stayed with him for forty years. He herded sheep. He married Jethro's daughter Zipporah and had two sons. One son was named Gershom which means refugee—the other Eliezer which means God of help.

Meanwhile the king of Egypt died and the Israelites continued to groan in slavery. One day while Moses was tending the flock he saw a bush that was burning, yet it did not burn up. Moses was quite amazed and went toward it and God spoke from the bush and said, "Take your shoes off your feet, for the ground you are standing is holy ground." Moses obeyed. God said "I am the God of your fathers." Then the Lord commanded Moses to go to Egypt to speak to Pharaoh to let His people go. It was three days journey into the wilderness...... Moses obeyed (ref. Exodus 2:11-25; 3:4-18).

> *13 And Moses said unto God, Behold, when I come unto the children of Israel, and shall say unto them, The God of your fathers hath sent me unto you; and they shall say to me, What is his name? what shall I say unto them? 14 And God said unto Moses, I AM THAT I AM: and he said, Thus shalt thou say unto the children of Israel, I AM hath sent me unto you. 15 And God said moreover unto Moses, Thus shalt thou say unto the children of Israel, The LORD God of your fathers, the God of Abraham, the God of Isaac, and the God of Jacob, hath sent me unto you: this is my name for ever, and this is my memorial unto all generations.30*
>
> (Exodus 3:13-15, KJV)

4. Moses talks to elders of Israel

God told Moses to call the elders of the people and tell them that God of Abraham, Isaac and Jacob is aware of their suffering and He will rescue them from the Egyptians. The Elders accepted the message; but the king of Egypt did not let the people go until God's hands forced him to. God promised when the Pharaoh let the people go, the Israelites would find favor in the Egyptian's eyes and would be given the wealth of the land, clothing and articles of silver and gold. Moses said, "What if the people do not believe me?"

God said, "Throw your staff down and it will become a serpent; grab its tail and it will be a staff. When you put your hand in your cloak it will become white like leprosy. Then put your hand back in your cloak it will be whole again. And, if they don't believe you then take some of the water from the Nile and pour it on dry ground and it will turn to blood."

Moses protested, "I am not good with words."

God answered, "Who made your mouth; is it not I? I will instruct you on what to say." Moses pleaded, "Send someone else."

---

[30] The Holy Bible: King James Version. Oak Harbor: Logos Research Systems, Inc., 1995.

The Lord was angry, "Alright, what about your brother, Aaron? He speaks well. And he is on his way to meet you. Talk to him and put the words into his mouth. I will be with both of you and instruct you both. Aaron will be the mouthpiece to the people; and you will tell him what to say."

So Moses returned home to Jethro, his father-in-law, and asked his permission to go and see his relatives in Egypt. It was granted. So Moses took his wife and sons, put them on a donkey and headed back to the land of Egypt. In his hand he carried the staff of God to perform all the miracles that God had shown him (ref. Exodus 4:1-29).

One night on the way to Egypt, the Lord confronted Moses and was about to kill him. But Zipporah took a flint knife to circumcise her sons to avoid Moses being killed because he had not been obedient in the manner of circumcision.

5. Moses and Aaron confront Pharaoh

The Lord had said to Aaron, "Go out into the wilderness to meet Moses." So Aaron went and met Moses and embraced him. Moses then told Aaron everything the Lord commanded and told the signs the Lord had command him to perform.

> *29 And Moses and Aaron went and gathered together all the elders of the children of Israel: 30 And Aaron spake all the words which the LORD had spoken unto Moses, and did the signs in the sight of the people. 31 And the people believed: and when they heard that the LORD had visited the children of Israel, and that he had looked upon their affliction, then they bowed their heads and worshipped.31*
>
> (Exodus 4:29-31, KJV)

After talking to the leaders of Israel, Moses and Aaron went and spoke to Pharaoh and said, "The Lord said, 'Let My people go so that they may have a festival unto Me, in My honor in the wilderness.'"

Pharaoh asked, "Who is the Lord?" He would not listen; he just hardened his heart and made the work harder for the Hebrews.

a. Ten plagues

Moses again approached Pharaoh and showed the signs of the staff becoming a snake then a staff again. Then he took staff and struck the water in the Nile and it turned to blood (March 7, 1463 BC) so there was no drinking water in the Nile or anyplace in Egypt.

There were a total of ten plagues in Egypt; they included frogs (March 16, 1463 BC) throughout the land, followed by lice (March 19, 1463 BC), then flies (March 20, 1463 BC). The plagues that attached the livestock of the Egyptians (March 23, 1463 BC) did not attack the livestock of the Israelites. Then there was the plague of festering boils (March 26, 1463 BC) that broke out on Egyptians and their animals. Next came the hail (March 27, 1463 BC) which wiped out all animals and people left outside as well as crops that were still standing. What the hail didn't destroy, the plagues of locusts (March 30, 1463 BC) destroyed (the remainder of the crops). After this came

---

[31] Ibid.

the plague of darkness (April 3-5, 1463 BC) that lasted for three days in Egypt. But where the Israelites lived, there was light.

During all this time after each judgment Pharaoh would repent to get the judgment removed but then harden his heart toward God and the Israelites. He would not let them go (ref. Exodus 7:15-25; 8:1-32; 9:1-35; 10:1-29).

After the darkness incident, Pharaoh shouted at Moses, "I am warning you never come back to see me again. The day you see my face you will die."

"Very well," Moses replied "I will never see your face again."

> *1 And the LORD said unto Moses, Yet will I bring one plague more upon Pharaoh, and upon Egypt; afterwards he will let you go hence: when he shall let you go, he shall surely thrust you out hence altogether. 2 Speak now in the ears of the people, and let every man borrow of his neighbour, and every woman of her neighbour, jewels of silver, and jewels of gold. 3 And the LORD gave the people favour in the sight of the Egyptians. Moreover the man Moses was very great in the land of Egypt, in the sight of Pharaoh's servants, and in the sight of the people. 4 And Moses said, Thus saith the LORD, About midnight will I go out into the midst of Egypt: 5 And all the firstborn in the land of Egypt shall die, from the firstborn of Pharaoh that sitteth upon his throne, even unto the firstborn of the maidservant that is behind the mill; and all the firstborn of beasts. 6 And there shall be a great cry throughout all the land of Egypt, such as there was none like it, nor shall be like it any more. 7 But against any of the children of Israel shall not a dog move his tongue, against man or beast: that ye may know how that the LORD doth put a difference between the Egyptians and Israel. 8 And all these thy servants shall come down unto me, and bow down themselves unto me, saying, Get thee out, and all the people that follow thee: and after that I will go out. And he went out from Pharaoh in a great anger.*[32]
>
> (Exodus 11:1-8, KJV)

6. Passover

While the Israelites were still in the land of Egypt, God gave the instructions for the Passover observance to Moses and Aaron (April 8, 1462 BC). They shared the instructions with the people. The Passover (April 10-14) was to be observed in this manner: "On the tenth day of this month select a one-year-old male sheep or goat with no defects for each family. Take special care of this chosen animal until the fourteenth day. Then the whole assembly of Israel must slaughter their animals at twilight. Then they are to take some of the blood and smear it on the sides and top of the doorframes of the house where they eat the animal. (This is a picture of Messiah's death that would cover the sins of all who believe.) The same night they must roast the whole animal over fire and eat it with salad greens and bread without yeast. Any left over meat that is not eaten before morning would be burned."

The instructions for eating this meal: "You need to be fully dressed, wear your sandals and carry your walking stick in hand. Eat the meal quickly for this is the Lord's Passover. On that night God will pass through the Land of Egypt and strike down every firstborn son and firstborn male

---

[32] Ibid.

animal. He will also execute judgment against all the gods of Egypt for He is Lord. The blood on your doorpost will serve as a sign, marking the house where you are staying—when He sees the blood He will pass over you and no plague of death will touch you when He strikes the Land of Egypt."

"This day is to be remembered throughout all generations" (ref. Exodus 12:14-27). So the people of Israel did as the Lord commanded through Moses and Aaron.

7. The nation of Israel is kicked out of Egypt

On that night at midnight (April 15, 1462 BC), the Lord struck down all the firstborn sons of the land of Egypt, from the firstborn of the Pharaoh, to the firstborn of the prisoner in the dungeon. Even the firstborn of their livestock died. So Pharaoh and all the officials and all the people of Egypt woke up during the night and loud crying was heard throughout the land of Egypt.

Pharaoh was so angry and upset he sent for Moses and Aaron during the night. He ordered, "Get out and take all the Israelites. Go, take your flocks and herds and be gone or we will all die."

The Israelites asked the Egyptians for clothing and articles of gold and silver. The Lord caused the Egyptians to look favorably on the Israelites, and they gave the Israelites whatever they asked for. So they stripped the Egyptians of their wealth (ref. Exodus 12:29-36).

8. From Egypt to the Red Sea to the wilderness

The people left Ramses and started for Succoth. God led them through the wilderness toward the Red Sea. From Succoth they came to Etham and the Lord went before them with a pillar of cloud which shielded them from the hot sun by day. At night it became a pillar of fire which gave them light and warmth. This allowed them to travel by day or by night as the Lord directed them. This was God's Shekinah glory marching toward Jerusalem.

Then the Lord told Moses to order the Israelites to camp by Pihahiroth between Migdol and the sea. Then Pharaoh would think the Israelites were confused. So Pharaoh's heart would be hardened and he would chase after them.

Pharaoh chased after the people of Israel with the forces of his army and all his troops and charioteers. As Pharaoh approached, the people of Israel panicked and they said to Moses,

"Why are you bringing us here to die in the wilderness.......we would be better off to be slaves in Egypt than corpses in the wilderness."

Moses told the people, "Don't be afraid, just stand still, and watch the Lord rescue you today. The Egyptians you see today will never be seen again. The Lord Himself will fight for you, relax" (ref. Exodus 12:37-51; 13:20-2; 14:3-20).

Then on April 17, 1462 BC, the Lord command Moses to have the people get moving. "Pick up your staff, raise your hand over the sea, and divide the water so the Israelites can walk on dry ground." Then the pillar of the cloud moved from the front of the camp to the rear, separating the Israelites from the Egyptians who were behind them.

21 And Moses stretched out his hand over the sea; and the LORD caused the sea to go back by a strong east wind all that night, and made the sea dry land, and the

waters were divided. 22 And the children of Israel went into the midst of the sea upon the dry ground: and the waters were a wall unto them on their right hand, and on their left. 23 And the Egyptians pursued, and went in after them to the midst of the sea, even all Pharaoh's horses, his chariots, and his horsemen. 24 And it came to pass, that in the morning watch the LORD looked unto the host of the Egyptians through the pillar of fire and of the cloud, and troubled the host of the Egyptians, 25 And took off their chariot wheels, that they drave them heavily: so that the Egyptians said, Let us flee from the face of Israel; for the LORD fighteth for them against the Egyptians. 26 And the LORD said unto Moses, Stretch out thine hand over the sea, that the waters may come again upon the Egyptians, upon their chariots, and upon their horsemen. 27 And Moses stretched forth his hand over the sea, and the sea returned to his strength when the morning appeared; and the Egyptians fled against it; and the LORD overthrew the Egyptians in the midst of the sea. 28 And the waters returned, and covered the chariots, and the horsemen, and all the host of Pharaoh that came into the sea after them; there remained not so much as one of them. 29 But the children of Israel walked upon dry land in the midst of the sea; and the waters were a wall unto them on their right hand, and on their left. 30 Thus the LORD saved Israel that day out of the hand of the Egyptians; and Israel saw the Egyptians dead upon the sea shore. 31 And Israel saw that great work which the LORD did upon the Egyptians: and the people feared the LORD, and believed the LORD, and his servant Moses.33

(Exodus 14:21-31, KJV)

The people were so excited they sang and shouted for joy.

1 Then sang Moses and the children of Israel this song unto the LORD, and spake, saying, I will sing unto the LORD, for he hath triumphed gloriously: the horse and his rider hath he thrown into the sea. 2 The LORD is my strength and song, and he is become my salvation: he is my God, and I will prepare him an habitation; my father's God, and I will exalt him. 3 The LORD is a man of war: the LORD is his name. 4 Pharaoh's chariots and his host hath he cast into the sea: his chosen captains also are drowned in the Red sea. 5 The depths have covered them: they sank into the bottom as a stone. 6 Thy right hand, O LORD, is become glorious in power: thy right hand, O LORD, hath dashed in pieces the enemy. 7 And in the greatness of thine excellency thou hast overthrown them that rose up against thee: thou sentest forth thy wrath, which consumed them as stubble. 8 And with the blast of thy nostrils the waters were gathered together, the floods stood upright as an heap, and the depths were congealed in the heart of the sea. 9 The enemy said, I will pursue, I will overtake, I will divide the spoil; my lust shall be satisfied upon them; I will draw my sword, my hand shall destroy them. 10 Thou didst blow with thy wind, the sea covered them: they sank as lead in the mighty waters. 11 Who is like unto thee, O LORD, among the gods? who is like thee, glorious in holiness, fearful in praises, doing wonders? 12 Thou stretchedst out thy right hand, the earth swallowed them.

---

[33] The Holy Bible: King James Version. Oak Harbor: Logos Research Systems, Inc., 1995.

13 Thou in thy mercy hast led forth the people which thou hast redeemed: thou hast guided them in thy strength unto thy holy habitation. 14 The people shall hear, and be afraid: sorrow shall take hold on the inhabitants of Palestina. 15 Then the dukes of Edom shall be amazed; the mighty men of Moab, trembling shall take hold upon them; all the inhabitants of Canaan shall melt away. 16 Fear and dread shall fall upon them; by the greatness of thine arm they shall be as still as a stone; till thy people pass over, O LORD, till the people pass over, which thou hast purchased. 17 Thou shalt bring them in, and plant them in the mountain of thine inheritance, in the place, O LORD, which thou hast made for thee to dwell in, in the Sanctuary, O Lord, which thy hands have established. 18 The LORD shall reign for ever and ever. 19 For the horse of Pharaoh went in with his chariots and with his horsemen into the sea, and the LORD brought again the waters of the sea upon them; but the children of Israel went on dry land in the midst of the sea.34

(Exodus 15:1-19, KJV)

9. God's provisions and laws

After a period of time, the Lord took care of the people's needs for water and for bread, manna, which fell daily except on the Sabbath because the Law of the Sabbath was given by God.

13 Speak thou also unto the children of Israel, saying, Verily my sabbaths ye shall keep: for it is a sign between me and you throughout your generations; that ye may know that I am the LORD that doth sanctify you. 14 Ye shall keep the sabbath therefore; for it is holy unto you: every one that defileth it shall surely be put to death: for whosoever doeth any work therein, that soul shall be cut off from among his people. 15 Six days may work be done; but in the seventh is the sabbath of rest, holy to the LORD: whosoever doeth any work in the sabbath day, he shall surely be put to death.35

(Exodus 31:13-15, KJV)

When the people craved meat, quail was provided. The people complained many times—forgetting God's provision for all their needs. Two months after the Israelites had left Egypt they arrived at the wilderness of Sinai. In the month of Abib (also known as Nisan) Moses received from God the laws for community living as well as the Ten Commandments.

1 And God spake all these words, saying, 2 I am the LORD thy God, which have brought thee out of the land of Egypt, out of the house of bondage. 3 Thou shalt have no other gods before me. 4 Thou shalt not make unto thee any graven image, or any likeness of any thing that is in heaven above, or that is in the earth beneath, or that is in the water under the earth: 5 Thou shalt not bow down thyself to them, nor serve them: for I the LORD thy God am a jealous God, visiting the iniquity of the fathers upon the children unto the third and fourth generation of them that

---

[34] Ibid.

[35] Ibid.

hate me; 6 And shewing mercy unto thousands of them that love me, and keep my commandments. 7 Thou shalt not take the name of the LORD thy God in vain; for the LORD will not hold him guiltless that taketh his name in vain. 8 Remember the sabbath day, to keep it holy. 9 Six days shalt thou labour, and do all thy work: 10 But the seventh day is the sabbath of the LORD thy God: in it thou shalt not do any work, thou, nor thy son, nor thy daughter, thy manservant, nor thy maidservant, nor thy cattle, nor thy stranger that is within thy gates: 11 For in six days the LORD made heaven and earth, the sea, and all that in them is, and rested the seventh day: wherefore the LORD blessed the sabbath day, and hallowed it. 12 Honour thy father and thy mother: that thy days may be long upon the land which the LORD thy God giveth thee. 13 Thou shalt not kill. 14 Thou shalt not commit adultery. 15 Thou shalt not steal. 16 Thou shalt not bear false witness against thy neighbour. 17 Thou shalt not covet thy neighbour's house, thou shalt not covet thy neighbour's wife, nor his manservant, nor his maidservant, nor his ox, nor his ass, nor any thing that is thy neighbour's.36

(Exodus 20:1-17, KJV)

The laws God gave varied from treatment of slaves to personal injury, property and the three annual festivals for the Lord:

1. Festival of Unleavened Bread
2. Festival of Harvest — First Fruits
3. Festival of Ingathering at End of Season

14 Three times thou shalt keep a feast unto me in the year. 15 Thou shalt keep the feast of unleavened bread: (thou shalt eat unleavened bread seven days, as I commanded thee, in the time appointed of the month Abib; for in it thou camest out from Egypt: and none shall appear before me empty:) 16 And the feast of harvest, the firstfruits of thy labours, which thou hast sown in the field: and the feast of ingathering, which is in the end of the year, when thou hast gathered in thy labours out of the field. 17 Three times in the year all thy males shall appear before the Lord GOD.37

(Exodus 23:14-17, KJV)

At this time the promises are given of God's presence and protection of Israel if they are obedient to God and do not make treaties with those in the land or serve their gods.

These laws were written in the book of the covenant and read aloud to the people. They promised to do everything the Lord commanded (ref. Exodus 15:23-27; 16:2-36; 19:1-25; 20:1-26; 21:22; 23:1-32; 24:3-8).

---

[36] Ibid.

[37] Ibid.

10. Moses visits God for forty days and nights

Then Moses climbed Mount Sinai and the cloud covered it. The glory of the Lord settled down on Mount Sinai and the cloud covered it for six days. On the seventh day the Lord called to Moses from inside the cloud. Then Moses disappeared into the cloud and climbed higher up the mountain and stayed for forty days and forty nights. The Lord told Moses the various things concerning the tabernacle that was to be built.

1. The offerings needed to build it (Exodus 25:3-9)
2. Plans for the ark of the covenant (Exodus 25:10-22)
3. Plans for the table (Exodus 25:23-30)
4. Plans for the lamp stand (Exodus 25:31-40)
5. Plans for the tabernacle which will have the above items (Exodus 26:1-37)
6. Plans for the altar of burnt offering outside the tabernacle (Exodus 27:1-8)
7. Plans for the courtyard (Exodus 27:9-19)
8. Light for the tabernacle (Exodus 27:20-21)
9. Clothing for the priests, who will be Aaron and his sons Nadab and Abihu, Eleazar and Ithamar (Exodus 28:1-5)
10. The ephod design for Aaron — the high priest (Exodus 28:6-14)
11. Design for the breast piece (Exodus 28:15-30)
12. Additional clothing for the priests
    a. robe (Exodus 28:31-35)
    b. medallion (Exodus 28:36-38)
    c. tunic of Aaron as well as sash (Exodus 28:39)
13. Aaron's sons' — special tunic, sashes and head coverings — priests' undergarments for Aaron and priests (Exodus 28:40-43)
14. Dedication of priests and promise of God's presence with them (Exodus 29:1-46)
15. Incense altar inside the holy place in front of curtain of the ark of the covenant of the holiest place.
16. Money to be raised for the tabernacle (Exodus 30:11-16)
17. Plans for the wash basins
18. The anointing oil formula and purpose
19. The incense for God's use
20.

Then the LORD spoke to Moses, saying: 2 a"See, I have called by name Bezalel the bson of Uri, the son of Hur, of the tribe of Judah. 3 And I have cfilled him with the Spirit of God, in wisdom, in understanding, in knowledge, and in all manner of workmanship, 4 to design artistic works, to work in gold, in silver, in bronze, 5 in cutting jewels for setting, in carving wood, and to work in all manner of workmanship. 6"And I, indeed I, have appointed with him dAholiab the son of Ahisamach, of the tribe of Dan; and I have put wisdom in the hearts of all the egifted artisans, that they may make all that I have commanded you.38

(Exodus 31:1-6)

21. Instructions for the Sabbath

12 The LORD then gave these further instructions to Moses: 13 "Tell the people of Israel to keep my Sabbath day, for the Sabbath is a sign of the covenant between me and you forever. It helps you to remember that I am the LORD, who makes you holy. 14 Yes, keep the Sabbath day, for it is holy. Anyone who desecrates it must die; anyone who works on that day will be cut off from the community. 15 Work six days only, but the seventh day must be a day of total rest. I repeat: Because the LORD considers it a holy day, anyone who works on the Sabbath must be put to death. 16 The people of Israel must keep the Sabbath day forever. 17 It is a permanent sign of my covenant with them. For in six days the LORD made heaven and earth, but he rested on the seventh day and was refreshed." 18 Then as the LORD finished speaking with Moses on Mount Sinai, he gave him the two stone tablets inscribed with the terms of the covenant,* written by the finger of God.39

(Exodus 31:12-18)

11. Israel forgets God and worships the golden calf

Now when the people saw that Moses adelayed coming down from the mountain, the people bgathered together to Aaron, and said to him, c"Come, make us lgods that shall dgo before us; for as for this Moses, the man who ebrought us up out of the land of Egypt, we do not know what has become of him." 2 And Aaron said to them, "Break off the fgolden earrings which are in the ears of your wives, your sons, and your daughters, and bring them to me."

3 So all the people broke off the golden earrings which were in their ears, and brought them to Aaron. 4 gAnd he received the gold from their hand, and he fashioned it with an engraving tool, and made a molded calf. Then they said, "This is your god, O Israel, that hbrought you out of the land of Egypt!" 5 So when Aaron saw it, he built an altar before it. And Aaron made a iproclamation and said, "Tomorrow is a feast to the LORD." 6 Then they rose early on the next day, offered burnt offerings, and brought peace offerings; and the people jsat down to eat and drink, and rose up to play. 7 And the LORD said to Moses, k"Go, get down! For your people whom you brought out of the land of Egypt lhave corrupted themselves. 8 They have turned aside quickly out of the way which mI commanded them. They have made themselves a molded calf, and worshiped it and sacrificed to it, and said, n'This is your god, O Israel, that brought you out of the land of Egypt!' " 9 And the LORD said to Moses, o"I have seen this people, and indeed it is a 2stiff-necked people! 10 Now therefore, plet Me alone, that qMy wrath may burn hot against

---

[38] The Holy Bible: The New King James Version. Nashville: Thomas Nelson, 1996, c1982.

[39] Holy Bible: New Living Translation. Wheaton: Tyndale House, 1997. (Ex 31:11-32:1).

them and I may 3consume them. And rI will make of you a great nation." 11 sThen Moses pleaded with 4the LORD his God, and said: "LORD, why does Your wrath burn hot against Your people whom You have brought out of the land of Egypt with great power and with a mighty hand? 12 tWhy should the Egyptians speak, and say, 'He brought them out to harm them, to kill them in the mountains, and to consume them from the face of the earth'? Turn from Your fierce wrath, and urelent from this harm to Your people. 13 Remember Abraham, Isaac, and Israel, Your servants, to whom You vswore by Your own self, and said to them, w'I will multiply your descendants as the stars of heaven; and all this land that I have spoken of I give to your descendants, and they shall inherit it forever.' " 14 So the LORD xrelented from the harm which He said He would do to His people. 15 And yMoses turned and went down from the mountain, and the two tablets of the Testimony were in his hand. The tablets were written on both sides; on the one side and on the other they were written. 16 Now the ztablets were the work of God, and the writing was the writing of God engraved on the tablets. 17 And when Joshua heard the noise of the people as they shouted, he said to Moses, "There is a noise of war in the camp." 18 But he said: "It is not the noise of the shout of victory, Nor the noise of the cry of defeat, But the sound of singing I hear." 19 So it was, as soon as he came near the camp, that ahe saw the calf and the dancing. So Moses' anger became hot, and he cast the tablets out of his hands and broke them at the foot of the mountain. 20 bThen he took the calf which they had made, burned it in the fire, and ground it to powder; and he scattered it on the water and made the children of Israel drink it. 21 And Moses said to Aaron, c"What did this people do to you that you have brought so great a sin upon them?" 22 So Aaron said, "Do not let the anger of my lord become hot. dYou know the people, that they are set on evil. 23 For they said to me, 'Make us gods that shall go before us; as for this Moses, the man who brought us out of the land of Egypt, we do not know what has become of him.' 24 And I said to them, 'Whoever has any gold, let them break it off.' So they gave it to me, and I cast it into the fire, and this calf came out." 25 Now when Moses saw that the people were eunrestrained (for Aaron fhad not restrained them, to their shame among their enemies), 26 then Moses stood in the entrance of the camp, and said, "Whoever is on the LORD's side—come to me!" And all the sons of Levi gathered themselves together to him. 27 And he said to them, "Thus says the LORD God of Israel: 'Let every man put his sword on his side, and go in and out from entrance to entrance throughout the camp, and glet every man kill his brother, every man his companion, and every man his neighbor.' " 28 So the sons of Levi did according to the word of Moses. And about three thousand men of the people fell that day. 29 hThen Moses said, 5"Consecrate yourselves today to the LORD, that He may bestow on you a blessing this day, for every man has opposed his son and his brother."40

(Exodus 32:1-29)

---

[40] <u>The Holy Bible: The New King James Version</u>. Nashville: Thomas Nelson, 1996, c1982. (Ex 32:1-29).

THE JEWISH YEAR

April (*Abib* or *Nisan*) Israel's first month of the year (Ex. 12:2; 13:4; 23:15; 34:18; Neh. 2:1; Esther 3:7). *1st day* of every month is called beginnings of months or new moons, a day of feasting, blowing of trumpets for a memorial before your God (Num. 10:10; 28:11-14; Ps. 81:3). *10th day,* the Passover lamb is chosen (Ex. 12:3-5). *14th day,* the Passover is eaten in the evening (Ex. 12:6-14; Lev. 23:5; Num. 9:2-5; 28:16; Ezek. 45:21). *15th to 21st* was the feast of the Passover. The first and last days of the feast, the 15th and the 21st, were Sabbath days, holy convocations, when no manner of work was to be done. All males 20 years old and upward must appear with a gift (Ex. 12:15-20; 23:14-17; Lev. 23:6-8; Num. 28:17-25; 2 Chr. 35:1). *21st* is a solemn assembly (Deut. 16:1-8, 16-17). [The 29th jubilee year, AD 29, Jesus died. He is our Passover (1 Cor. 5:7), slain to set us free from sin (Matt. 27:15; Mark 15:6; Luke 23:17; John 18:39).]	May (*Zif* or *Ziv*) 2nd. mo. (1 Kings 6:1). *1st day* of the month, new moon celebration. *14th,* the second Passover, is kept by those defiled by a dead body, or who were on a journey when the first Passover was kept (Num. 9:6-14).	June (*Sivan*) 3rd mo. (Esther 8:9). *1st day* of the month, new moon celebration. Pentecost Sunday falls during June 3 thru 9, fifty days after Passover Sabbath (a Saturday) (Lev. 23:10-21; Deut. 16:9-10). It is also called the feast of harvest (Ex. 23:16), and the feast of weeks, of the first fruits of wheat harvest (Ex. 34:22; Deut. 16:10). Each male must bring a gift (Deut. 16:16-17). Pentecost Sundays are circled in red.
	August (*Ab*) The 5th mo. (Ezra 7:8-9). *1st day* of the month, new moon celebration.	September (*Elul*) 6th mo. (Neh. 1:1; Zech. 7:1 *1st day* of the month, new moon celebration.
July (*Tammuz*). 4th mo. *1st day* of the month, new moon celebration	November (*Bul*) 8th mo. (1 Kings 6:38). *1st day* of the month, new moon celebration. God's 12-month calendar (1 Kings 4:7; Rev. 22:2)	December (*Chisleu*) 9th mo. (Neh. 1:1; Zech. 7:1) *1st day* of the month, new moon celebration. In the winter house the ninth month (Jer. 36:22). At Jerusalem was the feast of dedication. It was winter (John 10:22).
October (*Tishri*) 7th mo. (Ethanim, 1 Kings 8:2). *1st day,* new moon celebration. Of the twelve new moons, October 1 is the only holy convocation feast (Lev. 23:24; Num 29:1; Ps. 81:3). *10th day* the day of atonement, a day of afflicting the soul (fasting) (Lev. 16:29; 23:27, 29, 32). Every seventh year the law must be read before all Israel (Deut. 31:9-13; Jer. 34:9). *15th to the 21st,* the feast of tabernacles or feast of ingathering. They shall dwell in booths seven days (Ex. 23:14-17; Lev. 23:34-44; Deut. 16:13-17; Neh. 8:14). All males 0 years old and upward must appear with a gift (Ex. 23:4-17; Deut. 16:17). *22nd day,* the 8th day of the feast is a solemn assembly. Num. 29:35).		
	February (*Sebat*) 11th mo. (Zech. 1:7). *1st day* of the month, new moon celebration	March (*Adar*) 12th mo. (Esther 3:7; 13:8, 12). *1st day* of the month, new moon celebration. *14th and 15th,* Purim feast by decree of Queen Esther in 473 BC (Esther 9:17-32).
January (*Tebeth*) 10th mo. (Esther 2:16). *1st day* of the month, new moon celebration. 41		

---

41 1 <u>The Reese Chronological Bible.</u> The authorized edition of the original work by Edward Reese. Minneapolis: Bethany House Publishers, 1980. Page 23.

B. God establishes a place for Himself to dwell and a place for the people to worship

1. Tabernacle

The tabernacle is a separate and holy place where God dwelt with His people and revealed His will for Israel through Moses. Here the tablets of the Law were stored.
Here sacrifices were performed by the priest and people had their sins forgiven by God.

a. Exterior plan

The tabernacle was a portable tent. It was made from voluntary gifts of Israel. The materials are listed in Exodus 25:3-7; 35:4-15—such gifts as gold, silver, bronze; blue purple and scarlet material as well as fine embroidery; twined linen; goats' hair; dyed rams' skins and goats' skins; acacia wood; oil for lamps; spices; fragrant incense; stones for the ephod and breastplates.
The framework of the tabernacle was made up of forty-eight wooden frames fifteen feet high by twenty-seven inches wide covered with gold, over which were spread three coverings of goats' hair; rams' and goats' skins covered the entire structure. The wood used throughout the structure was acacia wood, known for its durability, covered with gold.
The court of the tabernacle was rectangular on an east to west plan. It was one hundred fifty feet long and seventy-five feet wide. The court was screened off from the camp of Israel by five white curtains, seven and one half feet high by one hundred feet in length and seventy- five feet in width, with curtains of fine linen supported on bronze pillars and attached by silver hooks. The hooks were made from the silver from the redemption money for each male over twenty years in the camp of Israel. The amount for redemption was half a shekel for each male. There were 13,605 shekels for the redemption of all of the sons of Israel except the tribe of Levi—which were holy and were priests unto the Lord.
In the courtyard stood the altar of burnt offering for sacrifice and the laver for cleansing of the priests.
The entrance to the court was through the gate on the east side.
Inside the courtyard was located the altar of bronze. The fire on this altar was never to go out. Here sin offerings were presented. The altar was a hollow chest of acacia wood covered with bronze. It was seven and one half feet wide by seven and one half feet long and four and one half feet high. The altar was carried by bronze poles in bronze rings (Exodus 27:1-8).
The laver was also in the courtyard. Here the priests washed themselves to prepare for their service in the tabernacle. The laver was made of highly polished brass or brass mirrors.

b. Interior plan

The sanctuary, or tabernacle, was located toward the west end of the courtyard.
The area of the most holy place was thirty feet by thirty feet. The holy place was sixty feet by thirty feet; the two were separated by a curtain with embroidered cherubim. The holy place had three pieces of furniture; (1) the table of showbread; (2) the golden lamp stand and (3) the golden altar of incense. This was made of acacia wood covered with gold and ornamentation. Rings and

poles were made for carrying. A number of accessories were made for the table. There were gold plates for bread (twelve loaves of bread which were changed weekly). Dishes for frankincense and vessels for wine offerings were also on the table of showbread. It was located on the west side of the holy place.

On the south side was a golden, seven-branched lamp stand. It was made of pure gold. It had a central shaft with six branches. All were adorned with almonds and flowers. The lamps gave a continuous light. All accessories of the lamp stands were of gold, such as snuffers, snuff dishes and vessels for holding the olive oil for the lamps.

In front of the curtain to the holy of holies was the altar of incense. Perpetual sweet- smelling incense was offered on it at night and in the morning, which symbolized the prayers of the priest of God. Only special incense could be placed on this altar. The altar of incense was a small altar constructed of acacia wood and overlaid with gold. It was one and one half feet square and three feet high. Rings and poles were made for it to be carried when moved during the wilderness march.

The holy of holies was the smallest part of the sanctuary— yet it was the most significant because of the ritual that was carried out there on the Day of Atonement. Here God Himself dwelt in the holiest of all. This was represented by the Shekinah cloud on the innermost sanctuary resting on the mercy seat of the ark of the covenant.

The ark of the covenant was the only piece of furniture in the holy of holies. It was 3¾ feet by 2¼ feet by 2¼ feet. It contained the Ten Commandments, the pot of manna and Aaron's rod that budded. The ark was covered with pure gold. Resting on the ark was a solid slab of gold called the mercy seat. At the ends of the lid were figures of gold, the cherubim. Their faces were toward the mercy seat and their wings touched overhead. Between the cherubim the Shekinah glory (or presence) of the God of Israel dwelt visibly.

The Tabernacle of Moses
(Ark of Covenant)

The Ark of the Covenant was placed in the holy of holies of the tabernacle.

The Shekinah glory of God filled the 10' x 10' x 10' cubical area of the Holy of Holies with the Ark of the Covenant and covered the earth floor with the veil.

The ark was never seen by the people on the wilderness walk (Numbers 4:44-45).42

When it was carried by the priests during the wilderness wandering, it was covered; hidden from the view of the common people.

The Cloud of Glory

A cloud covered the Tent of the Congregation, and the glory of the Lord filled the Tabernacle Ex 40:34. The Lord led Israel by a Cloudy Pillar of Fire out of Egypt to the Promised Land. The cloud gave them light and heat by night and shade from the heat of the day.

When the cloud brought Israel to Mt. Sinai, the cloud settled on the Mount and the Voice of God spoke to the nation out of the cloud at the Feast of Pentecost (Ex 19:9-19, Deu. 5:22).

The glory cloud showed the way of Israel as they journeyed in the wilderness until they came to the Land of Canaan.

---

[42] Conner, Kevin J. The Tabernacle of Moses. Portland: Bible Temple Publishing, 1975. Page 104.

After Solomon's Temple was built, the Glory Cloud dwelt upon the Ark of the Covenant in the holy of holies in the Temple (1 Kings 8:10-11; 2 Chronicles 5:13-14).

"The tragic end of the history of the cloud in the Old Testament, relative to the nation of Israel, is seen in the fact that the Glory-cloud eventually departed from the Temple which had become polluted with filthy abominations. God allowed this Temple to be destroyed because of these defilements. [Read Eze. 10:1-22] and compare with [1 Corinthians 3:16-17; 6:19-20]. The Glory cloud could never again return to a material Temple"43

The next time Shekinah glory was seen was in Yeshua when He walked the earth. Later, the glory is revealed in the Holy Spirit that lives in the believers of the church of Yeshua.

The people were allowed into the court of the tabernacle; there they took care of their sin offerings. The priests were allowed into the holy place to offer prayers and incense while the high priest was allowed into the holy of holies one day a year, on the Day of Atonement, to offer the blood of atonement on the mercy seat.

2. Transporting the tabernacle

When the tabernacle and camp moved, it was in an orderly procession moved by the Levites of various families. As long as the cloud hovered over the sanctuary, the camp remained stationary. When the cloud moved up from the sanctuary, a silver trumpet blast herald the breaking of camp, the priest took down the veil and covered the ark with it...... All the furniture was to be wrapped. The Kohathites carried all the pieces that were transported by poles. (Such as the ark and two altars) The Gershonites were entrusted with the curtains of the tabernacle, the tent of meeting with it covers, screen, and handling of the court, the screen, the altar and its equipment. The Merarites transported the frames, bars, pillars and bases of the tabernacle proper and pillars and bases of the court. The Kohathites son of Levites marched in the middle of the nation with six tribes before them and six behind.44

The rest of the disassembled structure was carried in six covered wagons each drawn by two oxen.

3. The attire of the priests

The tabernacle was a thing of beauty when it was completed. The priests and high priests also were made to a thing of beauty, befitting the beauty of the tabernacle and worthy of the presence of God.

All the priests wore white linen garments, as well as white turbans to symbolize the righteousness of God. Even the high priest laid aside his beautiful garments to wear the simple priestly garments on the Day of Atonement in the holy of holies, to sprinkle the blood on the mercy seat of the ark.

What Aaron, the high priest, wore spoke of Messiah and showed he was set apart for the service of God. He wore garments made of blue, purple and scarlet; an ephod; a beautifully woven

---

43 Ibid.

44 "Tabernacle." The Zondervan Pictorial Encyclopedia of the Bible. Tenney, Merrill C. General Editor. Vol. V (Q- Z). Grand Rapids: Zondervan Publishing House, 1975. Page 577.

girdle. On the bottom edge of the robe of the ephod were golden bells and pomegranates which could be heard from the holy place by the people outside the temple area.

The miter on his head said "Holinesses unto the Lord." This has to do with the inner life set aside for God's service.

The high priest also wore a breastplate which was like a vest. It had twelve different stones to represent the twelve tribes of Israel. It was beautiful. There was also a place where the *Urim* and *Thummim* were placed. They had something to do with predictions concerning God's will.

C. After forty years in the wilderness and the death of Moses, Joshua became the new leader

Before Moses' death on March 6, 1423 BC, Joshua was chosen by God to lead the children of Israel into the land of Canaan. Joshua was one of two men who believed God would keep His promise and deliver the land of Canaan into Israel's hand, regardless of the obstacles that they would face. Joshua and Caleb believed in God's faithfulness, while the rest of Israel did not believe and refused to go and take the land which God had promised them. So as a result of unbelief, that whole generation of Israel died in the wilderness. This was over a period of forty years. This journey should have taken only several weeks.

Moses saw a glimpse of the Promised Land from Mount Nebo on March 6, 1423 BC, the day he died. Israel mourned for Moses for a month. Then Joshua led the people on April 4, 1423 BC to cross the Jordan River. Three of the tribes had their inheritance on the east side of the Jordan while the other nine tribes were on the west side of the Jordan. The campaign took many years. Caleb received a special inheritance in Canaan because of his special faithfulness and obedience to God. The remainder of the inheritance was divided among the remaining tribes. Remnants of other nations remained in the land of Israel which would later prove to be thorns in the Israelites' side.

In the process of Israel taking over Canaan, they overthrew six nations—among them were the Hittites, Amorites, Canaanites, Perizzites, Hivites, Jebusites (ref. Joshua 12:8).

CHAPTER FIVE

Israel as a Nation

A. Background of Israel's history to King David

After Joshua's death, God gave the people judges to rule the people for a period of time.
At this time, the nation was a theocracy. The nation was ruled by God through judges. During the period of judges, Israel repeatedly fell into apostasy and tabernacle services were performed in a "religious" way, not from a heartfelt need. In Samuel's time, the people decided to bring the ark of the covenant from Shiloh (1 Samuel 4:1-22). The outcome was tragic: the Philistines captured the ark and later returned it when the Philistines were overcome with boils and tumors. They returned the ark with images of gold mice and gold tumors. After the ark was restored by the Philistines, it remained at Kiriath-Jearim (1 Samuel 7:1-2). Samuel presided over the religious exercises of the nation. There he offered burnt and peace offerings.

The time of the judges lasted through the time of Samuel, the prophet. Then the people desired a king so that they would be like other nations. So God gave them Saul, the son of Kish of the tribe of Benjamin. He ruled for forty years. Saul was the people's choice because he was outwardly strong, tall and handsome, and led the people into battle like the other nations around them. After God removed Saul, He made David, son of Jesse, their king. David was God's choice. He testified concerning David, "I have found David, son of Jesse, a man after My own heart. He will do everything I want him to do."

From David's descendants, the promised Messiah would come and walk in human flesh...... God with us. God's plan marches on.

After the children of Israel crossed the Jordan River, a place was found for the sacred tabernacle near Jericho at Gilgal. It was then moved to Shiloh in Ephraim.

After David captured Jebus (later called Jerusalem) and built himself a palace, he prepared a place for the ark and tabernacle of God on Zion (2 Samuel 6:17 ff; 1 Chronicles 16:1). David pitched a tent for the ark which he brought to Jerusalem. The ark was delivered by the priests. With

David's removal of the ark to Jerusalem there was both a tabernacle with its altar at Gibeon and one with the ark in Jerusalem, both to soon be replaced by the temple.

B. David chooses Solomon to be King

David had many sons and daughters but shortly before David's death, Adonijah, David's son, had rallied the people of Israel and all the king's sons to come to a feast where he would be made king. All were invited except Solomon—(David's son) — and Bathsheba his mother. Bathsheba and the prophet Nathan were talking. They were discussing Solomon's and her fates. Bathsheba had been promised by David that Solomon would be made king after David's death.

Bathsheba told the prophet of the promise but they both realized the dangerous situation. Both Bathsheba and Solomon would be put to death if Adonijah became king.

The prophet advised Bathsheba to go to the king and remind him of his promise to crown Solomon king, since Adonijah was planning on taking the throne of David, his father. It was the king, David's, desire that his son Solomon would have the throne because of God's promise that Solomon would build His temple.

The prophet promised to follow Bathsheba shortly after she spoke to the king to confirm the urgency of the matter. Bathsheba went and aroused the king from bed and reminded him of his promise and the urgency of doing it quickly. Then the prophet Nathan followed her and told the king of Adonijah's plan to become king. King David commanded that Solomon be summoned. He was taken to the tabernacle. There he was made king and the people rejoiced and Adonijah heard the noise of celebration and became afraid for his life when he heard that Solomon was made king.

David was joyful that he had lived to see his son Solomon anointed king. He knew he was God's choice. David charged his son to take care of several judgments against several people, including Adonijah. His other charge was to build the temple on Mount Moriah where David had purchased the field.

C. David's preparation for the temple

The location of Solomon's temple is identified with the threshing floor of Ornan (2 Chronicles 3:1), also known as Mount Moriah, the area of the sacrifice of Isaac by Abraham (Genesis 22:2). Here David established the location of the altar of the temple.[45]

David paid for Ornan Cave and the threshing floor to erect the altar of God. It was on this site that David sacrificed to Yahweh (1 Chronicles 1:28). It was here that he determined the location of the altar of Israel (1 Chronicles 22). David was not allowed to build the temple because David was a man of war and the time was not right. Solomon, David's son, who was a man of peace, would build the temple.

The inspiration for the temple plan and structure came to David from Yahweh when He had given him rest from all his enemies (2 Samuel 7:1-3). David assembled all the officials of Israel (1 Chronicles 28:1) and commissioned them and his son Solomon to build the temple. After this charge, he gave the pattern of the temple that he received from God to Solomon to follow. He also

---

[45] The Zondervan Pictorial Encyclopedia of the Bible. Tenney, Merrill C. General Editor. Vol. V (Q-Z). Grand Rapids: Zondervan Publishing House, 1975. Page 626.

gave the pattern of worship and the right way to know and fellowship with Him for the people and the priests.46

The Lord had promised David that his son Solomon would build the temple David desired to build; he had collected various supplies for the structure. Among the things he collected were gold, silver, copper, wood, fabric of various kinds plus the temple furnishings.

After this time, David amassed a great deal of materials for the building project. There were one hundred thousand talents of gold (18 million pounds), one million talents of silver (94 million pounds) plus from his own fortune for gilding and plating ornamentation one thousand talents (188 pounds) of gold of Ophir, a most prized gold, and seven thousand talents of refined silver (658,000 pounds). The officers gave five thousand talents (940,000 pounds) and ten thousand darics or 194 pounds of gold, and ten thousand talents (470,000 pounds) of silver. Brass (a crude alloy of copper) amounted to eighteen thousand talents (13.536 million pounds) and of iron one hundred thousand talents (75.2 million pounds), if iron is based on the values of a talent of copper.

Other people gave precious jewels of unknown quantities. Weights were specified and established for many articles of furniture (1 Chronicles 28:13-19) by David to indicate the size and pattern of articles that had been fixed by Yahweh.

David also prepared stones in the quarry. There were iron nails without number, cedar for framing and paneling (1 Chronicles 22:1-4) to which Solomon was free to add more as needed. Craftsmen also were found to contribute their skills to building the house of Yahweh (1 Chronicles 22:15).

The people from all stations of life were willing to build the temple as God had directed. The pattern of the temple, the size of furniture, implements, ritual and manner of worship was God's design, not man's.

D. Solomon's reign

Solomon agreed to do his father's will. He started his reign shortly before his father's death. After David's death, the Lord appeared to Solomon and asked him what he wanted more than anything else. Solomon replied he desired to have wisdom so that he could rule his people wisely. God granted his wish and gave him also riches, long life, and peace from enemies during his reign.

1. Building the temple

Solomon became a wise ruler as well as a great architect and planner. He began to take the plans of his father and to gather the materials needed for the temple structure.

First he commissioned stonecutters to cut the stones from the rock quarries according to specifications to fit in the temple. They would be cut and chiseled at the quarry so that not a sound of a hammer or chisel was heard at the site of the temple.

King Hiram of Tyre, a friend of King David's, was pleased that such a wise son like Solomon was made king in David's place. He promised to send cedar wood and provide labor to build the temple, and also to help with the design in metals such as brass, gold and silver, as well as oversee the overall structure of the temple.

---

[46] Ibid. Page 627.

David's temple was started May 2, 982 BC by Solomon and finished seven years later in November 975 BC. This was 480 years after the people of Israel were rescued from slavery in the land of Egypt. The dimensions of the temple were ninety feet long, a width of thirty feet and forty-five feet high. The house was made of finished stone. There was no hammer or any tool heard in the house while it was being built.

When he finished the house, it was covered with beams and boards of cedar. Then it was covered with fine gold with designs of palm trees and chains. It was also garnished with precious stones for beauty. The beams of the house, walls and doors were covered with gold, and engravings of cherubim were on the walls. The temple was three stories high with many rooms.

The porch before the house was thirty feet long by fifteen feet wide. It was also overlaid with gold.

Windows were added to add light to the structure. There were also storage rooms around the outer edge of the temple and in the interior. The most holy place was thirty feet by sixty feet. All the walls were covered with cedar that had been carved with knobs and flowers; then it was covered with gold. Even the nails were overlaid with gold.

In the holy of holies there were two cherubim carved of olive trees, each fifteen feet high. They faced inward, one on each wall of the inner house. Their wings went forward and touched each other and they were also overlaid with gold. A veil that separated the holy of holies from the holy place was made of fine linen of blue, purple and crimson, with cherubim woven into it.

Walls and floors were covered with cedar and engraved. Then they were covered with gold. The doors were made of olive wood. They were carved with carvings of cherubim and palm trees and open flowers. They were all covered with gold.

Solomon took an additional three years to make the furnishings of the temple.

975-972 BC

First two pillars were made that were twenty-seven feet high. The chapiter of brass on top of the pillar was seven and one half feet high. They were decorated with lilies, pomegranates, chain works and networks.

The pillars were put on the porch of the temple—one on the right hand side of the porch and one on the left side. The right hand was called *Jachin* (3199 *he will establish*) and the left was called *Boaz* (1162 *strength*) (ref. 1 Kings 6:2-36 NLT).

> *2 The Temple that King Solomon built for the Lord was 90 feet long, 30 feet wide, and 45 feet high. 3 The foyer at the front of the Temple was 30 feet wide, running across the entire width of the Temple. It projected outward 15 feet from the front of the Temple. 4 Solomon also made narrow, recessed windows throughout the Temple. 5 A complex of rooms was built against the outer walls of the Temple, all the way around the sides and rear of the building. 6 The complex was three stories high, the bottom floor being 7 1/2 feet wide, the second floor 9 feet wide, and the top floor 10 1/2 feet wide. The rooms were connected to the walls of the Temple by beams resting on ledges built out from the wall. So the beams were not inserted into the walls themselves. 7 The stones used in the construction of the Temple were pre-finished at the quarry, so the entire structure was built without the sound of*

hammer, ax, or any other iron tool at the building site. 8 The entrance to the bottom floor was on the south side of the Temple. There were winding stairs going up to the second floor, and another flight of stairs between the second and third floors. 9 After completing the Temple structure, Solomon put in a ceiling made of beams and planks of cedar. 10 As already stated, there was a complex of rooms on three sides of the building, attached to the Temple walls by cedar timbers. Each story of the complex was 71/2 feet high. 11 Then the Lord gave this message to Solomon: 12 "Concerning this Temple you are building, if you keep all my laws and regulations and obey all my commands, I will fulfill through you the promise I made to your father, David. 13 I will live among the people of Israel and never forsake my people." The Temple's Interior 14 So Solomon finished building the Temple. 15 The entire inside, from floor to ceiling, was paneled with wood. He paneled the walls and ceilings with cedar, and he used cypress for the floors. 16 He partitioned off an inner sanctuary—the Most Holy Place—at the far end of the Temple. It was 30 feet deep and was paneled with cedar from floor to ceiling. 17 The main room of the Temple, outside the Most Holy Place, was 60 feet long. 18 Cedar paneling completely covered the stone walls throughout the Temple, and the paneling was decorated with carvings of gourds and open flowers. 19 Solomon prepared the inner sanctuary in the rear of the Temple, where the Ark of the Lord's covenant would be placed. 20 This inner sanctuary was 30 feet long, 30 feet wide, and 30 feet high. Solomon overlaid its walls and ceiling with pure gold. He also overlaid the altar made of cedar. 21 Then he overlaid the rest of the Temple's interior with pure gold, and he made gold chains to protect the entrance to the Most Holy Place. 22 So he finished overlaying the entire Temple with gold, including the altar that belonged to the Most Holy Place. 23 Within the inner sanctuary Solomon placed two cherubim made of olive wood, each 15 feet tall. 24 The wingspan of each of the cherubim was 15 feet, each wing being 71/2 feet long. 25 The two cherubim were identical in shape and size; 26 each was 15 feet tall. 27 Solomon placed them side by side in the inner sanctuary of the Temple. Their outspread wings reached from wall to wall, while their inner wings touched at the center of the room. 28 He overlaid the two cherubim with gold. 29 All the walls of the inner sanctuary and the main room were decorated with carvings of cherubim, palm trees, and open flowers. 30 The floor in both rooms was overlaid with gold. 31 For the entrance to the inner sanctuary, Solomon made double doors of olive wood with five-sided doorposts. 32 These doors were decorated with carvings of cherubim, palm trees, and open flowers, and the doors were overlaid with gold. 33 Then he made four-sided doorposts of olive wood for the entrance to the Temple. 34 There were two folding doors of cypress wood, and each door was hinged to fold back upon itself. 35 These doors were decorated with carvings of cherubim, palm trees, and open flowers, and the doors were overlaid with gold. 36 The walls of the inner courtyard were built so that there was one layer of cedar beams after every three layers of hewn stone.47

(1 Kings 6:2-36, NLT)

---

[47] Holy Bible: New Living Translation. Wheaton: Tyndale House, 1997.

The foundation of the temple was laid in the month of *Ziv* (April—May) during the fourth year of Solomon's reign. The entire building was complete in the month of *Bul* (October- November) during the eleventh year of Solomon's reign. It took seven years (982-975 BC) to complete the temple. It was based on the plan of the tabernacle that was in the wilderness.

2. Furnishing for the temple

The designer of metal objects for worship and the ornaments of the temple were overseen by Hiram, who was a skilled craftsman in bronze from Tyre. He was half Israelite of the Tribe of Naphtali.

Hiram completed everything King Solomon assigned him to make for the temple.

1. Two pillars
2. Two bowl-shaped capitals on top of the pillars
3. Two networks of interwoven chains that decorated the capitals
4. Four hundred pomegranates that hung from the chains, on each of the chain networks that decorated the capitals on top of the pillars
5. Ten water coils holding ten basins
6. The sea and twelve oxen under it — The brim of the sea was decorated with lilies and it held three thousand baths. The sea is where the priests cleansed themselves.
   a.) Hiram also made ten bronze water carts that were six feet long by six feet wide by four and one half feet tall. They were ornately decorated. They were used to hold water; they held 220 gallons of water each. Five water carts were on the south side of temple and the other five were on the north side for the priest to wash anything needed for the sacrifices. The sea was placed on the southeast corner of the temple courtyard.
   b.) After the furnishings were completed, Hiram made lavers, shovels, ash buckets, pots and flesh hooks (which were used for sacrifices)......they were made of bright brass.

The vessels and articles of furniture made from gold were the table of showbread, the candle-sticks, bowls, snuffers, basins, spoons, the incense censers and the ark of the covenant.

7. The ash buckets, the shovels and the bowls
8. The altar of brass, which was in the courtyard, was thirty feet by thirty feet and fifteen feet high, where sacrifices were preformed daily. A molten sea for cleansing was fifteen feet in diameter; it stood on twelve oxen—three on the north, three on the west, three on the south, and three on the east. Their hind parts were inward and all were looking outward.

1. Solomon also made all the furnishing of the temple of the Lord.
2. Golden altar
3. Gold table for the bread of the presence
4. Lamp stands of solid gold
5. five on the south side
6. five on the north side in front of the most holy place
7. Flower decorations, lamps and tongs, all of gold
8. Solid gold small bowls, lamp snuffers, regular bowls, dishes and incense burners

9. The doors of the entrance of the most holy place and of the main room of the temple with their fronts overlaid with gold.

King Solomon finished all his work on the temple of the Lord. Then he brought all the gifts his father David had dedicated for the Lord's temple—the silver, the gold and various articles—and he stored them in the treasuries of the Lord's temple.

3. Dedicating the temple

After the temple was completed, Solomon summoned the elders and leaders of Israel to Jerusalem. They were to bring the ark of the covenant and all the holy vessels that were in the tabernacle during the Feast of Tabernacles, which is in the month of Ethanim (late September- October or early November).

October 14, 972 BC

The ark of the covenant was placed in the holy of holies; under the outstretched wings of the cherubim. There was nothing on the ark except the two stone tablets of the Ten Commandments which Moses put there at Mount Horeb when the Lord made a covenant with the children of Israel when they came out of Egypt.

When all the elders of Israel arrived, the priests picked up the ark and came with the Levites and brought the ark of the Lord along with the tent of meeting and the sacred items that had been in it.

There was much praising of God by the Levites with trumpets and cymbals, as they sang praises to God; saying, "He is good and His mercy endures forever." Then the cloud—the Shekinah glory of God's presence—filled the house.

So the priests could not minister in the temple because the glory of the Lord filled the house of God (ref. 1 Kings 8:1-11).

Afterward, King Solomon and the entire congregation of Israel sacrificed many animals before the presence of the ark. After this, the priests carried the ark of the Lord into the most holy place and placed it beneath the wings of the cherubim.

When the priests came out of the holy place, a thick cloud filled the temple of the Lord (God's presence was revealed). The priests could not continue their service because of the cloud; for the glorious presence of the Lord filled the temple.

Then Solomon prayed, "O Lord, You have said that You would live in a thick cloud of darkness. Now I have built a glorious temple for You, a place where You can live forever. Then Solomon stood before the altar of the Lord, before the whole congregation of Israel. He lifted his hands toward heaven and prayed.

> *23 He prayed, "O LORD, God of Israel, there is no God like you in all of heaven or earth. You keep your promises and show unfailing love to all who obey you and are eager to do your will. 24 You have kept your promise to your servant David, my father. You made that promise with your own mouth, and today you have fulfilled it with your own hands. 25 And now, O LORD, God of Israel, carry out your further promise to your servant David, my father. For you said to him, 'If your descendants guard their behavior as you have done, they will always reign over Israel.' 26 Now,*

O God of Israel, fulfill this promise to your servant David, my father. 27 "But will God really live on earth? Why, even the highest heavens cannot contain you. How much less this Temple I have built! 28 Listen to my prayer and my request, O LORD my God. Hear the cry and the prayer that your servant is making to you today. 29 May you watch over this Temple both day and night, this place where you have said you would put your name. May you always hear the prayers I make toward this place. 30 May you hear the humble and earnest requests from me and your people Israel when we pray toward this place. Yes, hear us from heaven where you live, and when you hear, forgive. 31 "If someone wrongs another person and is required to take an oath of innocence in front of the altar at this Temple, 32 then hear from heaven and judge between your servants—the accuser and the accused. Punish the guilty party and acquit the one who is innocent. 33 "If your people Israel are defeated by their enemies because they have sinned against you, and if they turn to you and call on your name and pray to you here in this Temple, 34 then hear from heaven and forgive their sins and return them to this land you gave their ancestors. 35 "If the skies are shut up and there is no rain because your people have sinned against you, and then they pray toward this Temple and confess your name and turn from their sins because you have punished them, 36 then hear from heaven and forgive the sins of your servants, your people Israel. Teach them to do what is right, and send rain on your land that you have given to your people as their special possession. 37 "If there is a famine in the land, or plagues, or crop disease, or attacks of locusts or caterpillars, or if your people's enemies are in the land besieging their towns—whatever the trouble is—38 and if your people offer a prayer concerning their troubles or sorrow, raising their hands toward this Temple, 39 then hear from heaven where you live, and forgive. Give your people whatever they deserve, for you alone know the human heart. 40 Then they will fear you and walk in your ways as long as they live in the land you gave to our ancestors. 41 "And when foreigners hear of you and come from distant lands to worship your great name—42 for they will hear of you and of your mighty miracles and your power—and when they pray toward this Temple, 43 then hear from heaven where you live, and grant what they ask of you. Then all the people of the earth will come to know and fear you, just as your own people Israel do. They, too, will know that this Temple I have built bears your name. 44 "If your people go out at your command to fight their enemies, and if they pray to the LORD toward this city that you have chosen and toward this Temple that I have built for your name, 45 then hear their prayers from heaven and uphold their cause. 46 "If they sin against you—and who has never sinned?—you may become angry with them and let their enemies conquer them and take them captive to a foreign land far or near. 47 But in that land of exile, they may turn to you again in repentance and pray, 'We have sinned, done evil, and acted wickedly.' 48 Then if they turn to you with their whole heart and soul and pray toward the land you gave to their ancestors, toward this city you have chosen, and toward this

Temple I have built to honor your name, 49 then hear their prayers from heaven where you live. Uphold their cause 50 and forgive your people who have sinned against you. Make their captors merciful to them, 51 for they are your people—your special possession—whom you brought out of the iron-smelting furnace of Egypt. 52 "May your eyes be open to my requests and to the requests of your people Israel. Hear and answer them whenever they cry out to you. 53 For when you brought our ancestors out of Egypt, O Sovereign LORD, you told your servant Moses that you had separated Israel from among all the nations of the earth to be your own special possession."48

(1 Kings 8:23-53)

After Solomon finished making these prayers and petitions to the Lord, he knelt with his hands stretched to heaven and blessed the entire congregation of Israel.

After Solomon prayed, he blessed Israel, then fire came down from heaven and consumed the burnt offering and sacrifices. The children of Israel saw the fire which came down and they gave glory to the Lord.

1 Now when Solomon had made an end of praying, the fire came down from heaven, and consumed the burnt offering and the sacrifices; and the glory of the LORD filled the house. 2 And the priests could not enter into the house of the LORD, because the glory of the LORD had filled the LORD'S house. 3 And when all the children of Israel saw how the fire came down, and the glory of the LORD upon the house, they bowed themselves with their faces to the ground upon the pavement, and worshipped, and praised the LORD, saying, For he is good; for his mercy endureth for ever.49

(2 Chronicles 7:1-3, KJV)

56 Praise the LORD who has given rest to his people Israel, just as he promised. Not one word has failed of all the wonderful promises he gave through his servant Moses. 57 May the LORD our God be with us as he was with our ancestors; may he never forsake us. 58 May he give us the desire to do his will in everything and to obey all the commands, laws, and regulations that he gave our ancestors. 59 And may these words that I have prayed in the presence of the LORD be before him constantly, day and night, so that the LORD our God may uphold my cause and the cause of his people Israel, fulfilling our daily needs. 60 May people all over the earth know that the LORD is God and that there is no other god. 61 And may you, his people, always be faithful to the LORD our God. May you always obey his laws and commands, just as you are doing today.50

(1 Kings 8:56-61) (ref. 2 Chronicles 6:1-42)

---

[48] Holy Bible: New Living Translation. Wheaton: Tyndale House, 1997. (1 Ki 8:22-53).

[49] The Holy Bible: King James Version. Oak Harbor: Logos Research Systems, Inc., 1995.

[50] Holy Bible: New Living Translation. Wheaton: Tyndale House, 1997.

After this the king and all Israel made many offerings of cattle, sheep and goats. And so the king and all the people of Israel dedicated the temple of the Lord.

October 8-23, 972 BC. This was the ninth jubilee year. The sacrifice and public festival was called for by the Lord, and the people rejoiced.

(2 Chronicles 8) Solomon finished the house of the Lord and it was perfect.

Then Solomon and all Israel celebrated the Festival of Tabernacles in the presence of the Lord. The celebration lasted fourteen days in all. Seven days for the dedication of the altar and seven days for the Feast of Tabernacles. Then Solomon sent the people home. They blessed the king and went home joyful because the Lord had been good to His servant David and His people Israel by giving them a wise king.

4. The Lord's appearance to Solomon

After Solomon finished building the temple of the Lord and the palace, the Lord appeared to Solomon a second time. The Lord said to him:

> *3 ...... "I have heard your prayer and your request. I have set apart this Temple you have built so that my name will be honored there forever. I will always watch over it and care for it. 4 As for you, if you will follow me with integrity and godliness, as David your father did, always obeying my commands and keeping my laws and regulations, 5 then I will establish the throne of your dynasty over Israel forever. For I made this promise to your father, David: 'You will never fail to have a successor on the throne of Israel.' 6 "But if you or your descendants abandon me and disobey my commands and laws, and if you go and worship other gods, 7 then I will uproot the people of Israel from this land I have given them. I will reject this Temple that I have set apart to honor my name. I will make Israel an object of mockery and ridicule among the nations. 8 And though this Temple is impressive now, it will become an appalling sight for all who pass by. They will scoff and ask, 'Why did the LORD do such terrible things to his land and to his Temple?' 9 And the answer will be, 'Because his people forgot the LORD their God, who brought their ancestors out of Egypt, and they worshiped other gods instead. That is why the LORD has brought all these disasters upon them.'"51*

(1 Kings 9:3-9)

The priests offered sacrifices, according to the commandment of Moses, on the Sabbath, during new moons, and on solemn feasts. Solomon approved the various services and ministries to the various families of Levites according to the order of his father David had set up. The celebrations were Passover (Feast of Unleavened Bread), Feast of Tabernacles and Day of Atonement. The temple acted as a unifying force for Israel. They had three annual festivals that the men came to before their God and to remember His great blessing to them.

---

51 Ibid.

5. The summary of Solomon's life.

Solomon was the wealthiest man in the world and continues to acquire greater wealth year by year especially silver and gold. Solomon also acquired two thousand horses for which he had built four thousand stalls.

He also had many foreign wives (seven hundred) and three hundred concubines. In time, his wives turned his heart from the Lord. In his old age he worshiped other gods instead of being completely faithful to the Lord his God, as his father David had been.

> *The Lord was very angry with Solomon since he had been warned by Yahweh about worshiping these gods but Solomon would not listen. So the Lord said to him. "Since you have not kept my covenant, I will take the kingdom from your son and give it to one of your servants. I will let your son be king of one tribe, Judah, for the sake of my servant David and Jerusalem my chosen city."*
>
> (ref. 1 Kings 11:9-13)

> *Solomon disobeyed God in three areas which the king of the people should not do: 15 you shall surely set a king over you whom the LORD your God chooses; one from among your brethren you shall set as king over you; you may not set a foreigner over you, who is not your brother. 16 But he shall not multiply horses for himself, nor cause the people to return to Egypt to multiply horses, for the LORD has said to you, 'You shall not return that way again.' 17 Neither shall he multiply wives for himself, lest his heart turn away; nor shall he greatly multiply silver and gold for himself. 18 "Also it shall be, when he sits on the throne of his kingdom, that he shall write for himself a copy of this law in a book, from the one before the priests, the Levites. 19 And it shall be with him, and he shall read it all the days of his life, that he may learn to fear the LORD his God and be careful to observe all the words of this law and these statutes.*[52]
>
> (Deuteronomy 17:15-19, NKJV)

1. Acquiring wealth (making that his god)
2. Acquiring many horses (becoming dependent on self for military might instead of God)
3. Acquiring many wives (should be faithful to one wife)

After the building of the temple in Jerusalem, Solomon lived twenty-seven more years until his death in 945 BC. Later in life he had disobeyed God. He worshiped Baal and Ashtoreth, the gods his wives worshiped, instead of the one true God. These things took his eyes off of God as his source. As a result, the kingdom of Israel was divided in 945-929 BC. Rehoboam became king of Judah and Benjamin, while Jeroboam I became king of Israel, which is made up of the following tribes: Simeon, Reuben, Gad, Ephraim, Issachar, Naphtali, Manasseh, Asher, Zebulon and Dan.

Solomon ruled Israel for forty years. When he died, he was buried in the city of David and his son Rehoboam became king over Judah and Benjamin. Jeroboam ruled the other ten tribes, which departed from God and worshiped two golden calves.

---

[52] The Holy Bible: The New King James Version. Nashville: Thomas Nelson, 1996, c1982.

(So in Solomon's life God's presence and leading could be seen in the two visions of God to Solomon and the wisdom God had given him to rule the people.)

God's presence could be seen at the temple in the cloud in the holiest place, as well as the presence of the ark of the covenant that was located under the cherubim in the holy of holies.

God continues to march through time and space, looking for a people who will love and obey Him.

E. From the death of Solomon, to the destruction of the temple, to the destruction of Babylon by Darius the Mede, and Cyrus, the Persian

1. The kings of Judah

After the death of Solomon, the kingdom of Israel became divided. There was the northern kingdom of Israel and the southern kingdom of Judah. In Judah there were a total of nineteen kings. There were eight good kings. Among these there were King Asa, who ruled forty-one years; Jehoshaphat ruled twenty-five years; Jehoash ruled forty years; Amaziah ruled twenty-nine years; Uzziah ruled fifty-two years; Jothan ruled sixteen years; Hezekiah ruled twenty-nine years and Josiah ruled thirty-one years. he other eleven kings were very evil and worshiped the pagan gods like the people around them. Some of the kings sacrificed their children in fire to Molech. The Lord was so fed up with Judah that He had Judah taken into captivity in Babylon in 586 BC during the reign of Zedekiah, who was a very evil king. This captivity happened after the fall of Jerusalem and the complete destruction of the temple in Jerusalem.

852 BC

After Judah had many years of evil kings, Joash became king for forty years. He became ruler at the age of seven. He was under the tutelage of Jehoiada, the priest who had a godly influence on his life and the life of the nation. It was through his influence that there were revivals in the nation. The Baals and images were destroyed. The worship of the true God was restored at the temple after a time. Joash had a desire to remodel the temple of God so he encouraged the people to give toward the remodeling of the temple—the priests were not cooperating.

> *4 And Jehoash said to the priests, All the money of the dedicated things that is brought into the house of the LORD, even the money of every one that passeth the account, the money that every man is set at, and all the money that cometh into any man's heart to bring into the house of the LORD, 5 Let the priests take it to them, every man of his acquaintance: and let them repair the breaches of the house, wheresoever any breach shall be found. 6 But it was so, that in the three and twentieth year of king Jehoash the priests had not repaired the breaches of the house. 7 Then king Jehoash called for Jehoiada the priest, and the other priests, and said unto them, Why repair ye not the breaches of the house? now therefore receive no more money of your acquaintance, but deliver it for the breaches of the house. 8*

And the priests consented to receive no more money of the people, neither to repair the breaches of the house.53

(2 Kings 12:4-8, KJV)

829 BC Jehoiada had a chest with a hole placed near the altar of the temple. There the people gave freely for the work of the temple. The money was used to pay the mason, hewers of stone and to repair the breaches of the temple. When the house was repaired, the extra money was brought to the king and Jehoiada. It was used to make the vessels for the house— both vessels of gold and silver, as well as the special spoon used in service. Burnt offerings were made to the Lord all the days of Jehoiada, the priest (ref. 2 Kings 12:9-16; 2 Chronicles 24:8-14).

Jehoash did what was right in the sight of the Lord all the days of his life.

In 813 BC Joash was slain by his servants while he was in his house of Millo. Amaziah, his son ruled in his place.

2. The kings of Israel

The kingdom of Israel, which is north of Judah, had nineteen kings. They were all evil. Israel was taken into captivity by the Assyrians in 722 BC. This took place during the reign of Hoshea.

The prophets during the reign of the kings in both kingdoms played an important part in trying to get the kings, as well as the people, to obey God and worship Him alone and not their idols. The people of Israel were told of the impending doom, as well as the promise of a Messiah in the future. Among the many prophets were Elijah, Elisha, Isaiah, Micah, Hosea, Daniel and Jeremiah.

723 BC Hosea (ref. Hosea 7:8:16; 10:13-16) and Amos (ref. Amos 9:1-10) spoke of the captivity coming to Israel. Zephaniah (ref. Zephaniah 1:1-23) and Jeremiah spoke of the captivity and destruction of Jerusalem.

Samaria, in Israel, was besieged for three years (723-721 BC) by King Shalmeser of Assyria. The people were captured and taken to Assyria and from there they were scattered throughout the world.

The reason for Israel's downfall can be seen in:

7 For so it was, that the children of Israel had sinned against the LORD their God, which had brought them up out of the land of Egypt, from under the hand of Pharaoh king of Egypt, and had feared other gods, 8 And walked in the statutes of the heathen, whom the LORD cast out from before the children of Israel, and of the kings of Israel, which they had made. 9 And the children of Israel did secretly those things that were not right against the LORD their God, and they built them high places in all their cities, from the tower of the watchmen to the fenced city. 10 And they set them up images and groves in every high hill, and under every green tree: 11 And there they burnt incense in all the high places, as did the heathen whom the LORD carried away before them; and wrought wicked things to provoke the LORD to anger: 12 For they served idols, whereof the LORD had said unto them, Ye shall not do this thing. 13 Yet the LORD testified against Israel, and against Judah, by all the prophets, and by all the seers, saying, Turn ye from your evil ways, and keep my

---

[53] The Holy Bible: King James Version. Oak Harbor: Logos Research Systems, Inc., 1995.

commandments and my statutes, according to all the law which I commanded your fathers, and which I sent to you by my servants the prophets. 14 Notwithstanding they would not hear, but hardened their necks, like to the neck of their fathers, that did not believe in the LORD their God. 15 And they rejected his statutes, and his covenant that he made with their fathers, and his testimonies which he testified against them; and they followed vanity, and became vain, and went after the heathen that were round about them, concerning whom the LORD had charged them, that they should not do like them. 16 And they left all the commandments of the LORD their God, and made them molten images, even two calves, and made a grove, and worshipped all the host of heaven, and served Baal. 17 And they caused their sons and their daughters to pass through the fire, and used divination and enchantments, and sold themselves to do evil in the sight of the LORD, to provoke him to anger. 18 Therefore the LORD was very angry with Israel, and removed them out of his sight: there was none left but the tribe of Judah only.[54]

(2 Kings 17:7-18, KJV)

(ref. 2 Kings 17:6; 18:10-11)

3. Judah's downfall and captivity — destruction of Jerusalem and the temple

After Israel's fall, Judah felt like they were spared any judgment. False prophets tried to make the people believe God would not judge Judah and take her into captivity. They were giving the people false hope even though they were worse than Israel.

The true prophets told of God's judgment for their idolatry, for not honoring the Sabbath day, and also for not honoring the Sabbatical years (letting the land rest from plowing and planting). They did not trust God to provide a bumper crop to take care of the Sabbatical year and the next year's food until the harvest.

God would take them from the land for seventy years to give the land the rest it should have had since the people had been in the land of Israel. Even though judgment was promised on the people by the prophets, they also gave the people hope that God would take care of them during their captivity.

(God's wrath and mercy is showing as He is marching through Judah's history.)

God had promised the restoration of Judah and Jerusalem (ref. Zephaniah 3:14-20).

3 For thus saith the LORD to the men of Judah and Jerusalem, Break up your fallow ground, and sow not among thorns. 4 Circumcise yourselves to the LORD, and take away the foreskins of your heart, ye men of Judah and inhabitants of Jerusalem: lest my fury come forth like fire, and burn that none can quench it, because of the evil of your doings. 5 Declare ye in Judah, and publish in Jerusalem; and say, Blow ye the trumpet in the land: cry, gather together, and say, Assemble yourselves, and let us go into the defenced cities. 6 Set up the standard toward Zion: retire, stay not: for I will bring evil from the north, and a great destruction. 7 The lion is come up from his thicket, and the destroyer of the Gentiles is on his way; he is gone forth from his place to make thy land desolate; and thy cities shall be laid waste, without

---

[54] The Holy Bible: King James Version. Oak Harbor: Logos Research Systems, Inc., 1995.

an inhabitant. 8 For this gird you with sackcloth, lament and howl: for the fierce anger of the LORD is not turned back from us. 9 And it shall come to pass at that day, saith the LORD, that the heart of the king shall perish, and the heart of the princes; and the priests shall be astonished, and the prophets shall wonder. 10 Then said I, Ah, Lord GOD! surely thou hast greatly deceived this people and Jerusalem, saying, Ye shall have peace; whereas the sword reacheth unto the soul. 11 At that time shall it be said to this people and to Jerusalem, A dry wind of the high places in the wilderness toward the daughter of my people, not to fan, nor to cleanse, 12 Even a full wind from those places shall come unto me: now also will I give sentence against them. 13 Behold, he shall come up as clouds, and his chariots shall be as a whirlwind: his horses are swifter than eagles. Woe unto us! for we are spoiled. 14 O Jerusalem, wash thine heart from wickedness, that thou mayest be saved. How long shall thy vain thoughts lodge within thee? 15 For a voice declareth from Dan, and publisheth affliction from mount Ephraim. 16 Make ye mention to the nations; behold, publish against Jerusalem, that watchers come from a far country, and give out their voice against the cities of Judah.55

(Jeremiah 4:3-16, KJV)

18 Thy way and thy doings have procured these things unto thee; this is thy wickedness, because it is bitter, because it reacheth unto thine heart. 19 My bowels, my bowels! I am pained at my very heart; my heart maketh a noise in me; I cannot hold my peace, because thou hast heard, O my soul, the sound of the trumpet, the alarm of war. 20 Destruction upon destruction is cried; for the whole land is spoiled: suddenly are my tents spoiled, and my curtains in a moment. 21 How long shall I see the standard, and hear the sound of the trumpet? 22 For my people is foolish, they have not known me; they are sottish children, and they have none understanding: they are wise to do evil, but to do good they have no knowledge. 23 I beheld the earth, and, lo, it was without form, and void; and the heavens, and they had no light. 24 I beheld the mountains, and, lo, they trembled, and all the hills moved lightly. 25 I beheld, and, lo, there was no man, and all the birds of the heavens were fled. 26 I beheld, and, lo, the fruitful place was a wilderness, and all the cities thereof were broken down at the presence of the LORD, and by his fierce anger. 27 For thus hath the LORD said, The whole land shall be desolate; yet will I not make a full end. 28 For this shall the earth mourn, and the heavens above be black: because I have spoken it, I have purposed it, and will not repent, neither will I turn back from it. 29 The whole city shall flee for the noise of the horsemen and bowmen; they shall go into thickets, and climb up upon the rocks: every city shall be forsaken, and not a man dwell therein. 30 And when thou art spoiled, what wilt thou do? Though thou clothest thyself with crimson, though thou deckest thee with ornaments of gold, though thou rentest thy face with painting, in vain shalt thou make thyself fair; thy lovers will despise thee, they will seek thy life.56

(Jeremiah 4:18-30, KJV)

---

[55] The Holy Bible: King James Version. Oak Harbor: Logos Research Systems, Inc., 1995.

[56] Ibid.

23 But this thing commanded I them, saying, Obey my voice, and I will be your God, and ye shall be my people: and walk ye in all the ways that I have commanded you, that it may be well unto you. 24 But they hearkened not, nor inclined their ear, but walked in the counsels and in the imagination of their evil heart, and went backward, and not forward.57

(Jeremiah 7:23-24, KJV)

27 Therefore thou shalt speak all these words unto them; but they will not hearken to thee: thou shalt also call unto them; but they will not answer thee. 28 But thou shalt say unto them, This is a nation that obeyeth not the voice of the LORD their God, nor receiveth correction: truth is perished, and is cut off from their mouth.58

(Jeremiah 7:27-28, KJV)

1 Oh that my head were waters, and mine eyes a fountain of tears, that I might weep day and night for the slain of the daughter of my people.59

(Jeremiah 9:1, KJV)

9 And the LORD said unto me, A conspiracy is found among the men of Judah, and among the inhabitants of Jerusalem. 10 They are turned back to the iniquities of their forefathers, which refused to hear my words; and they went after other gods to serve them: the house of Israel and the house of Judah have broken my covenant which I made with their fathers. 11 Therefore thus saith the LORD, Behold, I will bring evil upon them, which they shall not be able to escape; and though they shall cry unto me, I will not hearken unto them. 12 Then shall the cities of Judah and inhabitants of Jerusalem go, and cry unto the gods unto whom they offer incense: but they shall not save them at all in the time of their trouble60

(Jeremiah 11:9-12, KJV)

They had a break of about twenty years between the first and last deportation of Judah's captives before Jerusalem and the temple were destroyed. Several prophets warned of God's judgment (628-604 BC) (606 BC — July 9, 586 BC).

The law of the sabbatical year began 1415 BC. This was to be observed every seven years. At the time of the capture of Jerusalem by King Nebuchadnezzar of Babylon, seventy sabbatical years had passed which had not been kept by the people. Jeremiah prophesied that Judah would be in Babylon for seventy years to allow the land of Israel to have the seventy years of rest which it was due.

8For thus saith the LORD of hosts, the God of Israel; Let not your prophets and your diviners, that be in the midst of you, deceive you, neither hearken to your

---

[57] The Holy Bible: King James Version. Oak Harbor: Logos Research Systems, Inc., 1995.

[58] Ibid.

[59] Ibid.

[60] Ibid.

dreams which ye cause to be dreamed. 9For they prophesy falsely unto you in my name: I have not sent them, saith the LORD. 10For thus saith the LORD, That after seventy years be accomplished at Babylon I will visit you, and perform my good word toward you, in causing you to return to this place.61

(Jeremiah 29:8-10, KJV)

Jeremiah also prophesied about the capture of Judah and Jerusalem by King Nebuchadnezzar of Babylon. The capture of Judah took a total of twenty years.

During the third year of the reign of Jehoiakim, Nebuchadnezzar, King of Babylon, besieged Jerusalem 606 BC. In 605 BC was the first deportation from Judah. At this time, the vessels from the temple were taken to Babylon and placed in the treasure house of his god. The king also had certain choice people of the children of Israel and the kings and princes taken to Babylon. Among those taken to Babylon was Daniel who was steadfast with the Lord and did not submit to the Babylonian ways. The Lord raised him up to prominence in Babylon where he served four kings over a span of approximately seventy-plus years.

During the twenty-year siege of Judah, Jeremiah the prophet warned of God's judgment because of their worshipping of other gods and breaking the Sabbath.

6 Therefore, behold, the days come, saith the LORD, that this place shall no more be called Tophet, nor The valley of the son of Hinnom, but The valley of slaughter. 7 And I will make void the counsel of Judah and Jerusalem in this place; and I will cause them to fall by the sword before their enemies, and by the hands of them that seek their lives: and their carcases will I give to be meat for the fowls of the heaven, and for the beasts of the earth. 8 And I will make this city desolate, and an hissing; every one that passeth thereby shall be astonished and hiss because of all the plagues thereof. 9 And I will cause them to eat the flesh of their sons and the flesh of their daughters, and they shall eat every one the flesh of his friend in the siege and straitness, wherewith their enemies, and they that seek their lives, shall straiten them. 10 Then shalt thou break the bottle in the sight of the men that go with thee, 11 And shalt say unto them, Thus saith the LORD of hosts; Even so will I break this people and this city, as one breaketh a potter's vessel, that cannot be made whole again: and they shall bury them in Tophet, till there be no place to bury. 12 Thus will I do unto this place, saith the LORD, and to the inhabitants thereof, and even make this city as Tophet: 13 And the houses of Jerusalem, and the houses of the kings of Judah, shall be defiled as the place of Tophet, because of all the houses upon whose roofs they have burned incense unto all the host of heaven, and have poured out drink offerings unto other gods.62

(Jeremiah 19:6-13, KJV)

---

[61] Ibid.

[62] Ibid.

As a result, Jeremiah was marked and put into prison.

> *2 And the LORD sent against him bands of the Chaldees, and bands of the Syrians, and bands of the Moabites, and bands of the children of Ammon, and sent them against Judah to destroy it, according to the word of the LORD, which he spake by his servants the prophets. 3 Surely at the commandment of the LORD came this upon Judah, to remove them out of his sight, for the sins of Manasseh, according to all that he did; 4 And also for the innocent blood that he shed: for he filled Jerusalem with innocent blood; which the LORD would not pardon63*

> (2 Kings 24:2-4, KJV)

In December 598 BC began the second deportation of 3,023 captives. In March 16, 598 BC was the third deportation of 10,000 captives, including King Jehoiachin and his family, as well as the prophets Ezekiel and Mordecai.

All the men of might, as well as craftsmen and smiths, and all who were strong to go to war, were brought to Babylon.

597 BC After King Jehoiachin left Judah, Zedekiah, his brother was made king. He was evil and reigned eleven years in Jerusalem.

Jeremiah was faithful and warned of the captivity of Babylon to Zedekiah and the people remaining in Judah.

> *1 The word which came unto Jeremiah from the LORD, when king Zedekiah sent unto him Pashur the son of Melchiah, and Zephaniah the son of Maaseiah the priest, saying, 2 Enquire, I pray thee, of the LORD for us; for Nebuchadnezzar king of Babylon maketh war against us; if so be that the LORD will deal with us according to all his wondrous works, that he may go up from us. 3 Then said Jeremiah unto them, Thus shall ye say to Zedekiah: 4 Thus saith the LORD God of Israel; Behold, I will turn back the weapons of war that are in your hands, wherewith ye fight against the king of Babylon, and against the Chaldeans, which besiege you without the walls, and I will assemble them into the midst of this city. 5 And I myself will fight against you with an outstretched hand and with a strong arm, even in anger, and in fury, and in great wrath. 6 And I will smite the inhabitants of this city, both man and beast: they shall die of a great pestilence. 7 And afterward, saith the LORD, I will deliver Zedekiah king of Judah, and his servants, and the people, and such as are left in this city from the pestilence, from the sword, and from the famine, into the hand of Nebuchadnezzar king of Babylon, and into the hand of their enemies, and into the hand of those that seek their life: and he shall smite them with the edge of the sword; he shall not spare them, neither have pity, nor have mercy. 8 And unto this people thou shalt say, Thus saith the LORD; Behold, I set before you the way of life, and the way of death. 9 He that abideth in this city shall die by the sword, and by the famine, and by the pestilence: but he that goeth out, and falleth to the Chaldeans that besiege you, he shall live, and his life shall be unto him for a prey. 10 For I have set my face against this city for evil, and not for good, saith*

---

[63] Ibid.

the LORD: it shall be given into the hand of the king of Babylon, and he shall burn it with fire. 11 And touching the house of the king of Judah, say, Hear ye the word of the LORD; 12 O house of David, thus saith the LORD; Execute judgment in the morning, and deliver him that is spoiled out of the hand of the oppressor, lest my fury go out like fire, and burn that none can quench it, because of the evil of your doings. 13 Behold, I am against thee, O inhabitant of the valley, and rock of the plain, saith the LORD; which say, Who shall come down against us? or who shall enter into our habitations? 14 But I will punish you according to the fruit of your doings, saith the LORD: and I will kindle a fire in the forest thereof, and it shall devour all things round about it.64

(Jeremiah 21:1-14, KJV)

8 And many nations shall pass by this city, and they shall say every man to his neighbour, Wherefore hath the LORD done thus unto this great city? 9 Then they shall answer, Because they have forsaken the covenant of the LORD their God, and worshipped other gods, and served them.65

(Jeremiah 22:8-9, KJV)

He also condemned those who were in authority who did not take care and protect the people from harm.

Jeremiah prophesied that the people who were taken into Babylon would be divided into two parts......one group would be blessed and return to Judah to reestablish the nation and the temple, while the other group would be scattered throughout the earth. The sword, pestilence and famine would follow them.

1 The LORD shewed me, and, behold, two baskets of figs were set before the Temple of the LORD, after that Nebuchadnezzar king of Babylon had carried away captive Jeconiah the son of Jehoiakim king of Judah, and the princes of Judah, with the carpenters and smiths, from Jerusalem, and had brought them to Babylon. 2 One basket had very good figs, even like the figs that are first ripe: and the other basket had very naughty figs, which could not be eaten, they were so bad. 3 Then said the LORD unto me, What seest thou, Jeremiah? And I said, Figs; the good figs, very good; and the evil, very evil, that cannot be eaten, they are so evil. 4 Again the word of the LORD came unto me, saying, 5 Thus saith the LORD, the God of Israel; Like these good figs, so will I acknowledge them that are carried away captive of Judah, whom I have sent out of this place into the land of the Chaldeans for their good. 6 For I will set mine eyes upon them for good, and I will bring them again to this land: and I will build them, and not pull them down; and I will plant them, and not pluck them up. 7 And I will give them an heart to know me, that I am the LORD: and they shall be my people, and I will be their God: for they shall return unto me with their whole heart. 8 And as the evil figs, which cannot be eaten, they are so evil; surely thus saith the LORD, So will I give Zedekiah the king of Judah, and his

---

[64] Ibid.

[65] Ibid.

princes, and the residue of Jerusalem, that remain in this land, and them that dwell in the land of Egypt: 9 And I will deliver them to be removed into all the kingdoms of the earth for their hurt, to be a reproach and a proverb, a taunt and a curse, in all places whither I shall drive them. 10 And I will send the sword, the famine, and the pestilence, among them, till they be consumed from off the land that I gave unto them and to their fathers.66

(Jeremiah 24:1-10, KJV)

In 597 BC Jeremiah wrote a letter to those who were deported to Babylon.

4 Thus saith the LORD of hosts, the God of Israel, unto all that are carried away captives, whom I have caused to be carried away from Jerusalem unto Babylon; 5 Build ye houses, and dwell in them; and plant gardens, and eat the fruit of them; 6 Take ye wives, and beget sons and daughters; and take wives for your sons, and give your daughters to husbands, that they may bear sons and daughters; that ye may be increased there, and not diminished. 7 And seek the peace of the city whither I have caused you to be carried away captives, and pray unto the LORD for it: for in the peace thereof shall ye have peace. 8 For thus saith the LORD of hosts, the God of Israel; Let not your prophets and your diviners, that be in the midst of you, deceive you, neither hearken to your dreams which ye cause to be dreamed. 9 For they prophesy falsely unto you in my name: I have not sent them, saith the LORD. 10 For thus saith the LORD, That after seventy years be accomplished at Babylon I will visit you, and perform my good word toward you, in causing you to return to this place. 11 For I know the thoughts that I think toward you, saith the LORD, thoughts of peace, and not of evil, to give you an expected end. 12 Then shall ye call upon me, and ye shall go and pray unto me, and I will hearken unto you. 13 And ye shall seek me, and find me, when ye shall search for me with all your heart. 14 And I will be found of you, saith the LORD: and I will turn away your captivity, and I will gather you from all the nations, and from all the places whither I have driven you, saith the LORD; and I will bring you again into the place whence I caused you to be carried away captive.67

(Jeremiah 29:4-14, KJV)

The Lord promised to those who were dispersed throughout the world in the future: 18 Thus saith the LORD; Behold, I will bring again the captivity of Jacob's tents, and have mercy on his dwelling places; and the city shall be builded upon her own heap, and the palace shall remain after the manner thereof. 19 And out of them shall proceed thanksgiving and the voice of them that make merry: and I will multiply them, and they shall not be few; I will also glorify them, and they shall not be small. 20 Their children also shall be as aforetime, and their congregation shall be established before me, and I will punish all that oppress them. 21 And their nobles shall be of themselves, and their governor shall proceed from the midst of them;

---

66 The Holy Bible: King James Version. Oak Harbor: Logos Research Systems, Inc., 1995.

67 Ibid.

and I will cause him to draw near, and he shall approach unto me: for who is this that engaged his heart to approach unto me? saith the LORD. 22 And ye shall be my people, and I will be your God.68

(Jeremiah 30:18-22, KJV)

Ezekiel, the prophet, saw visions of Jerusalem's abominations: September 5, 592 BC

1 Then I looked, and, behold, in the firmament that was above the head of the cheru-bims there appeared over them as it were a sapphire stone, as the appearance of the likeness of a throne. 2 And he spake unto the man clothed with linen, and said, Go in between the wheels, even under the cherub, and fill thine hand with coals of fire from between the cherubims, and scatter them over the city. And he went in in my sight. 3 Now the cherubims stood on the right side of the house, when the man went in; and the cloud filled the inner court. 4 Then the glory of the LORD went up from the cherub, and stood over the threshold of the house; and the house was filled with the cloud, and the court was full of the brightness of the LORD'S glory. 5 And the sound of the cherubims' wings was heard even to the outer court, as the voice of the Almighty God when he speaketh. 6 And it came to pass, that when he had commanded the man clothed with linen, saying, Take fire from between the wheels, from between the cherubims; then he went in, and stood beside the wheels. 7 And one cherub stretched forth his hand from between the cherubims unto the fire that was between the cherubims, and took thereof, and put it into the hands of him that was clothed with linen: who took it, and went out.69

(Ezekiel 10:1-7, KJV)

22 Then did the cherubims lift up their wings, and the wheels beside them; and the glory of the God of Israel was over them above. 23 And the glory of the LORD went up from the midst of the city, and stood upon the mountain which is on the east side of the city.70

(Ezekiel 11:22-23, KJV)

Ezekiel also saw the destruction of Israel as well as the departure of the Shekinah glory of God's presence. He also saw the destruction of their leaders because of their rebellion against God and the pollution of His Sabbath. They would be judged by the sword. Jerusalem would be judged because of the sins of the people and its leaders (ref. Ezekiel 22:1-31).

January 10, 589-587 BC
The city of Jerusalem was besieged by King Nebuchadnezzar of Babylon during the reign of King Zedekiah of Judah.
January 15, 588 — 833 captives were taken from Jerusalem. Ezekiel prophesied against sur-rounding nations, including Tyre and Egypt, which were later conquered by Babylon.

---

[68] Ibid.

[69] Ibid.

[70] Ibid.

Jeremiah was imprisoned in a dungeon 587 BC and later King Zedekiah set him loose to dwell in the court of the prison, so he was given food to eat until there was none.

In 586 BC, by an act of faith, Jeremiah purchased a field as a sign to the people that they would return to Judah and have their own lands to own and live in (ref. Jeremiah 32:6-45).

Jeremiah dwelt in the court of the prison until the fall of Jerusalem on July 9, 586 BC. King Zedekiah fled, but he was captured by the Babylonians. His sons were slain, then his eyes were put out and he was deported to Babylon.

August 7-10 586 BC, the temple and great houses and the walls of the city were destroyed by fire. Jerusalem was plundered for the fifth time by Nebuchadnezzar. Only the poor were left behind to tend the fields (ref. 2 Kings 25:8-10; 2 Chronicles 10:19).

> *12 Now in the fifth month, in the tenth day of the month, which was the nineteenth year of Nebuchadnezzar king of Babylon, came Nebuzaradan, captain of the guard, which served the king of Babylon, into Jerusalem, 13 And burned the house of the LORD, and the king's house; and all the houses of Jerusalem, and all the houses of the great men, burned he with fire: 14 And all the army of the Chaldeans, that were with the captain of the guard, brake down all the walls of Jerusalem round about.71*
>
> (Jeremiah 52:12-14, KJV)

The temple furnishings and treasures were taken to Babylon.

> *13 And the pillars of brass that were in the house of the LORD, and the bases, and the brasen sea that was in the house of the LORD, did the Chaldees break in pieces, and carried the brass of them to Babylon. 14 And the pots, and the shovels, and the snuffers, and the spoons, and all the vessels of brass wherewith they ministered, took they away. 15 And the firepans, and the bowls, and such things as were of gold, in gold, and of silver, in silver, the captain of the guard took away. 16 The two pillars, one sea, and the bases which Solomon had made for the house of the LORD; the brass of all these vessels was without weight. 17 The height of the one pillar was eighteen cubits, and the chapiter upon it was brass: and the height of the chapiter three cubits; and the wreathen work, and pomegranates upon the chapiter round about, all of brass: and like unto these had the second pillar with wreathen work.72*
>
> (2 Kings 25:13-17, KJV)

In the sixth deportation, the priests were captured and taken. Jeremiah was left behind and lamented the fate of Jerusalem. 586 BC He took care of the poor people who were left behind (ref. Lamentation 1-5; Jeremiah 40:6-12).

The captivity was from 586-516 BC. During this time, there was no temple. At this time, Gedaliah became governor of Judah. Then in October 586 BC he was assassinated by Ismael.

Ismael then tried to take the people in Judah to the land of the Ammonites, and some to Egypt. Jeremiah prophesied the destruction of those Jews who dwelled in Egypt. Anmon, Moab, Philishia, Zedon and Tyre......all these nations later fell to Nebuchadnezzar's invasions.

---

[71] Ibid.

[72] Ibid.

4. Ezekiel's vision — Israel to be restored to their land.

Ezekiel has a vision that the valley of dry bones which is Israel will be restored to life in their land. He also sees the future temple of God and all its glory.

The fall of Babylon was prophesied:

> *11 And this whole land shall be a desolation, and an astonishment; and these nations shall serve the king of Babylon seventy years. 12 And it shall come to pass, when seventy years are accomplished, that I will punish the king of Babylon, and that nation, saith the LORD, for their iniquity, and the land of the Chaldeans, and will make it perpetual desolations. 13 And I will bring upon that land all my words which I have pronounced against it, even all that is written in this book, which Jeremiah hath prophesied against all the nations. 14 For many nations and great kings shall serve themselves of them also: and I will recompense them according to their deeds, and according to the works of their own hands.73*

(Jeremiah 25:11-14, KJV)

5. Babylon falls (ref. Jeremiah 50, 51).

Then Babylon fell when Belshazzar was king and had a wild party using the golden vessels taken out of the temple of God which was in Jerusalem. The king, his princes, wives and concubines drank from them celebrating the gods of gold, silver, brass, iron, wood and stone.

> *5 In the same hour came forth fingers of a man's hand, and wrote over against the candlestick upon the plaister of the wall of the king's palace: and the king saw the part of the hand that wrote. 6 Then the king's countenance was changed, and his thoughts troubled him, so that the joints of his loins were loosed, and his knees smote one against another. 7 The king cried aloud to bring in the astrologers, the Chaldeans, and the soothsayers. And the king spake, and said to the wise men of Babylon, Whosoever shall read this writing, and shew me the interpretation thereof, shall be clothed with scarlet, and have a chain of gold about his neck, and shall be the third ruler in the kingdom. 8 Then came in all the king's wise men: but they could not read the writing, nor make known to the king the interpretation thereof. 9 Then was king Belshazzar greatly troubled, and his countenance was changed in him, and his lords were astonied. 10 Now the queen, by reason of the words of the king and his lords, came into the banquet house: and the queen spake and said, O king, live for ever: let not thy thoughts trouble thee, nor let thy countenance be changed: 11 There is a man in thy kingdom, in whom is the spirit of the holy gods; and in the days of thy father light and understanding and wisdom, like the wisdom of the gods, was found in him; whom the king Nebuchadnezzar thy father, the king, I say, thy father, made master of the magicians, astrologers, Chaldeans, and soothsayers; 12 Forasmuch as an excellent spirit, and knowledge, and understanding, interpreting of dreams, and shewing of hard sentences, and dissolving of*

---

73 Ibid.

doubts, were found in the same Daniel, whom the king named Belteshazzar: now let Daniel be called, and he will shew the interpretation. 13 Then was Daniel brought in before the king. And the king spake and said unto Daniel, Art thou that Daniel, which art of the children of the captivity of Judah, whom the king my father brought out of Jewry? 14 I have even heard of thee, that the spirit of the gods is in thee, and that light and understanding and excellent wisdom is found in thee. 15 And now the wise men, the astrologers, have been brought in before me, that they should read this writing, and make known unto me the interpretation thereof: but they could not shew the interpretation of the thing: 16 And I have heard of thee, that thou canst make interpretations, and dissolve doubts: now if thou canst read the writing, and make known to me the interpretation thereof, thou shalt be clothed with scarlet, and have a chain of gold about thy neck, and shalt be the third ruler in the kingdom. 17 Then Daniel answered and said before the king, Let thy gifts be to thyself, and give thy rewards to another; yet I will read the writing unto the king, and make known to him the interpretation. 18 O thou king, the most high God gave Nebuchadnezzar thy father a kingdom, and majesty, and glory, and honour: 19 And for the majesty that he gave him, all people, nations, and languages, trembled and feared before him: whom he would he slew; and whom he would he kept alive; and whom he would he set up; and whom he would he put down. 20 But when his heart was lifted up, and his mind hardened in pride, he was deposed from his kingly throne, and they took his glory from him: 21 And he was driven from the sons of men; and his heart was made like the beasts, and his dwelling was with the wild asses: they fed him with grass like oxen, and his body was wet with the dew of heaven; till he knew that the most high God ruled in the kingdom of men, and that he appointeth over it whomsoever he will. 22 And thou his son, O Belshazzar, hast not humbled thine heart, though thou knewest all this; 23 But hast lifted up thyself against the Lord of heaven; and they have brought the vessels of his house before thee, and thou, and thy lords, thy wives, and thy concubines, have drunk wine in them; and thou hast praised the gods of silver, and gold, of brass, iron, wood, and stone, which see not, nor hear, nor know: and the God in whose hand thy breath is, and whose are all thy ways, hast thou not glorified: 24 Then was the part of the hand sent from him; and this writing was written. 25 And this is the writing that was written, MENE, MENE, TEKEL, UPHARSIN. 26 This is the interpretation of the thing: MENE; God hath numbered thy kingdom, and finished it. 27 TEKEL; Thou art weighed in the balances, and art found wanting. 28 PERES; Thy kingdom is divided, and given to the Medes and Persians. 29 Then commanded Belshazzar, and they clothed Daniel with scarlet, and put a chain of gold about his neck, and made a proclamation concerning him, that he should be the third ruler in the kingdom.[74]

(Daniel 5:5-29, KJV)

That night Babylon fell to Darius the Mede and Cyrus who entered the city of Babylon on October 29, 539 BC by way of the river gate. The river had been diverted so that it was an easy

---

[74] The Holy Bible: King James Version. Oak Harbor: Logos Research Systems, Inc., 1995.

entrance into the city despite the fact that the city was otherwise impossible to enter. The city was surrounded by high and wide walls as well as a fortress.

CHAPTER SIX

Life in Babylon

A. Daniel

Daniel was a Jewish boy who was taken into exile in Babylon as a young teenager during the first deportation. When he became a man, the Lord used him in a mighty way. Daniel was one of the leaders of the Babylonia government under the leadership of various rulers. Among them were Nebuchadnezzar, Belteshazzar and Darius of the Medes. Daniel's influence was felt over Babylon for a period of over seventy years.

Daniel was beloved of the Lord. The Lord used Daniel to interpret visions of others and also have visions from God. One vision from the Lord in particular revealed the future of Israel and the Gentile world.

1. Seventy sevens — the seventy weeks of Daniel

> 24 *"Seventy 5weeks are determined*
> *For your people and for your holy city,*
> *To finish the transgression,*
> *6To make an end of sins,*
> *gTo make reconciliation for iniquity,*
> *hTo bring in everlasting righteousness,*
> *To seal up vision and prophecy,*
> *iAnd to anoint 7the Most Holy.*
> *25 "Know therefore and understand,*
> *That from the going forth of the command*
> *To restore and build Jerusalem*
> *Until jMessiah kthe Prince,*
> *There shall be seven weeks and sixty-two weeks;*
> *The 8street shall be built again, and the 9wall,*
> *Even in troublesome times.*

> 26 *"And after the sixty-two weeks*
> *lMessiah shall lbe cut off, mbut not for Himself;*
> *And nthe people of the prince who is to come*
> *oShall destroy the city and the sanctuary.*
> *The end of it shall be with a flood,*
> *And till the end of the war desolations are determined.*
> *27 Then he shall confirm pa 2covenant with qmany for one week;*
> *But in the middle of the week*
> *He shall bring an end to sacrifice and offering.*
> *And on the wing of abominations shall be one who makes desolate,*
> *rEven until the consummation, which is determined,*
> *Is poured out on the 3desolate"*75
> (Daniel 9:24-27)

"Seventy weeks" does not mean weeks of seven days any more than it means weeks of seven years or seven other periods of time. The Hebrew word for "seven" is shabua—which means "a unit of measure." It would be comparable to our word *dozen*. When it stands alone, it could be a dozen of anything—a dozen eggs, a dozen bananas. So here, Seventy Weeks means seventy sevens. It could be seventy sevens of anything. It could be units of days or months or years. In the context of this verse it is plain that Daniel has been reading in Jeremiah about *years*, seventy years. Jeremiah had been preaching and writing that the captivity would be for seventy years. The seventy years of captivity were the specific penalty for violating seventy sabbatic years. That would be seventy sevens, a total of 490 years. In those 490 years, Israel had violated exactly seventy sabbatic years; so they would go into captivity for seventy years. "to fulfill the word of the LORD by the mouth of Jeremiah, until the land had enjoyed her Sabbaths: for as long as she lay desolate she kept Sabbath, to fulfill three-score and ten years" (2 Chron. 36:21).

One week = Seven years
Seventy weeks = Four hundred ninety years
Seventy weeks divided into three periods:
Seven weeks—Sixty-two weeks—One week

Now Daniel was puzzled as to how the end of the seventy years of captivity would fit into the long period of Gentile world dominion which the visions in chapters 7 and 8 had so clearly indicated. He obviously thought that at the end of the seventy years his people would be returned to the land, the promised Messiah would come, and the kingdom which had been promised to David would be established. How could both be true? It appeared to him, I am sure, to be an irreconcilable situation created by these seemingly contradictory prophecies.

The Seventy Weeks, or the seventy sevens, answer two questions. Israel's kingdom will not come immediately. The seventy sevens must run their course. These seventy sevens fit into the Times of the Gentiles and run concurrently with them. They are broken up to fit into gentile times. The word for *determined* literally means "cutting off." These seventy sevens are to be cut off, as the following verses will indicate. The seventy sevens for Israel and the Times of the Gentiles will

---

75 <u>The Holy Bible: The New King James Version</u>. Nashville: Thomas Nelson, 1996, c1982. (Da. 9:24-27).

both come to an end at the same time, that is, at the second coming of Christ. This is important to know in the correct understanding of the prophecy.76

The Seventy Weeks concern "thy people," meaning the people of Daniel. That would be Israel. And they concern "thy holy city," which can be none other that Jerusalem. Six things are to be accomplished in those Seventy Weeks or 490 years. We will see as we progress in our study that sixty-nine of the "weeks" have already passed, and one "week" is yet to be fulfilled.

Here are the six things to be accomplished:

1. "To finish the transgression." This refers to the transgression of Israel. The cross provided the redemption for sin—for the sin of the nation, but not all accepted it. Today the word has gone out to the ends of the earth that there is a redemption for mankind. But in the last "week" we are told that God says, "And I will pour upon the house of David, and upon the inhabitants of Jerusalem, the spirit of grace and of supplications......" (Zech. 12:10). And in Zechariah 13:1 "In that day there shall be a fountain opened to the house of David and to the inhabitants of Jerusalem for sin and for uncleanness." That has not been opened yet. All you have to do is to look at the land of Israel and you will know this has not been fulfilled.

2. "To make an end of sins." The national sins of Israel will come to an end at the second coming of Christ. They are just like any other people or any other nation. They are sinners as individuals and as a nation. They have made many mistakes as a nation (so have we), but God will make an end to that.

3. "To make reconciliation for iniquity." During this period of Seventy Weeks, God has provided a redemption through the death and Resurrection of Christ. This, of course, is for Jew and Gentile alike.

4. "And to bring in everlasting righteousness" refers to the return of Christ at the end of the 490 years to establish the kingdoms.

5. "To seal up the vision and prophecy" means that all will be fulfilled, which will vindicate this prophecy as well as all other prophecies in Scripture.

6. "To anoint the most Holy" has reference to the anointment of the holy of holies in the millennial Temple about which Ezekiel spoke (Ezek. 41-46).

Know therefore and understand, that from the going forth of the commandment to (445 BC) restore and to build Jerusalem unto the Messiah the Prince shall be seven weeks, (49 years) and threescore and two weeks: (plus 434 years) the street shall be built again, and the wall, even in troublous times. And after threescore and two weeks shall Messiah be cut off (crucified), but not for himself: and the people of the prince that shall destroy the city and the sanctuary; and the end thereof shall be with a flood, and unto the end of the ware desolations are determined.

And he shall confirm the covenant with many for one week: and in the midst of the week he shall cause the sacrifice and the oblation to cease, and for the over-spreading of abominations he shall make it desolate, even until the consummation, and that determined shall be poured upon the desolate.

(Dan. 9:25—27)77

---

76 McGee, J. Vernon. Thru the Bible. Vol. III (Prov. — Mal.). Pasadena: Thru the Bible Radio, 1981. Pages 586-587.

77 Ibid. Pages 587-588.

The starting point for this period of 490 years is essential to the correct understanding of the prophecy. Since this period is projected into the Times of the Gentiles, it must fit into ecular history and originate from some date connected with the Times of the Gentiles. Of course there have been many suggestions for a starting point: the decree of Cyrus (see Ezra 1:1-4); the decree of Darius (see Ezra 6:1-12); the decree of Artaxerxes (at the seventh year of his reign—Ezra 7:11-26); but I feel that the decree of Artaxerxes in the twentieth year of his reign (Neh. 2:1-8) meets the requirements of verse 25. The commandment to rebuild the city of Jerusalem was issued in the month Nisan 445 BC. That, then will be our starting point.

The first seven weeks of forty-nine years bring us to 397 BC and to Malachi and the end of the Old Testament. These were "troublous times," as witnessed to by both Nehemiah and Malachi.

Sixty-two weeks, or 434 years, bring us to the Messiah. Sir Robert Anderson in his book, *The Coming Prince*, has worked out the time schedule. From the first of the month Nisan to the tenth of Nisan (April 6) AD 32, are 173,880 days. Dividing them according to the Jewish year of 360 days, he arrives at 483 years (69 sevens). On this day Jesus rode into Jerusalem, offering himself for the first time, publicly and officially, as the Messiah.

After 69 weeks, or 483 years, there is a time break. Between the sixty-ninth and Seventieth Week two events of utmost importance are to take place:

1. Messiah will be cut off. This was the crucifixion of Christ, the great mystery and truth of the gospel: "From that time forth began Jesus to shew unto his disciples, how that he must go unto Jerusalem, and suffer many things of the elders and chief priests and scribes, and be killed, and be raised again the third day" (Matt. 16:21). "That whosoever believeth in him should not perish, but have eternal life" (John 3:15).
2. Destruction of Jerusalem, which took place in AD 70, when Titus the Roman was the instrument.

The final "week" (the seventieth), a period of seven years, is projected into the future and does not follow chronologically the other sixty-nine. The time gap between the sixty-ninth and seventieth weeks is the age of grace—unknown to the prophets (Eph. 3:1-12; 1 Pet. 1:10-12). The Seventieth Week is eschatological; it is the final period and is yet unfulfilled.

"The prince" is a Roman; he is the "little horn" of Daniel 7; he is "the beast" of Revelation 13. After the church is removed from the earth, he will make a covenant with Israel. Israel will accept him as her Messiah, but in the midst of the "week" he will break his covenant by placing an image in the Temple (Rev. 13). This is the abomination of desolation. What Israel thought to be the Millennium will turn out to be the Great Tribulation (Matt. 24:15-26). Only the coming of Christ can end this frightful period (Matt. 24:27-31).[78]

B. Cyrus of Persia

1. Edict to rebuild the temple in Jerusalem

Cyrus (*the sun*) was the founder of the Persian Empire. He was the son of Cambyses, a Persian of the royal family of the Achaemenedae. When he grew up to manhood, his courage and genius

---

[78] Ibid. Pages 588-589.

placed him at the head of the Persians. His conquests were numerous. He defeated and captured the Median king BC 559. Babylon fell before his army and ancient dominions of Assyria were added to his empire BC 538. The prophet Daniel lived in the court of the king. The edict of Cyrus to rebuild the temple can be found in 2 Chronicles 36: 22-23; Ezra 1:1-4; 3:7; 4:3; 5:13, 17; 6:3.

> *28 That saith of Cyrus, He is my shepherd, and shall perform all my pleasure: even saying to Jerusalem, Thou shalt be built; and to the Temple, Thy foundation shall be laid.79*
>
> (Isaiah 44:28, KJV)

Prophecy concerning Cyrus was given two hundred years before his birth. He is designated as "my shepherd." This is the only instance where a pagan potentate is given such a title. He was identified to be a man of responsibility who would return the nations of Israel to her Lord.

> *1 Thus saith the LORD to his anointed, to Cyrus, whose right hand I have holden, to subdue nations before him; and I will loose the loins of kings, to open before him the two leaved gates; and the gates shall not be shut.80*
>
> (Isaiah 45:1, KJV)

He carried out the will of God and delivered the Israelites from captivity and permitted them to return to the land of promise. He also encouraged the Israelites who did not return to send gifts of gold, silver and precious things with those who did go back to be used in the temple worship.

In this respect Cyrus was a Gentile messiah of Israel and a vague foreshadowing of the One to come. He also opened the gates of Babylon that shut Israel from returning to Palestine. They were free to return to their homeland.

> *3 And I will give thee the treasures of darkness, and hidden riches of secret places, that thou mayest know that I, the LORD, which call thee by thy name, am the God of Israel. 4 For Jacob my servant's sake, and Israel mine elect, I have even called thee by thy name: I have surnamed thee, though thou hast not known me. 5 I am the LORD, and there is none else, there is no God beside me: I girded thee, though thou hast not known me.81*
>
> (Isaiah 45:3-5, KJV)

The rich treasure which Babylon had taken from Jerusalem fell to Cyrus. God chose Cyrus because he knew the Lord. It is reasonable to conclude that Cyrus came to know the living and true God.

---

[79] The Holy Bible: King James Version. Oak Harbor: Logos Research Systems, Inc., 1995.

[80] Ibid.

[81] Ibid.

2 Thus saith Cyrus king of Persia, The LORD God of heaven hath given me all the kingdoms of the earth; and he hath charged me to build him an house at Jerusalem, which is in Judah.82

(Ezra 1:2, KJV)

God charged Cyrus to build him a house at Jerusalem which is in Judah (Ezra 5:13). The emphasis of the book of Ezra is upon the rebuilding of the temple. In the book of Nehemiah the emphasis is on the rebuilding of the walls of Jerusalem.

The book of Ezra is about seventy years after 2 Chronicles; the seventy years of captivity are over and the return to the land of Israel is signaled. The return to the land of Israel under Ezra took place about fifty years after the return of Zerubbabel. Nehemiah returned about fifteen years after Ezra.

Decree of Cyrus 536 BC:

1 Now in the first year of Cyrus king of Persia, that the word of the LORD by the mouth of Jeremiah might be fulfilled, the LORD stirred up the spirit of Cyrus king of Persia, that he made a proclamation throughout all his kingdom, and put it also in writing, saying, 2 Thus saith Cyrus king of Persia, The LORD God of heaven hath given me all the kingdoms of the earth; and he hath charged me to build him an house at Jerusalem, which is in Judah. 3 Who is there among you of all his people? his God be with him, and let him go up to Jerusalem, which is in Judah, and build the house of the LORD God of Israel, (he is the God,) which is in Jerusalem. 4 And whosoever remaineth in any place where he sojourneth, let the men of his place help him with silver, and with gold, and with goods, and with beasts, beside the freewill offering for the house of God that is in Jerusalem.83

(Ezra 1:1-4, KJV)

2. Edict to return to Judah and build the temple

a. The people are challenged to build the temple.

22 Now in the first year of Cyrus king of Persia, that the word of the LORD spoken by the mouth of Jeremiah might be accomplished, the LORD stirred up the spirit of Cyrus king of Persia, that he made a proclamation throughout all his kingdom, and put it also in writing, saying, 23 Thus saith Cyrus king of Persia, All the kingdoms of the earth hath the LORD God of heaven given me; and he hath charged me to build him an house in Jerusalem, which is in Judah. Who is there among you of all his people? The LORD his God be with him, and let him go up.84

(2 Chronicles 36:22-23, KJV)

---

[82] Ibid.

[83] Ibid.

[84] Ibid.

13 But in the first year of Cyrus the king of Babylon the same king Cyrus made a decree to build this house of God.85

(Ezra 5:13, KJV) 539 BC

b. Then the people respond to the challenge.

5 Then rose up the chief of the fathers of Judah and Benjamin, and the priests, and the Levites, with all them whose spirit God had raised, to go up to build the house of the LORD which is in Jerusalem. 6 And all they that were about them strengthened their hands with vessels of silver, with gold, with goods, and with beasts, and with precious things, beside all that was willingly offered.86

(Ezra 1:5-6, KJV)

Then Cyrus the king brought forth the vessels of the Lord which Nebuchadnezzar had taken from Jerusalem and gave them to Mitredath, the treasurer, and gave account of them to Sheshbazzar, the Prince of Judah. Cyrus said to take these vessels into the temple at Jerusalem which would be built; and he gave the dimensions of the building to be made— forty-five feet high, ninety feet wide, ninety feet long, which is about the same size as Solomon's temple. It was to be built on the same site as the previous temple, but it would not be as elaborate (ref. Ezra 5:14-16).

3 In the first year of Cyrus the king the same Cyrus the king made a decree concerning the house of God at Jerusalem, Let the house be builded, the place where they offered sacrifices, and let the foundations thereof be strongly laid; the height thereof threescore cubits, and the breadth thereof threescore cubits; 4 With three rows of great stones, and a row of new timber: and let the expenses be given out of the king's house: 5 And also let the golden and silver vessels of the house of God, which Nebuchadnezzar took forth out of the Temple which is at Jerusalem, and brought unto Babylon, be restored, and brought again unto the Temple which is at Jerusalem, every one to his place, and place them in the house of God.87

(Ezra 6:3-5, KJV)

In the spring 536 BC a remnant of the people returned, including Zerubbabel. There were a total of 49,897 people and priests and Levites who returned to Judah. Many of the people brought offerings for the temple. The altar was set up on October 1, 536 BC. The procedure for the offering of the burn offerings was written in the Law of Moses. The offerings were given morning and evening. They also kept the Feast of Tabernacles, offering for new moons and all the set feasts of the Lord.

Then they gave money to the masons and carpenters and food to those of Tyre and Zidon who brought cedar trees from Lebanon to the Sea of Joppa according to the grant that they had with Cyrus king of Persia.

---

[85] Ibid.

[86] Ibid.

[87] Ibid.

In May 535 BC the work of the foundation of the temple was laid. There was great celebration with praising and giving thanks to the Lord because He is good and His mercy endures forever. The people shouted and praised God because the foundation was laid. But, many of the priests and Levites and the ancient men who had seen Solomon's house wept after seeing the foundation of this house, while many other people shouted aloud for joy. There was so much noise from the shouts of joy and the noise of weeping of people it was impossible to discern what was going on from a distance (ref. Ezra 3:1-13).

> *1 How amiable are thy tabernacles, O LORD of hosts! 2 My soul longeth, yea, even fainteth for the courts of the LORD: my heart and my flesh crieth out for the living God. 4 Blessed are they that dwell in thy house: they will be still praising thee. Selah. 5 Blessed is the man whose strength is in thee; in whose heart are the ways of them.*88

(Psalm 84:1-2, 4-5, KJV)

> *10 For a day in thy courts is better than a thousand. I had rather be a doorkeeper in the house of my God, than to dwell in the tents of wickedness.*89

(Psalm 84:10, KJV)

> *1 O give thanks unto the LORD, for he is good: for his mercy endureth for ever. 2 Let the redeemed of the LORD say so, whom he hath redeemed from the hand of the enemy.*90

(Psalm 107:1-2, KJV)

> *1 Make a joyful noise unto God, all ye lands: 2 Sing forth the honour of his name: make his praise glorious. 3 Say unto God, How terrible art thou in thy works! through the greatness of thy power shall thine enemies submit themselves unto thee. 4 All the earth shall worship thee, and shall sing unto thee; they shall sing to thy name. Selah.*91

(Psalm 66:1-4, KJV)

3. The Samaritans cause trouble over the temple

Now when the enemies (Samaritans) of Judah and Benjamin heard they were building a temple unto the Lord God of Israel, they were angry. They approached Zerubbabel, and the chief of the fathers said, "We want to help since we serve your God and have given sacrifices to Him since the time when Esarhaddon, king of Assur brought them here." But the leaders of Israel said, "You are not to help build the house of our God. Only we are to build the temple as King Cyrus of Persia commanded us."

---

[88] The Holy Bible: King James Version. Oak Harbor: Logos Research Systems, Inc., 1995.

[89] Ibid.

[90] Ibid.

[91] Ibid.

Then the Samaritans caused trouble for them as they were building the temple. They hired counselors against them to frustrate their purpose all the days of Cyrus, king of Persia, even until the reign of Darius, king of Persia. Cyrus died at seventy years in 529 BC at the beginning of the reign of Ahasuerus. Rehum, the chancellor, and Shimshai, the scribe of the Samaritans, wrote a letter against Jerusalem saying, "Let it be know unto the king that the Jews are in Jerusalem, building that rebellious and bad city, and have set up the walls and joined the foundations. If this city is built, they will not pay toll and tribute, thus damaging the revenue of the king. If you search the records of your fathers, you will find that this city is a rebellious city and is hurtful unto kings; and they have rebelled in the past. For this reason, this city was destroyed. If this city is built again, and the walls set up, you shall have no control on this side of the river."

Then King Ashaueras sent answer to Rehum and Shimshai, the scribe. "I have made a search of the records. I give to you this commandment to cause the builders not to build the city until another commandment be given." Then the work of the house of God which was in Jerusalem stopped until the second year of the reign of Darius, king of Persia. The reign of Darius I was from 522-485 BC (ref. Ezra 4:6-24).

4. The prophets encourage the people to build the temple

September 1, 521 BC
Then the prophets Haggai and Zechariah, the son of Berekiah, the son of Iddo, prophesied to the Jews that were in Judah and Jerusalem, encouraging them to build their temple. They had been living in fancy houses while the temple lay at waste. Haggai said to Zerubbabel, the son of Shealtiel, governor of Judah, and to Joshua, the son of Jehozadak, the high priest, saying:

> *2 Thus speaketh the LORD of hosts, saying, This people say, The time is not come, the time that the LORD'S house should be built. 3 Then came the word of the LORD by Haggai the prophet, saying, 4 Is it time for you, O ye, to dwell in your cieled houses, and this house lie waste? 5 Now therefore thus saith the LORD of hosts; Consider your ways. 6 Ye have sown much, and bring in little; ye eat, but ye have not enough; ye drink, but ye are not filled with drink; ye clothe you, but there is none warm; and he that earneth wages earneth wages to put it into a bag with holes. 7 Thus saith the LORD of hosts; Consider your ways. 8 Go up to the mountain, and bring wood, and build the house; and I will take pleasure in it, and I will be glorified, saith the LORD. 9 Ye looked for much, and, lo, it came to little; and when ye brought it home, I did blow upon t. Why? saith the LORD of hosts. Because of mine house that is waste, and ye run every man unto his own house. 10 Therefore the heaven over you is stayed from dew, and the earth is stayed from her fruit.[92]*
>
> (Haggai 1:2-10, KJV)

September 24, 521 BC
Then Zerubbabel and Joshua, and all the remnant of the people obeyed the voice of the Lord their God and the words of Haggai as the Lord their God to build the house of the Lord because

---

[92] <u>The Holy Bible: King James Version</u>. Oak Harbor: Logos Research Systems, Inc., 1995.

they had a mind to work. They came and did the work in the house of the Lord of hosts, their God as He requested (ref. Haggai 1:1-10; Ezra 5:2; Haggai 1:11-15).

October 21, 521 BC

Haggai spoke to Zerubbabel and Joshua and the people and said, "Who of you saw this house in its first glory? Is this one now in comparison nothing? Be strong, people, for the Lord has promised He will fill this house with glory, as well as with silver and gold. 'The glory of this latter house shall be greater than the former,' saith the Lord of Hosts 'and in this place will I give peace saith the Lord of hosts'" (ref. Haggai 2:1-9).

November 521 BC.

Then Zechariah, the son of Berekiah, the son of Iddo, the prophet, said, "The Lord was very displeased with your ancestors. Don't be like them. When the prophets told them to turn from their evil ways, they did not obey" (ref. Zechariah 1:1-6).

5. The search for edict of Cyrus to build the temple

December 24, 521 BC

Haggai again encouraged the people, so work resumed on the temple with leadership of Zerubbabel. The foundation was laid and then the temple was finished. Even though there was opposition to their building the temple, the building progressed. Tatnai, Shethaiboznai and Aphaisochites sent a letter to Darius to see if the Jews had a right to build the temple. "Was there a decree made by Cyrus to build this house of God at Jerusalem? Please let us know concerning this matter" (ref. Ezra 6; Haggai 2:10-23; Ezra 5:3-17).

Then Darius, the king, made a search of the house records and found, at the palace of Achmetha in the province of Medes, a roll which was written; and Darius added to the decree.

> *6 Now therefore, Tatnai, governor beyond the river, Shetharboznai, and your companions the Apharsachites, which are beyond the river, be ye far from thence: 7 Let the work of this house of God alone; let the governor of the Jews and the elders of the Jews build this house of God in his place. 8 Moreover I take a decree what ye shall do to the elders of these Jews for the building of this house of God: that of the king's goods, even of the tribute beyond the river, forthwith expenses be given unto these men, that they be not hindered. 9 And that which they have need of, both young bullocks, and rams, and lambs, for the burnt offerings of the God of heaven, wheat, salt, wine, and oil, according to the appointment of the priests which are at Jerusalem, let it be given them day by day without fail: 10 That they may offer sacrifices of sweet savours unto the God of heaven, and pray for the life of the king, and of his sons. 11 Also I have made a decree, that whosoever shall alter this word, let timber be pulled down from his house, and being set up, let him be hanged thereon; and let his house be made a dunghill for this. 12 And the God that hath caused his name to dwell there destroy all kings and people that shall put to their*

hand to alter and to destroy this house of God which is at Jerusalem. I Darius have made a decree; let it be done with speed.93

(Ezra 6:6-12, KJV)

Then Tatnai, Shetharboznai and their companions did help with some of the supplies that would be needed for worship. So, the Jews built the temple and they prospered through the prophesying of Haggai and Zechariah. So they built and finished the temple according to the commandment of the God of Israel and according to the decrees of Cyrus and Darius and Artaxerxes, king of Persia (ref. Ezra 6:13-14).

6. The temple completed and dedicated

On March 3, 517 BC the temple was completed, which was the sixth year of the reign of Darius the king (ref. Ezra 6:15).

April 516 BC
The temple was dedicated by the children of Israel, the priests, Levites and the children of the captivity (ref. Ezra 6:16-18). It was a time of joy. It was at this time they set up the priests in their divisions and the Levites in their courses for their service to the Lord, as it was written in the book of Moses.

April 14-21, 516 BC
Passover was celebrated by all the Jews who separated themselves from the uncleanness of their heathen neighbors and practices (ref. Ezra 19-22).

C. Artaxerxes' decrees for Jews who return to Israel to take money and temple treasures for temple worship

Ezra 459 BC
Artaxerxes, king of Persia, gave to Ezra, the priest and scribe, a decree "that all of the people of Israel, priests and Levites in my realm which are so willing to go of their own free will to go to Jerusalem. I will give silver and gold to be taken with you to be offered unto the God of Israel whose home is in Jerusalem. Also freewill offering will be given for the Lord."

With the money received from the king of Persia and the Jews living in Persia, the purchase of animals such as cattle, rams, lambs for meat offerings and their drink offerings were provided for the Lord's temple service.

"The vessels will be given for the service of the house of God of Jerusalem. Whatever else you need, you can get out of the king's treasure. Also, the priests, Levites, singers, porters or ministers of this house shall not be taxed. You, Ezra, set up rulers and judges to rule the people, as well as those who know the Law of your God, and teach them to those who don't know God's Law. Whosoever doesn't do the Law of your God, you are to do speedy judgment; whether it be death, banishment, confiscation of goods or imprisonment. You decide" (ref. Ezra 7:1-28).

---

93 The Holy Bible: King James Version. Oak Harbor: Logos Research Systems, Inc., 1995.

1. Ezra chosen to lead in the journey to Israel

Ezra was quite thankful and praised God for finding favor with the king. Ezra prepared for the journey on April 1, 548 BC.

First Ezra searched among the Levites until he found a man of understanding who was of the sons of Mahli, the sons of Levi and Sherebiah. He and his sons and brethren made a total of thirty-eight priests who would serve in the priesthood. Also 220 Nethinims would work in the service of the priest (ref. Ezra 8:16-20).

2. Ezra prays for protection

April 9-11, 458 BC
Ezra proclaimed a fast when they approached the river of Ahava. There they prayed for protection of all the people, as well as the little ones, and for all their provisions and temple treasure they were taking with them. Ezra was afraid to request a band of soldiers and horsemen to protect them against the enemy on the way because he had told the king, "The hand of our God is upon all who seek Him; but His power and wrath is against all that forsake Him." So they fasted (ref. Ezra 8:21-30).

3. Temple treasures delivered. The people celebrate and repent for their sins.

The temple treasures were given to the Levites and priests to carry to Jerusalem to the house of God on April 12, 458 BC.

The journey began on August 1, 458 BC. The procession reached Jerusalem. There Ezra prepared his heart to seek the Law of the Lord and to teach Israel its statues and judgments.

On August 4, 458 BC, the treasury of the Lord's house was put into the hands of Meremoth, the son of Uriah, the priest, as well as Eleazar, Jozabad and Noadiah. They recorded all of the purchases and possessions received into the treasury.

Then the people celebrated by having burnt offerings unto the Lord, as well as sin offerings. Ezra prayed and confessed the sins of the people and he wept. Many of the people also wept for their sins.

Ezra's next reform was to condemn marriages to the heathen and their children. Those who repented and left their heathen mates were restored to fellowship with God. Ezra emphasized that they should only be married to their own people and not marry outside these people because the heathen would cause them to worship foreign gods, the very thing that caused God to put His people into captivity (ref. Ezra 7:6-10; Ezra 9:5; 10:1-44).

After the temple was built and the homes of those who lived in or near Jerusalem were completed (twenty years later), a protective wall was built around Jerusalem.

D. Decrees of Artaxerxes to build the walls of Jerusalem

December 445 BC

1. Nehemiah concerned for Jerusalem

Nehemiah was in Shusham, the palace, and he heard from Hanani with other men from Judah that the remnant that was left in Jerusalem was in great affliction and reproach because the wall of Jerusalem was broken down and the gates had been burnt with fire.

2. Nehemiah commissioned to build the walls for Jerusalem

After Nehemiah heard these things, he was very burdened, so he wept and mourned many days. He also fasted and prayed to God for wisdom.

> *Then I said, "O LORD, God of heaven, the great and awesome God who keeps his covenant of unfailing love with those who love him and obey his commands, 6 listen to my prayer! Look down and see me praying night and day for your people Israel. I confess that we have sinned against you. Yes, even my own family and I have sinned! 7 We have sinned terribly by not obeying the commands, laws, and regulations that you gave us through your servant Moses. 8 "Please remember what you told your servant Moses: 'If you sin, I will scatter you among the nations. 9 But if you return to me and obey my commands, even if you are exiled to the ends of the earth, I will bring you back to the place I have chosen for my name to be honored.' 10 "We are your servants, the people you rescued by your great power and might. 11 O Lord, please hear my prayer! Listen to the prayers of those of us who delight in honoring you. Please grant me success now as I go to ask the king for a great favor. Put it into his heart to be kind to me." In those days I was the king's cup-bearer.94*
>
> (Nehemiah 1:5-11, NLT)

In April of 445 BC Nehemiah was sad when he went to serve before the king, which was not his custom. The king asked, "Why are you sad?"

Nehemiah told him the condition of Jerusalem, "The city of my ancestors lies in waste and the gates have been burnt with fire."

So the king asked, "What would you like to do?"

Nehemiah made a silent prayer to God. Then he said to the king, "If it pleases the king please send me to Judah to rebuild the city walls where my ancestors are buried."

The king asked him, "How long will you be gone and when will you return?" Nehemiah told him and the king agreed to his request. Then Nehemiah was appointed governor of Judah.

Nehemiah asked the king to send a letter to Asaph, the keeper of the King's forest, requesting lumber to be used to make beams for gates. Nehemiah also requested letters to the governors beyond the Euphrates River, to allow for safe passage until he arrived in Judah. The king agreed. The king also sent captains of the army and horsemen for protection (ref. Nehemiah 2:3-9; 5:14).

---

[94] Holy Bible: New Living Translation. Wheaton: Tyndale House, 1997.

1 And it came to pass in the month Nisan, in the twentieth year of Artaxerxes the king, that wine was before him: and I took up the wine, and gave it unto the king. Now I had not been beforetime sad in his presence. 2 Wherefore the king said unto me, Why is thy countenance sad, seeing thou art not sick? this is nothing else but sorrow of heart. Then I was very sore afraid, 3 And said unto the king, Let the king live for ever: why should not my countenance be sad, when the city, the place of my fathers' sepulchres, lieth waste, and the gates thereof are consumed with fire? 4 Then the king said unto me, For what dost thou make request? So I prayed to the God of heaven. 5 And I said unto the king, If it please the king, and if thy servant have found favour in thy sight, that thou wouldest send me unto Judah, unto the city of my fathers' sepulchres, that I may build it. 6 And the king said unto me, (the queen also sitting by him,) For how long shall thy journey be? and when wilt thou return? So it pleased the king to send me; and I set him a time. 7 Moreover I said unto the king, If it please the king, let letters be given me to the governors beyond the river, that they may convey me over till I come into Judah; 8 And a letter unto Asaph the keeper of the king's forest, that he may give me timber to make beams for the gates of the palace which appertained to the house, and for the wall of the city, and for the house that I shall enter into. And the king granted me, according to the good hand of my God upon me. 9 Then I came to the governors beyond the river, and gave them the king's letters. Now the king had sent captains of the army and horsemen with me.95

(Nehemiah 2:1-9, KJV)

14 Moreover from the time that I was appointed to be their governor in the land of Judah, from the twentieth year even unto the two and thirtieth year of Artaxerxes the king, that is, twelve years, I and my brethren have not eaten the bread of the governor.96

(Nehemiah 5:14, KJV)

This decree of Artaxerxes was 445 BC — the twenty years of his reign—when the seventy weeks of Daniel began.

August 1-3, 444 BC

They proceeded on their journey. When they arrived, Sanballot the Horonite and Tobiah the servant of the Amorites heard it. They were not pleased that anyone should seek the welfare of the people of Israel.

After Nehemiah had been in Jerusalem three days, he inspected the ruins at night alone. He told no one what he was doing.

---

[95] The Holy Bible: King James Version. Oak Harbor: Logos Research Systems, Inc., 1995.
[96] Ibid.

3. Nehemiah encourages the Jews to build the wall

August 4, 444 BC

The next day Nehemiah talked to the people and encouraged them saying, "Jerusalem is a waste and the gates are burnt. Come; let us build up the wall of Jerusalem so we will no longer be a disgrace." The people agreed and they were ready to build. Sanballot and Tobiah came by and mocked them. But the people continued to build the wall. Various sections were built by different families; some were priestly families as well as the common people (ref. Nehemiah 2:11-18).

4. The enemies try to stop the building

After a period of time, Sanballot and Tobiah came by with their brethren and the army of Samaria and saw the work in progress. Sanballot stated, "Will these feeble Jews fortify themselves and revive the stones out of the heaps of rubbish which was burned? Even if they do build, if a fox goes across, it will break down the wall" (ref. Nehemiah 2:19-20).

5. The Jews persevere and the wall is completed

Now the people prayed to God: "Even though we are despised, may You judge them by putting them in captivity." So the people continued to build. Each section joined the next as the various builders worked to join their work to the next person's. The people had a mind to work.

After a period of time, Sanballot and Tobiah and their people heard that the walls were going up and the gaps in the walls were being closed; they were furious. They conspired to come together and fight against Jerusalem and hinder the construction of the wall.

The Jews prayed and were watchful day and night for their enemies. The people became discouraged. Nehemiah encouraged them with the promise that God would protect them from their enemies. From that time, half of the people worked while the other half held weapons. They agreed that when they heard the sound of the trumpet, the people would all go to that part of the wall to fight. The people also agreed to stay in Jerusalem to protect the city instead of going home (ref. Neh. 2:19-20; 3:1-32; 4:1-23; 5:1-19; 6:1-14).

The wall was completed, despite Tobiah's interference on September 25, 444 BC. It took fifty-two days. When the Jews' enemies heard that the wall was finished, they were downcast and they perceived that this work was by the power of God.

After the wall was built, the doors were installed. Porters opened them when the sun was hot and shut them when it was dusk. They were also left closed on the Sabbath day.

6. Various families were encouraged to live in and around Jerusalem

The city was large and there were a small amount of people in it, so Nehemiah encouraged many families of the Levites, and others, to live in Jerusalem and other nearby towns (ref. Nehemiah 6:15-19; 2:17-7:73; 11:1-36; 1 Chronicles 9:2-34).

7. Ezra reads the Law of Moses and the people repent

After the wall was built, on October 1, 444 BC the people gathered before the water gate in Jerusalem. There Ezra read the Law of Moses to the people. The people were very attentive to what God said in His law. The people understood. They wept and repented when they saw their sins. Ezra and Nehemiah told the people to rejoice and feast and share of their meals with those in need. "Remember, the joy of the Lord is your strength."

8. The dedication of the wall and celebration of the Feast of Tabernacles

October 2, 444 BC

It was found in the Law of Moses that the children of Israel should dwell in booths on the seventh month. It was published in all their cities as well as Jerusalem. "Go to the mount and fetch branches to make booths to dwell in" (ref. Nehemiah 8:9-15). So from October 15 — 21 444 BC, the people built booths upon the roofs of their houses and in their courtyards, as well as the courtyard of God's house, and dwelt there for a week. This was known as the Feast of Tabernacles. During the feast, Nehemiah read the book of the Law. On the eighth day there was a solemn assembly (ref. Nehemiah 8:16-18).

On October 24 the people assembled with fasting and wearing sack cloth. So the people of Israel separated themselves from all strangers and stood and confessed their sins and the iniquities of their fathers. They also stood and read the law and worshipped God.

The wall was dedicated with the priest, singers, Levites and the people purified and ready with much celebration (ref. Nehemiah 9:1-37).

9. Nehemiah returns and cleans the temple

433 BC

Nehemiah returned to Babylon during the thirty-second year of Artaxeres', king of Babylon's, reign. Then he returned to Jerusalem in 432 BC.

There he found that Tobiah had a chamber in the courts of the house of God. This made Nehemiah angry, so he threw out Tobiah and his baggage and then the temple was purified.

There were other reforms. Tithing and worship were reestablished, Sabbath keeping was reinstituted and the priesthood was cleansed (ref. Nehemiah 13:10-31).

PART II

INTER-TESTAMENT PERIOD

CHAPTER SEVEN

The Maccabean Revolt

A. Antiochus Epiphanies desires to Hellenize the world — Judaism outlawed

In 204 BC, the last strong Ptolemy ruler and their rivals, the Seleucid kings, began to control Palestine. The Seleucid line of conquerors was one of the four Greek generals who carved up Alexander the Great's enormous empire after his mysterious death in 323 BC. It was Antiochus the Great that took Palestine from a weak king in Egypt. His son, Antiochus Epiphanies I (whose name means *God manifested*) (the little horn of Daniel 8) wanted to make a great empire for himself. His goal was to Hellenize the world and make the Greek culture the way of life for all people. In Palestine he replaced spiritual priests with heathen ones. He outlawed Judaism and such practices as circumcision, Sabbath keeping and the eating of kosher food, as well as following the laws of Moses. He desecrated the temple by offering an unclean animal (pig) on the altar of God. He sprinkled all implements in the temple with the broth of a sow, completely defiling the sanctuary. He also abolished the worship of Y'hweh. He set up pagan worship with its sacrilege and immorality. He stole all of the temple treasure and took them to Greece.

In 168 BC, Antiochus Epiphanies forced the Jews to sacrifice on heathen altars to heathen gods (Daniel 11:21-35, KJV). He is a symbol and forerunner of the Antichrist that the angel Gabriel had described to the prophet Daniel concerning the abomination of a king who would put a stop to the sacrifices and desecrate the sanctuary. The deeds of this ruler provided a backdrop for Yeshua's description of another king yet to come, who would enter the temple, call himself god and defile the sanctuary in the last days (ref. Daniel 8:9-27).

B. The family of Maccabeus revolts

The Jews prepared to oppose the decrees of this king. Matthias, an aged priest, objected out of his supreme concern for the Jewish people who risked losing all the knowledge of the one true God. He was raised in a family of warriors from the priestly line of Aaron; he killed a few Syrian officers. His son, Judas Maccabeus, became the Jews' military leader (ref. Daniel 11:32-36). Many battles were fought by the Maccabees.

Thousands of Jews were killed in the conflict between them and the Greeks. Among those killed was Judas Maccabeus. His two brothers, Jonathan and Simon, led the fight to bring political independence and religious freedom back to the Jews. Israel began to make alliances with Rome at this time to help guarantee its independence.

C. Defiled temple cleansed and dedicated

Once Judas and his brethren and an army realized that the enemies had retreated, they decided to go up and cleanse and dedicate the sanctuary of the temple. They went up Mount Zion. There they saw that the sanctuary was desecrated, the altar profaned, the gates burned up, and shrubs were growing in the courtyard. They rent their clothes and wept.

Priests, who were pure and loved God's Law, cleaned the sanctuary and took the defiled stones of the altar and building into an unclean place. They took new whole stones according to the law and built a new altar and cleaned the sanctuary and courts. They made new holy vessels and brought the candlestick, the altar, burnt offerings, incense and the table. And upon the altar they burned incense, and the lamps that were upon the candlestick were lit to give light in the temple. Loaves of bread were set upon the table. A new veil was installed in the holy place. They finished all the work which they had begun.

Then on December 25, 164 BC, the priests relit the lights that were on the menorah and offered incense upon the altar. The priests then rose up and offered sacrifices, according to the law, upon the new altar of burnt offering which they had made. They dedicated the sanctuary with songs, cithems, harps and cymbals. Then all the people fell on their faces and worshipped and praised God. The God of heaven had given them good success, so they kept the dedication of the altar eight days and offered burnt offerings with gladness. Moreover, Judas and his brethren, with the whole congregation of Israel, ordained that the days of dedication of the altar should be kept in their season from year to year for eight days, starting with the twenty-fifth day of December (also known as the twenty-fifth day of Kislev). This is also known as the feast of Hanukkah or the Festival of Lights. It signifies the cleansing and lighting of the holy place.[97]

As a result of the Maccabees' victory, for the first time in 400 years, Israel became a semi-independent state free to worship the God of Israel as the Bible instructed.

Later John Hyrcanus, Matitiyahu's (Mattathias) grandson became ruler of Israel with Hellenistic leanings (of loving the Greek life style), the very thing his grandfather and family had fought so hard to vanish. He was both priest and king.

During his reign the two parties of Pharisees and the Sadducees came into their own. The Pharisees were legalistic and their God was form, ritual, and tradition which the Sadducees who originally believed the Word back slid into the pagan-influenced Greek way of life.

John Hyrcanus extended his reign eastward past the Dead Sea. He demanded the Edomites convert to Judaism and forced their sons to be circumcised. A century later, an Edomite convert by the name of Herod became King of the Jews. After Herod the Great became king, he beheaded the last of the high priests descending from the original Maccabees. It was this Herod who slayed all the babies under two in Bethlehem when Yeshua was born.

[98]Yeshua also celebrated this feast during His ministry (ref. John 10:22).

---

[97] The Apocrypha, The King James Version. Edited by Manuel Komroff. New York: Tudor Publishing Company, 1937.

[98] Sorko-kam, Shera. "A Hanukkah Story." 1937. Israel Report. Dec. 2007. Page 3.

It was later in the Talmud that the story about the oil miraculously lasting eight days until fresh oil could be consecrated became a legend and is repeated every year until this day.99,100

[99] The Apocrypha, The King James Version. Edited by Manuel Komroff. New York: Tudor Publishing Company, 1937.

[100] Sorko-kam, Shera. "A Hanukkah Story." Page 4.

CHAPTER EIGHT

Herod's Temple

A. Herod's temple is larger than Solomon's

When Herod had begun his grand project, the priesthood, suspicious that this cosmopolitan king intended to destroy the Temple and build no replacement—or worse, erect some profanation in its place—had resisted his plans. To prove that his intentions were honorable, Herod hired 10,000 laborers and ordered 1,000 wagons built for hauling stone. Moreover, to allay their fears that the most sacred areas of the new Temple might be profaned by non-priestly hands, he had 1,000 priests trained as masons and carpenters. (About 80 years later, during the reign of Nero in Rome, some of the work that these inexpert craftsmen had done was to collapse and need replacement.)

We have some idea of the glories of Herod's Temple, however, principally from Josephus, who, as a young man, lived among the priests in Jerusalem before the Temple was destroyed.[101]

Outdoing Solomon

From the writings of Josephus we learn that Herod wanted to rival the opulence and size of Solomon's Temple, and that he assumed it to have been twice as high as the existing Second Temple. And we know that, in order to accommodate the huge Court of the Gentiles around the Temple, he, in effect, enlarged the Temple Mount by building supporting structures into the deep valleys that border it. The entire complex—bounded by a wall that has been estimated at 840 feet long on the south, 945 feet long on the north, 1,410 fee long on the east, and 1,455 feet long on the west—covered almost 30 acres. The vast undertaking was not completed in Herod's lifetime (nor, indeed, for many decades after his death), but the Temple structure itself had been built in about a year and a half, faithful to the traditional Solomonic design in the arrangement of its rooms.

The walls and the double doors of the two-story sanctuary were covered in gold and topped with golden vines and clusters of golden grapes that were according to Josephus, "as tall as a man." Suspended before the doors was a spectacular tapestry that had been woven in Babylon; its multicolored design was a panorama of the universe. Within the building was an altar for incense, a golden menorah (a seven-branched lamp stand), and a table for the holy bread, or shewbread. Each

---

[101] "Jesus and His Times." <u>Reader's Digest</u>. Pleasantville: The Reader's Digest Association, Inc., 1987. Page 129.

Sabbath, 12 loves of unleavened bread were laid out in rows upon this table, along with fragrant frankincense, and were consecrated as an offering to God. The entrance to the innermost room of the Temple, the Holy of Holies, was always kept covered by a double veil, and into this empty, windowless room—an exact cube of 30 feet—daylight was never allowed to enter.102

B. Various parts of the temple and temple worship

The Court of the Gentiles

Here, non-Jews were allowed to bring offerings to be sacrificed by priests at the great altar.

The Temple was a tourist attraction; foreign kings, merchants, and servants alike visited the Court of the Gentiles and gazed in wonder at the building about which the Talmud, the book of Jewish law and commentary, was later to say: "He who has not seen the Temple of Herod has never in his life seen a beautiful building."

The Court of the Women

—So named because women were allowed to go no closer to the sanctuary and its altar. Here they would immediately have found companionship; the area was well known as a social gathering place, in many ways the heart of the Jewish community. Voices would be raised in greeting and in laughter as friends met friends; and today many families and traveling groups, having been separated among the crowds in the Court of the Gentiles, would be searching one another out.

Preachers and would-be prophets came here to exhort believers with their personal visions of truth. Scribes and scholars met here to discuss religious issues and debate points of religious law while students—even children—listened, learned, and perhaps asked questions. And here Jews could speak openly of their hopes and longings for the Messiah, the promised one, who was expected by many to deliver them from the Romans, whose soldiers stood nervous guard outside.103

The Temple treasury

Adding to the activity in the Court of the Women were the 13 chests of the Temple treasury, each shaped like a shofar, or ram's-horn trumpet, open to receive the various offerings given to defray the costs of sacrifice. The money would be transferred to one of the numerous treasury chambers built into the inner forecourt of the Temple, each for a distinct purpose. The Shekel Chamber held an enormous, constantly growing treasure—half-shekel annual dues imposed upon all Jewish men. In the Chamber of Utensils was a great store of gold and silver vessels for use in the worship services. Funds in the Chamber of Secrets were secretly handed out to "the poor of good family." Private individuals, too, could bring their money to the treasury for safekeeping.

In each of the four corners of the Court of the Women was a separate walled enclosure that served a special purpose. One was for storage and inspection of wood, for no wormy wood was to be used in the altar fire. A second held oil and wine for use in the services. A third was reserved for

---

102 Ibid. Page 130-132.

103 Ibid. Page 133.

lepers who believed themselves cured; here they were inspected by priests, and if they were found to be cured, they would purify themselves in a mikveh. Then, to complete the process of purification, they would make a burnt offering in atonement for the time that they had spent outside God's service. The fourth enclosure was set aside for Nazirites, the "dedicated" or "consecrated" ones, who were forbidden to drink wine, cut their hair, or approach a dead body.104

The Altar

The high altar, made of unfinished stone that had never been touched by metal tools, each of its four corners decorated with a horn-shaped projection.

Tradition had it that nearby, perhaps beneath the inner sanctum of the sanctuary, was the sacred rock upon which Abraham, at God's command, had prepared to sacrifice his son Isaac.

The rites of sacrifice

Animal sacrifice was central to the rituals of the Temple. On a normal day, the Temple priests' public duties began at dawn with the burnt offering of a lamb and ended 8 ½ hours later with the sacrifice of another. Each animal's throat was cut and its blood was ceremonially splashed against the altar. Both animals were butchered and the parts were burned in the altar fire in such a way as to maintain a continuous offering to God.

In addition, on every day except the Sabbath, there was a steady flow of private sacrifices, ranging from bulls to pigeons. Many were guilt or sin offerings, meant to remove an impurity or to atone for a misdeed; these were generally burnt offerings, in which the animal's flesh was reduced to ashes on the altar. Other sacrifices were peace offerings, made on such occasions as a family reunion, the recovery from an illness, the sealing of a private pact, or the harvesting of first fruits. In these, only parts of the animal—the entrails, some fatty tissue, and perhaps the kidneys—were burned, and the remainder of the meat was later eaten by the priests and by the offerer. In all offerings, the animal's blood (said to contain the essence of its life) belonged to God and had to be smeared on the horns of the altar or dashed against its sides or base, depending on the nature of the offering. The skins of sacrificial animals were the property of the priests. Although no private offerings were made on the Sabbath, the priests sacrificed two additional lambs as community offerings.

The institution of animal sacrifice had been a part of Judaism since the earliest times, an acknowledgment that all life belonged to God. In ancient times the patriarch of a family had performed the sacrifices himself, often upon a "high place," such as a raised platform or an altar constructed on a mountaintop.

Even after David and Solomon had centered religious activity in Jerusalem, sacrifices were still being made in many of the high places. It was not until after the return from the Babylonian Captivity that the rituals of sacrifice became the province of the Temple.

Only domestic animals that were raised for food were acceptable for sacrifice—cattle, goats, sheep, pigeons, and doves—and they had to be free from blemish, injury, disfigurement, and disease. For private offerings, the believer's rank and wealth were important in determining which animal was acceptable; where a high priest would have to offer a young bull to atone for a sin or

---

104 Ibid. Pages 133-134.

impurity, a king would offer a ram, a merchant or landowner a goat or a lamb, and a poor person a pair of birds. A very poor man might offer only a small measure of fine flour. Most animal sacrifices were accompanied by cereal offerings, consisting of cakes made from wheat flour and drink offerings of wine. From the cereal offerings, too, the priests received a portion for their own use.

A team of priests, each with a precisely assigned role, was in charge of the entire sacrificial process. The roles were chosen by casting lots; one priest would be assigned as the slaughterer, another would sprinkle blood on the altar, another would clear away the ashes, and so on. In most sacrifices, the worshiper simple laid his hand on the offering and perhaps announced the reason for the sacrifice before the animal was taken by a Levite to be slaughtered by a priest at a spot near the north side of the high altar. If the sacrifice was in atonement for a civil wrong, such as fraud, robbery, or other infringement of property rights, a confession of the crime and full restitution (plus a 20 percent fine) had to precede the offering of a burnt sacrifice. If the victim was no longer alive, the prescribed payment had to be made to the Temple priests. No one had to pay for the privilege of making a sacrifice, as did worshipers in most other Temples of the day. The right to sacrifice at the Temple in Jerusalem was basic; wood for the altar was supplied free.105

Instructions give to Moses

Priests were distinguished by their dress when serving at the Temple. Over white linen underclothing, he wore an ankle-length, seamless tunic of white linen, bound at the waist by a long girdle. On his head was a white linen hat. The high priest, depicted at the right, wore a blue headdress and over the priest's white tunic he wore a blue robe fringed with golden bells and pomegranates. Upon his shoulders was a vest-like ephod, embroidered with bands of gold, purple, scarlet, and blue. On his chest was a gold purse inset with 12 gemstones, representing the tribes. In an earlier day, the Urim and the Thummim—two ceremonial objects that were used to divine God's will—were kept in such purses. All priests went barefoot in the Temple.106

The preparations on the Temple Mount would be different for Passover than for any other day. The normal day's rituals would finish an hour early, and the remainder of the afternoon would be given over to the orderly slaughter of thousands of lambs. The Temple precincts would be crowded with pilgrims holding lambs, waiting for the gates to reopen after the final burnt offering had been made. Then about a third of the multitude would be admitted, and—to the sharp, piercing sound of a shofar—the gate would be closed behind them. The sacrificers would confront a long row of priests, each holding a bowl of gold or silver; behind each of these priests would be more priests, forming a line to the altar. When a worshiper reached on of the front rank of priests, he would use a sharp knife to open the carotid artery in the neck of the lamb he held and would drain the blood into the priest's bowl. The bowl would then be passed back to another priest, who would replace it with an empty bowl of the same precious metal and pass the full bowl on until it reached the altar. There the blood would be splashed on the base of the altar, and the empty bowl would begin its return journey through the hands of the same priests to be refilled.107

When all of this group's lambs had been killed and flayed, the gates would be reopened and a second wave of sacrificers would enter to repeat the process. The third and final wave would

---

105 "Jesus and His Times." <u>Reader"s Digest</u>. Pleasantville: The Reader"s Digest Association, Inc., 1987. Page 135.

106 Ibid. Page 136.

107 Ibid. Page 137.

include all the pilgrims still waiting in the courts. Throughout the long ritual, the voices of Levite singers would be raised, singing from the Psalms to the accompaniment of reed pipes and other instruments.

The sacrificers would return with the prepared lambs to their families,—or perhaps to groups of friends or fellow travelers—and there the lambs would be roasted and eaten, along with unleavened bread and bitter herbs. In the course of the meal, the story of the Exodus would be retold.

The remaining days of Passover week—known as the Feast of Unleavened Bread—were linked not only to the story of the Exodus but also to an agricultural festival that traditionally marked the beginning of the grain harvest. During this solemn week, no leavened bread (nor anything else that contained yeast) could be eaten.108

The Day of Atonement

The most solemn day of the year was the fast of Yom Kippur, the Day of Atonement, when the high priest himself administered all Temple services and went before the Lord to offer atonement for the sins of the nation. Although it was not one of the ordained pilgrim festivals, Yom Kippur preceded Succoth by only five days, and so many Jews assembled in Jerusalem for both the fast and the feast.

For this critically important service, the high priest had to prepare with great care. To avoid the possibility of ritual impurity, he would leave his home and enter a special apartment in the Temple seven days before the Day of Atonement. During this week, every step of the prescribed ritual would be studied and reviewed in detail, for it was of utmost importance that no mistake be made.

On the night before the service, he would maintain a vigil in the company of several other priests, who would read Scripture with him and help him to stay awake. Meanwhile, in case anything should happen to him, another priest was also being made ready to take his place.

When, on the Day of Atonement, the high priest entered the Holy of Holies for the first time, it was a dramatic moment. After passing between the two curtains that covered the entrance, he heaped incense on the coals he carried, and the room filled with smoke. Before presenting himself to the people, he prayed. "But he did not prolong his prayer," says the Mishnah, the book of law, "lest he put Israel in terror."109

The high priest wore special vestments for Yom Kippur, and in the course of the long day of ritual he would change them several times, bathing 5 times and washing his hands and feet 10 times. Early in the ritual, he would ceremoniously cast lots to choose between two goats— one to be offered as a burnt sacrifice, the other to be driven into the fearsome Judean Wilderness to die as a "scapegoat." He would confess that he himself had committed sins and would sacrifice a young bull as an offering for those sins and for the collective sins of all priests.

Then as the people followed his movements in apprehensive silence, fearful that he and they would be met with divine wrath, he would make his annual entrance into the Holy of Holies, there—in the name of all Israel and on their behalf—to offer atonement in the presence of God. Three times the high priest would go into the empty room, wherein, it was believed, God's presence would be made manifest, and at each reemergence, the people would breathe a collective

---

108 Ibid. Pages 137-138.

109 McGee, J. Vernon. Thru the Bible with J. Vernon McGee. Vol. 1 (Ex.). Pasadena: Thru the Bible Radio, c 1981. Page 318.

sigh of relief. The first time, he would make an offering of incense, filling the room with aromatic smoke. The second time, he would sprinkle the chamber with some of the blood of the young bull he had sacrificed earlier. Before his third and final entry he would sacrifice the goat that had been chosen for the purpose, and then he would sprinkle the chamber with some of the goat's blood.

Returning to the altar, the high priest would then lay his hands on the scapegoat and make confession for all the people, transferring their sins onto the animal. At the end of each confession, he would speak the Lord's name aloud—the only time the hallowed word could properly be spoken. Then the people formed a pathway through which another priest led the scapegoat toward the desert. It was taken to a deep ravine some 12 miles from Jerusalem, and there pushed over a steep cliff. The news of the animal's death was relayed by signals back to the high priest, and after he had performed a few final ceremonies, the day was concluded with a great rejoicing. Atonement had been made for the year; it was time to go back home and try with renewed faith and determination to live truly by the laws of God.110

Administration of the Temple complex was tightly controlled by a permanent staff of Temple officers, who supervised all operations, including the training and ongoing evaluation of the priests who held services. ......the proper functioning of this holy place required discipline, specialization, and attention to detail.111

The high priest

Of all these Temple servants, it was the high priest who carried the most authority. By definition he was a leader of the people and by law he was the head of the Sanhedrim, the council of authorities empowered to make judgments in Jewish religious and legal disputes. He was not required to officiate at daily Temple services, but he had the exclusive right and duty to perform certain services, such as that which took place on the Day of Atonement. He was generally preferred for such others as Passover, Succoth, and the burning of the red heifer.

The last sacrifice took place on the Mount of Olives, near a *mikveh* built especially to purify the high priest for the ceremony. The ashes from the ritual were collected and kept in a repository. As needed, ashes would be added to spring water to make lustral water, which was used in the ritual purification of someone, usually a priest, who had been contaminated by contact with a dead body. Priests took great care to avoid such contamination, and so lustral water was rarely needed; moreover, only a small amount of ash was required to make it. Hence, the burning of the red heifer occurred infrequently—some authorities say only seven times in the history of the Jews.

The high priesthood at the time of Christ was no longer a lifetime post, nor was its holder a member of the Zadokite clan. The last legitimate Zadokite, Onias III, had been replaced by his own brother in 175 BC at the order of the Seleucid ruler Antiochus IV. Three years later, the brother had been replaced by a non-Zadokite, Menelaus. About 20 years of turmoil and confusion had followed, in the course of which the next rightful Zadokite heir, Onias IV, had fled to Egypt and there, under the sponsorship of the Egyptian ruler, had built his own Temple. Finally, during Succoth in 152 BC, the Hasmonean ruler Jonathan—of a priestly but non-Zadokite family—had assumed the high priesthood himself, thus combining the secular and religious authorities of the land in his own person. The Hasmoneans had continued to hold both offices until the dynasty was destroyed

---

110 "Jesus and His Times." <u>Reader's Digest</u>. Pleasantville: The Reader's Digest Association, Inc., 1987. Pages 139-140.

111 Ibid. Page 141.

by Herod the Great, who instituted the practice of appoint ting high priests as he saw fit. After his death the Roman authorities continued to appoint new high priests at frequent intervals, choosing from among a few aristocratic families.112

For this reason the chosen man for the high priesthood was contaminated because he was not of the line of Zadok as required by the Law.

Spiritual Cleansing

The purpose of immersion in a mikveh, or watertight ritual bath, was to cleanse the spirit, not the body. A mikveh could not be portable—many were cut from living rock—and had to contain some free-running water, usually spring water or rainwater. The Temple had several mikvehs for priests, including at least two reserved for the high priest. Public mikvehs also existed near the Temple Mount; worshipers had to be cleansed before entering holy ground.113

There also would have been representatives from the many synagogues that existed in Jerusalem. And among the pilgrims from around the world would have been scribes, scholars, teachers, and intellectual leaders of far-flung communities. The festivals gave them the chance to exchange views. Here, amid the buzz and roar of human activity, they met with one another and with their counterparts in Jerusalem to debate, to teach, and to learn. From the exchanges there continually emerged, if not agreement, an ongoing awareness of the vital multiplicity of the Jewish faith.

Hence, the gathering of world Jewry that took place at the pilgrim festivals was more than an observance of ancient sacrificial rituals, more even than a reaffirmation of faith. It was an important element in maintaining the powerful continuity at the heart of Judaism. It served the common people in a similar way. Here Jews saw how other Jews were faring throughout the known world— still pious and devoted to their spiritual home, though speaking different languages and displaying the clothing and behavior of many lands. The pilgrims took home with them the tales of what they had seen; and the fact that a Jew might be a middle-class Babylonian, a prosperous Greek trader, or a landowning Egyptian did much to widen the horizons of those who lived in the cities, towns, and villages of Palestine.

They all had a chance to show how they were living their Jewish life.114

---

112 Ibid. Page 150

113 Ibid Page 141.

114 Ibid. Page 144

PART III

NEW TESTAMENT PERIOD

CHAPTER NINE

Yeshua (Jesus of Nazareth)

A. Background of Yeshua

In the fullness of time, God sent forth His son, born of a woman, conceived by the Holy Spirit of God. He, Jesus, (Yeshua) is the tabernacle of the Holy Spirit.

In Daniel 9:24-27 the Lord prophesied the time of the coming of the Jewish Messiah until the time the prince is to be cut off (see graph on page 176).

The Messiah had to be born approximately thirty-three years prior to being cut off for the sins of the people.

1. Forerunner's prediction

The prediction for the birth of the Messiah starts with the announcement of the birth of the forerunner, John the Baptist. His parents Zachariah and Elizabeth were godly people, advanced in age and had no children—both of the line of Aaron—the tribe of Levi. Zachariah was a priest of the order of Abiujah; Zachariah went to the Temple to serve as priest. This took place during the reign of King Herod of Judea during the week of Abia according to the Jewish calendar. This corresponds with June Thirteenth through Nineteenth according to our Julian calendar. It was at this time that Zachariah was serving in the Temple when an angel appeared to him.

The angel Gabriel appeared to Zachariah and gave to him the message that God had heard his prayer and that he would have a son in due season by his wife Elizabeth and they would call his name John. He did not believe, so he was struck dumb until the child John was born and circumcised.

It took Zacharias two to three days to get home since he and Elizabeth lived in the Judean hills, anywhere from eight to twenty miles south of the Temple. He arrived home June Twenty-third or Twenty-fourth and John the Baptist was conceived.115

2. Gabriel's announcement of Messiah's birth

> *26 Now in the sixth month the angel Gabriel was sent by God to a city of Galilee named Nazareth, 27 to a virgin abetrothed to a man whose name was Joseph, of the house of David. The virgin's name was Mary. 28 And having come in, the angel said to her, b"Rejoice, highly favored one, cthe Lord is with you; 5blessed are you among women!" 29 But 6when she saw him, dshe was troubled at his saying, and considered what manner of greeting this was. 30 Then the angel said to her, "Do not be afraid, Mary, for you have found efavor with God. 31 fAnd behold, you will conceive in your womb and bring forth a Son, and gshall call His name JESUS. 32 He will be great, hand will be called the Son of the Highest; and ithe Lord God will give Him the jthrone of His kfather David. 33 lAnd He will reign over the house of Jacob forever, and of His kingdom there will be no end."116*

Then the angel, Gabriel, approached Mary of Nazareth who was engaged to Joseph. He told her she would conceive and have a son who would be savior of mankind. He also told her that her cousin Elizabeth was with child. Mary and Joseph were both of royal linage.

> *14 Therefore the Lord Himself will give you a sign: hBehold, the virgin shall conceive and bear ia Son, and shall call His name jImmanuel.117*

Mary was of the line of Nathan, Bathsheba and David's son, while Joseph was of the direct line of Kings through the line of David and Bathsheba through his son Solomon's line. (Mary was approached by the angel between December 23rd and 24th). The conception was possible December 24th after 6:00 p.m. or December 25 according to the Jewish Calendar.

(Mary conceived Yeshua, by the Holy Spirit, on Christmas December 25.) Shortly after this, Mary took leave of her family to spend time with her cousin Elizabeth who was six months pregnant living in the hill country of Judea.118

When Elizabeth and Mary met, Elizabeth's baby leapt in her womb causing her to say:

> *42 Then she spoke out with a loud voice and said, "Blessed are you among women, and blessed is the fruit of your womb! 43 But why is this granted to me, that the mother of my Lord should come to me? 44 For indeed, as soon as the voice of your greeting sounded in my ears, the babe leaped in my womb for joy. 45 Blessed is she*

---

115 -Prophetic Observer. Oklahoma City: Southwest Rodeo Church, December 1995.

116 The Holy Bible: The New King James Version. Nashville: Thomas Nelson, 1996, c1982. (Lk. 1:13-26).

117 Ibid. (Is 7:14).

118 -Prophetic Observer. Oklahoma City: Southwest Rodeo Church, December 1995.

who believed, for there will be a fulfillment of those things which were told her from the Lord." 119

(Luke 1:42-45, NKJV)

Mary responded:

46 And Mary said: t"My soul 9magnifies the Lord, 47 And my spirit has urejoiced in vGod my Savior. 48 For wHe has regarded the lowly state of His maidservant; For behold, henceforth xall generations will call me blessed.120

(Luke 1:46-48)

3. John's birth (forerunner)

After a few months Elizabeth gave birth to a baby boy and Zachariah began to speak. He confirmed that the name of the child was to be John, and he praised God for His mercies. The people wondered what kind of child he would be. Although John the Baptist was not Elijah, he fulfilled the prophecies that the forerunner of Messiah would perform.

4. Yeshua is born

Mary returned home to Nazareth, advanced in her pregnancy. Joseph was beside himself when he realized Mary's condition. While he was thinking of divorcing Mary quietly, the angel Gabriel came to Joseph in a dream and encouraged him saying, "Don't be afraid to take Mary as your wife. The child she carries was conceived by the Holy Spirit. His name shall be Yeshua for He shall deliver His people from their sin." Joseph awoke from his dream. After he saw Mary, he told her of his dream and that he was willing to claim the child as his own and fulfill his covenant of marriage to Mary as prescribed in Jewish law (ref. Matthew 1:20-21).

In time, a proclamation of Cesar Augustus of Rome was given that all the world was to enroll in the city of their ancestry in order to be taxed.

As the time of Mary's delivery of her first born son approached, Caesar Augustus put out a law that all the known world was to be registered. Everyone was to return to the city of their ancestors and be registered for tax purposes. This caused Mary and Joseph to make a journey to Bethlehem when it was prophesied.

2 But you, O Bethlehem Ephrathah, who are little to be among the clans of Judah, from you shall come forth for me one who is to be ruler in Israel, whose origin is from of old, from ancient days.121

(Micah 5:2, RSV)

---

[119] The Holy Bible: The New King James Version. Nashville: Thomas Nelson, 1996, c1982.

[120] Ibid.

[121] The Holy Bible: The Revised Standard Version. Oak Harbor: Logos Research Systems, Inc., 1971.

It is wonderful how God causes godless men to fulfill His plan. This was around the Feast of Tabernacles, which is in September/October, the time the lambs are born — while Yeshua was to become the Lamb of God; the One in whom God's presence dwelt.

As recounted in Luke 2:8-16, Joseph took Mary, who was nine months pregnant, with him to Bethlehem, Judah. There was no exception, even for those who were with child, to comply with the order of Emperor Augustus.

This historical date for the decree of Caesar was in the fall—the first day of the Feast of Tabernacles which fulfills John 1:14:

> *14 And the Word was made flesh, and dwelt among us, (and we beheld his glory, the glory as of the only begotten of the Father,) full of grace and truth.122*
>
> (John 1:14, KJV)

The fullness of time had come which Micah the Prophet had foretold.

> *2 But thou, Bethlehem Ephratah, though thou be little among the thousands of Judah, yet out of thee shall he come forth unto me that is to be ruler in Israel; whose goings forth have been from of old, from everlasting.123*
>
> (Micah 5:2, KJV)

It was in a stable in Bethlehem that Yeshua was born. His birth was announced by angels to shepherds who came and honored Him at His birth. Yeshua came into the world with a lowly birth so that those who were outcasts, as well as those who ranked high in society, could have equal access to Him (ref. Luke 2:1-20).

It is interesting to note that the genealogy of Mary and Joseph both go back to King David. Mary's father was through the line of Nathan—Bathsheba's son, and Joseph through the line of Solomon— also of the line of Bathsheba (ref. Matthew 1:2-38; Luke 3:23b-38). Their son, Yeshua, was the rightful heir of the throne of Israel which can be seen through the genealogy. He was also of the Aaronic priestly line which can be seen on Mary's side. She and her cousin were of the tribe of Levi—Mary's and Elizabeth's mothers were sisters. Therefore, Yeshua is both the King of Kings and High Priest.

> *26 Now in the sixth month the angel Gabriel was sent by God to a city of Galilee named Nazareth, 27 to a virgin abetrothed to a man whose name was Joseph, of the house of David. The virgin's name was Mary.124*

The genealogy of God's Messiah is David to Solomon to Rehoboam to Jeconiah to Zerubbabel to Jesus of Nazareth, the only begotten Son of God. Only Jesus of Nazareth can be King Messiah.

The difference between the genealogy of Luke and Matthew can be seen in Luke following the priestly lineage. The Royal families intermarried several times. The first merging was when the

---

[122] The Holy Bible: King James Version. Oak Harbor: Logos Research Systems, Inc., 1995.

[123] Ibid.

[124] The Holy Bible: The New King James Version. Nashville: Thomas Nelson, 1996, c1982. (Lk. 1:26-27).

high priest married Elisheba, a daughter of Judah (Ex 6:23). Elisheba's brother Naashar carried on the royal lineage (Matt 1:4)

The next uniting of the two families occurred when David married Bathsheba who was a priestess. Luke's account lists several high priests. Lastly, Joseph of Judah's family married Mary who was of the priestly family of Aaron; Mary was a priestess as was her cousin Elizabeth (Luke 1:5, 36). She was also of the line of David through Nathan his son.

John the Baptist's father Zechariah was a high priest. He burned incense (Ex 30:7) as well as brought the blood of atonement for the people on Yon Kippur. It was at this time that Gabriel appeared to Zechariah.[125]

At the time that Yeshua came onto the scene, Rome was the world power. Rome's empire was from 63 BC — AD 476.

---

[125] The Reese Chronological Bible. The authorized edition of the original work by Edward Reese. Minneapolis: Bethany House Publishers, 1980. Pg 1250.

The 70 WEEKS of DANIEL 9[126]

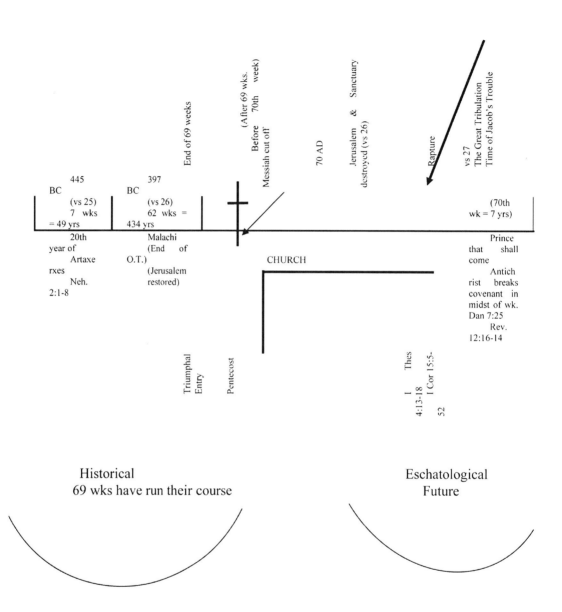

Historical
69 wks have run their course

Eschatological
Future

B. Childhood of Yeshua

October 3, 5 BC

When Jesus was eight days old He was circumcised and His name was called Yeshua (*Jesus*, which means *Savior*) as He was called by the angel before He was conceived in the womb. Then He was brought by His parents, Mary and Joseph, to the temple to be presented to the Lord. His parents offered a sacrifice of two young pigeons because they were poor and could not afford to offer a ram.

[126] McGee, J. Vernon. Thru the Bible with J. Vernon McGee. Vol. III (Prov. — Mal.). Pasadena: Thru the Bible Radio, c 1981. Pages 588.

At this time, there was an elderly man named Simeon who was waiting for God's promise to him, that he would see the Lord's promised Messiah (*God incarnate*) before he died. The day that Yeshua was presented in the temple, Simeon was led by the Holy Spirit to go to the temple. There he took the child in his arms and blessed Him. He thanked God for being allowed to see His redemption before he died.

> *28 Then took he him up in his arms, and blessed God, and said, 29 Lord, now lettest thou thy servant depart in peace, according to thy word: 30 For mine eyes have seen thy salvation, 31 Which thou hast prepared before the face of all people; 32 A light to lighten the Gentiles, and the glory of thy people Israel. 33 And Joseph and his mother marvelled at those things which were spoken of him. 34 And Simeon blessed them, and said unto Mary his mother, Behold, this child is set for the fall and rising again of many in Israel; and for a sign which shall be spoken against; 35 (Yea, a sword shall pierce through thy own soul also,) that the thoughts of many hearts may be revealed.127*

(Luke 2:28-35, KJV)

Then an elderly prophetess named Anna, the daughter of Phaniel, of the tribe Asher, came and saw the child at the temple and gave thanks to God.

In 4 BC, wise men from the East came to see the promised King of Kings who would be born of the Jewish people. They went to King Herod and asked where the King of the Jews had been born because, "We have seen His star in the East and have come to worship Him."

King Herod was upset and asked the scribes and priests where the Messiah was to be born. They said, "Bethlehem of Judea, as written by the prophet" (Matthew 2:6).

Then Herod asked the wise men when the star had appeared. They told him and then he said, "Go and find the child, let me know where He is and I will worship Him also."

The wise men left the king and saw the star in the East and it stood over the house where the young child was. They gave Him gifts of gold (because He was a king), frankincense (because He was a priest) and myrrh (to show His sacrificial death).

The wise men were shown in a dream not to return to Herod, so they departed into their country another way.

That night an angel of the Lord appeared to Joseph in a dream saying, "Arise and take the child and His mother and flee into Egypt until I tell you it is safe to return, for Herod will seek the young child to destroy Him."

> *1 When Israel was a child, then I loved him, and called my son out of Egypt.128*

(Hosea 11:1, KJV)

When Herod saw that the wise men did not return to report the whereabouts of the child, he became violent. He had all the children that were in Bethlehem from two years old and younger destroyed.

---

127 The Holy Bible: King James Version. Oak Harbor: Logos Research Systems, Inc., 1995.

128 The Holy Bible: King James Version. Oak Harbor: Logos Research Systems, Inc., 1995.

17 Then was fulfilled that which was spoken by Jeremiah the prophet, saying, 18 In Rama was there a voice heard, lamentation, and weeping, and great mourning, Rachel weeping for her children, and would not be comforted, because they are not.129

(Matthew 2:17-18, KJV)

After Herod's death, an angel appeared to Joseph in a dream, while he was in Egypt, saying, "It is safe to return to Israel for those that sought the child's life are dead." However, when Joseph heard that Archelaus was reigning in Judea, he was afraid. He was warned by God in a dream to live in the parts of Galilee and dwell in the city called Nazareth. It was spoken by the prophets that the Messiah would be called a Nazarene (ref. Matthew 2:1-23).

So Yeshua grew strong, both physically and spiritually, and He was filled with wisdom. The grace of God was upon Him. This was seen when He went with His parents when He was twelve years old for the feast of Passover in Jerusalem. When the feast of Passover was complete, Yeshua's parents started their journey home to Nazareth, thinking that Yeshua was in the company of their friends and family. They looked for Him but could not find Him. So they returned to Jerusalem. After three days of searching for Him, they found Him sitting with the doctors of the laws listening to them and asking them questions. All that heard Him were amazed at His understanding and answers. His mother approached Him and said, "Son, You had us worried about You. How could You treat us this way?"

Then Yeshua replied, "Why were you looking for Me? Didn't you realize I must be about My Father's business?" Mary and Joseph did not understand what He said but Yeshua returned to Nazareth with them, and Mary kept these sayings in her heart.

And Yeshua continued to increase in wisdom and stature and in favor with God and man. (Yeshua spent the next eighteen years in Nazareth being subject to His parents and learning the carpentry trade) (ref: Luke 2:40-52).

C. Adulthood of Yeshua

1. Baptism of Yeshua

In August 19 AD, Caesar Augustine died and Tiberius reigned in his stead in Rome. It was during the fifteenth year of the reign of Tiberius Caesar. Pontius Pilate was governor of Judea and Herod was tetrarch of Galilee, and his brother was tetrarch of Ituraea of the region of Trachonitis, and Lysaneas the tetrarch of Abilene.

Annas and Caiaphas were high priests. It was at this time that the word of the Lord came to John, son of Zechariah, in the wilderness and he came preaching and baptizing for repentance for the remission of sins.

4 As it is written in the book of the words of Esaias the prophet, saying, The voice of one crying in the wilderness, Prepare ye the way of the Lord, make his paths straight. 5 Every valley shall be filled, and every mountain and hill shall be brought

---

[129] Ibid.

low; and the crooked shall be made straight, and the rough ways shall be made smooth; 6 And all flesh shall see the salvation of God.130

(Luke 3:4-6, KJV)

In April 25 AD, John, Yeshua's cousin, came on the scene. He was preaching in the wilderness of Judea; he was the last of the Old Testament prophets. He said, "Repent, for the kingdom of heaven is at hand." Many came to hear John—some were of the religious class (the Pharisees and Sadducees)—John warned them to repent and do the works of righteousness and not rely on the fact that they had social or religious status.

The common people were encouraged to be honest in their dealings with one another and to sin no more. John was preaching that One would come after him whom he was not worthy of...... "and He will baptize you with the Holy Spirit and with fire" (ref: Matthew 3:7-10; Luke 3:7-14; Matthew 3:1-6; Mark 2:1-6; Luke 3:1-6; John 1:6-18; Matthew 3:11-12; Mark 1:7-8; Luke 3:15-18; John 1:19-28).

After a few months, Yeshua came from Nazareth of Galilee to be baptized by John in the Jordan River. When Yeshua was praying and baptized, the heaven was opened and the Holy Spirit descended in a bodily shape like a dove upon Him, and a voice from heaven said, "You are My beloved son. I am well pleased with You." John saw this and stated that this was the Son of God (Matthew 3:13-17; Mark 1:9-11; Luke 3:21-22; John 1:29-34).

Four hundred eighty-three years elapsed between the time of Jerusalem's reestablishment and the appearance and baptism of Yeshua (ref: Daniel 9:25).

2. Temptation of Yeshua

February AD 25

After Yeshua's baptism, He was led away by the Spirit of God into the wilderness with the wild beasts. The angels ministered to Him. There He was to be tempted by Satan. He fasted in the wilderness for forty days and forty nights; afterwards He was hungry. Then Satan said, "If You are the Son of God, command this stone that it be made bread."

Yeshua replied, "It is written, 'Man shall not live by bread alone, but by every word out of the mouth of God.'"

Then Satan took Yeshua to a high mountain to show Him all the kingdoms of the world in a moment. Then he said, "You can have all of this if You worship me."

Yeshua said, "It is written, 'Thou shall worship the Lord your God and Him only shall you serve.'"

Then Satan took Him to Jerusalem and set Him on the pinnacle of the temple and said, "If You are the Son of God, cast Yourself down, for it is written, 'He shall give His angels charge over You to keep You, and in their hands they shall lift You up in case You should dash Your foot against a stone.'"

Then Yeshua answered, "It is written, 'You shall not tempt the Lord your God.'"

Then Satan ended his temptation and departed from Him for a season (ref. Matthew 4:1-11; Mark 1:12-13; Luke 4:1-13).

---

[130] The Holy Bible: King James Version. Oak Harbor: Logos Research Systems, Inc., 1995.

137

D. Yeshua's ministry

1. Choosing His disciples

Yeshua started His ministry first by picking His first disciples. Among them were Andrew, Philip and Nathanael. These were John's disciples. Later Simon Peter came to Jesus (ref. John 1:35-42; John 1:43-51).

March AD 25

About this time there was a wedding in Cana of Galilee and the host had run out of wine for the celebration. Mary, the mother of Yeshua, asked Him to take care of the problem. She told the servants to do whatever Yeshua wanted them to do.

Yeshua told them to fill the six water pots of stone which were two to three firkins each (two to three gallons a piece) with water. The servants took the water to the host. He tasted it and it had turned to wine. This was the first miracle of Yeshua (ref. John 2:1-11).

Yeshua's early ministry showed God's righteous anger when He was at the Jewish Passover, April 14, AD 26, in Jerusalem. He drove out the money changers and those who sold animals. He said, "You are not to make My Father's house into a house of merchandise." This was an example of the zeal for God's house to be for worship, not merchandising.

The Jewish leaders were angry and asked, "Why are You doing this?"

He replied, "Destroy (Me) this temple and in three days I will raise this temple up." They did not understand (ref. John 2:13-22).

Yeshua went from place to place ministering and healing the people and sharing God's love as well as His judgment in the form of parables. He journeyed from Judea to Galilee to Samaria. He was rejected by those He grew up with in Nazareth (ref. Luke 4:16-30).

After leaving Nazareth, He went to Capernaum. While Jesus was at Capernaum, He was walking by the Sea of Galilee. There He called four fishermen to be fishers of men. They left their nets and followed Him. They were Simon-Peter and Andrew. Then James and John, the sons of Zebedee, were also called. While Jesus ministered with His four disciples, He healed the sick in body and spiritually, as well as mentally. They were freed of sickness, as well as evil spirits.

> *17 That it might be fulfilled which was spoken by Esaias the prophet, saying, Himself took our infirmities, and bare our sicknesses.*[131]
>
> (Matthew 8:17, KJV)

Lepers and paralytics were healed. The Pharisees were angry with Yeshua because He would heal on the Sabbath, and also He ate with publicans and sinners. Yeshua said, "The well don't need a doctor but the sick do" (ref. Matthew 9:12).

In time Yeshua selected twelve of all those who followed Him to be His disciples. They were Simon, called Peter; James and John, Sons of Zebedee; Andrew; Philip; Bartholomew and Matthew. There were Thomas and James, the sons of Alpheus; Thaddeus and Simon the Canaanite. Last but not least, was Judas Iscariot who later betrayed Yeshua so He would be crucified. After the disciples were all chosen (ref. Mark 3:13-19; Luke 6: 12-16), Yeshua went up on a mountain and

---

[131] The Holy Bible: King James Version. Oak Harbor: Logos Research Systems, Inc., 1995.

when He saw the multitudes, Yeshua preached the Sermon on the Mount (ref. Matthew 5:1-7:28; Luke 6:20-49). In this discourse He was teaching the people how to live in God's kingdom.

2. Various healings and forgiveness

After Jesus returned to Capernaum, a centurion (a Roman soldier and commander of one hundred men) begged Yeshua to heal his servant. But he did not feel worthy for Yeshua to come to his house to heal him so he said, "Just speak the word and I know my servant will be healed." Yeshua marveled at his faith.

Yeshua said, "Go thy way and as thou hast believed, let it be done for you." His servant was healed in the same hour (ref. Matthew 8:5-13; Luke 7:1-10).

In Nain Yeshua raised a widow's son from the dead. Later, Lazarus of Bethany, a friend, of Yeshua, was raised from the dead after being dead for four days (ref. Luke 7:11-17; John 11:1-46).

August 27 AD
Yeshua was preaching to the multitude and mentioned that John the Baptist was the greatest of those who were born of men, but that he that is least in the kingdom of God would be greater than he. This was shared after John the Baptist was killed by Herod and his wife Herodious (ref. Matthew 11:2-18; Luke 7:18-30).

September 27 AD
While Yeshua was at a Pharisee's dinner party, He was anointed by a woman who was a sinner. She brought an alabaster box of costly ointment. She was weeping and washed Yeshua's feet with her tears and dried them with her hair and kissed His feet and anointed them with the ointment. She showed her love to Yeshua because she was forgiven much by Him (ref. Luke 7:36-50).

3. Yeshua tours Galilee — various miracles

October AD 27, Yeshua again toured Galilee.

During this time, He preached parables about what the kingdom of God was like. He showed the need for harvesters, as well as the danger of the Word of God being snatched from the one who seeks to believe. Yeshua also showed how the kingdom of God is like a treasure that is priceless (ref. Matthew 13:1-23; Mark 4:1-25; Luke 8:4-18; Matthew 13; 4:46).

Yeshua showed He had God's power when He stilled the Sea of Galilee by rebuking the violent waves that would cover the ship He and His disciples were in.

> *39 And he arose, and rebuked the wind, and said unto the sea, Peace, be still. And the wind ceased, and there was a great calm. 40 And he said unto them, Why are ye so fearful? how is it that ye have no faith? 41 And they feared exceedingly, and said one to another, What manner of man is this, that even the wind and the sea obey him?* 132

(Mark 4:39-41, KJV)

---

[132] The Holy Bible: King James Version. Oak Harbor: Logos Research Systems, Inc., 1995.

November AD 27

After calming the waves, Yeshua and His disciples crossed the sea to the country of Gadarenes. There they met two men possessed with demons. The devils begged Him to please cast them into the herd of swine. Yeshua said, "Go," and they went into the herd of swine. The pigs, out of fear, ran violently down a steep cliff into the sea. The keepers of the swine fled and brought back the whole city and begged Yeshua to leave their coast because they had lost their livelihood in the hog business (ref. Matthew 8:28-34; Mark 4:1-20; Luke 8:26-39).

December AD 27

Yeshua returned to Galilee. There He healed Jairus' daughter and raised her from the dead. He also healed a women who had an issue of blood flowing for twelve years. It was her faith that restored her when she touched the hem of His garment, believing that was all she needed to do (ref. Matthew 9:18-26; Mark 5:21-43; Luke 8:40-56).

On Yeshua's third tour of Galilee, He sent His disciples, whom He was training, out two by two to go into the nearby community and preach the gospel of repentance. He warned of persecution, as well as the cost and rewards of being a disciple (ref. Matthew 9:35-38; Matthew 10:1-42; Mark 6:7-13; Luke 9:3-6).

April 28 AD

After the death of John the Baptist by Herod the tetrarch (March AD 27), Yeshua went to a desert place and a multitude of men, women and children gathered around. Yeshua was moved with compassion and healed their sick. When it was getting late, the disciples encouraged Yeshua to dismiss the crowd so they could buy food to eat for they were hungry. Jesus said they could stay; "Feed them."

The disciples replied, "All we have is five loaves and two fishes." Yeshua commanded the multitude to sit down on the grass. Then He blessed the bread and fishes and gave it to the disciples to give to the multitude. They did all eat and were satisfied and there were twelve baskets full of fragments from the meal; there were five thousand men beside women and children. Then Yeshua dismissed the people (ref. Matthew 14:13-21; Mark 6:30-44; Luke 9:10-17; John 6:1-13).

Yeshua ordered His disciples to get into a boat and go to the other side to Bethsaida. While He went to pray, He told them He would meet them later. There arose a storm on the sea that was fierce. It was the fourth watch (three o'clock a.m.) when Jesus went to them walking on the sea. The disciples were fearful when they saw Him. They thought He was a ghost. Jesus said, "Don't be afraid, it is I."

Peter requested to walk to Him. Yeshua allowed him, but when Peter saw how violet the wind was, he was fearful. Then he said, "Lord, save me!"

Immediately Yeshua put out His hand and said, "Why did you doubt?" After they entered the ship the wind ceased.

The disciples worshiped Him and said, "Truly, You are the Son of God" (ref. Matthew 14:22-33; John 6:14-21; Mark 6:45-52).

While Yeshua and the disciples were in Gennesaret, many came to touch the hem of Yeshua's garment and were healed of various diseases. The people followed Yeshua to Capernaum, May AD 28 (ref. Matthew 14:34-36; Mark 6:53-56). There He shared that He is the bread of life which came down from heaven. Many could not handle His teaching and left Him. Only those whom God had chosen stuck by Him and believed (ref. John 6:22-71).

June 28 AD

While on the coast of Tyre and Sidon, a foreign women, a Syrophenician, begged Yeshua to heal her demon-possessed daughter. She showed her faith by comparing herself to a dog that only gets the crumbs from his master's table. Yeshua healed the child because of her faith (ref. Matthew 15:21-28; Mark 7:24-30).

There was an uprising among the religious Jews. They demanded a sign to prove that Yeshua was the Messiah. Yeshua said "There will be no sign given to this adulterous generation except the sign of Jonah who was in the belly of the whale for three days and nights" (ref. Matthew 15:39; 16:1-4).

4. Peter proclaims Yeshua is the Son of God

August AD 28

While Yeshua was on the coast of Caesarea Philippi, He asked His disciples who the Son of man is. Peter answered and said, "Thou art the Christ, the Son of the living God."

Yeshua replied, "Blessed are you for flesh and blood did not reveal this to you, but My Father who is in heaven. Upon this confession will I build My church and the gates of hell shall not prevail against it." Yeshua commanded the disciples to tell no one about this thing (ref. Matthew 16:13-20; Mark 8:27-30; Luke 9:18-21).

After this time, Yeshua began to show His disciples that He was going to Jerusalem to suffer many things from the elders and chief priests and scribes. He would also be killed and rise again on the third day. He also told the disciples the need to give up their own self-life, take up the cross and follow Yeshua (ref. Matthew 16:21-28; Mark 8:31-38; Luke 9:23-27).

After this, several days later, Peter, James and John went with Yeshua to a high mountain to pray. Yeshua was transfigured and His face shone like the sun and His clothing was white like light. Then Moses and Elijah were seen talking to Yeshua by Peter after awaking from a deep sleep.

Peter said, "I am glad we were here to see this wonderful appearance. Let us build three booths; one for You, one for Moses and one for Elijah."

Then a cloud passed by and they heard a voice saying, "This is My beloved Son; hear what He has to say." After the voice was gone, Yeshua was alone. He told them not to tell anyone what they had seen (ref. Matthew 17:1-13; Mark 9:2-13; Luke 9:28-36).

5. Yeshua warns His disciples of His death and betrayal

While the disciples and Yeshua dwelt in Galilee, Yeshua said, "The Son of man shall be betrayed into the hands of men and they shall kill Him. The third day, He shall rise again." The disciples did not understand and were afraid (ref. Matthew 17:22-23; Mark 9:30-32; Luke 9:44-45).

Yeshua shared with the disciples that the greatest in the kingdom of heaven is one who comes to God with simple faith like a child (ref. Matthew 18:1-5; Mark 9:34-37; Luke 9:46-48).

He also shared the importance of forgiving their brothers for trespasses without number. He also spoke of prayer. "If two or three are gathered together in My name, there am I in the midst of them for any prayer request" (ref. Matthew 18:15-20).

October 14-21, 28 AD

During the Feast of Tabernacles, while Yeshua was in Jerusalem, tension built between Yeshua and the rulers of the Jews. The rulers considered Him a mad man and believed He should be killed, while the common people believed He was the Messiah (ref. John 7:1-53).

On the last day of the feast, Yeshua stood up and cried out, "If any man thirst, let him come to Me and drink. He that believeth on Me, as the scripture has said, shall receive the Holy Spirit" (ref. John 7:37-39). Many people heard and believed this was the prophet whom they were to look for.

15 The LORD your God will raise up for you a prophet like me from among you, from your brethren—him you shall heed— 16 just as you desired of the LORD your God at Horeb on the day of the assembly, when you said, 'Let me not hear again the voice of the LORD my God, or see this great fire any more, lest I die.' 17 And the LORD said to me, 'They have rightly said all that they have spoken. 18 I will raise up for them a prophet like you from among their brethren; and I will put my words in his mouth, and he shall speak to them all that I command him. 19 And whoever will not give heed to my words which he shall speak in my name, I myself will require it of him.133

(Deuteronomy 18:15-19, RSV)

Moses saw that Messiah would be more important than He was to Israel.

6. Similarities between Moses and Yeshua

- Both were leaders, prophets, priests, lawgivers, teachers
- Both spent early years in Egypt
- Both were rejected by relatives later accepted as leader
- Each one the wisest of their day
- Both confront demonic powers and were able to subdue them
- Moses appointed seventy rulers over Israel (the beginning of the Sanhedrin) ...Yeshua sent seventy disciples to teach the nations
- Neither one remained in the tomb
- Both fasted for forty days and faced spiritual crises on the mountain top
- Moses stretched his hand and commanded the Red Sea to allow the children of Israel to cross ... Yeshua rebuked waves of the Sea of Galilee to be still
- Both faces shone with the Glory of Heaven
- Moses rescued Israel from the dead religion of pagan Egypt ... Yeshua rescued Israel from the dead letter of the law of tradition.
- They both cured lepers and showed their authority through miracles they performed before many witnesses.
- Moses conquered the enemy of Israel the Amalekites with his upraised arms ... Yeshua conquered our great enemy sin and death with His upraised arms on the cross.
- Moses lifted the brazen serpent to heal his people ...Yeshua was lifted upon the cross to heal all believers of their sin.

---

[133] The Holy Bible: The Revised Standard Version. Oak Harbor: Logos Research Systems, Inc., 1971.

- The people were ungrateful and rebellious against the leadership of both.
- Moses and Yeshua died on a hill.
- Moses promised another Prophet would come ...Yeshua promised the Holy Spirit would come.
- In the month of Nisan (March-April) on the fourteenth day — the feast of Passover, both Moses and Yeshua freed all who trusted them.
- On the seventeenth day of the Feast of First fruits, Moses brought about the resurrection of the children of Israel as they passed through the Red Sea ...On the anniversary of that day, Yeshua became the first fruits of the resurrection as He arose from the dead.
- Fifty days later on the Feast of Pentecost, God gave to Moses and the people the Torah, the Law......Fifty days after His resurrection, God gave the church the great gift of the baptism of the Holy Spirit.134

December 14-15, 28 AD

After the Feast of Dedication (also known as Hanukkah), which is during December, Yeshua set His face to go to Jerusalem (ref. John 10:22). There He would face His destiny. On His way He sent out seventy men, two by two, to go to the various towns and villages to share God's news of the Kingdom in areas where He would come to. The seventy returned to Yeshua excited about what God had done (ref. Luke 10:1-24).

Then Yeshua showed He was the light in this dark world. "When the Son of man is lifted up then You will know I am the promised One and that I do nothing of Myself but what the Father has taught Me" (ref. John 8:12-30).

7. Yeshua's parables and miracles

December 28 AD

On Yeshua's travels He and His disciples stayed at the house of Mary and Martha in Bethany. This became their home base whenever they were in the Jerusalem area. While they were there, Yeshua healed a man born blind. He put clay on his eyes. Then He told him to go to the pool of Siloam and wash his eyes. The blind man did what he was told and he was healed. This caused quite a stir among the religious leaders. They could not believe the miracle nor could they believe that Yeshua was the promised Messiah. They cast the blind man from the synagogue because of his testimony that Yeshua had healed him (ref. John 9:35-41).

Yeshua told the people He is the good shepherd. He takes care of the sheep and knows each one. "There are many thieves and hirelings who flee when danger comes and do not care for the welfare of the sheep. My sheep hear My voice and know Me. They will not be plucked from My hand" (ref. John 10:29-38).

Yeshua called judgment against the Pharisees. Their plot thickened to kill Yeshua after He raised Lazarus from the dead (ref. John 11:37-54).

Yeshua then shared parables that showed the importance of being in right standing with God and not relying on the riches of the world. They also spoke of using our stewardship wisely. They also showed that the kingdom of heaven is like a mustard seed. It is also like a great banquet that is

---

134 Jeffrey, Grant R. Prophecies of Heaven the Last Frontier. New York: Bantam Books. Pages 82 and 83.

being prepared for guests who were invited and refused to come so that the poor and sinners were invited instead (ref. Luke 12:35-48; Luke 13:18-21, Luke 14:7-24).

January 28 AD

"When you wish to come into the kingdom, you need to count the cost. You need to be prepared" (ref. Luke 14:25-35).

February 28 AD

While Yeshua was spending time with tax collectors and sinners, He taught that the kingdom of heaven is like finding something that was lost and that is precious to the Father. We are like a valuable coin. Regardless whether we are a son or daughter who is a prodigal or a religious snob, He rejoices over anyone who is restored to Him (ref. Luke 15:1-32).

The kingdom of God will come quietly like it did during the days of Noah. There was harvesting, eating, drinking and marrying until the flood came and destroyed all except those who were in the ark (ref. Luke 17:26-30).

The kingdom of heaven is like a landowner who hired people throughout the day. They all received the same wage because they will all receive the same benefit of being in the kingdom regardless of how long they labored for God. But their reward will be according to what their works were, whether they are good or evil works (ref. Luke 17:1-10; Luke 16:19-31).

8. Yeshua's march to Jerusalem toward His sacrificial death

March 28 AD

After this time, Yeshua went to Jerusalem and talked to His twelve disciples and said to them,

> *33...... Behold, we go up to Jerusalem; and the Son of man shall be delivered unto the chief priests, and unto the scribes; and they shall condemn him to death, and shall deliver him to the Gentiles: 34 And they shall mock him, and shall scourge him, and shall spit upon him, and shall kill him: and the third day he shall rise again.135*

> (Mark 10:33-34, KJV)

> *34 And they understood none of these things: and this saying was hid from them, neither knew they the things which were spoken.136*

> (Luke 18:34, KJV)

> *24 Seventy weeks of years are decreed concerning your people and your holy city, to finish the transgression, to put an end to sin, and to atone for iniquity, to bring in everlasting righteousness, to seal both vision and prophet, and to anoint a most holy place. 25 Know therefore and understand that from the going forth of the word to restore and build Jerusalem to the coming of an anointed one, a prince, there shall be seven weeks. Then for sixty-two weeks it shall be built again with squares*

---

[135] The Holy Bible: King James Version. Oak Harbor: Logos Research Systems, Inc., 1995.

[136] Ibid.

and moat, but in a troubled time. 26 And after the sixty-two weeks, an anointed one shall be cut off, and shall have nothing; and the people of the prince who is to come shall destroy the city and the sanctuary. Its end shall come with a flood, and to the end there shall be war; desolations are decreed. 27 And he shall make a strong covenant with many for one week; and for half of the week he shall cause sacrifice and offering to cease; and upon the wing of abominations shall come one who makes desolate, until the decreed end is poured out on the desolator.137

(Daniel 9:24-27, RSV)

The seventy weeks of Daniel are seventy weeks of years which are equal to 490 years. It started at the decree of Artaxerxes in the twentieth year of his reign to rebuild the walls of the city of Jerusalem. It was the month of Nisan or April 445 BC. The first week of years is forty-nine years which brings it to 397 BC. Sixty-two more weeks of years is 434 years more. This brings us to when Messiah Yeshua rode into Jerusalem to offer himself as God's lamb, the Messiah. The Messiah was cut off. The day He arrived in Jerusalem on a donkey's colt was April 6, AD 32. (That is 173,850; divided by the Jewish year of 360 days that is 483 years or sixty-nine weeks of years.)

It was in 70 AD that Titus the Roman destroyed Jerusalem and its temple. The final week or seventieth week of Daniel's prophecy is a period of seven years which is future and is yet to be fulfilled during the great tribulation and the end of this current period know as the last days.

9. The last week — Passover week

Last week — April 1, AD 29

The twenty-ninth jubilee year

a. Yeshua and His disciples in Bethany

When the Jewish Passover was near, many of the people went to Jerusalem. Six days before Passover, Yeshua and the disciples went to Bethany where Mary and Martha lived as well as Lazarus who was raised from the dead (ref. John 11:55-57).

The chief priests were angry and were plotting on how they could put Lazarus as well as Yeshua to death, since it was by Lazarus' testimony of his resurrection that many of the Jews believed in Yeshua. They were jealous and angry that their authority was challenged.

While Yeshua and the disciples were at the table eating, Mary anointed the feet of Yeshua with one pound of spikenard, which is a very costly ointment. She then wiped His feet with her hair and the odor of the ointment filled the house. Judas Iscariot, who was the treasurer, said,

"Why was this not sold and given to the poor?" He said this because he was a thief and kept the money bag.

Then Yeshua said, "Let her alone. She is preparing Me for My burial. The poor you will always have with you but I will not always be here" (ref. John 12:2-8)

---

[137] The Holy Bible: The Revised Standard Version. Oak Harbor: Logos Research Systems, Inc., 1971.

b. A donkey and colt found for Yeshua

A week before Yeshua's crucifixion (Tuesday sunset to Wednesday sunset), Yeshua and the disciples were near Jerusalem by the villages of Bethage and Bethany. Yeshua told two disciples to go into the village and find a donkey and her colt with her. "Bring the colt to Me. If any person objects, tell them that the Lord has need of them."

c. Palm Sunday

(Fourth day before Passover, *Nisan* 11, Saturday sunset to Sunday sunset [Palm Sunday]) So the disciples brought the colt to Yeshua. He sat on it and rode to Jerusalem. This was done according to scripture.

> *4 All this was done, that it might be fulfilled which was spoken by the prophet, saying, 5 Tell ye the daughter of Sion, Behold, thy King cometh unto thee, meek, and sitting upon an ass, and a colt the foal of an ass.138*
>
> (Matthew 21:4-5, KJV)

A great multitude spread their garments on the way and spread banners from the trees along the way crying, "Hosanna to the Son of David: Blessed is He that cometh in the name of the Lord. Hosanna in the highest" (ref. Zechariah 9:9).

Some of the Pharisees said to Him, "Master, rebuke Your disciples."

He answered and said, "I tell you if they hold their peace, the stones would immediately cry out." Yeshua then beheld the city and wept saying, "If they had known Your peace, but this is hid from their eyes." Then He prophesied against the city (ref. Matthew 21:1-11; Luke 19:42; John 12:12-19).

> *43 For the days shall come upon thee, that thine enemies shall cast a trench about thee, and compass thee round, and keep thee in on every side, 44 And shall lay thee even with the ground, and thy children within thee; and they shall not leave in thee one stone upon another; because thou knewest not the time of thy visitation.139*
>
> (Luke 19:43-44, KJV)

This was fulfilled in 70 AD when Titus the Roman and his army destroyed the city and the temple.

d. Yeshua cleanses the temple

Then Jesus went into the temple of God and cast out all that bought and sold. He overthrew the tables of the money changers and said unto them, "My house shall be called the house of prayer; but you have made it a den of thieves" (ref. Matthew 21:12-17; Mark 11:15-48).

---

[138] The Holy Bible: King James Version. Oak Harbor: Logos Research Systems, Inc., 1995.

[139] Ibid.

The blind and the lame came to Him in the temple and He healed them. The children cried in the temple, "Hosanna to the Son of David." The chief priests and scribes were sore displeased. They sought to destroy Him.

> *16 And said unto him, Hearest thou what these say? And Jesus saith unto them, Yea; have ye never read, Out of the mouth of babes and sucklings thou hast perfected praise?140*
>
> (Matthew 21:16, KJV)

e. Scribes and Yeshua lock horns

Then Jesus entered into Jerusalem and into the temple. When evening came, He went to Bethany with the twelve.

When Yeshua returned to Jerusalem, the scribes demanded to know by what authority He did His miracles and spoke His teaching. Yeshua answered:

> *4 The baptism of John, was it from heaven, or of men? 5 And they reasoned with themselves, saying, If we shall say, From heaven; he will say, Why then believed ye him not? 6 But and if we say, Of men; all the people will stone us: for they be persuaded that John was a prophet. 7 And they answered, that they could not tell whence it was. 8 And Jesus said unto them, Neither tell I you by what authority I do these things.141*
>
> (Luke 20:4-8, KJV)

1) More parables

Then Yeshua spoke several parables. Among those was this one: There were two sons who were asked by their father to work in his vineyard. One refused, repented, then went later while the other said he would and did not. The lesson of this parable was that the harlots and publicans who repented will enter the kingdom of God before the religious and the self- righteous rulers who would not repent and do God's bidding (ref. Matthew 21:28-32).

The next parable Yeshua spoke was about a certain man who planted a vineyard and while in a far away country leased it out to husbandmen. The landowner sent a servant to get his part of the proceeds. The husbandmen beat him and sent him away with nothing. They gave the same treatment to several other servants who were sent.

Then the owner sent his son thinking they would respect him when they saw him. When the husbandmen saw him they decided to kill him so they could take his inheritance. "When the owner shall come, he will destroy those evil men and give the vineyard to others" (ref. Matthew 21:33-46; Mark 12:1-12; Luke 20:9-19).

> *17 And he beheld them, and said, What is this then that is written, The stone which the builders rejected, the same is become the head of the corner? 18 Whosoever*

---

140 Ibid.

141 The Holy Bible: King James Version. Oak Harbor: Logos Research Systems, Inc., 1995.

shall fall upon that stone shall be broken; but on whomsoever it shall fall, it will grind him to powder. 19 And the chief priests and the scribes the same hour sought to lay hands on him; and they feared the people: for they perceived that he had spoken this parable against them.142

(Luke 20:17-19, KJV)

2) More interchange

The Pharisees took counsel on how they might trap Yeshua in His talk (ref. Mark 12:13-17; Luke 20:20-26).

16 And they sent out unto him their disciples with the Herodians, saying, Master, we know that thou art true, and teachest the way of God in truth, neither carest thou for any man: for thou regardest not the person of men. 17 Tell us therefore, What thinkest thou? Is it lawful to give tribute unto Caesar, or not? 18 But Jesus perceived their wickedness, and said, Why tempt ye me, ye hypocrites? 19 Shew me the tribute money. And they brought unto him a penny. 20 And he saith unto them, Whose is this image and superscription? 21 They say unto him, Caesar's. Then saith he unto them, Render therefore unto Caesar the things which are Caesar's; and unto God the things that are God's. 22 When they had heard these words, they marvelled, and left him, and went their way.143

(Matthew 22:16-22, KJV)

The Sadducees, who say there is no resurrection, asked Yeshua a question: "Moses says if a man dies who has no children, his brother shall raise up seed unto his brother" (ref. Mark 12:18-33). Now there was a situation where:

25 ......there were with us seven brethren: and the first, when he had married a wife, deceased, and, having no issue, left his wife unto his brother: 26 Likewise the second also, and the third, unto the seventh. 27 And last of all the woman died also. 28 Therefore in the resurrection whose wife shall she be of the seven? for they all had her. 29 Jesus answered and said unto them, Ye do err, not knowing the scriptures, nor the power of God. 30 For in the resurrection they neither marry, nor are given in marriage, but are as the angels of God in heaven. 31 But as touching the resurrection of the dead, have ye not read that which was spoken unto you by God, saying, 32 I am the God of Abraham, and the God of Isaac, and the God of Jacob? God is not the God of the dead, but of the living 33 And when the multitude heard this, they were astonished at his doctrine.144

(Matthew 22:25-33, KJV)

---

[142] Ibid.

[143] Ibid.

[144] Ibid.

35 And Jesus answered and said, while he taught in the Temple, How say the scribes that Christ is the Son of David? 36 For David himself said by the Holy Ghost, The LORD said to my Lord, Sit thou on my right hand, till I make thine enemies thy footstool. 37 David therefore himself calleth him Lord; and whence is he then his son? And the common people heard him gladly. 38 And he said unto them in his doctrine, Beware of the scribes, which love to go in long clothing, and love salutations in the marketplaces.145

(Mark 12:35-38, KJV)

After the Sadducees were silenced, Pharisees asked Yeshua, "What is the greatest commandment in the law?"

37 Jesus said unto him, Thou shalt love the Lord thy God with all thy heart, and with all thy soul, and with all thy mind. 38 This is the first and great commandment. 39 And the second is like unto it, Thou shalt love thy neighbour as thyself. 40 On these two commandments hang all the law and the prophet.146

(Matthew 22:37-40, KJV)

Yeshua asked the Pharisees, "Whose Son is the Messiah?"
They answered, "The Son of David."
Yeshua said to them, "How can David when he is in spirit call Him Lord when He says:

44 The LORD said unto my Lord, Sit thou on my right hand, till I make thine enemies thy footstool? 45 If David then call him Lord, how is he his son? 46 And no man was able to answer him a word, neither durst any man from that day forth ask him any more questions.147

(Matthew 22:44-46, KJV)

The religious rulers were angry while the common people heard Him gladly.

Then Yeshua blasted the Pharisees and scribes for making the Law of Moses more complicated than God had intended. The Law was meant to be a blessing; but, the Pharisees had added stipulations that it made very hard for the common people to bear.

They also were so concerned for the details of the Law that they forgot mercy and faith. Outwardly they appeared to be righteous, but they were full of hypocrisy and iniquity, as their forefathers, who killed the prophets God sent to them (ref. Matthew 23:1).

f. Yeshua speaks of the signs of the end of times

When Yeshua and His disciples looked at the stones of the temple, the disciples were quite impressed. Yeshua said, "There shall not be left one stone upon another. They shall all be thrown down."

---

[145] Ibid.

[146] Ibid.

[147] Ibid.

The disciples asked, "When shall these things be and what shall be the sign of Your coming and the end of the world?"

Yeshua spoke of the signs of the end of times (ref. Matthew 24; Mark 13; Luke 21). These are the signs:

1. Many deceivers claiming to be Messiah
2. Wars and rumors of wars
3. Nations shall rise against each other
4. Famines, pestilence, earthquakes in various places
5. Many believers will be killed for Yeshua's sake

> *11 But when they shall lead you, and deliver you up, take no thought beforehand what ye shall speak, neither do ye premeditate: but whatsoever shall be given you in that hour, that speak ye: for it is not ye that speak, but the Holy Ghost.148*
>
> (Mark 13:11, KJV)

> *12 But before all these, they shall lay their hands on you, and persecute you, delivering you up to the synagogues, and into prisons, being brought before kings and rulers for my name's sake.149*
>
> (Luke 21:12, KJV)

6. People will hate and betray one another
7. Rise of many false prophets
8. Iniquity shall abound
9. Love of many will grow cold
10. The gospel of the kingdom shall be preached into all the world then the end shall come
11. He that endures to the end shall be saved
12. The abomination of desolation shall sit in the holy place which is the desecration of the temple—flee and don't turn back.
13.

> *11 And from the time that the continual burnt offering is taken away, and the abomination that makes desolate is set up, there shall be a thousand two hundred and ninety days.150*
>
> (Daniel 12:11, RSV)

> *27 And he shall make a strong covenant with many for one week; and for half of the week he shall cause sacrifice and offering to cease; and upon the wing of abomina-*

---

148 Ibid.

149 Ibid.

150 The Holy Bible: The Revised Standard Version. Oak Harbor: Logos Research Systems, Inc., 1971.

tions shall come one who makes desolate, until the decreed end is poured out on the desolator.151

(Daniel 9:27, RSV)

14. Sun and moon will be darkened, men's hearts shall fail for fear when these things are happening — stars shall fall from heaven
15. Messiah shall return in the clouds with power and glory. All the people shall mourn.
16. At the sound of the trumpet, the angels shall gather the elect from all ends of the earth.
17. It shall be like the days before the flood, the people were eating, drinking, marrying until the day Noah entered into the ark. There was violence everywhere. (It will be a surprise, they weren't expecting this; so shall be the coming of the Son of man.) His coming is imminent and He will judge all people; so be alert.
18. Israel will be reestablished before His return as seen in the parable of the fig tree. When Israel is a nation again, which is the fig tree, that generation shall not pass until these things are past. No one knows the day or hour when this shall happen, not even the angels, or the Son, only the Father (ref. Mark 13:32). It is now sixty years since the birth of Israel which was May 14, 1948.

The kingdom of heaven will be like ten virgins. Five were wise and five were foolish. The wise were prepared with the light (Holy Spirit) while the five foolish did not have enough light when the bridegroom came (ref. Matthew 25:1-13).

The kingdom of heaven is like a man who was going on a long trip and divided his goods among his servants to be stewards of those goods. Then they could trade and increase his property. To the more skilled he gave five talents; the least skilled received one talent. The gentleman returned to get an account of what they earned. They all received an increase of their talents except the servant who had one and didn't do anything with it. Those who used their talents he rewarded. The one who wasted his talent was judged and punished (ref. Matthew 25:14-30).

The kingdom will be a time when Yeshua will come in His glory and separate His sheep from the goats (who do not love Him and do His will) (ref Matthew 25:35-46).

32 And before him shall be gathered all nations: and he shall separate them one from another, as a shepherd divideth his sheep from the goats: 33 And he shall set the sheep on his right hand, but the goats on the left. 34 Then shall the King say unto them on his right hand, Come, ye blessed of my Father, inherit the kingdom prepared for you from the foundation of the world.152

(Matthew 25:32-34, KJV)

g. Final plot to kill Messiah

It was (Monday sunset to Tuesday sunset—*Nisan* 13) two days before the Feast of Passover when Yeshua said He was to be betrayed and crucified.

---

[151] Ibid.

[152] The Holy Bible: King James Version. Oak Harbor: Logos Research Systems, Inc., 1995.

At this time the chief priests and scribes and elders of the people and Caiaphas the High Priest gathered together to figure a crafty way to kill Yeshua.

They were afraid to do it on Passover lest the common people would rebel (ref. Matthew 26:1-5; Luke 22:1-2; Mark 14:1-2).

On the same day, Yeshua was in Bethany in the house of Simon the leper eating dinner. A woman came with an alabaster box with precious ointment. She poured the ointment on His head. The disciples were indignant and said this was a waste. This ointment could have been sold and the proceeds given to the poor.

Yeshua responded, "She has done a wonderful thing to me. The poor will always be with you, but I will not always be here. She has anointed My body for My burial. Wherever this gospel is preached, what she has done will be told in memory of her kindness" (ref. Matthew 26:6-13; Mark 14:3-9).

After this time, Satan entered into Judas Iscariot who went to the chief priests to betray Yeshua to them. They promised to give Judas thirty pieces of silver if he would betray Yeshua at a time when He was away from the multitude. (This is the price of a female slave.) So Judas went away until an opportune time came (ref. Matthew 26:14-16; Mark 14:10-11; Luke 32:3-6).

Certain Greeks came to the feast and sought out Yeshua. Yeshua said, "The Son of man shall be glorified." He also spoke of His death and Resurrection, as well causing all men to come to Him.

24 Verily, verily, I say unto you, Except a corn of wheat fall into the ground and die, it abideth alone: but if it die, it bringeth forth much fruit. 25 He that loveth his life shall lose it; and he that hateth his life in this world shall keep it unto life eternal. 26 If any man serve me, let him follow me; and where I am, there shall also my servant be: if any man serve me, him will my Father honour. 27 Now is my soul troubled; and what shall I say? Father, save me from this hour: but for this cause came I unto this hour. 28 Father, glorify thy name. Then came there a voice from heaven, saying, I have both glorified it, and will glorify it again. 29 The people therefore, that stood by, and heard it, said that it thundered: others said, An angel spake to him. 30 Jesus answered and said, This voice came not because of me, but for your sakes. 31 Now is the judgment of this world: now shall the prince of this world be cast out. 32 And I, if I be lifted up from the earth, will draw all men unto me. 33 This he said, signifying what death he should die. 34 The people answered him, We have heard out of the law that Christ abideth for ever: and how sayest thou, The Son of man must be lifted up? who is this Son of man? 35 Then Jesus said unto them, Yet a little while is the light with you. Walk while ye have the light, lest darkness come upon you: for he that walketh in darkness knoweth not whither he goeth. 36 While ye have light, believe in the light, that ye may be the children of light. These things spake Jesus, and departed, and did hide himself from them.153

(John 12:24-36, KJV)

37 But though he had done so many miracles before them, yet they believed not on him: 38 That the saying of Esaias the prophet might be fulfilled, which he spake, Lord, who hath believed our report? and to whom hath the arm of the Lord been

---

153 The Holy Bible: King James Version. Oak Harbor: Logos Research Systems, Inc., 1995.

revealed? 39 Therefore they could not believe, because that Esaias said again, 40 He hath blinded their eyes, and hardened their heart; that they should not see with their eyes, nor understand with their heart, and be converted, and I should heal them. 41 These things said Esaias, when he saw his glory, and spake of him. 42 Nevertheless among the chief rulers also many believed on him; but because of the Pharisees they did not confess him, lest they should be put out of the synagogue: 43 For they loved the praise of men more than the praise of God. 44 Jesus cried and said, He that believeth on me, believeth not on me, but on him that sent me. 45 And he that seeth me seeth him that sent me. 46 I am come a light into the world, that whosoever believeth on me should not abide in darkness. 47 And if any man hear my words, and believe not, I judge him not: for I came not to judge the world, but to save the world. 48 He that rejecteth me, and receiveth not my words, hath one that judgeth him: the word that I have spoken, the same shall judge him in the last day. 49 For I have not spoken of myself; but the Father which sent me, he gave me a commandment, what I should say, and what I should speak. 50 And I know that his commandment is life everlasting: whatsoever I speak therefore, even as the Father said unto me, so I speak.154

(John 12:37-50, KJV)

Even though the Greeks accepted Yeshua, the Jewish leaders rejected Him.

1) Messianic prophecies seen in Passover week

The Passover season reveals many Messianic prophecies concerning Yeshua's last week of His life on Earth. In Daniel 9, it speaks of the time when Messiah will be killed. In Zechariah 9, we are told of Messiah's triumphal entry into Jerusalem. In Psalm 41, we see that Messiah would be betrayed by a friend. In Zechariah 11, we are told He would be sold for thirty pieces of silver. And in Isaiah 53, we see the details of Yeshua's sufferings — He would be wounded for our sins and transgressions — His hands and feet would be pierced.

2) Passover meal and the betrayer revealed

The day of preparation for Passover day, Tuesday, April AD 29:
When the first day of Passover had arrived, when the lamb was to be killed, Yeshua sent Peter and John to go and prepare the Passover meal for them to eat (ref. Mark 14:12-16; Matthew 26:17-19).

9 And they said unto him, Where wilt thou that we prepare? 10 And he said unto them, Behold, when ye are entered into the city, there shall a man meet you, bearing a pitcher of water; follow him into the house where he entereth in. 11 And ye shall say unto the goodman of the house, The Master saith unto thee, Where is the guest-chamber, where I shall eat the passover with my disciples? 12 And he shall shew

---

154 Ibid.

you a large upper room furnished: there make ready. 13 And they went, and found as he had said unto them: and they made ready the Passover.155

(Luke 22:9-13, KJV)

When evening had arrived, Yeshua was sitting down with the twelve disciples eating the Passover. Then He spoke that one of them was going to betray Him. Then He revealed who it was by giving the sop to Judas Iscariot. Most of the disciples, except the betrayer Judas Iscariot, did not get it. Judas went and did his dirty deed (ref. Matthew 26:20-25; Mark 14:18-21).

21 When Jesus had thus said, he was troubled in spirit, and testified, and said, Verily, verily, I say unto you, that one of you shall betray me. 22 Then the disciples looked one on another, doubting of whom he spake. 23 Now there was leaning on Jesus' bosom one of his disciples, whom Jesus loved. 24 Simon Peter therefore beckoned to him, that he should ask who it should be of whom he spake. 25 He then lying on Jesus' breast saith unto him, Lord, who is it? 26 Jesus answered, He it is, to whom I shall give a sop, when I have dipped it. And when he had dipped the sop, he gave it to Judas Iscariot, the son of Simon. 27 And after the sop Satan entered into him. Then said Jesus unto him, That thou doest, do quickly. 28 Now no man at the table knew for what intent he spake this unto him. 29 For some of them thought, because Judas had the bag, that Jesus had said unto him, Buy those things that we have need of against the feast; or, that he should give something to the poor. 30 He then having received the sop went immediately out: and it was night. 31 Therefore, when he was gone out, Jesus said, Now is the Son of man glorified, and God is glorified in him. 32 If God be glorified in him, God shall also glorify him in himself, and shall straightway glorify him. 33 Little children, yet a little while I am with you. Ye shall seek me: and as I said unto the Jews, Whither I go, ye cannot come; so now I say to you. 34 A new commandment I give unto you, That ye love one another; as I have loved you, that ye also love one another. 35 By this shall all men know that ye are my disciples, if ye have love one to another.156

(John 13:21-35, KJV)

3) Institution of Communion to celebrate Yeshua's death and Resurrection

Yeshua used the Passover meal with the unleavened bread (or matzo) and the wine to show how to celebrate and remember His death and Resurrection. He took the matzo, which was broken and pierced in half, to show this was a picture of His body that was broken for them (like the lamb slain) to give its life, and the piercing of the matzo showed how His body would be pierced. They were to take and eat. He then took the cup of wine and gave thanks, for this was the blood of the new covenant for the forgiveness of sins for many (ref. Matthew 6:26-29; Mark 14:22-25; Luke 22:14-23).

---

155 Ibid.

156 Ibid.

23 For I have received of the Lord that which also I delivered unto you, That the Lord Jesus the same night in which he was betrayed took bread: 24 And when he had given thanks, he brake it, and said, Take, eat: this is my body, which is broken for you: this do in remembrance of me. 25 After the same manner also he took the cup, when he had supped, saying, This cup is the new testament in my blood: this do ye, as oft as ye drink it, in remembrance of me. 26 For as often as ye eat this bread, and drink this cup, ye do shew the Lord's death till he come.157

(1 Corinthians 11:23-26, KJV)

After this, Yeshua settled a dispute among the disciples as to who is greatest in the kingdom. He said that He as chief is one who serves His brethren, not one who lords over others. Then Yeshua showed an example of greatness. He took the lowest job at the meal and washed the feet of His disciples. Peter objected. Yeshua said, "I need to wash your feet or you will have no part in Me."

Peter replied, "Please wash my hands, head, as well as my feet."

10 Jesus saith to him, He that is washed needeth not save to wash his feet, but is clean every whit: and ye are clean, but not all. 11 For he knew who should betray him; therefore said he, Ye are not all clean. 12 So after he had washed their feet, and had taken his garments, and was set down again, he said unto them, Know ye what I have done to you? 13 Ye call me Master and Lord: and ye say well; for so I am. 14 If I then, your Lord and Master, have washed your feet; ye also ought to wash one another's feet. 15 For I have given you an example, that ye should do as I have done to you. 16 Verily, verily, I say unto you, The servant is not greater than his lord; neither he that is sent greater than he that sent him. 17 If ye know these things, happy are ye if ye do them.158

(John 13:10-17, KJV)

Yeshua said, "One who I have chosen has betrayed Me."

18 I speak not of you all: I know whom I have chosen: but that the scripture may be fulfilled, He that eateth bread with me hath lifted up his heel against me. 19 Now I tell you before it come, that, when it is come to pass, ye may believe that I am he.159

(John 13:18-19, KJV)

Yeshua said, "You will turn against Me tonight, for it is written, I will kill the shepherd and the sheep of the flock (which is you) will be scattered abroad."

Peter answered, "I will not turn against You."

Yeshua answered him. "This night before the cock crows you shall deny Me three times" (ref. Matthew 26:31-35; Mark 14:27-31; Luke 22:31-38; John 13:36-38).

---

[157] Ibid.

[158] Ibid.

[159] Ibid.

4) Yeshua comforts His disciples

Then Yeshua shared that they should not be upset about the future, "For in the Father's house there are many mansions. I am preparing a place for each one of you. Then I will come back to you and take you with Me. I am in the Father and He is in Me. The words I speak are His. My works are His."

> *12 Verily, verily, I say unto you, He that believeth on me, the works that I do shall he do also; and greater works than these shall he do; because I go unto my Father. 13 And whatsoever ye shall ask in my name, that will I do, that the Father may be glorified in the Son. 14 If ye shall ask any thing in my name, I will do it. 15 If ye love me, keep my commandments.160*

(John 14:12-15, KJV)

Then Yeshua promised that the Holy Spirit would come to them, after He was gone, to live in them. He would show them the truth of God's Word and how to live. "I am in My Father and you are in Me and I am in you."

"You need to love Me. As a result of your love you will be obedient to Me. The Holy Spirit will live in you and teach you all things, and He will bring to your mind whatever I have said to you. I promise you the peace of God in all situations. I am going away to the Father — rejoice and believe in who I am when you see all that I have told you has come to pass."

Then Yeshua compared Himself to a vine — we are the branches. Every branch that bears fruit will go through pruning to encourage and to bear more fruit. Pruning is painful, but produces results in a believer's life.

Then Yeshua warned that those who are in Messiah will face persecution because they are hated by the world. "The world hates Me as well as they hate the Father who sent Me" (ref. John 15:24-27).

Yeshua also comforted the disciples by telling them He had to go away so that the comforter (Holy Spirit) could come to them. His duty is to reprove the world of sin, and of unrighteousness and of judgment. The Spirit will guide in all truth. He will glorify Yeshua.

"For a little while you will not see Me and yet a little while you shall see Me."

> *20 Verily, verily, I say unto you, That ye shall weep and lament, but the world shall rejoice: and ye shall be sorrowful, but your sorrow shall be turned into joy.161*

(John 16:20, KJV)

> *22 And ye now therefore have sorrow: but I will see you again, and your heart shall rejoice, and your joy no man taketh from you. 23 And in that day ye shall ask me nothing. Verily, verily, I say unto you, Whatsoever ye shall ask the Father in my*

---

160 Ibid.

161 Ibid.

name, he will give it you. 24 Hitherto have ye asked nothing in my name: ask, and ye shall receive, that your joy may be full.162

(John 16:22-24, KJV)

Then Yeshua prayed for His own disciples

1 These words spake Jesus, and lifted up his eyes to heaven, and said, Father, the hour is come; glorify thy Son, that thy Son also may glorify thee: 2 As thou hast given him power over all flesh, that he should give eternal life to as many as thou hast given him. 3 And this is life eternal, that they might know thee the only true God, and Jesus Christ, whom thou hast sent. 4 I have glorified thee on the earth: I have finished the work which thou gavest me to do. 5 And now, O Father, glorify thou me with thine own self with the glory which I had with thee before the world was. 6 I have manifested thy name unto the men which thou gavest me out of the world: thine they were, and thou gavest them me; and they have kept thy word. 7 Now they have known that all things whatsoever thou hast given me are of thee. 8 For I have given unto them the words which thou gavest me; and they have received them, and have known surely that I came out from thee, and they have believed that thou didst send me. 9 I pray for them: I pray not for the world, but for them which thou hast given me; for they are thine. 10 And all mine are thine, and thine are mine; and I am glorified in them. 11 And now I am no more in the world, but these are in the world, and I come to thee. Holy Father, keep through thine own name those whom thou hast given me, that they may be one, as we are. 12 While I was with them in the world, I kept them in thy name: those that thou gavest me I have kept, and none of them is lost, but the son of perdition; that the scripture might be fulfilled. 13 And now come I to thee; and these things I speak in the world, that they might have my joy fulfilled in themselves. 14 I have given them thy word; and the world hath hated them, because they are not of the world, even as I am not of the world. 15 I pray not that thou shouldest take them out of the world, but that thou shouldest keep them from the evil. 16 They are not of the world, even as I am not of the world. 17 Sanctify them through thy truth: thy word is truth. 18 As thou hast sent me into the world, even so have I also sent them into the world. 19 And for their sakes I sanctify myself, that they also might be sanctified through the truth. 20 Neither pray I for these alone, but for them also which shall believe on me through their word; 21 That they all may be one; as thou, Father, art in me, and I in thee, that they also may be one in us: that the world may believe that thou hast sent me. 22 And the glory which thou gavest me I have given them; that they may be one, even as we are one: 23 I in them, and thou in me, that they may be made perfect in one; and that the world may know that thou hast sent me, and hast loved them, as thou hast loved me. 24 Father, I will that they also, whom thou hast given me, be with me where I am; that they may behold my glory, which thou hast given me: for thou lovedst me before the foundation of the world. 25 O righteous Father, the world hath not known thee: but I have known thee, and these have known that thou

---

[162] Ibid.

hast sent me. 26 And I have declared unto them thy name, and will declare it: that the love wherewith thou hast loved me may be in them, and I in them.163

(John 17:1-26, KJV)

h. To Gethsemane to be betrayed

Then Yeshua and His disciples sang a hymn and went out into the Mountain of Olives. There they went to a place called Gethsemane and Yeshua said unto the disciples, "Stay here while I go and pray."

Then He took Peter, James and John with Him. He told them "My soul is exceedingly sorrowful. My death is near. Watch and pray with Me." Yeshua went apart and prayed (ref. Luke 22:39-46; Matthew 26:30-46).

> *36 And he said, Abba, Father, all things are possible unto thee; take away this cup from me: nevertheless not what I will, but what thou wilt. 37 And he cometh, and findeth them sleeping, and saith unto Peter, Simon, sleepest thou? couldest not thou watch one hour? 38 Watch ye and pray, lest ye enter into temptation. The spirit truly is ready, but the flesh is weak. 39 And again he went away, and prayed, and spake the same words. 40 And when he returned, he found them asleep again, (for their eyes were heavy,) neither wist they what to answer him. 41 And he cometh the third time, and saith unto them, Sleep on now, and take your rest: it is enough, the hour is come; behold, the Son of man is betrayed into the hands of sinners. 42 Rise up, let us go; lo, he that betrayeth me is at hand.164*

(Mark 14:36-42, KJV)

Then Judas Iscariot came with a great multitude that had swords and staves. They were the chief priests, elders of the people and Roman soldiers (ref. Matthew 26:30-46; Luke 22:47-53; John 18:2-9).

> *43 And immediately, while he yet spake, cometh Judas, one of the twelve, and with him a great multitude with swords and staves, from the chief priests and the scribes and the elders. 44 And he that betrayed him had given them a token, saying, Whomsoever I shall kiss, that same is he; take him, and lead him away safely. 45 And as soon as he was come, he goeth straightway to him, and saith, Master, master; and kissed him. 46 And they laid their hands on him, and took him. 47 And one of them that stood by drew a sword, and smote a servant of the high priest, and cut off his ear. 48 And Jesus answered and said unto them, Are ye come out, as against a thief, with swords and with staves to take me? 49 I was daily with you in the Temple teaching, and ye took me not: but the scriptures must be fulfilled. 50 And they all forsook him, and fled. 51 And there followed him a certain young man, having a linen cloth cast about his naked body; and the young men laid hold on him: 52 And he left the linen cloth, and fled from them naked. 53 And they led Jesus away to the*

---

163 Ibid.

164 The Holy Bible: King James Version. Oak Harbor: Logos Research Systems, Inc., 1995.

high priest: and with him were assembled all the chief priests and the elders and the scribes.165

(Mark 14:43-53, KJV)

i. Judgment of Yeshua

1) Under Annas

Then the multitude and the captains and officers of the Jews took Jesus and bound Him. He was led away to Annas, the father-in-law of Caiaphas, who was the high priest that year.

Now Caiaphas told the Jewish leaders that it was expedient that one man should die for the people (like the Passover lamb for the atonement of their sins).

The high priest asked of Yeshua's teaching (ref. John 18:12-19).

20 Jesus answered him, I spake openly to the world; I ever taught in the synagogue, and in the Temple, whither the Jews always resort; and in secret have I said nothing. 21 Why askest thou me? ask them which heard me, what I have said unto them: behold, they know what I said. 22 And when he had thus spoken, one of the officers which stood by struck Jesus with the palm of his hand, saying, Answerest thou the high priest so? 23 Jesus answered him, If I have spoken evil, bear witness of the evil: but if well, why smitest thou me?166

(John 18:20-23, KJV)

The soldiers that held Yeshua mocked Him and struck Him.

63 And the men that held Jesus mocked him, and smote him. 64 And when they had blindfolded him, they struck him on the face, and asked him, saying, Prophesy, who is it that smote thee? 65 And many other things blasphemously spake they against him.167

(Luke 22:63-65, KJV)

Many false witnesses came forward at the council to try to put Yeshua to death. Finally two false witnesses said:

61......This fellow said, I am able to destroy the Temple of God, and to build it in three days. 62 And the high priest arose, and said unto him, Answerest thou nothing? what is it which these witness against thee? 63 But Jesus held his peace. And the high priest answered and said unto him, I adjure thee by the living God, that thou tell us whether thou be the Christ, the Son of God. 64 Jesus saith unto him, Thou hast said: nevertheless I say unto you, Hereafter shall ye see the Son of man sitting on the right hand of power, and coming in the clouds of heaven. 65 Then the

---

[165] Ibid.

[166] Ibid.

[167] The Holy Bible: King James Version. Oak Harbor: Logos Research Systems, Inc., 1995.

high priest rent his clothes, saying, He hath spoken blasphemy; what further need have we of witnesses? behold, now ye have heard his blasphemy. 66 What think ye? They answered and said, He is guilty of death. 67 Then did they spit in his face, and buffeted him; and others smote him with the palms of their hands, 68 Saying, Prophesy unto us, thou Christ, Who is he that smote thee? 168

(Matthew 26:61-68, KJV)

Peter followed Yeshua at a distance while He was being led to the high priest's palace. He went in and sat with the servants to see what would happen to Him (ref. Mark 14:53-65; Luke 22:54-65).

Three different people approached Peter and asked if he had been with Yeshua of Nazareth. He denied it three times. Then the cock crowed twice and Peter remembered that Yeshua had said to him, "Before the cock crows twice, you will deny Me three times." Then he wept and fled the scene (ref. Matthew 26:58-72; Luke 22:55-62; John 18:15-27; Mark 4:54-72).

The next day, Wednesday, the council asked:

67 Art thou the Christ? tell us. And he said unto them, If I tell you, ye will not believe: 68 And if I also ask you, ye will not answer me, nor let me go. 69 Hereafter shall the Son of man sit on the right hand of the power of God. 70 Then said they all, Art thou then the Son of God? And he said unto them, Ye say that I am. 71 And they said, What need we any further witness? for we ourselves have heard of his own mouth. 169

(Luke 22:67-71, KJV)

When it was early in the morning, the chief priests and elders of the people took counsel against Yeshua to put Him to death. Then they bound Him and delivered Him to Pontius Pilate, the governor (ref. Matthew 27:1-14; Mark 15:2-5; Luke 23:1-5; John 18:28-38).

After Judas Iscariot, who betrayed Yeshua, saw that Yeshua was condemned to death, he repented. He brought the thirty pieces of silver, which the priests and elders had given to him for betraying Yeshua,

4 Saying, I have sinned in that I have betrayed the innocent blood. And they said, What is that to us? see thou to that. 5 And he cast down the pieces of silver in the Temple, and departed, and went and hanged himself. 6 And the chief priests took the silver pieces, and said, It is not lawful for to put them into the treasury, because it is the price of blood. 7 And they took counsel, and bought with them the potter's field, to bury strangers in. 8 Wherefore that field was called, The field of blood, unto this day. 9 Then was fulfilled that which was spoken by Jeremy the prophet, saying, And they took the thirty pieces of silver, the price of him that was valued, whom they of the children of Israel did value; 10 And gave them for the potter's field, as the Lord appointed me. 170

(Matthew 27:4-10, KJV)

---

168 Ibid.

169 Ibid.

170 Ibid.

The money was used by the priests to purchase the potter's field (ref. Acts 1:18-19).

2) Under Pontius Pilate

When Yeshua stood before Pilate, the governor asked, "Are You the king of the Jews?" "You said It."

> *36 Jesus answered, My kingdom is not of this world: if my kingdom were of this world, then would my servants fight, that I should not be delivered to the Jews: but now is my kingdom not from hence. 37 Pilate therefore said unto him, Art thou a king then? Jesus answered, Thou sayest that I am a king. To this end was I born, and for this cause came I into the world, that I should bear witness unto the truth. Every one that is of the truth heareth my voice. 38 Pilate saith unto him, What is truth? And when he had said this, he went out again unto the Jews, and saith unto them, I find in him no fault at all.171*

(John 18:36-38, KJV)

When the chief priest accused Him of many things, He did not answer anything and Pilate marveled.

Then Pilate said, "I find no fault in this man" (ref. Matthew 27:11-14; Mark 15:2-5, Luke 23:1-5; John 18:28-38).

When Pilate heard that Yeshua was from Galilee, he knew He was of Herod's jurisdiction. So he sent Yeshua to Herod who was at Jerusalem.

3) Under Herod

When Herod saw Yeshua, he was glad. He hoped to see some miracle done by Him. He asked many questions, but Yeshua said not a word. Herod and his men of war put a gorgeous robe on Yeshua and mocked Him and sent Him again to Pilate. (That day Pilate and Herod became friends) (ref. Luke 23:6-12).

4) Under Pilate

Then Pilate called together the chief priests and rulers of the people, saying, "I have examined Him and find no fault in this man—neither does Herod. I will just scourge Him then release one prisoner at Passover. Shall I release Barabbas or the king of the Jews?"

The people yelled, "Release Barabbas." Barabbas was a murderer and robber.

Then Pilate asked, "What should I do with Yeshua?" (whom he wanted to release). The people cried, "Crucify Him."

Then Pilate asked, "What evil has He done? I find no cause of death in Him. I will chastise Him and let Him go." Then the people yelled all the more to crucify Him.

Then Pilate gave the sentence the people required and he released Barabbas (ref. Matthew 27:15-26; Mark 15:6-15; Luke 23:13-40; John 18:39-40).

---

[171] Ibid.

Then the soldiers of Pilate took Yeshua into the praetorian and stripped Him and put on a scarlet robe. Then they crowned Him with a crown of thorns on His head and gave Him a reed as a scepter for His right hand. They bowed their knees before Him and mocked Him, saying: "Hail, King of the Jews." After they mocked Him, Yeshua was brought before Pilate and the people.

After Pilate said he found no fault in Him, the Jews answered, "We have a law, and by our law, He ought to die because He has made Himself the Son of God."

> *8 When Pilate therefore heard that saying, he was the more afraid; 9 And went again into the judgment hall, and saith unto Jesus, Whence art thou? But Jesus gave him no answer. 10 Then saith Pilate unto him, Speakest thou not unto me? knowest thou not that I have power to crucify thee, and have power to release thee? 11 Jesus answered, Thou couldest have no power at all against me, except it were given thee from above: therefore he that delivered me unto thee hath the greater sin. 12 And from thenceforth Pilate sought to release him: but the Jews cried out, saying, If thou let this man go, thou art not Caesar's friend: whosoever maketh himself a king speaketh against Caesar.*[172]

(John 19:8-12, KJV)

It was about the third hour, which is nine o'clock a.m. our time, on the preparation day of Passover (Wednesday). Pilate said, "Behold your King."

But the people said, "Crucify Him."

Pilate said unto them, "Shall I crucify your King?"

The chief priests answered, "We have no king but Caesar." They took Yeshua away to be crucified (ref. John 19:1-16; Matthew 27:27-31; Mark 15:16-19).

j. Crucifixion of Yeshua

Was Jesus Christ Crucified on Good Friday? ……..Does It Make Any Difference?

Nisan 14—The Lord's Passover (Israel's Passover Preparation Day)

Tuesday —6:00 p.m. (First Watch): Jesus observed Passover in the Upper Room with His Apostles (No lamb, because Jesus Himself was to be the Lamb).

Tuesday—9:00 p.m. (Second Watch): Jesus arrested and taken to Caiaphas to be judged.

Tuesday—12:00 midnight (Third Watch): Jesus judged and found guilty of blasphemy to the Sanhedrin.

Wednesday—9:00 a.m. (third hour): Jesus nailed to the cross.
Wednesday—12:00 noon: darkness over the earth to the ninth hour.
Wednesday—3:00 p.m. (ninth hour): Jesus died and gave up the ghost.

---

[172] The Holy Bible: King James Version. Oak Harbor: Logos Research Systems, Inc., 1995.

Nisan 15—Israel Passover Day—First Day of Unleavened Bread

Wednesday—6:00 p.m. Jesus' body placed in tomb.
Wednesday—6:00 p.m. to 6:00 p.m. Thursday; Jesus' body was in the tomb—one night and one day (24 hours)

Nisan 16—Second Day of Unleavened Bread
Thursday—6:00 p.m. to 6:00 p.m. Friday: Jesus' body lay in the tomb for the second night and second day (total now 48 hours).

Nisan 17—Third Day of Unleavened Bread
Friday—6:00 p.m. to 6:00 Saturday: Jesus' body lay in the tomb for the third night and third day (total now 72 hours).

"For as Jonas was three days and three nights in the whale's belly; so shall the Son of man be three days and nights in the heart of the earth" (Matt. 12:40).

Jesus arrived in Jerusalem on the eve of Nisan 9 because He came to fulfill the Father's will that He would be the Lamb of God who would take away the sins of the world; lambs chosen for Passover must be separated from parents for seven days before the Day of Preparation.

Jesus was anointed by Man on Nisan 10 for His death, because a sacrificial lamb must be chosen (anointed) on this day, four days before the Passover. Nisan 10 the year Christ was crucified was indicated to be a Saturday Sabbath. Four days later, on Wednesday, Jesus was crucified.

Jesus not only must have fulfilled every specific prophecy, but also every example and type, else He could not have been the Messiah.173

After the soldiers mocked Yeshua, they took off the purple robe and put His clothes on Him and led Him away to be crucified. While Yeshua was carrying the cross, the soldiers compelled Simon of Cyrene to help bear the cross of Yeshua to a place in Hebrew called Golgotha (ref. Matthew 27:32-34; Mark 15:20-23; Luke 23:26-32, John 19:17).

Nine o'clock AM — Twelve o'clock pm
When they came to the place called Calvary, Yeshua was crucified with two malefactors—one on the right and one on the left.

The title put on Yeshua's cross was written "Jesus of Nazareth the King of the Jews." This was written in Hebrew, Greek and Latin. The chief priests objected to the sign but Pilate said, "What I have written, I have written." Then the soldiers who crucified Yeshua cast lots for His vestures, and divided His clothes into four parts.

24 They said therefore among themselves, Let us not rend it, but cast lots for it, whose it shall be: that the scripture might be fulfilled, which saith, They parted my raiment among them, and for my vesture they did cast lots. These things therefore the soldiers did.174

(John 19:24, KJV)

---

173 "Was Jesus Christ Crucified on Good Friday? Does it Make Any Difference?" The Gospel Truth. Page 20.

174 The Holy Bible: King James Version. Oak Harbor: Logos Research Systems, Inc., 1995.

There were some who stood reviling Him. "If You are the Son of God.......come down from the cross. He saved others, Himself He cannot save. If He be the king of Israel, let Him come down from the cross and we will believe Him." The thieves with Him also reviled Him (ref. Matthew 27:35-44; Mark 15:24-32; Luke 23:33-43; John 19:18-27).

Near the cross stood Mary, Yeshua's mother, and her sister, Mary, the wife of Cleophas, and Mary Magdalene. When Yeshua saw His mother and John, the disciple He loved, standing nearby, He said to His mother, "Woman, behold your son." Then He said to His disciple, "Behold thy mother." From that hour John took care of her in his home.

Twelve o'clock — Three o'clock p.m.

From twelve o'clock to three o'clock there was darkness over all the land. Then Jesus cried out, "My God, My God why have You forsaken me?" (ref. Matthew 27:45-50; Mark 15:33-37; Luke 23:44; John 19:28-30).

When the darkness struck, the veil separating the holy place from the holiest place in the temple. The vail was torn from the top to the bottom to show that man now had access to God's presence. It also showed that God tore the veil, not man.

After this Jesus said, "I thirst." So a sponge with vinegar and hyssop was put to His mouth. He said, "It is finished."

At three o'clock p.m. Yeshua cried out with a loud voice and said, "Father, into Thy hands I commit My spirit." After He said this, He gave up His spirit and died (ref. Matthew 27:45-50; Mark 1533-37; Luke 23:44-46; John 19:28-37).

It was the preparation for the Passover Sabbath—the same day the Passover lamb is killed for the sins of the people. The leaders of the Jews felt the bodies should not remain on the cross. So they begged Pilate to break the legs of those who were crucified that they might be taken down from the cross. So the soldiers broke the legs of the two thieves crucified with Yeshua. But when they came to Yeshua they did not break His legs because He was already dead.

One soldier pierced his side and out came blood and water.

Archeological research was done on the precise spot of Yeshua's crucifixion. This is the general location as the information referred to above. A drill was used to penetrate some 30 feet of rock at this historic place. Water flowed from this location underground into the Patrick cistern named after the researcher. As was speculated, there is a water passage through the rock into the cistern used for sacrificial rites. This place is called Jeremiah's grotto under Calvary.

In the course of research traces of blood were found on the drill bit used. This blood contained only 24 chromosomes and no X chromosome. This indicates an unusual male and its makeup cannot be that of animals. Human cells are normally made up of 48 chromosomes. This blood sample was tested in a U.S. laboratory.

Not having an alternative explanation, it doesn't take a lot of imagination to link this half number and its location to Yeshua. It makes a certain amount of sense in view of Genesis 3:15. This verse speaks of the seed of a woman and not that of a man.

Twenty-four chromosomes suggest a human being whose earliest embryonic meiosis/mitosis cell division was different. This could possibly be an evidence confirming a virgin birth as predicted in Isaiah 7:14. No one is offering another speculation about how there could be blood with all of its other features, but only have half the usual number of this genetic makeup.

Such archeology was done under rules specified by the Israel Antiquities Authority and took place between1979-89. Wyatt Archeological Research Inc. undertook it and Ron Wyatt found three holes, 13 inches square and three feet deep on Golgotha, cut into the rock. He claimed these were sockets for Roman crosses.

After four years of careful exploration a small entrance into a chamber was discovered. It measured twenty-two feet deep by fourteen feet wide and eight feet high. When they took samples of the dried blood to the Jewish authorities Department of Antiquities, three Israeli rabbis visited the site. One collapsed and was taken to a hospital. A second died and a third was murdered that night.

Israeli authorities sealed the chamber, because it could cause Orthodox Jews to want to build the Third Temple and this could lead to a blowing up of the Dome of the Rock and start a holy war. Jewish rabbinical leaders and non-believers discount Wyatt as sincere, but delusional.

Wyatt has gone to be with the Lord, but his work continues through an associate who assisted him throughout this research His name is Hal Bryan, who is convinced of the validity of this work. Many skeptics deny it and seek to discredit the discoveries in one way or another. Still, certain physical facts cannot be denied and have been verified by the governmental Ministry.

Science can confirm faith, but it cannot create it. Perhaps, your faith parallels mine that a small portion of Yeshua's blood has remained embedded in the rock until this age, when science is capable of examining the DNA. Other drops of bloody residue could have seeped down below the rock. It then would have gone through the water passage, which flowed into the cistern below, the place of Temple sacrifice and was used there. My faith does not require that this be so, but why shouldn't God be able to even satisfy every physical requirement of His sacrificial system, as well as its spiritual accomplishment?[175]

For these things are written that scripture should be fulfilled: "A bone of Him shall not be broken." Another scripture said: "they shall look on Him who they have pierced" (ref. Matthew 27:45-50; Mark 33:46; John 19:28-37).

Then the veil of the temple was rent from top to bottom after a violent earthquake. The graves were opened and many bodies of the saints, which slept, arose. They went into the holy city and appeared to many. Now when the centurions watching Yeshua saw the earthquake and the things being done, they were fearful and said, "Truly this was the Son of God. He was certainly a righteous man." Many women followed from Galilee and ministered; among them were Mary Magdalene, Mary the Mother of James and Joses and Salome. They saw what was happening to Yeshua (ref. Matthew 27:51-55; Mark 15:38-41; Luke 23:47-49).

k. Burial of Yeshua

That evening Joseph of Arimathaea, who was a disciple of Yeshua, went to Pilate and begged for the body of Yeshua. Then Pilate commanded that the body be delivered.

Then Joseph took the body and wrapped it in a clean linen cloth and laid it in a new tomb hewn out of rock. He rolled a large stone over the entrance of the sepulcher and then he departed. That was the day of preparation before the Passover feast which was a very important Sabbath celebration.

Mary Magdalene and Mary the Mother of Joses saw where Yeshua was buried so that they could return with the spices to complete the burial process on Sunday morning (ref. Matthew 27:57-61; Mark 15:42-47; Luke 23:50-56; John 19:38-42).

---

[175] Messianic Jewish Alliance. Number 136. Rancho Mirage: Messianic Jewish Alliance. Page 2-3.

The next day after the preparation, the chief priests and Pharisees came to Pilate and asked that a guard be put at the tomb for three days and seal the stone. "Yeshua said while He was alive 'after three days I shall arise again.' Just in case His disciples come by night and steal His body and say to the people 'He is risen from the dead' and they spread a lie" (ref. Matthew 27:62-66).

l. Resurrection of Yeshua

On the first day of the week at dawn came Mary Magdalene and Mary the mother of James and Salome. They came to bring sweet spices to anoint Yeshua's body. When they arrived, they found that the stone had been rolled away by a great earthquake. An angel of the Lord had descended from heaven and rolled back the stone from the door and sat, and his countenance was like lightening and his raiment white as snow.

The guards were at the tomb when the earthquake came and the angels rolled away the stone in front of the grave. The guards came to the city and told the chief priests what had happened. Then the elders assembled and took counsel. They gave large sums of money to the soldiers to tell the people that Yeshua's disciples came by night and stole His body while they were sleeping. "If this story comes to the governor's ears, we will talk to him and protect you." So the guards took the money and did as they were told. This saying is reported among Jews until this day (ref. Matthew 28:11-15).

The women found the stone had been rolled away. When they entered, they could not find the body of Yeshua. Two young men in shining garments said, "Do not be afraid. Why are you seeking the living among the dead? He is not here; He is risen. Behold He is going before you to Galilee. He told you that the son of man must be delivered into the hands of sinful men and be crucified and on the third day rise again." They remembered His word.

"Go and tell His disciples and Peter that He is going to Galilee and you shall see him" (ref. Matthew 28:1; Mark 18:1; Matthew 28:2-8, Luke 24:1-8; John 20:1).

Mary Magdalene, Joanna, Mary the Mother of James and other women told the disciples about Yeshua being resurrected and alive. The word seemed like a fairytale, so they did not believe.

Then Peter and John decided to check out the women's story and went to the sepulcher. Then Peter looked in and saw the linen wrapped together in a place by itself, separated from the napkin for His head. When they saw the sepulcher, they believed.

They did not know the scripture that He must rise again from the dead (ref. Luke 24:9-12; John 20:2-10).

m. The many appearances of Yeshua after His resurrection

Yeshua appeared first to Mary Magdalene out of whom He had cast seven devils, when she was at the tomb weeping. She looked into the tomb and saw two angels, one at the head and the other at the feet of where the body of Yeshua had lain. They said to her, "Why are you weeping?"

"Because they have taken away my Lord and I don't know where they have put Him." Then she turned and saw Yeshua, but didn't recognize Him. Yeshua asked, "Why are you crying?" She thought it was the gardener.

She said, "Sir, if you have moved Him, tell me where you laid Him and I will take Him away."

Then Yeshua said, "Mary."

She recognized him and said, "Master."

Then Jesus told her, "Don't touch Me, I have not ascended to My Father; but tell My brethren and say unto them I am ascending to My Father and your Father and to My God and your God."

So Mary Magdalene reported these things to the disciples (ref. John 20:11-18). Christ also appeared to other women (ref. Matthew 28:9-10).

Yeshua appeared to two men on their way to Emmaus. He was not recognized. They were discussing Yeshua of Nazareth, who was mighty in word and deed before God and man. They told Him how the chief priests and rulers delivered Him to be condemned to death and had Him crucified. "We thought this was the One who would redeem Israel. It is three days since this happened. Certain women said they saw angels which said that He is alive."

Then Yeshua said, "Oh fools and slow of heart to believe all that the prophets had spoken." Then He began from Moses and all the prophets to explain to them all the scriptures concerning Himself.

As the company drew near the village, Yeshua was constrained to stay and share a meal with them. As they sat at the meal He broke the bread and blessed it and gave it to them. Their eyes were opened and they recognized Him and He vanished out of their sight (ref. Luke 24:13-32).

Then Yeshua appeared to the eleven disciples. They were terrified. "Look at My hands and My feet; handle Me—a spirit does not have flesh and bones." Then He ate a piece of broiled fish to prove He was not a spirit.

Then Jesus said to them, "Peace be unto you; as My Father sent Me so send I you." Then He breathed on them and said, "Receive the Holy Spirit. Whosoever sins you remit, they are remitted unto them, and whosoever sins you retain are retainable."

Thomas, called Didymus, was not with them when Jesus came. So he did not believe their report. He said, "Until I see in His hands the print of the nails and put my finger into the print of the nails and thrust my hand into His side I will not believe" (ref. Mark 16:14; Luke 24:26-43; John 20:19-25).

Eight days later Yeshua appeared to the disciples and Thomas through closed doors. Then He said to Thomas, "Touch My hands and thrust your hand into My side. Don't be faithless, but believe." Then Thomas touched Him and answered, "My Lord and My God."

Yeshua said to him, "Thomas, because you have seen, you believe; blessed are those who have not seen, yet believe" (ref. John 20:19-29).

After these things had happened, Yeshua showed Himself to the disciples at the Sea of Tiberius. There were gathered together Simon Peter, Thomas call Didymus, Nathanael, the sons of Zebedee and two other disciples. They decided to go fishing at night. By the next day they had caught nothing.

The next morning Yeshua stood on the shore, but the disciples did not recognize Him. Then Jesus said, "Did you catch anything?"

They answered, "No." Then He said to them to cast the net on the right side of the ship. They obeyed but they were not able to bring in the nets themselves because of the multitude of fishes, so they called their partners in another ship to come help with their catch. They had caught 153 fish and the nets had not broken. This was a miracle.

Yeshua said unto them after preparing a meal of bread and fish, "Come and dine." This was the third time that Yeshua showed Himself to the disciples (ref. John 21:1-24).

Yeshua gave the great commission to the disciples at a mountain in Galilee when Yeshua came to them. They saw Him and worshiped Him.

18 And Jesus came and spake unto them, saying, All power is given unto me in heaven and in earth. 19 Go ye therefore, and teach all nations, baptizing them in the name of the Father, and of the Son, and of the Holy Ghost: 20 Teaching them to observe all things whatsoever I have commanded you: and, lo, I am with you alway, even unto the end of the world. Amen.176

(Matthew 28:18-20, KJV)

17 And these signs shall follow them that believe; In my name shall they cast out devils; they shall speak with new tongues; 18 They shall take up serpents; and if they drink any deadly thing, it shall not hurt them; they shall lay hands on the sick, and they shall recover.177

(Mark 16:17-18, KJV)

After this He was seen of about five hundred brethren at once (ref: 1 Corinthians 15:6).

44 And he said unto them, These are the words which I spake unto you, while I was yet with you, that all things must be fulfilled, which were written in the law of Moses, and in the prophets, and in the psalms, concerning me. 45 Then opened he their understanding, that they might understand the scriptures, 46 And said unto them, Thus it is written, and thus it behooved Christ to suffer, and to rise from the dead the third day: 47 And that repentance and remission of sins should be preached in his name among all nations, beginning at Jerusalem. 48 And ye are witnesses of these things. 49 And, behold, I send the promise of my Father upon you: but tarry ye in the city of Jerusalem, until ye be endued with power from on high.178

(Luke 24:44-49, KJV)

3 To whom also he shewed himself alive after his passion by many infallible proofs, being seen of them forty days, and speaking of the things pertaining to the kingdom of God: 4 And, being assembled together with them, commanded them that they should not depart from Jerusalem, but wait for the promise of the Father, which, saith he, ye have heard of me. 5 For John truly baptized with water; but ye shall be baptized with the Holy Ghost not many days hence. 6 When they therefore were come together, they asked of him, saying, Lord, wilt thou at this time restore again the kingdom to Israel? 7 And he said unto them, It is not for you to know the times or the seasons, which the Father hath put in his own power. 8 But ye shall receive power, after that the Holy Ghost is come upon you: and ye shall be witnesses unto me both in Jerusalem, and in all Judaea, and in Samaria, and unto the uttermost part of the earth.179

(Acts 1:3-8, KJV)

---

[176] The Holy Bible: King James Version. Oak Harbor: Logos Research Systems, Inc., 1995.

[177] Ibid.

[178] Ibid.

[179] Ibid.

n. Yeshua's ascension

The last appearance and the ascension was on Thursday, May 26 AD 29.

19 So then after the Lord had spoken unto them, he was received up into heaven, and sat on the right hand of God. 20 And they went forth, and preached every where, the Lord working with them, and confirming the word with signs following. Amen.180

(Mark 16:19-20, KJV)

50 And he led them out as far as to Bethany, and he lifted up his hands, and blessed them. 51 And it came to pass, while he blessed them, he was parted from them, and carried up into heaven. 52 And they worshipped him, and returned to Jerusalem with great joy: 53 And were continually in the temple, praising and blessing God. Amen.181

(Luke 24:50-53, KJV)

9 And when he had spoken these things, while they beheld, he was taken up; and a cloud received him out of their sight. 10 And while they looked stedfastly toward heaven as he went up, behold, two men stood by them in white apparel; 11 Which also said, Ye men of Galilee, why stand ye gazing up into heaven? this same Jesus, which is taken up from you into heaven, shall so come in like manner as ye have seen him go into heaven. 12 Then returned they unto Jerusalem from the mount called Olivet, which is from Jerusalem a sabbath day's journey.182

(Acts 1:9-12, KJV)

There were many more things concerning Yeshua that are not written, but what is written is that you might believe Yeshua is the Messiah, the Son of God; and that believing you might have eternal life through His name. It was in Yeshua that the Shekinah glory of God's presence had come to dwell among mankind (ref. John 20:30-31).

25 And there are also many other things which Jesus did, the which, if they should be written every one, I suppose that even the world itself could not contain the books that should be written. Amen.183

(John 21:25, KJV)

---

[180] Ibid.

[181] Ibid.

[182] Ibid.

[183] Ibid.

CHAPTER TEN

The Early Church

A. The birth of the Church

The birth of the church and the presence of God were revealed by the Holy Spirit in the believers and in their lives.

After the death and resurrection of Yeshua, Yeshua made many appearances to the disciples and other believers during the forty days before His ascension into heaven.

Yeshua shared many of the scriptures from the Old Covenant (Torah, prophets and writings) which spoke of His birth, life, death, Resurrection, as well of His ascension. He also spoke of the things pertaining to the kingdom of God.

Yeshua commanded His followers that they should not depart from Jerusalem, but wait for the promise of the Holy Spirit in the near future. He told them, "The Holy Spirit shall come upon you: and you shall be My witnesses both in Jerusalem, in all of Judea, and unto Samaria, as well as into the uttermost parts of the world" (ref. Acts 1:3-8).

May 26, AD 29
After the Lord spoke to them, Yeshua was received up into heaven and sat at the right hand of God (ref. Mark 16:20).

On Sunday, June 5, AD 29
On the day of the feast of Pentecost, there were about 120 followers who were one in spirit. They were sitting together in an upper room. Suddenly a sound came from heaven like a rushing mighty wind. It filled the room. Then there appeared cloven tongues like fire which sat upon each one of them. They were all filled with the Holy Spirit and began to speak in other languages as the Spirit gave them the ability to speak. The Church was born and the Holy Spirit indwelt in mankind who were believers in Yeshua as their Savior and Redeemer.

A multitude of people came together and were amazed because each man heard the gospel concerning Yeshua's life, death and Resurrection and the need for them to receive Messiah Yeshua in their lives for the forgiveness of sin in each man's own individual language where he was born.

The following language groups were present: Parthian, Medes, Elamites, Mesopotamian, Cappadocia, Judea, Asia, Crete, Arabia, Phrygian, Pamphylia and parts of Libya, and Rome. These were Jews and Jewish proselytes from these various areas. Some who heard were amazed while others said they were drunk (ref. Acts 2:1-13). Then Peter stood up and preached:

14 But Peter, standing up with the eleven, lifted up his voice, and said unto them, Ye men of Judaea, and all ye that dwell at Jerusalem, be this known unto you, and hearken to my words: 15 For these are not drunken, as ye suppose, seeing it is but the third hour of the day. 16 But this is that which was spoken by the prophet Joel; 17 And it shall come to pass in the last days, saith God, I will pour out of my Spirit upon all flesh: and your sons and your daughters shall prophesy, and your young men shall see visions, and your old men shall dream dreams: 18 And on my servants and on my handmaidens I will pour out in those days of my Spirit; and they shall prophesy: 19 And I will shew wonders in heaven above, and signs in the earth beneath; blood, and fire, and vapour of smoke: 20 The sun shall be turned into darkness, and the moon into blood, before that great and notable day of the Lord come: 21 And it shall come to pass, that whosoever shall call on the name of the Lord shall be saved. 22 Ye men of Israel, hear these words; Jesus of Nazareth, a man approved of God among you by miracles and wonders and signs, which God did by him in the midst of you, as ye yourselves also know: 23 Him, being delivered by the determinate counsel and foreknowledge of God, ye have taken, and by wicked hands have crucified and slain: 24 Whom God hath raised up, having loosed the pains of death: because it was not possible that he should be holden of it. 25 For David speaketh concerning him, I foresaw the Lord always before my face, for he is on my right hand, that I should not be moved: 26 Therefore did my heart rejoice, and my tongue was glad; moreover also my flesh shall rest in hope: 27 Because thou wilt not leave my soul in hell, neither wilt thou suffer thine Holy One to see corruption. 28 Thou hast made known to me the ways of life; thou shalt make me full of joy with thy countenance. 29 Men and brethren, let me freely speak unto you of the patriarch David, that he is both dead and buried, and his sepulchre is with us unto this day. 30 Therefore being a prophet, and knowing that God had sworn with an oath to him, that of the fruit of his loins, according to the flesh, he would raise up Christ to sit on his throne; 31 He seeing this before spake of the resurrection of Christ, that his soul was not left in hell, neither his flesh did see corruption. 32 This Jesus hath God raised up, whereof we all are witnesses. 33 Therefore being by the right hand of God exalted, and having received of the Father the promise of the Holy Ghost, he hath shed forth this, which ye now see and hear. 34 For David is not ascended into the heavens: but he saith himself, The LORD said unto my Lord, Sit thou on my right hand, 35 Until I make thy foes thy footstool. 36 Therefore let all the house of Israel know assuredly, that God hath made that same Jesus, whom ye have crucified, both Lord and Christ.184

(Acts 2:14-36, KJV)

---

[184] The Holy Bible: King James Version. Oak Harbor: Logos Research Systems, Inc., 1995.

When the people heard, they were convicted in their hearts and asked what they needed to do. Peter replied, "Repent and be baptized in the name of Yeshua for the remission of sins and you shall receive the gift of the Holy Spirit."

They obeyed. On that day, three thousand people were added to the Church (ref. Acts 2:37-47).

41 Then they that gladly received his word were baptized: and the same day there were added unto them about three thousand souls. 42 And they continued sted-fastly in the apostles' doctrine and fellowship, and in breaking of bread, and in prayers.185

(Acts 2:41-42, KJV)

In the early Church, the believers were filled with God's power and presence. It was revealed in their lives. Their behavior was no longer sinful, but godly. The Law of God was in their hearts and was worked out in their daily lives. The disciples preached and taught in the name of Yeshua. People were also healed of various diseases and infirmities. It was like Yeshua had multiplied Himself into all the believers in Church. This made the priests and rulers of the people very angry. The priests tried to get the disciples and early believers to be silent in using the name of Yeshua when they healed the sick and preached the Word. Some of the believers were put into prison, while others were martyred like Stephen for his faith.

Because of the persecution, many of the believers scattered from the area of Jerusalem to the areas of Samaria, Judea and Damascus. There they spread the message of Yeshua and the Resurrection (ref. Acts 3:8-14).

B. Saul, the persecutor of the Church, becomes Paul, the apostle

AD 37

Saul was one of the Pharisees who persecuted the Church of Yeshua in Jerusalem. He was so zealous that he went to the high priest to get permission to go to Damascus to bring back, bound, any believers that might be found, to Jerusalem (ref. Acts 8:1-4; 9:1-2).

As Saul came near to Damascus, he was blinded by a bright light shining from heaven (God's Shekinah glory). He fell and heard a voice saying, "Saul, why are you persecuting Me?"

Saul answered, "Who are You, Lord?"

The Lord answered and said, "I am Yeshua who you are persecuting." Then Saul trembled and said, "What should I do?"

The Lord answered, "Go into Damascus and it will be told to you what you shall do."

The men who were with Saul heard the voice, but saw no one.

When Saul arose from the ground, he was blind and had to be led into the city of Damascus. There he fasted and prayed for three days (ref. Acts 9:3-9).

Meanwhile, in that city there was a godly disciple named Ananias. He had a vision. The Lord told him to go lay hands on Saul and restore his sight.

Ananias objected, saying, "I have heard of all the evil this man has done in persecuting the saints in Jerusalem and how he plans on doing the same here in Damascus."

---

[185] Ibid.

The Lord replied, "Don't worry. He is a chosen vessel for Me. He shall witness of Me to the Gentiles and kings, as well as the children of Israel. I will show him what he will suffer for My name's sake."

Ananias went to the house where Saul was and he laid hands on him and said. "Brother, Saul, the Lord, even Yeshua, which appeared to you, has sent me to you so that you will receive your sight and be filled with the Holy Spirit."

Immediately scales fell from Saul's eyes and he received his sight and then was filled with the Holy Spirit. Then he was baptized.

Saul then broke his fast and ate (ref. Acts 9:10-19).

While Saul was with the disciples, he preached in the synagogues that Yeshua was the Son of God. All who heard him were amazed.

The Jewish leaders in that area took counsel to kill Saul, who was also known as Paul; but, the disciples helped Paul to escape by lowering him in a basket at night, down the city wall (ref. Acts 9:20-25).

AD 38-40 Paul went for a period of several years into Arabia. There he grew in wisdom and grace in God's Word. There the Lord was his teacher.

C. Paul's influence on the early Church and on the Bible

Paul became the greatest influence on the Christian Church. His teachings are included in the New Covenant or New Testament part of the Bible. Paul wrote thirteen letters that are included in the Bible. Among these are:

Books	When Written
Romans	56 AD
1 & 2 Corinthians	55 AD
Galatians	48 AD

Ephesians	61 AD
Philippians	61 AD
Colossians	61 AD
1 & 2 Thessalonians	52 AD
1 & 2 Timothy	62 AD & 67 AD
Titus	65 AD
Philemon	61 AD

These letters were written during the years of his ministry and missionary journey 48 AD— 67 AD.[186]

God's presence is seen in the writings of Paul the apostle. Some of the topics he covered which reflected God's character in the believers' lives were the eleven fruits of the Spirit which are love, joy, peace, long suffering, gentleness, goodness, faith, meekness, temperance, righteousness and

---

[186] Jensen, Irving L. Jensens' Survey of the New Testament. Chicago: Moody Press, Copyright 1981. Page 237.

truth. (Reference Gal.5: 22, 23, Ephesians 5:9) He also covered the armor of God. This is what every Christian should have to protect him against the wiles of the devil, the enemy of God.187

> *11 Put on the whole armour of God, that ye may be able to stand against the wiles of the devil. 12 For we wrestle not against flesh and blood, but against principalities, against powers, against the rulers of the darkness of this world, against spiritual wickedness in high places. 13 Wherefore take unto you the whole armour of God, that ye may be able to withstand in the evil day, and having done all, to stand. 14 Stand therefore, having your loins girt about with truth, and having on the breastplate of righteousness; 15 And your feet shod with the preparation of the gospel of peace; 16 Above all, taking the shield of faith, wherewith ye shall be able to quench all the fiery darts of the wicked. 17 And take the helmet of salvation, and the sword of the Spirit, which is the word of God: 18 Praying always with all prayer and supplication in the Spirit, and watching thereunto with all perseverance and supplication for all saints.188*

(Ephesians 6:11-18, KJV)

Paul wrote in 1 Corinthians 14:1 that we should desire the spiritual gifts. There are nine gifts listed in 1 Corinthians 12:8-10:

1. Word of Wisdom
2. Knowledge
3. Faith
4. Gifts of Healing
5. Miracles
6. Prophecy
7. Discerning of Spirits
8. Tongues
9. Interpretation of tongues189

Paul also wrote of the nine ministries God gave to the church
Exhorters (Romans 12:4,8)
Those with a definite ministry (Romans 12:4,8)
Apostles (1 Corinthians 12:28)
Prophets(1 Corinthians 12:28)
Teachers(1 Corinthians 12:28)
Helpers (1 Corinthians 12:28)
Administrators (1 Corinthians 12:28)
Evangelists to perfect and edify the body of Christ (Ephesians 4:11-12)

---

[187] Meredith, J.L. Meredith Book of Bible Lists. Minneapolis: Bethany House Publishers, 1980. Pages 188-189.

[188] The Holy Bible: King James Version. Oak Harbor: Logos Research Systems, Inc., 1995.

[189] Meredith, J.L. Meredith Book of Bible Lists. Minneapolis: Bethany House Publishers, 1980. Page 188.

Pastors for the work of ministry and the help to perfect and edify the body of Christ (Ephesians 4:11-12)190

D. Paul's background

Paul was born around the time Christ was born in the City of Tarsus of the province of Cilicia. Paul's father was a native of Palestine. He was a Roman citizen and a merchant by trade. He was a strict Pharisee. His mother was probably a devout woman. Paul had at least one sister and nephew (Ref: Act 23:16).

Paul's trade was that of tent making. He may have gone to the university in Tarsus. His rabbinical training was under Gamaliel at Jerusalem.

After Paul's rabbinical training, he probably served in the synagogues outside of Palestine. He returned to Jerusalem some time after Yeshua's ascension. He soon became the leader of the persecution of the church. At the height of his opposition, he was converted to Christ around AD 33 on the road to Damascus (Ref: Acts 9:1-19A).

Later, Paul became a leader and expositor of the Gospel of Christ.191

E.Paul's missionary journeys

Paul made three different missionary journeys in the Mediterranean area of the Roman Empire. The first one was in 47-48 AD in the known Southeast Asia Minor area. He covered fifteen hundred miles (Acts 13:1-14:28). His second journey was in Macedonia, Achaia in 47-52 AD. He covered three thousand to four thousand miles (Acts 15:36-18:22). The third journey was in Western Asia Minor in 52-56 AD covering four thousand miles (Acts 18:23-21:17). During these journeys, Luke, the physician, went with him. He wrote the accounts of the early Church and the ministry of Paul, the apostle, in the book of Acts. He also wrote an account of the life of Christ in the Gospel of Luke.

Paul's mission field became peoples of all nations, races and religions. They came from all walks of life, from the commoner to the kings of nations.

Later Paul was imprisoned a couple of times by the Roman government. When he had his final trial in Rome, it was brief. According to tradition, he was beheaded in 67 AD; but the writings of Paul, which were inspired by the Holy Spirit, live on in the hearts of Christians over the centuries. Even today, the Lord uses His word to comfort and teach the believers.

F. Other apostles important in the early Church

There were other key apostles that helped build the Church through their witnessing and leadership. They also contributed to the writing of Scripture. There was James, the half brother of Jesus, who was one of the leaders of the Church in Jerusalem. He wrote the book of James 45 AD. Peter was a leader of the Church in Jerusalem and he wrote the letters of 1 and 2 Peter, 64 AD and 67 AD. Luke, the beloved physician who traveled with Paul, wrote the books of Luke and Acts. Matthew wrote the book of Matthew. John, who was the beloved disciple of Yeshua while He was

---

190 Ibid. Pages 188-189.

191 Jensen, Irving L. Jensen's Survey of the New Testament. Chicago: Moody Bible Institute, 1981. Pages 236-237.

on the earth, later wrote the Gospel of John, the letters of 1, 2, and 3 John in 95 AD and also the book of Revelation in 96 AD. Revelation speaks of the end times world situation, God's judgment on the earth, as well as the judgment that will fall on Israel and her restoration. It also speaks of Yeshua's return and a new heaven and Earth. It also speaks of Yeshua's one thousand year earthly reign on Earth...the final judgment of mankind. It also speaks of the judgment of Satan and his angels.

It is interesting to note that most of the Scriptures were written before the destruction of Jerusalem and its temple in 70 AD.

The Church age, which began at Pentecost, has continued over two thousand years into the present. It will continue until the Church is taken out of the world to be with Yeshua in the heavenlies. Later in the millennial kingdom, He rules the earth from Jerusalem. After the millennial kingdom, we will be with Yeshua in the heavenly New Jerusalem to rule and reign with Him. God is still marching through time to His eternal destiny with His redeemed people that have been saved by Him since Creation to the present.

CHAPTER ELEVEN

Destruction of the Second Temple

A. Introduction to the destruction of the temple

DAY OF CALAMITY, DAY OF CELEBRATION
By David Brickner, Executive Director

Tisha b' Av (literally the ninth day of the Jewish calendar month called Av), is a day of remembrance in the Jewish religion. While it is not one of the Holy Days commanded in the Bible, according to tradition, both the first and second Temples were destroyed on the ninth of Av. And so, my Jewish people spend the day fasting, lamenting this great loss and praying for the holy Temple to be restored. This year, Tisha b' Av falls on August 10th.

TISHA B'AV [192]

NAME:	TISHA B'AV (The Ninth of Av) pronounced Tee-shub-buh-AHV
DATE:	August 2 on the 2000 calendar and Av, 9 on the Jewish calendar
COMMEMORATES:	The day on which, according to tradition, the first Temple was destroyed. Tradition assigns these other sorrowful occurrences in Jewish history to this day:

---

[192] Brickner, David. "Day of Calamity, Day of Celebration." <u>Jews for Jesus - Newsletter</u>. Vol. 12:5760. San Francisco: Jews for Jesus International, August 2000.

	Moses broke the tablets of the Law upon seeing the people worshiping the Golden Calf. God determined that the people freed from slavery in Egypt would not be allowed to enter the Promised Land due to rebelliousness. The second Temple in Jerusalem was destroyed in AD 70. The Jewish community in Spain was expelled in 1492.
SCRIPTURE REFERENCE:	Jeremiah 52:12,13 (Date given as 10th)
OBSERVANCE:	A time of national mourning. On the Ninth of Av, the person does not eat from sunset to the nightfall of the following day. Community: (In Israel) mourning and weeping in prayer at the Wailing Wall (the only portion of the Temple wall still standing). Synagogue: Reading from the book of Lamentations in a dirge- like chant. Worshipers in Orthodox synagogues remove shoes and sit on low stools or on the floor as a symbol of mourning. Home: The meal before the fast includes eggs, which are often symbolic of mourning.

B. The true significance of the temple was God's promise to Israel

And there I will meet with you, and I will speak with you from above the mercy seat, from between the two cherubim which are on the ark of the Testimony, about everything which I will give you in commandment to the children of Israel...... This shall be a continual burnt offering throughout your generations at the door of the tabernacle of meeting before the Lord, where I will meet you to speak with you.

(Exodus 25:22; 29:42)

The two pillars of God's promise were His presence and His provision. He would dwell in the midst of His people and speak with them. He would provide atonement for their sins, forgive them and make them holy. That atonement was secured through the blood of the animal sacrifices offered on the altar. All of this was to be accomplished in the Temple.

The sacrifices were a way to acknowledge and illustrate the consequence of disobeying God. That consequence was death. God has zero tolerance for sin. But His righteousness and judgment are tempered by His other perfections, especially His mercy and grace. The sacrifices provided a way for God to extend that mercy and grace—by allowing a substitute. The animal died in place of the transgressor. In an agrarian economy, those animals were expensive and not sacrificed lightly. The whole event was a drama of the highest order and the Temple was the stage that God provided for the enactment. Only in that holy place would God allow this most profound experience. The Temple was Israel's heartbeat, the center of her life-giving encounter with God's presence and provision of atoning power.

Many of Jesus' activities and teachings took place in and around that Temple. He made some of His most controversial comments concerning it, such as: "'......Destroy this Temple, and in three days I will raise it up.' Then the Jews said, 'It has taken forty-six years to build this Temple, and will You raise it up in three days?' But He was speaking of the Temple of His body" (John 2:19-21).

By identifying Himself as the Temple, Jesus was claiming to fulfill God's purpose and promise concerning the Temple. In one brief, profound statement Jesus announced that He was the very presence of God once so evident in the Temple. Jesus not only identified Himself with God's presence in the Temple, but with God's provision of the Temple sacrifice. Jesus' statement would have been outlandish if the second part of Jesus' prediction had not come true. But He did rise from the dead after three days, as promised, proving that His sacrifice for sin was acceptable once and for all. This was God's plan all along. All the years of animal sacrifices pointed to a time when an innocent person would willingly take the punishment for the sins of the people: something that an animal could never do. The very sacrifice that God did not require Abraham to follow through with his son Isaac, God Himself made when He sent His own son Jesus to die for us.

Jesus made another prediction regarding that second Temple, an ominous prediction but one that would also serve to confirm His claims concerning His own life and work:

"Then Jesus went out and departed from the Temple, and His disciples came up to show Him the buildings of the Temple. And Jesus said to them, 'Do you not see all these things? Assuredly, I say to you, not one stone shall be left here upon another, that shall not be thrown down'" (Matthew 24:1,2).

Jesus clearly predicted the destruction of the second Temple. Titus and his Roman legions fulfilled that prediction as they marched into Jerusalem and destroyed not only the Temple, but the entire city. As awful as this national tragedy was, it did point back to the claims of Jesus of Nazareth. Thousands of Jewish people had already placed their faith in Y'shua (Jesus) and when that second Temple was destroyed in AD 70, thousands more followed. Yet most of my Jewish people did not. And so it remains to this day.

Therein lies my burden and that of Jews for Jesus. The greatest calamity of Jewish history was not the destruction of the Temple which had been made with hands, but the emptiness of so many hearts in which God wants to dwell. Until my people recognize Jesus as the Messiah, those whom God desires to have for His Temple are void of God's presence and His provision of atonement. This should cause all those who love the God of Israel to mourn. I plan to spend August 10th fasting and praying over the greatest calamity ever to befall my Jewish people—the rejection of their Savior.193

C. The destruction of Jerusalem and Herod's temple 70 AD by Titus

It was in 70 AD when Vespasian was Caesar. Titus of Rome marched with two legions, which is twelve thousand soldiers plus cavalry, against Jerusalem and destroyed the wall and homes of the city and the temple. Titus tried to spare the temple and just break down the walls and door of the temple in order to enter. It was on the eighth month, which is AB (or the seventeenth day of *Nisan*—April 12th) [it is also called *Beth Av*] that Titus gave orders to use battering rams to be used against the western wall of the temple. After six days without ceasing, the wall remained firm. When the soldiers tried to climb over the walls, the Jews killed them. When Titus perceived that his endeavor to spare a foreign temple turned out to have his soldiers killed, he gave orders to

---

193 Brickner, David. "Day of Calamity, Day of Celebration." Jews for Jesus - Newsletter. Vol. 12:5760. San Francisco: Jews for Jesus International, August 2000.

set the gates of the temple on fire. The fire melted the silver which covered the gates. The wood underneath, which was quite dry, caused the fire to spread itself suddenly in and around the temple. The people who were caught in the fire were amazed and did nothing and died in the temple blaze. The fire burned for two days. The next day, Titus commanded that chosen men should go through the ruins and put out the fire.

Then the Jews fought the chosen men of Caesar who were in the town of Antonia. Titus sent for reinforcements and overcame the Jews. The Jews then locked themselves in the inner court of the temple. Titus decided to storm the temple. The next day, early in the morning, Titus, with his whole army, encamped around the temple. This was the same day, the ninth day of *AB*, that the former temple was burnt by the king of Babylon in 569 BC.

One of the soldiers accidentally took something that was burning and threw it into a golden window where there was a passage to rooms that were around the holy house on the north side. As the flames went upward, the Jews tried to stop the fire.

Titus was told that the temple was on fire. Caesar ordered the fire to be put out, but the soldiers did not hear. The fire spread. When the soldiers saw all the gold, their hope of plunder as well as their hatred of the Jews caused them to go wild. So the temple was burned down without Caesar's approval.

For the same month and day were now observed as I said before......the holy house was burnt formerly by the Babylonians. Now the number of years that passes from its first foundation, which was laid by King Solomon, till its destruction which happened in the second year of the reign of Vespasian, are called to be one thousand one hundred and thirty, besides seven months and fifteen days; from the second building of it which was done by Haggai, in the second year of Cyrus the King till it destruction under Vespasian, there were six hundred and thirty-nine years and forty-five days.194

This was 569 BC.

The Jews were warned of the impending doom but did not heed the warning. There was a star resembling a sword, which stood over the City and a comet that continued a whole year......."195

Before the Jews rebellion and before the commotions which preceded the war the people...... came to the feast of unleavened bread on the eight day of Nissan April and at the 9th hour of the night so great a light shone round the altar and the holy house that it appeared to be as bright (as) day-time; which light seemed to be a good sign to the unskilled, but was so interpreted by the sacred scribes as a portend to those events that followed. At the same Passover festival, a heifer was sacrificed. As she was led by the priest to be sacrificed, a lamb was brought in the midst of the Temple. Moreover, the eastern gate of the inner court of the Temple |which was of brass and vastly heavy, and had been with difficulty shut by twenty men, and rested upon a basis armed with iron, and had bolts fastened very deep into the firm floor, which was there made of one entire stone|, was seen to be opened of its own accord about the sixth hour of the night. Now those that kept watch in the Temple came running to the captain of the Temple and told him of it; who then came up thither and not without great difficulty was able to shut the gate again......the gate was opened

---

194 <u>Josephus Complete Works</u>. Translated by William Whiston. Grand Rapids: Kregel Publications. Page 581.

195 Ibid. Page 582

for the advantage of their enemies......this signal foreshowed the desolation that was coming up on them.196

The prophecy, made by Yeshua thirty-seven years before, had been fulfilled. One Roman Centurion was heard to say that there was not one stone left upon another and that there was no sign that the place had ever been inhabited (ref. Mark 13:2).

> *2 But he answered them, "You see all these, do you not? Truly, I say to you, there will not be left here one stone upon another, that will not be thrown down." 197*
>
> (Matthew 24:2, RSV)

After the Temple was destroyed, the city was destroyed by fire and plundered by the soldiers. The Jews fled to the desert and scattered.198

The first temple, as well as the second temple, was destroyed on the 9th day of the month of *AB*. This shows that God has complete and total control over the destiny of mankind and the events of history. All of this happened after the death of Paul the Apostle and the completion of the writing of the New Testament letters to the church, except the writings of John the Apostle.

After this time, the gospel has gone all over the world for the last two thousand years. God continues to march on in time into eternity to the New Jerusalem to bring a people who love and obey Him completely into His kingdom.

---

196 Ibid.

197 The Holy Bible: The Revised Standard Version. Oak Harbor: Logos Research Systems, Inc., 1971.

198 Josephus Complete Works. Translated by William Whiston. Grand Rapids: Kregel Publications. Page 582

PART IV

CHURCH AGE AND RISE OF ISRAEL AS A NATION

CHAPTER TWELVE

Jerusalem a Stumbling Block to the World

A. Background to the Jews returning to Israel and other important events and dates

1. Timeline

1867	Last restriction of Jewish residence in Jerusalem was removed. Many Jews moved there.
1878	Establishment of *Petah Tikvah* in Judea and *Rosh Pinnah* in Galilee by religious Jews. These were the first Jewish villages in Palestine in our times.
1879	Eliezer Ben-Yehuda advocated a national rebirth in Palestine.
1880	RETURN TO ZION: The New *Yishuv* began in *Erez* (land of) Israel. This was the secular, nationalist community whose goal was to build an economy based on Jewish labor and agriculture. Prior to 1880, the Old *Yishuv* of mostly Orthodox Jews were opposed to all modern trends and depended on contributions from abroad (*halukkah*) to exist. Ottoman rule had opposed Jewish participation in economic life. About 12,000 Jews lived in Jerusalem then.
1881	Ben-Yehuda moved to *Erez* Israel and began to revive the Hebrew language.
1881-82	Pogroms in southern Russia hit about 100 Jewish communities. Massacres and arson became endemic. 199
1882	First *Aliyah* (ascent)—Jewish immigration to Holy Land on a large scale.
1893	Term "Zionism" coined.

---

199 Kremers, Mari F. "Review of Dates." <u>God Intervenes in the Middle East</u>. Page 274.

January 1895	The Dreyfus Affair—A French court martial accused the innocent Jewish Captain Dreyfus of high treason and Parisian mob rioted against him.
1895	Anti-Semitic riots and election of a mayor on an anti-Semitic platform in Vienna.
August 29, 1897	First World Zionist Congress in Basel, Switzerland, led by Dr. Theodor Herzl, the founder of Zionism.
Xxxx	Armistice between Old and New *Yishuv* in Israel.
1900	World Zionist Congress met.
January 1, 1901	Modern Pentecostalism began with the outpouring of the Holy Spirit on Agnes Ozman in Bethel Bible School in Topeka, Kansas.
1902	World Zionist Congress met. Collapse of British offer of land in Sinai for the Jews.
1902, 1903, 1905, 1906	New wave of Russian pogroms against Jews.
1903	World Zionist Congress met. No agreement on British offer of Uganda as a place of refuge for Jews.
November 1903-1905	Welsh Revival led by Evan Roberts.
1904	World Zionist Congress met. Abandoned Uganda plan.
August 1, 1914 (Av 9)	Germany declared war on Russia.
1914-1918	WORLD WAR I. 200

October 31, 1917	British offensive took Beersheba, Gaza, and Jaffa from Turks.
November 2, 1917	Balfour Declaration favoring "a National Home for the Jewish people" in Palestine.
December 10 (Kislev 25), 1917 *Hanukkah*	English General Allenby took Jerusalem from Turks without firing a shot, ending 400 years of Turkish rule in Palestine.
1917-1947	BRITISH PERIOD in Palestine.
1920	League of Nations established.
1920	England received the British Mandate of Palestine from League of Nations.

[200] Ibid. Page 275

April 24, 1920	Balfour Declaration approved by the Allies' Conference at San Remo.
1921	Winston Churchill, British Secretary of the Colonies, signed 77.6% of Palestine over to Arabs, creating Transjordan. This was the first partition of Palestine.
July 1922	The League of Nations confirmed Transjordan's boundaries. President Woodrow Wilson, a Christian Bible student, protested this arbitrary partition, as he was concerned abut Biblical boundaries.
July 24, 1922	League of Nations incorporated the Balfour Declaration into British Mandate of Palestine.
1927	Recognition of future state of Israel by a Protestant denomination in their creed: "This millennial reign will bring the salvation of national Israel" (General Council of Assemblies of God, Constitution Article V-Item 14 on "The Millennial Reign of Christ").201
1928	British recognized Transjordan as independent state.
1933	*Humanist Manifest I* signed.
January 30, 1933	Adolf Hitler made chancellor; consolidated his power within 6 months.
1934-1945	The Third *Reich*—German government under Hitler.
1935	Vast oil fields discovered in Saudi Arabia. It has larger oil reserves than any area of similar size in the world.
1936-1939	Major Arab uprisings in Palestine.
July 7, 1937	British Peel Commission: three-way partition plan and restriction on European Jews escaping to Palestine and on Jewish land purchases.
August 1937	Nazi reorganization of four concentration camps in Germany.
1938	About 30,000 Jews taken to German concentration camps.

1938	Pan-Arab Conference in Cairo adopted policy that all Arab states and communities would prevent development of Zionist state.
March 1938	Hitler annexed Austria.
July 1938	President Franklin D. Roosevelt organized a conference of 32 nations at Evian-les- Bains, France, to rescue Jews in the Third *Reich*. Most countries refused to help, which Hitler interpreted as approval of his "Final Solution" (killing all Jews).

---

[201] Ibid. Pages 276-277

November 9, 1938	Crystal Night (*Kristallnacht*)-Nazis looted and burned 119 Jewish synagogues and 7,500 shops in Germany, causing economic ruin for the Jews.202
May 17, 1939	British MacDonald White Paper abandoned Peel Partition Plan and Balfour Declaration policy. The White Paper severely restricted Jewish immigration and land purchase in Palestine and left Jews in Europe to their fate.
September 1, 1939	German invasion of Poland.
1939-1945	WORLD WAR II.
1939-1945	THE HOLOCAUST: Six million Jews murdered by Nazis.
January 2, 1942	Palestinian Jews joined Allies to fight Nazis. Amin al-Husseini, the Islamic Mufti of Jerusalem, collaborated with the Nazis as proven at the 1946 Nuremberg trials. British refused immigration to Jewish survivors from Europe.
May 8, 1945	V-E DAY — VICTORY IN EUROPE.
June 16, 1945	First test of the atomic bomb—White Sands, New Mexico.
September 2, 1945	V-J DAY — VICTORY OVER JAPAN. End of World war II.

1945	Many Jews immigrated to Palestine after the war.
October 24, 1945	Establishment of the United Nations, to which most nations belong.
1945	Arab League formed.
1946	Transjordan granted complete independence by Britain.
Spring 1947	Bedouins discovered Dead Sea scrolls in Qumran caves.203
April 1947	British government turned Palestine problem over to U.N.
May 1947	Special session of U.N. General Assembly convened to deal with Palestine. They appointed U.N. Special Committee on Palestine (UNSCOP) to study issue.
July 1947	British refused to allow the "*Exodus 1947*" to dock at Haifa with its survivors of Nazi death camps. This became a world-renowned symbol of Jewish need for a homeland.

---

[202] Ibid. Page 277

[203] Ibid. Page 278

Saturday November 29, 1947	PALESTINE PARTITION PLAN gained a majority vote in United Nations. Israel was granted 16.1% of original 1920 British Mandate of Palestine, or the equivalent of one tenth of 1% of the total land of the 21 Arab nations. Arabs did not accept a Jewish state, and planned to take all of Palestine by force.
1948	National Council of Churches organized.
Friday May 14, 1948	PROCLAMATION OF INDEPENDENCE OF ISRAEL. Government established.
12:01 a.m. May 15, 1948	British withdrew the last of their forces and government from Jerusalem.
Saturday May 15, 1948	Armies of Egypt, Transjordan, Syria, Lebanon, Saudi Arabia, and Iraq attacked the new state. Eight months of warfare ensued. Israel's Provisional Government remained in Tel Aviv.
1948-1977	Labor Party in full control of government
1948-1951	Mass immigration of Jews to Israel.
January 7, 1949	WAR OF INDEPENDENCE ended by cease-fire: Jerusalem was divided between Israel on the west and Jordan on the east. Arab League declared "a permanent state of war" against Israel.204

1949-1967	Jordan denied Israeli access to Temple Mount in East Jerusalem.
May 14, 1949	Israel admitted to United Nations.
October 1, 1949	Communist government in China.
1949	Billy Graham's First Crusade.
1949	North Atlantic Treaty Organization (NATO) was formed to prevent Russia from taking over Western Europe. The Council of Europe was organized.
October 1949	Communists rule East Germany.
January 23, 1950	West Jerusalem was proclaimed the capital of Israel and seat of the Knesset.
April 1950	Transjordan changed its name to "Jordan" after annexing the West Bank. Only Britain and Pakistan recognized the annexation *de jure*.

---

[204] Ibid. Page 279

1951	Six nations formulated European Coal and Steel Community (ECSC) (Precursor of the European Community — E.C.).
October 1956	WAR: Israel, supported by Britain and France, launched preemptive attach on Arab neighbors. Cease-fire came on November 5.
1957	Treaty of Rome. European Community's Parliament set up. Members to be voted to office by direct suffrage in the future. European Economic Community (EEC) and European Atomic Energy Community (Euratom) established.
1958	World Bible Conference in Jerusalem sponsored by Israeli government, Increasing emphasis on Jewish cultural and spiritual heritage.
November 14, 1960	Creation of Organization of Petroleum Exporting Countries (OPEC), After World War II, the world's need for oil became an issue in international politics. Important oil discoveries were made in Iran in 1908; Iraq in 1927; Saudi Arabia in 1935. The Middle East has about three-fifths of the world's oil resources.205

1967	Spain repealed 1492-Edict of Expulsion of the Jews. Jews could now obtain legal recognition as a religious body in Spain.
Monday June 5, 1967 (Iyyar 26)	SIX-DAY WAR began. Israel bombed airfield of Egypt, Syria, Jordan and Iraq. Jordan seized U.N. headquarters in Jerusalem and attacked Israel. (Jesus ascended on Iyyar 26, 30 AD)
Wednesday June 7, 1967	JERUSALEM UNITED: Israel took Temple Mount and entire city.
Saturday June 10, 1967	Cease-fire—Israel gained East Jerusalem with Temple Mount, West Bank, Gaza, Sinai, and Golan Heights.
1967	Israel united all of Jerusalem as their capital. Their claim is still unrecognized by the United Nations.
1967	The Soviet Union and Eastern European satellites, except Romania, severed diplomatic relations with Israel.
1967	Billy Graham first preached in the Communist countries of Eastern Europe.
1967 onward	Soviet propaganda was the main source of anti-Semitic material.
1967 onward	Archaeology now possible on Temple Mount and all Jerusalem.

---

[205] Ibid. Page 280

1967	ECSC, EEC, Euratom merged to form European Community (E.C.).
1968	E.C. abolished all tariffs between members. Common tax on imported goods.
1968	Formation of the Club of Rome, an international body that seeks solutions to earth's problems. 100 leaders meet regularly.206

1972	Euthanasia legalized in Holland.
1973	*Humanist Manifesto II.*
January 22, 1973	Supreme Court legalized abortion in United States in *Roe v. Wade.*
October 6 (Tishri 10), 1973	*YOM KIPPUR WAR*: Egyptians and Syrians attacked on two fronts.
November 11, 1973	Cease-fire signed on Armistice Day.
November 1973	Most African nations broke relations with Israel due to Arab oil concerns.
November 10, 1975	37th anniversary of "Crystal Night" (November 9, 1938)—United Nations passed a resolution condemning Zionism as a form of racism.
November 19, 1977	By visiting Jerusalem, Anwar Sadat acknowledged the Jewish state. His subsequent Peace Treaty with Israel prevented Egypt from joining other Arab nations to attack Jews. Without Egypt, the Arab neighbors did not invade Israel.
December 1977	Syria broke ties with Egypt.
1977-90	Coalition governments in Israel between liberal Labor Party and conservative Likud.
September 17, 1978	Camp David Peace Accords were signed by Begin and Sadat and witnessed by Carter.
March 26, 1979	Israel signed a Peace Treaty with Egypt and returned Sinai to Egypt. The boundary line was east of El Arish.
1979	Ayatollah Khomeini came to power in Iran. A fervent believer in anti-Semitic classic, *Protocols of the Elders of Zion.* He called America "the Great Satan."

---

[206] Ibid. Page 281

June 7 and 10, 1979	First election of "The Assembly," the parliament of the E.C.207
July 16, 1979	Saddam Hussein assumed undisputed power in Iraq after a coup.
July 20, 1980	First Global Conference of the Future.
July 30, 1980	After an Israeli law which formally recognized Jerusalem as the capital of Israel, foreign embassies left that city. Those of El Salvador and Costa Rica are the only ones there today.
September 1980	Iraq invaded Iran.
December 9, 1987	Palestinian *intifada* (uprising) began.
1988	Israel defines "who is a Jew" for the purposes of the Law of Return to that land (also in 1984 and 1990).

May 1988	A flask of 1900-year-old persimmon oil of a kind used to anoint Judah's kings, was found in a cave near the Dead Sea.208
August 1988	Iran-Iraq War ended with cease-fire.
December 1988	Palestinian Liberation Organization (P.L.O.) recognized Israel and renounced terrorism. U.S. opened dialogue with P.L.O.
1989	U.S. and Egypt attempted to bring Israel and Palestinians to peace table.
January 1989	George bush became U.S. President. His policy was not as supportive of Israel as previous presidents.
November 9, 1989	Berlin Wall came down exactly 51 years after "Crystal Night" (Nazi destruction of Jewish property in Germany).
December 1989	Egypt and Syria restored diplomatic relations after 12 years, marking the end of Egypt's ostracism in Arab world.
1989-1990	Collapse of Soviet regimes in Eastern Europe.

[207] Ibid. Page 282

[208] Ibid. Page 283

March 15, 1990	Collapse of Labor-Likud coalition government due to a 60-60 vote deadlock in the *Knesset*.

April 1990	Saddam Hussein threatened to burn half of Israel.
May 30-*Shavuot*, 1990	Israeli forces blocked attack by Palestinian gunboats on Tel Aviv beach.
June 1990	U.S. suspended dialogue with the P.L.O.
June 11, 1990	Conservative Likud government took office in Israel.209
August 1990	Saddam Hussein annexed Kuwait and the Allied forces mobilized for war.
October 2, 1990	Unification of West and East Germany.
October 1990	Israel distributed gas masks to citizens.
October 8-*Sukkot*, 1990	Palestinians attacked Jewish worshippers at "Western Wall," Jerusalem. Jewish police fire on Palestinians.
February 1991	Iraq launched 39 Scud missiles against Israel and several against Saudi Arabia.
February 27, 28, 1991 (*Adar* 13 and 14)	Allies defeated Saddam Hussein's army in 100 hours by midnight of the 27th and celebrated victory the next day. On these two days, the Feast of *Purim*, Jews still celebrate their defeat of Haman and their enemies in 473 BC in Persia (Esth. 9:17). "Many Orthodox Jews believed that the war against Iraq was the beginning of the coming of Messiah" (*The Washington Post*, March 2, 1991, p.B-6).
April 1, 1991	Israel's new entry restrictions cut in half the number of Palestinians working in Israel. Their standard of living has plummeted due to Gulf War and *intifada*.210

2. Clocks ticking to the imminent return of the Lord

1 But of the times and the seasons, brethren, ye have no need that I write unto you. 2 For yourselves know perfectly that the day of the Lord so cometh as a thief in the night. 3 For when they shall say, Peace and safety; then sudden destruction cometh upon them, as travail upon a woman with child; and they shall not escape. 4 But ye,

---

[209] Ibid. Page 284

[210] Ibid. Page 285

brethren, are not in darkness, that that day should overtake you as a thief. 5 Ye are all the children of light, and the children of the day: we are not of the night, nor of darkness. 6 Therefore let us not sleep, as do others; but let us watch and be sober. 7 For they that sleep sleep in the night; and they that be drunken are drunken in the night. 8 But let us, who are of the day, be sober, putting on the breastplate of faith and love; and for an helmet, the hope of salvation. 9 For God hath not appointed us to wrath, but to obtain salvation by our Lord Jesus Christ, 10 Who died for us, that, whether we wake or sleep, we should live together with him.211

(1 Thessalonians 5:1-10, KJV)

There are at least eight clocks ticking that are all pointing towards a major event coming in the year 2012. We do not know the date of the rapture, we believe it is imminent. We believe Christ could come at any moment. However, there is something big coming in the year 2012. Again, lest we be misunderstood, we do NOT know when the rapture is going to occur, but we want to share with you eight clocks that are ticking away and they all point towards a major event-taking place in 2012. It is possible that these events could be events that take place at the middle of the 7-year Tribulation. They could also be events that take place at the rapture, or it is possible they are all things that happen but do not mean anything at all.

In light of the fact that we believe the Bible teaches there will be 6000 years of human history, and then a 1000 year Sabbath rest, we have to be very close to the rapture. We believe we are near the year 2000 of the New Testament Age on God's calendar. God does not use the solar calendar; He uses the 360-day prophetic calendar. It is right now somewhere close to the year 2000 on God's calendar if you start with Calvary to the present with 360-day years. The New Testament did not start at the birth of Christ, it started at Calvary.

We want to share with you eight clocks that are ticking towards a major event in the year 2012. These events certainly line up with Scripture as far as the Tribulation in concerned, but you will have to use your own judgment as to what these clocks may mean. We are to see the day approaching and be prepared for the rapture. It is like a couple when they find out they are going to have a baby. They are very excited, they begin telling others that they are expecting, they begin preparing their home for the new arrival, but they do not pack the suitcase until after the 8th or 9th month when the "signs" begin to appear. My friend, we believe the signs all point to the fact that we are near the end of that 9th month and we had better have the bags packed and the gas tank full!

There are eight clocks a tickin' that all point towards an event in 2012:

Daniels's Clock

Daniel's clock is ticking away. Daniel talked about the revived Roman Empire that will be ruled by the Antichrist. We are on the verge of that right now. The term "global" is a household word even now. We hear about global markets, global currency, global trade, and global unity. The whole world is tied together through the internet, stock market, and trade. Daniel's 70th week is just a trumpet sound away. The whole world is now ready for globalism. Look at the following quotes concerning "globalism."

---

[211] <u>The Holy Bible: King James Version</u>. Oak Harbor: Logos Research Systems, Inc., 1995.

"Globalization is the central reality of our time. It is coming and you can't stop it."

- Bill Clinton State of the Union Address, January, 2000

"If one world encapsulates the changes we are living through, it is globalization. It is the future of the world as we know it."

-Former secretary general of the United Nations, Kofi Annan

Back in the year 2000, the prime ministers of great Britain, the Netherlands, Sweden, and the chancellor of Germany all banded together to collectively write, "We all embrace the potential of globalization. It is the future of the world as we know it."

"The New Left Takes on the World" Washington Post, September 6, 2000, p. A19

Asteroid Clock

Did you know there is a huge asteroid headed towards the earth in 2012? Could this be one of the events of the Tribulation? Our government is taking it quite seriously. They say it is huge, and they are very concerned about the damage it could cause. This thing is coming closer than any they have ever tracked. We read that NASA is building some sort of weapon in hopes of shooting at it and diverting it.

Nostradamus Clock

We realize Nostradamus may not have even been a saved man, but he said that World War III would take place between 2008—2012. It may not mean anything, but it is another clock ticking.

Mayan Indian Clock

The Mayan Indians were not Christians. They were non believers, but they built the most sophisticated calendar ever built without calculators or computers. They said the end of the world was December 21, 2012! They said this hundreds of years ago. Scientists have found that they were 100% right about one thing though. They knew that our solar system would pass the edge of the equator in the middle of the rift at the outer edge of the Milky Way Galaxy on December 21, 2012. (Use the internet to find detailed information on the Mayan Indian Doomsday Clock.) Scientist today are not real sure what it will do because there are going to be strange gravitational pulls on the earth, but nobody is real sure what is going to happen. This certainly could be part of the Tribulation wouldn't you agree? We do not know if it means anything, but it is a clock ticking.

Many people and ancient cultures over the centuries have wondered if December 21, 2012 is history's final day. Even a modern economics computer program predicted that the year 2012 is the date for catastrophe or the end of the world. Among those that predicted the end of history were:

- The Hopi Indians of American Southwest have taught that the world would one day be covered with a "spider web" (the World Wide Web?!) and the final day of history would be December 21, 2012.
- The "Web-bot" computer designed to make predictions for worldwide financial investments has predicted that catastrophes will increase around the world culminating in the year 2012.

- The ancient Roman Sybil, a prophetess who predicted the birth of Jesus, also predicted that human history would end in 2012.
- "I ching," an ancient Chinese Book called "Book of Changes," also predicted a coming doomsday in 2012.

Is it possible that God spoke through pagan sources concerning the same timeline for the latter days as presented in the Bible?[212]

According to the Bible, we are living in the time of the final stage before the Lord's return to set up His millennial kingdom. There are many signs now in the process of being fulfilled, such as the prophecies of Yeshua in Matthew 24. Other signs of the end of times are the establishment of Israel as a nation in 1948 and the establishment of the European Union where the Antichrist will rule.

The final sign that we are in the final generation before Yeshua sets up His millennial kingdom is that Jerusalem was recaptured on June of 1967 by the Jews. The countdown for the return of Yeshua began.

The average life span of the generations that lived from the time of Adam to Yeshua is fifty-two years.

Year Jerusalem recaptured
+ 52   years of average generation
End of tribulation?
- 7   for years of tribulation
2012 is the year where something cataclysmic is predicted to happen

During this time, the temple will be rebuilt on the Temple Mount under the direction of the Antichrist who has made a false peace between the Arabs and the Israelites for a period of seven years. During this time, God's judgment will reign on all mankind and the earth.

In the middle of this time, the Antichrist will proclaim himself as god. The Jews will reject him as the Messiah and the Antichrist will have an all-out war on the Jews and also the tribulation believers living at that time.

The Lord's return for His Church can happen at anytime now that the stage has been set. The Word has promised the Church will be saved out of the tribulation.

Church Age Clock

If you study the Seven Churches mentioned in Revelation chapter two and three, you will find that they are not only literal churches that existed in John's day, but also that they are also prophetic of the seven periods of the Church Age.

---

[212] Van Impe, Drs. Jack and Rexella. <u>History's Final Day?</u> DVD. Troy: Jack Van Impe Ministries International. ©2008.

Chart of the Seven Ages of Church History:

Ephesus	Means desirable one — 1st
Smyrna	Comes from the word myrrh, signifying suffering......100-300
Pergamos	Means marriage, as in married to the state or world......300-500
Thyatira	Means continual sacrifice, (works, mass, ceremonies, dark ages, etc.) 500-1500
Sardis	Means remnant.....and we see this during the reformation period...... 1500-1700
Philadelphia	Brotherly love...... Great awakenings, revivals, Edwards, Whitefield...... 1700-1901
Laodicean	The rights of the people......just look around today! 1901- Rapture

*Dates are approximate

Brief Summary of the Seven Ages of the Church

The church in Ephesus represents the first 100 years of history, also called the Apostolic Age. This is during the days of the Apostles, including Paul's missionary journeys.

The church in Smyrna represents the next 200 years from 100-313 when Constantine showed up. It is said that Polycarp, a convert of John, was the pastor in Smyrna. History gives us record of ten Roman Emperors who persecuted the church during this time. Compare that to Revelation 2:10 *Fear none of those things which thou shalt suffer: behold, the devil shall cast some of you into prison, that ye may be tried; and ye shall have tribulation ten days......* Nero was the first of those ten wicked emperors who brought terrible persecution to the church. In AD 156 Polycarp was given the choice to revile Christ or be burned at the stake to which he made this famous reply: *"Eighty and six years have I served him and He never did me any harm; how then can I blaspheme my King and my Saviour?"* The church in Pergamos represents the age from 313 to 590. Pergamos is defined "marriage." The Church united with the state or the world if you will. The church became the state religion, and the political leader, Constantine, became the religious leader. Much of Catholic doctrine stems from this age, including the practice of the doctrines of Balaam and the Nicolaitans. The church in Thyatira represents the age from 590-1500's also known as "The Dark Ages." The name Thyatira means "continual sacrifice." It symbolizes the works, ceremonies, and rituals such as "the mass" and Mary worship and good deeds that were added to the gospel. The church in Sardis represents the Reformation Age from 1500-1700 during the times of Luther, Calvin, and others. The printing press was invented in 1550 with a Bible being the first complete book ever printed! The Bible in the hands of the common man soon opened many of the people's eyes to the truth. Be very careful about following someone who thinks that the Bible is a book for the "clergy" and not the common man. 2 Peter 1:20-21 *Knowing this first, that no prophecy of the scripture is of any private interpretation. For the prophecy came not in old time by the will of man: but holy men of God spake as they were moved by the Holy Ghost.*

The church in Philadelphia covers 1700's-1901 and is the time of great revivals and the two great awakenings. Philadelphia means "brotherly love." God raised up some great men like George Whitefield, and Jonathan Edwards, who preached the famous sermon "Sinners in the Hands of an Angry God." Men like Spurgeon and Moody shook whole continents for God in the 1800's! America arose as the Christian nation of the world. To this day, she still sends out more fundamental Christian missionaries than any other nation.

The church in Laodicea covers 1901 until the rapture. This age is by far the worst of them all. ...... What a shame, but just look at Revelation 3:14-20 and see if it is not describing our churches today. There has not been much revival to speak of since 1901. Our churches are cold, our people are pleasure seekers, proud, unfaithful, covetous, and of very little conviction. Our churches are rocked by sin and immorality, people are easily offended, and preachers are either running off with the secretary or refusing to preach against sin. We had better get ready, the trumpet is about to sound, and the rapture could occur at any moment, all things are now ready. How about you, are you ready to meet the Lord?

Nuclear Clock

For the first time ever, in our generation, the world has the capability to destroy itself. Never before has that been possible. When George Washington read the following passage in 1776, do you suppose it made much sense to him as he looked at his old flintlock?

> *For then shall be great tribulation, such as was not since the beginning of the world to this time, no, nor ever shall be. And except those days should be shortened, there should no flesh be saved: but for the elect's sake those days shall be shortened.*
>
> (Matthew 24:21-22)

7000 Year Clock

If the world is going to last 6000 years, and then God has a Sabbath rest, then we are at the door! We believe there have been 3993 years from Adam to Calvary. 7 years of Old Testament are yet to come during the Tribulation, or Daniel's 70th week. You see, all 70 of those weeks of years mentioned are Old Testament.

> *Seventy weeks are determined upon thy people and upon thy holy city, to finish the transgression, and to make an end of sins, and to make reconciliation for iniquity, and to bring in everlasting righteousness, and to seal up the vision and prophecy, and to anoint the most Holy.*
>
> (Daniel 9:24)

When Messiah was "cut off" at Calvary, Israel's clock stopped, and the New Testament Age clock began. If we use the 360-day, year clock that God uses, we are now very close to the end of that 2000-year clock that started at Calvary. The 7-year Tribulation will complete the 4000-year-Old Testament clock, and we are near the end of the New Testament clock, leaving the 1000 year Millennium to complete the 7000 years of human history. We are almost at the door my friend; you had better have your bags packed and the gas tank full! In fact, maybe we had better leave the car running!

Israel's Clock

Now learn a parable of the fig tree; When his branch is yet tender, and putteth forth leaves, ye know that summer is nigh: So likewise ye, when ye shall see all these things, know that it is near, even at the doors. Verily I say unto you, This generation shall not pass, till all these things be fulfilled.

(Matthew 24:32-34)

Most people believe the fig tree represents Israel. This passage is a prophecy about the restoration of the nation of Israel, which took place in 1948. However, they got Jerusalem in the six-day war of 1967. A generation is somewhere around 40 years. Brethren, we are near the end of this clock as well.

These are eight clocks a'ticking. We are sure there are others. We did not even mention that the Iranian president mentioned recently that the Muslim Messiah would be coming up out of the well within two years! Is he possibly a candidate for the Antichrist?

How is your "clock?" Are you redeeming the time that God has given you? Are you busy for the Lord? This is no time to be backslidden! If you are ever going to do something for God, you better get doing it!213

B. Israel's birth and its struggles

This is the Last Generation

Since the birth of Israel on May 14, 1948, a series of remarkable events have set the stage for Israel to fulfill the ancient dream of rebuilding the holy sanctuary. We can confidently await the coming again of Jesus Christ in our lifetime. Jesus warned His disciples that the rebirth of Israel, the budding of the fig tree, would be the major prophetic sign that He will return within the same generation. "When ye shall see all these things, know that it is near, even at the doors. Verily I say unto you, This generation shall not pass, till all these things b e fulfilled." (Matthew 24:33-34).214

Ezekiel foretold that Israel, after two thousand years of being in dispersion throughout the world, would become a nation in one day. Israel would also rebuild the temple. These two events would lead to the return of Yeshua and set up His millennial kingdom on Earth.

---

213 Goodwin, Dan (Evangelist), and Pastor Bill Waughn. "A Seven-fold Promise of His Soon Coming." Faith Baptist Church Publications. Goodwin Publishers, Copyright 2008. Pages 56-66.

214 Jeffrey, Grant R. The New Temple and the Second Coming. Colorado Springs: Waterbrook Press. Page 183.

21 And say unto them, Thus saith the Lord GOD; Behold, I will take the children of Israel from among the heathen, whither they be gone, and will gather them on every side, and bring them into their own land: 22 And I will make them one nation in the land upon the mountains of Israel; and one king shall be king to them all: and they shall be no more two nations, neither shall they be divided into two kingdoms any more at all.215

(Ezekiel 37:21-22, KJV)

DESPITE CENTURIES OF PERSECUTION and attempts from many quarters to exterminate them, the Jews have at last regained their home, 59 years ago— May 14, 1948-the State of Israel became a reality. Since then the history of the region has been marked by military, political, and ideological conflict. The news from the region over the intervening years has presented harrowing scenes and has significantly raised the fear of widespread conflict in the Middle East.216

Originally, the Arabs were agreeable to Israel being a nation.

It was in 1896 Theodor Herzl wrote a pamphlet entitled, "The Jewish State" which aroused an intense longing for the Jews to return to Israel. Herzl was influenced by Christian Zionist who believed prophecies. Another step toward the rebirth of Israel was taken at the end of World War I when the Allied Powers dismembered the Turkish Empire, which had sided with Germany in the war.

In 1917 British foreign secretary Arthur Balfour wrote his famous Balfour Declaration, which favoured 'the establishment in Palestine of a national home for the Jewish people.' The declaration specified that the establishment of a Jewish nation must not 'prejudice the civil and religious rights of existing non-Jewish communities in Palestine, or the rights and political status enjoyed by Jews in any other country." The Balfour agreement was endorsed on July 24, 1922, by the Council of the League of Nations (the forerunner of the United Nations) plus fifty-two nations, including the United States, and for a short time even some Arab leaders.

Emir Faisal ibn Hussein, the leader of the Arab Kingdom, met several times with the Zionist leader, Dr. Chaim Weizmann. One of their declarations, signed in 1919, stated that "the surest means of working out the consummation of their national aspirations is through the closest possible collaboration in the development of the Arab State and Palestine (the Jewish Homeland.") In 1919 Emir Faisal wrote to Zionist leader Felix Frankfurter, a U.S.

Supreme Court Judge, declaring, "We Arabs, especially the educated among us, look with the deepest sympathy on the Zionist movement....... Our two movements complete one another. The Jewish movement is national and not imperialist. Our movement is national and not imperialist, and there is room in Syria [which at that time included all of Palestine] for us both."

These friendly sentiments were not shared by all Arabs and had all but died out by 1948, when Israel officially became a nation once again. Almost immediately an alliance of Arab nations invaded Israel and for more than a year Israel and the surrounding nations were at war. A peace agreement was brokered, but it would not last. In 1967, after the Arab states prepared once again to attack, Israel regained control of the Temple Mount in the Six-Day War. In 1973 the Israelis again defended their land against a surprise Arab attack during the brief Yom Kippur War. Limited

---

[215] The Holy Bible: King James Version. Oak Harbor: Logos Research Systems, Inc., 1995.

[216] Israel at War at Peace. The Bible Standard. Vol. Extra 101.Chester Springs: Bible Standard Ministries. Page 6-7.

attacks have marked the past thirty years, with terrorist groups such as the Palestinian Liberation Organization, Hamas, and Hezbollah launching attacks against Israeli citizens.

As we can see on any newscast today, terrorism and Middle Eastern hatred of Israel is escalating. These actions will culminate in a battle predicted in Scripture.217

Though the superficial reason for the present hostility is the deep resentment felt against Israel because of that state's occupation of Palestinian allotted territory, there are deeper, more ancient reasons. Much of this trouble has at its root a principle of hatred for Israel: the nation and its people. It is no secret that in many Arab capitals the presence of the Jewish state is an unacceptable offense. This animosity can trace its roots to Biblical times, and the family hostility between two distinct branches of Abraham's family: Isaac and Ishmael. Although the conflict at the present time is primarily between the Palestinian fighters and the Israeli State, it is too simple to view it only in those terms. Neither is it simply a battle between Muslim and Jew for there are Palestinian Christians joining forces against what they regard as the occupying force. In addition, there are nations whose dislike of Israel springs from different cultural reasons, and whose heritage is Christian.218

ABRAHAM: A REVERED ANCESTOR Abraham, the ancient father of the faithful, is claimed by Jews, Muslims, and Christians alike, each group holding him high as a righteous servant of the Most High God. The Koran correctly identifies Abraham as the father of the Jews and who was not a Christian (The Koran, Sura II, v. 134); he was in fact a Hebrew and the forerunner of the Semitic people, which includes both Jews (through Isaac) and Arabs (through Ishmael). The discord between Sarah and Hagar provoked by Ishmael's disdain for Isaac, and the subsequent casting out of Hagar and her son, set the pattern for the centuries of hostility between the two branches of Abraham's offspring which followed (Gen. 21: 9-21).

The Scriptures record that Abraham was emotionally troubled by this quarrel between his wife and Hagar, his concubine, because he also loved Ishmael. It is important to keep this in mind when we view the present-day struggle between Jew and Palestinian. God loves the Palestinians and the Arab people. He promised that the offspring of Ishmael would be a great people (verse 13 and 18). Indeed, under the Ottoman Empire, the Arab nations were among the most influential powers of the time. Through their culture and literary advancement they disseminated great wisdom and were the envy of the world; while western countries were mired in medieval darkness, Arab civilization was immersing itself in high learning and scholarship. The Christian response was to attack them in the unholy Crusades. The Ottoman Empire collapsed shortly after the First World War, and the prophetic time had come for Israel to cast off the yoke of foreign oppressors, and through it all a rich legacy of Arab culture still remained.219

1. In remembrance of the Holocaust

Israel at 60: Blinded in Part, Sees in Part by Shira Sorko-Ram

Sixty years ago this month a nation was born in a day — but at great cost. Emaciated Jews from 1945 to 1948, stumbled out of Europe's death camps liberated by the Allies, but they had no

---

[217] Jeffrey, Grant R. The New Temple and the Second Coming. Pages 170-171.

[218] Israel at War at Peace. The Bible Standard. Vol. Extra 101.Chester Springs: Bible Standard Ministries. Page 6-7.

[219] Ibid. Page 6-7.

place to go. Their homes and possessions were destroyed or confiscated and their family members murdered. Many of the survivors believed that the only place in the world they might find safety would be back in their ancient homeland — the land of Israel.

But there was only one catch. The British army had conquered the Holy Land at the end of World War I, and for the thirty-one critical years they controlled Israel's ancient land, they did all in their power to keep Jews from entering so-called Palestine (from the word Philistine). Their close ties with the Arab world and its oil was persuasive enough for them to impose increasingly strict quotas for Jews entering Israel each year. Arabs were free to settle the land, but the quota for Jews was absurd.

Decimated and heavily weighted with flashbacks of Nazi slaughter, all through WWII and after, Jews attempted to board rickety boats and land secretly on deserted beaches, trying desperately to avoid the British occupying forces who were there to put them back on boats to Europe. Those who succeeded (most did not) to set their feet on the holy ground in the middle of the night, were met by local Jews in the underground who gave them guns and told them they must fight for their lives — or another Holocaust was awaiting them — this one by the surrounding Arab nations.

The pitifully small number of 46,000 Holocaust survivors who were admitted into the land after World War II (plus those who were smuggled in) celebrated with the local Jewish community Israel's Declaration of Independence on May 14, 1948 — 60 years ago. Most of these recent immigrants hadn't yet learned much Hebrew, and many knew none at all. But when five Arab armies invaded the newborn nation the next day, all able men and women took up whatever weapons they had. 6,000 Jews died in that war, some of them because they could not understand their officers' commands.

> *As for your birth......when I passed by you and saw you squirming in your blood, I said to you in your blood, "Live!"*
>
> (Ezekiel 16:7)

Sixty years ago, 600,000 Jews lived in this land. Some came from families who had inhabited the Promised Land for many generations — Safed, Tiberius, Jaffa, Hebron and above all, Jerusalem. There were always Jews living in the Holy Land, though most were wanderers among the nations of the world.

Why didn't the Jews flee to Israel before World War II?

When Hitler rose to power in the 1930's, and the black clouds gathered over the millions of Jews living in Europe and Russia, a few sniffed the wind, saw the present danger and heeded the call. Instead of declaring the ancient hope, "Next year in Jerusalem," at Passover, they decided, "This year." Of those who left Europe, some 150,000 made it to Palestine between 1933—1935.

But as a rising Hitler became more brazen against the Jews, hundreds of thousands who recognized the danger would have made their escape but were heartlessly blocked from coming to Palestine. The British saw that few nations were ready to take in the European Jews and feared that the Holy Land would be flooded with millions of them. They cold- bloodedly directed their navy to intercept the few desperate boatloads of Jews that managed to flee Europe before the war started. The refugees were stopped in the water and turned back to Nazi-controlled Europe by the British navy.

The demons of World War II ascended out of the pit. Now it was too late. As the ovens burned, the gates of British-occupied Palestine were mercilessly locked tight, stranding 6,000,000 Jews in Europe who went to their deaths.

Unless you look at the situation close-up, you cannot possibly comprehend the heinous sins done to the Jewish people by the Allies — especially Britain. One small incident: A group of Jews hired a dilapidated boat called the Struma, which quickly developed a leak and a malfunction in the engine. It was allowed into a Turkish port, and the Turks worked long and hard for two months to get the British to give the passengers visas to Palestine. The British absolutely refused, and relentlessly pressured Turkey not to take them either!

Finally a tug boat simply pulled the boat out into the sea where suddenly an unexplained explosion blew the ship out of the water and 763 women, men and children perished. Only one man survived.

No doubt England itself survived the war because of the praying men and women of Great Britain who interceded day and night on behalf of their nation and for the Jewish people.

After the war ended, 70,000 Jews boarded more ramshackle boats and were smuggled into the Holy Land, as the British even after the death of 6,000,000 Jews, continued to block their immigration except for a tiny quota. Still, here and there, another boatload of more souls landed in the dead of night at some isolated beach, silently following their Jewish guides to evade the British. Their descendants are here in Israel today.

I will take you one from a city and two from a family, and I will bring you to Zion.

(Jeremiah 3:14)

Waves of Jews Began Coming Home in Early 1900's

Around the turn of the 20th century, only some 40,000 Jews lived in Israel. (There are many different numbers given by various sources.) They faced abject poverty, famine roving marauders and expulsion by the Turks. But steadily, every year, in the early 1900's, because of persecution in Russia and Eastern Europe, they kept coming.

But what they found was a land despised and forsaken of men. A land of no trees, of desert, and in Galilee, a land of malaria-ridden swamps. A lonely land with few inhabitants.

They cleaned the swamps. They fought the roving bands of Arabs. And the emerging local Arab leaders continued to attack under the permissive eye of British rulers. Still, before the British cut off Jewish immigration in 1939, 450,000 Jews had come home.

The Atlantic Monthly wrote in its July 1919 magazine:

"There is no chapter in the colonizing history of any people finer than the story of these Jewish pioneers. They came to Palestine ignorant of agriculture, ignorant of the land, ignorant of the people, miserably equipped. The (Turkish, then British) government laid its dead hand on all development. It was only by stealth, and with the assistance of baksheesh (money), that a house or a shelter could be erected. There was no security for land property or life, and fever and pestilence raged. The settlers had to compete with native labor accustomed to a very low standard of life. They had to make their own roads, furnish their own police, their own schools their own sanitary apparatus; and while the government of Palestine offered them nothing but the privilege of paying taxes, the governors of the countries from which colonists came extended them no protection."

The Jewish immigrants created an enterprise unknown anywhere else in the world. Under the harsh conditions of a barren land and dangerous neighbors they created the kibbutz — a communal society where a group of people built their houses together, ate together, built factories together, farmed together, and even had special homes in the kibbutz for the children. Though the structure of the kibbutz has radically changed in modern times in the direction of a normal village, the kibbutz was a vehicle that had a tremendous impact in building a Jewish state from scratch. Many of Israel's most well-known politicians and military officers were raised on a kibbutz.

Now here is an interesting point that is crucially important to understand.

Wherever Jews settled, Arab immigration grew exponentially. "The Arabs who went to Palestine sought economic opportunity created by the Zionists. As Europeans, the Zionist brought with them to Palestine resources and skills far in advance of anything possessed by the local population. Jews initiated advanced economic activities that created jobs and wealth and drew Arabs" (http://www.danielpipes.org/article/1110).

May 15, the Day after Independence Day

Nevertheless, when the new Prime Minister, David Ben Gurion, declared Israel an independent state, the Islamic nations had absolutely no intention of permitting such a state to rise out of the ashes of this devastated people. Egypt, Syria, Transjordan, Lebanon and Iraq immediately invaded Israel. Their intentions were declared by Azzam Pasha, Secretary General of the Arab League: "This will be a war of extermination and a momentous massacre which will be spoken of like the Mongolian massacres and the Crusades" (Jewish Virtual Library, The 1948 War, Mitchell Bard).

For reasons only God can give, the Jews survived. Both Jews and Arabs fought until exhausted, and the 1949 Cease Fire was signed by all. However, Arab attacks continued without cessation. The Islamic god categorically refused to accept the reestablishment of a Jewish state on the land God gave Abraham, Isaac and Jacob.

But with the signing of the Declaration of Independence, the Jews in Arab countries began to suffer great persecution. Arab riots broke out, and Jewish property was burned and looted. Jews lost their holdings, their bank accounts were frozen and their property confiscated. 856,000 Jews from Arab countries fled for their lives, forced to leave their property behind. (In comparison, about 700,000 Arabs fled from Palestine when the five Arab nations invaded Israel in 1948). In three years, the population of Israel doubled, and by 1957 900,000 Jews had found refuge in Israel because the new State had opened its gates to all Jews. Israel absorbed them all.

The Israeli Personality

The souls of the Jews who came to Israel from the Holocaust were marred and broken. Most became hardened atheists. They reasoned that if there were a God, He would not have let the Holocaust happen. There are still 250,000 Holocaust survivors alive in Israel today. Not only they, but their children and the children's children bear scars.

Some European ultra-Orthodox Jews managed to escape to the Holy Land before the death trains caught them. They are haters of Christianity. They see Christians as Nazis, or as the Russian- Orthodox priests who slaughtered Jews in Russia in the pogroms. They see Christians as the Spanish inquisitors who drove a million Jews out of Spain. They see Christians as the Crusaders galloping towards Jewish towns and burning down synagogues full of Jews.

But I am very angry with the nations.....for while I was only a little angry, they furthered the disaster.

(Zechariah 1:15)

They see Jews who believe in Yeshua as descendants of the above—traitors to the Jewish people, betrayers of the God of Israel, followers of a Man who caused His disciples to become the modern Hamas — enemies of the Jewish people. In persecuting us they think that they are offering service to God.

The World Views Israel as Negative

Today there are just over 5,500,000 Jews living in Israel — fewer than the number killed in the concentration camps. The nation has seen continuous war for 60 years — in her cities and along her borders.

A BBC poll released on April 2 found Israel to be the second most disliked country in the world. Only Iran is seen as surpassing Israel in unpopularity with Pakistan coming in as a close third. As the Jerusalem Post described it, "Welcome to the Axis of the Unloved." The nation with the most negative feelings toward Israel is Egypt with an incredible 94% of the population. (And we have a peace agreement with Egypt?!) Israel was seen as playing a harmful role in the world by more than half of the 17,000 respondents who were questioned in 34 countries.

Israelis have watched with incredulity the monster of Islamic tyranny rise — not only with bombs and guns, but with sophisticated skills to manipulate the world media as its greatest ally. Israel has watched in amazement and unbelief as virtually the whole world, through the united Nations, has turned against Israel.

Israel has witnessed the top universities in the western world and the east, join the haters of Israel by placing hordes of professors who preach and teach the up-and-coming generation of world leaders the illegitimacy of Israel, the occupiers, who built their nation on another's land.

Israel watches the Middle East burn as Europe and the U.S. fiddle over which sanctions to impose on Iran and her nuclear installations — (which sanctions are best — the nations ponder — the weak ones or the weaker ones?). Iran is already invading Israel — through Hizbullah and Hamas. It is no secret — these terrorists are trained in Iran and their weapons are coming from Iran.

In a little anger I hid My face from you a moment; But with everlasting lovingkindness I will have compassion on you, Says your redeemer.

(Isaiah 54:8)

There are areas of spiritual reality that Israel sees better than any country in the world. She understands the existential threat of Islamic theology. She understands, as no one else does, that the spiritual powers that revealed the Koran to Mohammed are planning a complete takeover of the world.

Confused

There is one area where Israel has been blinded — the most important of all. Satan has seen to it that Jewish people associate Yeshua, the King of the Jews, the Redeemer of Israel, as the Person most responsible for the persecution of the Jewish people over the last 2,000 years.

Therefore, she is confused as she sees Evangelical Christians from America, Canada, Britain, Germany, Japan, Korea, South America and even the islands of the sea, becoming the only friends left in the whole wide world who support Israel.

How can it be? What has happened to Christianity that has caused it to evolve from a fierce enemy of the Jews to the only friend left? What happened to all the liberals and the leftists, the intelligencia of the nations that were her best friends? Where did they all go?

And Christians of all people! Jews have felt more uncomfortable around Christians than any other group of people anywhere! How is she to respond to the outreached hand of her new friends?

Some Jews, like President of the Union for Reform Judaism, Eric H. Yoffie, has warned everyone to stay away from Christians. Besides the constant fear of all Jews that Christians want to convert them to Christianity, he says the differences in theology between Reform Judaism and Evangelical Christianity are simply a gap too wide to bridge. Gay lifestyle and abortions are championed by the secular (Reform) Jewish community in the Diaspora, who after thousand of years of persecution instinctively believe that freedom to believe whatever you want and to do whatever you want is the best climate for Jews to survive.

Jews have long memories. Those who are alive are survivors.

Revolution in the Air

But here is where the Orthodox Jewish community — especially in Israel — comes to the fore. Their theology agrees in many areas with Evangelical Christianity. The Orthodox are against abortion, gay lifestyle, and believe that this land was given to the Jewish people — as do Christian Zionists. And there are many other Israelis and Jews from the Diaspora of all persuasions who are saying, "We really can't be picky about our friends. If Christians are reaching out to us, we are willing to accept their friendship." This is an enormous paradigm shift if the way Israelis perceived Christians in the past.

Furthermore, Israelis are seeing that Arab Christians living in the land are very very different than Muslim Arabs. As a whole, Christian Arabs have received the revelation of God's love for the Jewish people and His plan to plant them back in this land. Evangelical Arab Christians understand that one day the Jews will return wholeheartedly to their God and usher in the Kingdom of God where the King will rule from Jerusalem.

The differences between Muslim and Evangelical Arabs are growing starker. Christian Arabs in the Palestinian Authority are themselves fiercely persecuted. And you cannot imagine the deep, all-consuming hatred the Muslim Palestinians have for Israelis. Westerners simply do not experience this kind of passionate, burning hatred. You have to hear it to believe it. We are inundated with their rage pouring forth on the BBC, CNN or when interviewed in Israeli TV.

And the hatred will not change because the Palestinians are teaching their children from birth to see Israel has a hideous, monstrous occupier, murderers who kill babies and children, thieves who have stole Palestinian land — although the Palestinians as a people only appeared in human history a generation ago and they have never ever had their own land.

Even though the United Nations miraculously endorsed Israel's right to birth a nation on her ancient homeland on November 29, 1947, the Arabs did not accept it, do not accept it and will not accept it in the future.

Judaism Searches for Holiness

Many Jews seek to live a holy life before God, but alas, their forefathers have led them astray. Instead of opening their hearts to all of God's redemptive revelation, they have walked in the way of their fathers, choosing ritual and tradition over intimate relationship.

> *You too have done evil, even more that your forefathers; for behold, you are each one walking according to the stubbornness of his own evil heart, without listening to Me.*
>
> (Jeremiah 16:12)

Religious Jews still talk to God today, but they do not know He wants to talk to them. Orthodox Jews relate to the Biblical text only in reference to what ancient and modern rabbinical authorities say it means. Thus the great, deep veil over the eyes of the Jewish people concerning Yeshua, the only Hope of Israel.

There is not yet the concept of the God of Israel dwelling inside a life. The Jewish people don't understand the meaning of, *"I will give you a new heart and a new spirit......and I will put My Spirit within you......" Ezekiel 36:26*

Today, they seek Judaism as their savior. Repentance is a turning back to Judaism. But one day, their eyes will turn to God.

> *In those days and at that time, declares the Lord, the sons of Israel will come, they and the sons of Judah as well; they will go along weeping as they go, and it will be the Lord their God they seek......that they may join themselves to the Lord in an everlasting covenant that will not be forgotten.*
>
> (Jeremiah 50:4-5)

Today in Israel's 60th year, the Messianic Jewish community has been mandated one of the most important assignments of all ages — to pour Light and Life into the darkness covering our people towards the Messiah. We are the light. We have been given the truth of God's Word.

But we are considered a sect, Jews who have lost their way. Rejection by the general public and harassment and even expulsion by the Orthodox establishment are our daily bread. Many Jewish public figures who have embraced Christians — some wholeheartedly — still despise the Jews who are followers of Yeshua.

> *But how will they call on Him in whom they have not believed? And how shall they believe in Him whom they have not heard (in a way that they understand what is being said about Yeshua)? And how will they hear without a preacher? And how shall they preach unless they are sent?*
>
> (Romans 10:14-15)

Israel still has a calling. And since the gifts and the calling of God are irrevocable, Israel will one day be a light to the gentiles, and their acceptance of their Savior will cause the dead to rise.

What will their acceptance be but life from the dead?

(Romans 11:15)

Isn't it interesting that God has promised to redeem all Israel and turn her back to Himself when He pours out His Spirit and washes away all her guilt? And isn't it equally interesting that God will bless whatever nation stands with Israel, and prays for her peace, but curse the nation that opposes her?

Note: This year Israel's Independence Day will be celebrated on the evening of May 7 and all day May 8, according to the Hebrew calendar.220

2. Early history of the modern state

The modern history of the nation of Israel has its roots in ancient prophecy. During, the first decade of its existence since 1948, Israel's chief source of income was from Germany in the form of war reparations and indemnity payments to individuals which resulted from the holocaust. In addition, the new state received grants from the United States. These ended in 1959 and were followed by a series of loans.

Israel's population tripled during those years and by the end of 1957 stood at nearly 2,000,000 including over 200,000 Arabs. Its present population is approximately 6,500,000. Its proclamation of independence had declared: "The State of Israel will be open to the immigration of Jews from all countries of their dispersion." According to Ben-Gurion, the first Prime Minister, about 1,000,000 immigrants from 79 countries arrived in Israel in this first decade (Jer. 30:2,3,10,11).

Ezekiel chapter 37, with its vision of reassembled and revitalized skeletons, is a wonderful portrayal of the Jewish people, under the influence of Zionism coming back to "life" after their centuries of homeless dispersion.*221*

a. "Fishers and hunters"

Since Jer. 16: 14-16 is one of the clearest Bible passages describing Israel's regathering to the Holy Land, we will examine it in this connection: "Therefore behold, the days are coming," says the LORD, "that it shall no longer be said, 'The LORD lives, that brought up the children of Israel from the land of Egypt,' "but, 'The LORD lives, that brought up the children of Israel from the land of the north, and from all the lands where He had driven them.' For, I will bring them back into their land which I gave unto their fathers. Behold, I will send for many fishermen," says the LORD, "and they shall fish them; and afterward I will send for many hunters, and they shall hunt them from every mountain, and from every hill, and out of the holes of the rocks."

We understand that the "land of the north" is Russia, where at the end of the 19th century nearly one-half of the Hebrew race resided. "All the lands" seems to refer to the other countries in which were found large enclaves of Jews, such as Poland, Germany, Romania, and Hungary.

---

[220] Sorko-Ram, Shira. "Israel at 60: Blinded in Part, Sees in Part." Maoz Israel Report. May 2008. Pages 1-3, 6-9.

[221] Israel at War at Peace. The Bible Standard. Vol. Extra 101.Chester Springs: Bible Standard Ministries. Page 7.

1) The "fishers"

From about 1878, in harmony with His promise in Jer. 16: 16, God sent "fishers" to draw His scattered people back to their homeland. Their bait was Zionism which embraced the philosophy of the return of the Jewish people to their ancient homeland in Palestine much despised by many in and out of Israel today. Many statesmen - Jews and Christians -and other influential figures were involved in promoting the cause of Zionism, especially following the work of Theodore Herzl and the Zionist Congress of 1897. The message of Zionism appealed to many Jews and they came from afar to claim their ancient land. Others remained where they were until they were pursued by the "hunters."

2) The "hunters"

Probably the most frightful chapter of the modern age has been the vicious persecution and attempted extermination of the Jewish people by the Nazi regime of Adolf Hitler. Utterly cruel and single-minded in his determination to wipe the Jews off the face of the earth, his barbarism redefined the word "holocaust" and blotted western civilization with a stain that cannot be removed or forgotten.

What the appeal of Zionism could not do, persecution accomplished, driving Jews by the thousands to Palestine and forcing the rest of the world to wake up to the claims and ancient rights of these people. The Holocaust gave a determination for survival and an identity to the Jewish people in away that no other event in their history of dispersion has ever done.

3. The Six-Day War

Born in the tumult of war, when they were attacked by the Combined Arab nations whose motto was to exterminate them and to drive them out of Palestine, the young state's existence was again threatened in June 1967. The Arab world, led by Egypt's President, Gamel-Abdul Nasser, renewed its war against Israel. Israel's victory in that conflict resulted in her acquisition of more territory. In fact, the remarkably swift "six-day" war left her in control of the West Bank, the Gaza Strip, the Sinai Peninsula, and the Golan Heights. Most important, Israeli forces captured Old Jerusalem. Jews were again in control of King David's city. These are the acquisitions which aggravate the dispute today. Though Israel has relinquished the Sinai Peninsula, it still occupies the Golan Heights (claimed by Syria) and now occupies parts of the West Bank. Of Israel's 6.5 million population, about 128,000 are Israeli settlers in the West Bank, the Golan Heights, and East Jerusalem. Some refer to the West Bank as Judea and Samaria, the Biblical names for the region.222

Israel is mostly urban and the majority of Israeli citizens are Jewish. The term "Jewish" conveys the thought of nationality, ethnic origin: Israel is Jewish by religion and ethnicity and Israeli by citizenship, but because they have come from all over the world, the Jewish population contains considerable racial, cultural, and ethnic diversity. More than half of Israeli Jews are Israel-born (Sabras), but their parents or grandparents came from more than 100 different countries, even as the Scriptures indicate when speaking of the regathering of the scattered people. (Deut. 30: 1-3; Jer. 32: 37). Bonding together an immigrant population of such diverse cultures, languages, and racial

---

[222] " Israel at War at Peace." The Bible Standard. Vol. Extra 101.Chester Springs: Bible Standard Ministries. Page 7.

characteristics has been a tremendous challenge to the leaders of the new state, and their success may well be due in large part to the ever-present threat of enemies from without and from within.

As complex as are the reasons for the plight of the Palestinian people, it apparently suits the Arab countries to use their plight as a public rebuke to Israel. However, in the pursuit of peace between Israel and the Palestinian Arabs, both sides are urged to make painful compromises, and while there is no evidence of the latter's making any concessions, Israel has repeatedly relinquished territories won in the various conflicts with her aggressors. The 'Land for Peace" policy has so far proved to be a delusion, and it remains to be seen whether the political and security issues can be worked out successfully. The dreadful fear remains that no matter what Israel does, no matter how much territory she concedes, she will still find herself unpopular and threatened with destruction by her neighbors. The history of the Jewish people does not cement well for a future unattended by Divine Providence.

4. The present situation

As noted, the gradual acquisition of territory through warfare has brought to Israel and her Palestinian neighbors the trouble that we see today. However, it is fair to note that Israel took territory as spoils of war -war which was forced upon her.

With the passing of Yasser Arafat, and the changing of the Presidency of the Palestinian Authority, the world at large had hoped that the tanks and mortars and bombers would be diminished, but it is evident to us and what the Israeli's themselves fail to clearly see, is that no matter how much territory is relinquished to the Palestinians they will always ask for more. Their aim is not, so much, that they need more land, for no amount of land will satisfy them, but they do not and will never accept Israel's right to exist in the region, under any conditions. The following report of the Israel National News Service (March 2006) from the speech of Palestine's Hamas Leader substantiates the above stand: Speaking at a gathering after the death of the head of the Palestinian National Council, Khaled Alfahom, Mash'al emphasized the importance of the "Palestinian spirit" in winning the historic battle against Zionism.

The following are excerpts from his speech: "Ben-Gurion [Israel's first prime minister] hoped that subsequent generations of Arabs will forget [their defeat in the 1948 War of Independence, commonly referred to by them as] the catastrophe. Israel knows that today they have to contend with an Arab generation that is stronger than in the past. They will see future generations waving the banner of Islam. Palestine's liberation will come with the help of Allah, until it is attained by the last soldier, woman, and child, despite resistance by Israel and the United States... Jerusalem will become Arab and Muslim again, including all the places holy to Islam and Christianity. Today, we are close to attaining Palestinian national rights... We and the Zionists have been brought together by destiny. If they want a fight, we'll be there; if they want a war we're ready; if they want a conflict we'll be there however long it takes. We have more determination than Israel...We'll defeat it, with the help of Allah, and we'll liberate the land."

The elections in Gaza brought to power the Hamas terrorist group and with this came more suicide bombings and rocket attacks on Israel. In recent months, Gaza has taken a back seat to Hizbullah operating in Southern Lebanon and the resultant rocket attacks as far south into Israel as Haifa. According to British Telegraph, the Arab Jewish conflict has now shifted to Iran, who, it is alleged, has banded together with the Hizbullah terrorist group to further afflict Israel. It is said that Iran has used Israel's withdrawal from southern Lebanon a few years ago, to set up a sophisticated intelligence gathering operation to identify targets in northern Israel. A solid group of recently constructed control towers and monitoring stations built by Hizbullah insurgents along the entire Lebanon-Israel border has been placed less that 300 feet from Israel Defence Forces positions. This, together with recently supplied weapons for the terrorists-including mortars and rockets with a 30 mile range, continue to pose a threat and harassment to Israel. IDF crossed the boarder into Lebanon and attempted to remove the Hizbullah strongholds but withdrew before the job was finished. Now, the UN has deployed peace keeping troops, from many countries and a number of them are Muslin countries, into Southern Lebanon until such time as the Lebanese government can be responsible for keeping Hizbullah from occupying the area.223

a. The sixtieth anniversary of Israel's independence

8 Who hath heard such a thing? who hath seen such things? Shall the earth be made to bring forth in one day? or shall a nation be born at once? for as soon as Zion travailed, she brought forth her children.224

(Isaiah 66:8, KJV)

The first day of remembrance is the Holocaust Memorial Day which honors six million Jews who were murdered during the time of the Holocaust.

Israel's Independence day is also remembered when Israel was prophetically re-born as a nation on May 14, 1948. Many who live in Israel today have lost all or most of their relatives. The Jewish people don't realize that was an attack by Satan himself through the instrument of Hitler.

This is what the Lord says through the prophet Jeremiah concerning the survival and existence of the Jewish period:

35 Thus saith the LORD, which giveth the sun for a light by day, and the ordinances of the moon and of the stars for a light by night, which divideth the sea when the waves thereof roar; The LORD of hosts is his name: 36 If those ordinances depart from before me, saith the LORD, then the seed of Israel also shall cease from being a nation before me for ever.225

(Jeremiah 31:35-36, KJV)

11 Then he said unto me, Son of man, these bones are the whole house of Israel: behold, they say, Our bones are dried, and our hope is lost: we are cut off for our parts. 12 Therefore prophesy and say unto them, Thus saith the Lord GOD; Behold, O my people, I will open your graves, and cause you to come up out of your graves, and bring you into the land of Israel. 13 And ye shall know that I am the LORD, when I have opened your graves, O my people, and brought you up out of your graves, 14 And shall put my spirit in you, and ye shall live, and I shall place you in

---

[223] " Israel at War at Peace." The Bible Standard. Vol. Extra 101.Chester Springs: Bible Standard Ministries. Page 7, 14-15.

[224] The Holy Bible: King James Version. Oak Harbor: Logos Research Systems, Inc., 1995.

[225] Ibid.

*your own land: then shall ye know that I the LORD have spoken it, and performed it, saith the LORD.*226

(Ezekiel 37:11-14, KJV)

On May 14, 1948 the United Nations approved that the Jewish homeland which was under British control would become a nation. Within twenty-four hours, on May 15, 1948, Israel became a nation. Five Arab neighboring nations invaded the nation to wipe out the Jewish nation. They were Egypt, Syria, Transjordan, Lebanon and Iraq. This war lasted about fifteen months. During this war, God was with the Jewish people and only six thousand Jewish lives were lost.

Scripture speaks of Israel's spiritual rebirth which is starting to take place.

*25 Then will I sprinkle clean water upon you, and ye shall be clean: from all your filthiness, and from all your idols, will I cleanse you. 26 A new heart also will I give you, and a new spirit will I put within you: and I will take away the stony heart out of your flesh, and I will give you an heart of flesh. 27 And I will put my spirit within you, and cause you to walk in my statutes, and ye shall keep my judgments, and do them. 28 And ye shall dwell in the land that I gave to your fathers; and ye shall be my people, and I will be your God. 29 I will also save you from all your unclean-nesses: and I will call for the corn, and will increase it, and lay no famine upon you. 30 And I will multiply the fruit of the tree, and the increase of the field, that ye shall receive no more reproach of famine among the heathen.*227

(Ezekiel 36:25-36, KJV)

It is the Messianic Jews and Christians who are living in Israel that are reaching these unbelieving Jews so that they will come to know that Yeshua is their long awaited Messiah. A special prophetic Hebrew Bible is being translated to be distributed in Israel to show the unbelieving Jews that Yeshua is the long awaited Messiah.228

This month of May is the sixtieth year of Statehood of Israel. During this time there have been many miracles of building and planting and establishing the vision of a homeland called Israel. During this time World war II Holocaust survivors found a home. New immigrants during these years have come from all nations of the world. Once again Jewish children are playing in the streets of Jerusalem as Isaiah prophesied. The "dead" Hebrew language has become the speech of Israel. The pioneers have built the old waste place and repaired the cities that were destroyed in the past (Isaiah 62:4).

These past sixty years have been a time of heartache and joy. The land has become united and fruitful in spite of the many wars that have been fought with its neighbors.

The Diamond commemorates the sixtieth anniversary "Israel is God's diamond. It is being cut and polished and is being made ready to be present to the soon-coming Messiah."

Israel's very survival is a wonder. This nation is threatened with nuclear destruction by Shiite Iran, its South Western cities find themselves being pummeled by Gazan rockets launched by Hamas, and the Syrian armed Islamic armies of Hezbollah challenges its Northern borders. The

---

[226] Ibid.

[227] Ibid.

[228] Messianic Prophecy Bible Project. Tulsa. May 2008. Page 2-5

Palestinian authority is also growing stronger assisted by the United States. Its goal is to recover all land "occupied by Israel." The EU, the UN and the US and Russia are demanding the re-division of this land to bring peace. Israel's own leaders are weak and indecisive. Just this week Defense Minister Barak pulled the IDF out of the forty settlements in the West Bank, to please the U.S. State Department. The settlers have been disarmed a week ago. Barak has told these settlements that if they want protection they must hire private security services. PM Olment is drafting a plan to offer "compensation" for those who leave their homes......Israeli intelligence Major General Amos Yadlin warned the Cabinet that Hamas are planning a massive holiday attack. Pray that Hamas schemes will bear no fruit. Pray for a quiet, peaceful sixtieth Independence Day.229

PA Urges Palestinians to "Return" to Israel on the 60th Anniversary

The Jerusalem Post reports: "The Palestinian Authority is planning to mark Israel's 60th anniversary by calling on all Palestinians living abroad to converge on Israel by land, sea and air.

The plan, drawn by Ziad Abu Ein, a senior Fatah operative and deputy Minister for Prisoners' Affairs in the Palestinian Authority, states that the Palestinians have decided to implement United Nations Resolution 194 regarding the refugees.

Article 11 of the resolution, which was passed in December 1948, says that 'refugees wishing to return to their homes and live at peace with their neighbors should be permitted to do so at the earliest practicable date, and that compensation should be paid for the property of those choosing not to return and for loss of or damage to property which, under principles of international law or in equity, should be made good by the Governments or authorities responsible.'

The initiative is the first of its kind and is clearly aimed at embarrassing Israel during the anniversary celebrations by highlighting the issue of the 'right of return' for the refugees.

Entitled 'The Initiative of Return and Coexistence,' the plan suggests that the PA has abandoned a two-state solution in favor of one state where all Arabs and Jews would live together.

The Palestinians, backed by all those who believe in peace, coexistence, human rights and the UN resolutions;, shall recruit all their energies and efforts to return to their homeland and live with the Jews in peace and security,' the plan says.

Fulfilling the right of return is a human, moral and legal will that can't be denied by the Jews or the international community. On the |60th| anniversary of the great suffering, the Palestinian people are determined to end this injustice.

Abu Ein's initiative, which has won the backing of many PA leaders in Ramallah, calls on all Israelis to welcome the Palestinians 'who will be returning to live together with them in the land of peace.'

The plan calls on the refugees to return to Israel on May 14, 2008 with their suitcases and tents so that they could settle in their former villages and towns. The refugees are also requested to carry UN flags upon their return and to be equipped with their UNRWA-issued ID cards.

The Arab countries hosting Palestinian refugees are requested to facilitate the return of the refugees by opening their borders and allowing them to march toward Israel. The plan specifically refers to Jordan, Syria, Lebanon and Iraq, who governments are asked to provide logistic support to allow the refugees to carry out their mission.

---

229 Ibid. Pages 3.

Palestinian refugees living in the US, EU, Canada and Latin America are requested to use their foreign passports to fly to Ben-Gurion Airport from May 14-16. The plan calls for the Palestinians to hire dozens of boats flying UN Flags that will converge on Israeli ports simultaneously...... (Regardless of what the Palestinians and any other leaders state, God's Word states that Israel belongs to the Jews eternally and mentions it 120 times.)230

C. Israel's blessings

ISRAEL, CHANNEL OF BLESSING

Israel has been revived and has become again an independent nation. This summer a record breaking number of Jews from North America made their Aliyah to Israel, even in the face of the war. We believe that the long-promised time of Israel's real exaltation as the channel of Messianic blessing to mankind is not too far off. Even though there shall be another great spasm of tribulation as this Old World passes away and a New Order is generated; it is, as the prophets declare "the time of Jacob's trouble" that has not yet run its full course and must do a further purifying work among Israelis and also among the Arab states and the world at large (Jer. 30: 1-7; Isa. 2: 2-5). These things shall not hinder us as the Lord's people from rejoicing in the symbolic New Heavens and New Earth, which God declares He is going to establish in human society-"We, according to his promise, look for new heavens and a new earth, in which righteousness dwells" (Isa. 65: 17-19; 2 Pet. 3: 13).

1. The certainty of God's promises

God's promises are sure of fulfillment. This present evil world does not have God's full blessing and as a result will not be the recipient of the Divine promises. God's projected blessings will be fully realized in His Millennial Kingdom here on earth, which is yet future, and the new order of affairs will be in operation at that time. It is certain that the Palestinian people will eventually have a happy and settled future in store for then, but they will, in the meantime have to learn to accept God's arrangement for the bestowal of these benefits. The Divine arrangement is that these blessings will come through the medium of Israel as the chief nation of earth in the next age. Everyone, all mankind including ourselves, who attain to the earthly phase of the Kingdom will have to become submissive to Christ's rule that will be in place in that Day. For the present, God is working out His will through His chosen Israel. This is not to say that Israel is a paragon of virtue. Many of its people are secular and care little for the promises given to Abraham and their forefathers. We do not, therefore, expect them to behave in a righteous manner. But God's love for this people is not conditioned on their righteousness, but on His promises. The Apostle Paul makes it plain that Israel is beloved for the fathers' sake (Rom. 11: 28, 29).

God loves His people Israel, though they are blinded to His plans and purposes for them. And so it is with all who pledge allegiance to Abraham's God. There is no perfection in self. All—Jew, Muslim, Gentile— must come to believe in and accept the Son of God, the Messiah, Christ Jesus. For most Jews this, for the present, is unacceptable, for they trust the Law and their traditions. For most Muslims this arrangement is even a more difficult vault to surmount, for their writings

---

230 Van Impe, Jack. Intelligence Briefing. Troy: Jack Van Impe Ministries, Inc., May 2008. Pages 5.

teach that Allah has no offspring. For the vast majority of the world, mired in materialism or the day-to-day grind of a self-filled existence, it is beyond their understanding that they are in need of salvation.

Just as Abraham's hand was stayed from killing his son, Isaac, so the enemies of Israel, be they Arab or Gentile, will be thwarted in their attempt to destroy the Jewish people. "No weapon that is formed against you shall prosper" wrote Israel's prophet, Isaiah (54: 17). There is no suicide bomber, no missile, no fighter plane or rocket that can thwart and separate God's people from the land which He has given them. Whether a Palestinian state becomes a reality remains to be seen, but the God of Abraham, Isaac, and Jacob will not permit it at the expense of Israel's existence.[231]

2. Ezekiel's vision of Israel

1948

The prophecy in Ezekiel remind us of his great prophecy that we are approaching the "age of redemption......the age of Messiah."

> *The LORD took hold of me, and I was carried away by the Spirit of the LORD to a valley filled with bones. 2 He led me around among the old, dry bones that covered the valley floor. They were scattered everywhere across the ground. 3 Then he asked me, "Son of man, can these bones become living people again?" "O Sovereign LORD," I replied, "you alone know the answer to that." 4 Then he said to me, "Speak to these bones and say, 'Dry bones, listen to the word of the LORD! 5 This is what the Sovereign LORD says: Look! I am going to breathe into you and make you live again! 6 I will put flesh and muscles on you and cover you with skin. I will put breath into you, and you will come to life. Then you will know that I am the LORD.'" 7 So I spoke these words, just as he told me. Suddenly as I spoke, there was a rattling noise all across the valley. The bones of each body came together and attached themselves as they had been before. 8 Then as I watched, muscles and flesh formed over the bones. Then skin formed to cover their bodies, but they still had no breath in them. 9 Then he said to me, "Speak to the winds and say: 'This is what the Sovereign LORD says: Come, O breath, from the four winds! Breathe into these dead bodies so that they may live again.'" 10 So I spoke as he commanded me, and the wind entered the bodies, and they began to breathe. They all came to life and stood up on their feet—a great army of them. 11 Then he said to me, "Son of man, these bones represent the people of Israel. They are saying, 'We have become old, dry bones—all hope is gone.' 12 Now give them this message from the Sovereign LORD: O my people, I will open your graves of exile and cause you to rise again. Then I will bring you back to the land of Israel. 13 When this happens, O my people, you will know that I am the LORD. 14 I will put my Spirit in you, and you will live and return home to your own land. Then you will know that I am the LORD. You will see that I have done everything just as I promised. I, the LORD, have spoken!" Reunion of Israel and Judah 15 Again a message came to me from the LORD: 16 "Son of man, take a stick and carve on it these words: 'This stick represents Judah*

---

[231] "Israel at War at Peace." <u>The Bible Standard</u>. Vol. Extra 101.Chester Springs: Bible Standard Ministries. Page 15.

and its allied tribes.' Then take another stick and carve these words on it: 'This stick represents the northern tribes of Israel.' 17 Now hold them together in your hand as one stick. 18 When your people ask you what your actions mean, 19 say to them, 'This is what the Sovereign LORD says: I will take the northern tribes and join them to Judah. I will make them one stick in my hand.' 20 Then hold out the sticks you have inscribed, so the people can see them. 21 And give them this message from the Sovereign LORD: I will gather the people of Israel from among the nations. I will bring them home to their own land from the places where they have been scattered. 22 I will unify them into one nation in the land. One king will rule them all; no longer will they be divided into two nations. 23 They will stop polluting themselves with their detestable idols and other sins, for I will save them from their sinful backsliding. I will cleanse them. Then they will truly be my people, and I will be their God. 24 "My servant David will be their king, and they will have only one shepherd. They will obey my regulations and keep my laws. 25 They will live in the land of Israel where their ancestors lived, the land I gave my servant Jacob. They and their children and their grandchildren after them will live there forever, generation after generation. And my servant David will be their prince forever. 26 And I will make a covenant of peace with them, an everlasting covenant. I will give them their land and multiply them, and I will put my Temple among them forever. 27 I will make my home among them. I will be their God, and they will be my people. 28 And since my Temple will remain among them forever, the nations will know that I, the LORD, have set Israel apart for myself to be holy."232

(Ezekiel 37:1-28, NLT)

The vision of the valley of dry bones……this vision describes the experience of the Jewish people who were slaughtered and persecuted for two thousand years in the graveyard of the nation. Then Ezekiel prophesized to those bones of the Jews that "breath come into them and they lived and stood on their feet and were a great army." The Lord commanded, "I will open your graves and cause you to come up out of your graves and bring you into the land of Israel."

3. Ezekiel's vision fulfilled

Over sixty years ago there were less than fifty thousand Jews living in Israel. Today there are about five million Jews who have returned to fulfill God's Word. The prophet Isaiah says:

……and from north and south. I will bring my sons and daughters back to Israel from the distant corners of the earth.233

(Isaiah 43:6, NLT)

The children of Israel have been brought back to their land to meet their coming Messiah.

---

[232] Holy Bible: New Living Translation. Wheaton: Tyndale House, 1997.

[233] Ibid.

We are the first generation to see many specific prophecies fulfilled in our lifetime than in the previous two thousand years. In addition, to the return of the Jews to the land, we have seen a nation born in one day on May 15, 1948.

> *Who has ever seen or heard of anything as strange as this? Has a nation ever been born in a single day? Has a country ever come forth in a mere moment? But by the time Jerusalem's birth pains begin, the baby will be born; the nation will come forth.234*
>
> (Isaiah 66:8, NLT)

Ezekiel predicted, "I will multiply the fruit of the tree and the increase of the field" and said that "this land that was desolate is become like the Garden of Eden" (ref. Ezekiel 36, 30, 35).

This tiny desert nation now blossoms like a rose and provides ninety percent of the citrus fruit in Europe. The pure fertilizers from the Dead Sea salts now produce awesome yields from the previously parched desert soil.

The Ezekiel tablets are the book of Ezekiel written on stone tablets that were hidden away and later found with other temple artifacts in one of the caves in the Israeli desert.

It is interesting to note that the discovery of Ezekiel's tablets coincides with the mass migration into Israel.

> *When I bring them home from the lands of their enemies, my holiness will be displayed to the nations. 28 Then my people will know that I am the LORD their God— responsible for sending them away to exile and responsible for bringing them home. I will leave none of my people behind. 29 And I will never again turn my back on them, for I will pour out my Spirit upon them, says the Sovereign LORD.235*
>
> (Ezekiel 39:27-29, NLT)

Another fascinating prophecy by Zephaniah speaks of Hebrew being the language of the people of Israel when they are brought back to their land.

> *9 For then will I turn to the people a pure language that they may all call upon the name of the LORD, to serve him with one consent.236*
>
> (Zephaniah 3:9, KJV)

The amazing thing about this prophecy is, even during the time of Yeshua, Hebrew was only used by the scribes and priests for religious purposes in temple. Greek and Aramaic was the language of the people. Today, Hebrew is spoken in Israel by the common man.

---

[234] Ibid.

[235] Ibid.

[236] The Holy Bible: King James Version. Oak Harbor: Logos Research Systems, Inc., 1995..

D. Signs of the later times before Yeshua returns

1. Like the days of Noah and of Lot

As far as the signs of the last days relating to morality and the social order, Jesus referenced the "days of Noah" and the "days of Lot." We read in the sixth chapter of Genesis that in the days of Noah violence filled the Earth, and women were prostituted by the "sons of God," who many theologians conclude to have been fallen angels. Today, crime is practically out of control. According to government statistics printed in the 1997 *World Almanac*, there are now five million men and women either in prison or on parole.

In the cities of the plains where Lot lived, homosexuality was the preferred sexual order. Under the Law of Moses, homosexual behavior deserved the death penalty. In the New Testament, homosexuality is identified as the most vile and abominable sin humans can commit, and if allowed to go unchecked will destroy any nation (Roman.1). Today, homosexuals receive preferred treatment over heterosexuals.237

In both the Old and New Testaments, God not only informs us that homosexuality will destroy a nation, but it is even forbidden to allow it within society: "Who knowing the judgment of God, that they which commit such things are worthy of death, not only do the same, but have pleasure in them that do them" (Rom. 1:32).

Conclusion

There are many other events that occurred in 1997 that signal the soon coming of our Lord Jesus Christ. The Scriptures point out that the most tragic thing about warnings from God is that people take no heed of them. Jesus lamented that Israel knew "not the time of their visitation." Jesus said of the flood and the judgment upon Sodom and Gomorrah, "they knew not" until the judgment came. This meant they cared not—they took no heed. This certainly described the condition of the pacified, psychologized church membership of today.

> *Knowing this first, that there shall come in the last days scoffers, walking after their own lusts, and saying, 'Where is the promise of his coming? For since the fathers fell asleep, all things continue as they were from the beginning of the creation.' For this they willinkgly are ignorant......*
>
> (2 Peter 3:3-5)

2. Seven signs to show we are in the generation of Messiah's return.

There are seven signs that need to be fulfilled to signal the second return of Messiah Yeshua to the earth with His saints to rule in Jerusalem. (The rapture of all believers is imminent.)

The signs began with the establishment of the European Union. The European Union was started in 1948 with three nations. Then in 1956, the Treaty of Rome as signed. The size of the

---

237 Hutchings, Noah. "Days of Noah Signs of Times of Later Times before Christ Returns." Prophetic Observer. Oklahoma City: Southwest Radio Church, Dec.1997, c. 1997. Page 3-4.

boundaries of the European Union has increased to more nations. Eventually, the influences will become global.

The European Union will have open boarders, a common currency and a united political purpose and all inclusive boarders.

Until recently the leadership of European Union was established on a rotating basis of the member nations of six months each. Recently they are planning on having a permanent president to take over leadership.

The New World Order was born on November 10, 2009 at 4:25 in Brussels Belgium. Herman VanKampury was elected as its first permanent president.

Quote from Canadian Prime Minister, Charles McVey:

> *The New World Order has arrived and is in place, but needs a Governance (or a leader to rule.)*

Kissinger said, "Obama is primed to create NewWorld Order" Jan, 2, 2009.

There are "Conflicts across the globe and an international respect for Barack Obama have created the perfect setting for establishment of the New World Order." Kissinger told PBS Interviewer Charles Rose last year.

Obama is trying to set forth his peace plan with the Non Proliferation Treaty. It will not work a no nation can bring peace. Only Yeshua can bring true peace to the world when He returns to set up His millennial kingdom.

The New World Order is made up of 247 nations. They will be divided into ten regions or divisions as prophecies in Daniel 2 and Revelations 13. Among these divisions will be North America, South America, Europe, Austrilia, China and Africa.

Several of the early church fathers felt that after the earth is divided into ten regions that Yeshua would return and set up His Millinnial Kingdom. Among the early church fathers who were impressed by the Holy Scriptures were Baravalas (100 A.D.) Dranius and Justin Martin 140 A.D. Jerome who wrote the Latin Vulgate Bible, used the expression that when the earth is divided into ten divisions, Yeshua would set up His Millinnial Kingdom and judge the nations. (Revelations 19:1-20:4)238

In time, the world dictator, the antichrist, will come out of the European Union to present a seven-year peace treaty with Israel. Then the Third Temple in Israel will be assembled. After three and a half years, the antichrist will defile the Temple and then persecute the Jews and the believers in Yeshua.

The second sign of the return is the Universal I.D. system that will be in place. It will be world wide in scope. It will be used as identification also to buy or sell food etc. and for employment purposes, as well as for tracking the whereabouts of each person on the planet. Currently the I.D. is a chip to be placed in a credit card.

The I.D. for the United States' citizens was currently scheduled for May 2008 but has been changed to May 2009.

Eventually, the I.D. will be an implant on the hand or forehead when the world dictator comes into power.

---

[238] Jack Van Impe president (T.V. program) performer, writer, moderator, Jack Van Impe Ministries Producer, Trinity Broadcasting Network. December 16,2009.

16 It forced all the people, small and great, rich and poor, free and slave, to be given a stamped image on their right hands or their foreheads, 17 so that no one could buy or sell except one who had the stamped image of the beast's name or the number that stood for its name. 18 Wisdom is needed here; one who understands can calculate the number of the beast, for it is a number that stands for a person. His number is six hundred and sixty-six.239

(Revelation 13:16-18, NABWRNT)

The third sign is Israel, which is the fig tree, will be reestablished as a nation in May 14, 1948 when Messiah returns.

32 Now learn this parable from the fig tree: When its branch has already become tender and puts forth leaves, you know that summer is near. 33 So you also, when you see all these things, know that it is near—at the doors! 34 Assuredly, I say to you, this generation will by no means pass away till all these things take place. 35 Heaven and earth will pass away, but My words will by no means pass away. 36 But of that day and hour no one knows, not even the angels of heaven, but My Father only. 37 But as the days of Noah were, so also will the coming of the Son of Man be. 38 For as in the days before the flood, they were eating and drinking, marrying and giving in marriage, until the day that Noah entered the ark, 39 and did not know until the flood came and took them all away, so also will the coming of the Son of Man be. 40 Then two men will be in the field: one will be taken and the other left. 41 Two women will be grinding at the mill: one will be taken and the other left.240

(Matthew 24:32-41, NKJV)

Scripture says that Israel will be born in a day.

Who has heard such a thing?
Who has seen such things?
Shall the earth be made to give birth in one day?
Or shall a nation be born at once?
For as soon as Zion was in labor,
She gave birth to her children.241

(Isaiah 66:8, NKJV)

The fourth sign is Jerusalem shall be under the control of Israel. It has been over two thousand years since Jerusalem has been under Israel's control.

In 1967 Jerusalem was captured from the Arabs by the Israeli Army.

---

[239] Confraternity of Christian Doctrine. Board of Trustees. The New American Bible : Translated from the original languages with critical use of all the ancient sources and the revised New Testament. Confraternity of Christian Doctrine, 1996, c1986.

[240] The Holy Bible: The New King James Version. Nashville: Thomas Nelson, 1996, c1982.

[241] Ibid.

24 And they will fall by the edge of the sword, and be led away captive into all nations. And Jerusalem will be trampled by Gentiles until the times of the Gentiles are fulfilled.242

(Luke 21:24, NKJV)

The fifth sign is Russia shall become a strong nation and will unite with the Muslim nations to war against Israel (Reference Ezekiel 38 and 39).

The sixth sign is that China will become a strong warring nation and will come with an army of two hundred million soldiers from the Far East to fight against Israel in the Battle of Armageddon.

12 Then the sixth angel poured out his bowl on the great river Euphrates, and its water was dried up, so that the way of the kings from the east might be prepared. 13 And I saw three unclean spirits like frogs coming out of the mouth of the dragon, out of the mouth of the beast, and out of the mouth of the false prophet. 14 For they are spirits of demons, performing signs, which go out to the kings of the earth and of the whole world, to gather them to the battle of that great day of God Almighty. 15 "Behold, I am coming as a thief. Blessed is he who watches, and keeps his garments, lest he walk naked and they see his shame." 16 And they gathered them together to the place called in Hebrew, Armageddon.243

(Revelation 16:12-16, NKJV)

The seventh sign is the rise of Islamic hatred of Israel as they terrorize the Jewish nation.

1 Do not keep silent, O God!
Do not hold Your peace,
And do not be still, O God!
2 For behold, Your enemies make a tumult;
And those who hate You have lifted up their head.
3 They have taken crafty counsel against Your people,
And consulted together against Your sheltered ones.
4 They have said, "Come, and let us cut them off from being a nation, That the name of Israel may be remembered no more."244

(Psalm 83:1-4, NKJV)

It is quite evident, as you see the Muslim Nations desiring to get rid of Israel as a nation. The nations of the world are taking away the land Israel has. It also is shown in their planning of taking Jerusalem away from Israel as well as the division of Jerusalem. God is not pleased. God promises to judge all nations that take part in the division of Jerusalem and the Land of Israel which God gave to Israel as a permanent possession.245

---

[242] Ibid.

[243] Ibid.

[244] Ibid.

[245] Van Impe, Jack Presents (TV Program) (Performer/writer/moderator) Jack Van Impe Ministries (Producer). Trinity Broadcasting Network. (2008, April 10).

3. Human tracking devices

a. human tracking devices debated

Critics of Microchip Implants Fear Big Brother Surveillance.
By Todd Lewan
Associated Press

CityWatcher.com, a provider of surveillance equipment, attracted little notice itself—until a year ago, when two of its employees had glass-encapsulated microchips with miniature antennas embedded in their arms.246

The radio frequency identification tags, which are as long as two grains of rice and as thick as a toothpick, was used as means of clearance into various areas of secured entry. You put your arm under a scanner and it allows entrance of special access to various secure rooms or file privileges. The downside is that it is a tracking device that lets big brother know where you are, what your personal records are, and even what you are thinking.

Some Christian critics saw the implants as the fulfillment of a biblical prophecy that descries an age of evil, which humans are forced to take the 'Mark of the Beast' on their bodies to buy or sell anything.

The Bible tells us that God's wrath will come to those who take the Mark of the Beast. He said, "Those who refuse to accept the Satanic chip 'will be saved,' Gary Wohlscheid said."247

RFID, in Steinhardt's opinion, 'could play a pivotal role in creating that surveillance society.'

In design, the tag is simple: A medical-grade glass capsule holds a silicon computer chip, a copper antenna and a 'capacitor' that transmits data stored on the chip when prompted by an electromagnetic reader.

Implantations are quick, relatively simple procedures. After a local anesthetic is administered, a large-gauge hypodermic needle injects the chip under the skin on the back of the arm, midway between the elbow and the shoulder.

'It feels just like getting a vaccine—a bit of pressure, no specific pain,' said John Halamaka, an emergency physician at Beth Israel Deaconess Medical center in Boston.

He got chipped two years ago, 'so that if I was ever in an accident, and arrived unconscious or incoherent at an emergency ward, doctors could identify me and access my medical history quickly.'

......there are consequences to having an implanted identifier.

Indeed, as microchip proponents and detractors readily agree, Americans' mistrust of microchips and technologies like RFID runs deep. Many wonder:

- Do the current chips have global positioning transceivers that would allow the government to pinpoint a person's exact location, 24-7? (No; the technology doesn't yet exist.)
- But could a tech-savvy stalker rig scanners to video cameras and film somebody each time they entered or left the house? (Quite easily, though not cheaply. Currently, readers cost $300 and up.)

---

246 Lewan, Todd "Human Tracking Devices Debated." The Fresno Bee. Associated Press, Sunday, July 22, 2007.
247 Ibid

- How about thieves? Could they make their own readers, aim them at unsuspecting individuals, and surreptitiously pluck people's IDs out of their arms? (Yes. There's even a name for it –'spooking.')
- What's the average life span of a microchip? (About 10-15 years.)
- What if you get tired of it before then — can it be easily, painlessly removed? (Short answer: No.)

Presently, Steinhardt and other privacy advocates view the tagging of identity documents — passports, diver's licenses and the like — as a more pressing threat to Americans' privacy than the chipping of people. Equipping hospitals, doctors' offices, police stations and government agencies with readers will be costly, training staff will take time, and, he said, 'people are going to be too squeamish about having an RFID chip inserted into their arms, or wherever.'248

b. ID to be set up in the United States very soon

I am stunned—The Lord was leading me to offer you our blockbuster video Global ID: 666— then as I was preparing to write to you, the news broke:

As Congress prepared to pass a major military spending bill, one member of Congress quietly slipped in a provision for "Real ID"—requiring driver's licenses to contain a microchip......for tracking your movements wherever you go!

Now we get word that the FBI is embarking on a $1 billion project to build a database of people's faces, fingerprints, and palm patterns.

Oh, how could anyone question the truth of God's Word! The Scripture is so clear. After we're gone, the world leader comes to power in Rev. 13:1. A religious leader in Rev. 13:11 promotes the politician and promotes the mark.

It's here! You and I are living in the time that the book of Revelation prophecies.

"Real ID" will mean employers banned from hiring you without the chip. Banks and financial institutions would be banned from doing business with you without the chip. According to the language of the law, people born on or after December 1, 1964, will have to obtain a "Real ID" (the exact date of implementation is being negotiated) — but those born earlier aren't off the hook...... we just have three more years to get our "Real ID"!249

The chipped I.D. will be a means of keeping track of every individual who carries it.

- Big Brother has arrived to create the greatest surveillance system in history.
- Echelon in England, as part of the European Union, records three billion phone calls and email transmissions daily in every language.
- ALSO – The U.S.A., China, and Japan are in a race to build computers performing 1,000 trillion calculations per second – that's 146,000 pieces of information on each member of the human race globally.
- Presently, six subversive organizations are working to control the world through an elaborate spy system.

---

248 Ibid

249 Jack Van Impe. Troy: Jack Van Impe Ministries, Inc. Newsletter dated April 5, 2008.

Who is behind the I.D. chip

- Global leaders promoting this monstrous plan. They are:
  - The Club of Rome.
  - The New Age movement
  - The United Nations
  - The European Union headquartered in Brussels, Belgium.
  - The Illuminati, whose tentacles reach throughout the world.
  - The Council on Foreign Relations comprised of the elite from various nations including most of our U.S. Congressmen and Senators.
  - The Trilateral Commission, which infiltrates governments and promotes the CFR agenda.
  - The Bilderbergs formed a few years ago, and is so secretive that at a recent meeting, guards were reportedly instructed to shoot intruders!

In 85 fast-paced minutes, we reveal the astonishing truth about the coming world dictator—whose arrival is imminent—and how the tentacles of his global government system will very soon entangle and ensnare the entire world!

But this is barely the beginning. Global ID: 666 is going to "blow you away" with the documentation of the one-world government and one-world religion which will rule all six billion of the world's citizens. It will reveal to you:

Mark-of-the-Beast technology is already here!

- How former Soviet leader Mikhail Gorbachev is promoting the one-world government right here in North America!
- What the Mark of the Beast will enable people to do—and what they won't be able to do if they don't have it!
- What the European Union is planning for world domination!
- How a "one-world religion" will be established to promote the one-world government. A recent news report stated: "God is dead in Europe."
- How New-Agers, guided by spiritism, are getting involved in political issues to help usher in their New World Order.
- How two sinister organizations are involved in setting the stage—both headquartered in Brussels, Belgium.
- How the world dictator will attempt to track every human being on the planet and how close to fruition this entire plan already is!
- The U.S. Senate voted to begin the ID process May 12, 2008. It has been postponed until 2009. Did our TV program and video contribute to the postponement?[250]

The establishment of one-world government will affect billions—because Daniel 2:44 says, 'And in the days of these kings shall the God of heaven set up a kingdom, which shall never be destroyed......' This is the coming of Messiah, the return of our Christ who destroys this Antichrist

---

[250] Ibid.

system and rules and reigns for 1,000 years (II Thessalonians 2:8; Revelation 20:4)! In the new video, I share some amazing dates when all of this could possibly happen!251

Information World Control

What lies ahead for civilization? What does the Bible predict? Guided by the Holy Spirit, the prophet states in Daniel 8:23 and 12:4 that knowledge and scientific advancement will be used by an international despot to control the nations of the world.

After the Rapture of the church of Jesus Christ, this leader—called the Antichrist—will take control of a newly-built Jewish Temple in the Holy Land. He will proclaim himself as the awaited Messiah and claim that he is God! Second Thessalonians 2:4 describes his action by stating that the Antichrist *opposeth and exalteth himself above all that is called God, or that is worshipped; so that he as God sitteth in the Temple of God, shewing himself that he is God.* The world will accept his proclamations out of fear. Yes, as world war is about to be unleashed upon the earth, this global charmer will convince humanity that he has the answers to the world's ills—that he alone can bring peace. Thus, on the basis of peace negotiations between Israel and many nations (Daniel 9:27), he will be accepted.

I believe that the Antichrist will enslave and control earth's billions through a sophisticated computer fashioned in his likeness. Thus, he will be able to have all the facts on every member of the human race at his fingertips. With unerring precision, he will know who received his orders, obeys his commands, and honors his laws. Modem computers are already storing information on members of the human race. Now, what about these computers? One of the greatest physicists to live, Stephen Hawking, of England—and he's comparable to Einstein, a genius—said that we have made man in our image through the computers, and they are alive. Computers are alive! Think of it! And then there's Professor Montanago, who said that this device is alive, for whenever you combine biological cells with silicon in electrical equipment, it lives. In his book, "Techno Futures," James Canton of technotu.com outlines the top computer trends for the 21st century. Computers will become powerful extensions of human beings, designed to augment intelligence, learning communications, and productivity. Computers will become intuitive—they will learn, recognize, and know what we want, who we are, and even what we desire. They're alive! Computers will have digital senses—speech, sight, smell, and hearing—enabling them to communicate with humans and other machines.

The international dictator will use such a computer, fashioned after his likeness (Revelation 13:14), to enslave the inhabitants of earth. He will effectively do this through commerce—the buying and selling of products.

Revelation 13:16, 17 states, *And he causeth all, both small and great, rich and poor, free and bond, to receive a mark in their right hand, or in their foreheads: And that no man might buy or sell save he that had the mark, or the name of the beast, or the number of his name.* This forthcoming computer of the ages will give the Antichrist all the information necessary for him to govern the world. Its memory bank will know the number, record and history of every living person! This number will definitely include "666" in one manner or another (Revelation 13:18).

I believe it will be a prefix, such as 666-7, 666-300, etc. Every individual credit card number must have some differentiation to distinguish one person from another. If all credit cards were

---

251 Ibid.

identical, there would be mass confusion. Similarly, there will be some variance along with the "666" marking.

Some students of Bible prophecy theorize that this number will actually be composed of the international, national and area computer codes presently in use (or being implemented) plus an individual number, such as the person's Social Security Number. The present international computer code is "6", and this is anticipated to expand to "666." The national computer identification code for the United States is "110." Within our nation are many area codes presently used for telephone communication. Thus, by using each of these codes in sequence, ending with the Social Security or other assigned number, every man, woman, and child within our borders could be individually identified. Such a number might be 666-110-212-419-27-2738.

Now I want to report a startling mathematical equation which was worked out on current computers by Col. Henry C. MacQueen, Sr., of Saratoga, California. He took the three six- digit units, which, with their permutations of numbers came out to N-60, and multiplied them by three. I don't expect you to understand the depth of the statement which I am about to make because I personally can only repeat what the computers revealed. I, too, am unable to grasp the enormity of the following figures. I state them to show you that each of earth's six- and-one-half-billion inhabitants could possess his own personal number through the permutations of the figures described as "666". In fact, the computers arrived at the conclusion that 46,834,995,519,212,567,931,529,902,559,000 (forty-six nonillion, eight hundred thirty-four octillion, nine hundred ninety-five septillion, five hundred nineteen sextillion, two hundred-twelve quintillion, five hundred sixty-seven quadrillion, nine hundred thirty-one trillion, five hundred twenty-nine billion, nine hundred-two million, five hundred fifty-nine thousand) human beings could each have his own number. Six hundred sixty-six, with its permutations, fits the bill, even if trillions more should be born!

$$$ versus "666"

The world's current monetary system is creating havoc among bankers. In America alone, the annual check processing cost is millions! What a waste! Cash causes even greater problems as graft; bribery, corruption, and crime sweep the world. Leaders are crying, "Away with cash and eliminate crime!" *The American Bar Magazine* reports that "crime would be virtually eliminated if cash became obsolete. Cash is the only real motive for 90 percent of the robberies. Hence, its liquidation would create miracles in ridding earth's citizens of muggings and holdups."

In connection with a cashless society, plans are being laid internationally to make a numbers system feasible. This explains the strange lines and figures known as the Universal Product Code on virtually every item of merchandise sold today. The metric system is also being promoted and installed at a cost of billions of dollars by international bankers. Their aim is the establishment of a one-world government! This government will control human beings through computerized numbers for all people. Presently, no one knows how each of us spends our cash. Once every transaction is credited to a person's number, however, "Big Brother" will know everything about everyone through computers!

What a profound statement in the light of Bible prophecy! In 1973 in Brussels, Belgium, a handful of people had an ambitious idea, and the Society for Worldwide Interbank Financial Tele communication (SWIFT) started their mission of creating a shared worldwide data processing and communications link and a common language for international financial transactions. As of December 2007, SWIFT has linked 8,332 financial institutions in 208 countries.

Any computer system in the world can be hooked into the mother computer in Luxembourg (whose major links are located in Brussels, Belgium). This information is doubly interesting when one realizes that Brussels is the headquarters of the EWU Common Market nations and NATO. In all probability, the present preparations may be part of the formation of the final ten-kingdom federation of nations prophesized in Daniel 2 and Revelation 13.

Let us now consider how the number "666" could become functional in such a mechanized society. Suppose to every person in the world we assigned a single credit card and individual identification number? The *Knight News Service* of Miami, Florida, reports that bankers believe "most shoppers would exchange the wallet full of credit cards they now carry for a single, all purpose card and number."

We see, then, that a world number is feasible in the near future. However, this is a problem. A person could be kidnapped or killed for the numbered card. Because of this, some are advocating the insertion of a number on one's body—one that would not mar, scar, or detract from a person's features. It would be a laser-beam tattoo, invisible to the human eye but clearly visible under an infrared light. Others are promoting a microchip that will be implanted in the hand or body.

A world ruler will arise with the new system. This beast is described in Revelation 13:7-8, 16-17: *Power was given him over all kindreds, and tongues, and nations. And all that dwell upon the earth shall worship him......And he causeth all, both small and great, rich and poor; free and bond, to receive a mark in their right hand, or in their foreheads: And that no man might buy or sell, save he that had the mark, or the name of the beast, or the number of his name.*

One day soon, all buyers and sellers—the consumer and the producer alike—will be required *to receive a mark in their right hand, or in their foreheads* (Revelation 13:16). This requirement can only be initiated and enforced by the Antichrist himself! It is the goal of the global leaders to chip every human being in the world by 2017.

I believe that when the Antichrist makes his debut and officially institutes the number "666" internationally, we Christians will be gone. Paul makes this fact emphatically clear in 2 Thessalonians 2:3-8. In verses 6-8, he informs the saints that the Antichrist cannot mount his throne until the hinderer—the Holy Spirit—is removed: *And now ye know what withholdeth* [or what holds back the Antichrist's coming to power] *that he might be revealed in his time......only he who now letteth* [hindereth] *will let* [hinder], *until he be taken out of the way.*

After the restrainer's removal, then shall that wicked one be revealed. The Antichrist cannot reign until the Holy Spirit's restraining influence is removed (I Corinthians 3:16, 6:10). This restraining influence consists of believers in who hearts the Spirit dwells. Christ must come to call His own out of this world before the leader of the one-world government assumes power.252

---

[252] Van Impe, Dr. Jack. "Information and World Control." Perhaps Today. Troy: Jack Van Impe Ministries, Inc. Newsletter dated May/June, 2008. Pages 3-5.

E. Building the third temple

1. Background

A TRIBULATION SCENARIO

I am going to present here a possible scenario of how things may work out during the Tribulation period. Keep in mind once again that we have been given certain prophecies by God. So we know they're going to take place.

Sometimes, it seems difficult to believe they will take place. But by looking at the Word of God and comparing it to current events, we begin to see patterns developing that seem to make their fulfillment more plausible. But it is only when the actual biblical fulfillment comes to fruition that we will know exactly how God saw it would work.

Anyhow, we do know that the Rapture will take place. I believe it will be before the seven- year Tribulation. The time of the gentiles will have been fulfilled and God is now focusing on Israel for the final week of Daniel's prophetic seventy weeks.

Probably at the beginning of this time period the Antichrist will sign a covenant with Israel and other nations, guaranteeing Israel's safety. Israel is deceived by the Antichrist and False Prophet and believes the age of her messianic redemption has arrived. A Third Temple is built, perhaps next to The Dome of the Rock and the Mosque al-Aksa. Maybe the Antichrist and False Prophet will even convince the Jews to allow a "Christian" church to be erected on the Temple Mount as well.

So for a time Israel is living in peace with world and is worshiping and making sacrifices in her cherished Temple.

Near the middle of the Tribulation, however, things begin to sour in this age of peace and prosperity. The Russian army from the north, along with other nations, mostly Muslim, start heading towards Israel which is now a land of "unwalled villages" (Ezekiel 38:11). It is the true God who comes to Israel's rescue and destroys this northern army.

Israel recognizes her God and is now fully aware that she has been following the wrong general. The Antichrist, in his anger, goes into the Temple and in an act of self-deification, proclaims that he is God (II Thess. 2:4). This act is known as the abomination of desolation.

It appears that it is at this point when the utopian kingdom created by man comes to an end and all hell breaks loose. Revelation 13:4-8 tells us:

> *5 And there was given unto him a mouth speaking great things and blasphemies; and power was given unto him to continue forty and two months. 6 And he opened his mouth in blasphemy against God, to blaspheme his name, and his tabernacle, and them that dwell in heaven. 7 And it was given unto him to make war with the saints, and to overcome them: and power was given him over all kindreds, and tongues, and nations. 8 And all that dwell upon the earth shall worship him, whose names are not written in the book of life of the Lamb slain from the foundation of the world.*

(Revelation 13:4-8)

It could also be that at this point the mark of the beast is enforced. It will be a sign of allegiance to the beast because God warns in Revelation 14:9-11:

9 And the third angel followed them, saying with a loud voice, If any man worship the beast and his image, and receive his mark in his forehead, or in his hand, 10 The same shall drink of the wine of the wrath of God, which is poured out without mixture into the cup of his indignation; and he shall be tormented with fire and brimstone in the presence of the holy angels, and in the presence of the Lamb: 11 And the smoke of their torment ascendeth up for ever and ever: and they have no rest day nor night, who worship the beast and his image, and whosoever receiveth the mark of his name.

(Revelation 14:9-11)

The final generation of man will not be so wise, however. God's wrath will be manifested against those who worship the beast and take his mark through "the seven last plagues" (Revelation 15:1)253

1 And I saw another sign in heaven, great and marvellous, seven angels having the seven last plagues; for in them is filled up the wrath of God.

(Revelation 15:1)

2. Wealth of Israel to be restored

The wealth of the Dead Sea is to be used to restore His people's wealth to that of King David's and King Solomon's day to be used in part to pay for the construction of the third temple.

a. Treasures from the sea

PROPHESIED TREASURES FROM THE DEAD SEA

Throughout the Scriptures we find numerous prophecies that refer to God placing treasures for Israel within the seas. For many centuries these predictions seemed unlikely to ever be fulfilled. However, since the rebirth of Israel, scientists and engineers have developed enormous mineral resources from the Dead Sea. The Bible includes the following prophecies:

They shall call the people unto the mountain; there they shall offer sacrifices of righteousness: for they shall suck of the abundance of the seas, and of treasures hid in the sand.

(Deuteronomy 33:19)254

And I will give thee the treasures of darkness, and hidden riches of secret places, that thou mayest know that I, the Lord, which call thee by thy name, am the God of Israel.

(Isaiah 45:3)

---

253 Patti Lalonde. "Building the Third Temple." <u>This Week in Bible Prophecy Inc</u>. Vol. 3/Issue 4. St. Catharines: This Week in Bible Prophecy Inc., April 1995. Page 224.

254 Jeffrey, Grant R. <u>The New Temple and the Second Coming</u>. Colorado Springs: Waterbrook Press. Page 171.

O thou that dwellest upon many waters, abundant in treasures, thine end is come, and the measure of thy covetousness.

(Jeremiah 51:13)

In the 1930's the British Mandate authorities allowed a British company known as Potash Ltd. to set up a pumping and extraction plant that would recover some of the extraordinary mineral wealth from the dead Sea—wealth that had been hidden by God as 'the treasures of darkness, and hidden riches of secret places' (Isaiah 45:3). The company pumped a slush-like supersaturated liquid from a depth of two hundred feet at the northern end of the Dead Sea. The liquid moved through a thirty-inch pipe some twelve hundred feet up the side of mountains to the west of the Dead Sea. The company had scraped out enormous evaporation pans near the top of a mountain. Five huge pools were arranged in a cascade-like series, with each evaporation pan spilling over to the next lower pool.

The unusually high temperatures and high winds of the area cause the slush-like material to evaporate, producing extremely pure sodium chloride (table salt, which is highly valuable.) The residue was poured into the next evaporation pool and after evaporation produced magnesium chloride (used in the manufacture of aluminum). Each additional evaporation pool produced another chemical separation: calcium chloride, potassium chloride, and finally magnesium bromide. When I searched the Internet to determine the current values of the amount of chemicals that have been calculated to exist in the Dead Sea, I arrived at these incredible figures (see table).

Chemical	Est Billion Tons	Price per Ton	Total Value
Magnesium chloride	22	$290	$6.38 trillion
Sodium chloride	11	$450	$4.95 trillion
Calcium chloride	5	$350	$1.75 trillion
Potassium chloride	2	$85	$170 billion
Magnesium bromide	1	$1,280	$1.28 trillion
Total Estimate	41		Over $14 trillion

Annual addition of potassium chloride to Dead Sea: 40,000 tons*
(*This amount is more than enough to replenish the annual harvest.)

To place this $14 trillion value in perspective, it is virtually equal to the annual gross national product of the United States.

The Lord has not only brought His people back to their land, but He is motivating them to restore its ancient fertility and wealth as it was in the days of King David and King Solomon.[255]

---

[255] Ibid. Pages 171-173.

3. a. The Orthodox view of Messiah and the temple

The rabbinic view of the messiah will be a man of prophetic anointing like Elijah, a military victor like David, and a wise politician like Solomon......He will be a Jewish man with a charismatic personality, who is a leader within rabbinic orthodoxy and who will lead Israel in political unity and military victory. The rabbinic council would simply have to identify such a hero, and give him their divine stamp of approval.256

An international war will break out against Israel involving Russia and the Arab states. A miraculous victory for Israel will take place. A strong orthodox power base will recognize a leader from the war as the messiah. He will serve as a combination king, prime minister and chief rabbi.

Unity and peace will be brought to the country. In the aftermath of war, a stunned peace settles over the Middle East and Europe. The Temple Mount area is cleansed. Sacrifices are begun. Construction of Temple is begun.

Money will pour in from all over the world for the Temple. Tourists and religious pilgrims from around the world come to Israel. Israel emerges as an international leader, both economically and politically. God's grace and favor is unmistakably upon the nation.

Jewish believers in Yeshua in Israel are preaching openly in the streets accompanied by miracles. The orthodox establishment brands them as a cult and tries to imprison them, but popular resistance won't allow it. Miracles and persecution are happening at the same time.257

Purpose of the End Time Temple

1. To serve as a sign of God's power both to the scattered and re-gathered of the nation of Israel.
2. It will serve as a stumbling block to everyone of humanistic orientation.
3. To cleanse religious hypocrisy from the Temple and people.
4. It will be a place of unity, purity, beauty and worship. Yeshua called it "My father's house."258

The hope of two thousand years — which was prayed by all observant Jewish men.

b. The hope of two thousand years

The Jewish prayer service is repeated by all observant men twice daily, morning and evening. Generally speaking, the men gather together in the synagogue both before work and after: The central part of that twice-a-day prayer service is a list of eighteen prayers call the *"shmonah-esreh"* or the *"Eighteen."*

To follow the orthodox way of thinking, it is significant to notice the order of certain of these prayers:

---

256 Juster, Dan and Keith Intrater. "Israel, the Church and the Last Days. (Rebuilding the Temple)." The Orthodox Messiah. Page 230.

257 Ibid. Page 235.

258 Ibid. Page 236.

The tenth prayer requests the re-gathering of the Jewish people from the four corners of the earth back to the land of Israel.

The fourteenth prayer asks for the return of the city of Jerusalem to the Jewish people. The fifteenth prayer asks for the coming of the messiah.

The seventeenth prayer asks for the rebuilding of the Temple with the restoration of the Temple worship system.

Isn't that significant? Notice the order: the regathering to Israel — the recapture of Jerusalem — the coming of the Messiah — the rebuilding of the Temple. There you have it: Israel, then Jerusalem, then Messiah, then the Temple.

This prayer has been said by orthodox Jewish men all over the world in unison and agreement twice daily for nearly two thousand years. Imagine the effect of that. Their hopes of two thousand years are in the process of coming to pass. Let us pray for their eyes to be opened to the truth of Messiah Yeshua in these last days.[259]

4. Preparations for the temple

a. Background

The second Temple was destroyed on the Ninth day of Av (August) in AD 70 by General Titus, son of Emperor Vespasian.

The first Temple was built by King Solomon around 1000 BC and destroyed by the Babylonians in 586 BC.

The second Temple was built by the Jews in their return to Jerusalem 536 BC after the Babylonian captivity. It was expanded by Herod starting in 18 BC and was finished a few years before its destruction in 70 AD.

The third Temple will be built on the ancient foundation that Solomon put in place over three thousand years ago.

The rebuilding of the third Temple is important in end time prophecies. Scripture makes it clear that before Messiah returns, the Third Temple of God must stand again on the original location on the Temple Mount.

Preparations for the rebuilding the Temple is now in progress. The Temple must once again occupy its place on the Temple mount before the events of the last days can take place.[260]

> *Now learn a lesson from the fig tree. When its buds become tender and its leaves begin to sprout, you know without being told that summer is near. 33 Just so, when you see the events I've described beginning to happen, you can know his return is very near, right at the door. 34 I assure you, this generation will not pass from the scene before all these things take place.[261]*

(Matthew 24:32-34, NLT)

---

[259] Ibid. Page 240.

[260] Jeffrey, Grant R. New Temple and Second Coming. Colorado Springs: Waterbrook Press. Page 3 and 4.

[261] Holy Bible: New Living Translation. Wheaton: Tyndale House, 1997.

b. Tensions regarding rebuilding the third temple

There are religions and political tensions that stand in the way of the rebuilding of the Temple such as the Moslem Dome of the Rock and the fear of treading on the area where the Holy of Holies is located.

Another reason the Jews cannot rebuild the Temple or resume worship in the Temple is because the Sanhedrin Court, the highest body of Jewish lawmakers, is reconvened. It is necessary to reestablish the Levitical priesthood. The Sanhedrin is the only religious body to determine the correct location of the Temple and to reinstitute the ancient rituals and to oversee the many details related to the Temple ritual and worship.262

One of Yeshua's prophecies indicates that the Sanhedrin will be fulfilling its duties in the last days. Messiah warned His disciples about the coming persecution in Jerusalem during the Tribulation. He told them to pray that their flight from the city would not be "on the Sabbath day." (Matthew 24:20)

The reason for this commandment against performing works on the Sabbath:

> *Remember to observe the Sabbath day by keeping it holy. 9 Six days a week are set apart for your daily duties and regular work, 10 but the seventh day is a day of rest dedicated to the LORD your God. On that day no one in your household may do any kind of work. This includes you, your sons and daughters, your male and female servants, your livestock, and any foreigners living among you.263*
>
> (Exodus 20:8-10, NLT)

The ancient Sanhedrin had determined that any travels on the Sabbath that exceeded one thousand paces was considered work. If an invasion force should attack on the Sabbath, the Jews in Jerusalem limited their travel to one thousand paces would ensure their destruction. Christ's prophecy implies that the Sanhedrin will exist in the last days and will have the authority to enforce such a religious rule. In the Book of Acts 7:12, Luke wrote that the distance from the Mount of Olives to the Temple Mount is one thousand paces.264

c. The command to rebuild the temple

Israel has been without a temple for over 1900 years. During this time devout Jews living in exile prayed that they would live to see their temple rebuilt in their days. They longed for the Lord to return His Shekinah glory and divine presence in the sanctuary in Jerusalem.

Finally after nineteen centuries, today's generation has been given the task of making these ancient dreams come true.

The rebuilding of the Temple is central to the Messianic hopes of the Jewish people. God never rescinded His command that Israel build a sanctuary for Him.

---

262 Jeffrey, Grant R. New Temple and Second Coming. Pages 4 and 5.

263 Holy Bible: New Living Translation. Wheaton: Tyndale House, 1997.

264 Jeffrey, Grant R. New Temple and Second Coming. Pages 5 and 6.

I want the people of Israel to build me a sacred residence where I can live among them.265

(Exodus 25:8, NLT)

His command is still in force today.

The Lord gave Moses the precise blueprint for His earthly sanctuary, the tabernacles and it was used as the basic design of Solomon's Temple and later the second Temple. It will also be used for the basic design of the Tribulation (or third Temple) Temple which can be built at anytime soon. The Temple was patterned and objects of worship are made according to the eternal Temple in heaven.266

I want the people of Israel to build me a sacred residence where I can live among them. 9 You must make this Tabernacle and its furnishings exactly according to the plans I will show you.267

(Exodus 25:8-9, NLT)

They serve in a place of worship that is only a copy, a shadow of the real one in heaven. For when Moses was getting ready to build the Tabernacle, God gave him this warning: "Be sure that you make everything according to the design I have shown you here on the mountain."268

(Hebrews 8:5, NLT)

Yeshua mentioned the existence of the "Holy Place" in a future Temple when he told His disciples about the events of the last days and the Great Tribulation. He warned that "when ye therefore see the abomination of desolation, spoken of by Daniel, the prophet, standing in the Holy place, let them which are in Judea flee into the mountains (Matthew 24:15-16).

The "abomination that maketh desolate" would stand in the Temple of God in Jerusalem.

His army will take over the Temple fortress, polluting the sanctuary, putting a stop to the daily sacrifices, and setting up the sacrilegious object that causes desecration.269

(Daniel 11:31, NLT)

From the time the daily sacrifice is taken away and the sacrilegious object that causes desecration is set up to be worshiped, there will be 1,290 days.270

(Daniel 12:11, NLT)

---

[265] Holy Bible: New Living Translation. Wheaton: Tyndale House, 1997.

[266] Jeffrey, Grant R. New Temple and Second Coming. Colorado Springs: Waterbrook Press. Pages 6 and 8.

[267] Holy Bible: New Living Translation. Wheaton: Tyndale House, 1997.

[268] Ibid.

[269] Ibid.

[270] Ibid.

Both of these prophecies suggest that the Third Temple will be built before the antichrist comes to power and takes control of Europe and the surrounding Mediterranean nations.

Satan will spiritually defile the Holy Place of the rebuilt Temple by directing his antichrist to violate the Holy of Holies at the beginning of the last three and a half years of the Tribulation. The False Prophet, the antichrist's partner, will then demand that the antichrist be worshipped as "god" in the rebuilt Temple.

The Third Temple will be built on the most passionately contested piece of real estate on earth. Architectural plans and re-creating of precious vessels to be used in Temple worship, as well as the searched for the lost treasurer of the ancient Temple, are in progress that will be necessary to reinstate sacred worship and animal sacrifice.[271]

After nineteen centuries of praying and waiting, the Jews are finally being given the historic task of making their ancient dreams come true. The generation alive today will see the temple of God once again standing in Jerusalem, and the returning Messiah, Yeshua, ruling from the throne of David.

TRIBULATION TEMPLE

Would a rebuilt temple be blasphemous?

Since Israel has been reestablished, efforts to rebuild the temple are in progress. There are varying views on the right of the temple being built.

Some Christian theologians contend that it would be blasphemous for a new Jewish Temple to be rebuilt. Based on statements in the book of Hebrews which speak of Christ's work on the cross, they contend that His act satisfied once and for all time that which the Temple sacrifice only foreshadowed. According to this reasoning, the rebuilding of a third Temple would deny that Jesus' atoning work on the cross made the Temple sacrifice void.

No true Christian would deny that Jesus' work on the cross abolished the need for Temple sacrifice. Christians who look with interest to the Jews rebuilding their Temple are not in any way denying Christ's saving work through His death. Rather, (BC 21) [they view of rebuilding of the Temple as a prophetic sign of the times. The Jews will rebuild the Temple, in part, because of their rejection of Jesus as the Messiah, but what they do in unbelief will fulfill God's sovereign plan of having a Temple in Jerusalem for the Antichrist to defile.

Christians who are excited about recent Jewish developments to rebuild the Temple in no way compromise orthodox Christian belief, since they do not see it as relating to the forgiveness of sins, once and for all accomplished in Christ. Instead they see it as related to God's prophetic plan.][272]

This is also the pattern of every exodus of the Jewish people After each exodus, the Jewish people did not just come home to their Promised Land, but eventually the Temple was built so that God could dwell in the midst of His City and His Land — among His People. After the first Exodus from Egypt, Solomon's Temple was built to which the Lord came in such power and glory that the priests could not even continue to minister before His awesome presence. After the second Exodus from Babylon, the Temple of Zerubbabel was built, the Temple which Jesus succinctly called the House of His Father.

---

[271] Jeffrey, Grant R. New Temple and Second Coming. Pages 8 and 9.

[272] Ice, Thomas and Randall Price. "Tribulation and Beyond." Ready to Rebuild. Eugene: Harvest House Publishers, 1992. Pages 202, 203.

He will not come to a mosque, nor to a Western Wall—He will come "suddenly to His House His Temple."

Now we have come to the third homecoming of the Jewish people, from all the countries where they had been scattered.

And again this exodus will be climaxed in the building of the Third Temple, fulfilling the words of the Prophet Isaiah: "And it shall come to pass in the last days that the mountain of the LORD's Temple will be established as chief among the mountains; it will be raised above the hills, and all nations will stream to it. And many people shall go and say, 'Come, and let us go up to the mountain of the LORD, to the house of the God of Jacob, and he will teach us of his ways, and we shall walk in his paths: for out of Zion shall go forth Torah, and the Word of God from Jerusalem'" (Is.2:23).273

d. Location of the temple to be determined and conflict with Arab neighbors.

The locations of the former temples were previously thought to be at the sight of the Dome of the Rock; however, during the last few years, Jewish archaeologists have made discoveries on and beneath the Temple Mount that pinpoints the original location of Solomon's temple. The site is north of the Dome of the Rock. These findings are the work of very dedicated archeologists and historians.

Amid the recent turmoil and destruction in Israel, these archeological and historical experts have persevered in their work, and it has proved fruitful indeed. *The Jerusalem Post Internet Edition (2/7/2007)* posted a story about an announcement from Hebrew University's Prof. Joseph Patrich. He asserts that by investigating an ancient cistern on the Temple Mount, and comparing its location to Mishnaic writings describing practices within the Temple, the precise location of the Second Temple can be identified. Significantly, this new research places the Dome of the Rock in the outer confines of the Temple Courts, not within the Temple proper which means the Temple can be built without disturbing the Dome of the Rock.

The Wyatt foundation has continued the late Ron Wyatt's research regarding the location of the Ark of the Covenant and of Golgotha. Between February 2003 and August 2005, workers and volunteers used radar and subsurface interface radar techniques to guide a series of digs. Artifacts and buildings dating to the time of King David and Solomon were unearthed, including a tunnel believed to have been used by the prophet Jeremiah to bring the Ark of the Covenant and other Temple vessels to safety during the Babylonian siege.274

On February 7, 2007, there was a Jerusalem Post article generally not covered by the Western Press. Professor Joseph Patrich of Hebrew University pinpointed the exact location of the Second Jewish Temple. It was found to be in a more Southeasterly and diagonal angle relative to the Eastern wall of the Temple Mount and not perpendicular to it, as had previously been assumed. Also, the location of the laver and a ramp have been seen and identified.

This research was based upon the findings of a large underground cistern mapped by British engineer Sir Charles Wilson in 1966. This giant reservoir for water drainage measured 4.5 meters wide and 54 meters long. As measured now, it could hold up to 12,000 gallons of water.

---

273 Vander Hoeven, William. "When will Messiah Come." Jewish Voice Today. Page 6.

274 "Jewish Year 5768." Messianic Times. Vol. 17 #2, (May/June 2007).

Examining the location and configuration of this underground pool, together with rabbinical writings in the Mishna about passageways and daily rituals, tells us that these waters were used in the daily purification rites. These sacrificial duties were carried out by the priests on the ancient altar of sacrifice. The water was brought up by a waterwheel mechanism from the cistern.

Patrick said his research indicates that the rock, over which the Dome of the Rock was built in the 7th Century, is actually outside of the confines of the Temple itself. It is this rock that Muslims believe to be the spot from which Muhammad ascended to heaven, although this is not stated specifically in the Koran.275

Other recent archeological findings include the exact site of the Pool of Siloam in the City of David, and a ramp used by the Second Temple priests to ascent from the ritual cleansing areas into the Temple proper *(The Jerusalem Post, 3/27/2006)*. *Haaretz* published a report by Nadav Shragai stating that archeologists Ronny Reich and Eli Shukron unearthed a wide road that led to the Temple. *Israel National News* published a story on March 13, 2007 on the excavation of a religiously observant community in Jerusalem, where a mikvah, utensils, and a gold coin depicting Trainus Caesar (98-117 CE) were found. This is the first discovery revealing Jewish life in Jerusalem after the destruction of the Second Temple. These discoveries are significant because years of ambiguity and uncertainty have caused conflict regarding the location of the Temple site, as well as denial of the right of the Jewish people to the land the Temple once occupied.

There is very real effort to suppress history and even bury the growing mountains of evidence. Members of the Islamic community have admitted, at great personal risk, that the existence of the Jewish Temples has been denied by Muslim leaders for years, in spite of generations of Waqf (Temple Mount caretakers) stories testifying to the truth (*World Net Daily*, Aaron Klein, 6/14/2006). The Dome of the Rock represents a past victory that the Muslim community can embrace. To them, the existence of the Dome justifies Arab claims to the land of Israel; it is proof that Jerusalem was once a Muslim city, and must be again.

But with each new find, archeologists have chipped away at the very center of Arab, and especially Palestinian, claims to the land of Israel. Having proof of the historical accuracy of the Scriptures regarding the existence and functioning of the Temple in Jerusalem would once again establish the right of the Jewish people to the land of Israel, especially Jerusalem. Both Jews and Arabs have known this for many years; it is hoped for by Israel but dreaded by Arabs.276

At this moment, negotiations are in progress to bring peace for the Jewish people and its neighbors. It will be the spirit of antichrist who is influenced by Satan, the father of lies, who will be able to come up with a solution acceptable for Jews and the Arabs to live in peace. When this happens, the question of Jerusalem's Temple Mount and the rebuilding of the temple will be solved.

1) The placement of the temple

In order to build the Temple, it is believed the exact location of the former two Temples must be correctly identified. One reason is because the site for the Temple was divinely appointed. Another is because there appears to be a continuity between Temples — each being built with its Holy of Holies enclosing the same protrusion of Mount Moriah known as Even ha-Shetiyah ("The

---

275 Liberman, Paul. Israel Archeology. Number 136. Rancho Mirage: International Messianic Jewish Alliance. Pages 1-2.

276 "Jewish Year 5768." Messianic Times. Vol. 17 #2, (May/June 2007).

Foundation Stone"). Since it was upon this stone that the Ark of the Covenant had been set and the Shekinah (Divine Presence) had descended, departed, and promised to return, it is thought that no other place can be substituted.

The Temple Mount platform, built so it supports the Temple and its courts, has been preserved down through the centuries. While this has limited the area for the search for the original site, it is impossible to resolve the matter due to the lack of complete access to the site. Nevertheless, based on many evidences that can be discerned without archaeological investigation, three major theories of location have been advanced.

One theory put forth by Tel Aviv architect, Tuvia Sagiv, based on accounts in ancient sources and topographical elevations, argues that the Temple was situated at the southwestern corner of the platform near to where the Al Aqsa Mosque is today.

Another theory, with both traditional support and the consensus of Israeli archaeologists, is that the Temple stood exactly where the Dome of the Rock is today.

A more popular theory is that of Hebrew University physicist Asher Kaufmann. His research, relying upon details given in *Middot*, computations of angles of line-of-sight between the Mt. of Olives (where the red heifer was sacrificed) and the eastern court of the Temple where the Great Altar stood, as well as physical clues discovered around the outside of the platform (now destroyed or hidden by the Muslims), concludes that the Temple was built on the northwestern corner of the platform, only about 330 feet from the Muslim Dome of the Rock. He believes that bedrock identifiable within a small cupola at this site, known in Arabic as the Dome of the Tablets, was the Foundation Stone within the Holy of Holies.[277]

There is a dark spot on the western wall that is the actual ashes from the burning of the temple on the night of *Av* in AD 70. If Israel can prove conclusively that the original temple stood in this open area north of the Dome of the Rock, then it is conceivable they could rebuild the temple there without disturbing the Muslim dome. This can be seen in Revelation 11:1-2.

> *1 And there was given me a reed like unto a rod: and the angel stood, saying, Rise, and measure the Temple of God, and the altar, and them that worship therein. 2 But the court which is without the Temple leave out, and measure it not; for it is given unto the Gentiles: and the holy city shall they tread under foot forty and two months.*[278]
>
> (Revelation 11:1-2, KJV)

It is interesting to note that "the court which is outside the temple" would correspond to the court of the Gentiles of the ancient temple. If this research is correct, the Dome of the Rock is in the court of the Gentiles.

2) The politics of the temple

The issue of rebuilding the Temple has been at the forefront of the Arab-Israeli conflict, though often downplayed. The Islamic Authority (called in Arabic the *Wakf*), which maintains rigid con-

---

[277] Price, Dr. L. Randall. "Will There be a Third Temple." Phoenix: Jewish Voice Today. January/February 2004. Page 4.

[278] The Holy Bible: King James Version. Oak Harbor: Logos Research Systems, Inc., 1995.

trol of the Temple Mount, blamed the Israeli government for starting a fire in the Al Aqsa mosque in 1969 in order to destroy the structure and rebuild the Temple, despite the fact that a mentally unstable member of a Christian cult actually set the blaze.

Ever since, the Muslims have assumed that every incursion in or near the area — whether for archaeological or religious purposes—has been for the same purpose. For this reason, riots followed: an excavation to uncover the subterranean Western Wall tunnel in 1982, a demonstration by the Temple Mount Faithful in 1990 in which 17 were killed, excavations to reveal the Herodian street next to the Western Wall in 1995, and the opening of an exit tunnel to the Hasmonean tunnel in 1996, in which 58 were killed.[279]

a) Tunnels under the city of Jerusalem

The city of Jerusalem is fortified by large series of tunnels and underground chambers, cisterns for large storage of water and storage rooms for food and supplies as well as for temple storage and ritual baths. This area has fortified the city of Jerusalem for thousands of years. During that time there have been at least twenty-seven invasions of Jerusalem.

This city under Jerusalem is carved out of solid rock. The limestone under the city was soft enough to chisel when it was first exposed to air. In a few years the tunnel wall would become as hard as any stone.

(1) Temple Mount tunnel dispute

ISRAELIS, IN NIGHTIME MOVE,
OPEN TEMPLE MOUNT TUNNEL
by Barton Gellman, Washington Post

JERUSALEM, September 24 — Israel carried out a surprise predawn excavation under heavy guard today to complete a long-disputed tunnel below the edge of the Temple Mount, a site sacred to Jews and Muslims alike. Arab leaders reacted in out-rage, and stone-throwing Palestinian youths battled police through much of the day, briefly driving Jewish worshippers from the Western Wall.

It was the latest of several military-style operations by Israel's new Likud Party-led government to alter the face of East Jerusalem, where the Arab population is predominant and Palestinians seek to build the capital of their hope-for state.

The political stakes were higher today because the Temple Mount—where two of Islam's most revered mosques, al-Aqsa and the gold-leafed Dome of the Rock, rise over the remains of Judaism's Second Temple—is the rallying point for religious nationalist on both sides. The rival claims have recent history of bloodshed exceeded only by those involving the Tomb of the Patriarchs in the West Bank city of Hebron, where adherents of the two faiths are also struggling for control of ancient real estate.

'If there's a message here, the only message is that, "Hey guys, we are not playing games here,'" Jerusalem Mayor Ehud Olmerf, a senior Likud figure, told reporters, after posing hoe in

---

[279] Price, Randall. "Time for a Temple? Jewish Plans to Rebuild the Temple." Israel My Glory. Westville: The Friends of Israel, Gospel Ministry, Inc., December/January 1997/1998. Pages 16-19.

hand for photographers during the night, 'We will not agree that everything that happens in Jerusalem will be subject to negotiation, because we are the sovereign of the city.'

Prime Minister Binyamin Netanyahu, who gave the final order for the work and left immediately afterward on a European diplomatic tour, said the tunnel, which is intended primarily to provide greater access by tourists to artifacts of ancient eras, will be a boon to Arabs as much as Jews.

There were no serious injuries in today's fighting, which began when crowds of young Palestinians challenged Israeli police guarding the newly cut tunnel exit in the Old City's Muslim Quarter. Palestinians later burned a car and a truck on Salahedin Street in the commercial heart of East Jerusalem and heaved stones from atop the Temple Mount toward Jews praying at the Western Wall.

Similar clashes in 1990, which began with a plan by Jewish extremists to lay a symbolic cornerstone for new construction on the Temple Mount, ended in the deaths of 17 Palestinians under police gunfire. Israeli security forces continued to deploy in unusual numbers tonight.

The manner of today's excavation, which was concealed from the Islamic religious trust that runs the mosques on the Temple Mount, reflected Netanyahu's preference for displays of power on matters touching the governance of Jerusalem. Heavy equipment and border police armed with assault rifles moved quietly into place after midnight Monday. They sealed the area from passers by as they cut through the last 10 feet of stone and built a vault-like swinging metal door.

Palestinian leader Yasser Arafat speaking to reporters in Gaza, said he had been unable to sleep after learning of the excavations. He described them as 'extremely dangerous' and said they were part of a campaign to 'change the characteristics of the city' and to appropriate Muslim sites.

'This is a crime, a big crime, against our religious and holy places,' he said, 'and it is completely against the peace process.'

The 534-yard tunnel, which retraces an ancient roadway rediscovered in 1987, skirts the western foundation of the Temple Mount. The path it traces was at ground level when King Herod's rebuilt Second Temple was razed by the Romans in the 1st Century but was covered by successive layers of construction and debris in the nearly two millennia since.

The tunnel has been nearly finished for years and already was open to tourists by appointment with a guide. No more than a yard wide in places, the pathway opens into enormous subterranean vaults and displays a spectacular succession of artifacts from the Hasmonean, Herodian, Roman, Mamluk and Crusader eras.

Its only entrance and exit until today was a gateway at the northern edge of the Western Wall plaza. Today's excavation opened it at the other end, directly onto the Via Dolorosa, the path that Jesus is said to have taken on his way to crucifixion.

Those last few feet of digging will allow an enormous increase in human traffic. Two- way touring through the narrow bottlenecks kept the volume of visitors until now at 70,000 a year. Israel's Tourism Ministry estimated today that the new arrangement 'will now afford an opportunity for about 400,000 tourists of all faiths to visit the fascinating site each year.'

The unmistakable subtext for all concerned was the struggle for political and practical control of the eastern half of Jerusalem, which Israel captured from Jordan in 1967. Palestinian and foreign officials, including senior Americans who asked not to be quoted directly, contrasted the new government's muscular step today and its accelerated construction of Jewish housing in the Israeli-occupied West Bank with the absence of any concrete stop to deliver on negotiated promises to Arafat's Palestinian Authority.

Israeli opposition leaders endorsed that view. Tel Aviv Mayor Roni Milo, a Likud moderate, said it was foolish of Netanyahu to force the issue of the Temple Mount before withdrawing Israel's army from most of Hebron, as required six months ago by treaty. In Cairo, the 22-nation Arab League said it was 'following with anger what the Israeli authorities are doing' to 'wipe out Arab and Islamic sites.'

Netanyahu, however, speaking to Israeli reporters during his flight to Europe, said: 'Anyone who has been in the Western Wall tunnel, as I was a year ago, could only be excited to his very soul. We are simply touching the rock of our existence, without exaggeration, and I think that this is important to Jerusalem, important to Palestinian merchants [in the Muslim Quarter], who in their hearts, even if they don't say so, know that their position has improved incomparably' *(Washington Post, 9/26/96)*.280

---

[280] Barton Gellman. "Israelis, in Nighttime Move, Open Temple Mount Tunnel." Washington Post. Rpt. in End- Time Handmaidens & Servants. Jasper: End-Time Handmaidens, Inc., October 1996.

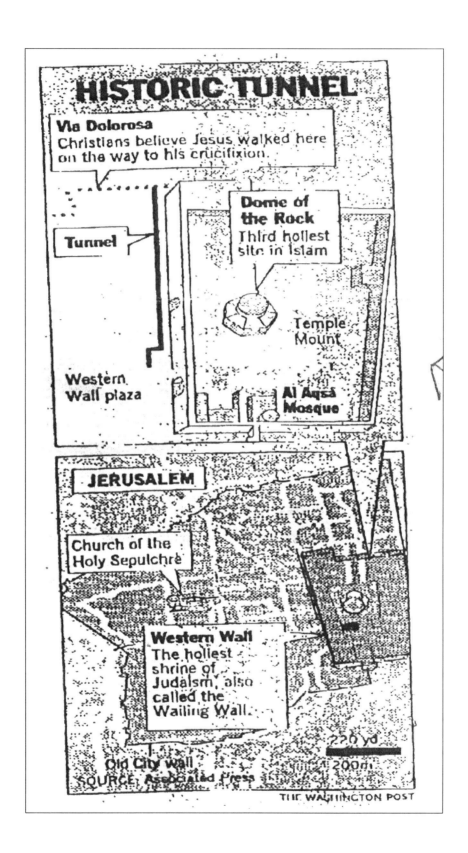

Jerusalem's tunnel and the Temple Mount

JERUSALEM ......

The Wall Street Journal —front page — reported Palestinian violence sparked by a 'tunnel on Jerusalem's Temple Mount.' The Washington Post explained that 'it should come as no surprise that violent passions were aroused by Israel's tampering with the ground beneath the Dome of the Rock and Al-Aqsa Mosque.' Peter Jennings, whose pro-Palestinian bias is notorious, parroted the charge. He reported, 'Muslims say the tunnel cuts under their compound and call it a crime against Islam.' Fully a week after the tunnel was opened, the National Public Radio reported that the Palestinians 'claim the project threatens the stability of the Al-Aqsa Mosque.'

Their claims were a lie.

The tunnel is 450 yards long. Along the route there are ancient, hand-chiseled cisterns, narrow passages, an arch that supported the bridge across the Tyropean Valley allowing the priests access to the Temple area from the upper city, and the original Herodian foundation stones upon which the western (wailing) wall was built. Up until September, only three or four hundred people a day could enter the tunnel because they had to return back the same way through areas that could only accommodate one-way pedestrian traffic. Israel, without disturbing or infringing on anyone's rights, broke through at the northern end of the tunnel to provide an exit. Now, as many as four thousand people a day can visit this very important biblical site.

The real issue is not about a tunnel that has been purported to infringe on Muslim sites. What is really at stake is world opinion of who has the historical right to control the Temple Mount itself. The Arab/Muslim sites are situated on top of the Temple Mount, but the Arabs are well aware of the Jewish history that lies beneath —predating the Arab sites by nearly 1500 years. The ability to walk through the tunnel from one end and exit through another now provides an important view of Jewish history for the entire world to see.[281]

(2) Destruction of the Temple Mount

*TERRIBLE DESTRUCTION ON THE TEMPLE MOUNT: Recently the legal advisor of the Israeli Government visited the Temple Mount and was shocked to see the terrible destruction which the Arabs together with the Islamic Movement in Israel are engaged in. This visit came after The Temple Mount and Land of Israel Faithful Movement made a petition to the Supreme Court asking that the destruction being performed by the Arabs in the beautiful halls, called the Hulda Halls, be immediately stopped. These halls were the main entrance for millions of pilgrims during the Second Temple period. His report after the visit had to be an answer to the petition by the Faithful. The report also shocked all the Israel people and everyone in the world who heard about it.

In the report, he wrote that the Arabs had dug 10 metre deep over a large area next the so- called Solomon's Stables in order to build a new entrance to the Solomon's Stables after they had built a mosque in the Stables which is the biggest in the Middle East. Solomon's Stables were never actually stables but were halls which were part of the Second Temple complex which were built by

---

[281] "Jerusalem's Tunnel and the Temple Mount: Rioting, Bloodshed, and World Condemnation." <u>Zion's Fire, Middle East News & World Views</u>. Vol. 7, number 6. Orlando: Zion's Hope Inc., Nov/Dec 1996. Page 22.

King Herod and were used for the worship in the Temple. The first barbaric destruction and new building in the area was when the function of the area was changed and the mosque built. Along with this work they destroyed monuments which had remained after the destruction of the Temple in 70 CE. This destruction and building of the mosque is a part of the Arab activities to destroy any Jewish identity on the Temple Mount and any evidence which had remained for 2000 years since the Temple existed on this holy hill. Their goal is to completely convert the Temple Mount and to make it into a completely Islamic site. The so-called 'Palestinian Authority' is responsible for this vandalism and in reality they even control the Temple Mount directly under the orders of terrorist murderer, Arafat. They very well know the deep significance of this holy hill to the Jewish people, Israel and all the world. They know the desire of everyone to purify the Temple Mount from the foreign pagan worshippers who make this abomination against the G-d of Abraham, Isaac and Jacob Who consecrated this place to be His house. They know that the G-d of Israel will remove them from this place as He removed all the foreign enemies and pagan worshippers who robbed this most holy place from the people of Israel and judged them and removed them from history. They are trying to stop the march of the G-d and people of Israel back to the house of G-d and to the place which is and will for ever be their very focus, their heart and their soul. They do it in such a barbaric way without any respect for G-d, the Creator and Father of all of us and they are lifting their hands against His holy house and site. We know that, like all the enemies of G-d and Israel who lifted their hands against G-d and His holy house, they will be judged by G-d Himself.

At the time of writing, they continue this destruction and the building of the mosque. Many thousand cubic metres of earth are being taken away by trucks (yesterday there were 120 trucks) which are working day and night to accomplish this work quickly before they are stopped. This work is done with no regard to any holy archaeological remains from the Temple. The earth is thrown in the Kidron Valley, east of the Temple Mount; so much earth has been placed there that a new hill has been formed. They throw the earth together with the remains and friends of the Faithful Movement who have gone to check the situation have found many archaeological remains which have been destroyed. The heads of the Antiquities Authority in Jerusalem stated yesterday after they had checked the destruction that the Arabs are making the greatest destruction since the destruction of the Temple itself in 70 CE. It is like a destruction of the Third Temple. Everyone who has seen this barbaric destruction and the terrible damage that has been caused to the remains of the Temple started to cry and to mourn and tore their garments in despair. A deep sorrow came to the hearts of the Israelis especially when they see that nobody does anything to stop it. Unfortunately the Israeli Government is in a position of terrible weakness and they are afraid to challenge the Arabs and stop the work even though they have the legal and godly right and duty to do so. It is such a tragedy to see the Israeli Government, which has all the strength and ability to stop this barbaric destruction, in this position of weakness and fear of Arab or Islamic human reactions but not of the Almighty G-d of Israel and the Universe. It is a tragedy to see the silence of the great powers in the world, including the UN, who are supposed to be Christians and this most holy site should be very holy and important to them as well. All of them prefer the Arab oil, money, votes in the UN and other materialistic advantages that they believe the Arabs can give them if they remain silent rather than the Almighty G-d Who will give them His moral value and laws. They continue their hypocritical behaviour of taking the Temple Mount, Jerusalem and the land which G-d gave in an eternal covenant and give it to their materialistic allies, the Arabs and the Moslems.

The Temple Mount and Land of Israel Faithful Movement is now in a state of great sorrow and sadness because of this terrible destruction and the critical situation on the Temple Mount, Jerusalem and the land of Israel. But this will never break us or stop our activities. More than this, we feel deeply the criticalness of this time and G-d is giving us strength and encouragement to intensify and double our activities. We reject all this weakness and hypocrisy. As real soldiers of G-d we are ready to fight and struggle for Him, for His Name, for His Word and for His most holy site and house. We are ready to sacrifice everything in our lives for Him and we trust in Him completely. The first step that the Movement made was on Tuesday 7th, December when we marched and demonstrated against this barbaric destruction and for G-d and His house. On the same early morning, the Faithful made an urgent petition to the Supreme Court of Israel asking that the destruction be immediately stopped, that the site be restored to its original state (if this is still possible after such a destruction) or as close to that state as possible and to immediately arrest all those involved in the destruction and illegal building of the mosques and bring them to court. We are doing our best to ensure that this petition will be considered soon and we wonder why up to today this has still not been done. We have also called on the Israeli people and the Israeli leadership to throw off their weakness and fulfill their godly duty. G-d will never forgive anyone who does not do this. The Israeli people is full of sorrow and anger and from all sides they are calling on the Government to fulfill its duty. We are looking forward to this occurring before it is too late.

We continue to trust only in the G-d of Israel and the Universe and he will be with us. Nobody can stop His determination to redeem His holy site, the Temple Mount, Jerusalem, the people and land of Israel and all mankind. We shall be with Him in this critical and great moment. The Temple Mount and Land of Israel Faithful Movement will continue to share with you the Developments in this situation (Temple Mt Faithful 12-14-99).[282]

THE TEMPLE MOUNT

THE TEMPLE MOUNT: Many of you have read my vision concerning the Temple Mount in Jerusalem, and some of you have heard me preach on it. Something very strategic is happening there now. I had heard about it for several months, and just a week ago, when we were in Jerusalem, I saw it with my own eyes. The southern wall of the Temple Mount is beginning to bulge out. The Muslims who control the site, which they call Haram as-Sharif, say extensive digging at the compound in recent months has created more prayer room for worshippers (Muslim), and has not harmed anything of historical value. Israeli archaeologist counter that the work has caused irreversible damage to what Jews call the Temple Mount, the site of the ancient Jewish Temples, dating back 3,000 years, and the spot where the latest Mideast bloodletting erupted last September, 2000. The Temple Mount is the holiest site in Judaism, where the first and second Temples stood before their destruction in 586 BC and AD 70, respectively. Some Israelis claim the Muslims' excavations in the compound are designed to rob the Jews of any future claims to the hilltop by destroying remains of the two Temples.

---

[282] <u>End-Time Handmaidens & Servants (Newsletter)</u>. Jasper: End-Time Handmaidens, Inc., December 17, 1999. Pages 7-8.

There are claims that they have taken out 20,000 tons of fill and trucked them to garbage dumps without any archeological supervision. The battle over the digging intensified in August, 2001, with each side blaming the other for an ominous 35-foot-wide bulge in the southern wall that raised fears of a collapse. Israeli architects blame the bulge on the Waqf's work, which began 21 months ago, and has so far added praying room for up to 10,000 worshippers by removing dirt from the two unused underground structures beneath Al Aqsa Mosque. Both are now tiled and lighted and carpeted. The Palestinians say Israeli archeological digs around the outside base of the wall are to blame for the bulge in the wall which holds up the southern end of Al Aqsa, just around the corner from what is often pointed out as the pinnacle of the Temple where Satan tempted Jesus. It is not far from the Western Wall, where Jews are allowed to pray. If the wall collapses it will destroy the Al Aqsa Mosque and possibly also the Dome of the Rock which is near to it. The bulge is easy to see from the southeast corner of the wall.283

b). Bulging Temple Mount wall threatens to buckle

The Messianic times, Bulging Temple Mount Wall Threatens to buckle, Rebekah Kolber, November 2002, page 8-9

JERUSALEM — Fear that heavy stone blocks could rain down on Muslim worshippers is concerning the Israeli government as archeologists report that the southern wall of the Temple Mount in Jerusalem's Old City is in imminent danger of collapse.

The fear is that such a disaster, as well as causing death and injury, could ignite further violence in the Land. A bulge extending some 450 square feet mars the wall built by King Herod more than 2,000 years ago. According to the Antiquities Authority of the State of Israel, it measures just over one hundred thirty-five feet by a little more than three feet.

'The wall will collapse,' said Dr. Eilat Mazar, a Hebrew University archeologist who has carried out archeological work in the Old City and examined the southern wall of the Temple Mount at the request of the Israeli government.

Mazar created an uproar when she spoke out publicly on Israel Radio earlier this year about this issue, which has been cloaked in secrecy since the Antiquities Authority began structural engineering tests in August 2001.

'The area is a sensitive issue,' Jerusalem mayor Ehud Olmert explained, 'Violence has resulted from much less [than a collapse of the wall.].'

In the event of a collapse, stones weighing hundreds of pounds could crash onto Muslim worshipers inside the Temple Mount area.

According to the mayor's office, the stones could fall on those in the open courtyard area or the event could lead to a structural collapse that could cause the al-Aksa mosque, also in the southern area of the Temple Mount, to fall as well.

The danger of a collapse increases at this time of the year when hundreds of thousands of Muslims will be gathering on the Temple Mount during the holy month of Ramadan, further stressing the fragile structure, archeologists say.

The area inside the Temple Mount directly surrounding and to the side of the growing bulge, beneath the Mount platform and toward its southeast corner, is known as Solomon's Stables.

---

283 End-Time Handmaidens & Servants (Newsletter). Jasper, End-Time Handmaidens, Inc., Oct/Nov 2001. Page 3-4

There were no stables here at any time and the pillars, which caused the Crusaders to give the area its name, were not there at the time of Solomon. Rather, these were the pillars of Herod's Temple.

The colonnade remained as it was at the time of the Second Temple until 1996. The Arabs have dug beneath the al-Aksa Mosque and carved up the ruins of Solomon's Stables and the Eastern Huldah Gate. The once-ornamental Huldah passageway with its marble pillars was cemented over and the pillars of Solomon's Stables have been covered.

After the removal of 6,000 tons of earth and much transformation of these two underground Second Temple period structures the area now houses the largest mosque in Israel. The underground al-Marawani Mosque extends over 1.5 acres and is capable of holding 15,000 (some say 10,000) worshippers. It could collapse as well according to the Temple Mount Faithful web site.

It was possible that the extensive construction work involved had led to the southern wall weakening, said Shuka Dorfman, director-general of the Antiquities Authority.

The Wakf, the Muslim religious trust that runs the Temple Mount, has continued to conduct extensive digging in this area, most notably during the past year. Dorfman refused to confirm that this is the cause of the bulge, citing the need for further tests by structural engineers, but he acknowledged that the damage to the wall worsened significantly this past year.

Wakf director Adnan Husseini, who previously claimed that reports of damage to the southern wall were 'fabrication,' now says, 'Our workers are continually trying to repair the problem and are 20 percent done.'

The Wakf refuses to deal with the Israeli government on this and other issues, prohibits Jewish people from entering the Temple Mount area and continues to authorize construction projects that destroy archeological treasures.

Despite whatever work is being done by the Wakf, the bulge continues to grow according to the Temple Mount Faithful.

Although Husseini insists the wall is stable, archeologists warn that the heavy stone blocks lining the Temple Mount are in danger of collapsing. 'There are serious grounds for the apprehension that it could collapse.' Olmert told Israel Radio. 'We have reached the moment of truth.'

When the bulge began to protrude noticeably during the summer of 2001, Internal Security Minister Uzi Landau proposed that police remove all the heavy building tools in place on the Temple Mount including the stone-cutting machine used by the Wakf for the past two years."[284]

Prime Minister Ariel Sharon rejected the proposal but is convening a forum of ministers and government officials to discuss what could be taken to curb the site's destruction.

This forum could decide to continue trying to work with the Wakf, or it could declare the southern wall in danger of immediate collapse. The latter option would empower the Jerusalem Municipality to halt Wakf-approved construction projects and remove construction vehicles from the Mount itself.

While officials scramble for ways to fix the wall, others are waiting for it to fall.

'Let the wall collapse along with the [al-Aksa] mosque. This is the hand of God,' said Gershon Salomon, leader of the Jerusalem-based Temple Mount Faithful organization, which advocates rebuilding the Temple and bringing back sacrifices.

---

[284] Kolber, Rebekah. "Bulging Temple Mount Wall Threatens to Buckle." The Messianic Times. November 2002. Page 8

'This is a fulfillment of the prophecies of the redemption of the Temple Mount and Israel, ' he said. 'It is so sad that everyone who looks for the reason for the bulge |is| too blind to understand this prophetic fact,' said Salomon.

Rick Ridings, director of the Jerusalem worship and intercession ministry, Succat Hallel, also sees the hand of God in this situation. He regularly leads prayer teams in the area of the Temple Mount.

'For about three years we've been led to pray the words of Isaiah 30:12-13. We began praying this before people really knew about the crack,' said Ridings.

'We were praying about the spiritual prison of Islam, not really thinking about it as a literal thing.'

Ridings believes the event could lead many Muslims to question their faith and perhaps turn to Yeshua. 'If it were to collapse it would be a clear judgment on Islam,' he said.285

c). The Temple Mount for sale

BEDFORD, TX — According to unnamed sources with the Israeli government, Israel is prepared to cede control of the Temple Mount to the Palestinians in an effort to reach a lasting peace agreement with the ever insatiable, always unreliable PLO.

In talks with Mahmoud Abbas, it is reported that Prime Minister Ehud Olmert presented a plan that would relinquish control of the holiest site to all Judaism to the Muslims. Other sites near the Mount would be controlled by a consortium of Jews, Christians and Muslims. The Western Wall, the remaining relic of the last Temple, would remain under Israeli control.

The PLO has stated repeatedly that no negotiations with Israel would be acceptable unless control of the Temple Mount was given over to the Palestinians.

Would a move such as this actually appease the Palestinian Authority, or would it just be an inducement for an already insatiable appetite for Jewish lands?

The disposition of the Temple Mount has long been the point of contention in negotiations between Israel and Palestine.

Apparently, Israel is now ready to put that issue on the table. A similar offer was made to Yasser Arafat in January of 2000, an offer that would have given Arafat almost everything he wanted, including ninety-eight percent of the territory of Judea, Samaria, and Gaza, all of East Jerusalem except for the Jewish and Armenian quarters, Palestinian sovereignty over the Temple Mount, conceding only the right of Jews to pray there, and a compensation fund of $30 billion.

Arafat chose the route of launching yet another intifada against the Jewish people. Diplomats within the EU are pushing for a final agreement to be reached. U.S. Secretary of State Condoleezza Rice has been pressing Abbas and Olmert to iron out their differences and have a workable plan.

In recent meetings between the two men, the concessions have, as always, been very one-sided: Olmert has ordered the release of 178 members of the Al Aqsa Martyrs Brigades (a wing of Fatah — the terrorist organization that has been responsible for the many suicide bombings in Israel during the past 36 months.)

Olmert is being pressed to release another 206 terrorists and remove security checkpoints that are essential in stopping these heinous attacks against the Jewish people.

---

285 Ibid. Page 9.

In yet another concession to the Palestinians, the IDF has turned patrolling duties in the West Bank over to Palestinian policemen (simply a more acceptable word for "terrorists.")

What has the Palestinian Authority given up in these talks? Nothing!

As is the norm, Israel is the one doing the giving. Any receiving for Israel is on the end of a terrorist's rocket launcher or suicide bomb. Nothing has changed to insure peace for Israel.

The Jews laid claim to the Temple Mount in the Tenth Century BC when King Solomon built the first resplendent Temple.

The Muslims were Johnny-come-lately residents, having built the Dome of the Rock on top of the Temple Mount in 681 AD. For all of the protestations that the Temple Mount belongs to the Palestinians, the city of Jerusalem is not mentioned in the Koran.

Islamic tradition marks it as the spot where Muhammad purportedly took his midnight journey to heaven. The location was marked simply by the phrase "the fartherest mosque." Only much later was the city pinpointed as Jerusalem.

Israel has been pressured in the past to relinquish land and the results have been catastrophic. Bethlehem, for example, has become a terrorist stronghold where it is unsafe for Christians to travel. Gaza has been returned to the PLO because of U.N. pressure; now Iran, through its proxy, HAMAS, controls the area and is making life miserable for everyone— Jews and Palestinians alike.

The pressure on Prime Minister Olmert is enormous. The danger of the land-for-peace initiative being led by the U.S. is that if it fails, the rockets will fall......and they will fall on Israel.

The terrorists will begin attacking and killing Jews in yet another attempt to bring Israel to its knees. Their excuse will be that they are attempting to liberate the Temple Mount. If that succeeds, it will only embolden the terrorists to launch attacks in even greater numbers.

Michael D. Evans is the author of the #1 New York Times bestseller, The Final Move Beyond Iraq, www.beyondiraq.com.286

e. Need for resumption of ancient sacrificial system

Daniel prophesied that the rebuilt temple would serve as the center of Israel's worship— complete with the resumption of the ancient animal sacrificial system. In his seventy weeks (see Daniel 9:24-27), he predicted that the last great world dictator—the Antichrist—would arise within the area of the ancient Roman Empire and would eventually rule the revived empire, including western Europe, North Africa and the Middle East.

(Daniel 2:40-45; 7:7-8) He declared that this world dictator would sign a seven-year security treaty with Israel.

> *He will make a treaty with the people for a period of one set of seven, but after half this time, he will put an end to the sacrifices and offerings. Then as a climax to all his terrible deeds, he will set up a sacrilegious object that causes desecration, until the end that has been decreed is poured out on this defiler.287*

(Daniel 9:27, NLT)

---

286 Evans, Michael D. "The Temple Mount for Sale." Save Jerusalem Newsletter. Michael D. Evans, Editor, June 14, 2008.

287 Holy Bible: New Living Translation. Wheaton: Tyndale House, 1997.

After three and a half years the world leader would violate the treaty and would enter the holy of holies and defile the rebuilt temple by claiming he is god, causing the ceasing of daily sacrifices.

In order for a ceasing of the daily sacrifices, the daily morning and evening sacrificial system has to be reinstated. The last sacrifice was in the summer of AD 70 shortly before the Roman legions surrounded the second temple and destroyed it.

Yeshua warned that Antichrist will defile the holy of holies (ref. Matthew 24:15-16).

Paul also warned that the son of perdition (Antichrist) will exalt himself so that he would be worshipped as god (2 Thessalonians 2:3-4).

The altar of sacrifice will be built east of the site where the third temple will stand.

1) The uniqueness of the altar's site

1. The altar [is to be constructed] in a very precise location; it may never be changed; as it is written, "This is the altar for the burnt offerings of Israel."

Yitzchak our Patriarch was prepared to be sacrifice on [the future site of the *Beis*] *HaMikdash*; as it is written, "Go to the land of Moriah," and it is written in *Divrei HaYomim*. "And Shlomo began building G-d's house in Jerusalem, on Mount Moriah, where [G-d] appeared to David his father, in the place where David prepared on the threshing floor of Ornan, the Jebusite."

2. It is universally accepted that the site on which David and Solomon built the altar on the threshing floor of Ornan, is the location on which Avraham built the altar on which he prepared Yitzchak for sacrifice.

On this location, Noah built [an altar] when he emerged from the ark. On this location, Cain and Able offered [their] sacrifices. And Adam, the first man, offered a sacrifice on this location after he was created [Indeed,] he was created from this very spot; as our Sages said, "Adam was created from the place from which he [would be granted] atonement."288

2) Passover to be celebrated in Jerusalem

*TEMPLE MOUNT FAITHFUL: Passover Sacrifice in Jerusalem — On April 10, the Temple Mount and Land of Israel Faithful Movement, together with the Chai v'Kaiyam organization, intend to hold a Passover sacrifice on the Temple Mount. This will be done on an altar which is already prepared. We have asked the government of Israel to grant us permission to hold the sacrifice on the Temple Mount this year.

Israel is now in her midst of her third redemption — the biggest of them all. The G-d of Israel returned Jerusalem and the Temple Mount to us through major miracles. Now He expects us to renew this sacrifice immediately, even before the Temple is rebuilt. Our tradition teaches us that once the sacrifice is reintroduced the redemption of Israel will be accomplished, and the Third Temple will be built and Mashiach ben David will come. This was and is the dream and desire of all the generations of Israel since the destruction of the second Temple as well as so many people all over the world. We are not allowed to disappoint the G-d of Israel and all those generations. We are not allowed to neglect what G-d commanded us to do especially at this time.

---

288 Schneerson, Lubavitcher and Rebbe Rabbi Menachem M. "The Uniqueness of the Altar's Site." Analytical Studies. Seek out the Welfare of Jerusalem. Adapted from Likkutei Sichos Vol. XIX, Parshas Re'eh. Brooklyn: 1994. Pages 49-50.

We want the government of Israel to fulfill the expectations of the G-d of Israel and the Israeli people with no fear of what the enemies of Israel and other powers will do to try to prevent it. The G-d of Israel will not allow them to touch Israel, especially when Israel is doing His will. Only He controls the destiny of Israel and He is determined to accomplish His prophetic plans with the people and the land of Israel. The day when the Passover sacrifice is performed will be a big day in the eyes of G-d and in the life of the people and land of Israel and many people all over the world.

The Temple Mount and Land of Israel Faithful Movement is determined to hold this sacrifice whether or not the government grants their permission. If permission is not granted to enter the Temple Mount, then the sacrifice will be performed in the City of David before the Southern gates of the Temple Mount, the main gates used by the Israelites to enter the Temple Mount during time of the First and Second Temples. Even though the Passover sacrifice has to be performed on the Temple, we shall sacrifice it in the City of David as a symbolic act and as a first step for the fulfillment of this important commandment. It will also be a message to the Israeli government and to the people of Israel that we are living at a time of godly redemption and we are not allowed to disappoint G-d and history through spiritual and political weakness. We have to trust G-d's promises and not fear His enemies. By this act we want to open the gate to a new godly era in the life of Israel and all the nations exactly as we attempted to lay the cornerstone on the Temple Mount.

The City of David has a special and deep significance in the life of the land of Israel. King David was the greatest king of Israel who liberated Jerusalem, bought the Temple Mount, built an altar to the honor of the G-d of Israel on this Hill and prepared it for the building of the First Temple by his son, King Solomon. This is the reason why we decided to hold this sacrifice in this holy place. It will be done without an altar but exactly according to all the details of G-d's commandment for the Passover sacrifice. It is only on the Temple Mount that sacrifice can be performed on an altar. We hope the Israeli government will at least grant us the permission to perform the sacrifice in this place. If not, we shall perform it on a hill close to the Temple Mount and the City of David from where the Temple Mount and site of the Holy of Holies can be clearly seen.

We are determined to perform this sacrifice this year and we pray and act that it will be performed on the Temple Mount. This unique and exciting sacrifice has to be performed according to the commandments of the G-d of Israel on the day before the first day of Passover. It must be done from midday until midnight. It has to be eaten in the special family Seder in Jerusalem. This is the night when the G-d of Israel punished the Egyptians with the tenth plague, killing the firstborn sons of the Egyptians and passing over the homes of the children of Israel. On the same night G-d took the Israelites from Egypt out of slavery to freedom. G-d commanded us to remember this forever and to know that He is the eternal Savior and Father of Israel.289

f. Temple to be built before Messiah returns

John suggested that the third temple was a temple of God in Revelation 11:1-2. So it had to be built by Jews to be a genuine holy temple.

God declared that the Temple must be rebuilt before Messiah returns to earth and cleanses the sanctuary. Both of these events will occur in the generation that witnessed the return of the Jews to their Promised Land in 1948. King David prophesied:

---

289 End-Time Handmaidens & Servants (Newsletter). Jasper: End-Time Handmaidens, Inc., March 26, 1998. Page 5.

For the LORD shall build up Zion; He shall appear in His glory290

(Psalm 102:16, NKJV).

Yeshua promised His disciples that the generation that witnessed the budding of the fig tree (the rebirth of Israel) would also see the coming of the Son of Man.

32 Now learn this parable from the fig tree: When its branch has already become tender and puts forth leaves, you know that summer is near. 33 So you also, when you see all these things, know that it is near—at the doors! 34 Assuredly, I say to you, this generation will by no means pass away till all these things take place.291

(Matthew 24:32-34, NKJV)

The fig tree was well known as a symbol of Israel, as the eagle is the symbol of America and the maple leaf a symbol of Canada.292

According to Psalm 90:10, the length of a typical lifetime or natural generation is seventy to eighty years. The most logical interpretation of Christ's prophecy is about the generation is those who were alive in 1948 will see the fulfillment of the prophecies regarding the rebuilding of the Temple and Yeshua's return (reference Matthew 24:32-34).293

A move to break ground for the third temple would risk inciting a brutal global jihad. Despite the Islamic opposition to any Jewish building on the Temple Mount, the Lord prophesied that the Jewish exiles would in the last days, return to their Promised Land and rebuild the temple as prophesied by Ezekiel the prophet.

26 Moreover I will make a covenant of peace with them, and it shall be an everlasting covenant with them; I will establish them and multiply them, and I will set My sanctuary in their midst forevermore. 27 My tabernacle also shall be with them; indeed I will be their God, and they shall be My people. 28 The nations also will know that I, the LORD, sanctify Israel, when My sanctuary is in their midst forevermore.294

(Ezekiel 37:26-28, NKJV)

God will change the hearts of the Jewish leaders and the Islamic—Arab world as well as the rest of the world (ref. Ezekiel 38-39).

g. The Sanhedrin to be reestablished

Before Israel can rebuild the Temple the ancient Sanhedrin must be reestablished. The original Sanhedrin met for the last time in AD 453 in the town of Tiberius, Israel. It must reconvene to

---

[290] The Holy Bible: The New King James Version. Nashville: Thomas Nelson, 1996, c1982.

[291] Ibid.

[292] Jeffrey, Grant R. The New Temple and the Second Coming. Colorado Springs: Waterbrook Press. Page 91.

[293] Ibid.

[294] The Holy Bible: The New King James Version. Nashville: Thomas Nelson, 1996, c1982.

address rulings regarding sacred rituals, sacrifices, qualifications for membership in the Temple Levitical priesthood and other matters pertaining to the rebuilding of the Temple and the restoration of authentic Temple worship.

In accordance with the rules specified by Rabbi Moses Maimonides (AD 1200), seventy- one of the most highly respected Rabbis Israel received special ordination as the new Sanhedrin on October 13, 2004. The new Sanhedrin includes Orthodox Jewish leaders from every part of Israel, including two former chief rabbis of Israel—Ovadiah Josef, the former chief rabbi of the Sephardic Jews (Middle Eastern Jews) and Josef Elyashiv, the former chief rabbi of the Ashkenazi Jews (European Jews), Rabbi Elyashiv is considered by many top rabbis in Israel to be the true spiritual heir of Moses and therefore was in position of spiritual authority to ordain the seventy other religious leaders required for a full Sanhedrin Court.

The modern day Sanhedrin was formally convened in Jerusalem on January 20, 2005. The leader of the Sanhedrin, Rabbi Yeshai Ba'avad, declared that the rabbinic body would meet monthly to issue religious legal rulings. They have discussed several key ideas related to the building of the Third Temple, including the construction of an altar that would be used for the sacrifice of a lamb during a future Passover. Hundreds of Priests from the Tribe of Levi were authorized to begin training in the precise rituals of the ancient Temple sacrifices. They also reinstated the Sanhedrin's authority to announce the Rosh Hodesh, beginning which is of the lunar month of each month of the Jewish calendar.295

In January 2005, the Sanhedrin discussed the right place to build the third temple. The rabbinical council believes that the correct placement for the temple, according to scripture, is north of the Dome of the Rock, which is supported by scripture and significant archaeological discoveries. This would make it possible for the Israelites to build the third temple in an open area directly to the west of the sealed Eastern Gate.

h. Plans and preparations for the temple

Architects and engineers have been called with their plans and knowledge regarding the construction of the temple.

Donors will be needed to contribute funds to acquire building materials. (Costing billions, the third temple will be the most expensive building in history.)

One of the most intriguing needs is the "gathering and preparation of prefabricated disassembled portions to be stored and ready for rapid assembly, in the manner of King David." It is significant that God told David to quarry the stones off site and then transport the quarried limestone blocks to the Temple Mount. There they will be assembled silently, in respect of the sanctuary of the structure. Sanhedrin plans to quarry the necessary stone blocks off site and then quickly assemble the stones in silence on the Temple Mount when God provides a sign that the time has come.296

A number of Jewish rabbis and scholars have argued that it is presumptuous for Jews to make plans to build the Temple before the Messiah appears. They point to the word of the prophet Zechariah:

---

295 Jeffrey, Grant R. The New Temple and the Second Coming. Colorado Springs: Waterbrook Press. Pages 105-107.

296 Ibid. Page 110.

12 And speak unto him, saying, Thus speaketh the LORD of hosts, saying, Behold the man whose name is The BRANCH; and he shall grow up out of his place, and he shall build the Temple of the LORD: 13 Even he shall build the Temple of the LORD; and he shall bear the glory, and shall sit and rule upon his throne; and he shall be a priest upon his throne: and the counsel of peace shall be between them both.297

(Zechariah 6:12-13, KJV)

Zechariah's prophecy of the Messiah's role in building the Temple refers to the enormous millennial Temple that will be constructed following the battle of Armageddon. Therefore, there is no contradiction between Zechariah's prophecy of the Messiah building the Fourth Temple during the Millennium and the numerous other prophecies in both the old and new Testaments that refer to the Jews of Israel building the Third Temple prior to the antichrist defiling the sanctuary during the tribulation.298

i. Recovering lost temple treasures

A copper scroll was found in Qumran on the West side of the Dead Sea with many manuscripts written on leather and parchments in March of 1953.

The rolled-up scroll was made up of three copper sheets riveted together. The metal was quite corroded after being in the cave for over two thousand years. With the help of a Jeweler's saw, the roll was cut sideways and the scroll was carefully unrolled. The unknown author had chiseled Hebrew letters into the copper sheets. The copper scroll revealed a detailed list of sixty four secret locations where the Jewish Essene priests had hid gold and silver treasurer from the first and second Temple. The buried treasure mentioned on the list included a number of sacred Temple Vessels, manuscripts, gold and silver bullion, the oil of anointing, and the breastplate of the high priest.

The original Temple not only had the gold and silver Temple treasurer, but it served as a central bank for the nation, for both the government and private citizens.

The list is a basic account of the sacred Temple treasurers that were hidden away until they could be recovered for use in the third Temple.

A large portion of the annual Temple revenues were derived from the half-shekel Temple tribute demanded annually for every male citizen in Israel and Jews living outside of Israel, as well as the large numbers of proselytes who had embraced Judaism. The half-shekel was equal to two days wages for a typical laborer. This tribute accumulated each year and over the centuries produced an immense treasury.299

Among the sixty-four sites listed, three major areas described in the copper scroll include, areas near Qumran, in Southern Jerusalem centered on Mount Zion and an area east of the Jordan River in present-day Jordan. The areas were known to have been major centers of Essene settlements on activities.

---

[297] The Holy Bible: King James Version. Oak Harbor: Logos Research Systems, Inc., 1995.

[298] Jeffrey, Grant R. The New Temple and the Second Coming. Pages 110-111.

[299] Ibid. Pages 49-55.

It is not easy to match the described landmarks of these areas to present-day terrain, due to the changes of the physical features of the land since the copper scroll was written two thousand years ago.

j. Gathering and making temple tools

Every job has its tools of the trade. The doctor need his medical equipment, the lawyer his law books, the farmer his machinery for planting and harvesting, the painter his rollers and brushes, and the bricklayer his trowel.

The priest will also need their special tools in the future Jerusalem Temple.

According to those who look forward to the rebuilding of the Third Temple, it is expected to employ some estimated 28,000 priests and 4,000 Levites, all of whom must have the proper equipment to carry out their respective tasks in the service of the Sanctuary.

Tools can normally be purchased, but where does one go to buy tools for a Temple that has not existed for 2,000 years? What store would manufacture and supply such tools for a profession that today cannot even use them?

While there is no shop to which prospective priests can go, the tools of their trade, nevertheless, now exist and are being produced in increasing quantity.

On Dec. 5, 1999 the Temple Institute publicly unveiled one of three of its newest Temple vessels. A six-foot golden menorah takes center stage in the Jewish Quarter within the ancient causeway of pillars left from Byzantine Jerusalem's Cardo. The wax mold for this menorah had been displayed with the Institute's collection of vessels in their visitor center for some years while the finances were being raised to purchase the amount of gold needed to make the cast.

The seven-foot, seven-branch Menorah has been re-created by the Temple Institute out of pure gold costing $250,000. This is to give light in the sanctuary.

According to the Biblical injunction, the menorah must be made from one solid piece of gold, which would have been cost prohibitive. Therefore, the menorah is hollow and gold plated, yet still meeting the Biblical requirements since it was wholly immersed in molten gold as 'one piece.'300

The altar of incense is currently being made by Jewish craftsmen. Vessels for the interior of the temple also being constructed will include the table of showbread, as well as the laver for cleansing of the priest's hands and feet.

> *18 Thou shalt also make a laver of brass, and his foot also of brass, to wash withal: and thou shalt put it between the tabernacle of the congregation and the altar, and thou shalt put water therein. 19 For Aaron and his sons shall wash their hands and their feet thereat.301*

(Exodus 30:18-19, KJV)

Recovering the sacred objects from the second Temple are key in the rebuilding the Temple. Among these are the ashes of the Red Heifer and the oil of anointing.

The altar of burnt offering will be rebuilt prior to the actual third temple construction.

---

300 Price, Dr. Randall. "Groups Collecting Temple 'Tools.'" The Messianic Times. Vol. 10, Num. 2. Summer 2000. Page 20.

301 The Holy Bible: King James Version. Oak Harbor: Logos Research Systems, Inc., 1995.

After a lot of research, many articles have been made. Among those articles is the Mizank, used to collect the blood of the sacrifice which is immediately applied to the horns of the altar. This is done daily. This shows our need to apply the blood of Yeshua to our hearts daily.

k. Anointing oil

The oil of anointing was made up of fine ingredients that the Bible requires for the anointing of Israel's priests and anointing the temple furnishings; and is also used as the fragrance on the oblation to create a sweet-smelling aroma. God commanded Moses to create the oil of anointing using five ingredients:

> *Collect choice spices—12½ pounds of pure myrrh, 6¼ pounds each of cinnamon and of sweet cane, 24 12½ pounds of cassia, and one gallon of olive oil. 25 Blend these ingredients into a holy anointing oil. 26 Use this scented oil to anoint the Tabernacle, the Ark of the Covenant 302*

(Exodus 30:23-26, NLT)

Haggai, in 520 BC, wrote:

> *Use this oil also to anoint Aaron and his sons, sanctifying them so they can minister before me as priests. 31 And say to the people of Israel, "This will always be my holy anointing oil."303*

(Exodus 30:30-31, NLT)

The anointing oil was discovered in Cave 11 and was analyzed. It was composed of the five ingredients exactly as God commanded Moses. Carbon-14 radioactive dating indicated the oil was almost 2,000 years old and it was from the second temple. The Talmud declares that a drop of this special oil will cause water to turn milky white. The Israel Museum verified that the oil did turn water milky white.

One of five ingredients of the oil is the rare persimmon or balsam oil. There were only two groves in the whole of the Middle East where the precious balsam trees grew—one in Jericho and the other in a wadi near EnGedi on the west side of the Dead Sea.

When it was apparent that the Romans were going to destroy Jerusalem and the temple, the priests burned the two groves of balsam trees to keep them out of the hands of the Romans. Without the balsam groves, there is no way that the anointing oil can be recreated.

After the anointing oil was used in the tabernacle and later the first and second temples, the oil of anointing disappeared when the Romans destroyed the second temple.

The discovery of the ancient pot of oil will be used in the new Temple building and worship. In time, Yeshua will be anointed as Israel's Messiah by the high priest, using the consecrated oil of anointing, when he returns in glory to save Jerusalem from the armies of the antichrist. Yeshua

---

[302] Holy Bible: New Living Translation. Wheaton: Tyndale House, 1997.

[303] Ibid

will cleanse the Third Temple and establish His Kingdom forever. When Yeshua returns, the oil of anointing will be used to usher in His Messianic rule.304

Two chief rabbis of Israel are in possession of the ancient clay jar that contains the oil of anointing from the second temple. This points to the imminent coming of the Messiah.

1. The ark of the covenant

There is a need for the finding of the Ark of the Covenant which symbolizes the presence of God and also God's unbreakable relationship with Israel. When the Ark is rediscovered, it will be a rallying cry for Jews in other countries to return to Israel.

In the last days, the antichrist will find the Ark—a tremendous temptation to capture and use as a prop for his own political and religious goals. After his initial victories over his enemies, "then shall he (antichrist) return into his land with great riches; and his heart will be against the holy covenant and he shall do exploits and return to his own land" (Daniel 11:28). The first fulfillment of the prophecy of the Antichrist is related to the Syrian tyrant King Antiochus IV. In 1682 BC, a secondary fulfillment points to the future antichrist's defilement of the Third Temple, an act referred to as the abomination of desolation by Daniel and Yeshua. The antichrist will hate the Ark of the Covenant because it is the symbol of God's unbreakable relationship with Israel.305

The ark, which has been missing for thousands of years from Israel, will be found and placed in the holy of holies of the temple. The ark will play a major role in inspiring the Jews to build the third temple.

The original ark of the covenant was covered with gold inside and out. It was forty-five inches by twenty-seven inches by twenty-seven inches with a mercy seat of pure gold as the lid of the ark. The Lord said His divine presence would dwell within the ark forever.

The ark will play a pivotal role in our future according to Jeremiah 3:15-17.

> *15 And I will give you pastors according to mine heart, which shall feed you with knowledge and understanding. 16 And it shall come to pass, when ye be multiplied and increased in the land, in those days, saith the LORD, they shall say no more, The ark of the covenant of the LORD: neither shall it come to mind: neither shall they remember it; neither shall they visit it; neither shall that be done any more. 17 At that time they shall call Jerusalem the throne of the LORD; and all the nations shall be gathered unto it, to the name of the LORD, to Jerusalem: neither shall they walk any more after the imagination of their evil heart.306*
>
> (Jeremiah 3:15-17, KJV)

Before the return of Messiah, Israel will once more visit the ark of the covenant. When Messiah comes, the ark will no longer be the central focus of Israel's worship. The prophecy implies that this sacred object will play a crucial role in the leading up to the rebuilding of the temple and the coming of Messiah.

---

304 Jeffrey, Grant R. The New Temple and the Second Coming. Pages 56-58.

305 Ibid. Page 143.

306 The Holy Bible: King James Version. Oak Harbor: Logos Research Systems, Inc., 1995.

The Ark of the Covenant in Ethiopia

Deep within a complex of underground passages beneath the ancient Church of Zion, in Aksum in northern Ethiopia, is a secret passage that leads to a highly guarded hiding place for the most sacred object in human history. For three thousand years—from the time of King Solomon—this passage to the Holy of Holies has been protected by royal priestly guards of the ancient Ethiopian Jewish monarchy. The last ruling monarch of Ethiopia was Emperor Haile Selassie, who called himself "the conquering Lion of Judah." The city of Aksum was the ancient capital of the kingdom of the Queen of Sheba.

Within this underground Temple are seven concentric rings of interior circular walls. An ordinary Ethiopian Coptic priest can worship within the areas of the first to the fourth rings. Only the highest priests and the Emperor can enter the fifth and sixth innermost ring. The final seventh central walled circular room is the secret Holy of Holies. The Ethiopians claim that the Holy Ark of the Covenant with the Mercy Seat and Shekinah Glory of God has lain in this sacred room of their Temple for three thousand years. Only one person is allowed to enter this room and he is the Guardian of the Ark. This Ethiopian priest-guard is chosen at the age of seven, the age of understanding, from the priestly family. He is trained as a child, in his age of innocence and agrees to guard the Ark for the rest of his life, never seeing the light of day or living a normal life. This guardian fasts for 225 days every year according to the Ethiopian Jewish sacred festival calendar. He prays, meditates and guards the sacred Ark with his life. He never leaves this Holy of Holies until the day of his death, when he is replaced by another chosen Guardian. Each day the High Priest enters the sixth innermost ring to bring the Guardian his food.

The Ethiopian monarchy is the oldest continuous royal dynasty in history. It begins with the Queen of Sheba and her son, Menelik the First, the offspring of her marriage to King Solomon of Israel, and continues until the late Emperor Haile Selassie. Prince Menelik the First was educated in Israel. When He returned home at the age of 19, he secretly took with him the Ark of the Covenant, where Ethiopian tradition says it remains. The Ethiopian Royal Chronicles claim he left a perfect replica of the Ark in the Holy of Holies.

After the rebirth of Israel in 1948, the Israeli government enjoyed very close relations with Emperor Haile Selassie and supplied considerable technical support and aid to Ethiopia. The royal family has told me that Israeli government representatives helped Ethiopia on many occasions and that Israeli agents repeatedly asked the Emperor about the Ark of the Covenant in Aksum. They suggested that, since Israel had returned from captivity and the Temple Mount was recaptured, it was time for the Ethiopians to return the Ark to its ancient resting place in a rebuilt Temple in Jerusalem. The Emperor is reported to have replied: "In principle, I agree that the Ark should be returned to the Temple, but the correct time has not yet come." He felt that God would reveal the right time for the return of the Ark to Jerusalem.[307]

During the mid 1990's a secret mission was carried out toward the end of the Ethiopian Civil war. Negotiations took place between Israeli intelligence agents and Ethiopia's Marxist generals concerning the Ark of the Covenant. The Ethiopian military leaders demanded a bribe of tens of millions of dollars to allow the ark to be taken to Israel. A number of wealthy Jews donated the necessary funds. Suitcases containing the ransom money were delivered to the corrupt officials who promptly left Ethiopia at the end of the civil war to fly to Switzerland. However, unknown to

---

[307] Jeffrey, Grant R. Heaven the Last Frontier. Pages 101, 102, 105.

the deporting Marxist officials with suitcases contained counterfeit U.S. dollars. The Israeli agents phoned the Swiss banks to inform them of the counterfeit nature of the currency. Israel then took the real money raised by Jewish donors and gave it to the neighboring Eritrean rebels who had just conquered the Ethiopian capital of Addis Ababa. Since the fleeing officials had looted the country's treasury, these funds were desperately needed by the new Ethiopian government.

An elite team of Israeli Special Forces flew unmarked cargo planes into the northern providence of Gorier and secretly entered the city of Aksum at night during the chaos of the closing days of the civil war. Each of the Israelis were handpicked soldiers and each was a descendant of the tribe of Levi. According to the Law of Moses, only trained Levites were to carry the Ark of the Covenant (Reference Numbers 4:15).

Apparently secret negotiations had been held with Ethiopia's senior religious leaders as well as the surviving members of the royal family (in light of Emperor Silesia's earlier agreement that the Ark should return to Israel.) The special troops removed the ark from the underground treasury beneath the Church of Saint Mary of Zion. The Levites carried the Ark, with its special blue covering into a military cargo plane using staves to hoist it on their shoulders in the Biblically prescribed manner. After arriving in Israel, the Ark was taken to a secure location near Jerusalem, where it will be held until the time comes to place it within the Holy of Holies of the Third Temple. It is said that a replica of the Ark of the Covenant was placed in Ethiopian Holy of Holies in Aksum, thus repeating history.

Many Orthodox rabbis believe the Ark of the Covenant is now back in Israel in a secret vault until God gives the signal to rebuild the Temple.308

In Isaiah 18 there is a clear indication that the ark will be brought from Ethiopia in the end of times.

> *1 Woe to the land shadowing with wings, which is beyond the rivers of Ethiopia: 3 All ye inhabitants of the world, and dwellers on the earth, see ye, when he lifteth up an ensign on the mountains; and when he bloweth a trumpet, hear ye. 7 In that time shall the present be brought unto the LORD of hosts of a people scattered and peeled, and from a people terrible from their beginning hitherto; a nation meted out and trodden under foot, whose land the rivers have spoiled, to the place of the name of the LORD of hosts, the mount Zion.309*
>
> (Isaiah 18:1,3,7, KJV)

The announcing of the return of the ark of the covenant to the holy of holies of the rebuilt third temple will signal for Israel the final ushering in of the Messianic Era. Only time will reveal the true role of the ark of the covenant in the events that will surround the rise of the Antichrist and the return of Yeshua as Israel's Messiah.

Schlomo Goren - **Secrets of location of the Ark of Covenant**
Rabbi Schlomo Goren, an important figure in the recent unfolding of the prophetic scenario in Israel, died at age 77 late in October 1994. From 1972 until 1983 Mr. Goren was Israel's Ashkenazic [of Eastern European origin] chief rabbi. Before becoming a chief rabbi of Israel, he rose

---

308 Jeffrey, Grant R. The New Temple and the Second Coming. Pages 159-161.

309 The Holy Bible: King James Version. Oak Harbor: Logos Research Systems, Inc., 1995.

to be his country's chief military chaplain and, in that capacity, became the first person to lead a prayer service at the Western Wall after Israeli soldiers captured East Jerusalem in the 1967 Arab-Israeli war. When the Israeli troops arrived at the wall, which is the most sacred site in Judaism, Rabbi Goren blew a *shofar*, or ram's horn, in celebration according to a November 3, 1994, article in the *New York Times*. Born in Poland, he was taken to what was then *Palestine* in 1925, studied at Hebrew University, and became chief rabbi of Tel Aviv before rising to chief rabbi of Israel.

The first of several significant events in Goren's life that interest the prophecy scholar occurred immediately after the capture of the Temple Mount area in the 1967 Arab-Israeli war. According to Dr. Randall Price in his recent book, *In Search of Temple Treasures*, Goren "was placed in charge of the Temple Mount and immediately assigned a corps of engineers a two-week task of measuring and mapping the area. He also opened a synagogue on the Mount and brought Torah scrolls, prayer books, and other items of worship in expectation of revival of Jewish presence at the site. Goren's state of euphoria was short- lived, however. Within four weeks, Israel had officially relinquished control of the Temple Mount to the Arabs as a conciliatory gesture. What might have led to immediate restoration of Temple worship in Jerusalem disintegrated before the eyes of the once-exultant rabbi.

Fourteen years later, Goren participated in the excavation of a tunnel behind Warren's Gate beneath the site where the ancient Temple had stood. After a year and a half of secret digging beneath the third most holy site in Islam, Goren and Rabbi Meir Yehuda Getz may have been within a few feet of the area containing the ancient Ark of the Covenant and other Temple Treasures. With the passage of time, however, the clandestine operation began to lose its cloak of secrecy and, when the excavation may have been less than thirty or forty yards from the ancient artifacts, a Muslim mob descended on the archaeological dig and closed it down immediately. Arabs quickly sealed Warren's Gate with plaster, precluding any further excavations. In 1992 the plaster was "reworked" to make it blend into rough natural rock adjacent to it in order to suppress questions by pilgrims visiting the Holy Land.

Both Goren and Getz claimed to know the precise location of the Ark of the Covenant. However, Goren has now taken this secret to his grave, fearing that disclosure might threaten the security of the Ark and other Temple treasures. Such a discovery, had it been made public, would have clearly validated Jewish claims on the Temple Mount and might have inspired Jews to clamor for the rebuilding of the Temple on what is now Arab property.310

m. The plans for the temple

According to Temple Institute spokesman Rabbi Chaim Richman, detailed blueprints for the Third Temple have existed for the past four years. The plans were necessarily drawn according to the primary sources for this information: the Bible, Josephus, and *Middot*. Additions to these ancient specifications have included the use of electricity and other modern improvements that agree with *Halacha* (the *Law*).311

---

[310] Ingraham, David A. and Schlomo Goren. "Keeping Time on God's Prophetic Clock." <u>Prophetic Observer</u>. Oklahoma City: Southwest Radio Church, Jan. 1995, c. 1994. Page 4.

[311] Price, Randall "Time for a Temple? Jewish Plans to Rebuild the Temple." <u>Israel My Glory</u>. Westville: The Friends of Israel, Gospel Ministry, Inc. December/January 1997/1998. Page 15.

Other structures pertaining to the Temple's function have also been planned or actually built. Under the auspices of Rabbi Shlomo Goren, the 70-seat Supreme Court building that housed the Sanhedrin in Temple times has again been constructed.

According to Goren, its present location adjacent to the Temple Mount is correct for the restored Temple complex as envisioned by the Prophet Ezekiel, which is to be 30 times larger than that of previous Temples. The legal stipulations that the Sanhedrin will use to govern Israel's relationship to the rebuilt Temple and its services have already been researched and are in the process of being published (the first volume in 1986) by the Research Center for Jewish Thought under the direction of Yoel Lerner.

The Preparations for the Temple

Since 1987, a group of rabbinical researchers, designers, and craftsmen, under the direction of Rabbi Yisrael Ariel, have been creating in the Jewish Quarter of Jerusalem what they call a "Temple-in-waiting." Their efforts have resulted in computerized visualizations and blueprints for the Third Temple and the production of ritually qualified vessels, garments, and other items necessary for a restoration of the Temple services. Known as the Temple Institute, this organization has been at the forefront of the publication of Third Temple research. Among the items that have been or are in the process of being created are: apparel for the high priest (his eight-layered woven robe, the golden crown worn on his head, and his jeweled breastplate bearing the names of the tribes of Israel); priestly garments and the blue- purple dye (*tchelet*) for the priestly *tsitsit* (fringes on the prayer shawl); the eleven sacrificial incense spices, urns, ewers, incense pans, forks, shovels, and carts (for burnt offerings); the gold and silver *mizrak* (vessels used to dispense sacrificial blood on the altar); the golden laver, flasks, and measuring cups (used in the libation offerings); vessels for the meal offerings; the lottery boxes (for the Day of Atonement); the mortar and pestle and the stone vessel (*kelal*) for grinding and holding the purifying ashes of the red heifer; the golden menorah (lamp stand); cleaving instruments and oil pitchers for replenishing the oil for its light; silver trumpets (for assembling Israel at the Temple); and the barley altar.

While a replica of the Ark of the Covenant is prominently displayed in the Temple Institute's visitor center, spokesmen for the Institute publicly state that they believe the original still exists in a secret chamber located under the Temple Mount beneath the site of the Holy of holies. When access to the site is possible and all other ritual requirements have been met, they expect it to be recovered and take its place within the restored Temple.

n. The priests for the temple

1) DNA of the priests

The third temple will require a trained priesthood of Levites and Cohanim. Cohanim are direct descendants of Aaron, the high priest. Scientists have found a special variation of the "Y" chromosome that is shared by Jews from this priestly sub-tribe.

Hundreds of scripture verses command Israel to continue with the temple worship system forever (ref. Ezekiel 40-48, Daniel 9:24-27; Zechariah 14) and predict that Israel will be restored to its Promised Land and carry out the ancient temple worship forever.

Orthodox Yeshivas in Jerusalem have trained more than five hundred young Jewish men who are descended from the tribe of Levi to fulfill the duties of temple worship and sacrifice. Many have also been trained in worship rituals and have learned to play the recreated musical instruments such as the ancient trumpets and lyre.

According to rabbinic tradition, even though the genealogical records of the Temple were lost and Jews were scattered throughout Gentile lands, those of the tribe of Levi were forbidden to alter their names (which connoted their priestly heritage) when assimilated into foreign cultures. Thus, we continue to this day to have Levis and Cohens and derivatives of those names. Recently, a more scientific test to verify those of priestly lineage has appeared. In studies of male Jews claiming descent from Aaron, it was found that they as a group uniquely carry an aberration of the Y chromosome. Because each person's DNA is as individual as a fingerprint, this characteristic linked these men together as a separate and identifiable group that must be traced back to an original ancestor.

However, even without such information to identify priests, Rabbi Nachman Kahane, head of the Young Israel Synagogue (the closest synagogue to the Western Wall, located in the Muslim Quarter) and The Institute for Talmudic Commentaries maintain a computerized list of all known candidates in Israel. Other Orthodox organizations in Israel are helping to educate this priesthood. The Yeshiva founded by Motti Dan Hacohen, known as *Ateret* Cohanim, trains its students in the order of priestly service. The yeshiva states that it is not interested in activist attempts to enter the sacred precincts, but, with its sister organization *Atara Leyoshna*, it has aggressively attempted to acquire numerous Arab properties in the Muslim Quarter next to the Temple Mount in order to establish a "Jewish presence" in preparation for rebuilding the Temple.

Link to the High Priest - The Bible tells us that in the last days the sacrificial system of worship will be reinstituted in Israel. By Tobie Sanders

In order for the sacrificial system of worship to be reinstituted in Israel, the priesthood will have to return. To do this, the lineage of the priestly order would have to be known. It has been said that Jews can trace their lineage back several centuries even to the point of knowing what area of property in the land of Israel belonged to their family line. The line of the priests has been kept even more intact. Now the scientific world is recognizing that the priestly line shows the accuracy of the Scriptures.

The Thursday, January 2, 1997, edition of the *Daily Oklahoman* presented an article titled, "Rabbis Linked Genetically to Aaron." It said:

"Scientists have shown the Jewish priesthood has been passed down the male line for thousands of years, supporting biblical accounts dating it back to the appointment of the first Israelite high priest 3,300 years ago. In a letter to the latest edition of *Nature* magazine, published Tuesday, the scientists said they carried out tests on 188 unrelated rabbis from Israel, North America, and Britain. The composition of Y chromosomes—which are inherited from the father—in the samples taken from the rabbis were markedly different from the lay Jews. Studies have shown chromosomal variations between Jewish communities in different part of the world, at least in part because of the genetic mixture with neighboring non-Jews. But the study showed Y-chromosome composition in rabbis was similar wherever they were, suggesting a common origin."

There is now proof that the Jewish priesthood has been passed down the male line for thousands of years. Both Ashkenazi and Sephardic have been found to share a variation of the Y chromosome, linking them as descendants of Aaron, the High Priest, who lived 3,300 years ago.312

This was the result of a study conducted by Professor Karl Skorecki, a senior nephrologist at Rambam Hospital in Haifa and head of molecular medicine at the Technion's medical school, along with colleagues in Haifa, London and Arizona. Their finding was published in the British science Journal 'Nature.'

The researchers took samples of genetic material from unrelated Jewish men in the three countries and asked them whether they were from the priestly tribe. Tissue was taken by swabbing the inside of their cheeks.

The phenotypes of 188 secular and religious Jews, who said they were Kohanim (priests of the tribe of Levi), were found to be very different from those who said they were not.

It is believed that about 5 percent of the seven million male Jews around the world belong to the priestly tribe. This means 350,000 altogether, or about 100,000 to 120,000 in Israel alone.

Researchers in Israel, London, and Arizona found a preponderance of the YAP, DYS19B haplotype in Kohanim of both Ashkenazi and Sephardic origin (as well as a few Yemenites), but not in the non-Kohanim.

Any differences in the gene structure would reflect molecular-biological changes due to mutations; these are useful in calibrating the rate of mutations in the genes and observing human molecular evolution. Skorecki added: "The Y chromosome, carried only by men, is passed patrilineal; mitochondrial DNA is transmitted by the mother's X chromosomes" *(Jerusalem Post, January 11, 1997, #1888).*

Now that they can prove who the priesthood is, it looks like everything is lining up for the fulfillment of the scriptures that the offering of sacrifices will begin again (Era 2:62-63; Ezra 6:18; Ezekiel 45:15-25).313

Exodus 28:P1 says: 'And take thou unto thee Aaron thy brother, and his sons with him, from among the children of Israel, that he may minister unto me in the priest's office, even Aaron, Nadab and Abihu, Eleazar and Ithamar, Aaron's sons.' This would tend to agree, along with the Jewish calendar, with the time frame of 3,300 years ago when the priesthood was established.

We have read reports of the priesthood being reestablished in Israel today. Many have wondered how the Jews could be sure true Levitical priests were actually performing the duties of the office. The Bible tells us in Leviticus 17:11 that 'the life of the flesh is in the blood.' In this case, the blood has come about as the method for detection and confirmation showing the life of the priesthood through the centuries. The Jews have never been in doubt who the Levites are, no matter how much they might have been scattered across the earth.314

---

312 Sanders, Tobie. "Link to the High Priest." Bible in the News. Vol. 2. Oklahoma City: Southwest Radio Church, February 1997. Page 14.

313 End-Time Handmaidens & Servants (Newsletter). Jasper: End-Time Handmaidens, Inc., February 1997.

314 Sanders, Tobie. "Link to the High Priest." Bible in the News. Vol. 2, Oklahoma City: Southwest Radio Church, February 1997. Page 14.

2) 2,574-year-old sin bars priest from temple service

Today, signs throughout Jerusalem announce the coming of Messiah. Yeshivas on Mt. Moriah are training priests and Levites for resuming sacrificial worship; other yeshivas are weaving priests' clothing out of pure linen, while silversmiths and metal workers fashion vessels for the Temple, and musical instruments are made to announce the Messiah's appearance. Ancient biblical laws regarding the Sabbath and personal cleanliness are being strengthened so that observing Jews may be ready for standing on holy grounds on Mt. Moriah.

The last eight chapters of Ezekiel describe requirements for Temple worship when the Messiah appears, and we read from verses 15-17, 22 from the 44th chapter: "But the priests the Levites...... shall enter into my sanctuary, and they shall come near to my table, to minister unto me...... And it shall come to pass, that when they enter in at the gates of the inner court, they shall be clothed with linen garments......Neither shall they take for their wives a widow, nor her that is put away; but they shall take maidens of the seed of the house of Israel."

When the Lord appears in the Temple the priests must be dressed according to the law and not have married a divorced woman or a woman with sin in her life. Considering these requirements for priests today who are getting ready for Temple worship, the article that appeared in the *Daily Oklahoman* of December 17, 1994, dateline Israel, is most interesting:

"Rabbis have ruled a couples' 1982 marriage illegal because of sin committed by the wife's family 2,500 years ago, news reports said Sunday. Shoshana Hadad and Masoud Cohen could also face criminal charges for misleading the rabbi who married them, the Religious Affairs Ministry said. The ruling is based on a historical rumor. Rabbis believe a distant ancestor of Hadad, a Tunisian immigrant, illegally married a divorcee in about 580 BC, Israel Television said. That transgression marked the entire family. Rabbis decreed that their daughters for generations — including Shoshana Hadad — could never marry a Cohen. Cohens are descendants of the original Jewish Temple priests."

Should the Messiah come, Masoud Cohen will not only be barred from serving in the Temple, he and his wife may be sent to jail for a sin committed by the wife's relative 2,574 years ago. Masoud's sin was claiming that he was still a priest who could serve in the Temple and be pure enough to stand before Messiah. Israel is serious about getting ready for the Kingdom Age.315

3) Blue dye for the garments of the high priests

Since the day of the Second Temple, the crucial ingredients needed for the blue dye had been lost. This was important for proper Temple worship. This dye was produced from a rare mollusk found in the Mediterranean Sea. This sea creature was thought to be extinct. However in the late 1990's, Israeli divers discovered the mollusk, the hillazon snail (Murex trunculus), in the Red Sea.

A thick liquid is extracted from a gland in the mollusk to produce a rich blue dye. The Temple Institute in Jerusalem has created a supply of the blue dye, which will be used to create the garments required in Temple worship. The un-spun wool for the priestly robe is dipped in to this liquid turning the wool a bright green. When the now green wool is exposed to light it takes on a rich blue

---

[315] "2,574-Year_old Sin Bars Priest From Temple Service. Keeping Time On God's Prophetic Clock." <u>Prophetic Observer</u>. Oklahoma City: Southwest Radio Church, Jan. 1995, c. 1994. Page 4.

color. Once it dries, the wool is spun by craftsmen into a blue thread that is incorporated into the garments worn by the high priest.

The blue dye is also used to produce the tsitsit or fringes worn by observant Jewish males in the Temple.316

The linen robes are being made like those commanded in Exodus 39:27-29. These are for the Levite and Cohanim Priests. The robes are constructed from a special 6-ply linen thread. The sash which goes around the waist is more than fifty-five feet long.317

The Temple Institute has prepared more than one hundred of the sacred worship vessels and hundreds of priestly garments to be worn by Levites in future temple services.

The breastplate was made for the high priest; it was a four-inch square of heavy gold. Twelve different stones were placed in it. There were four rows with three stones in each row. Each was a different gem stone. The breastplate was used to reveal the will of God with the *Urim* and *Thummin*.

o. Waters of purification

The Purification for the Temple

According to the rabbis of the Temple Movement, in order for a Temple to be rebuilt today, those who would enter the area of sanctity and perform the holy tasks must first be ritually pure. Because all Jews have become ceremonially unclean in the *Diaspora (Dispersion)*, the only means to reverse this condition and establish a functioning priesthood is through the ashes of the red heifer (described in Num. 19).

This year, a red heifer was born in Israel—the first in 2,000 years. There is some debate concerning its legitimacy due to the presence of several white hairs. Nevertheless, other qualified red heifers have been secured from Mississippi rancher Clyde Lott. These have already been approved by Israeli authorities for import and are now awaiting transport to Israel. Because the Jewish sage Maimonides taught that there had been nine red heifers between the beginning of the Tabernacle and the end of the Second Temple, and that when the tenth arrived it would be prepared by the Messianic King, a special urgency is attached to this recovery by leaders of the Temple Institute, such as Rabbi Chaim Richman.318

Only water of purification with the ashes of the red heifer is needed to clean the site where the third temple will stand. The foundation stones were defiled by sin and possibly from the presence of dead men's bones in the earth below.

The water of purification is also used to purify the priests and sacred objects from spiritual defilement resulting from contact with death. However, the priest who obediently offers the red heifer would himself become unclean until evening. The water of purification was applied with hyssop on those who had contract with death. They were considered unclean for a week and could not participate in the community/marriage and especially temple worship unless they were cleansed according to Numbers 19:

---

[316] Jeffrey, Grant R. The New Temple and the Second Coming. Page 113.

[317] Ibid. Page 127.

[318] Price, Randall. "Time for a Temple? Jewish Plans to Rebuild the Temple." Israel My Glory. Westville: The Friends of Israel, Gospel Ministry, Inc., December/January 1997/1998. Pages 16-19.

2 This is the ordinance of the law which the LORD hath commanded, saying, Speak unto the children of Israel, that they bring thee a red heifer without spot, wherein is no blemish, and upon which never came yoke: 5 And one shall burn the heifer in his sight; her skin, and her flesh, and her blood, with her dung, shall he burn: 9 And a man that is clean shall gather up the ashes of the heifer, and lay them up without the camp in a clean place, and it shall be kept for the congregation of the children of Israel for a water of separation: it is a purification for sin.319

(Numbers 19:2, 5, 9, KJV)

In addition to the spiritual significance of the water of purification, it had the ability to destroy germs and stop infection.

The waters of purification contained the ashes of the heifer's body combined with cedar, hyssop and scarlet thread. The cedar oil would irritate the skin. This encouraged people to vigorously rub the solution into their hand. The hyssop oil is an effective antiseptic and antibacterial agent used to protect the people against diseases.

The prophet Ezekiel confirmed that the waters of purification from the red-heifer sacrifice will be used to cleanse the future temple and the Jewish people.

25 Then will I sprinkle clean water upon you, and ye shall be clean: from all your filthiness, and from all your idols, will I cleanse you.320

(Ezekiel 36:25, KJV)

p. The red heifer

The main purpose of the sacrifice of the red heifer was to cleanse the Temple Mount and the priesthood.

2 This is the ordinance of the law which the LORD hath commanded, saying, Speak unto the children of Israel, that they bring thee a red heifer without spot, wherein is no blemish, and upon which never came yoke: 3 And ye shall give her unto Eleazar the priest, that he may bring her forth without the camp, and one shall slay her before his face: 9 And a man that is clean shall gather up the ashes of the heifer, and lay them up without the camp in a clean place, and it shall be kept for the congregation of the children of Israel for a water of separation: it is a purification for sin.321

(Numbers 19:2-3, 9, KJV)

The red heifer was to be without blemish. Her blood was to be sprinkled opposite the entrance to the tabernacle during the time the Israelites wandered in the wilderness. When the temple was later completed, the sacrifice of the red heifer was on a plateau on the western slope of the Mount of Olives......across from the holy of holies......in line with the Eastern Gate of the city.

---

[319] The Holy Bible: King James Version. Oak Harbor: Logos Research Systems, Inc., 1995.

[320] Ibid.

[321] Ibid.

The ceremonial burning of the red heifer has only occurred seven times according to the Mishna:

By Moses
By Ezra
Five times after the destruction of the second temple

Each time the ashes which remained from the previous sacrifice were added to the new ashes to provide a perpetual sacrifice.

The animal was completely burned with cedar wood, hyssop and scarlet within the bonfire on the plateau. Afterward, the priest would gather the ashes in a clay vessel and return to the temple. There ashes were then sprinkled on the surface of the water in a large cistern to provide "waters of purification" that would purify the people from ritual defilements.

The sacrifice of the red heifer symbolically points to Messiah Yeshua and His sacrifice on the cross. He was sacrificed outside the city of Jerusalem. So was the red heifer. Usually male animals are sacrificed, not females; the red heifer was the only female animal the Law commanded to sacrifice. Interestingly, our Messiah was betrayed for thirty pieces of silver, the price of a female slave.

THE RED HEIFER

There was much excitement in Israel over the birth of a "Red Heifer" on a farm, in the village of Fkar Hasidim (which is near Haifa.) in late spring 1997.

A "pure" Red Heifer is very rare. It could not have a single white hair.

In order that the heifer will be accepted according to Torah requirements it will be at least two years old before it is used. It must be without blemish, be without defect, and it must have never worn a yoke otherwise it could be disqualified for sacrifice.

Once the red heifer has passed inspection, it is time to cleanse the Temple area and the foundation stones with the ashes of the red heifer. In preparation for sacrifice for the building of the Third Temple, the Sacrifice of the Red heifer must be performed outside the camp.

The blood of the heifer must be sprinkled seven times in front of the tabernacle; the entire heifer must be burned before the priest; cedar wood, hyssop and a scarlet thread are added to the fire.[322]

The Water of Purification is then prepared by a priest who is clean. He will gather the ashes and add water, then store the mixture outside the camp in a clean place. The Water of Purification is not only for ritual cleansing. It has medical benefits as well.

The only real obstacle to the rebuilding of the Temple is not the missing ashes, but political access to the Temple Mount.[323]

Just as Zechariah predicted, Jerusalem is indeed becoming a burdensome stone to all the nations of the earth. The rebuilding of the Temple will be another intensifying aspect in the present Middle East imbroglio.[324]

---

[322] "The Red Heifer." Koinonia House. Coeur d'Alene: Koinonia House. Page 9.

[323] Ibid. Page 11.

[324] Ibid.

> *2 Behold, I will make Jerusalem a cup of drunkenness to all the surrounding peoples, when they lay siege against Judah and Jerusalem. 3 And it shall happen in that day that I will make Jerusalem a very heavy stone for all peoples; all who would heave it away will surely be cut in pieces, though all nations of the earth are gathered against it.325*

(Zechariah 12:2-3, NKJV)

1) The search for the ashes of the red heifer

In 1981 I did a series of programs with Dr. Emil Gaverluk and Vendyl Jones relating to the "ashes of the red heifer." It was at this time that Jones was engaged in archaeological investigative work in the area of Qumran, Israel, at the northern end of the Dead Sea. One of the Dead Sea Scrolls, the Copper Scroll states: "On the way from Jericho to Succakah, by the River Ha Kippa in the tomb of Zadok the priest is the cave that has two openings. On the opening on the side of the north (the view is toward the east) dig two and one-half cubits under the plaster and there will be found the kalal and under it one book.

The "kalal" was the container of the ashes of the last, or ninth, red heifer. The "kalal," according to Mr. Jones, was a pot made of cow dung and clay. Other sources indicate the kalal was a stone pot. According to Rabbi Chaim Richman, the ashes of the red heifer were divided into three parts: (1) One part was in the Temple to be used for purification; (2) one in the woman's court to be saved as a memorial; and (3) one at the place of burning for purification of the priests at the next burning *(Mystery of the Red Heifer, 41)*It is also assumed hat the remains of the third portion would be put into the ashes of the subsequent red heifer to purify them—just in case they were not as pure as they should be.

Instructions in Numbers 19 for the particulars of the red heifer sacrifice don't mention the need for including ashes of the previous heifer in the ashes of the succeeding heifer. Although it is thought by some Jews that the Messiah will come when the tenth red heifer is sacrificed, this cannot be documented by Scripture.

From an Orthodox point of view, the only hope is the coming of the Messiah, just as Josephus reported He was the last hope of the Jews in AD 70. The growing aspiration of many religious Jews is to help the Messiah to come sooner by rebuilding the Temple. In order to initiate restored Temple worship, there must be the ashes of a pure red heifer. Therefore, there is no need to rebuild the Temple until such ashes are in evidence. Quoting from *The Mystery of the Red Heifer* (p.8), by Rabbi Richman:326

......be difficult for some to believe that a cow could be so important. But the truth, the fate of the entire world depends on the red heifer. For God has ordained that its ashes alone is the single missing ingredient for the reinstatement of biblical purity—and thereafter, the rebuilding of the Holy Temple.

Vendyl Jones believed that the Copper Scroll indicated that the ashes of the last red heifer were in cave #4, named the "Cave of the Column," at Wadi Hakippah. Jones, along with volunteer helpers from the United States, searched for the kalal that held the ashes for over a decade. He did

---

[325] The Holy Bible: The New King James Version. Nashville: Thomas Nelson, 1996, c1982.

[326] Hutchings, Noah. "The Ashes of the Red Heifer." Prophetic Observer. Vol. 4 #8-L-820. Oklahoma City: Southwest Radio Church, Aug. 1997, c. 1997. Page 1-2.

locate a vial of anointing oil and incense used in the Temple, but he did not find a kalal of heifer ashes. It is thought by some that before the Temple was destroyed in AD 70, and as Jones insists, that Essenes took vessels and items required for Temple worship either before or after it was destroyed, and hid them in sixty-seven places. If there were three kalals of ashes, then it is possible that one may still be buried under the Temple Mount, or hidden near the "place of burning" on Mt. Olivet.

The ordinance of the law commanding the sacrifice of a red heifer is found in Numbers 19:1-2:

> *And the Lord spake unto Moses and unto Aaron, saying, This is the ordinance of the law which the Lord hath commanded, saying, Speak unto the children of Israel, that they bring thee a red heifer without spot, where is no blemish, and upon which never came yoke.*

(Numbers 19:1-2)

It should be noted that this ordinance came from the Lord, by direct oral instruction from God Himself. Although this ordinance was not a part of the Ten Commandments, it was a commandment from the Lord.

This was a commandment specifically to the "children of Israel." It was never a commandment to the Gentiles.

The children of Israel were to bring a red heifer. A red heifer is simply a young red female bovine. Melody, the present red heifer in Israel, is the result of artificial insemination from a bull in Sweden. Clyde Lott in Mississippi is also breeding cattle for Israel, but whether either would be acceptable under the law would be questionable. Rabbi Richman gives two incidents where the red heifer sacrificed was purchased from Gentiles, so this would be a matter for the rabbinate to decide. It is also concluded that the red heifer must be born in Israel, and although this is not directly commanded in the ordinance of the law, it may be inferred.

2) Birth of a red heifer

October 16, 1989 the chief rabbi of Israel sent a team of scientists to Europe to obtain frozen embryos of a breed of red heifers that will be used to raise a pure red heifer on an Israeli cattle ranch.

KNEE JERK
REPORT FROM MICHAEL ALTER:

Knee Jerk: Some of you may have found the recent news astounding in regards to the reconstitution of the DAILY SACRIFICE in Jerusalem. I would like to give you some more background on this issue. About 3 years ago Clyde Lot conducted the sale of genetically engineered heifer embryos to the Temple Mount Faithful. These calves inutero was selected for their single characteristic of being head-to-toe red, as scriptures require.

It was planned that when the calves reach the age of 3 years old they would be ready for immediate sacrifice. In about 8 weeks the calves will start turning 3 years of age, thus the push to construct the altar immediately so that the sacrifices can begin on Rosh Hashanah.327

DAYSTAR INTERNATIONAL: *Jews Hail Birth of Red Cow as Sign to Start Third Temple* — The birth of the red heifer for the purification rites (Numbers 19:2-7) is being hailed as a sign from God that work can soon begin on building the third Temple. The birth of the red animal, to a black-and-white mother and a dun-colored bull, is being hailed as a miracle by activists who want to rebuild the Temple and prepare the way for the Jewish Messiah's entry to Jerusalem. "We have been waiting for 2,000 years for a sign from God, and now he has provided us with a red heifer," said one activist."328

Reverend Lott shared with us that it would be impossible to ship an acceptable red heifer to Israel, because it would first have to be marked with ink, and then with stapled tags in the ears, giving the record of inspection and vaccination. The Lord commanded that the red heifer be without spot or blemish. Reverend Lott hopes that one of his heifers might be shipped to Israel to give birth there to an acceptable heifer, or send impregnated eggs to be implanted in cows in Israel.

The present red heifer candidate in Israel has a few white hairs, and by biblical definition would not be acceptable. I asked our guide, Gila Trebeich, about this and she said that although there were a couple of white hairs, the roots of these hairs were red and the keepers were hoping that in due course, these also would turn red.

The final qualification for a red heifer to meet the Lord's requirements is that it must never have worn a yoke. Rabbi Richman contends that if someone even leaned on it, the heifer would have to be disqualified.

Under the law animals were sacrificed at the Passover and Yom Kippur, and there were daily or intermittent sacrifices of doves, pigeons, etc. Like the burning of the red heifer, all such sacrificial offerings in some way were to teach Israel of their need for a substitute eternal sacrifice, who once and for all would take away their sins (Rom.11).

Red is the color of sin:

Come now, and let us reason together, saith the Lord; though your sins be as scarlet, they shall be as white as snow; though they be red like crimson, they shall be as wool.

(Isaiah.1:18)

Red is also the color or blood, and the priest sprinkled the blood of the heifer seven times before the congregation.

The commandment that the red heifer was to do no labor signified that salvation is not of works, but by faith through God's grace (Eph. 2:8-9).329

And ye shall give her unto Eleazar the priest, that he may bring her forth without the camp, and one shall slay her before his face: And Eleazar the priest shall take

327 End-Time Handmaidens & Servants (Newsletter). Jasper: End-Time Handmaidens, Inc., August 9, 1996. Page 4.

328 Ibid.

329 Hutchings, Noah. "The Ashes of the Red Heifer." Prophetic Observer. Vol. 4 #8-L-820. Oklahoma City: Southwest Radio Church, Aug. 1997, c. 1997. Page 2.

*of her blood with his finger, and sprinkle of her blood directly before the tabernacle
of the congregation seven times: And one shall burn the heifer in his sight; her skin,
and her flesh, and her blood, with her dung, shall he burn......*

(Numbers 19:3-5)

Only a high priest could offer up blood for a sin offering, so in offering up His own blood, Jesus Christ became our eternal High Priest (Heb. 7:21).

The burning of the red heifer as a sin offering was a type of the sinner's eternal judgment in the Lake of Fire. The penalty for sin was satisfied in type.

*And the priest shall take cedar wood, and hyssop, and scarlet, and cast it into the
midst of the burning of the heifer.*

(Numbers 19:6)

Hyssop is a fragrant, leafy, hairy, vine plant that grows out of walls and above the ground in Israel. It was used by Moses as a symbol of purity, and it was the only plant that could be used to sprinkle the waters of purification. Scarlet is a symbol for sin, and the cedar is a representative wood for the cross. In the hyssop, cedar, and scarlet being cast into the fire as it burned the red heifer, we see a representation of Jesus Christ dying for the sins of the world:

*For he hath made him to be sin for us, who knew no sin; that we might be made the
righteousness of God in him.*

(2 Corinthians 5:21)

*And a man that is clean shall gather up the ashes of the heifer, and lay them up
without the camp in a clean place, and it shall be kept for the congregation of the
children of Israel for a water of separation: it is a purification for sin.*

(Numbers 19:9)

According to the Mishna and the Talmud, it became a serious matter of contention as to which man in Israel would be clean enough to gather the ashes of the red heifer, or to draw the water for purification, so pregnant women would actually give birth to their children within the Temple area. These children would never hear vulgar language, be near sinful acts, and even their feet would not touch the ground. An ox-drawn cart would carry them to the Spring of Siloam—all cleansed with the ashes of the red heifer in the water of separation and purification. The children would never get off the cart, but would lower purified stone vessels into the spring by attached strings. These were the precautions that the priests and Levites would take to carry out the type that foreshadowed the salvation that the Messiah would bring.330

---

330 Hutchings, Noah. "The Ashes of the Red Heifer." <u>Prophetic Observer</u>. Vol. 4 #8-L-820. Oklahoma City: Southwest Radio Church, Aug. 1997, c. 1997. Page 3.

q. Children wanted for future temple service

CHILDREN WANTED FOR FUTURE TEMPLE SERVICE: The Jews are preparing for the offering of the sacrifices, after almost 2000 years. This notice was sent out through the INS News Service-Israel.

An Ultra Orthodox Jewish sect is searching for parents willing to hand over newborn sons to be raised in isolation and purity, in preparation for the rebuilding of the Biblical Temple in Jerusalem. Only members of the Jewish priestly cast (Kohanim) need apply, according to the report in the Haaretz newspaper, dated March 1st. The Movement for Establishing the Temple wants to keep the children in a secluded compound in the hills of Jerusalem. The idea is to raise a child, who from the moment of birth will not touch the dead, not be under the same roof with the dead, and will not even be in a hospital, where the dead are also found, Yosef Elboim, the rabbi assigned to finding willing parents, told Haaretz. Once the boys turn 13 they will be able to slaughter and burn a sacred red heifer, literally a holy cow, and sprinkle its ashes on people, in a purification ritual last performed in Biblical times. This ritual is meant to cleanse those who have come into contact with the dead and prepare them for the reconstruction of the Temple that was destroyed in 70 AD. 'Today, when there is no one undefiled who can prepare the ashes in a state of purity, there is a problem, which we intend to solve with the help of priestly children,' Elboim said. Even if willing parents step forth, the sect will still face a major problem—finding an unblemished red heifer (Reuters).331

1) 'Samuels' sought for the third temple priesthood

With rising expectancy to rebuild the Third Temple in Jerusalem, Rabbi Yosef Elboim of the Movement for Establishing the Temple is asking for 20 parents to dedicate their unborn male children to a special program for producing a purified priesthood.

Hannah set the precedent for this when she presented her young son, Samuel, to Eli, the High Priest, to be raised for the priesthood (1 Samuel 1:24-28).

The Movement wants to raise newborn babies of Levitical descent in isolation to avoid contact with ritual defilement. This would be done by removing the chosen children to a secluded compound in the Jerusalem hills where they would be raised in a building specially constructed with elevated floors which prevent contact with the ground. This is thought important as ancient unmarked graves, which cause defilement, could be hidden in the ground.

Corpse-impurity is a ceremonial contamination preventing the priesthood from functioning today. Daily contact with the dead (people, animals, or insects) as well as with people or things in contact with them (for example: hospital workers) has put every Jew today into a state of ritual defilement.

The only remedy is the ritually cleansing ashes of the Red Heifer. No pure Red Heifers yet exist in Israel. Moreover, no one is in a state of purity to make the sacrifice of the red cow when it does exist.

The Haifa heifer, disqualified because of sprouting white hairs, nevertheless has been impregnated with imported Red Heifer semen in an attempt to yet produce the needed all-Red Heifer.

---

331 <u>End-Time Handmaidens & Servants (Newsletter)</u>. Jasper: End-Time Handmaidens, Inc., August 9, 1996. Page 3.

Rabbi Elboim will prepare the priest to offer the sacrifice when ready. Strict isolation from birth will be necessary so the boys have no possible way of contaminating themselves.

The compound for this project has been donated by the ultra-Orthodox Jewish Idea Yeshiva.

Four religious families in the Jerusalem area have been approached and at least one mother has volunteered her yet-to-be-born baby boy.

Rabbi Elboim claims 95 percent of the observances performed in the Temple can't be carried out because of ritual impurity. This project will reverse that impediment; when the boys reach their 13th birthdays they will be qualified to burn the Red Heifer and distribute its ashes.332

> *And he that gathereth the ashes of the heifer shall wash his clothes, and be unclean until the even: and it shall be unto the children of Israel, and unto the stranger that sojourneth among them, for a statute for ever.*
>
> (Numbers 19:10)

This sacrifice was a type of purification that would last forever, and not just for Israel, but for any strangers, meaning Gentiles. When the sin bearer came to fulfill the type, Israel clung to the type and refused to accept the truth.

> *He came unto his own, and his own received him not. But as many as received him, to them gave he power to become the sons of God, even to them that believe on this name.*
>
> (John 1:11-12)

Not only were the waters for purification (which contained a small amount of the ashes of the red heifer) used for cleansing and separation (sanctification) of the Temple, vessels, furnishing, priests, Levites, and even the congregation, we read in the ordinance that any Israelites who touched a dead body, or even came into close proximity to a dead body, must be sprinkled with the waters of purification. This signified that there is no death for those who have been purified by faith in the atoning blood of Jesus Christ (1 Cor. 15:54-57).

The water of purification containing the ashes of the red heifer for daily cleansing and sanctification was a definitive setting forth of the absolute truth of God that the blood wherewith we are saved from sin is the same blood wherewith we are daily cleansed from sins we commit either by commission or omission.333

r. Place of burning of the red heifer

The "place of burning," Miphkad Altar, is located just below the northern summit of the Mount of Olives, on a line from the entrance to the Temple through the Eastern Gate. There is now a problem in using the traditional "place of burning" to sacrifice a new red heifer. According to Ezekiel 44:1-4, the eastern Gate, which is closed will not be opened until the Messiah comes. Also,

---

[332] Price, Randall. "'Samuels' Sought for the Third Temple Priesthood." The Messianic Times, Vol. 9, number 1, spring 1998. Page 13.

[333] Hutchings, Noah. "The Ashes of the Red Heifer." Prophetic Observer. Vol. 4 #8-L-820. Oklahoma City: Southwest Radio Church, Aug 1997, c. 1997. Page 3.

the "place of burning" is in the possession of Arabs and Muslims and a sacrificial service to make possible the rebuilding of the Temple would start another holy war.

There is one popular view that Jesus Christ had to be sacrificed on the "place of burning" in order to fulfill the red heifer type and example. However, if Jesus were crucified on the Mount of Olives, the following would have to be considered:

- Everything that Jesus did on the Mount of Olives was duly noted by the writers of the Four Gospels. If Jesus were crucified on the Mount of Olives, the Gospel writers would have so stated.
- Two others accused of serious crimes were crucified with Jesus, and the Romans would not have willfully incurred Jewish anger by executing criminals on a Jewish holy site.
- Golgotha, the hill in the shape of a skull, is scripturally presented as the place where Jesus was crucified. This hill is just outside the city wall near the Damascus Gate—not on the Mount Olivet.
- We read in Hebrews 13:12 that Jesus shed His blood and suffered without the gate. In John 19:20 we read that Jesus was crucified "nigh" to the city, and we also read that the tomb where He was laid was "nigh" to where He was crucified. There is only one place that fits this description —Golgotha, just outside the wall, near the Damascus Gate, with a tomb of a rich man in a garden near Skull Hill.
- The Romans always crucified victims near a well traveled road, and the highway to the north exited from the Damascus Gate past Golgotha.

When the tenth red heifer is sacrificed, where will the burning take place? Before the Western Wall, on Mount Moriah, or even on Mount Zion, would be inside the city? Could it occur just outside the Damascus Gate at the foot of Golgotha where Jesus was crucified? Possibly.

Interest by world Jewry in the red heifer manifests a growing conviction that the coming of Israel's Messiah is imminent. The *Boston Globe* of April 6, 1997, in a story titled "Heifer's Appearance in Israel stirs Hopes, Apocalyptic Fears," observed:

"She stares out at the world through dewy eyes, stumbling on awkward legs, dipping into her trough with abandon, oblivious to the soaring hopes and apocalyptic fears that have spread with the news of her birth. Watched over by an armed guard in a skullcap and visited by rabbis and other seekers of meaning, this rust-colored six-month-old heifer is hailed as a sign of the coming of the Messiah and decried as a walking atom bomb. Of a variety believed extinct for centuries, the red heifer is seen by some as the missing link needed for religious Jews to rebuild their ancient Temple in Jerusalem. Sacrificing the animal in its third year and using its ashes in a purification rite would allow Jews to return 2,000 years later to the Temple site, a spot holy to both Jews and Muslims......Many fear that the calf's arrival could create an explosive situation."

The sacrificial ordinance of the red heifer is an object lesson in God sending His only begotten Son, Jesus Christ, into the world to be offered for us, in our place. Only when Jesus literally returns at the Battle of Armageddon will Israel understand the true meaning of this Old Testament typology (Rom. 11:25-28; Rev. 1:7; Matt. 24:15-27; Zech. 12:10).

To Christians, news relating to a red heifer in Israel means that Jesus Christ is coming back soon, and it is near, even at the doors. To non-Christians it means to either receive Jesus Christ as Lord and Savior or get ready for the seven-year time of judgment, a time which Jesus said would be "great tribulation, such as was not since the beginning of the world to this time, no, nor ever shall be" (Matt. 24:21).334

---

[334] Hutchings, Noah. "The Ashes of the Red Heifer." <u>Prophetic Observer</u>. Vol. 4 #8-L-820. Oklahoma City: Southwest Radio Church, Aug 1997, c. 1997. Page 4.

CHAPTER THIRTEEN

Stage Set for the Tribulation and Reign of Antichrist

A. Two timelines of events

Possible Sequence of Key Prophetic Events

1948	Rebirth of Israel.
1967	Israel captures old city of Jerusalem and the Temple Mount.
1973	Yom Kippur War: Israel survives invasion from Syria, Egypt, Jordan, Iraq.
1980	+ The Temple Institute researches and begins creation of vessels for temple worship
2005	The Sanhedrin is reconvened for the first time since AD 425. The temple location is determined by the Sanhedrin. Priests are trained in temple sacrifice.

ANTICIPATED PROPEHTIC EVENTS

__?__ The Russian-Islamic alliance will attack Israel but will be defeated supernaturally.

__?__ Israel will build the third temple and resume the ancient temple worship.

__?__ The ten nations (see Daniel 2:40-45) in Europe and surrounding Mediterranean nations will unite, forming the revived Roman Empire.

__?__ A world dictator, the Antichrist, will rise to power over the revived Roman Empire and extend his global rule through military victories and peace treaties.

__?__ The Antichrist will sign a seven-year security treaty with Israel (see Daniel 9:24-27).

__?__ Halfway through the seven years, the Antichrist will stop the daily temple sacrifice (see Daniel 12:11). The Antichrist will violate the holy of holies of the third temple.

__?__ Someone will assassinate the Antichrist; then he will rise from the dead and claim to be god, demanding worship as such. He will introduce the mark of the beast system.

__?__ The Antichrist's forces will attach righteous Jews and Gentiles who refuse to worship him.

__?__ Nations from Asia ('kings of the east') will lead a revolt against the Antichrist raising a 200 million troop army and crossing Asia to engage in a massive military confrontation with the western military forces of the Antichrist.

__?__ The battle of Armageddon will occur seven years after the Antichrist signs the treaty with Israel.

__?__ Jesus Christ will defeat both armies to save Israel. He will enter through the sealed Eastern Gate of the Temple Mount into the rebuilt temple. He will cleanse the sanctuary.

__?__ Christ will establish His millennial kingdom from the throne of David in Jerusalem. Gentile nations will send representatives to the temple to acknowledge their eternal allegiance to Christ (see Zechariah 14:16).335

Section Two: Coming Events — Proposed

Future days are suggested because coming Biblical events seem to fulfill the last three Feasts of Israel

	A. The Invasion of Israel
Rosh Hashanah Judgment Day (*Tishri* 1)— Year 1	The invasion will be brief, since God will disarm the invaders (Ezek. 39:3). The whole attack may be over in six days, as was the Six-Day War. The invaders will be destroyed in Israel.
Tishri 6 — Year 1	At the end of the invasion, half of the Christians (Matt. 25:1-9) will go forth immediately to call the world to repent, accept the righteousness that Jesus Christ offers, and expect to be *"caught up"* by Jesus Christ to escape God's coming wrath.
Tishri 6 — Year 1	Israel also will go forth immediately to bury the dead and cleanse the land for seven months (Ezek. 38:12-14).
	B. The Seven-Year Transition to Messiah's Rule (Rule of Antichrist

---

335 Jeffrey, Grant R. The New Temple and the Second Coming. Colorado Springs: Waterbrook Press. Pages 189-190.

336 Kremers, Mari F. "Review of Dates." God Intervenes in the Middle East. Pages 286-287.

	The First Three-and-One-Half Years
Tishri 10 — Year 1	Yom Kippur; God's two witnesses will appear and do powerful miracle in Israel for 1,260 days. An exceptional leader *"will confirm a covenant with many"* (in Israel) for one seven-year period. This will be the start of his seven-year reign and the transition to Messiah's rule on earth. Many Jews will go to Israel believing him to be their Messiah. 336
Tishri 15-21 — Year 1	Inauguration of Israel's king.
Iyyar (May/June) —Year 1	The Temple may be started right after the seven months of cleansing the land and after Passover. (Iyyar was also the month in which the work on both prior Temples was begun)......A man thought to be Messiah must be present to authorize the construction of the Temple. There must be peace with the Moslems for this to happen.
Sivan 20 or *Tammuz*	Israel brings forth her progeny, the 144,000 (Rev. 12:1-5), 280 days (average human gestation) after leader confirms a covenant. This encompasses Tishri 10 to Sivan or

20—Year 1	*Tammuz* 20, depending on whether there is an added month that year.
Sivan 20 or *Tammuz* 20—Year 1	The leader of Israel will become ruler of the E.C.
Tishri—at start of Year 3	The Temple may be completed after 18 months of construction.
Tishri—8-21- Year 3 Feast of Tabernacles	Dedication of the Temple may take two weeks if done in keeping with that of Solomon's Temple (1 Kin.8:65f; 2 Chr. 7:8f) and at the start of the Israeli leader's 3rd year in office.
Tishri—22-Year 3	*Shemini Atzeret*—Final Assembly on the eight day of the Feast of Tabernacles (*Sukkot*) and the end of the dedication. The Temple may then be used for 18 months for worship before the sacrificial system is halted in the middle of the leader's 4th year in office.337

---

[337] Ibid. Page 287.

[338] Ibid.

About Mid-point— Year 4	The false messiah of Israel ("Caesar" of the E.C.) will receive a fatal wound from a sword but yet will live. The whole world will be astonished and will follow him after he arises as the beast (Rev. 13:3, 12, 14).338
The Second Three-and-One-Half Years	
Nisan 10— Year 4 The Midpoint	The exact midpoint of the seven years of transition will be a fateful day. The 144,000 Jewish servants of our God are *"caught up"* and enter heaven, led by Messiah. They are called *"firstfruits of God and the Lamb"* (Rev. 14:4). (On the same day, the Israelites entered the Promised Land under Joshua.) The families of these men will be protected by God for the remaining 1,260 days in the desert (Rev. 12:6, 14).
Nisan 10— Year 4	God's two witnesses will be killed by *"the beast"* (Rev. 11:7) after completing their assigned 1,260 days.
Nisan 10— Year 4	The Messianic pretender of Israel ("Caesar" of the E.C.) will stop the Temple sacrifices, declare himself to be God, and demand worship of his image in the Temple. The Jews will realize this man is the prophesied false messiah and flee (Dan. 9:27; 2 Thess. 2:4; Rev. 13:14f) He will become dictator for 42 months (1,260 days) of the world, which is divided up into ten regions. Each area will have a king, who gives his authority to the dictator (Rev 13:1, 5; 17:12f). He arises from the sea of humanity.
Nisan 10— Year 4	The false prophet will emerge and exercise the beast's authority, making the people of earth worship the beast and his image. The false prophet will perform great miraculous signs and deceive those who reject the real Messiah (Rev. 13:11ff).339
Nisan 10— Year 4	"The woman" (the families of the 144,000) is flown to the place prepared for her by God in the desert, where she will be taken care of for the 1,260 days of wrath (Rev. 12:6, 14). Those in Judea flee to the mountains (Matt. 24:16ff; cf. Rev. 12:17).
Nisan 10— Year 4	THE GREAT TRIBULATION: The wrath of Almighty God will start on earth, and extend for three-and-a-half years.

339 Ibid. Pages 288-289.

Nisan 14— Passover— Year 4	A breath from God will bring the two witnesses to life in Jerusalem. They will be "called up" to heaven immediately. People worldwide will see them ascent (via television). Within the same hour, an earthquake in Jerusalem kills 7,000 people and one-tenth of the city will collapse (Rev. 11:11f.
From the Midpoint to the end of the 7 years	The false prophet will force people to receive the mark of the beast on the forehead or right hand in order to buy or sell. Of those who are not beheaded by the beast, half of unrepentant mankind are killed by sword, famine, plague, wild beasts, and troops (Rev. 6:8; 9:15).
The 7th year	The last year that the nations trample upon Jerusalem (Rev. 11:2).
Before the end of the 7th year	The marriage and wedding supper of Messiah and His Bride (Rev. 19:7ff; Matt. 22:2-14; 25:10; Eph. 5:31f. This has its roots in Is. 54:5-7; Hos. 2:19f).340
Tishri 1— *Rosh Hashanah* — Year 8	The beast, the ten kings, and their armies from all nations may begin to assemble at the Plain of Jezreel at Armageddon (*Har Mageddon*—Mount of Megiddo-Rev. 16:16) on the same day a few nations invaded Israel seven years before. They will attack Jerusalem.
Tishri 10— *Yom Kippur*— Year 8	Israel's Deliverer will be *"revealed from heaven in blazing fire"* (2 Thess 1:7). He will be seen by all eyes as He descends (Rev. 1:7). The Mount of Olives, just east of the Temple, will split from east to west when His feet touch down upon it. Jesus Christ brings His angelic hosts and all His saints with Him. He fights the armies gathered to make war against Him. The Antichrist and false prophet will be cast into lake of fire. Satan will be bound and thrown into the Abyss for 1,000 years. The kings of the earth and their armies will be slain (Zech. 14:2f, 12; Rev. 19:11f). CHRIST AS HIGH PRIEST. The First Resurrection concludes with: The Old Testament people written in the book of life. (Dan. 12:1, 2, 13). The post-Rapture Christians who had been beheaded by the Antichrist (Matt. 24:30; Mark 13:26; Rev. 20:4ff).

Tishri 10— *Heshvan* 10—Year 8	All levels of Israeli society will mourn and grieve bitterly as for an only child when they look upon their Redeemer with His pierced hands and feet (Zech. 12:10; Is. 53:5; Ps. 22:16). This will include the clans of David (political leadership), Nathan (the prophets) Levites (the priests), Shimei, and all the rest (Zech 12:12ff). Shimei represents the ones who have cursed the Lord's anointed (2 Sam. 16:5). The traditional mourning period lasts 30 days.

	JUDGMENT OF THE SURVIVORS ON EARTH: King Messiah will judge the nations for their treatment of the least of His brethren, *"whoever does the will of my Father in heaven"* (Matt. 12:50.341
Tiishri 10 — Tishri 1 — Entire 8th year	THE JUBILEE YEAR OF RESTORATION—(Yobel) beginning on Yom Kippur has probably not been celebrated in Israel since the days of Jeremiah (before Jewish exile into Babylon). At the end of the time decreed for Daniel's people and their city, everlasting righteousness will be brought in and the land of Israel will be returned to the Jewish tribes.
Tishri 15-21 Sukkot— Year 8	INAUGURATION OF THE KING IN HIS KINGDOM to dwell (shaken) with His people permanently. The Feast of Tabernacles looked backward to the tabernacles or shelters (sukkot) in which the Israelites dwelt in the wilderness after they left Egypt.
Heshvan 10—Year 8	Israel's mourning period will conclude Daniel's 1,290 days (1,260 of wrath and 30 days of mourning—Dan. 12:11).342

B. The war of Gog and Magog

Prophetic signposts clearly indicate we are quickly approaching the final turning point— the Second Coming of Jesus Christ to set up His kingdom.342

Prior to that long-awaited event, a great battle will take place in which the Lord will protect Israel from a massive invading army.

An unprecedented military alliance will form, led by Russia. The alliance will be made up of Islamic nations, including virtually all Middle Eastern Arab and Islamic states, North African states, Central Asian (former southern U.S.S.R.) states, plus Iran and a number of Asian nations.

---

340 Ibid. Pages 290-291.

341 Ibid. Page 290.

342 Jeffrey, Grant R. The New Temple and the Second Coming. Page 173.

In Ezekiel 38:2-6 God prophesied in great detail the names of the ancient nations that will invade Israel. Magog is identified as Russia by both Josephus and Herodotus, ancient Jewish and Greek historians respectively. The prophecy specifically names Iran (Persia), Ethiopia, and Libya in North Africa. The names Gomer and Togarmah are believed to refer to nations of Central Asia.

The alliance will attack Israel in an overpowering attempt to annihilate the chosen people. The prophet Ezekiel declared that God will employ supernatural means to defend Israel in this war, the coming War of Gog and Magog. The Lord will intervene to destroy 85 percent of the Russian-Islamic army be means of fire and brimstone, plague, madness, and the greatest earthquake in history (see Ezekiel 38:19-22; 39:1-2,6).

The devastation will be so vast that cities around the world will be shaken. The global earthquake will cause buildings, bridges, and walls to crumble.

The Scriptures prophesy that it will take seven months just to bury the fallen soldiers, and it will take seven years for Israel to burn the weapons of the invaders. Out of this profound global crisis, a political, military, and religious transformation will occur. God says, 'And they shall know that I am the Lord God' (Ezekiel 28:24). With Russia and its Islamic allies militarily devastated, the political-military balance of the world will be transformed.

Many Christians wonder how the United States will align itself at the time of the War of Gog and Magog. I believe we will see a major shift in American foreign policy in the near future, with America withdrawing from its role as world policeman to adopt a policy of isolationism. The massive reduction (virtually 50 percent) in the size of the U.S. military during the Clinton administration and the natural war-weariness from the continuing wars in Iraq and Afghanistan may explain why there is so little specific prophecy about America in the last days.343

Another reason America is not mentioned in prophecy is because as a nation we have fallen away from God. America is being judged in its losing control of its economic life.

Right now, America is facing an economic "perfect storm."

This past March (2008), the American financial system nearly collapsed. Bear Stearns, one of the nation's top financial institutions, had to be rescued from bankruptcy by the Federal Bank. *The Wall Street Journal*, a newspaper not prone to alarmism, blared the startling headline: "Fed saves American Financial System From *Collapse*."

The Fed had to pour $30 billion into the deal initially, to stave off a panic that would have sunk this nation into the worst economic depression in its history. To date, more that $300 billion has been put into the system to save it.

Ten years ago, I wrote a book entitled, *America's Last Call: On the Brink of a Financial Holocaust*. In that book, I warned of the following events:

There would be a meltdown of the bond market.
God's judgment would strike suddenly on the U.S. economy.
A brief, false sense of prosperity would precede the coming economic collapse. (This short flicker of prosperity would be God's final mercy before the chastening to come.)
There would be a real estate meltdown, with a market made up of mostly sellers and very few buyers. Multitudes would lose their homes to repossession.
There would be an ominous rise of homosexual power.
A sudden storm of confusion would take place on Wall Street.

---

343 Ibid. Pages 173-175.

God's watchmen and prophets would be silenced.

The U.S. dollar would collapse.

America would lose control of its economy. To date, China has loaned America hundreds of billions of dollars. We have become the world's number one debtor nation, no longer in control of our finances.344

If this seems far-fetched, think about the radical changes that will take place in the United States after the Rapture. All born-again Christians will be instantly transferred to heaven, vacating their positions in government, education, business, the church, and the military. When the salt is removed, spiritual rot will quickly set in. As America finds itself without the Christian leadership that has been the foundation of its greatness for several centuries, the balance of geopolitical and military power will shift dramatically to Europe and the Pacific Rim nations. As the Bible prophesies, the focus of world events will turn to the Middle East, Israel, and the revived Roman Empire of Europe and North Africa.

The Scriptures prophesy that, following the supernatural defeat of the Russian and Islamic armies when they attempt to annihilate Israel, the nations of the European Union and the Middle East will step into the political-military vacuum created by the elimination of both Russia's and Islamic military power. Both Daniel and the book of Revelation contain prophecies that point to the revival of the Roman Empire as the world's next superpower (Daniel 2:40-45; 7:23-25; Revelation 13:1,7).345

40 And the fourth kingdom shall be strong as iron: forasmuch as iron breaketh in pieces and subdueth all things: and as iron that breaketh all these, shall it break in pieces and bruise. 41 And whereas thou sawest the feet and toes, part of potters' clay, and part of iron, the kingdom shall be divided; but there shall be in it of the strength of the iron, forasmuch as thou sawest the iron mixed with miry clay. 42 And as the toes of the feet were part of iron, and part of clay, so the kingdom shall be partly strong, and partly broken. 43 And whereas thou sawest iron mixed with miry clay, they shall mingle themselves with the seed of men: but they shall not cleave one to another, even as iron is not mixed with clay. 44 And in the days of these kings shall the God of heaven set up a kingdom, which shall never be destroyed: and the kingdom shall not be left to other people, but it shall break in pieces and consume all these kingdoms, and it shall stand for ever. 45 Forasmuch as thou sawest that the stone was cut out of the mountain without hands, and that it brake in pieces the iron, the brass, the clay, the silver, and the gold; the great God hath made known to the king what shall come to pass hereafter: and the dream is certain, and the interpretation thereof sure.346

(Daniel 2:40-45, KJV)

---

[344] Wilkerson, David. "The Most Important Issue of This Hour." World Challenge Pulpit Series. Lindale: © 2008 World Challenge, Inc. May 12, 2008. Page 1.

[345] Jeffrey, Grant R. The New Temple and the Second Coming. Pages 173-175.

[346] The Holy Bible: King James Version. Oak Harbor: Logos Research Systems, Inc., 1995.

23 Thus he said, The fourth beast shall be the fourth kingdom upon earth, which shall be diverse from all kingdoms, and shall devour the whole earth, and shall tread it down, and break it in pieces. 24 And the ten horns out of this kingdom are ten kings that shall arise: and another shall rise after them; and he shall be diverse from the first, and he shall subdue three kings. 25 And he shall speak great words against the most High, and shall wear out the saints of the most High, and think to change times and laws: and they shall be given into his hand until a time and times and the dividing of time.347

(Daniel 7:23-25, KJV)

1 And I stood upon the sand of the sea, and saw a beast rise up out of the sea, having seven heads and ten horns, and upon his horns ten crowns, and upon his heads the name of blasphemy. 7 And it was given unto him to make war with the saints, and to overcome them: and power was given him over all kindreds, and tongues, and nations.348

(Revelation 13:1, 7, KJV)

We are entering a dangerous period of history. In spite of a heightened desire for peace, there is little reduction in the vast armaments available to dictators, terrorists, and rogue nations. With friendly nations withdrawing from their traditional stance of active support of American foreign policy, Europe is truly uniting for the first time since the fall of the Roman Empire more than fifteen centuries ago. A united Europe will be an economic, political, and military colossus on the transformed world stage once the prophesied global dictator rises to seize power in Europe. Each of the major players described in prophecy is moving into its appointed place to fulfill the prophecies concerning the birth pangs of the Messianic Age, the coming Great Tribulation, and the return of Christ.

We are commanded to remain alert and live each day in the awareness that Christ is coming soon:

For when they shall say, Peace and safety; then sudden destruction cometh upon the, as travail upon a woman with child; and they shall not escape. But ye, brethren, are not in darkness that that day should overtake you as a thief. Ye are all the children of light, and the children of the day; we are not of the night, nor of darkness. Therefore let us not sleep, as do others, but let us watch and be sober.

(1 Thessalonians 5:3-6)349

---

[347] Ibid.

[348] Ibid.

[349] Jeffrey, Grant R. The New Temple and the Second Coming. Colorado Springs: Waterbrook Press. Pages 175-176.

C. The Rapture of the Church

1. Signs prophesied by Yeshua and their fulfillment
Get Revived—He's Coming!

False Christs

In Matthew 24:3, Jesus was asked, *When shall these things be? And what shall be the sign of thy coming* [to earth], *and of the end of the world* [or Age of Grace]? He replied in verse 5, *Many shall come in my name, saying, I am Christ; and shall deceive many.* Has it happened? Since the year 1900, more than 1,100 false Christs have appeared on the scene.

Eventually, a false Christ will proclaim himself as the true Christ and become accepted on an international scale. The Bible predicts such an hour in 2 Thessalonians 2:4.

This internationally defied dictator will inaugurate a world peace program which holds the world spellbound for 42 months, or 3 ½ years. Then, in the middle of the seven-year period of Tribulation, he breaks all of his pledges and destroys his contractual obligations with Israel (see Daniel 9:27).

At this time, Russia begins a world war as she invades Israel (see Ezekiel 38 and 39). This war involves all nations (see Zechariah 14). This is God's outline from the Bible.

First the international dictator establishes global peace, and, when the world believes that Utopia has arrived, the bottom falls out of the hopes and aspirations. *For when they shall say, Peace and safety; then sudden destruction cometh upon them* (1 Thessalonians 5:3). A conference held to reduce nuclear weaponry may be the beginning of the end. This thought leads to the next sign Christ mentioned.

Wars and Rumors of Wars

From this proclamation one sees that the world can expect nothing but rivalry and battles until the Antichrist produces the false peace of the Tribulation era. There have been over 100 limited wars fought since the end of the Second World War, and presently one out of every four nations on earth is engaged in conflict.

Soon, we will experience the greatest global confrontation in the annals of history, for we are marching toward Armageddon at this very moment.

The Red Horse of the Apocalypse is about to appear. Revelation 6:4 states, *There went out another horse that was red: and power was given to him that sat theron to take peace from the earth, and that they should kill one another: and there was given unto him a great sword.* The signs abound—come quickly, Lord Jesus.

Famines

Christ added in Matthew 24:7, *And there shall be famines, and pestilences.* According to the World Food Programme, hunger and poverty claim 25,000 each day, 854 million people do not have enough food to eat—this is more than the population of the United States, Canada, and the European Union. The number of chronically hungry people worldwide is growing at an average of four million people per year. And every five seconds, a child dies because they are hungry.

Soon the voice of Revelation 6:6 will sound: *A measure of wheat for a penny......*A measure in Bible times was a quart, and a penny was a day's wages. Imagine a loaf of bread for a day's labor! It's coming — and soon!

Pestilences

AIDS and Avian flu have arrived and could destroy millions in the near future. Pestilence, the twin sister of hunger, is also on the rampage. Malaria, West Nile Virus, and Japanese Encephalitis are deadly diseases that are carried by the common mosquito. Malaria still kills millions around the globe annually. It is estimated that there are more than 300 million people in Africa who are infected with it.

The West Nile Virus is relatively new to the United States, with its first known appearance taking place in New York City in the summer of 1999. Since then, it has rapidly spread westward, infecting birds, humans, and horses. In 2004, the Centers for Disease Control and Prevention (CDC) reported more than 2,500 cases in the U.S. with 100 deaths. In 2003, there were more than 9,800 reported cases with more than 250 deaths.

Japanese Encephalitis is transmitted by mosquitoes that have fed on infected pigs and birds and then feed on humans. In 2005, Japanese Encephalitis killed over 1,000 people in India in just a few months' time. Biologists say that this is one of the 'most scary' diseases to contract because even though it is not often fatal, it does often cause brain damage in those who contract it.

Yes, the insect world is multiplying unbelievably. Entomologists estimate that the number has now climbed to one quintillion, representing five million different species. In fact, if a person could weigh all insects together, their combined weight would be 12 times that of the entire human race. Undoubtedly, the pestilence that Jesus predicted will soon rear its head in monstrous proportions and world hunger will be felt by every country on earth. This, along with what comes out of the bottomless pit in Revelation 9:2 (causing the plague of verse 3), is just around the corner. Listen to the prediction: *There came out of the smoke locusts upon the earth: and unto them was given power, as the scorpions of the earth have power.* Their purpose is to destroy and kill.

Earthquakes

Jesus also said, [There shall be] *earthquakes, in divers places* (Matthew 24:7).

Men foolishly say, "We've always had earthquakes. How can this be a sign?" Get ready, Mr. Skeptic! The Lord made this prediction around 30 AD. From the year He made the statement until 1959, a total of 24 major earthquakes were recorded. Since 1960, however, more than 96 major quakes have jostled the earth. Think of it—24 major quakes in 1,959 years, and over 96 in 48 years. Since I am of 2010 there have been major earthquakes weekly, some were around the world. The birth pains for the soon return of Yeshua for His church. How quickly could the hour of Tribulation soon engulf the world!

Signs in Space

Verses 27-30 of Matthew 24 tell us:

> *For as the lightning cometh out of the east, and shineth even unto the west; so shall also the coming of the Son of man be. For wheresoever the carcass is, there will the eagles be gathered together. Immediately after the tribulation of those days shall the sun be darkened, and the moon shall not give her light, and the stars shall fall from heaven, and the powers of the heavens shall be shaken: And then shall appear the sign of the Son of man in heaven.*

Luke adds to this account in chapter 21:25-26:

> *And there shall be signs in the sun, and in the moon, and in the stars and upon the earth distress of nations, with perplexity; the sea and the waves roaring; Men's hearts failing them for fear, and for looking after those things which are coming on the earth: for the powers of heaven shall be shaken.*

Now watch it. These signs point to the close of the Tribulation Hour because they signal the return of the King to earth. Verse 27 says, *Then shall they see the Son of man coming in a cloud with power and great glory.* This is the coming of Christ to set up His glorious millennial reign (see Revelation 20:6).

As stated previously, these space signs, which are to take place at the conclusion of the Tribulation Hour, or almost seven years after the believers' departure via the Rapture, are already showing partial fulfillment. Humans walking, driving, and planting a flag on the moon certainly make one realize that the signs are for 21st century citizens. Had one made such a prediction at the turn of the 20th century, he would have become a candidate for a mental institute.

Today, space activity has become so commonplace that no one even talks about the first step Neil Armstrong took on the moon in 1969.

To the argumentative skeptic who ridiculously states, "Oh, we have always had signs—nothing has changed. It's the same as it was in Grandma's day," I say, "Get your head out of the sand, Mr. Ostrich, and fix your eyes on the heavenlies. The space age is with us, and Christ's prophecies are occurring with such alarming rapidity that only a hardened heart could doubt it."

What do all these alarming facts signify? Jesus said, *When ye shall see all these things, know that it is near, even at the doors* (Matthew 24:33).

Are you ready? Are you winning others and preparing them for Christ's return? Let's live by the Holy Spirit's warning in Romans 13:11-12:

> *And that, knowing the time, that now it is high time to awake out of sleep: for now is our salvation nearer than when we believed. The night is far spent, the day is at hand: let us therefore cast off the works of darkness, and let us put on the armour of light.*

If ever believers needed to be living in a constant state of revival, it is now.350

Pope Benedict XVII on Easter Sunday, April 4, 2010 preached to his congregation that they need to be ready for the rapture. It is coming soon.351

2. Israel's temple and God's judgment

The plans for the rebuilding of the Temple gives ample proof we are rapidly approaching the final days of this era. First the Temple must be rebuilt; then the daily sacrifices must begin. Then the antichrist can enter the Holy of Holies. These preparations for the Temple show how close we are to the rapture of the church, the Great Tribulation, and the coming of the Messiah.352

The Church will not be subject to the wrath of God—which will be the judgment of God upon a sinful world for a period of 1,260 days or three and one-half years. The Church (or the bride of Christ) will be raptured to be with Yeshua who will receive His bride, the Church; and she will remain with Him forever. The Rapture or catching up of the saints will take place seven years before Messiah returns to Earth to rule in the millennial kingdom.

Those who are in the grave, as well as those who are alive who are in His will, will be raised to be with Him in heaven, to be judged for their works whether they are good like gold, silver or precious jewels, or are worthless and are wood, hay or stubble, to be judged by fire. Those whose works survive the fire will be honored by the Lord. If there are no good works, the believer will come to heaven saved by the blood of Yeshua but with no rewards of crowns. This judgment will take place during the great tribulation.

During the great tribulation many Jews and Gentiles will become believers. Many of these will be martyred for their faith and also because they will not take the mark of the Antichrist on the hand or forehead in order to buy and sell. Those who survive the great tribulation will be gathered at the end of the tribulation before the start of the millennial kingdom.

D. The bema judgment seat of Christ

At the bema judgment seat of Christ all the believers who ever lived will be judged according to their works of holiness and righteousness in their lives. It will take place in heaven after the Rapture of the Church. This judgment will not affect their salvation. Their lives will be judged by Yeshua on the basis of their works and heart attitude to see if there is real spiritual gold. The Lord has promised eternal rewards for those who have lived in holiness and obedience to His commands.

To rule and reign with Yeshua is part of the reward which belongs to the Christians in the Millennium and the new earth. Every believer has an opportunity to qualify for positions of leadership in the world by our obedience to Yeshua today.

There are five crowns that we as believers can receive:

---

[350] Van Impe, Dr. Jack. "Get Revived—He's Coming!" Lighting New Fires Inner Circle Report. Troy: Jack Van Impe Ministries. April 2008

[351] Jack Van Impe Presents (T.V Program, performer, writer, moderator) Jack Van Impe Ministries (Producer) Trinity Broadcasting Network. April 17, 2010.

[352] Jeffrey, Grant R. Heaven the Last Frontier. New York: Bantam Books, 1990.

1. The crown of life — for those who withstand tribulation and martyrdom for Christ — did not deny Him.

> *10 Do not be afraid of what you are about to suffer. I tell you, the devil will put some of you in prison to test you, and you will suffer for ten days. But be faithful, even if you have to die, and I will give you the crown of life..353*
>
> (Revelation 2:10, NCV)

2. The crown of glory — those who served as leaders and overseers of the flock with a right spirit of Yeshua

> *Now I have something to say to the elders in your group. I also am an elder. I have seen Christ's sufferings, and I will share in the glory that will be shown to us. I beg you to 2 shepherd God's flock, for whom you are responsible. Watch over them because you want to, not because you are forced. That is how God wants it. Do it because you are happy to serve, not because you want money. 3 Do not be like a ruler over people you are responsible for, but be good examples to them. 4 Then when Christ, the Chief Shepherd, comes, you will get a glorious crown that will never lose its beauty.354*
>
> (1 Peter 5:1-4, NCV)

1. The crown of rejoicing — to the one who brings others to Yeshua for salvation
2. The crown of righteousness—this crown to be given to all Christians that long for the return of Christ.

> *8 Now, a crown is being held for me—a crown for being right with God. The Lord, the judge who judges rightly, will give the crown to me on that day—not only to me but to all those who have waited with love for him to come again.355*
>
> (2 Timothy 4:8, NCV)

1. The incorruptible crown—crown of purity is for those who overcome in their daily spiritual struggles which they wage in their lives.

> *25 All those who compete in the games use self-control so they can win a crown. That crown is an earthly thing that lasts only a short time, but our crown will never be destroyed. 26 So I do not run without a goal. I fight like a boxer who is hitting something—not just the air. 27 I treat my body hard and make it my slave so that I myself will not be disqualified after I have preached to others.356*
>
> (1 Corinthians 9:25-27, NCV)

---

[353] The Holy Bible: New Century Version , Containing the Old and New Testaments. Dallas: Word Bibles, 1991.

[354] Ibid.

[355] Ibid.

[356] Ibid.

After the judgment of the believers, which will take place during the seven years of the tribulation, there will be the wedding feast for the bride of Christ and all the guests who will be at the feast. Among the guests will be those who are believers of Yeshua during the tribulation. The brethren of Yeshua will be the Jews who believe during the tribulation. These will be those who enter the messianic kingdom.

E. The coming of Antichrist

The third temple will be built before the Antichrist appears and takes control of the ten nations or regions of the revived Roman Empire and later the nations of the world.

Daniel foresaw in his vision of the seventy weeks that this coming world dictator would make a covenant (or peace treaty) for seven years (which is the beginning of the great tribulation).

> *24 A period of seventy sets of seven has been decreed for your people and your holy city to put down rebellion, to bring an end to sin, to atone for guilt, to bring in everlasting righteousness, to confirm the prophetic vision, and to anoint the Most Holy Place. 25 Now listen and understand! Seven sets of seven plus sixty-two sets of seven will pass from the time the command is given to rebuild Jerusalem until the Anointed One comes. Jerusalem will be rebuilt with streets and strong defenses, despite the perilous times. 26 After this period of sixty-two sets of seven, the Anointed One will be killed, appearing to have accomplished nothing, and a ruler will arise whose armies will destroy the city and the Temple. The end will come with a flood, and war and its miseries are decreed from that time to the very end. 27 He will make a treaty with the people for a period of one set of seven, but after half this time, he will put an end to the sacrifices and offerings. Then as a climax to all his terrible deeds, he will set up a sacrilegious object that causes desecration, until the end that has been decreed is poured out on this defiler.357*

> (Daniel 9:24-27, NLT)

Three and half years after the initial covenant signing, the dictator will break the treaty and enter the temple to defile it. No one is allowed in the temple except the priest. Only the high priest is allowed in the holy of holies and only on the Day of Atonement.

> *"The time will come when you will see what Daniel the prophet spoke about: the sacrilegious object that causes desecration standing in the holy place" — reader, pay attention!358*

> (Matthew 24:15, NLT)

The tribulation temple will be a false temple that preparations are in the process of being made. It will be a false temple because God's presence is not there. Here the Antichrist, who will have united with all the major religions of the world when this happens, will solve the problems of the

---

[357] Holy Bible: New Living Translation. Wheaton: Tyndale House, 1997.

[358] Ibid.

Temple Mount disagreements between the Jews and Arabs. At first he will appeal to both Jews and Muslins.

> *4 who opposes and exalts himself above all that is called God or that is worshiped,*
> *so that he sits as God in the Temple of God, showing himself that he is God.359*
>
> (2 Thessalonians 2:4, NKJV)

He will pose as a replacement for the Messiah, fooling both the Jew and Muslin. Then after he pronounces that he is god and desecrates the temple, the Jews will realize that they followed the wrong person.

The rebuilding of the temple will be an exciting milestone in the coming prophetic scenario. Yeshua said:

> *28 Now when these things begin to happen, look up and lift up your heads, because*
> *your redemption draws near.360*
>
> (Luke 21:28, NKJV)

Yeshua rightly prophesied, "if another comes in his own name you will receive him" (John 5:43).

> *3 Let no man deceive you by any means: for that day shall not come, except there*
> *come a falling away first, and that man of sin be revealed, the son of perdition; 4*
> *Who opposeth and exalteth himself above all that is called God, or that is wor-*
> *shipped; so that he as God sitteth in the Temple of God, shewing himself that he*
> *is God. 5 Remember ye not, that, when I was yet with you, I told you these things?*
> *6 And now ye know what withholdeth that he might be revealed in his time. 7 For*
> *the mystery of iniquity doth already work: only he who now letteth will let, until he*
> *be taken out of the way. 8 And then shall that Wicked be revealed, whom the Lord*
> *shall consume with the spirit of his mouth, and shall destroy with the brightness of*
> *his coming: 9 Even him, whose coming is after the working of Satan with all power*
> *and signs and lying wonders, 10 And with all deceivableness of unrighteousness in*
> *them that perish; because they received not the love of the truth, that they might be*
> *saved. 11 And for this cause God shall send them strong delusion, that they should*
> *believe a lie.361*
>
> (2 Thessalonians 2:3-11, KJV)

The man of sin will be revealed; he will proclaim himself to be god and sit in the temple of God. The Antichrist not only sits in the temple, but is in the temple of the heart of the people. Their hearts will be so deceived by the lies of Satan, that they will, without hesitation, accept him in their hearts. So they will harden their hearts to God's truth.

---

[359] The Holy Bible: The New King James Version. Nashville: Thomas Nelson, 1996, c1982.

[360] Ibid.

[361] The Holy Bible: King James Version. Oak Harbor: Logos Research Systems, Inc., 1995

God's judgment will be coming on the earth, yet there will be no repentance. They will even blaspheme the very God who is able to forgive.

> *15 And the kings of the earth, and the great men, and the rich men, and the chief captains, and the mighty men, and every bondman, and every free man, hid themselves in the dens and in the rocks of the mountains; 16 And said to the mountains and rocks, Fall on us, and hide us from the face of him that sitteth on the throne, and from the wrath of the Lamb.362*
>
> (Revelation 6:15-16, KJV)

> *20 And the rest of the men which were not killed by these plagues yet repented not of the works of their hands, that they should not worship devils, and idols of gold, and silver, and brass, and stone, and of wood: which neither can see, nor hear, nor walk: 21 Neither repented they of their murders, nor of their sorceries, nor of their fornication, nor of their thefts.363*
>
> (Revelation 9:20-21, KJV)

> *9 And men were scorched with great heat, and blasphemed the name of God, which hath power over these plagues: and they repented not to give him glory. 10 And the fifth angel poured out his vial upon the seat of the beast; and his kingdom was full of darkness; and they gnawed their tongues for pain, 11 And blasphemed the God of heaven because of their pains and their sores, and repented not of their deeds.364*
>
> (Revelation 16:9-11, KJV)

ANTICHRIST, THE ARK, AND THE TEMPLE

At some point during the lifetime of this generation, at God's appointed time, the Third Temple will be built, possibly following the War of Gog and Magog. The Holy of Holies in the Third Temple will once again house the ark of the covenant, which was the major object in the Temple that pointed clearly to the second coming of the Messiah. The ark is a profound symbol to the Jews and a guarantee of God's unbreakable covenant with Israel. The presence of the ark also will factor into the evil that will be brought about by the Antichrist during the Tribulation.

A quick overview of the seven-year Tribulation period shows that there are two distinct sections: (1) During the first half (three and a half years), the Antichrist presents himself as the messiah—an economic, political, religious, and military genius who rules globally and supports Israel.365

---

[362] Ibid.

[363] Ibid.

[364] Ibid.

[365] Jeffrey, Grant R. The New Temple and the Second Coming. Pages 175-176.

THE MAN OF SIN

The feeling of Hasidic Jews is if the Messiah builds the Temple and gathers all the Jews back to Israel, then we shall know he is Moshiach. Moshiach will come by his accomplishments and not through his pedigree...... Both Jews and non-Jews will recognize that he is responsible for all the wonderful improvements in the world: an end to war, an end to hunger, an end to suffering, a change in attitude.

This new Jewish concept of the messiah then is that of a mortal man and a leader with sufficient charisma to capture and command the admiration of the world — if not its devotion. He will not be recognized by his lineage (as the biblical Messiah — a descendant of the Davidic dynasty but by his acts of global significance.

Yeshua said to the Jews, 'I am come in my Father's name and ye received me not. "If another shall come in his own name, him ye will receive." (John 5:43)

This is a prophetic prophecy of the coming antichrist. Many Jews in the days ahead will follow the wrong commander. Perhaps this imposter, heralding in an age of peace and tolerance and understanding will somehow convince the Jews to accept a gentile presence on the Temple Mount.366

> *Then I was given a reed like a measuring rod. And the angel stood, saying, "Rise and measure the Temple of God, the altar, and those who worship there. 2 But leave out the court which is outside the Temple, and do not measure it, for it has been given to the Gentiles. And they will tread the holy city underfoot for forty-two months.367*

(Revelation 11:1-2, NKJV)

To begin the second period of three and a half years, the Antichrist will stop the Temple sacrifice. He will then be assassinated, and to the wonder of all humanity, he will be satanically resurrected. He will proclaim that he is 'god' and will defile the Holy of Holies. This defilement of the Temple by stopping the daily sacrifice begins the second half of the seven-year Tribulation (see Matthew 24:21). The prophet Daniel confirms that the elimination of the daily sacrifice in the Temple by the orders of the Antichrist will begin the three-and-a-half-year period (1,290 days) that will constitute the "Great Tribulation," the terrible persecution of the Antichrist under the Mark of the Beast police totalitarian control system (Daniel 12:11; Revelation 13:16-18). That three-and-a-half-year period of the Great Tribulation will end with the cataclysmic battle of Armageddon and Jesus Christ's triumphant return in glory to set up His kingdom on earth.

The apostle Paul warned about the son of perdition 'who opposeth and exalteth himself above all that is called God, or that is worshipped; so that he as God sitteth in the Temple of God, shewing himself that he is God' (2 Thessalonians 2:4). This prophecy will be fulfilled when the Antichrist enters the Third Temple and defiles the restored Ark of the Covenant, possibly by touching it or sitting on the mercy seat or worse. This would qualify as the abomination of desolation mentioned by Daniel and by Jesus (see Matthew 24:15). The Antichrist's defilement of the Holy Place is so abominable that the wrath of God will be instantly poured out on Jerusalem. Christ referred to this

---

[366] "Building the Third Temple," This week in Bible Prophecy. St Catharines: This Week in Bible Prophecy Inc. Vol. 3. Issue 4. April 1995. Pages 15-16.

[367] The Holy Bible: The New King James Version. Nashville: Thomas Nelson, 1996, c1982.

time: 'When ye therefore shall see the abomination of desolation, spoken of by Daniel the prophet, stand in the holy place, (whoso readeth, let him nderstand:) then let them which be in Judaea flee into the mountains...... For then shall be great tribulation, such as was not since the beginning of the world to this time, no, nor ever shall be' (Matthew 24:15-16, 21).

When the Prince of Darkness defiles the Temple, many Jews will recognize that he is a false messiah. After the Antichrist defiles the Temple, someone will kill him with a sword. It may be a Jewish believer who breaks through his security and succeeds in stabbing him with a sword in the head or neck. John's description of the assassination suggests the Antichrist will succumb to a head or neck wound: 'I saw one of his heads as it were wounded to death; and his deadly wound was healed: and all the world wondered after the beast' (Revelation 13:3). Revelation 13:12 repeats that his 'deadly wound was healed.' Later in the chapter, John elaborates about the 'beast, which had the wound by a sword, and did live' (verse 14).

After Satan raises the Antichrist from the dead, the Antichrist's partner, the false Prophet, will use this incredible event—probably watched by billions on the Internet, CNN, and other media outlets—to convince the world that the Antichrist is the long-awaited messiah. Once the Antichrist consolidates his control of Jerusalem and the Middle East, the False Prophet will force the people living under the jurisdiction of his world government to worship the Antichrist as 'god.' The 666 mark of the beast will be globally enforced as a totalitarian police control system. Those who submit to worship the antichrist as 'god' will accept the 666 mark on their foreheads or right hands. The righteous ones who reject the 666 will not be able to buy or sell anything and will be forced to go underground to escape being beheaded by forces of the Antichrist (Revelation 20:4).

From that point until the battle of Armageddon, 1,260 days later, the world will be convulsed with spiritual and physical warfare between the forces of the Antichrist and the Jews and Gentiles, who resist them. The Temple will probably be the initial battleground as the righteous priests battle to the death against supporters of the antichrist. Revelation 12:17 warns that 'the dragon was wroth [enraged] with the woman [Israel; the people of Israel], and went to make war with the remnant of her seed, which keep the commandments of God, and have the testimony of Jesus Christ.'368

Israel will make the futile mistake and accept the false peace and the false Messiah and false temple Jesus prophesied, "......if another shall come in his own name you will receive him" (John 5:43).

Apostle Paul speaks about the day of the Lord and His coming to Earth; he writes:

> *Let no man deceive you by any means: for that day shall not come, except there come a falling away first, and that man of sin be revealed, the son of perdition, who opposes and exalts himself above all this is called God, or that is worshipped: so that he as God sitteth in the Temple of God, shewing himself that he is god.*
>
> (2 Thessalonians 2:3-4)

For this reason a temple must be built because the Antichrist will dwell in the hearts of people because they have been deceived by the lies of Satan. Their hardened hearts will not desire truth. So for this reason "......God will send them a strong delusion that they should believe a lie."

God will send great judgments of destruction on those who will not repent of their sins.

---

368 Jeffrey, Grant R. The New Temple and the Second Coming. Pages 176-179.

In Revelation 16, the people's hearts are so filled with the lie of Satan that they accept the Antichrist wholeheartedly and blaspheme the very God who forgives.

> *9 And men were scorched with great heat, and blasphemed the name of God, which hath power over these plagues: and they repented not to give him glory. 10 And the fifth angel poured out his vial upon the seat of the beast; and his kingdom was full of darkness; and they gnawed their tongues for pain, 11 And blasphemed the God of heaven because of their pains and their sores, and repented not of their deeds.369*

(Revelation 16:9-11, KJV)

F. The False Prophet

Prophecy in the regards to the False Prophet from the "Sacred Theology of the Catholic Church" there are these prophecies:

It was prophecies in 1226 A.D "there is coming a time in the Catholic Church there will be fighting between Cardinal against Cardinal, Bishop against Bishop. This may be the hour because of the struggle in the church concerning pedifiles.

This from the Sacred Theologies of the Catholic Church:

In 1443 A.D, the Arch Bishop of Ireland received a prophecy from God about the Popes that will rule from his time into the future. There would be 112 popes. He was given each ones name and ensignia.

Pope #110- Pope John Paul II. Present pope is #111-Pope Benedict XVI. Pope #112 Peter Romano (Peter of Rome).

This information comes from a current Vatican Magazine.

Pope John Paul the Venerable, we honor you. Pope Benedict the Good Shepherd, we love you. Peter the Roman, we await you. This pope will rule the church during WWW III, armagedon.

Pope Benedict XVI is 83 years old. The next pope can come at anytime. This pope will defect from the faith.

Quote Catholic Archbishops Sheen said:

> The false prophet will have a religion with out a cross, a religion with out a world to come, a religion to destroy religions. There will be a counterfeit church. Christ's Church will be one, and the false prophet will create the other, the false church will be worldly, economical and global. It will be a loose federation of churches and religions forming some type of global association, a world parliament of churches. It will be emptied of all divine content and will be the mystical body of the anti-christ. The mystical body on earth today will have its Judus decent and he will be the false prophet. Satan will recruit him from among our Bishops.

From the book "The Keys of This Blood" by Malachi Martin

Malachi Martin was quoting Bishop Fulton Sheen a great Jesuits. He knew his theology he was a close friend of Pope John Paul. Quote from Malachi Martin,

---

369 The Holy Bible: King James Version. Oak Harbor: Logos Research Systems, Inc., 1995.

"That day, when this false prophet comes on the scene of Revelations 13:11, Roman Catholics will have the spectacle of a Pope validly elected. Who cut the entire visibule body of the church lose from the traditional unity, and the papacy oriented apostolic structure that the church has always hithert believed, and thought was divinely established.

The shudder that will shake the Roman Catholic Body in that day wil be the shudder of its death and agony, for its pains will be from within itself, orchestrated by its leaders and its members. No outside enemy will have brought this about. Many will accept the New Regime. Many will resist. All will be fragmented. There will be no one on Earth to hold the fragmenting members of the visible Roman Catholic Body together as a living compact organization. Men will then be able to ask for the first time in the history of the church. Where is the visible body of the church that Christ founded? And there will be none.

Jack Van Impe asked,

Can a Bishop or Cardinal defect? Remember what happened at Notradome, a Jesuit school. Our president who is all for abortion and was honored with doctor's degrees. In order for the president to be honored, they had to cover up every religious symbol that referred to Christ. The same thing happened when the President went to speak at Georgetown University they also had to cover the religious symbols.

The false prophet (pope) could come from any liberal Catholic Bishop or Cardinal school around the world. The symbol of the false prophet is a lamb with a horn. The lamb symbolizes the Messiah but the horns shows that there will be a satan's influence. (Revelation 13:11)

The false prophet will emerge and exercise the beast authority, making the people of Earth to worship the beast and his image. The false prophet will perform great miraculous signs and deceive those who reject the real Messiah, Yeshua. (Revelation 13:88)

The people of the world await Peter Roma, the false prophet.370

Why two More Temples?

God will allow Antichrist to have his brief moment in history is to demonstrate that the way of evil is futile, fruitless, and fleeting. The dark reign of Antichrist over the land of Israel and the world from the third Temple for a meager three-and-a-half-year period will furnish a contrast with the light of Messiah's thousand-year reign. His kingdom will shine forth with true peace and lasting solutions to the problems of this world—problems which were initiated by mankind and which came to their ultimate fruition under the dominion of Antichrist. This lesson of history will be reinforced by the further contrasts of the third and forth Temples.

|The third Temple will be employed by Antichrist when he makes his false claims to be Messiah and sets up his false image in the Holy of Holies, defiling the sanctity of the Temple. This event will give rise to the final three-and-one-half years of the tribulation which will be the greatest

---

370 Jack Van Impe president (T.V. program) performer, writer, moderator, Jack Van Impe Ministries Producer, Trinity Broadcasting Network. December 16, 2009.

time of persecution Jews and Gentile believers have ever know. While the third Temple will be a last days Temple, it will not be the last, but will lead to the final Temple that planet Earth will see—the Messiah's millennial Temple, "the house of prayer for all the peoples" (Isaiah 56:7).371

G. Israel's purging and escape

Israel is set for an exodus greater than that of Egypt. When the Seventh Seal of the wrath of God is revealed from heaven, Israel will undergo her greatest testing and her deepest purification. It will last about 3 ½ years. It will be worse than the time of the Maccabees (1 Maccabees 1:41-62).

Installation of Gentile Cults
(Cp 2 Macc. 6.1 – 17; Mt 24.15; Mk 13.14)

> *41 Then the king wrote to his whole kingdom that all should be one people, 42 and that all should give up their particular customs. 43 All the Gentiles accepted the command of the king. Many even from Israel gladly adopted his religion; they sacrificed to idols and profaned the sabbath. 44 And the king sent letters by messengers to Jerusalem and the towns of Judah; he directed them to follow customs strange to the land, 45 to forbid burnt offerings and sacrifices and drink offerings in the sanctuary, to profane sabbaths and festivals, 46 to defile the sanctuary and the priests, 47 to build altars and sacred precincts and shrines for idols, to sacrifice swine and other unclean animals, 48 and to leave their sons uncircumcised. They were to make themselves abominable by everything unclean and profane, 49 so that they would forget the law and change all the ordinances. 50 He added, "And whoever does not obey the command of the king shall die." 51 In such words he wrote to his whole kingdom. He appointed inspectors over all the people and commanded the towns of Judah to offer sacrifice, town by town. 52 Many of the people, everyone who forsook the law, joined them, and they did evil in the land; 53 they drove Israel into hiding in every place of refuge they had. 54 Now on the fifteenth day of Chislev, in the one hundred forty-fifth year, they erected a desolating sacrilege on the altar of burnt offering. They also built altars in the surrounding towns of Judah, 55 and offered incense at the doors of the houses and in the streets. 56 The books of the law that they found they tore to pieces and burned with fire. 57 Anyone found possessing the book of the covenant, or anyone who adhered to the law, was condemned to death by decree of the king. 58 They kept using violence against Israel, against those who were found month after month in the towns. 59 On the twenty-fifth day of the month they offered sacrifice on the altar that was on top of the altar of burnt offering. 60 According to the decree, they put to death the women who had their children circumcised, 61 and their families and those who circumcised them; and*

371 Ice, Thomas and Randall Price. "Tribulation and Beyond." <u>Ready to Rebuild</u>. Harvest House Publishers. Pages 206-207.

they hung the infants from their mothers' necks. 62 But many in Israel stood firm and were resolved in their hearts not to eat unclean food.372

(1 Maccabees 1:41-62, NRSV)

It will be worse than when Hitler persecuted six million Jews by putting them in the gas chambers of Europe. This included men, women and children.

This tribulation will be the worse since the beginning of the world. Unless those days were shortened no flesh would be saved; but for the elect's sake those days will be shortened [For Israel's sake the days will be limited] (Matt 24:21,22).

Daniel 9:27 speaks of the antichrist who "in the midst of the week he shall cause the sacrifice and the oblation to cease." At this time he will break the peace treaty with Israel at the halfway point of the last seven years of Gentile history, and forbids them to exist as a Jewish state. Halfway into the seven-year Middle East treaty, the Antichrist will outlaw the practice of Judaism, as did the Syrian, Antiochus Epiphanies. He will also defile the Holy of Holies of the Temple and make the Temple desolate.373

During the Day of the Lord, which is during the last seven years of Gentile history, the Lord will break seven seals. They are as follows:

1. With the first seal came the Antichrist on the political scene, taking dominion through false peace in the Middle East.
2. With the second seal came war
3. With the third seal came famine
4. With the fourth seal came disease and death resulting from the wars.
5. With the fifth seal came the persecution of believers both of the Church and the nation of Israel.
6. With the sixth seal came cosmic disturbances, such as prolonged darkness and signs in the heavens with increased earthquakes on Earth.
7. There was silence in heaven for about one-half an hour getting ready for the trumpet judgments of God.

John writes of this time that the heaven will roll back like a scroll and men will run to the mountains looking for safety, "for the great day of His (God's) wrath is come: and who shall be able to stand?" (Revelation 6:17).

At this time God will send an angel to place His mark on 144,000 Jews from the twelve tribes of Israel and the church will be raptured (Reference Revelation 7:1-8).

9 After this I beheld, and, lo, a great multitude, which no man could number, of all nations, and kindreds, and people, and tongues, stood before the throne, and before the Lamb, clothed with white robes, and palms in their hands; 10 And cried with a loud voice, saying, Salvation to our God which sitteth upon the throne, and unto the Lamb. 14 And I said unto him, Sir, thou knowest. And he said to me, These are they

---

372 The Holy Bible : New Revised Standard Version. Nashville: Thomas Nelson, 1996, c1989.

373 Johnian, Mona. Life in the Millennium. Pages 86-87.

which came out of great tribulation, and have washed their robes, and made them white in the blood of the Lamb.374

(Revelation 7:9-10, 14, KJV)

H. Judgment of Gentile nations

The coming of the Messiah and the judgment of the nations will take place after the great tribulation of seven years.

After the great tribulation of the Jews and the world, Yeshua will return to Earth a second time and it will be visible to all who are on the earth during the tribulation. He will descend from heaven on the clouds riding on a white horse followed by the armies of heaven (Revelation 19:11, 14).

Yeshua will return to Israel in the same manner and same place in which He was taken into heaven:

11 Which also said, Ye men of Galilee, why stand ye gazing up into heaven? this same Jesus, which is taken up from you into heaven, shall so come in like manner as ye have seen him go into heaven.375

(Acts 1:11, KJV)

4 And his feet shall stand in that day upon the mount of Olives, which is before Jerusalem on the east, and the mount of Olives shall cleave in the midst thereof toward the east and toward the west, and there shall be a very great valley; and half of the mountain shall remove toward the north, and half of it toward the south.376

(Zechariah 14:4, KJV)

The Messiah will descend to Earth on the Mount of Olives opposite the Temple Mount, according to the prophet Zechariah (ref. Zechariah 14:3-4). Then a great earthquake will split the earth from the Mediterranean through the Mount of Olives to the Dead Sea. Yeshua will cross the Kidron Valley as He did on Palm Sunday almost two thousand years ago. The Battle of Armageddon will end in the triumphant victory of the heavenly army of Christ. He will set up His eternal rule from the city of Jerusalem which will ultimately produce the greatest blessings the world has ever known.

The prophet Ezekiel declared that the promised Messiah would enter the sealed Eastern Gate of the Temple Mount into the rebuilt sanctuary. The Bible tells the followers of Messiah that they will reign and rule with Messiah forever.

1 Afterward he brought me to the gate, even the gate that looketh toward the east: 2 And, behold, the glory of the God of Israel came from the way of the east: and his voice was like a noise of many waters: and the earth shined with his glory. 4 And the glory of the LORD came into the house by the way of the gate whose prospect

---

[374] The Holy Bible: King James Version. Oak Harbor: Logos Research Systems, Inc., 1995.

[375] Ibid.

[376] The Holy Bible: King James Version. Oak Harbor: Logos Research Systems, Inc., 1995.

*is toward the east. 5 So the spirit took me up, and brought me into the inner court;
and, behold, the glory of the LORD filled the house.377*

(Ezekiel 43:1, 2, 4, 5, KJV)

Amazingly this gate has been shut for many centuries. The Moslems, under Suleiman the Magnificent, built a large graveyard in front of the Eastern Gate to prevent Messiah from coming. In their religious belief a priest or holy man would be defiled by walking through a graveyard. They felt that this gravesite would prevent the Messiah from fulfilling Ezekiel's prophecy.

Yeshua returns to Earth from heaven to establish His kingdom. Yeshua's glory will include both His humanity and His divinity. He will at that time be Judge, King, Teacher, Shepherd and Redeemer of mankind. He will be revealed as the true "Son of David". He will show His righteousness, holiness, mercy and goodness as He rules the planet. He will receive the worship of mankind He rules. Finally Jerusalem will become the "City of Peace" because the Prince of Peace will rule forever. The oppression of the evil government prior to Yeshua's return will be replaced by the benevolent protection of a just and loving Savior.

The covenant which God made with Abraham and the kingdom promises to David, Solomon and the prophets, will be finally realized in the Millennial Kingdom. These promises of peace, justice, prosperity and eternal blessings for Israel and the nations will find fulfillment when Christ sets up His throne in Jerusalem. In addition to the material promises, the Lord promised a new covenant with Israel in which He would give them "a new heart," forgiveness of sin, and the infilling of the Spirit to the renewed nation. This promised kingdom will provide the fulfillment of all the hopes and dreams of the chosen people forever.378

The Jews will be gathered from the four corners of the earth to live in Israel.

Under the direction of Yeshua, the resurrected believers of the Church will provide the leadership for a just society among the nations.

The saints reign with Christ one thousand years.

*4 And I saw thrones, and they sat upon them, and judgment was given unto them:
and I saw the souls of them that were beheaded for the witness of Jesus, and for the
word of God, and which had not worshipped the beast, neither his image, neither
had received his mark upon their foreheads, or in their hands; and they lived and
reigned with Christ a thousand years. 5 But the rest of the dead lived not again until
the thousand years were finished. This is the first resurrection. 6 Blessed and holy is
he that hath part in the first resurrection: on such the second death hath no power,
but they shall be priests of God and of Christ, and shall reign with him a thousand
years.379*

(Revelation 20:4-6, KJV)

Land will bloom as a rose and the curse of sin will be removed from the earth.

---

377 Ibid.

378 Jeffrey, Grant R. Heaven the Last Frontier. New York: Bantam Books, 1990. Page 132.

379 The Holy Bible: King James Version. Oak Harbor: Logos Research Systems, Inc., 1995.

17 Is it not yet a very little while, and Lebanon shall be turned into a fruitful field, and the fruitful field shall be esteemed as a forest? 18 And in that day shall the deaf hear the words of the book, and the eyes of the blind shall see out of obscurity, and out of darkness.380

(Isaiah 29:17-18, KJV)

The nations of the world will face Yeshua at His judgment seat following their defeat at the Battle of Armageddon.

The armies of the Asian nations and the army of the nations of the West that will be left by the Antichrist, the leader of the revived Roman Empire in Europe, will fight in the Valley of Megiddo, also known as the Battle of Armageddon, to destroy Israel and each other in a bloody struggle for world supremacy. Yeshua will interrupt this battle by returning to Earth at that moment with His heavenly army of angels and Christian saints.

19 And I saw the beast, and the kings of the earth, and their armies, gathered together to make war against him that sat on the horse, and against his army.381

(Revelation 19:19, KJV)

Both armies will turn from fighting each other to fighting Yeshua and His army. They will be defeated in the greatest military disaster of history. The Bible states that the whole valley will be a river of blood and mud so that the horse will sink into "up to the horse's bridle."

Yeshua will destroy the Antichrist who caused Israel and the nations so much devastation and persecution.

8 And then shall that Wicked be revealed, whom the Lord shall consume with the spirit of his mouth, and shall destroy with the brightness of his coming: 9 Even him, whose coming is after the working of Satan with all power and signs and lying wonders.382

(2 Thessalonians 2:8-9, KJV)

The nations will be judged by Yeshua on the basis of their treatment of both the Jews and the Gentile believers according to Matthew 25:31-46. Those nations which protected God's people will be called "sheep nations." They will be preserved to enjoy the blessings of the millennial kingdom and eternity. Those nations which despised and persecuted the people of God will be judged as "goat nations"—those nations will cease to exist in the future.

31 When the Son of man shall come in his glory, and all the holy angels with him, then shall he sit upon the throne of his glory: 32 And before him shall be gathered all nations: and he shall separate them one from another, as a shepherd divideth his sheep from the goats: 33 And he shall set the sheep on his right hand, but the goats on the left. 34 Then shall the King say unto them on his right hand, Come, ye

---

[380] Ibid.

[381] Ibid.

[382] Ibid.

blessed of my Father, inherit the kingdom prepared for you from the foundation of the world.383

(Matthew 25:31-34, KJV)

Individuals left at this time will also be judged individually by God as the basis of their acceptance or rejection of the pardon of Yeshua's blood.

After the judgment of the Antichrist and the false prophet, Yeshua sits on His throne with the saints and His angels and judges the people left on the earth. The sheep, the righteous believers, will be separated to His right hand. Yeshua will then begin by honoring the believing dead, starting with the Old Testament saints, then the New Testament saints, those of the church age and then the tribulation saints. Yeshua honors each one and says, "Well done, good and faithful servant."

Revelation 5:10 tells us that Yeshua has redeemed us and has "made us kings and priests to our God; and shall reign on Earth." Leadership during the Millennium may be exercised in other areas besides governmental functions, such as education, hospitals and various social organizations. There must be nations in the future, both in the Millennium and the future new earth. If our countries will bless Israel and Gentile believers in Yeshua during the great tribulation when they are judged by Yeshua as a "sheep nation," they will be allowed to continue their existence under the King of God forever.

The unbelievers will go to His left (the goats). Yeshua will say, "Depart from Me, you cursed, into the everlasting fire prepared for the devil and his angels; for I was hungry and you gave Me no food; I was thirsty and you gave Me no drink. I was a stranger and you did not take Me in, naked and you did not clothe Me, sick and in prison and you did not visit Me."

The people will respond, "Lord, when did we see You hungry or thirsty or a stranger or naked or sick or in prison and did not minister to You?"

Yeshua will reply, "Assuredly I say to you inasmuch as <u>you did it not unto the least of My brethren</u> you did it not to Me. You will go away to everlasting punishment, but the righteous into eternal life."

Then a wide chasm will open in the earth and swallow them up. They will be cast into outer darkness and await the great white throne judgment after the Millennium. They were given many warnings, yet they continued to be lovers of themselves rather than of God.

A subgroup of the believers will be the Jewish believers which are a part of Yeshua's brethren who will go into the Millennium who believe in Messiah's redemptive work.

The second coming of Christ will accomplish several purposes of God. It will close the Church age and fulfill prophecies concerning the great and terrible day of the Lord (Joel 2:11; Malachi 4:5). It will show Messiah's rescue and fight for Israel.

2 For I will gather all nations against Jerusalem to battle; and the city shall be taken, and the houses rifled, and the women ravished; and half of the city shall go forth into captivity, and the residue of the people shall not be cut off from the city. 3 Then shall the LORD go forth, and fight against those nations, as when he fought in the day of battle.384

(Zechariah 14:2-3, KJV)

---

383 Ibid.

384 The Holy Bible: King James Version. Oak Harbor: Logos Research Systems, Inc., 1995.

At this time Gentile world power as well as Satan's rule over the earth through the Antichrist and the false prophet will end.

20 And the beast was taken, and with him the false prophet that wrought miracles before him, with which he deceived them that had received the mark of the beast, and them that worshipped his image. These both were cast alive into a lake of fire burning with brimstone.385

(Revelation 19:20, KJV)

1 And I saw an angel come down from heaven, having the key of the bottomless pit and a great chain in his hand. 2 And he laid hold on the dragon, that old serpent, which is the Devil, and Satan, and bound him a thousand years, 3 And cast him into the bottomless pit, and shut him up, and set a seal upon him, that he should deceive the nations no more, till the thousand years should be fulfilled: and after that he must be loosed a little season.386

(Revelation 20:1-3, KJV)

Messiah's second coming will also prepare Israel to enter His kingdom.

The Jewish people will be gathered, judged, cleansed, regenerated and established in their own land (Isaiah 27:12-13; Ezekiel 20:30-38, Ezek 36:25).

The surviving gentiles will also be prepared to enter the Millennial Kingdom. They too will be gathered and judged (Matthew 25:31-46) whether they are Jewish or Gentile, only those who are born again will enter the Messiah's Kingdom.387

---

385 Ibid.

386 Ibid.

387 LaHaye, Tim and Jerry B. Jenkins. "Kingdom Come." (last book in Left Behind Series) Carol Stream: Tyndale House Publishers, Inc. Pages xi-xlvi, 1-66, 343-356.

PART V

REIGN OF MESSIAH YESHUA

CHAPTER FOURTEEN

The Millennium

A. Timeline of Millennium

1. Coming events

Future days are suggested because coming Biblical events seem to fulfill the last three Feasts of Israel.

Kislev 25— Year 8	REDEDICATION OF THE MILLENNIAL TEMPLE 45 days after the mourning period is over appears to fall on the first day of Hanukkah, ("dedication")! It was the day the Second Temple was rededicated after the Maccabees seized it from Antiochus Epiphanies, the Syrian tyrant. Note: This follows Daniel's schedule: (1,290 + 45 = 1,335 days—Dan. 12:12).388
	C. The Millennium and Beyond
7th Millennium	One thousand years of peace under Messiah who will rule with an iron scepter (Ps. 2:9; Rev. 2:27; 19:15). The saints (Jews and Gentiles) will reign with Jesus (2 Tim. 2:12; Rev. 3:21) and be given authority over the nations (Rev.2:26). They will govern the 12 tribes of Israel (Matt. 19:28), administer cities (Luke 19:17ff), and ultimately judge the world and (fallen) angels (1 Cor. 6:2f).
End of 7th Millennium	Satan will be released briefly to test those born on earth during the millennium. A huge number will band together and rebel against God's authority. They will march across the earth and surround Jerusalem. Fire will come down from heaven and devour them. Then, Satan will be thrown into the lake of fire to join the beast and the false prophet. They will be tormented day and night forever (Rev. 20:7ff).

---

388 Kremers, Mari F. "Review of Dates." God intervenes in the Middle East. Pages 288-289.

After Man's Final Rebellion	The Resurrection of the wicked dead. The Great White Throne Judgment: (Rev. 20:11-15) (1) People who will not accept Messiah's covering of righteousness and forgiveness will stand before God's Judgment, clothed in their own self-will and deeds. (2) Fallen angels who have been waiting in darkness and chains (2 Pet. 2:4; Jude 6).
Post Judgment	At the start of the eight millennia: *"The heavens will disappear with a roar; the elements will be destroyed by fire, and the earth and everything in it will be laid bare (burned up, KJV)"* (2 Pet. 3:10; Matt. 24:35). *"Earth and sky fled from His presence"* (Rev. 20:11). There will be a new heaven, a new earth, and a new Jerusalem. There will be no more death, mourning, crying, or pain for the old……things shall pass away.390

B. The interval between Yeshua's second return and the beginning of the Millennium.

75-day interval

Daniel 12:11-12 indicates a seventy-five day interval between the glorious appearing of Christ on Earth after the Battle of Armageddon and the start of the thousand year kingdom.

> *And from the time that the daily sacrifice is taken away, and the abomination of desolation is set up, there shall be one thousand two hundred and ninety days. Blessed is he who waits, and comes to the one thousand three hundred and thirty-five days.*

Yeshua returns at the end of the seventieth week (Daniel 9:24-27) which is divided into 1,260 days each. A careful reading of the entire chapter of Daniel 12 tells us that Christ's return occurs at the end of the second set of 1,260 days.

Daniel 12:11 speaks of something accomplished at the end of 1,290 days……thirty days beyond the glorious appearing of Yeshua.

In Ezekiel 40:48, it tells us that the Lord will establish a temple during the Millennium. It is most likely during this thirty-day period. There the temple sacrifices will be restored.

Daniel 12:12 says "blessed are those who reach 1,335 days" which is an additional 45 days. The "blessed" are those who are qualified to enter the millennial messianic kingdom where Yeshua will be the chief ruler.

From this we conclude that the seventy-five-day interval is the time of preparation of the temple and for the kingdom. Since the earth had been destroyed during the judgments of the tribulation and the earth had been leveled except for the area surrounding Jerusalem, it seems logical that the Lord would renovate His Creation in preparation for the millennial kingdom.

During the seventy-five-day interval, Yeshua will set about recreating Eden on Earth. Every day the landscape will change from complete desolation to full-grown greenery— everything will be perfect from the plants, shrubs, trees, grasses, fields and orchards. The earth will teem with produce and animals of all kinds.

---

[389] Ibid. Page 292.

The newly-developed city of Jerusalem will see its boundary expand to accommodate the new temple, eighteen miles north of the city near Shiloh. It will be massive. A paved causeway will lead all the way from Jerusalem to the new temple where the courtyard alone will be larger than the old city had been......more than a mile square. The neighborhood for priests and Levites will encompass an area of forty to fifty miles, more than six times the size of greater London and ten times the circumference of the original ancient walled city. The reason for the immense size of the Millennium temple is because the entire population of the earth will make use of it at one time or another.

Isaiah the prophet foretold this time:

> *The parched ground shall become a pool, and the thirsty land springs of water; in the habitation of jackals, where each day, there shall be grass with reeds and rushes. A highway shall be there and a road shall be called the highway of Holiness. The unclean shall not pass over it, but it shall be for others.*

> *Whoever walks the road, although a fool, shall not go astray. No lion shall be there, nor shall any ravenous beast go upon it; it shall not be found there. But the redeemed shall walk there, and the ransomed of the Lord shall return and come to Zion with singing, with everlasting joy on their heads. They shall obtain joy and gladness and sorrow and sighing shall flee away. Isaiah 36:7- 10 KJV*

The desire for eating meat will be gone. The food will come from the bounty of the trees and bushes and vines as well as the harvest from the earth.

> *18 But be glad and rejoice forever in what I create;*
> *For behold, I create Jerusalem as a rejoicing,*
> *And her people a joy.*
> *19 I will rejoice in Jerusalem,*
> *And joy in My people;*
> *The voice of weeping shall no longer be heard in her,*
> *Nor the voice of crying.*
> *20 " No more shall an infant from there live but a few days,*
> *Nor an old man who has not fulfilled his days;*
> *For the child shall die one hundred years old,*
> *But the sinner being one hundred years old shall be accursed.*
> *21 They shall build houses and inhabit them;*
> *They shall plant vineyards and eat their fruit.*
> *22 They shall not build and another inhabit;*
> *They shall not plant and another eat;*
> *For as the days of a tree, so shall be the days of My people,*
> *And My elect shall long enjoy the work of their hands.*
> *23 They shall not labor in vain,*
> *Nor bring forth children for trouble;*
> *For they shall be the descendants of the blessed of the LORD,*
> *And their offspring with them.*
> *24 " It shall come to pass*

> *That before they call, I will answer;*
> *And while they are still speaking, I will hear.390*
> (Isaiah 65:18-24, NKJV)

> *9 At that time I will change the speech of the peoples to a pure speech, that all of*
> *them may call on the name of the LORD and serve him with one accord.391*
>
> (Zephaniah 3:9, NRSV)

The people will speak in Hebrew even though they don't know a word of it.

The light of the sun and moon will be brighter because they are supercharged by the Shekinah glory of Messiah Yeshua.

> *Moreover the light of the moon will be as the light of the sun, And the light of the*
> *sun will be sevenfold, as the light of seven days, in the day that the LORD binds up*
> *the bruise of His people and heals the stroke of their wound.392*
>
> (Isaiah 30:26, NKJV)

> *But be glad and rejoice forever in what I create; for behold, I create Jerusalem as*
> *a rejoicing, and her people a joy. I will rejoice in Jerusalem, And joy in My people;*
> *The voice of weeping shall no longer be heard in her, Nor the voice of crying. No*
> *more shall an infant from there live but a few days, or an old man who has not ful-*
> *filled his days; For the child shall die one hundred years old, But the sinner being*
> *one hundred years old shall be accursed.*
>
> (Isaiah 65:18-20, NKJV)

God will plant within you the desire and ability to do all that needs to be done yourself. Your prayers will be instantly heard. You will meet for worship with friends and loved ones as well as new acquaintances of all colors and nationalities. The animals will be at peace with one another as well as with man.

> *25 The wolf and lamb will feed together. The lion will eat straw like the ox. Poi-*
> *sonous snakes will strike no more. In those days, no one will be hurt or destroyed*
> *on my holy mountain. I, the LORD, have spoken!393*
>
> (Isaiah 65:25, NLT)

C. The wedding feast

The wedding takes place during the seven-year tribulation when the bride and the bridegroom become one. After the seventy-five days of Messiah's return, the celebration of the wedding of the

---

[390] The Holy Bible: The New King James Version. Nashville: Thomas Nelson, 1996, c1982.

[391] The Holy Bible : New Revised Standard Version. Nashville: Thomas Nelson, 1996, c1989.

[392] The Holy Bible: The New King James Version. Nashville: Thomas Nelson, 1996, c1982.

[393] Holy Bible: New Living Translation. Wheaton: Tyndale House, 1997.

lamb takes place and all who are in the kingdom are invited to come and partake. They will come from the East, the West, the South and the North to sit with the bride and with Yeshua.

Millions of people will come to the marriage supper. The bride of Yeshua will consist of all born-again believers from the time of Pentecost until the Rapture. Also present will be friends of the Bridegroom as well as the guests.

The banquet tables will be lined up for miles to take care of all who are invited to the feast. The guests may either sit or recline at the table as desired. The table will be filled with fresh fruits and vegetables that were harvested from the earth that was restored to the fruitfulness like the Garden of Eden.

The people who sit or recline to eat and drink and worship and sing and celebrate the introduction of the bride, her companions, and friends of the Bridegroom — including all of Israel — will be those who have been redeemed by their faith in God before the time of the Church or who have become tribulation saints.

In the sky will be the angels who sing praises and glory to the Lamb who was slain and now the Bridegroom who honors His own bride. His bride will feel loved and wooed by Yeshua with His everlasting love.

After the wonderful feast that will last for days, everyone will return to their own nations and towns to begin rebuilding their homes and towns, as well as infrastructures, such as mass communications, transportation such as airplanes, and computers to restore all the modern conveniences such as running water and electricity.

Many people will start building their homes and other beautiful dwellings from the raw materials such as wood and stone that Yeshua will provide in the renewed earth.

Each year representatives of all nations will make their annual sojourns to the temple in Jerusalem for the Feast of Tabernacles. Yeshua wants all the citizens of the world to enjoy the bounty of His new Creation.

> *16 And it shall come to pass, that every one that is left of all the nations which came against Jerusalem shall even go up from year to year to worship the King, the LORD of hosts, and to keep the feast of tabernacles.394*
>
> (Zechariah 14:16, KJV)

> *10 Sing and rejoice, O daughter of Zion: for, lo, I come, and I will dwell in the midst of thee, saith the LORD. 11 And many nations shall be joined to the LORD in that day, and shall be my people: and I will dwell in the midst of thee, and thou shalt know that the LORD of hosts hath sent me unto thee. 12 And the LORD shall inherit Judah his portion in the holy land, and shall choose Jerusalem again. 13 Be silent, O all flesh, before the LORD: for he is raised up out of his holy habitation.395*
>
> (Zechariah 2:10-13, KJV)

This starts when the children of Israel return to their country because God plans on dwelling with His people in Jerusalem.

---

394 The Holy Bible: King James Version. Oak Harbor: Logos Research Systems, Inc., 1995.

395 Ibid.

20 But the LORD is in his holy Temple: let all the earth keep silence before him.396
(Habakkuk 2:20, KJV)

Currently, God dwells in His holy temple in heaven but he will move to His holy temple in Jerusalem during the Millennium. Here the Father will acknowledge His Son.

The Lord has said to me, "You are my Son, today I have begotten you. Ask of me, and I will give you the nations for your inheritance, and the ends of the earth for your possession. You shall break them with a rod of iron; you shall dash them to pieces like a potter's vessel."

Serve the Lord with fear and rejoice. Kiss the Son lest He be angry and you perish in the way, when His wrath is kindled but a little. Blessed are all those who put their trust in Him.
Yeshua said:

Know that I am the Lord your God. I dwell in Zion on my holy mountain. Jerusalem shall be holy and no aliens shall ever pass through here again. Judah shall abide forever. For, I your Lord dwell in Zion. The Mountain of my house is hereby established and shall be exalted above the hills; all nations shall flow to it. Many shall say, "Come, let us go up to the mountain of the Lord to the house of the god of Jacob; and will teach us His ways and we shall walk in his paths, for out of Zion shall go forth the law, and my word from Jerusalem."

Those who are in the kingdom will realize that Yeshua is all that matters. There will be no jealousy, envy or sin. Their greatest joy will be in serving and worshiping their Lord, who brought them to Himself.

D. Life in the Millennium

Millennium is derived from the Latin words *mille* (1,000) and *annum* (year).

The Millennium is the time that Christ's kingdom, after the Rapture and tribulation, will take place and prior to the creation of a new heaven and Earth. During this time Yeshua will reign physically on Earth. His light will illumine the globe. His justice will prevail. It seems inconceivable that anyone will reject Him, yet scripture prophecy is clear in that when Satan is loosed for a season at the end of the Millennium, even though there are many believers on Earth, there will be those who will live for themselves and become the army of rebellion against God.

1. Israel in the Millennium
Israel's borders were fixed by God 4,000 years ago when He covenanted with Abraham. (Gen 15:18 quote.)

---

[396] Ibid.

18 In the same day the LORD made a covenant with Abram, saying, Unto thy seed have I given this land, from the river of Egypt unto the great river, the river Euphrates.397

(Genesis 15:18, KJV)

The land of Israel will eventually extend from Egypt to Iraq. His influence during the Millennium is going to be much larger. It will be world wide.

The Nations of the earth will send ambassadors to Israel seeking wisdom that will flow out of its government just as the ancient kings went to Solomon for the same reason.

Jerusalem, the capital of Israel and of the whole earth, will measure twelve miles square.398

Ezekiel saw the exact dimensions of the Millennial Sanctuary in Jerusalem from which Yeshua will rule the earth (ref. Ezekiel 43:10-12; 45:9; 47:13; 48:7; 48:23-29).

The vision of Ezekiel (chapters 40-48) — was a complete architectural rendering of God's future plans for the nation, the land and the individual tribes of the descendants of Isaac, Abraham's son.399

Messiah showed Ezekiel the pattern of His future home, and all the ordinances that would be conducted in it, including the sin offering as Israel once sacrificed for their sin. Throughout the millennium, Israel will be offering sacrifices to God as a reminder to themselves of the sacrifice Messiah paid for their salvation.400

The church of present believing Jews and Gentiles already accepted the sacrificial death and shed blood of Yeshua. In the Millennium the nation of Israel will acknowledge the same.

'And so all Israel will be saved as it is written……the delivered will come out of Zion, and He will turn away ungodliness from Jacob' (Romans 11:26).

When the Millennium first begins it will be filled with only believers. Then a new generation of children will be born; and the innocent children from the tribulation period will be there. They will all be sinners needing of forgiveness and salvation.

Many people will come from the East and West and sit down with Abraham, Isaac and Jacob in the millennial kingdom. The resurrected saints will not marry but those who reach the Millennium alive will marry and have children. The millennial kingdom will be made up of the resurrected saints with glorified bodies and those who came through the tribulation and have entered the millennial kingdom in their natural bodies will be able to marry and have children.

The children will be born into the world without birth pangs, and then must come to the place of their repentance and a decision to become followers of Christ.

These children will be raised in the nurture and admonition of the Lord, and they will live in the physical presence of Christ. They will also be influenced, not only by their immediate family, but by also every other person with whom they come into contact. If they do not receive the Lord into their hearts by the age of one hundred, God will annihilate them. Many parents will be praying and encouraging their children to receive the Lord, while some of the children of the tribulation

---

[397] The Holy Bible: King James Version. Oak Harbor: Logos Research Systems, Inc., 1995.

[398] Johnian, Mona. Life in the Millennium. Pages 83-84.

[399] Ibid. Page 85.

[400] Ibid. Page 86.

(the Gentiles—as well as children of the Millennium) will think God is cruel, who kills unbelievers who do not make Yeshua Lord of their lives.

Scripture is quite clear that at the end of one thousand years, Satan will be loosed from the bottomless pit; then he will tempt all the young people of all the nations. He will amass an army that will be as numerous as the sand on the seashores. Not only will there be young people choosing their own ways, but they will rebel against Yeshua and follow Satan.

No one born during the time of the kingdom will die before the age of one hundred. When someone dies at one hundred he will be considered young because everyone else will live for the entire Millennium. They will expose themselves as unbelievers. The only ones who die will be Gentiles who do not trust Christ for their salvation. The Jews will already have a heart for God.

This will be a time of general prosperity and health both for the Jew and the Gentile.

And when he comes, he will open the eyes of the blind and unstop the ears of the deaf. 6 The lame will leap like a deer, and those who cannot speak will shout and sing! Springs will gush forth in the wilderness, and streams will water the desert.401

(Isaiah 35:5-6, NLT)

There will be joy and songs of thanksgiving, and I will multiply my people and make of them a great and honored nation. 20 Their children will prosper as they did long ago. I will establish them as a nation before me, and I will punish anyone who hurts them.402

(Jeremiah 30:19-20 (NLT)

Distribute the land as an inheritance for yourselves and for the foreigners who have joined you and are raising their families among you. They will be just like native-born Israelites to you, and they will receive an inheritance among the tribes.403

(Ezekiel 47:22, NLT)

The house of Israel will be saved because of God's covenant with Israel. Jeremiah wrote:

"Behold the days are coming," says the Lord, "When I will make a new covenant with the house of Israel and the house of Judah. I will put my law in their minds, and write it on their hearts; and I will be their God and they shall be my people. No more shall every man teach his neighbor, and every man his brother saying, 'Know the Lord;' for they shall know me, from the least of them to the greatest of them. For I will forgive their iniquities, and their sin I will remember no more." "The day will come," says the LORD, "when I will make a new covenant with the people of Israel and Judah. 32 This covenant will not be like the one I made with their ancestors when I took them by the hand and brought them out of the land of Egypt. They broke that covenant, though I loved them as a husband loves his wife," says the LORD.

---

[401] <u>Holy Bible: New Living Translation</u>. Wheaton: Tyndale House, 1997.

[402] Ibid.

[403] Ibid.

*33 "But this is the new covenant I will make with the people of Israel on that day,"
says the LORD. "I will put my laws in their minds, and I will write them on their
hearts. I will be their God, and they will be my people. 34 And they will not need to
teach their neighbors, nor will they need to teach their family, saying, 'You should
know the LORD.' For everyone, from the least to the greatest, will already know
me," says the LORD. "And I will forgive their wickedness and will never again
remember their sins."404*

(Jeremiah 31:31-34, NLT)

The millennial kingdom starts out idyllic—even the animals will be at peace with each other
and mankind.

The animal kingdom will be at peace in the millennial kingdom.

> *The wolf also shall dwell with the lamb,*
> *The leopard shall lie down with the young goat,*
> *The calf and the young lion and the fatling together;*
> *And a little child shall lead them.405*
> (Isaiah 11:6, NKJV)

Towards the end, the Millennium will be populated by those who — against all odds, and all
reason—will spawn the fire of war that the sin would fuel.

The government will start with Yeshua in Jerusalem. His authority will extend to His prince,
David, the king of Israel. The apostles will judge over the twelve tribes. There will also be princes
with local judges under them, as well as counselors throughout the world. Last of all will be
the worthy Gentiles who made it through seven years of tribulation into the millennial kingdom.
Those who proved themselves worthy of Yeshua's honor He will honor as His worthy servants.
Other rulers of the people will be the resurrected saints—the saints who were given position in the
kingdom because their works on Earth were judged worthy.

2. The Millennium will begin sinless

The life in the kingdom will be purposefully active. In the Millennium the Lord declares that
man will have a just economy which will provide joyous and purposeful employment of the skills
of men.

The Gentile nations that survive God's purging will continue to live and operate as natural
people. They will work, build, marry and rear families. In all the nations, (civil), and religious laws
will be mandatory. They will marry and rear families and operate as natural people.406

> *2 In the last days, the Temple of the LORD in Jerusalem will become the most impor-*
> *tant place on earth. People from all over the world will go there to worship. 3 Many*

---

404 Holy Bible: New Living Translation. Wheaton: Tyndale House, 1997.

405 The Holy Bible: The New King James Version. Nashville: Thomas Nelson, 1996, c1982.

406 Johnian, Mona. Life in the Millennium. Pages 174-175.

nations will come and say, "Come, let us go up to the mountain of the LORD, to the Temple of the God of Israel. There he will teach us his ways, so that we may obey him." For in those days the LORD's teaching and his word will go out from Jerusalem. 4 The LORD will settle international disputes. All the nations will beat their swords into plowshares and their spears into pruning hooks. All wars will stop, and military training will come to an end.407

(Isaiah 2:2-4 (NLT)

8 The LORD hath sworn by his right hand, and by the arm of his strength, Surely I will no more give thy corn to be meat for thine enemies; and the sons of the stranger shall not drink thy wine, for the which thou hast laboured: 9 But they that have gathered it shall eat it, and praise the LORD; and they that have brought it together shall drink it in the courts of my holiness.408

(Isaiah 62:8-9, KJV)

The relationship with Yeshua and the people will be like it was with "Adam and Eve who walked with God in the cool of the day." Their relationship will be a daily walk with God which includes every aspect of their exciting and purposeful lives.

The interests and skills you have will be used in the kingdom. It will be a joyful life without fear or poverty.

13 Then shall the virgin rejoice in the dance, both young men and old together: for I will turn their mourning into joy, and will comfort them, and make them rejoice from their sorrow. 14 And I will satiate the soul of the priests with fatness, and my people shall be satisfied with my goodness, saith the LORD.409

(Jeremiah 31:13-14, KJV)

E. The millennial temple

1. Ezekiel's vision of the millennial temple

One of the most hotly debated questions related to the future Temple is who will build it, the Jewish people or the coming Messiah? Some Jewish sages held that God's command in the Torah demands that Israel must first rebuild the Temple. Exodus 25:8 declares, 'Let them make me a sanctuary; that I may dwell among them.' However, other authorities held that Israel should wait until the Messiah comes to build the Temple Himself. They pointed to the messianic message of the prophet Zechariah (6:12) where the prophet predicted: 'Behold the man whose name is The BRANCH; and he shall grow up out of his place, and he shall build the Temple of the Lord.'

The resolution of this apparent contradiction will be found in the fact that the Scriptures declare there must be two more Temples in Israel's future. The Third Temple will be built by the Jews in the near future on the Temple Mount. This Third Temple is the one that will be defiled by the Anti-

---

[407] Holy Bible: New Living Translation. Wheaton: Tyndale House, 1997.

[408] The Holy Bible: King James Version. Oak Harbor: Logos Research Systems, Inc., 1995.

[409] Ibid.

christ, launching the Great Tribulation. Finally, the Third Temple will be cleansed by the coming of Jesus Christ as Israel's great High Priest and Messiah following His victory over the Antichrist in the battle of Armageddon. The Fourth Temple, described by the prophets Ezekiel and Zechariah, will then be built by Jesus the Messiah during the millennial kingdom; thus fulfilling both prophecies (see diagram). The Temple built by the Messiah will be the fourth and eternal Temple for the Millennium. This millennial Temple will exceed even the glory of the Third Temple.

The millennial Temple will be enormous, with walls extending more than one mile in each direction. If fact, the Fourth Temple will be so large that it could not possibly fit on the existing Temple Mount or even within the boundaries of the walled Old City of Jerusalem. The land measurements given in Ezekiel (chapters 40-48) indicate that the Messiah will build the Fourth Temple approximately twenty-five miles north of the walled city of Jerusalem.

In every detail this Fourth Temple differs from the Third Temple that must be built by the Jews on the present Temple Mount. The Scriptures do not say whether the Third Temple will coexist with the millennial Temple during the Millennium. However, in light of Daniel's prophecies that Christ will cleanse and sanctify the Third Temple after the Antichrist's defilement, it appears that the newly rebuilt Third Temple will continue to be used for worship during the thousand-year rule of Christ on earth. Israel will finally enjoy its long-awaited peace under the reign of the Messiah.

Additionally, Ezekiel prophesied a thirteen fold division of the land from Dan to Beer-sheba during the Millennium, which will provide each of Israel's twelve tribes with a parallel portion of land stretching horizontally from the Mediterranean Sea to the great Euphrates River (see Ezekiel 48:1-35). Each strip will be 25,000 rods in width measuring north to south (225,000 feet, or 43.25 miles wide). In the center of Israel a special portion of land called the Prince's Portion will be reserved for use by the Nassi, the Messiah (see Ezekiel 45:1-4). The Prince's Portion will contain the new, enlarged city of Jerusalem and the Fourth Temple. The dimensions of the new city of Jerusalem will be a 4,500-rod square, about 7.75 miles on each side.

Dr. Alfred Edersheim, the author of *The Temple*, explained that according to tradition, the boundary line between the ancient tribal allotment of Judah and Benjamin ran directly through the Old City of Jerusalem and the Temple.5 Ezekiel describes the thirteenth portion of the land for the holy oblation (containing the millennial Temple, the new city of Jerusalem, and the Prince's Portion allotted to the Messiah) as lying between the tribal allotments of Judah and Benjamin once again (see Ezekiel 48:8-10,22). While the other tribes will enjoy possession of their tribal portion forever, the prophet declares that the Levites will not inherit land. Instead, they will dwell in the portion known as the holy oblation with their beloved Messiah and receive their income from the Temple.

THE SIZE OF THE MILLENNIAL TEMPLE

The new Temple Mount area in the Millennium will be enormous. The Bible states, 'There shall be for the sanctuary five hundred [rods] in length, with five hundred [rods] in breadth, square round about' (Ezekiel 45:2). A rod is equal to 6 cubits or 9 feet, when a cubit is defined as eighteen inches, so each side of the Fourth Temple will measure 4,500 feet—almost one mile long! The world has never seen such a massive structure. This measurement would yield a Temple area of 20.25 million square feet. For the sake of comparison, the Second Temple, built and enlarged by King Herod, was the largest Temple enclosure in history: it encompassed almost thirty-five acres. The entire Temple Mount area that survives today, remains thirty-five acres. In other words, Ezekiel's prophecy revealed that the future millennial Temple will be thirty-six times larges than the Second Temple!

The glory of this millennial Temple will be manifested in the eternal presence of the Shekinah Glory of God. Ezekiel had witnessed in his earlier vision (see Ezekiel 11:22-23) the tragic departure of the Shekinah Glory from Solomon's Temple because of Israel's spiritual rebellion. Fortunately, God's plan of redemption for Israel and the gentiles includes His promise that Jesus the Messiah will return in His glory to inhabit the Temple of God. When the Devine Presence dwells once again in Jerusalem, the Jews will take their position as God's chosen people in their Promised Land. Through Israel, God will bless all the nations of the world. God's promise was given through Ezekiel: 'Then will I sprinkle clean water upon you, and ye shall be clean: from all your filthiness, and from all your idols, will I cleanse you' (Ezekiel 36:25). The prophecies reveal that it will not be long until the Messiah will return to fulfill all that God has promised concerning the redemption of Israel.410

ISRAEL'S FOUR TEMPLES

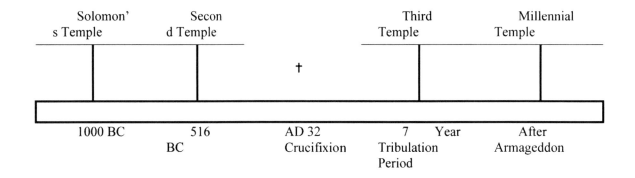

2. Ezekiel's city — a millennial vision

Ezekiel 40-48 describes Ezekiel's detailed vision of that future Temple and the rejuvenated land at the end of times. 'This vision was given Ezekiel in 25th year of captivity. Fourteen years after Jerusalem was destroyed (Ezekiel 40:1) 597 BC — 25 years = 572 BC and 586 BC — 14 years = 572 BC.411

1. The detailed plans showed all the porches, posts, chambers, room, courts, windows, altars with their detailed measurements.
2. Future temple will have beauty as well as functionality.

---

410 Jeffrey, Grant R. The New Temple and the Second Coming. Colorado Springs: Waterbrook Press. Pages 179-183.

411 Cohen, Dr. Gary G. "Zion's Fire. Ezekiel's City — A Millennial Vision." Middle East News & World Views. Orlando: Zion's Hope Inc., July/August 1998. Page 21.

3. There will be ceremonial sacrifices in the millennial temple (Ezekiel 40:39-43). God is conveying here through Ezekiel's word that forgiveness, acceptance and holiness, will be a part of His future provision for his people.412

4. There will be a renewed priesthood serving in this temple (Ezekiel 40:46; 42:13). 'There will be priests. They will take care of the holy altar and hence they must have been redeemed by God. Ezekiel 40:46 says they will be 'Zadok — Levi Priests. This emphasizes that the proper and true priestly line will be restored. They will be of the Cohen line.'413

5. There will be singing again in the temple (Ezekiel 40:44) 'chambers for the singer.' Joyous singing of holy praises to the true God of Grace will be restored.

6. The Shekinah glory will again fill this temple (Ezekiel 43:1-5). 'This implies that the nation would be restored to favor and again have God's peace and protection.'

7. God's name shall not again be defiled in the age of the millennial temple (Ezekiel 43:7).

8. The Eastern Gate is awaiting the Prince, the Messiah to enter it (Ezekiel 44:1-3). Messiah who entered the gate during His life on Earth will enter it again when He returns. Currently this gate has been sealed since the sixteenth century unto this day. It was sealed by Suleiman the Magnificent, the Turkish Sultan who rebuilt Jerusalem and its walls.

1 Then He brought me back to the outer gate of the sanctuary which faces toward the east, but it was shut. 2 And the LORD said to me, "This gate shall be shut; it shall not be opened, and no man shall enter by it, because the LORD God of Israel has entered by it; therefore it shall be shut. 3 As for the prince, because he is the prince, he may sit in it to eat bread before the LORD; he shall enter by way of the vestibule of the gateway, and go out the same way."414

(Ezekiel 44:1-3, NKJV)

9. No unsaved person shall enter into the millennial sanctuary (Ezekiel 44:9).

9 Thus saith the Lord GOD; No stranger, uncircumcised in heart, nor uncircumcised in flesh, shall enter into my sanctuary, or any stranger that is among the children of Israel.415

(Ezekiel 44:9, KJV)

10. The Sabbath shall again be observed in Israel (Ezekiel 46:1).

1 Thus saith the Lord GOD; The gate of the inner court that looketh toward the east shall be shut the six working days; but on the sabbath it shall be opened, and in the day of the new moon it shall be opened.416

(Ezekiel 46:1, KJV)

---

412 Ibid. Page 22.

413 Ibid.

414 The Holy Bible: The New King James Version. Nashville: Thomas Nelson, 1996, c1982.

415 The Holy Bible: King James Version. Oak Harbor: Logos Research Systems, Inc., 1995.

416 Ibid.

11. The Dead Sea will become part of a fresh water system in this new temple age (Ezekiel 47:1-12). Ezekiel witnesses water seeming to rise from beneath the temple area and then sees these waters rising and going eastward toward the Dead Sea. He is told that the waters shall be healed and that fishers shall stand upon it from En-gedi. En-gedi is on the western side of the Dead Sea about in the Middle......God says He will make it happen as part of the dynamic restoration of the land.417

12. The land will be re-divided again with the ancient tribes each assigned a tract (Exodus 47:13-48:30). Land will be parceled out by God, and peace will prevail.

13. The twelve gates of the millennial city shall be named for each of the twelve tribes (Ezekiel 48:31-34).

14. The name of the city shall be called "The Lord is there" (Ezekiel 48:35); in Hebrew this is "Jehovah Shammah." Ezekiel's blessed vision was of the millennial temple.418

3. More details concerning the temple and worship

The prophet Micah (740 BC) wrote about the Millennium temple:

> *In the last days, the Temple of the LORD in Jerusalem will become the most important place on earth. People from all over the world will go there to worship.419*
>
> (Micah 4:1, NLT)

Two centuries later Haggai (520 BC) wrote:

> *The future glory of this Temple will be greater than its past glory, says the Lord Almighty. And in this place I will bring peace. I, the Lord Almighty, have spoken!420*
>
> (Haggai 2:9, NLT)

> *Tell him that the LORD Almighty says: Here is the man called the Branch. He will branch out where he is and build the Temple of the LORD. 13 He will build the LORD's Temple, and he will receive royal honor and will rule as king from his throne. He will also serve as priest from his throne, and there will be perfect harmony between the two.421*
>
> (Zechariah 6:12-13, NLT)

---

417 Cohen, Dr. Gary G. "Zion's Fire. Ezekiel's City — A Millennial Vision." Middle East News & World Views. Orlando: Zion's Hope Inc., July/August 1998. Page 23.

418 Ibid. Page 22.

419 Holy Bible: New Living Translation. Wheaton: Tyndale House, 1997.

420 Ibid.

421 Ibid.

15 At that time I will bring to the throne of David a righteous descendant, and he will do what is just and right throughout the land.422

(Jeremiah 33:15, NLT)

The prophecy is in regards to the temple only. Yeshua bears the glory and will sit on the throne of David.

The gateway that will face east will be at the top of a set of stairs that are the width of the wall. Each gate chamber will be the same length and width as is the vestibule of the inside gate.

The eastern gateway will have three chambers on one side and three on the other—again all the same size.

From the front of the entrance gate to the front of the vestibule of the inner gate will be beveled window frames in the gate chambers and in their intervening archways on the inside of the gateway all around, likewise in the vestibules; and all around the inside on each gatepost will be palm trees.

In the outer court, thirty chambers will face a pavement that extends all the way around. These same features will appear on all four sides of the temple. Gateposts will face the outer court, and palm trees will stand on its gateposts on both sides and seven steps will lead up to it. There will be a chamber that has eight tables equipped for sacrificial offerings which will be to remind the people that Yeshua was the sacrificial Lamb. There the priests will slay the burnt offerings, the sin offerings and the trespass offering. There will also be four tables of hewn stone for the burnt offering, and on these they will lay the instruments with which they will slaughter the burnt offerings and the sacrifice. There will be hooks fastened around the room where the flesh of sacrifice will hang before it is put on the altar.

The offerings that will be acceptable will be a bull for sin offering, as well as ram or a kid of the goats. They all have to be without blemish so they can be used for the various sin and trespass offerings required by the Mosaic Law. The sacrificial altar will be located in front of the temple.

Outside the inner gate will be the chambers for the singers in the inner court. The chamber facing south will be for priests who have charge of the temple. The priests will be of the sons of Zadok of the tribe of Levi. They will minister to the Lord Yeshua.

Ezekiel also foretold the sacred vessels and linen robes would be prepared for use in future temple during the Millennium.

16 They shall enter into my sanctuary, and they shall come near to my table, to minister unto me, and they shall keep my charge. 17 And it shall come to pass, that when they enter in at the gates of the inner court, they shall be clothed with linen garments; and no wool shall come upon them, whiles they minister in the gates of the inner court, and within.423

(Ezekiel 44:16-17, KJV)

The sons of Zadok, who kept charge of God's sanctuary when the children of Israel went astray, shall come near to minister. No priest shall drink wine when he enters the inner court. They

---

[422] Ibid.

[423] The Holy Bible: King James Version. Oak Harbor: Logos Research Systems, Inc., 1995.

shall not take as a wife a widow or a divorced woman, but a virgin of the descendants of the house of Israel, or they may marry a widow of a priest.

They shall teach Yeshua's people the difference between holy and unholy and cause them to discern between the clean and unclean. They shall also teach His law and statues.

The beauty of the architecture of the most holy place will be breathtaking. The width of the structure will increase from the lowest story to the highest. The doors of the side chambers will open onto a terrace—one door toward the north, one the other toward the south. The three stories opposite the threshold will be paneled with wood from the ground to the windows embellished with cherubim and palm trees—a palm tree between cherub and cherub. Each cherub will have two faces, so that the face of a man is toward a palm tree on one side, and the face of a young lion toward a palm tree on the other side. This design will be throughout the temple all around.

The doorposts of the temple will be square, like the front of the sanctuary. The altar will be made of wood. It will be located in the holy of holies.

In the north and south courts there will be chambers on the opposite courtyard. The chambers will be built into the thickness of the wall. There will be a walk in front of them.

The north and south chambers are holy chambers where the priests approach the Lord with the most holy offerings. When the priests come out of the holy chamber, before they go to the people, they will remove their garment that they use for ministry, for they are holy. They must put on other clothing when they approach the people.

This is the law of temple: the whole area surrounding the mountaintop where the temple sits is most holy.

The outer gate of the sanctuary on the east is to remain shut because the Lord God of Israel has entered into it. As for the prince, he may sit and eat bread before the Lord, but he shall enter by the way of the vestibule of the gateway and go out the same way.

The purpose of the temple throughout Scripture has been to establish a location upon the earth for the presence of God to be revealed, and through the ritual, shows God's holiness to His people.

The new millennial law will contain a mixture of Mosaic-type laws with totally new non-Mosaic laws not found in the original 613 laws. Yeshua will be physically present, instead of the Shekinah glory with the ark of the covenant. The new temple will measure one square mile in area (Ezekiel 40:48-41:26) instead of the smaller Solomonic model (reference Ezekiel 40-48). This speaks of the temple size and the sacrificial system.

The sacrifices will not deal with sin, but will provide ritual cleansing of the priests, sanctuary and utensils. Only Yeshua's sacrifice on the cross can actually remove one's sin. The ceremonial uncleanness will be dealt with during the Millennium because Yahweh will be dwelling on Earth in the midst of a sinful and unclean people. This sacrificial system will be a temporary one which will last only one thousand years.

> *20 And thou shalt take of the blood thereof, and put it on the four horns of it, and on the four corners of the settle, and upon the border round about: thus shalt thou cleanse and purge it.*424

(Ezekiel 43:20, KJV)

---

424 The Holy Bible: King James Version. Oak Harbor: Logos Research Systems, Inc., 1995.

26 Seven days shall they purge the altar and purify it; and they shall consecrate themselves.425

(Ezekiel 43:26, KJV)

The atonement is specifically directed at the cleansing of the altar in order to make it ritually clean. The other uses of atonement have to do with the cleansing of objects so the ritual purity may be maintained for proper worship (Ezekiel 45:15, 17, 20).

It will serve as a memorial to Yeshua's once-for-all atoning work. In the same way the Lord's Supper includes this aspect (1 Corinthians 11:23-26).

The ark of the covenant will no longer be important because Yeshua will be present to be worshipped directly as the Messiah King.

16 And it shall come to pass, when ye be multiplied and increased in the land, in those days, saith the LORD, they shall say no more, The ark of the covenant of the LORD: neither shall it come to mind: neither shall they remember it; neither shall they visit it; neither shall that be done any more. 17 At that time they shall call Jerusalem the throne of the LORD; and all the nations shall be gathered unto it, to the name of the LORD, to Jerusalem: neither shall they walk any more after the imagination of their evil heart.426

(Jeremiah 3:16-17, KJV)

In the millennial temple service, the various temple sacrifices are specifically called "memorials" (Exodus 30:16; Leviticus 2:2, 9; 5:16; 24:7, Numbers 5:15, 18, 26). The millennial believers will observe the sacrifices as a memorial of Yeshua's sacrificial provision and death. The millennial temple and its rituals will serve to be a daily reminder of fallen man's need before a Holy God and a lesson about how this same God lovingly works to remove the obstacle of human sin for those who trust Him.

At the door of the temple there will be water flowing from under the threshold of the temple toward the eastern region. It will go down into the valley and enter the sea. When it reaches the sea, the waters will be healed. Wherever the river goes, it will heal the lands, and there shall be a great multitude of fish from En Gedi, to En Eglaim, to the great sea.

The land where the temple compound is located is holy to the Lord. The rest of the land of Israel will be for general use by the city, for dwellings and agriculture. The city shall be in the center. The produce shall be for the workers of the city who shall cultivate it.

Yeshua has made a covenant of peace with His people. It shall be an everlasting covenant. He will establish them and cause them to multiply. He will set His sanctuary in their midst forever. His tabernacle shall be with them. He will be their God and they shall be His people. The nations will also know that He is the Lord, and have sanctified Israel, since His sanctuary is in their midst forevermore. The name of the city from that day forward shall be: The Lord Is There.

The fourth temple (millennial temple) will be built by the Messiah approximately twenty- five miles north of the present city of Jerusalem.

---

[425] Ibid.

[426] Ibid.

12 And speak unto him, saying, Thus speaketh the LORD of hosts, saying, Behold the man whose name is The BRANCH; and he shall grow up out of his place, and he shall build the Temple of the LORD.427

(Zechariah 6:12, KJV)

The glory of the millennial temple will be the eternal presence of the Shekinah glory of God that will dwell there. Messiah will return in all His glory to inhabit the tabernacle of God forever. God's divine presence will once again dwell in Israel. Then the Promised Land will be a blessing to all the nations of the world. God's promise in the words of Ezekiel: "Then I will sprinkle clean water upon you and you shall be clean from all your filthiness and from all your idols, will I cleanse you" (ref. Ezekiel 36:25). In the near future the Messiah will come and fulfill all the great prophecies of the redemption of Israel and the Promised Land.

Then the man brought me back to the entrance of the Temple. There I saw a stream flowing eastward from beneath the Temple threshold. This stream then passed to the right of the altar on its south side. 2 The man brought me outside the wall through the north gateway and led me around to the eastern entrance. There I could see the stream flowing out through the south side of the east gateway. 3 Measuring as he went, he led me along the stream for 1,750 feet and told me to go across. At that point the water was up to my ankles. 4 He measured off another 1,750 feet and told me to go across again. This time the water was up to my knees. After another 1,750 feet, it was up to my waist. 5 Then he measured another 1,750 feet, and the river was too deep to cross without swimming. 6 He told me to keep in mind what I had seen; then he led me back along the riverbank. 7 Suddenly, to my surprise, many trees were now growing on both sides of the river! 8 Then he said to me, "This river flows east through the desert into the Jordan Valley, where it enters the Dead Sea. The waters of this stream will heal the salty waters of the Dead Sea and make them fresh and pure. 9 Everything that touches the water of this river will live. Fish will abound in the Dead Sea, for its waters will be healed. Wherever this water flows, everything will live. 10 Fishermen will stand along the shores of the Dead Sea, fishing all the way from En-gedi to En-eglaim. The shores will be covered with nets drying in the sun. Fish of every kind will fill the Dead Sea, just as they fill the Mediterranean! 11 But the marshes and swamps will not be purified; they will be sources of salt. 12 All kinds of fruit trees will grow along both sides of the river. The leaves of these trees will never turn brown and fall, and there will always be fruit on their branches. There will be a new crop every month, without fail! For they are watered by the river flowing from the Temple. The fruit will be for food and the leaves for healing.428

(Ezekiel 47:1-12, NLT)

God will cause a great river of healing, which will come from under the temple eastward toward the desert to the Dead Sea. God promises that the land shall be miraculously healed and

---

427 The Holy Bible: King James Version. Oak Harbor: Logos Research Systems, Inc., 1995.

428 Holy Bible: New Living Translation. Wheaton: Tyndale House, 1997.

the waters of the Dead Sea shall come alive with abundant fish. Then it shall be a place to spread forth the nets.

The prophet also tells that the land of Israel will finally enjoy its long-awaited peace under the reign of Messiah. He will rule from the throne of David in Jerusalem.

In the middle of Israel will be a portion called the "Prince's Portion" for the Messiah. This portion will also contain the new enlarged city with the fourth temple and *Terumah*, which will contain the temple and new city. Ezekiel describes the sacred plot of land that will be set aside for God on the north of the city as the *Terumah*.

> *When you divide the land among the tribes of Israel, you must set aside a section of it for the LORD as his holy portion. This piece of land will be 81/3 miles long and 62/3 miles wide. The entire area will be holy ground. 2 A section of this land, measuring 875 feet by 875 feet, will be set aside for the Temple. An additional strip of land 871/2 feet wide is to be left empty all around it. 3 Within the larger sacred area, measure out a portion of land 81/3 miles long and 31/3 miles wide. Within it the sanctuary of the Most Holy Place will be located. 4 This area will be a holy land, set aside for the priests who minister to the LORD in the sanctuary. They will use it for their homes, and my Temple will be located within it.429*

> (Ezekiel 45:1-4, NLT)

A curious feature of the prophecy shows that the old Temple will be between Judah and Benjamin while portion for the Temple city and Messiah home will be between Judah and Benjamin. While the other tribes will enjoy possession of their tribal portion forever, the prophet declares that the Levites will not inherit the land. They will dwell in the Prince's Portion with their Messiah and enjoy the tithes of the people as their reward and possession.430

4. Music in the Millennium

During the Millennium a magnificent choir of countless people will sing the song of Moses.

> *Then Moses and the people of Israel sang this song to the LORD:*
> *"I will sing to the LORD, for he has triumphed gloriously;*
> *he has thrown both horse and rider into the sea.*
> *2 The LORD is my strength and my song;*
> *he has become my victory.*
> *He is my God, and I will praise him;*
> *he is my father's God, and I will exalt him!*
> *3 The LORD is a warrior;*
> *yes, the LORD is his name!*
> *4 Pharaoh's chariots and armies,*
> *he has thrown into the sea.*
> *The very best of Pharaoh's officers*

---

[429] Ibid.

[430] Jeffrey, Grant R. Heaven the Last Frontier. New York: Bantam Books, 1990. Pages 204-205.

have been drowned in the Red Sea.
5 The deep waters have covered them;
they sank to the bottom like a stone.
6 " Your right hand, O LORD,
is glorious in power.
Your right hand, O LORD,
dashes the enemy to pieces.
7 In the greatness of your majesty,
you overthrew those who rose against you.
Your anger flashed forth;
it consumed them as fire burns straw.
8 At the blast of your breath, the waters piled up!
The surging waters stood straight like a wall;
in the middle of the sea the waters became hard.
9 "The enemy said, 'I will chase them,
catch up with them, and destroy them.
I will divide the plunder,
avenging myself against them.
I will unsheath my sword;
my power will destroy them.'"431
(Exodus 15:1-9, NLT)

A choir will sing the song of the Lamb:

Then I saw in heaven another significant event, and it was great and marvelous. Seven angels were holding the seven last plagues, which would bring God's wrath to completion. 2 I saw before me what seemed to be a crystal sea mixed with fire. And on it stood all the people who had been victorious over the beast and his statue and the number representing his name. They were all holding harps that God had given them. 3 And they were singing the song of Moses, the servant of God, and the song of the Lamb:

> *Great and marvelous are your actions, Lord God Almighty. Just and true are your ways, O King of the nation.432*

(Revelation 15:1-3, NLT)

The choir of 144,000 redeemed will sing a song only they know.

This great choir sang a wonderful new song in front of the throne of God and before the four living beings and the twenty-four elders. And no one could learn this song except those 144,000 who had been redeemed from the earth.433

(Revelation 14:3, NLT)

---

[431] Holy Bible: New Living Translation. Wheaton: Tyndale House, 1997.

[432] Ibid.

[433] Ibid.

Many of Psalms will be sung by those who desire God's blessing. Only God knows the heart of those who truly seek Him. Our primary responsibility is to 'give unto the Lord due his name.' Every person's life is to be a public worshiper of God.434 This comes before helping the poor, the hurting, and the hungry which are charitable, Christian deeds. God's dream is to have a people who love him above everything else.435

5. Feasts and Sabbaths

During the Millennium it will be a time of feasting and celebrating which are the purposes of holidays or Holy Days, which were to be set aside for worship and refreshing the total person.
There are eight feasts which the apostle Paul referred to. They are:

• Weekly Sabbath
• Feast of Passover
• Unleavened Bread
• First Fruits
• Feast of Pentecost
• Feast of Tabernacles
• Feast of Trumpets
• Feast of Atonement

These eight feasts of God are to be perpetual forever, and they hold a great significance for the believer in the days to come.
The Sabbath has now come to mean "a time to rest your mind and body now from the routine of work." A spiritual intention is far greater. The Bible tells us that Sabbaths range from:

1 day	Exodus 16:23-39
2 days	Leviticus 23:6-8
1 year	Leviticus 25:4
70 years	2 Chronicles 36:31
Eternity	Hebrews 4:9

Sabbath began in heaven. The first day God rested from natural work, Sabbath went into effect in eternity.
Sabbath is as simple as God's desire to fellowship with His man created in His image— also man's desire to draw life and strength from his creator through worship.

---

434 Johnian, Mona. Life in the Millennium. Pages 194-197.

435 Ibid.

"As surely as my new heavens and earth will remain, so will you always be my people, with a name that will never disappear," says the LORD. 23 "All humanity will come to worship me from week to week and from month to month.436

(Isaiah 66:22-23, NLT)

The Millennium will observe the Sabbath days and keep the feast of God.437

F. Justice system

Yeshua will teach the nations how to settle their differences peacefully. His policies are going to transform man's understanding of what it takes to prosper at living. But natural life will continue.438

(Mortal Gentiles who are alive at Yeshua's coming will have a role in governing themselves. Zechariah warns of the punishment upon the Gentile Nations that do not send representatives to Jerusalem each year during the Feast of Tabernacles.) They will be judged by a lack of rain.

In the end, the enemies of Jerusalem who survive the plague will go up to Jerusalem each year to worship the King, the LORD Almighty, and to celebrate the Festival of Shelters. 17 And any nation anywhere in the world that refuses to come to Jerusalem to worship the King, the LORD Almighty, will have no rain. 18 And if the people of Egypt refuse to attend the festival, the LORD will punish them with the same plague that he sends on the other nations who refuse to go. 19 Egypt and the other nations will all be punished if they don't go to celebrate the festival.439

(Zechariah 14:16-19, NLT)

This also confirms there will be unbelievers during the Millennium who will refuse to obey God's laws.

Internationally Yeshua will rule the nations. He will be the King of Kings. He will head up the central government of the entire world population.

Scripture speaks that King David will be raised up to sit on the throne of Israel as a prince under Yeshua.

4This is the message the LORD gave concerning Israel and Judah: 8 "For in that day, says the LORD Almighty, I will break the yoke from their necks and snap their chains. Foreigners will no longer be their masters. 9 For my people will serve the LORD their God and David their king, whom I will raise up for them.440

(Jeremiah 30:4, 8-9, NLT)

---

436 Holy Bible: New Living Translation. Wheaton: Tyndale House, 1997.

437 Johnian, Mona. Life in the Millennium. Pages 185-188.

438 Ibid. Pages 174-175.

439 Holy Bible: New Living Translation. Wheaton: Tyndale House, 1997.

440 Ibid.

And I, the LORD, will be their God, and my servant David will be a prince among my people. I, the LORD, have spoken!441

(Ezekiel 34:24, NLT)

This illustrates that Israel will be a long time without a king or prince, and without sacrifices, Temple, priests, or even idols! 5 But afterward the people will return to the LORD their God and to David's descendant, their king. They will come trembling in awe to the LORD, and they will receive his good gifts in the last days.442

(Hosea 3:4-5, NLT)

G. Parallels between King David and Yeshua

God made a promise to David that his kingdom and his throne would last forever. It was through Yeshua, a descendant of David, that Satan and his host of fallen angels were stripped of all legal right to govern the earth (ref. Colossians 2:15).443

David had a plan to build God a house, but God's plan for David was far greater. God would take David's house—his family line — and from it He would bring forth the eternal throne of His Savior. The Millennial throne began in David. There are many parallels between David and Yeshua.

1. David was thirty years old when he began to reign—Yeshua was thirty years old when He began to preach the coming kingdom.
2. David did not receive his full kingdom at first. He had a small following (2 Samuel 22:11, 12). At first Yeshua had only a remnant of followers—the common people (Mark 12:37).
3. David did not receive Jerusalem as his capital for six and one half years. Yeshua was rejected by Jerusalem at his first coming. His followers were only a remnant of Israel.

37 O Jerusalem, Jerusalem, thou that killest the prophets, and stonest them which are sent unto thee, how often would I have gathered thy children together, even as a hen gathereth her chickens under her wings, and ye would not!444

(Matthew 23:37, KJV)

4. David ruled over Israel for thirty-three years. Yeshua was crucified at age thirty-three. David ruled in Jerusalem one year for every year of Messiah's first coming.

5. David desired to build God a permanent house in Jerusalem

1 Now it came to pass, as David sat in his house, that David said to Nathan the prophet, Lo, I dwell in an house of cedars, but the ark of the covenant of the LORD

---

441 Ibid.

442 Ibid.

443 Johnian, Mona. "The Millennial Throne." Life in the Millennium. Page 101.

444 The Holy Bible: King James Version. Oak Harbor: Logos Research Systems, Inc., 1995.

remaineth under curtains. 4 Go and tell David my servant, Thus saith the LORD, Thou shalt not build me an house to dwell in.445

(1 Chronicles 17:1, 4, KJV)

Messiah will build the house of God in Jerusalem during the Millennium.

12 And speak unto him, saying, Thus speaketh the LORD of hosts, saying, Behold the man whose name is The BRANCH; and he shall grow up out of his place, and he shall build the Temple of the LORD: 13 Even he shall build the Temple of the LORD; and he shall bear the glory, and shall sit and rule upon his throne; and he shall be a priest upon his throne: and the counsel of peace shall be between them both.446

(Zechariah 6:12-13, KJV)

6. David restored the world of God to Israel by bringing the ark of the covenant back to Jerusalem.

12 And it was told king David, saying, The LORD hath blessed the house of Obededom, and all that pertaineth unto him, because of the ark of God. So David went and brought up the ark of God from the house of Obededom into the city of David with gladness. 13 And it was so, that when they that bare the ark of the LORD had gone six paces, he sacrificed oxen and fatlings. 14 And David danced before the LORD with all his might; and David was girded with a linen ephod. 15 So David and all the house of Israel brought up the ark of the LORD with shouting, and with the sound of the trumpet.447

(2 Samuel 6:12-15, KJV)

The Ark represented the Word of God—Yeshua.

1 That which was from the beginning, which we have heard, which we have seen with our eyes, which we have looked upon, and our hands have handled, of the Word of life.448

(1 John 1:1, KJV)

Just as David brought the ark of God's Word back into Jerusalem with a great processional of praise and worship, the Word will descend from heaven with the worship of a great multitude.

6 And I heard as it were the voice of a great multitude, and as the voice of many waters, and as the voice of mighty thunderings, saying, Alleluia: for the Lord God

---

[445] Ibid.

[446] The Holy Bible: King James Version. Oak Harbor: Logos Research Systems, Inc., 1995.

[447] Ibid.

[448] Ibid.

omnipotent reigneth. 13 And he was clothed with a vesture dipped in blood: and his name is called The Word of God. 16 And he hath on his vesture and on his thigh a name written, KING OF KINGS, AND LORD OF LORDS.449

(Revelation 19:6, 13, 16, KJV)

7. David conquered his enemies.

17 And the fame of David went out into all lands; and the LORD brought the fear of him upon all nations.450

(1 Chronicles 14:17, KJV)

Yeshua will conquer all nations

27 All the ends of the world shall remember and turn unto the LORD: and all the kindreds of the nations shall worship before thee.451

(Psalm 22:27, KJV)

8. David ruled with judgment and justice

15 And David reigned over all Israel; and David executed judgment and justice unto all his people.452

(2 Samuel 8:15, KJV)

Yeshua will rule by the same constitution.

6 For unto us a child is born, unto us a son is given: and the government shall be upon his shoulder: and his name shall be called Wonderful, Counsellor, The mighty God, The everlasting Father, The Prince of Peace. 7 Of the increase of his government and peace there shall be no end, upon the throne of David, and upon his kingdom, to order it, and to establish it with judgment and with justice from henceforth even for ever. The zeal of the LORD of hosts will perform this.453

(Isaiah 9:6-7, KJV)

9. David ruled over Israel from Jerusalem. Yeshua will rule Israel, and all the nations from Jerusalem.

7 And he said unto me, Son of man, the place of my throne, and the place of the soles of my feet, where I will dwell in the midst of the children of Israel for ever, and my

---

[449] Ibid.

[450] Ibid.

[451] Ibid.

[452] Ibid.

[453] Ibid.

holy name, shall the house of Israel no more defile, neither they, nor their kings, by their whoredom, nor by the carcases of their kings in their high places.454

(Ezekiel 43:7, KJV)

10. David's clothing proclaimed the coming priest-king office of Messiah.

27 And David was clothed with a robe of fine linen, and all the Levites that bare the ark, and the singers, and Chenaniah the master of the song with the singers: David also had upon him an ephod of linen.455

(1 Chronicles 15:27, KJV)

The linen ephod was the garment of priest and Levites who served in the Temple. Yet David was permitted by God to wear it as a type of Priesthood of Yeshua when He rules the earth as priest-King during the Millennium. The coming government of God during the millennium will be a combination of church and state. Every law will be weighted by a godly standard. God promised David.456

36 His seed shall endure for ever, and his throne as the sun before me. 37 It shall be established for ever as the moon, and as a faithful witness in heaven. Selah.457

(Psalm 89:36-37, KJV)

H. Two kingdoms

There are two kingdoms in the Bible. One that is limited in time, the other is universal. The universal Kingdom of God rules time, space, and creation. It will last forever. The Millennial Kingdom of Christ is earth wide. It is limited to one thousand years. Its purpose is to provide a transitional period between human government and eternity. This period of one thousand years is for the restoration of an earth and society devastated by sin. The Millennium is a phrase of the universal kingdom of God.

The world will keep trying to throw off all godly restraint. Paul wrote of Yeshua and said, "He must reign until he has put all enemies under his feet" (1 Cor 15:27). Without exception, every power in heaven and on earth, from the man in the cave to the most powerful leader of a nation will be brought into total subjection to the authority of the kingdom of heaven.

This is the primary purpose of the millennium period.458

Israel has been without a king almost 2,000 years and has been without a priesthood. The Millennium will restore it all.459

---

454 Ibid.

455 Ibid.

456 Johnian, Mona. "The Millennial Throne." Life in the Millennium. Pages 102-107.

457 The Holy Bible: King James Version. Oak Harbor: Logos Research Systems, Inc., 1995.

458 Johnian, Mona. "The Millennial Throne." Life in the Millennium. Page 108.

459 Johnian, Mona. Life in the Millennium. Pages 175-176.

Yeshua will rule under God. King David will rule under Yeshua, and under David will be the twelve apostles who will each rule over one of the twelve tribes of Israel.

> *27 Then Peter said to him, "We've given up everything to follow you. What will we get out of it?" 28 And Jesus replied, "I assure you that when I, the Son of Man, sit upon my glorious throne in the Kingdom, you who have been my followers will also sit on twelve thrones, judging the twelve tribes of Israel.460*
>
> (Matthew 19:27-28, NLT)

The earth will have both mortal and immortal residents living on it. We will work and interact with each other after His resurrection.461

I. Revolt and judgment of the rebellious nations

For a thousand years there will not be wars or rumors of wars, no nation rising against nation. But now an army will be raised by nations toward the end of the Millennium whose number is as the sand of the sea led by Satan. The army of the defiant and rebellious youth will greatly increase to be millions. They will finally be in place, gathering for a battle against Yeshua and His saints. These will be the youth who are under one hundred years old at the end of the Millennium. They will acquire warships, tanks, personnel carriers, bombs, rockets and all manner of battle parapher- nalia, as well as food and medical supplies. They will surround the whole expanse of the city of Jerusalem. Every nation on Earth will send its fighting forces to fight against Yeshua Messiah and His saints.

When the armies have been assembled, Satan will be released from the bottomless pit and will be in the midst of the army. He will be prepared to show himself and lead them. The cosmic battle of the ages between the forces of good and evil, light and darkness will begin.

Suddenly within the masses, Satan himself will come as a shining light, a gleaming sword raised high. He will shout, "I come to claim what has been rightfully mine since the dawn of time: the very throne of God." Yeshua, the King of Kings, Mighty God will rise to meet his challenge for the last time. Satan will advance toward the Temple and shriek: "charge!" Yeshua will quietly respond, "I am who I am." With that, the clouds will holler back and the heavens will open and mountains of flames will burst forth. Satan's entire throng of men, women, weapons, everything will be vaporized in an instant leaving around the holy mountain a ring of ash that will soon blow away in the breeze.462

Satan will stand alone and fall silently. Then Yeshua will speak:

> *12 How art thou fallen from heaven, O Lucifer, son of the morning! how art thou cut down to the ground, which didst weaken the nations! 13 For thou hast said in thine heart, I will ascend into heaven, I will exalt my throne above the stars of God: I will sit also upon the mount of the congregation, in the sides of the north: 14 I will ascend above the heights of the clouds; I will be like the most High. 15 Yet thou*

---

460 Holy Bible: New Living Translation. Wheaton: Tyndale House, 1997.

461 Johnian, Mona. Life in the Millennium. Page 177.

462 Johnian, Mona. "Kingdom Come." Life in the Millennium. Pages 455-457.

shalt be brought down to hell, to the sides of the pit. 16 They that see thee shall narrowly look upon thee, and consider thee, saying, Is this the man that made the earth to tremble, that did shake kingdoms; 17 That made the world as a wilderness, and destroyed the cities thereof; that opened not the house of his prisoners?463

(Isaiah 14:12-17, KJV)

13 Thou hast been in Eden the garden of God; every precious stone was thy covering, the sardius, topaz, and the diamond, the beryl, the onyx, and the jasper, the sapphire, the emerald, and the carbuncle, and gold: the workmanship of thy tabrets and of thy pipes was prepared in thee in the day that thou wast created. 14 Thou art the anointed cherub that covereth; and I have set thee so: thou wast upon the holy mountain of God; thou hast walked up and down in the midst of the stones of fire. 15 Thou wast perfect in thy ways from the day that thou wast created, till iniquity was found in thee. 16 By the multitude of thy merchandise they have filled the midst of thee with violence, and thou hast sinned: therefore I will cast thee as profane out of the mountain of God: and I will destroy thee, O covering cherub, from the midst of the stones of fire. 17 Thine heart was lifted up because of thy beauty, thou hast corrupted thy wisdom by reason of thy brightness: I will cast thee to the ground, I will lay thee before kings, that they may behold thee. 18 Thou hast defiled thy sanctuaries by the multitude of thine iniquities, by the iniquity of thy traffick; therefore will I bring forth a fire from the midst of thee, it shall devour thee, and I will bring thee to ashes upon the earth in the sight of all them that behold thee.464

(Ezekiel 28:13-18, KJV)

Inside the Temple King David cried in a loud voice, 'This is Messiah Yeshua, who, being in the form of God, did not consider it robbery to be equal with God, but made Himself of no reputation, taking the form of a bondservant and coming in the likeness of men. And being found in appearance as a man, He humbled Himself and became obedient to the point of death, even the death of the cross.'

Therefore God also has highly exalted Him and given Him the name which is above every name, that at the name of Yeshua every knee should bow, of those in heaven, and of those on earth, and of those under the earth, and that every tongue should confess that Yeshua is Lord to the glory of God the Father.

A seam in the cosmos opened at Yeshua's command. There Satan was thrown into the abbess where the beast and the false prophet were.465

After 1,000 years of God's presence and revival in a world of peace and prosperity, millions of people will still be rebellious against God and His authority over their lives. They will continue to resent the Kingdom constitution and standards. John says the numbers of the rebellious will be as the sand of the sea. These people will be sick of holiness as we are of ungodliness today. This

---

[463] The Holy Bible: King James Version. Oak Harbor: Logos Research Systems, Inc., 1995.

[464] Ibid.

[465] Holy Bible: New Living Translation. Wheaton: Tyndale House, 1997.

ungodly host of people from the four corners of the earth will join with Satan at the end of the thousand years and make war once again on Israel.466

John prophesied that after the Millennium, Satan would be released from the bottomless pit to lead in a final rebellion against God. He will be released for "a little season" to test mankind one last time. Many of those born during this period to natural men and women will choose to join this final rebellion of Satan. God will destroy Satan and his army with fire. God will transfer the people of Earth safely from the old earth to the new earth. They will be protected like Noah's family during the flood and they will live in peace forever in the new earth. Satan would then be cast into the lake of fire forever

1 And I saw an angel come down from heaven, having the key of the bottomless pit and a great chain in his hand. 2 And he laid hold on the dragon, that old serpent, which is the Devil, and Satan, and bound him a thousand years, 3 And cast him into the bottomless pit, and shut him up, and set a seal upon him, that he should deceive the nations no more, till the thousand years should be fulfilled: and after that he must be loosed a little season. 4 And I saw thrones, and they sat upon them, and judgment was given unto them: and I saw the souls of them that were beheaded for the witness of Jesus, and for the word of God, and which had not worshipped the beast, neither his image, neither had received his mark upon their foreheads, or in their hands; and they lived and reigned with Christ a thousand years. 5 But the rest of the dead lived not again until the thousand years were finished. This is the first resurrection. 6 Blessed and holy is he that hath part in the first resurrection: on such the second death hath no power, but they shall be priests of God and of Christ, and shall reign with him a thousand years. 7 And when the thousand years are expired, Satan shall be loosed out of his prison, 8 And shall go out to deceive the nations which are in the four quarters of the earth, Gog and Magog, to gather them together to battle: the number of whom is as the sand of the sea. 9 And they went up on the breadth of the earth, and compassed the camp of the saints about, and the beloved city: and fire came down from God out of heaven, and devoured them. 10 And the devil that deceived them was cast into the lake of fire and brimstone, where the beast and the false prophet are, and shall be tormented day and night for ever and ever.467

(Revelation 20:1-10, KJV)

J. The cleansing of heaven and Earth from sin

After the Millennium the existing earth and heavens will be cleansed with fire and renewed from the pollution of sin. There will be no sin in the new heaven and earth or in the New Jerusalem. Even heaven has experienced sin's pollution because of Satan appearing there before the throne of God. Heaven as well as Earth will be cleaned and renewed by fire.

---

[466] Johnian, Mona. Life in the Millennium. Page 179.

[467] The Holy Bible: King James Version. Oak Harbor: Logos Research Systems, Inc., 1995.

7 And that same word of God is keeping heaven and earth that we now have in order to be destroyed by fire. They are being kept for the Judgment Day and the destruction of all who are against God. 10 But the day of the Lord will come like a thief. The skies will disappear with a loud noise. Everything in them will be destroyed by fire, and the earth and everything in it will be burned up. 11 In that way everything will be destroyed. So what kind of people should you be? You should live holy lives and serve God, 12 as you wait for and look forward to the coming of the day of God. When that day comes, the skies will be destroyed with fire, and everything in them will melt with heat. 13 But God made a promise to us, and we are waiting for a new heaven and a new earth where goodness lives.468

(2 Peter 3:7, 10-13, NCV)

Satan will not die but will be thrown into the Lake of Fire which is located at the center of the earth among molten lava with the evil angelic hosts and the unbelievers who were judged at the Great White Throne Judgment. Satan was assigned to the Lake of fire.469

K. The great white throne judgment of unsaved mankind from Creation to the end of time and the judgment of Satan and his angels to be thrown into the lake of fire.

Descending from the heavens was Yeshua, sitting on a great white throne. He judges every man according to their works. Whosoever was not found written in the Book of Life was cast into the lake of fire with the devil and his angels.

1. Resurrection of the dead

On the earth, the resurrection of the bodies of all the men and women throughout history who died outside of Yeshua will be judged. All who are present will be judged by the works of their lives. Their deeds will stand in judgment against them for they did not repent in their hearts. He will judge their hearts and not their outward works.

21 Not all those who say that I am their Lord will enter the kingdom of heaven. The only people who will enter the kingdom of heaven are those who do what my Father in heaven wants. 22 On the last day many people will say to me, 'Lord, Lord, we spoke for you, and through you we forced out demons and did many miracles.' 23 Then I will tell them clearly, 'Get away from me, you who do evil. I never knew you.'470

(Matthew 7:21-23, NCV)

---

468 The Holy Bible: New Century Version , Containing the Old and New Testaments. Dallas: Word Bibles, 1991.

469 Johnian, Mona. Life in the Millennium. Pages 179-180.

470 The Holy Bible: New Century Version , Containing the Old and New Testaments. Dallas: Word Bibles, 1991.

5 But the rest of the dead lived not again until the thousand years were finished. This is the first resurrection.471

(Revelation 20:5, KJV)

12 And I saw the dead, small and great, stand before God; and the books were opened: and another book was opened, which is the book of life: and the dead were judged out of those things which were written in the books, according to their works. 13 And the sea gave up the dead which were in it; and death and hell delivered up the dead which were in them: and they were judged every man according to their works.472

(Revelation 20:12-13, KJV)

And anyone whose name was not found recorded in the Book of Life was thrown into the lake of fire.473

(Revelation 20:15, NLT)

And just as it is destined that each person dies only once and after that comes judgment.474

(Hebrews 9:27, NLT)

Only the unbelieving dead will be judged at the great white throne judgment of God for whatever evil works were done while he was on Earth. There are degrees or compartments in the underworld of greater or lesser torments according to their deeds.

2. The Bible teaches what hell is

1. located beneath the ocean floor (Job 26:5, 6)
2. divided into five departments: *tartarus* (1 Peter 3:19) "Paradise" which was emptied when Yeshua arose from the dead with His saints (Luke 16:19-31); hell (Matthew 16:18); the abyss or bottomless pit (Luke 8:26-31); the lake of fire (Revelation 20:6, 11-15)
3. It is a place of pain and sorrow (Psalm 18:15 and Psalm 116:3)

The Great White Throne Judgment will determine where — in which compartment the unbeliever and ungodly will spend eternity. Regardless where the lost reside, it will be a place of pain and sorrow, and in case any of the redeemed should be tempted to turn back from eternity, Isaiah said there will be an opening where we can look into hell as a continual warning against sin.

---

[471] The Holy Bible: King James Version. Oak Harbor: Logos Research Systems, Inc., 1995.

[472] Ibid.

[473] Holy Bible: New Living Translation. Wheaton: Tyndale House, 1997.

[474] Ibid.

And as they go out, they will see the dead bodies of those who have rebelled against me. For the worms that devour them will never die, and the fire that burns them will never go out. All who pass by will view them with utter horror.475

(Isaiah 66:24, NLT)

14 And death and hell were cast into the lake of fire. This is the second death.476

(Revelation 20:14, KJV)

Death and Hades were also cast into the lake of fire.

3. Three classes of mankind

At the end of the Millennium, and in eternity, there will be three classes of men; the lost who are condemned to the underworld; the natural saved who are the subjects of God's kingdom, and the resurrected saints who are rulers of the kingdom.

These three classes will be for eternity.477

4. Final judgment of two groups of sinners

GREAT WHITE THRONE

The great white throne judgment will occur after the Millennium and will involve the final judgment of the two groups of sinners:

1. the rebellious angels as well as Satan
2. all the wicked dead who ever lived as well as religious folk who did not accept Messiah's sacrificial death for their sins

11 And I saw a great white throne, and him that sat on it, from whose face the earth and the heaven fled away; and there was found no place for them. 12 And I saw the dead, small and great, stand before God; and the books were opened: and another book was opened, which is the book of life: and the dead were judged out of those things which were written in the books, according to their works. 13 And the sea gave up the dead which were in it; and death and hell delivered up the dead which were in them: and they were judged every man according to their works. 14 And death and hell were cast into the lake of fire. This is the second death. 15 And whosoever was not found written in the book of life was cast into the lake of fire.478

(Revelation 20:11-15, KJV)

---

[475] Holy Bible: New Living Translation. Wheaton: Tyndale House, 1997.

[476] The Holy Bible: King James Version. Oak Harbor: Logos Research Systems, Inc., 1995.

[477] Johnian, Mona. Life in the Millennium. Pages 181-182.

[478] The Holy Bible: King James Version. Oak Harbor: Logos Research Systems, Inc., 1995.

5. Satan and his angels judged

All the angels who joined Satan's rebellion will stand before the great white throne. There are two classes:

1. those who attempted physical relations with women are chained in darkness.

> *4 For if God spared not the angels that sinned, but cast them down to hell, and delivered them into chains of darkness, to be reserved unto judgment; 6 And turning the cities of Sodom and Gomorrha into ashes condemned them with an overthrow, making them an ensample unto those that after should live ungodly.*
>
> 479(2 Peter 2:4, 6, KJV)

2. the second group will be angels who would remain with Satan to do his bidding until Satan and all the angels are thrown in the lake of fire....... with Satan in the lake of "everlasting fire prepared for the devil and his angels" (Matthew 25:41).

The lake of fire was originally prepared for the devil and his angels. If man had never rebelled against God or if all men had repented of their sins, then the gates of hell would have never opened to mankind.

---

[479] Ibid.

CHAPTER FIFTEEN

The New Jerusalem

A. Description of the city

9 Then one of the seven angels who had the seven bowls filled with the seven last plagues came to me and talked with me, saying, "Come, I will show you the bride, the Lamb's wife." 10 And he carried me away in the Spirit to a great and high mountain, and showed me the great city, the holy Jerusalem, descending out of heaven from God, 11 having the glory of God. Her light was like a most precious stone, like a jasper stone, clear as crystal. 12 Also she had a great and high wall with twelve gates, and twelve angels at the gates, and names written on them, which are the names of the twelve tribes of the children of Israel: 13 three gates on the east, three gates on the north, three gates on the south, and three gates on the west. 14 Now the wall of the city had twelve foundations, and on them were the names of the twelve apostles of the Lamb. 15 And he who talked with me had a gold reed to measure the city, its gates, and its wall. 16 The city is laid out as a square; its length is as great as its breadth. And he measured the city with the reed: twelve thousand furlongs. Its length, breadth, and height are equal. 17 Then he measured its wall: one hundred and forty-four cubits, according to the measure of a man, that is, of an angel. 18 The construction of its wall was of jasper; and the city was pure gold, like clear glass. 19 The foundations of the wall of the city were adorned with all kinds of precious stones: the first foundation was jasper, the second sapphire, the third chalcedony, the fourth emerald, 20 the fifth sardonyx, the sixth sardius, the seventh chrysolite, the eighth beryl, the ninth topaz, the tenth chrysoprase, the eleventh jacinth, and the twelfth amethyst. 21 The twelve gates were twelve pearls: each individual gate was of one pearl. And the street of the city was pure gold, like transparent glass.

(Revelation 21:9-21, NKJV)

1. The glory of the New Jerusalem

22 But I saw no temple in it, for the Lord God Almighty and the Lamb are its temple. 23 The city had no need of the sun or of the moon to shine in it, for the glory of God illuminated it. The Lamb is its light. 24 And the nations of those who are saved shall walk in its light, and the kings of the earth bring their glory and honor into it. 25 Its gates shall not be shut at all by day (there shall be no night there). 26 And they shall bring the glory and the honor of the nations into it. 27 But there shall by no means enter it anything that defiles, or causes an abomination or a lie, but only those who are written in the Lamb's Book of Life.480

(Revelation 22:22-27, NKJV)

7 Let us be glad and rejoice, and give honour to him: for the marriage of the Lamb is come, and his wife hath made herself ready. 8 And to her was granted that she should be arrayed in fine linen, clean and white: for the fine linen is the righteousness of saints. 9 And he saith unto me, Write, Blessed are they which are called unto the marriage supper of the Lamb. And he saith unto me, These are the true sayings of God.481

(Revelation 19:7-9, KJV)

(v. 9) The bride, the Lamb's wife is identified as the Holy Jerusalem, descending out of heaven from God. (v. 10) The city is the wife of the Lamb she is beautifully adorned so is the church. The church is the bride of Messiah she will be at the Marriage supper of the Lamb (Revelation 21:9-10, KJV).

The city will be spotless and pure like the church after it is glorified. The city is compared to a bride in its beauty and intimate relationship to Christ, the Lamb of God. The bride figure is made up of both the individual who lives in the city as well as the New Jerusalem with its physical characteristics and beauty.482

The city will shine with the glory of God like the Shekinah Glory that filled the holy of holies in the Tabernacle and Temple. Its brightness 'was like a stone most precious, even like a jasper stone, clear as crystal (verse 12). The Jasper stone is like transparent crystal, similar to a diamond, who facets sparkle with every color of the rainbow. The jasper stone is "most precious" because of its beauty and cost and will be extensively used in making the New Jerusalem (verse 19).483

11 having the glory of God. Her light was like a most precious stone, like a jasper stone, clear as crystal.484

(Revelation 21:11, NKJV)

---

[480] The Holy Bible: The New King James Version. Nashville: Thomas Nelson, 1996, c1982.

[481] The Holy Bible: King James Version. Oak Harbor: Logos Research Systems, Inc., 1995.

[482] Levy, David. "The New Jerusalem." Israel My Glory. Westville: The Friends of Israel, Gospel Ministry, Inc., Apr/May 1999. Page 24.

[483] Ibid. Page 25.

[484] The Holy Bible: The New King James Version. Nashville: Thomas Nelson, 1996, c1982.

In eternity there will be no need for a Temple because God Himself will dwell in the midst of His people, who will have a direct, immediate and intimate communion with Him.

The city will have no need of creative light from the sun or moon because 'the glory of God did light it, and the Lamb is the light of it' (v. 23). God's glorious presence in the city will illuminate every corner of New Jerusalem; nothing will be hidden. All the 'nations......who are saved shall walk' in the physical and spiritual 'light (v. 24) of God's glory.'

2. The architecture of the city

The New Jerusalem that is described in Revelation 21 is what it will be in its eternal state. John mentioned that the walls of the New Jerusalem are 'great and high' (v. 12). The walls are not needed for defense because the city will have no enemies. The walls will be symbolic of God's protection and security and the exclusion of all that is evil.[485]

In vv. 25-26 — John mentioned the gates shall not be shut by day; for there shall be no night there. The kings shall bring glory and honor of the nations into it. 'The city will be open to all believers.. only the redeemed whose names are written in the Lamb's book of life' (v. 27) will be there......[486]

The City will have 12 gates, each one inscribed with the name of one of the tribes of Israel (v. 12)......an angel will be stationed at each gate as an honor guard stressing the security of both the city and God's glory (v. 12).[487]

There will be 'twelve gates' (v. 21) each made of one huge pearl attached to the city walls that will open into the streets made of 'pure gold' as it were transparent glass (v. 21). 'Each pearl gate will bear the name of one tribe of Israel, and these gates will never be closed.'[488]

The city will have 'twelve foundations' and in them the names of the twelve apostles of the Lamb.

There will be twelve foundations which are each made up of a different precious stone (v. 19-20). The precious stones for the city's foundations will be layered one on top of another in the following order:

1. Jasper stone — clear crystal like a diamond, brilliant
2. Sapphire — blue with gold flecks
3. Chalcedony — is a translucent milky or grayish quartz with colored stripes running through
4. Emerald — brilliant grass-green transparent variety of beryl
5. Sardonyx — is an onyx stone with alternating brown and white bands running through it
6. Sardius — translucent red stone — like ruby.
7. Chrysolite — gold in color, resembling a golden jasper stone
8. Beryl — a translucent blush or sea-green colored stone
9. Topaz — is a translucent yellow or yellow-green stone
10. Chrysoprasus — is a translucent apple-green stone.

---

[485] Levy, David. "The New Jerusalem." Page 25.

[486] Ibid. Page 26.

[487] Ibid. Page 25.

[488] Ibid.

11. Jacinth — is a translucent, bluish — smoke, violet colored stone
12. Amethyst — is a brilliant purple or violet transparent stone.489

The twelve foundations will be structured to refract the effulgence of God's glory and holiness. Such beauty will transcend anything mankind has seen since the inception of God's Creation.

(v. 15 & 16) The size of the city will be 1,500 miles on each side and 1,500 miles high. The city may be a perfect cube in shape. The walls will only be 216' high. (v.17)

The material used to build the walls of the city was pure gold, clear as glass (v. 18). The city of pure gold with walls of Jasper would look like a sparkling diamond which is designed to reflect the effulgence of God's radiant glory in every area of the city.490

3. It will be like the Garden of Eden

John the revelator shared the Paradise qualities of the New Jerusalem. It will be like the Garden of Eden before Adam and Eve sinned. The river of the water of life is clear as crystal proceeding out of the throne of God and of the Lamb (22:1). This will be a life-giving river, providing those living in the city with a deeper quality of spiritual life and symbolically portraying the eternal life manifested to them in eternity. This river will flow 'out of the throne of God and of the Lamb' (22:1) indicating that Yeshua will be enthroned with God the Father in eternity.

> *And he showed me a pure river of water of life, clear as crystal, proceeding from the throne of God and of the Lamb. 2 In the middle of its street, and on either side of the river, was the tree of life, which bore twelve fruits, each tree yielding its fruit every month. The leaves of the tree were for the healing of the nations. 3 And there shall be no more curse, but the throne of God and of the Lamb shall be in it, and His servants shall serve Him. 4 They shall see His face, and His name shall be on their foreheads.491*

(Revelation 22:1-4, NKJV)

In the New Jerusalem there is 'the tree of life' (v2) located in the middle of the street, whose branches will be large enough to spread on both sides of the river of life. The 'tree of life' will bear 'twelve kinds of fruits and yield her fruit every month' (v2). This tree will produce an annual harvest to twelve different fruits. The mention of twelve months would indicate that time will be calculated in eternity.492

The 'tree of life' is first seen in Genesis 3:22. Adam and Eve were driven from the Garden of Eden so that they could not partake of the tree of life. If they had eaten from the tree, they would have lived eternally in their natural bodies, which possessed the sin nature.493

---

489 Ibid.

490 Ibid.

491 The Holy Bible: The New King James Version. Nashville: Thomas Nelson, 1996, c1982.

492 Levy, David. "The New Jerusalem." Israel My Glory. Westville: The Friends of Israel, Gospel Ministry, Inc., Apr/May 1999. Page 26.

493 Ibid.

The leaves from the tree will provide 'healing for the nations' (v.2). The word healing comes from a Greek word that means therapeutic or health giving. There will be no disease in the New Jerusalem because the 'curse' (v3) will be removed; therefore, the leaves of the tree will enhance the joy of life in eternity.494

4. Yeshua's promise to build a place for the believers.

Let not your heart be troubled; you believe in God, believe also in Me. 2 In My Father's house are many mansions; if it were not so, I would have told you. I go to prepare a place for you. 3 And if I go and prepare a place for you, I will come again and receive you to Myself; that where I am, there you may be also.495

(John 14:1-3, NKJV)

Traditionally, the Church has always assumed this to mean that Jesus would be going back to heaven to prepare a place for the believers. At death we would then go there to live with Him forever, and heaven would be our home. But may I suggest that what Jesus was actually saying was this: Jesus was going back to the heavenly Jerusalem where He would prepare a glorious residence for each believer. Those who died before Jesus' return to earth would immediately occupy their residence. But there would be a generation that would not die, and Jesus must also prepare a home for them in the eternal city.

When the city is completed and all residences are built, He will come in the clouds and gather together all believers both in heaven and on earth, and as one great company we will descend back to earth for the end of human government and the celebration of the marriage feast. This marks the beginning of the Millennium. Then, for 1,000 years, the earth will undergo preparation to receive New Jerusalem—for the full consummation of the marriage, about which John wrote.

2 Then I, John, saw the holy city, New Jerusalem, coming down out of heaven from God, prepared as a bride adorned for her husband. 3 And I heard a loud voice from heaven saying, "Behold, the tabernacle of God is with men, and He will dwell with them, and they shall be His people. God Himself will be with them and be their God. 9 Then one of the seven angels who had the seven bowls filled with the seven last plagues came to me and talked with me, saying, "Come, I will show you the bride, the Lamb's wife." 10 And he carried me away in the Spirit to a great and high mountain, and showed me the great city, the holy Jerusalem, descending out of heaven from God, 11 having the glory of God. Her light was like a most precious stone, like a jasper stone, clear as crystal.496

(Revelation 21:2-3, 9-11, NKJV)

The Bride is New Jerusalem—the city of God, the throne of God, and the immortal saints of God, of all ages. According to Hebrews eleven, it is the city that has been prepared for all believers, from faithful Abel to the martyrs of the New Testament Church and until the moment of the Rap-

---

494 Ibid.

495 The Holy Bible: The New King James Version. Nashville: Thomas Nelson, 1996, c1982.

496 Ibid

ture. The Bride is not only buildings, nor is it only people. The Bride of Christ includes the full wedding party. Without the throne of God, the Bride is not complete. Without the people of God, the city is not complete. We need to see the full spectrum of God's plan if we will catch a preview of the marriage that is to come. I suggest that the consummation of the marriage of Christ with His bride will take place 1,000 years after the wedding supper [which in God's sight is one day, 2 Peter 3:8]. It will be a union for eternity.497

The universe is and will continue to be run from New Jerusalem. Whereas all nations will answer to earthly Jerusalem during the Millennium, in eternity all creation will answer to heavenly New Jerusalem.

A celestial phenomenon will one day occur in the heavens. At the end of the Millennium, a brilliant planet will begin to move from the outermost regions of creation toward the Milky Way. It will not be a comet that whizzes across the sky and then disappears into the darkness, but this planet will—as it were—move with pomp and majesty at a pace every eye can see. Accompanied by a heaven illuminated seven times brighter than we know today, this New Jerusalem planet will glide as a bride down the aisles of space until it reaches the longing sphere of its Eternal Groom.

And waiting on planet earth to receiver her will be the Son of God. Then forever, New Jerusalem with its saints, and the earth with its redeemed, will shine as two flawless, blue- white diamonds, bound together with Christ, in the mystery of the ages. It is the mystery of God's will which Paul says was God's 'good pleasure which he purposed Himself, that in the dispensation of the fullness of times He might gather together in one all things in Christ, both which are in Heaven and which are on the earth—in Him' (Ephesians 1:9, 10).498

B. Life in eternity

1. Yeshua blesses the believers

After death and Hades are cast into the lake of fire, the earth and its atmosphere will be judged by fire. All that remained will be the New Jerusalem and Yeshua on His throne. In an instant Yeshua will create a new earth and the holy city will descend. Yeshua will then bless those who made it through the millennial kingdom. Their old bodies will be restored to the bodies of their youth and they will be ready to enter the kingdom of heaven. The only thing that will matter to the people will be to praise and glorify Yeshua, the lover and Savior of their souls.

The billions who lived through the Millennium will ascend to the most beautiful and massive foursquare city of transparent gold. The elect and redeemed throughout the ages will gather into the New Jerusalem.

A loud voice from heaven will say:

> *Behold the tabernacle of God is with men, and He will dwell with them and they shall be His people. God Himself will be with them and be their God. And God will wipe away every tear from their eyes; there shall be no more death, nor sorrow, nor crying. There shall be no more pain, for the former things have passed away.*

---

[497] Johnian, Mona. "Epilogue: A Glimpse of Eternity." Life in the Millennium. Pages 200-202.

[498] Ibid. Pages 202-203.

Then Yeshua will say from the throne:

Behold, I make all things new. It is finished. I am the Alpha and the Omega, the Beginning and the End. I give of the foundation of the water freely to him who thirsts. But the cowardly, unbelieving, abominable, murderers, sexually immoral, sorcerers, idolaters and all liars have their part in the lake of fire which burns with fire and brimstone.

Yeshua will stand and faced the billions of believers, stretching wide His arms and announce:

You chose to believe in Me and accept My death on the cross for your sins. My Resurrection from the dead proved this sacrifice was acceptable to My Father. Therefore, on the basis of your faith, I invite you into the eternal city the Father and I have been preparing for you.

The new earth will be as majestic and beautiful as the original Garden of Eden. The great city will bear the very glory of God. His light will be like a most precious jasper stone, clear as crystal. She will have a great and high wall with twelve gates and twelve angels at the gates and the names written on them will be the names of the twelve tribes of Israel. There will be three gates on the east, three gates on the north, three gates on the south and three gates on the west.

2. Yeshua and the Lord God are the light and temple

There will be no temple in the New Jerusalem because the Lord God Almighty and the Lamb will be its temple. The city will have no need of sun or moon for there will be no more night. There will be no need for lamps or the light of the sun because the Lord God, the Lamb, will be the light. The only residents of the new heaven and new earth will be those who were written in the Lamb's Book of Life, and they shall reign forever and ever.

22 And I saw no temple therein: for the Lord God Almighty and the Lamb are the temple of it. 23 And the city had no need of the sun, neither of the moon, to shine in it: for the glory of God did lighten it, and the Lamb is the light thereof. 24 And the nations of them which are saved shall walk in the light of it: and the kings of the earth do bring their glory and honour into it. 25 And the gates of it shall not be shut at all by day: for there shall be no night there. 26 And they shall bring the glory and honour of the nations into it.[499]

(Revelation 21:22-26, KJV)

The ultimate end for the believer is not tribulation, destruction, judgment and suffering, but the unspeakable glory of God. God's and man's dreams are fulfilled where the Creator and His Creation, mankind, loves and obeys Him willingly.

---

[499] The Holy Bible: King James Version. Oak Harbor: Logos Research Systems, Inc., 1995.

3. Other references to the New Jerusalem

There are many references to the heavenly Jerusalem even outside of the book of Revelation. The heavenly Jerusalem has been the goal of all the saints since the earliest of times. Hebrews 11:8-10 reveal that 'by faith Abraham......looked for a city which hath foundations, whose builder and maker is God.' In Galatians 4:25-26 the Apostle Paul speaks of the present earthly Jerusalem and the 'Jerusalem which is above.'

In the book of Revelation the New Jerusalem is presented in conjunction with the eternal state. In Revelation 21:1-2 we read: 'And I saw a new heaven and a new earth: for the first heaven and the first earth were passed away; and there was no more sea. And I John saw the holy city, New Jerusalem, coming down from God out of heaven, prepared as a bride adorned for her husband.'

During the millennial reign of Christ on earth the New Jerusalem will be suspended over the earth. It will be the dwelling place of believers throughout all eternity. When the first heaven and the first earth pass away, the New Jerusalem will come down and, apparently, hang over the earth as a kind of satellite city. The city is a cube measuring 1500 miles wide, 1500 miles long, and 1500 miles high.

In the New Jerusalem there is no curse, sorrow, suffering, or pain. According to Revelation 21:24 people will be able to freely travel between this satellite city and the renewed earth, for the kings of the earth will bring their glory into this heavenly city.[500]

There are at least three heavens:

1. Atmosphere — above the earth
2. Heavenlies—among the stars, available to all spiritual creatures
3. Third Heaven which contains the angelic host, the New Jerusalem and the Throne of God[501]

Before the new heaven and new earth are renovated, the old earth will be destroyed by fire.

> *6 Whereby the world that then was, being overflowed with water, perished: 7 But the heavens and the earth, which are now, by the same word are kept in store, reserved unto fire against the day of judgment and perdition of ungodly men. 10 But the day of the Lord will come as a thief in the night; in the which the heavens shall pass away with a great noise, and the elements shall melt with fervent heat, the earth also and the works that are therein shall be burned up.*[502]
>
> (2 Peter 3:6-7, 10, KJV)

After the earth and the heavens are cleansed by fire, the heavenly city will come to Earth, the New Jerusalem. In that city, the glory of God will fill her with His divine presence. This will cause the whole city to glow with an internal light like a beautiful "Jasper stone, clear as crystal" (ref. Revelation 21:11).

---

[500] Bible in the News. N-199. Southwest Radio Ministries, Sept. 2007.

[501] Jeffrey, Grant R. Heaven the Last Frontier. New York: Bantam Books, 1990. Page 179-180.

[502] The Holy Bible: King James Version. Oak Harbor: Logos Research Systems, Inc., 1995.

4. Location of the New Jerusalem and the inhabitants currently in the New Jerusalem

The New Jerusalem is currently located in heaven. After the Millennium, the New Jerusalem will descend to the new earth where it will take its place among many new cities of the new earth. It will not be like other cities. It will be a very special place, the home of the bride of Christ.

The New Jerusalem is currently inhabited by the angels, the spirits of those who died in Yeshua, and also the Old Testament saints who were raised from the dead as part of the first fruits of the first resurrection when the graves were opened and the bodies of the dead saints were raised after Yeshua's Resurrection.

These resurrected saints ascended into heaven with Yeshua (Matthew 27:52-53). At the Rapture, the spirits of the departed saints who are already in the New Jerusalem will receive their resurrected bodies. Those who are raptured—caught up—their bodies will be transformed into a new glorified body like Yeshua. All those who are present in the New Jerusalem will be written in the Lamb's book of Life because they had accepted the pardon of sin offered by Yeshua.

The believers will have Yeshua's name written in their foreheads. They will have access to the pure river of life in the New Jerusalem which proceeds from the throne of God (Revelation 22:1). The tree of life will stand near the river and bear twelve fruits, a different fruit each month in their own season.

3 And I heard a great voice out of heaven saying, Behold, the tabernacle of God is with men, and he will dwell with them, and they shall be his people, and God himself shall be with them, and be their God. 4 And God shall wipe away all tears from their eyes; and there shall be no more death, neither sorrow, nor crying, neither shall there be any more pain: for the former things are passed away. 5 And he that sat upon the throne said, Behold, I make all things new. And he said unto me, Write: for these words are true and faithful. 6 And he said unto me, It is done. I am Alpha and Omega, the beginning and the end. I will give unto him that is athirst of the fountain of the water of life freely.503

(Revelation 21:3-6, KJV)

John ends the Book of Revelation with:

17 And the Spirit and the bride say, Come. And let him that heareth say, Come. And let him that is athirst come. And whosoever will, let him take the water of life freely. 18 For I testify unto every man that heareth the words of the prophecy of this book, If any man shall add unto these things, God shall add unto him the plagues that are written in this book: 19 And if any man shall take away from the words of the book of this prophecy, God shall take away his part out of the book of life, and out of the holy city, and from the things which are written in this book. 20 He which testifieth these things saith, Surely I come quickly. Amen. Even so, come, Lord Jesus.504

(Revelation 22:17-20, KJV)

---

[503] The Holy Bible: King James Version. Oak Harbor: Logos Research Systems, Inc., 1995.

[504] Ibid.

5. About the appearance of the New Jerusalem

The New Jerusalem, the home of the believer, will cover an area equal to half the size of the United States of America. It is shaped either as a cube or a pyramid. The wall around the city is 216 feet high with twelve gates around the city.......three on each side. Architects have calculated that for every believer from Adam to the present they would have a mansion over one half mile wide by one half mile in length.

The foundations of the walls of the city will be adorned with all kinds of precious stones in this order from the foundation up: jasper, sapphire, chalcedony, emerald, sardonyx, sardius, chrysolite, beryl, topaz, chrysoprasus, jacinth and amethyst. The streets of the city will be of pure gold, like transparent glass (ref. Revelation 21:16-21).

6. The attitude and occupation of the believers

The New Jerusalem will be the headquarters and home of the Church. We will reign and rule with Christ on Earth forever. The curse of sin will be eradicated from the planet. The earth will be a worldwide Garden of Eden. It will be a joyful place to live.

> *18 My people will be happy forever because of the things I will make. I will make a Jerusalem that is full of joy, and I will make her people a delight. 19 Then I will rejoice over Jerusalem and be delighted with my people. There will never again be heard in that city the sounds of crying and sadness.*505
>
> (Isaiah 65:18-19, NCV)

Eternity will not be a place of idleness, boredom, or wearisome labor, but one of joyful service and worship.

Believers will look on the face of God" (v4) because they will be in their glorified bodies. They will bear the seal of God's ownership showing they are citizens of the New Jerusalem.506

They will reign with God forever and ever. v5, Rev 3:21, Rev 5:10, Rev 20:4, 6 ......only eternity will reveal the exact role and responsibility of glorified believers in ruling and reigning over the universe. What a blessed new home that awaits believers in eternity.507

Life on the New Earth will be productive:

> *21 In that city those who build houses will live there. Those who plant vineyards will get to eat their grapes. 23 They will never again work for nothing. They will never again give birth to children who die young. All my people will be blessed by the LORD; they and their children will be blessed.*508
>
> (Isaiah 65:21, 23, NCV)

[505] The Holy Bible: New Century Version , Containing the Old and New Testaments. Dallas: Word Bibles, 1991.

[506] Levy, David. "The New Jerusalem." Israel My Glory. Page 26.

[507] Ibid.

[508] The Holy Bible: New Century Version , Containing the Old and New Testaments. Dallas: Word Bibles, 1991.

The natural men who survived Armageddon — both Jew and Gentile, will enjoy children, crops, cattle and fruit throughout eternity.

> *2 Dear friends, now we are children of God, and we have not yet been shown what we will be in the future. But we know that when Christ comes again, we will be like him, because we will see him as he really is. 3 Christ is pure, and all who have this hope in Christ keep themselves pure like Christ.509*

> (1 John 3:2-3, NCV)

7. The new heaven and earth will be the final home of the righteous sons of God.

The new heaven and the New Jerusalem will be the final home of all the righteous sons of God — Adam to the last member of the Church. We will have access to the "tree of life" with its twelve fruits and the pure river of life.

There will be seasons and months to provide variety of climate in our new home. There will be no night in the New Jerusalem because God Himself will illuminate the city of God.

> *5 There shall be no night there: They need no lamp nor light of the sun, for the Lord God gives them light. And they shall reign forever and ever.510*

> (Revelation 22:5, NKJV)

Revelation 7:9 promises we shall be clothed with white robes to symbolize the righteousness of God. John and Paul saw in their heavenly visions a wonderful paradise that contains the pure original forms of many things we enjoy on Earth.

God told Moses:

> *5 who serve the copy and shadow of the heavenly things, as Moses was divinely instructed when he was about to make the tabernacle. For He said, "See that you make all things according to the pattern shown you on the mountain."511*

> (Hebrews 8:5, NKJV)

In the book of Revelation, John describes Yeshua giving rewards to every man according to his works on Earth.

> *12 And behold, I am coming quickly, and My reward is with Me, to give to every one according to his work.512*

> (Revelation 22:12, NKJV)

---

509 Ibid.

510 The Holy Bible: The New King James Version. Nashville: Thomas Nelson, 1996, c1982.

511 Ibid.

512 Ibid.

6 and raised us up together, and made us sit together in the heavenly places in Christ Jesus, 7 that in the ages to come He might show the exceeding riches of His grace in His kindness toward us in Christ Jesus.513

(Ephesians 2:6-7, NKJV)

2 I know a man in Christ who fourteen years ago—whether in the body I do not know, or whether out of the body I do not know, God knows—such a one was caught up to the third heaven. 3 And I know such a man—whether in the body or out of the body I do not know, God knows— 4 how he was caught up into Paradise and heard inexpressible words, which it is not lawful for a man to utter.514

(2 Corinthians 12:2-4, NKJV)

One of the great joys of eternity will be getting together with long-lost friends and family who have passed on before us to await us in the eternal city. There will be no sorrow or pain. Even children who die before the age of accountability will be there, which is expressed by the faith of King David......that he would go to his infant son who had died (ref. 2 Samuel 12:23).

8. Music in heaven

There will be wonderful music in Heaven.

8 And the four beasts had each of them six wings about him; and they were full of eyes within: and they rest not day and night, saying, Holy, holy, holy, LORD God Almighty, which was, and is, and is to come. 9 And when those beasts give glory and honour and thanks to him that sat on the throne, who liveth for ever and ever, 10 The four and twenty elders fall down before him that sat on the throne, and worship him that liveth for ever and ever, and cast their crowns before the throne, saying, 11 Thou art worthy, O Lord, to receive glory and honour and power: for thou hast created all things, and for thy pleasure they are and were created.515

(Revelation 4:8-11, KJV)

8 And when he had taken the book, the four beasts and four and twenty elders fell down before the Lamb, having every one of them harps, and golden vials full of odours, which are the prayers of saints. 9 And they sung a new song, saying, Thou art worthy to take the book, and to open the seals thereof: for thou wast slain, and hast redeemed us to God by thy blood out of every kindred, and tongue, and people, and nation.516

(Revelation 5:8-9, KJV)

---

[513] Ibid.

[514] Ibid.

[515] The Holy Bible: King James Version. Oak Harbor: Logos Research Systems, Inc., 1995.

[516] Ibid.

There will be a one-hundred-million-voice choir in the New Jerusalem. The 144,000 will sing a new song of praise to God and to the Lamb. There will not only be beautiful music, but wonderful fragrances.

9. Animals in new heaven and new Earth

There will be animals in the new heaven and new earth.

> *25 Wolves and lambs will eat together in peace. Lions will eat hay like oxen, and a snake on the ground will not hurt anyone. They will not hurt or destroy each other on all my holy mountain," says the LORD.517*
>
> (Isaiah 65:25, NCV)

10. Life will be purposeful

The Bible describes our life in heaven as purposeful and joyful. We will serve God and rule with Him forever. Only eternity will reveal the exact role and responsibility of the glorified believers in ruling and reigning over the universe. What a blessed home awaits believers in eternity.

> *15 Therefore are they before the throne of God, and serve him day and night in his temple: and he that sitteth on the throne shall dwell among them.518*
>
> (Revelation 7:15, KJV)

> *3 And there shall be no more curse: but the throne of God and of the Lamb shall be in it; and his servants shall serve him: 4 And they shall see his face; and his name shall be in their foreheads. 5 And there shall be no night there; and they need no candle, neither light of the sun; for the Lord God giveth them light: and they shall reign for ever and ever. 6 And he said unto me, These sayings are faithful and true: and the Lord God of the holy prophets sent his angel to shew unto his servants the things which must shortly be done.519*
>
> (Revelation 22:3-6, KJV)

We shall be able to enjoy the beauty of God's creation of animals, waterfalls and forests, which will exist on the Earth during the Millennium and beyond. All the good things of Earth will continue to be experienced by those who survive the Tribulation and the Battle of Armageddon.

After the Millennium, sinless sons of Adam may even explore the other solar systems and populate other planets.520

Then the sinless natural sons of Abraham would finally fulfill the promise made to Abraham by God in the book of Genesis "In blessing I will bless thee, and in multiplying I will multiply

---

[517] The Holy Bible: New Century Version , Containing the Old and New Testaments. Dallas: Word Bibles, 1991.

[518] The Holy Bible: King James Version. Oak Harbor: Logos Research Systems, Inc., 1995.

[519] Ibid.

[520] Jeffrey, Grant R. Heaven the Last Frontier. New York: Bantam Books, 1990. Page 191.

thy seed as the stars of Heaven, and as the sand which is upon the sea shore......" (Gen. 22:17). Even the renovated New Earth would not hold an infinitely growing population such as the Bible describes. God might have created the infinite universe as a home for man under the rule of Yeshua and His Bride the Church.

All the spiritual and intelligent life of a vast universe will join in a song of worship to God.521

> *13 And every creature which is in heaven, and on the earth, and under the earth, and such as are in the sea, and all that are in them, heard I saying, Blessing, and honour, and glory, and power, be unto him that sitteth upon the throne, and unto the Lamb for ever and ever.522*
>
> (Revelation 5:13, KJV)

11. God is satisfied with His march throughout the ages

The privilege of becoming members of the bride of Christ, the Church, and participating in the marriage supper of the Lamb in heaven belongs to everyone who accepts His pardon for their sins.

> *7 Let us be glad and rejoice, and give honour to him: for the marriage of the Lamb is come, and his wife hath made herself ready. 8 And to her was granted that she should be arrayed in fine linen, clean and white: for the fine linen is the righteousness of saints. 9 And he saith unto me, Write, Blessed are they which are called unto the marriage supper of the Lamb. And he saith unto me, These are the true sayings of God.523*
>
> (Revelation 19:7-9, KJV)

So now God is satisfied. His march to the New Jerusalem is ended and His plan to have a people who love and obey Him from their heart is finally fulfilled. This beautiful relationship will continue throughout eternity.

---

[521] Ibid. Pages 192 and 193.

[522] The Holy Bible: King James Version. Oak Harbor: Logos Research Systems, Inc., 1995.

[523] Ibid.

CHAPTER SIXTEEN

Summary

A. Summary

God's march to the New Jerusalem started at the time that God created the heavens and earth. Then He created the angelic host who worshipped and served Him. One day sin entered into heaven; one special angel named Lucifer rebelled with one third of the angelic host against God Almighty. Lucifer, a created being, wanted to be like God and desired to be worshipped like God. He was therefore thrown out of heaven for his rebellion along with one-third of the angelic host who were foolish enough to be his followers.

As time passed, God was lonesome so He had a desire to create a creature who would worship Him and obey Him willingly from his heart. He created Adam and later his wife Eve. In time, they disobeyed God and sin entered their perfect paradise which God had created. God made a promise to Adam and Eve that the Messiah would come through the seed of the woman. He would die for their sins. But as a reminder of God's promised provision. God sacrificed a lamb for their sins. The lamb was to be a substitute for the Messiah until He would come. Then the Messiah would be their sacrificial Lamb. They were to make a sacrifice whenever they transgressed God's commandment. This reminder has continued over the centuries.

Many generations past after Adam's sin and in due time Noah, who was of the line of Seth who was Adam's third son, was born. Noah was a righteous man. Also his genealogy was perfect. It was not polluted by angelic intermarriage with the human race in his family tree. God commanded Noah to build an ark to house his family which included his wife and their three sons (Ham, Shem and Japheth) as well as their wives.

The ark would also be large enough to house a pair of every unclean creature or animal as well as seven pairs of every clean animal. There also needed to be enough room to take care of all their food.

It took 120 years to build the ark. During this time, Noah witnessed to his evil generation concerning God's judgment of a coming flood. They only laughed and mocked him. They had never seen rain.

Just before the flood came, the Lord God brought the animals to the ark. He told Noah and his family to enter the ark with the animals. Then the Lord closed the door of the ark.

The fountains of the deep broke and the heavens above released heavy rains. It rained forty days and nights. The waters rose over the highest mountains.

A little over a year later, God rested the ark on Mount Ararat and told Noah and his family to leave the ark. The animals also left the ark. God blessed Noah and his family as well as the animals and told them to be fruitful and multiply and fill the earth.

The Lord also gave Noah and his family and all generations that would follow the sign of the rainbow. This was a sign that He would never again destroy the earth by a flood.

After many generations, Abram, who was of the line of Shem (one of the sons of Noah), was called by God to leave Ur of the Chaldees. God promised to give Abram a land to him and his descendants. He also promised that he would be a father of a nation through his wife Sarai, even though they were quite old and childless.

In time, Abram and Sarah gave up waiting. Sarai suggested that Abram take Hagar, her hand-maiden, as a wife and let her bear a son for him.

Ishmael was born. Thirteen years later God spoke to Abram and promised him that Sarai would bear him a son by this time next year.

Isaac was born. He grew and when he was weaned, Ishmael mocked Isaac. Sarah was angry. She told Abraham to get rid of Hagar and her son since he was not to be heir with her son Isaac. Abraham was grieved—he loved Ishmael. This was the beginning of the Israeli and Arab conflict that has lasted many centuries even until now.

When Sarah was about 120, she died. Isaac was a young man. Abraham was concerned that Isaac should have a wife from among his relatives and not from the people of Canaan where he dwelt. So Abraham sent his servant to Ur to bring back Rebecca to be Isaac's wife.

After twenty years of marriage, Rebecca gave birth to twins. The eldest was Esau and the younger was Jacob. After Jacob stole the first-born blessing from his brother by deceiving his father, he fled to his Uncle Laban, who was Rebecca's brother, because Esau threatened to kill Jacob. There he settled down and took care of Laban's sheep. While he was at his Uncle Laban's, he married his two cousins, Rachel and Leah, and also their two maids, Bilhah and Zilpah. Twelve sons were born to them.

After about twenty years, Jacob fled the country with his family and his flocks that he had earned as his wages. His father-in-law followed Jacob, planning on killing him for taking all of Jacob's wives and children as well as his flocks. But God intervened. God told Laban in a dream not to do or say anything good or evil to Jacob. When Laban caught up with Jacob, they made a covenant between them. They went their separate ways. Jacob returned to Bethel in Canaan after leaving his father-in-law. There he dwelt for many years.

Joseph, the eldest son of Rachael, Jacob's favorite wife, was given a special coat. This made his older brothers envious. One day Joseph told his brothers about a dream he had—that he was to be a ruler over them. They became angry and were planning on killing him. But Judah suggested that they sell him to the Ishmaelite traders as a slave. These traders were going to Egypt. There Joseph was sold to Potiphar who made Joseph steward of his house. Potiphar's wife made continuous advances. In time, she caught Joseph alone. He fled and left his coat behind. She falsely accused Joseph of rape. As a result Joseph ended in prison— but God was there.

After a couple of years, Pharaoh dreamed two terrible dreams. He needed an interpreter. The butler remembered Joseph and told the Pharaoh about Joseph interpreting his dream.

Pharaoh summoned Joseph from prison and told him about the two scary dreams. Joseph replied, "God is the One who interprets dreams. Egypt is about to go through seven years of abundant harvests to be followed by seven years of famine." Then Joseph made several suggestions as to what might be done to prepare for this coming famine. Pharaoh was so pleased with him that he made Joseph second in command in Egypt.

When the famine came to Egypt, it also came to Joseph's family who were living in Canaan. When Jacob heard there was food in Egypt, he sent all his sons to Egypt except Benjamin. On their second trip to Egypt they also took their youngest brother Benjamin with them in spite of their father Jacob's objections. At that time Joseph revealed himself to his brothers.

Joseph and Pharaoh invited Joseph's family to come to Egypt to live in the land of Goshen where they would be provided for. Goshen would be suitable for them and their cattle. At that time, there were still five years left of the famine that God had promised.

During the famine, the children of Israel (Jacob) were well taken care of; however, the average citizen of Egypt had to barter everything they had over the period of the famine in order to get food. After the seven years of famine they had to give one-fifth of their harvest to Pharaoh yearly.

Shortly before the death of Israel, Israel blessed all of his sons and also the two sons of Joseph. He told each one what would happen in the future of each son. Judah was told that the Messiah would be his descendant. After his death, he was buried in Canaan, the burial place of Abraham. After Israel's death, Joseph's brothers were fearful that Joseph would take revenge on them for selling him into slavery. Joseph comforted them and said that God had sent him to Egypt ahead to provide for them.

Joseph lived until he saw his great-great-grandchildren. On his death bed, he made the children of Israel promise that when they left Egypt and returned to Canaan, they would take his bones and bury them in Canaan.

After a period of time, a Pharaoh arose that did not know about Joseph. He was worried because the children of Israel had multiplied to a large national threat. So, he put out an edict that all the male children of Israel were to be killed.

At this time Moses was born. After he was three months old, his mother put Moses in a reed basket in the Nile River. His sister followed the basket to see what would happen. Pharaoh's daughter saw the basket. When she opened the basket, she saw the child who was crying; she decided to adopt him. Moses' mother was hired to become a nurse to the child until he was weaned. Then he was taken into Pharaoh's palace to be raised as a prince.

When Moses was forty years old, he was burdened for the Hebrews. He killed an Egyptian while defending a Jewish slave. Then he fled to Midian to avoid being killed by Pharaoh for his crime.

While Moses dwelt in Midian, he married Zipporah the daughter of Jethro, who was a priest of Midian. Zipporah and Moses had two sons.

Moses made his living by tending his father-in-law's sheep. After Moses was in Midian forty years, he saw a burning bush that was not consumed. He approached the bush. There God spoke out of the bush and commissioned Moses to go to Egypt and free the children of Israel from slavery and take them to the Promised Land of Canaan.

Moses hesitated because he knew he would have to talk to Pharaoh and he was not a good speaker. So God agreed to let Moses' brother Aaron be the spokesman or priest.

God warned Moses that Pharaoh would harden his heart, in spite of all the plagues that would be sent on Egypt and its people, animals and harvest. But, after the last plague—the tenth—when God slayed all the first born of all the people of Egypt and their animals, the children of Israel were kicked out of the country. The children of Israel were spared the tenth plague because of the blood of the lamb that was put on their side door posts as well as the upper door post. It was to be a sign to the angel of death that those who were in this house were under the blood of the lamb. Those who were in the house were dressed in their traveling clothes ready to travel to the Promised Land while they were eating a Passover meal in honor of God's protection of the children of Israel.

Not a family in Egypt was exempt from someone of their family being killed after the death angel passed through Egypt. The Egyptians and Pharaoh were afraid and demanded that the children of Israel leave immediately.

Over two million Jews left Egypt and journeyed toward the Red Sea.

Then, the Pharaoh hardened his heart and realized his workforce was gone. He also thought he and his army would trap them and bring back the children of Israel and put them back into slavery.

God protected the people and their flock from the Egyptians. Under Moses direction, they miraculously crossed the Red Sea on dry ground. After they had all safely crossed, Pharaoh and his army followed, but were all destroyed when the sea returned to its place.

The journey to the Promised Land should have taken only a few weeks. But because of the people's rebellion against God and Moses, the children of Israel wandered in the wilderness for forty years. It took forty years for the older rebellious generation to die off, and a new generation was born that would go into the promised land of Canaan.

God took care of the needs of the people in the wilderness. They were given manna for food and water for them to drink as well as their flocks; a cloud by day to keep cool and a fiery cloud by night to keep them warm. This cloud also led them during their wilderness march. Their clothing and shoes never wore out during the forty-year journey in the wilderness.

Moses received from God the laws and the ordinances to govern the people's daily lives and conduct, as well as their spiritual lives. Moses received these laws from God on Mount Sinai.

Moses also received from God plans for the tabernacle which would be the center of Israel's worship. The priests were to be of the tribe of Levi. Aaron, Moses' brother, was to be high priest and his sons were also to serve in the tabernacle.

The tabernacle was an ornate collapsible structure. The furnishings were of gold. The large altar for sacrifices was brass. The ark of the covenant held the Ten Commandments, Aaron's rod that budded and a pot of manna. It was placed in the holy of holies of the tabernacle. It was here that the Shekinah glory of God dwelt on the mercy seat of the ark of the covenant.

The people were aware of God's presence in the camp. They knew He was in the tabernacle in the fiery cloud that led them by night, and also they could see the glow on Moses' face every time he spent time communing with God.

After forty years of wondering, God chose Joshua to replace Moses when the new generation had grown up and were eager to enter the Promised Land.

Moses was allowed to take a glimpse into Canaan from Mount Nebo shortly before Israel crossed into Canaan. Then Moses died on the mountain and God took him.

Joshua led the children of Israel across the Jordan at the flood season of the year. The priests were the first to step into the river carrying the ark of the covenant. Then, God caused the river to back up; the people crossed over on dry ground.

Israel then crossed the river and fought many battles and subdued most of their enemies. Then the land was divided among the twelve tribes. Three tribes received their inheritance on the east side of the Jordan while nine tribes received their inheritance on the west side.

The inheritance of the tribe of Levi was the Lord and various priest cities scattered throughout the land of Israel. They also received tithes and offerings from the people.

A period of a couple of hundred years passed since they entered the land of Canaan. During this time, the people were ruled by judges who were raised up by God to protect the people from their enemies. Not only were many of the judges warriors, but many expounded God's Law to the people.

The last judge to be raised by God was Samuel who was a priest. He was a just judge. He later anointed a king over the people because they wanted a king—his name was Saul. He was the people's choice. They wanted a champion to rule them.

Years later, Samuel anointed David of the tribe of Judah to be king. He was God's choice. After the death of Saul, David became king, first of the tribes of Judah and Benjamin and later of the rest of Israel.

During most of David's life he was a warrior. He was a man after God's own heart. One of his heart's desires was to build a temple for the Lord, but the Lord, through Nathan the prophet, told David he could not build the temple because he was a man of blood. However, his son Solomon would be the one who would build the temple. God gave David one other promise: It was that the Messiah would be one of his descendants.

Even though God told David he could not build the temple, he made many preparations for the temple. He purchased Mount Moriah to be the place where the temple was to be built. He gathered silver, gold, precious stones, fine wood and also quarried stone off site for the temple. He also had architectural plans, as well as the needed furnishings, ready for the temple.

In time, Solomon was made king while David was alive. Then David passed on his commission to build the temple to his son Solomon.

In time, Solomon built the temple, as directed by his father, and filled it with the furnishings his father left. Other furnishings were also made under Solomon's direction.

After the temple was completed, Solomon had a dedication for the temple. He also prayed, asking God to remember His people and forgive their sins. God answered his request by burning up the sacrifice on the altar with lightening. God also answered another request of Solomon to give him wisdom to rule his people wisely. Solomon became the wisest man that ever lived.

After Solomon's death, the kingdom of Israel became divided. His son Rehoboam ruled the southern kingdom which included Benjamin and Judah. It was in the southern kingdom where the city of Jerusalem and the temple were located. A rival ruler, Jeroboam, ruled the rest of the northern kingdom of Israel.

All the kings of Israel were wicked. They worshipped all the pagan gods of the land. The people of Israel were later captured and taken into captivity in 721 BC.

Judah wasn't much better than Israel. There were a few good kings; but most of them were evil and caused the people to sin by worshipping heathen gods. The prophets warned both Israel and Judah of God's coming judgment. Later the people of Judah were taken into captivity in Babylon in 586 BC. At that time the temple and the city of Jerusalem were destroyed.

The children of Judah sojourned in Babylon for seventy years. During this time Daniel, a Jew, was a ruler in the Babylonian court under several kings. Later he ruled in the court of Cyrus of Persia. Daniel was blessed by God, who showed Daniel what would happen to Israel in the future and also the end of times.

After seventy years of captivity of the Jews, Cyrus issued an edict that would allow the Jews who would go to return to Jerusalem and rebuild the temple. Some of the people responded to the challenge and returned to build the temple. The Samaritans living in the land caused the people to stop the work for twenty years. The prophets in Israel encouraged the people to build the temple. After the temple was built, it was dedicated to God.

It was King Artaxerxes who made a decree for any Jew who would return to Israel to take offerings and the temple treasure back to Israel to be used in the temple worship. Ezra was chosen to lead the people on their journey to deliver the treasure to Israel. When they arrived in Jerusalem, the people celebrated and repented for their sins and for the sins of their fathers who did not obey God's law.

Nehemiah, who was serving under King Artaxerxes, was commissioned to go back and rebuild the walls of Jerusalem. When Nehemiah arrived in Jerusalem, he surveyed the damage done to the city walls. He then encouraged the people to build the walls, in spite of the surrounding enemies who were trying to stop the process. It took fifty-three days to rebuild the wall, which was a miracle. This caused the enemies to realize that God was with the Jews.

After the walls were built, Ezra read the Law of Moses to the people and the people repented for their sins. Then the walls of the city were dedicated and they celebrated the Feast of Tabernacles.

There is a period of four hundred years from the time of the last prophet in Israel to the time of the New Testament. During this time, Antiochus Epiphanies took over the area of Israel. He had a desire to Hellenize the world, so he outlawed Judaism and forced the Greek culture on the Jews. He even desecrated the temple by sacrificing a pig on the altar. Among the laws forbidden by Antiochus Epiphanies was the celebrating of the Sabbath, circumcision and the eating of kosher food.

The family of Maccabaeus, who were priests, revolted with many of the people of Israel on their side, and they fought against Antiochus Epiphanies and won. They cleaned the temple and dedicated it to God in remembrance of the occasion. The Jews celebrate the Festival of Lights, also known as Hanukah. Shortly before the New Testament era, the family of Herod the Great was ruling in Israel. Herod the King of Judah desired to remodel the temple in Jerusalem so it would be larger and grander than Solomon's. It was started in 19 BC and finished shortly before its destruction by Titus in 70 AD. It was in that temple that God's presence was seen in Yeshua.

About 4 BC Yeshua, who was the prophesied Messiah, was born to Mary, a virgin who was engaged to Joseph. He was a carpenter of Nazareth. This birth took place in Bethlehem during the Feast of Tabernacles, when Rome had issued an edict that every person in the known world was to return to their families' ancestral place of birth. After Yeshua's birth, Joseph took Mary and the child to Egypt where they stayed for a couple years because of God's warning to Joseph in a dream that Herod was planning on killing all the babies two years old and younger in Bethlehem.

When Joseph returned to Israel with his family they went to Nazareth and settled there. There Yeshua grew in favor with God and man. There He worked in the carpenter trade until God, His Father, called Him, at age thirty, to His mission which was His destiny to be Savior of mankind.

One day, John the Baptist, Yeshua's cousin, was calling the people to repent and be baptized for their sins. Yeshua came and submitted to be baptized, in spite of John's objection that he himself needed to be baptized instead of Yeshua.

After Yeshua's baptism, He was led into the desert. There He fasted and was tempted by the devil three times.

Then Yeshua started His ministry of healings, forgiveness and teaching the people. During this time He chose twelve disciples. His ministry lasted about three years.

Yeshua told His disciples of His coming sacrificial death. They could not believe this would happen. They were expecting a King Messiah, not a suffering servant who would die for their sins.

The Sunday of the week of Passover Yeshua made a grand entrance into Jerusalem, riding on a colt of a donkey that had never been ridden. The people praised God and waved palm branches as He rode into Jerusalem.

While He was in Jerusalem, Yeshua cleansed the temple and preached to the people. The Scribes and the Pharisees locked horns with Yeshua. Then Yeshua spoke of the end of times. At this time the Pharisees and Judas Iscariot, a disciple of Yeshua, set up the final plot to kill Yeshua. It happened after the Passover meal. Judas Iscariot left and went to the priests and told them where they would find Yeshua that evening and how to recognize Him.

Meanwhile, Yeshua and the other disciples, after the meal, instituted the communion service to celebrate Yeshua's death and resurrection. Then Yeshua comforted His disciples. Then they sang a hymn and went to Gethsemane to pray. While Yeshua was praying, the other disciples slept. Then Judas Iscariot came with the priests and soldiers to betray Yeshua. Judah betrayed Yeshua with a kiss. Then He was taken to be judged first by the High Priest, then Pontius Pilate, and then Herod, and later again by Pilate.

The other disciples fled. Judas Iscariot later repented of his deed but committed suicide. Yeshua was crucified according to Psalm 22 and Isaiah 53. He was then buried in a rich man's tomb. After three days He arose from the grave, according to scripture, on Resurrection Sunday. He appeared to many of His disciples at various times for a period of forty days. He was seen by as many as five hundred people at a time. He ascended to heaven from Mount Olivet forty days after His Resurrection. He was seen by five hundred people.

Then one hundred and twenty of the people who believed in Yeshua stayed in an upper room in Jerusalem for ten days—which is the Feast of Pentecost or First Fruits. There they received the Holy Spirit as promised by Yeshua. The Spirit gave them boldness and the ability to speak in other languages, leading thousands to the Lord. Thus the Church was born.

After much persecution the Church scattered throughout the Roman Empire. One of the persecutors was Saul of Tarsus. Later Yeshua revealed Himself to Saul. Saul was converted and became Paul the apostle to the Gentiles. He journeyed all over the Roman Empire and led many Gentiles to the Lord. Later he was imprisoned and then killed for his faith. He was also the most prolific writer of the New Testament.

In 70 AD, because of the rebellion of the Jews, Titus destroyed the temple and the city of Jerusalem. The people of Israel were dispersed throughout the empire.

After two thousand years the Jews were put back into the land of Israel. It was after suffering many years of persecution and Hitler's holocaust. On May 14, 1948, Israel became a nation. From the day Israel was born, they have been in constant conflict with their Arab neighbors. They were also in the place where they were to be, according to God's time clock. On June 5, 1967, Israel captured the city of Jerusalem and the mountain where the temple of Solomon was located in the Six-Day War. Ezekiel had a vision of Israel's return to the land and the temple that would be rebuilt.

There are many signs that show that Yeshua's return is near. It will be like the days of Noah and Lot. There will be much violence and immorality. There will be an increase of natural calamities such as earthquakes and floods. There will be human tracking devices that will be used and knowledge will increase. Most important of all, the third temple will be rebuilt.

The third temple is now in the process of being built. The precise location on the mount has been established as to where the temple is to be built; the Sanhedrin has been reestablished. The gathering and the making of temple tools and artifacts are being completed. The anointing oil has been located. The ark of the covenant will be brought forth at the appointed time. The priests for the temple are being trained and their clothing is being prepared for worship.

The water of purification is being prepared, as well as the breeding of the pure red heifer. Special priestly children are being prepared who will offer the red heifer as a sacrifice when the time comes for the temple to be put on Mount Zion.

While all the temple preparations are going on, the stage is now being set for the coming of the Antichrist who will bring a false peace in the world after the Battle of Armageddon. He will fool the Muslims and Jews to believe that he is the Messiah. He will have a peace treaty with Israel for seven years so that Israel can build her temple. In the middle of the seven years, he will enter the holy of holies and defile the sanctuary and claim himself as God. Israel will realize that they were fooled and have followed the wrong man.

Before the Antichrist is revealed, the rapture or catching up of the saints to heaven by Yeshua will take place. Those who are alive and believe in Yeshua as well as those who died in Yeshua shall rise and be judged for leadership positions in the millennial kingdom, depending on their faithfulness to God while they lived on Earth.

During the seven years of tribulation, Israel will be purged and those who make it through the tribulation will be brought into Yeshua's presence and will realize that He is the Messiah. Israel as a nation will be saved and will go into the millennial kingdom with Yeshua.

When the tribulation wars are going on around Jerusalem, Yeshua with His saints will return to Earth. Those nations who were fighting each other will turn and fight Yeshua and His army to keep Him from establishing His kingdom on Earth. They will fail.

After the war, Yeshua will judge the Gentile nations on how they treated the Jews, as well as the tribulation saints. Those nations that treated the Jews and tribulation saints kindly will be allowed to remain as nations in the millennial kingdom. Those who did not treat Israel kindly will cease to exist as nations.

Individuals who are not believers will be put in a special place under the earth until the time they will face their final judgment at the end of the Millennium. There will be a short interval of a couple of months between Yeshua's second return and the beginning of the Millennium. During this period, Yeshua will renew the earth's geography as well as the landscape. There will be a change in land masses, as well as rivers, lakes and seas. The land will be a lush garden and there will be many animals and fruit-bearing trees and herbs.

The millennial temple and the city of Jerusalem will be built. The temple will be about one square mile in size, in order to be able to house all the people of the earth when need be for special feasts.

The wedding feast of the Lamb, (Yeshua) and His bride (the Church), will take place and all who are present at the banquet will be all the people who have been saved from the beginning of time to the second return of Messiah Yeshua. The people from the tribulation who come into the kingdom will be saved and will be able to marry and have children. The saints with glorified bodies will not marry and have children.

The children born in the Millennium will need to make Yeshua Lord of their lives before the age of one hundred or they will die as unbelievers on their one hundredth birthday. Even though Yeshua will be ruling and reigning over all the kingdoms of the earth, still at the end of the one thousand years, millions of youngsters who are less than one hundred years old will rebel under the leadership of Satan. They will surround Jerusalem and the saints of God to try to destroy Yeshua and His rule. A word spoken by Yeshua will cause them to be destroyed by fire and they will turn to ashes.

Ezekiel had a vision of the millennial kingdom where Messiah would be the Shekinah glory for the temple and the city. He also saw the temple and worship using much of the old temple worship and sacrifice to show how Messiah Yeshua fulfilled the various aspects of the service.

There will be music in the Millennium that will pay honor to Yeshua. Many of the Jewish feasts and Sabbaths will be kept, but they will have a much deeper meaning since Yeshua is the Lord of the Sabbath.

In the Millennium there will be a theocratic system of justice with Yeshua as its head. King David will be the king of Israel. The nations of the world will have their own government, but they will be answerable to Yeshua. Each year, representatives are to be sent from each nation at the Feast of Tabernacles. If they neglect to send a representative, that nation will be judged and not receive any rain.

At the end of Millennium, after the war of the rebellious ones, Satan and his angels will be sent to the lake of fire located in the bowels of the earth. He will be with the Antichrist and the false prophet. Then there will be the final judgment of the unbelievers and they will be sent into the lake of fire also. After the judgment of the unbelievers, and Satan and his angels, God will cleanse the heaven and earth from sin by fire. Then He will renew the earth and the heavens.

God has prepared a beautiful city for His children—the New Jerusalem. It is a massive four-square city of transparent gold where the elect and redeemed throughout the ages will live whose names are in the Lamb's Book of Life. There will be no need for lamps or sun or moon because Yeshua will be the light.

The new Jerusalem and the new earth will be like the Garden of Eden.

Life in eternity for the believers will be blessed. It will be a life with activity and purpose. There will be much praising and singing and rejoicing, as well as fellowship in heaven. Yeshua will be close to every believer in eternity. There will be constant communion between the Creator and His creature. It will even be better than it was for Adam and Eve with God before sin found its way into their paradise.

So God is satisfied—He has His special creature that loves and obeys Him willingly from his heart and not by force or obligation. God's march through the ages to the new Jerusalem will work out as He has planned and purposed in His heart, in spite of the work of Satan and mankind who tried to derail God's plan and purpose, of having the Messiah Yeshua (who is God to die for mankind's sins and saving him for eternity) to bring man into eternal fellowship, starting at the point he accepts Yeshua's sacrifice for himself.

B. Conclusions

Through the eons of time, God marched toward His goal! He wanted a creature that would love and obey Him willingly with his heart. His first Creation started with the angelic host. One third of the angels with Lucifer (Satan) as their leader rebelled against God. They are to be judged after the Millennium and thrown into the lake of fire. Some of Satan's angels are incarcerated and are in chains waiting for their final judgment.

After the angels were created, God created mankind (Adam and Eve). Satan decided to mess up God's plan and cause Adam and Eve to sin. They yielded to temptation so sin entered into the human race.

God had a backup plan and promised that the Messiah would come, who would die for their sins as a Passover Lamb. If they would believe in the promise as well as the finished work of God's forgiveness for their sins, they would be saved. As a result, their lives would be changed. Their names would be written in the Lamb's Book of Life. Then they would spend eternity with God in the eternal home He has prepared for them.

Many times throughout history, Satan tried to mess up God's plan of salvation by sin and persecution. He failed many times as God continues to work out His will and He continues His march toward the new Jerusalem with His chosen ones.

Those who do not believe will be condemned and will spend eternity in the lake of fire that was prepared for the devil and his angels.

The ultimate end for the believer is not tribulation, destruction, judgment and suffering, it is the unspeakable glory of God. God's and man's dream for eternity is fulfilled where the Creator and His Creation, mankind, loves and obeys Him willingly. There will be the closeness like Adam and Eve experienced in the Garden of Eden on a continuous basis. There will be peace and fulfillment for all eternity starting now—not only between the Creator and His Creation—but between their fellow man in their eternal home, the New Jerusalem.

God is satisfied. His march to the New Jerusalem is ended and His plan to have a people who love and obey Him from their hearts is finally fulfilled. This beautiful relationship will last throughout eternity.

C. Recommendations

1. How to know you will be in God's eternal home

Dear Friend,
If you wish to be a part of the heavenly new Jerusalem, you need to first know that you are a sinner and you are not able to be right with God on your own merit. You must believe that Yeshua as the Passover Lamb died for your sins. He arose from the grave and ascended into heaven and sits at the right hand of His Father. If you do, pray to ask Yeshua into your heart and forgive your sins.

Here is a suggested prayer:

Dear God, I confess I have sinned against You and I am truly sorry for it. Messiah Yeshua (Jesus), please come into my heart and cleanse me with Your blood. Thank You for doing this according to Your Word. Make me the kind of person You want me to be. I ask in Your name Yeshua, Amen.524

Does this prayer express the desire of your heart? If it does, please pray it now.

Now thank Him by faith for doing this. Some people have emotional experiences; others do not. Thank Him for coming into your heart on the authority of the Scripture.

Did you invite the Messiah into your heart and life? Did you really mean it? Then where is Yeshua?

God says:

---

[524] "Have You Ever Heard of the Five Jewish Laws?" The Messianic Jewish Movement International Inc. Bethesda:

Because ye have taken my silver and my gold and have carried into your temples my goodly pleasant things.525

(Joel 3:5, KJV)

God is not a man that he should lie. He is not a human, that he should change his mind. Has he ever spoken and failed to act? Has he ever promised and not carried it through?526

(Numbers 23:19, NLT)

The moment that you ask Messiah Yeshua into your heart and life as an act of faith, God does many wonderful things for you including the following:

Your sins are atoned for (forgiven).

All of us have strayed away like sheep. We have left God's paths to follow our own. Yet the LORD laid on him the guilt and sins of us all.527

(Isaiah 53:6, NLT)

You receive righteousness (right-standing-with-God by faith).

And Abram believed the LORD, and the LORD declared him righteous because of his faith.528

(Genesis 15:6, NLT)

Look at the proud! They trust in themselves, and their lives are crooked; but the righteous will live by their faith.529

(Habakkuk 2:4, NLT)

You enter into a personal relationship with God and you become a child of God!

"This covenant will not be like the one I made with their ancestors when I took them by the hand and brought them out of the land of Egypt. They broke that covenant, though I loved them as a husband loves his wife," says the LORD.530

(Jeremiah 31:32, NLT)

You receive eternal life!

---

[525] The Messianic Jewish Movement International Inc. 1974. Page 15.

[526] Holy Bible: New Living Translation. Wheaton: Tyndale House, 1997.

[527] Holy Bible: New Living Translation. Wheaton: Tyndale House, 1997.

[528] Ibid.

[529] Ibid.

[530] Ibid.

5 Because ye have taken my silver and my gold, and have carried into your temples my goodly pleasant things.531

(Joel 3:5, KJV)

2 Many of those whose bodies lie dead and buried will rise up, some to everlasting life and some to shame and everlasting contempt.532

(Daniel 12:2, NLT)

God's Holy Spirit (Ruach Ha-Kadesh) enters your life.

And I will give them singleness of heart and put a new spirit within them. I will take away their hearts of stone and give them tender hearts instead.533

(Ezekiel 11:19, NLT)

Then I will pour out a spirit of grace and prayer on the family of David and on all the people of Jerusalem. They will look on me whom they have pierced and mourn for him as for an only son. They will grieve bitterly for him as for a firstborn son who has died.534

(Zechariah 12:10, NLT)

You begin the abundant life and the exciting adventure for which God created you......to know God and to make Him known.

11 He made darkness his secret place; his pavilion round about him were dark waters and thick clouds of the skies.535

(Psalm 18:11, NLT)

"But you are my witnesses, O Israel!" says the LORD. "And you are my servant. You have been chosen to know me, believe in me, and understand that I alone am God. There is no other God; there never has been and never will be.536

(Isaiah 43:10, NLT)

How to grow in God's abundant life:

Confess any future sins to God and forsake them.

---

[531] The Holy Bible: King James Version. Oak Harbor: Logos Research Systems, Inc., 1995.

[532] Holy Bible: New Living Translation. Wheaton: Tyndale House, 1997.

[533] Ibid.

[534] Ibid.

[535] The Holy Bible: King James Version. Oak Harbor: Logos Research Systems, Inc., 1995.

[536] Ibid.

People who cover over their sins will not prosper. But if they confess and forsake them, they will receive mercy.537

(Proverbs 28:13, NLT)

Pray to God and praise (thank) God much!

The LORD hates the sacrifice of the wicked, but he delights in the prayers of the upright.538

(Proverbs 15:8, NLT)

Read God's Word two or three times daily.

But they delight in doing everything the LORD wants; day and night they think about his law.539

(Psalm 1:2, NLT)

Memorize Bible verses.

Open my eyes to see the wonderful truths in your law.540

(Psalm 119:18, NLT)

Fellowship at least weekly with other Bible believers.

Then those who feared the LORD spoke with each other, and the LORD listened to what they said. In his presence, a scroll of remembrance was written to record the names of those who feared him and loved to think about him.541

(Malachi 3:16, NLT)

---

[537] Holy Bible: New Living Translation. Wheaton: Tyndale House, 1997.

[538] Holy Bible: New Living Translation. Wheaton: Tyndale House, 1997.

[539] Ibid.

[540] Ibid.

[541] Ibid.

Appendix A

Outline of Book

Appendix B

LIST OF TABLES

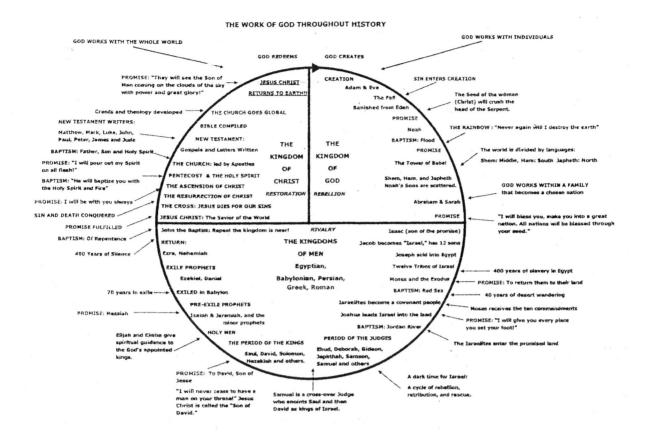

Fig. #1

This diagram is designed to give a quick overview of the history of God at work in our world. It begins with Creation and moves through God's relationship with individuals, then a family (ethnicity) and then with the entire world. In the beginning God Creates, and at the end God completely Redeems his creation when Christ returns to reign as King of kings and Lord of lords. There are three main teaching points in the diagram. They are as follows.

1. THE PROMISES OF GOD: There are at least ten promises throughout history that I have recorded here. Most of them point directly to Jesus who fulfills them all! Nine of these promises have been fulfilled, but the last is yet to come. Since God has fulfilled all of his promises until now, there is no reason to believe that he will not fulfill the final one!

2. BAPTISMS: As I moved through history I began to see baptism as a very significant event in the life of God's creation. Each baptism (of which there are six) represents the leaving behind of an old life, being cleansed or filled, and taking on a brand new life in relationship to God! These re crisis moments in the lives of those who pass through them. Their lives are never the same after having experienced God's baptizing work.

3. KINGDOMS: I have divided the circle into three kingdoms, which in reality are only two, for the kingdom of God and of Christ are one in the same. I only do this for historical purposes. In the italicized print I have three words. *REBELLION, RIVALRY, and RESTORATION.* This describes the relationship of God and his creation. Under the first, "The kingdom of God" we see people relating to God as the authority in their lives. Many rebelled against God, but they still knew that God was God and king! But a subtle shift happens after the tower of Babel incident. At Babel the community of earth joined forces to rebel against God, but after Babel, kingdoms and cultures sprang up, creating their own gods and their own forms of worship. These kingdoms became Rival Kingdoms, "The Kingdoms of Men." Now rebellion added a new twist, rivalry. The kingdom of Christ comes to restore the reign of God in the hearts and lives of those who would make him king.

542

---

[542] Turner, Pastor Benjamin of Boise Five Mile Church of the Nazarene, Boise, Idaho.

Fig. #2

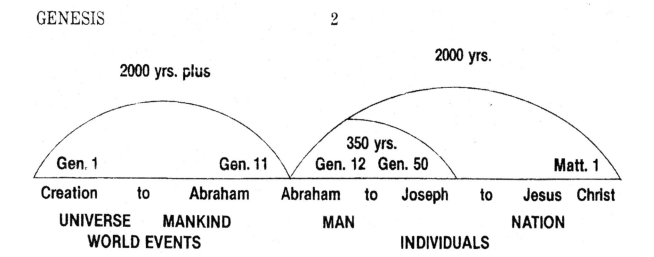

GENESIS   2

543

543 McGee, J. Vernon, Thru the Bible with J. Vernon McGee. Vol. 1 (Gen-Deu.). Pasadena: Thru the Bible Radio, c 1981. Page 2.

Fig. #3

ANCIENT RULERS			
Kings of Egypt		The Ptolemies.	
(Dates after Flinders Petrie, "History of Egypt.")		Ptolemy I. Soter	306 -285
		Ptolemy II. Philadelphus	285 -247
	BC	Ptolemy III. Euergetes I.	247 -222
Menes	4777- 4715	Ptolemy IV. Philopator I.	222 -204/205
Khufu (Cheops)	3969- 3908	Ptolemy V. Epiphanies	204/ 205-181
		Ptolemy VI. Eupator	181
Twelfth Dynasty		PtolemyVII. Philometor I.	181 -146
Amenemhat I.	2778- 2748	Cleopatra I. (regent)	181 -173
Usertesen I.	2758- 2714	PtolemyVIII. Philometor II.	146
Amenemhat II.	2716- 2681	Ptolemy IX. Euergetes II.	146 -117
Usertesen II.	2684- 2660	Ptolemy X. Soter II.	117 -107
Usertesen III.	2660- 2622	Ptolemy XI. Alexander I.	107 -88
Amenemhat III.	2622- 2578	Soter II. (again)	88- 81

Two kings	2578-2565	Ptolemy XII. Alexander II.	81
		Ptolemy XIII. Auletes	81-58
Eighteenth Dynasty		Berenice IV. (queen)	58-55
Aahmes I.	1587-1562	Auletes (again)	55-52
Amenhotep I.	1562-1541	Cleopatra VI.	52-49
Thothmes I.	1541-1516	Ptolemy XIV., Cleopatra's brother	52-48
Thothmes II.	1516-1503	Cleopatra VI. (again)	48-30
Hatasu (queen)	1503-1481	Ptolemy XV., Cleopatra's brother	48-45

Thothmes III.	1481-1449	Ptolemy XVI., Cleopatra's son	45-30
Amenhotep II.	1449-1423		
Thothmes IV.	1423-1414	Kings of Assyria.	
Amenhotep III.	1414-1383	Tiglath-Pileser I.	112 0-1100
Five kings	1383-1328	Tiglath-Pileser II.	950 -930
		Asur-dan II.	930 -911
Nineteenth Dynasty		Ramman-Nirari II	911 -890

Rameses I.	1328-1326	Tukulti-Nindar	890 -884
Seti I.	1326-1300	Asurnazirpal	884 -860
Rameses II.	1300-1234	Shalmaneser II.	860 -824
Mineptah	1234-1214	Shamas-Rimmon IV.	824 -811
Five kings	1214-1202	Ramman-Nirari III.	811 -782
		Shalmaneser III.	782 -772
Shishak	952-930	Asur-dan III.	772 -754
		Asur-nirari	754 -745
Twenty—sixth Dynasty		Tiglath-Pileser III. (Phul)	745 -727
Psammetichus I.	664- 610	Shalmaneser IV. Or V.	727 - 722/721
Necho II.	610-594	Sargon	721 -722-705
Psammetichus II.	594-589	Sennacherib	705 -681
Uahabra	589-570	Esarhaddon	681 -669
Aahmes II.	570-526	Asurbanipal	668 -626
Psammetichus III.	526-525	Two Kings	626 -606

Kings of Babylon		Roman Emperors	
	BC	Augustus	27 BC-14 AD

Cyrus	559-529	Tiberius	14-37
Cambyses	529-522	Caligula	37-41
Darius Hystaspes I	522-485	Claudius I.	41-54
Xerxes I	486(5)-465(4)	Nero	54-68
Artaxerxes Longimanus	465(4)-425(4)	Galba	68-69
Xerxes II.	425(4)	Otho	69
Darius Nothus II	425(4)-423-404	Vitellius	69
Artaxerxes Mnemon	405-361(59)	Vespasian	70-79
Artaxerxes III.	361(59)-338	Titus	79-81
Arses	338-336	Domitian	81-96
Darius Codomanus	336-330	Nerva	96-98
Kings of Macedonia (Greece)			
Amyntas II	394-370		
Alexander II.	369-368		
Ptolemy I	368-365		
Perdiccas III.	365-359		
Amyntas III	359		
Philip II	359-336		
Alexander III. (Macedonian empire)	336-323		

544

---

544 The Reese Chronological Bible. The authorized edition of the original work by Edward Reese. Minneapolis: Bethany House Publishers, 1980. Pages 843-844.

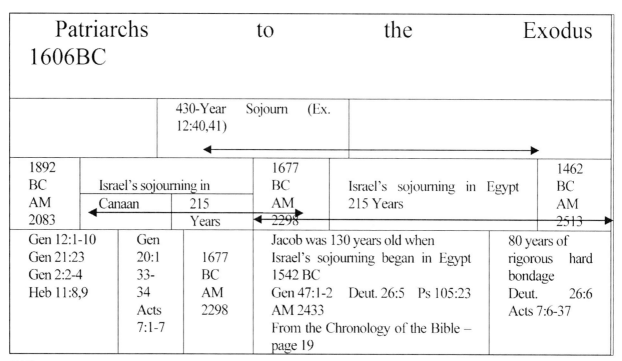

Patriarchs 1606BC		to		the		Exodus
		430-Year Sojourn (Ex. 12:40,41)				
1892 BC AM 2083	Israel's sojourning in		1677 BC AM 2298	Israel's sojourning in Egypt 215 Years		1462 BC AM 2513
	Canaan	215 Years				
Gen 12:1-10 Gen 21:23 Gen 2:2-4 Heb 11:8,9	Gen 20:1 33-34 Acts 7:1-7	1677 BC AM 2298	Jacob was 130 years old when Israel's sojourning began in Egypt 1542 BC Gen 47:1-2 Deut. 26:5 Ps 105:23 AM 2433 From the Chronology of the Bible – page 19		80 years of rigorous hard bondage Deut. 26:6 Acts 7:6-37	

545

Fig. #4

545 Reese, Edward and Frank R. Klossen. The Reese Chronological Bible. Minneapolis: Bethany House Publishers 1975 ©, 1980. Page 118.

Fig. #5

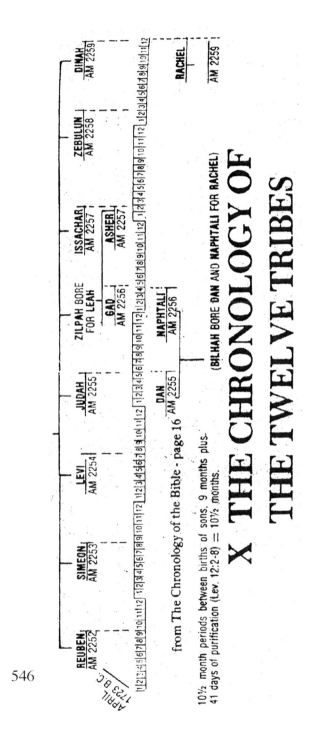

X THE CHRONOLOGY OF THE TWELVE TRIBES

546

[546] Reese, Edward and Frank R. Klossen. The Reese Chronological Bible. Minneapolis: Bethany House Publisher 1975 © 1980, page 672.

Fig. #6

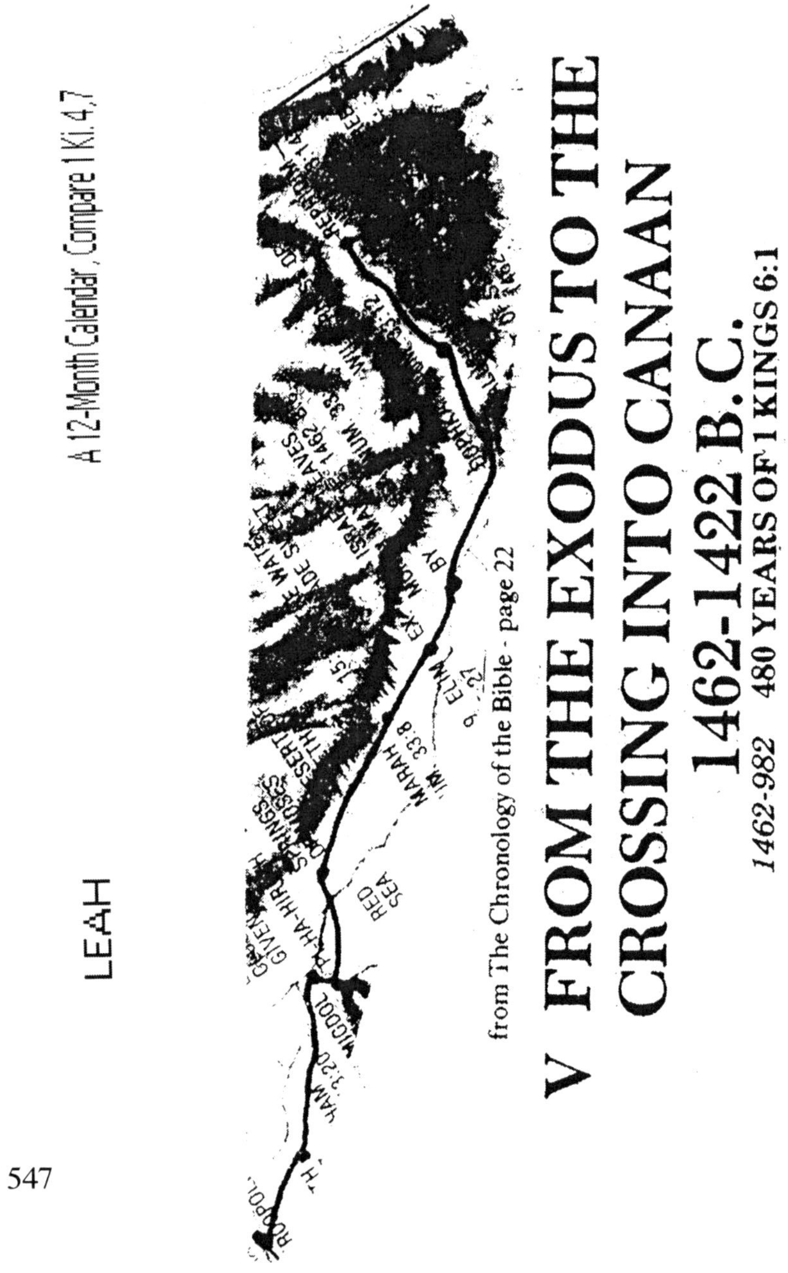
A 12-Month Calendar, Compare 1 Ki. 4,7
LEAH
547
from The Chronology of the Bible - page 22
V FROM THE EXODUS TO THE
CROSSING INTO CANAAN
1462-1422 B.C.
1462-982 480 YEARS OF 1 KINGS 6:1
RED SEA
MARAH
33:8
ELIM
MIGDOL

---

547 Reese, Edward. The Reese Chronological Bible. ©1977. Minneapolis: Bethany House publishers 1980. Page 140.

Fig. #7

SIX PERIODS OF JEWISH HISTORY BEFORE CHRIST

400 B.C.	334	324	204	165	63	5 B.C.
PERSIAN	ALEXANDRIAN	EGYPTIAN	SYRIAN	MACCABEAN	ROMAN	

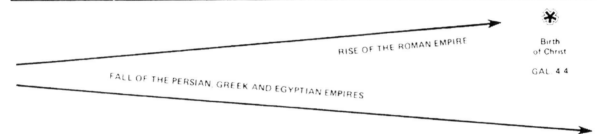

RISE OF THE ROMAN EMPIRE

Birth
of Christ

GAL. 4 4

FALL OF THE PERSIAN, GREEK AND EGYPTIAN EMPIRES

548

548 Jensen, Irving L. Jensen's Survey of the Old Testament. Chicago: Moody Press. 1981. Page 47.

Fig. #8

985 The First Year of Solomon's Reign
  984
    983
      982   The fourth year of Solomon's reign 480 years after exodus (1 Kings 6:7).
        981
          980 The eleventh year (1 Kings 6:38). The eighth month
            979 BUL (November) the temple was completed.
              978
                977
                  976
1 Kings 6:38 11th year— 975 —The eighth month Bul (November) the temple was completed
1 Kings 8:2-8 7th month— 974 —God's ark was brought into the temple (2 Chronicles 5:1-8)
See Levitcus 25———— 973 —The 49th year a sabbatical year of celebration.
Jubilee Year————— 972 —Solomon's dedication was completed[549]

---

[549] Reese, Edward and Frank R. Klossen. The Reese Chronological Bible. Minneapolis: Bethany House Publishers 1975 ©, 1980. Page 588.

Fig. #9

550

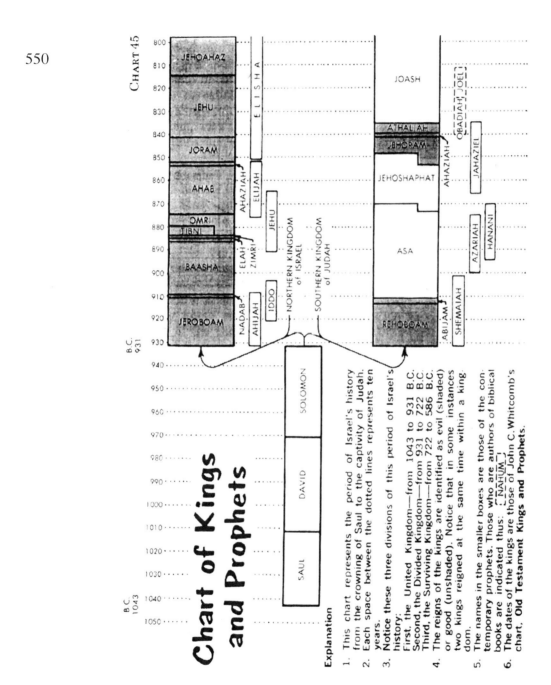

550 Jensen, Irving L. Jensen''s Survey of the Old Testament. Chicago: Moody Press. 1978. Page 188.

395

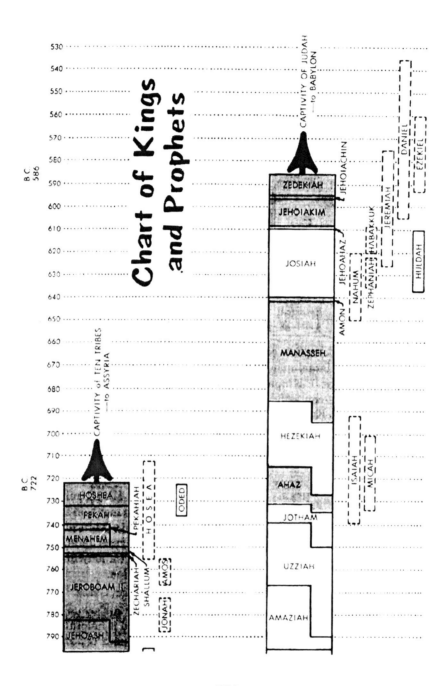

Chart of Kings and Prophets

551

551 Jensen, Irving L. Jensen''s Survey of the Old Testament. Chicago: Moody Press. 1978. Page 189.

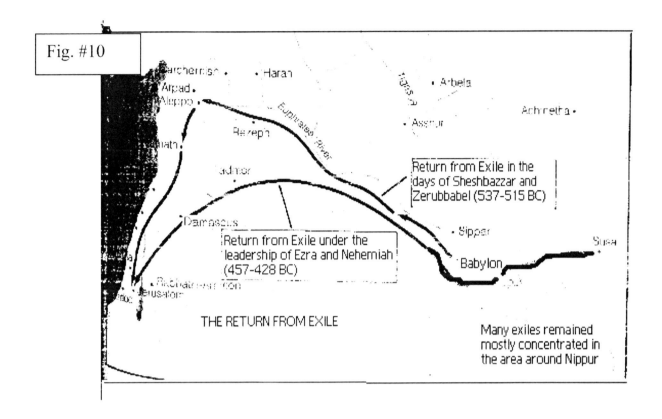

Fig. #10

Return from Exile in the days of Sheshbazzar and Zerubbabel (537-515 BC)

Return from Exile under the leadership of Ezra and Nehemiah (457-428 BC)

THE RETURN FROM EXILE

Many exiles remained mostly concentrated in the area around Nippur

552

---

552 Tenney, Merrill C. The Zondervan Pictorial Encyclopedia of the Bible. Vol. 10, D-G. Grand Rapids: The Zondervan Corporation. ©1975, 1976. Page 427.

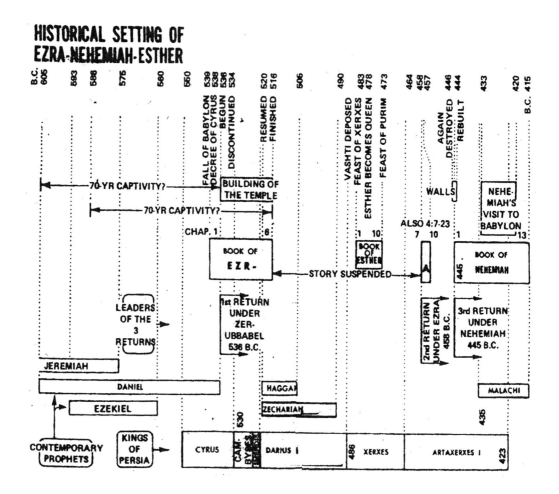

553

Fig. #11

---

553 Jensen, Irving L. Jensen.'s Survey of the Old Testament. Chicago: Moody Press. 1978. Pages 220-221.

Fig. #12

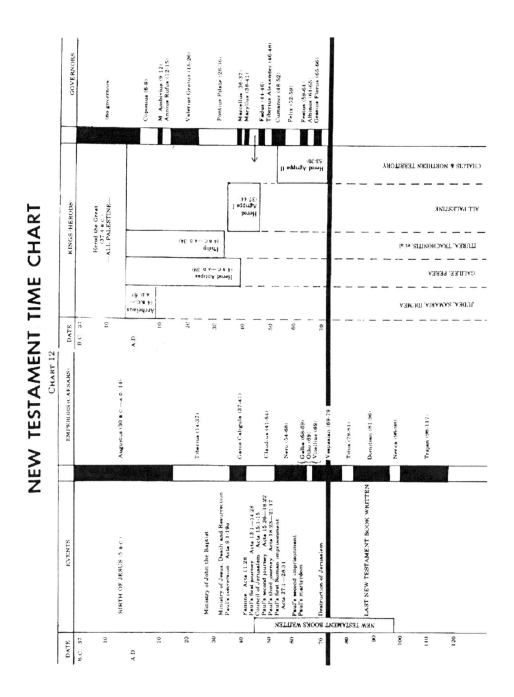

554

[554] Jensen Irving L. Jensen's Survey of the New Testament Chicago: Moody Press 1987, Pg. 61-61

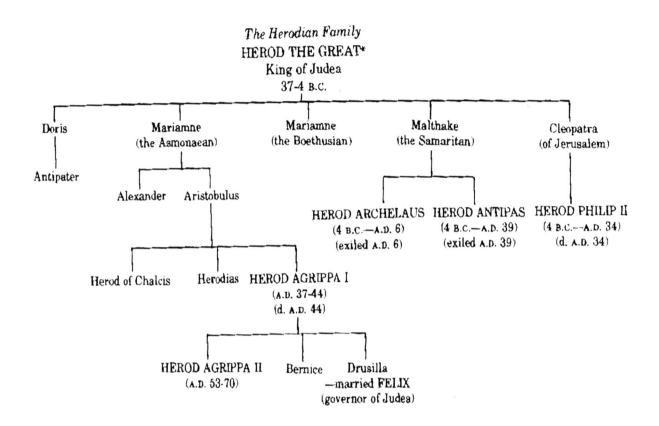

The Herodian Family
HEROD THE GREAT*
King of Judea
37-4 B.C.

* Names of kings noted in the New Testament are capitalized

555

Fig. #13

---

555 Jensen, Irving L. Jensen''s Survey of the New Testament. Chicago: Moody Press. 1981. Appendix A.

Fig. #14

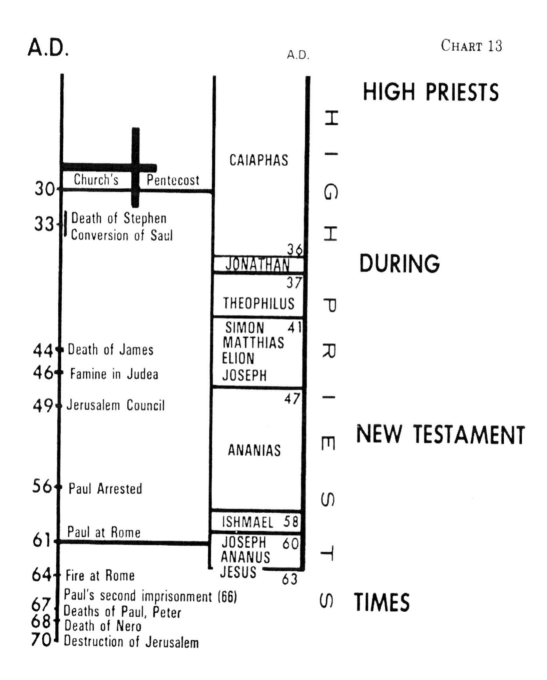

CHART 13

A.D.   A.D.

HIGH PRIESTS

CAIAPHAS

30— Church's | Pentecost

33— Death of Stephen
Conversion of Saul

36
JONATHAN   **DURING**
37
THEOPHILUS

SIMON   41
MATTHIAS
ELION

44— Death of James   JOSEPH

46— Famine in Judea   47

49— Jerusalem Council

ANANIAS   **NEW TESTAMENT**

56— Paul Arrested

ISHMAEL 58
Paul at Rome
61—   JOSEPH   60
ANANUS
64— Fire at Rome   JESUS
63
67— Paul's second imprisonment (66)
Deaths of Paul, Peter   **TIMES**
68— Death of Nero
70— Destruction of Jerusalem

H I G H   P R I E S T S

556

556 Jensen, Irving L. Jensen.'s Survey of the New Testament. Chicago: Moody Press. 1981. Page 62.

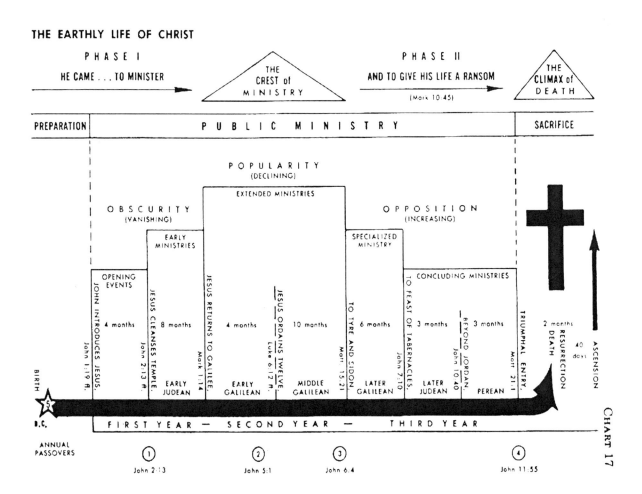

557

Fig. #15

---

557 Jensen, Irving L. Jensen's SUIVey of the New Testament. Chicago: Moody Press. 1981. Page 104.

Fig. #16

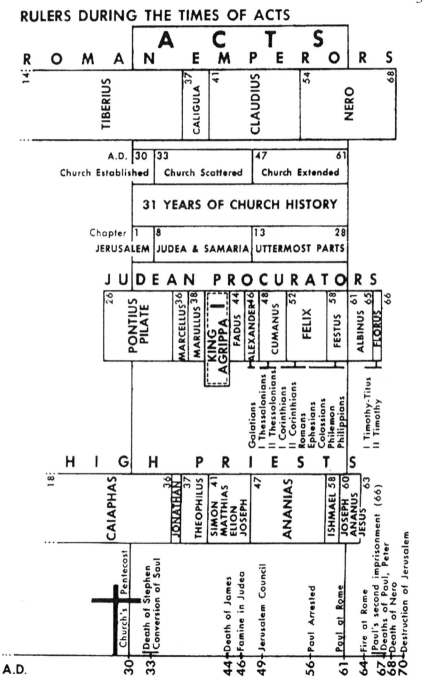

558 Jensen, Irving L. Jensen.'s Survey of the New Testament. Chicago: Moody Press. 1981. Page 208.

Fig. #17

CANONICAL ORDER
OF N.T. BOOKS

559

HISTORY	1. MATTHEW 2. MARK 3. LUKE 4. JOHN 5. ACTS	
E P I S T L E S	6. ROMANS 7. 1 CORINTHIANS 8. 2 CORINTHIANS 9. GALATIANS 10. EPHESIANS 11. PHILIPPIANS 12. COLOSSIANS 13. 1 THESSALONIANS 14. 2 THESSALONIANS } **to churches** 15. 1 TIMOTHY 16. 2 TIMOTHY 17. TITUS 18. PHILEMON } **to individuals**	**P A U L I N E**
	19. HEBREWS 20. JAMES 21. 1 PETER 22. 2 PETER 23. 1 JOHN 24. 2 JOHN 25. 3 JOHN 26. JUDE	**NON-PAULINE**
VISIONS	27. REVELATION	

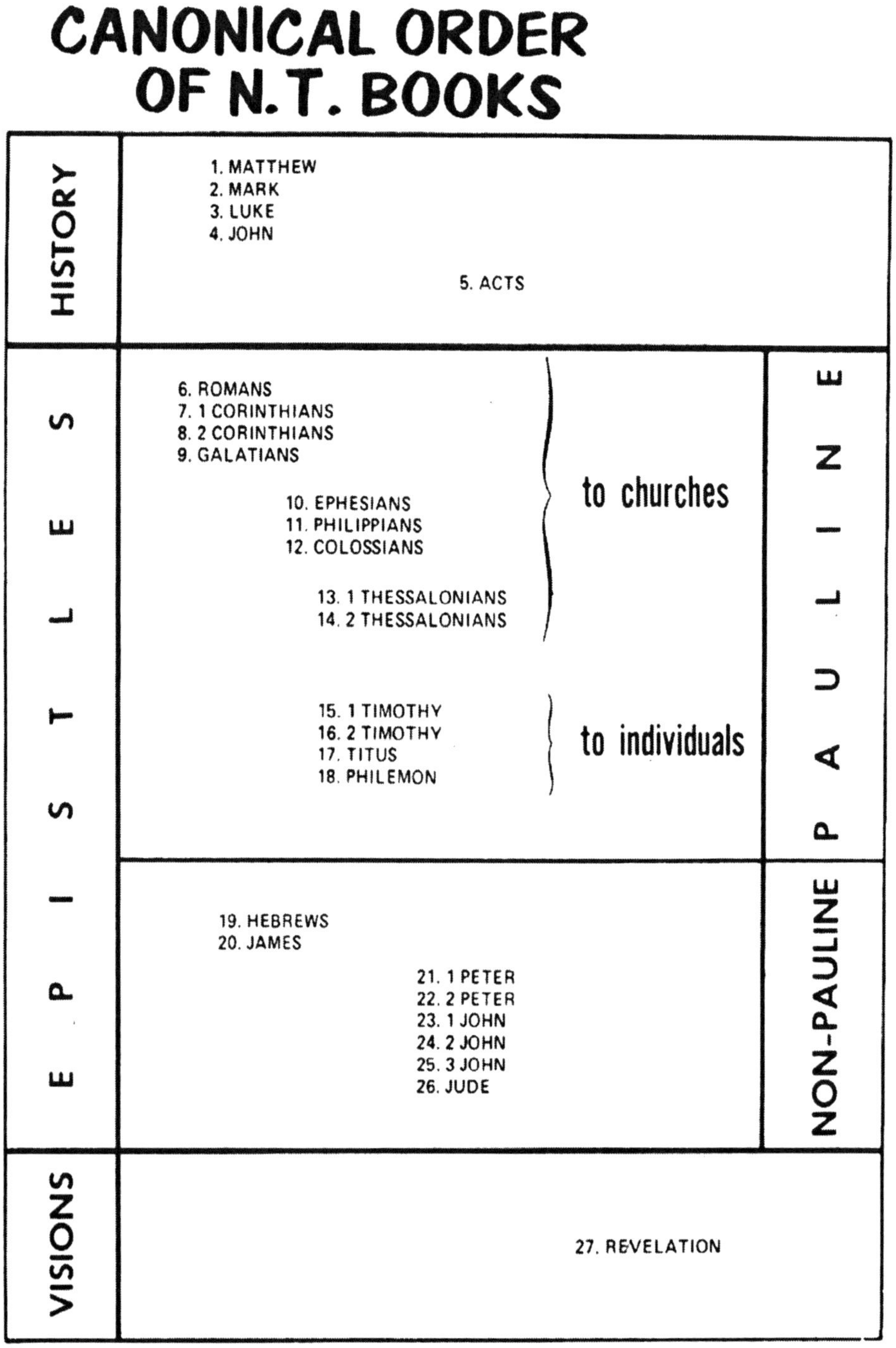

559 Jensen, Irving L. Jensen's Survey of the New Testament. Chicago: Moody Press. 1981. Page 23.

Fig. #18

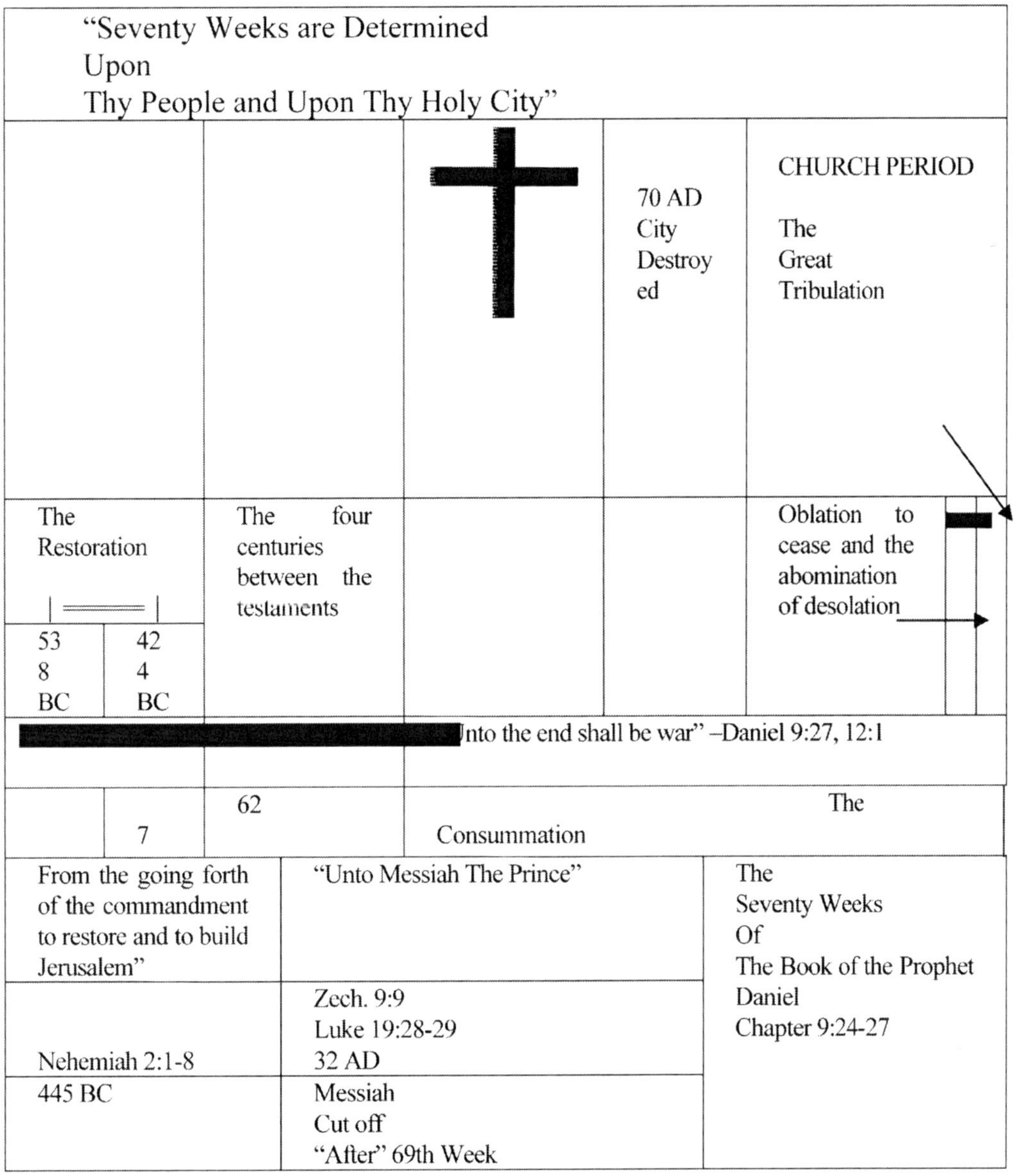

"Seventy Weeks are Determined Upon Thy People and Upon Thy Holy City"				
		✝	70 AD City Destroyed	CHURCH PERIOD The Great Tribulation
The Restoration |═══| 538 BC 424 BC	The four centuries between the testaments			Oblation to cease and the abomination of desolation
████████████████ Unto the end shall be war" –Daniel 9:27, 12:1				
7	62	Consummation		The
"From the going forth of the commandment to restore and to build Jerusalem"	"Unto Messiah The Prince"			The Seventy Weeks Of The Book of the Prophet Daniel Chapter 9:24-27
Nehemiah 2:1-8 445 BC	Zech. 9:9 Luke 19:28-29 32 AD Messiah Cut off "After" 69th Week			

560

560 The Zondervan Pictorial Encyclopedia of the Bible. Ed. Merrill C. Tenney. Vol. 2, (D-G). Grand Rapids: The Zondervan Corporation, ©1975, 1976.

Fig. #19

Second
Coming
Of
Christ,
First
Resurrection

Great
White
Throne
Judgment

Church Period

Satan Bound
Millennium

New Heaven
and Earth

Great Tribulation

A little season

Armageddon

Gog & Magog

561

---

[561] The Zondervan Pictorial Encyclopedia of the Bible. Ed. Merrill C. Tenney. Vol. 2 (D-G). Grand Rapids: The Zondervan Corporation, ©1975, 1976. Page 357.

HISTORICAL SETTING OF REVELATION   Chart 120

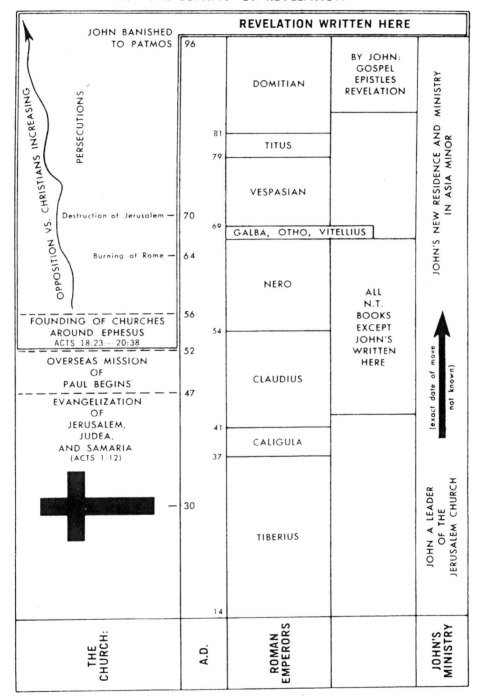

562

562 Jensen, Irving L. Jensen's Survey of the New Testament. Chicago: Moody Press. 1981. Page 495.

Appendix C.

LIST OF MAPS

Map   Page

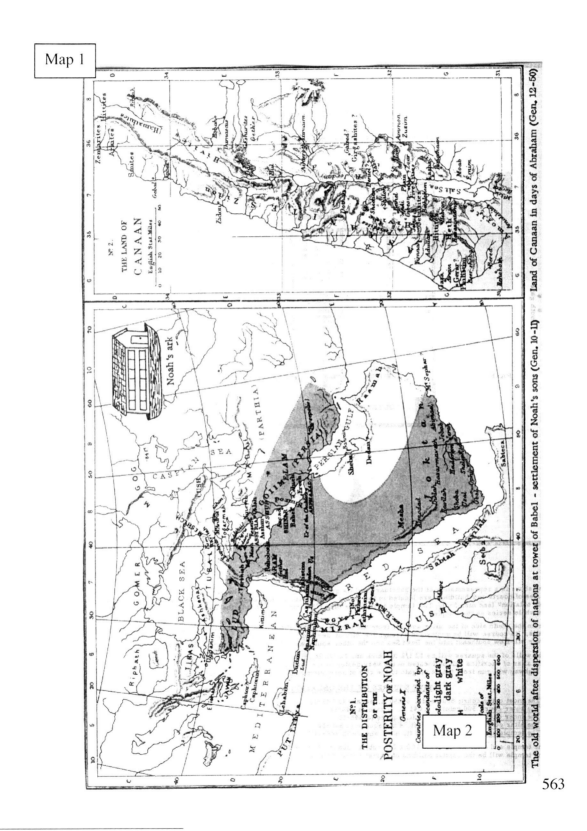

Map 1

Map 2

The old world after dispersion of nations at tower of Babel – settlement of Noah's sons (Gen. 10-11)   Land of Canaan in days of Abraham (Gen. 12-50)

563

[563] Dake, Fenis Jennings. Dake's Annotated Reference Bible. Lawrenceville: Dake Bible Sales, Inc. ©1963-1991. Charts and Map Section.

Map 3

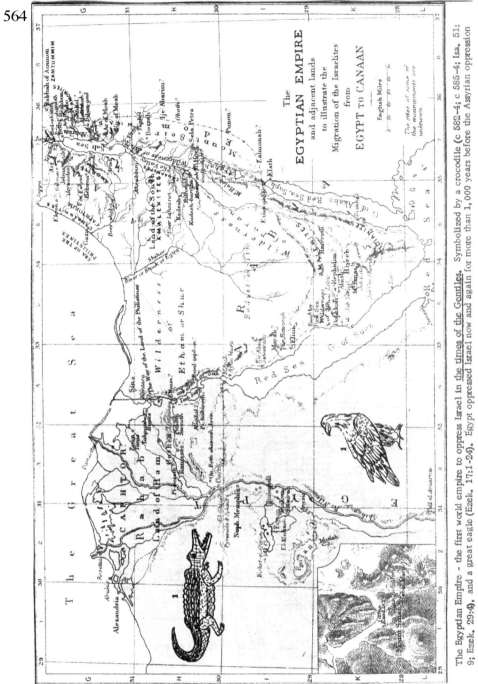

564 Dake, Fenis Jennings. Dake.'s Annotated Reference Bible. Lawrenceville: Dake Bible Sales, Inc. ˝1963-1991. Charts and Map Section.

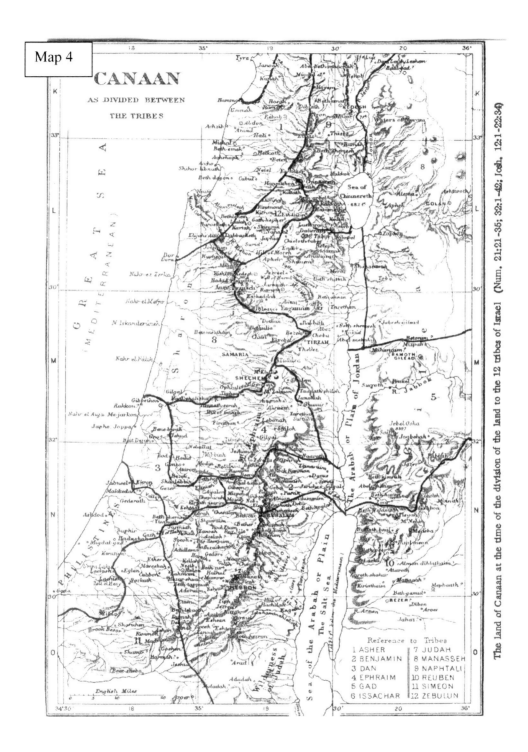

565

565 Dake, Fenis Jennings. *Dake's Annotated Reference Bible.* Lawrenceville: Dake Bible Sales, Inc. ©1963-1991. Charts and Map Section.

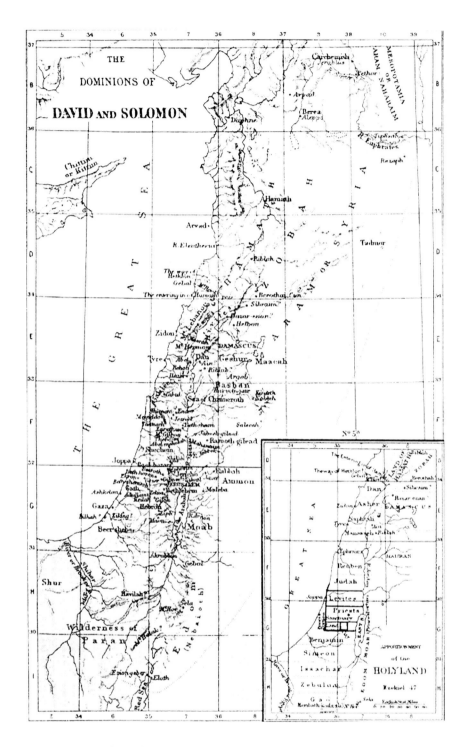

This map shows the empire of David and Solomon — the greatest kingdom of Israel in all history. The small map (5-a) shows the division of the land to the 12 tribes and the holy oblation as in the Millennium (Ezek. 45:1-48:35)566

---

566 Dake, Fenis Jennings. Dake's Annotated Reference Bible. Lawrenceville: Dake Bible Sales, Inc. ©1963-1991. Charts and Map Section.

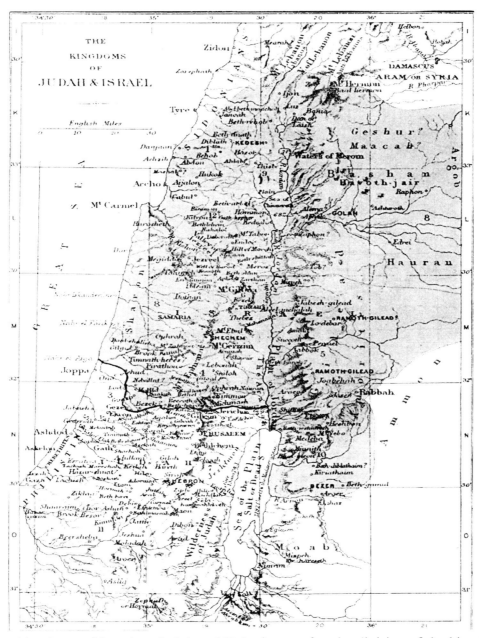

The two kingdoms of Israel — Judah and Ephraim — after the division of the kingdom at the death of Solomon (1 Kings 12). The division continued for 260 years — until the captivity of the 10 tribes to Assyria (2 Kings 17).567

---

567 Dake, Fenis Jennings. Dake's Annotated Reference Bible. Lawrenceville: Dake Bible Sales, Inc. ©1963-1991. Charts and Map Section

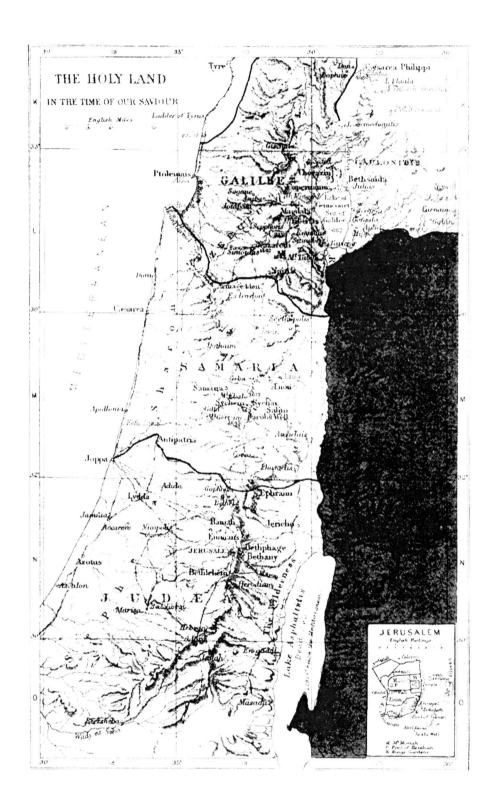

568

[568] Dake, Fenis Jennings. Dake's Annotated Reference Bible. Lawrenceville Dake Bible Sales, Inc. ©1963-1991.

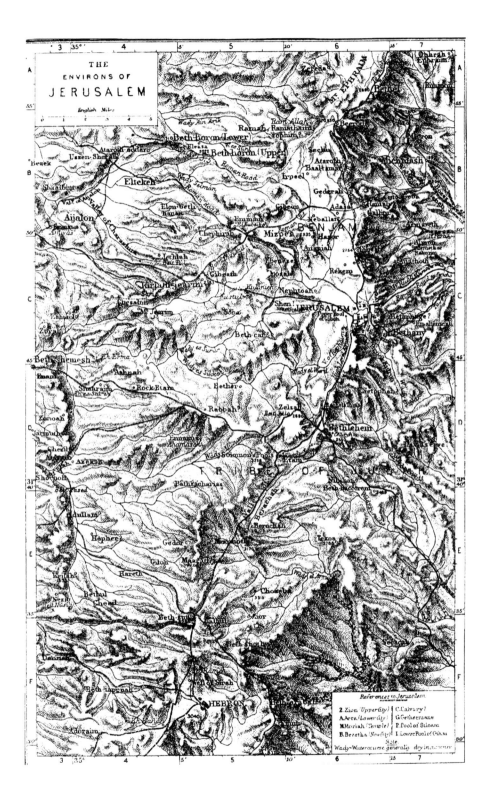

569

[569] Dake, Fenis Jennings. Dake's Annotated Reference Bible. Lawrenceville: Dake Bible Sales, Inc. ©1963-1991.

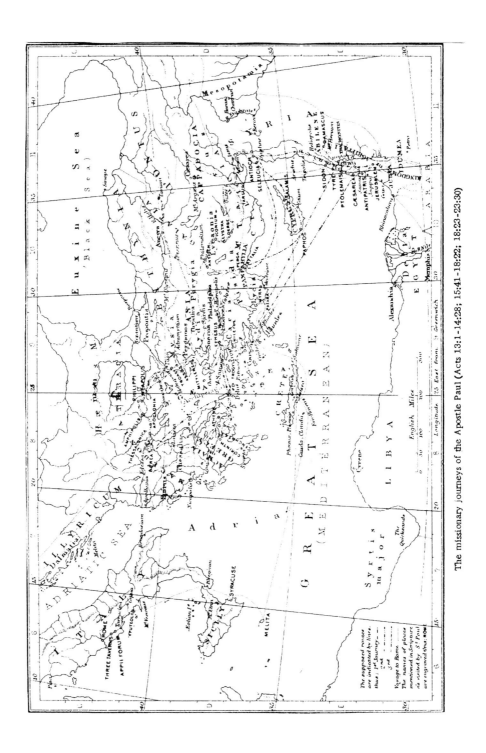

The missionary journeys of the Apostle Paul (Acts 13:1-14:28; 15:41-18:22; 18:23-23:30)

570

---

570 Dake, Fenis Jennings. Dake.'s Annotated Reference Bible. Lawrenceville: Dake Bible Sales, Inc. ˝1963-1991. Charts and Map Section.

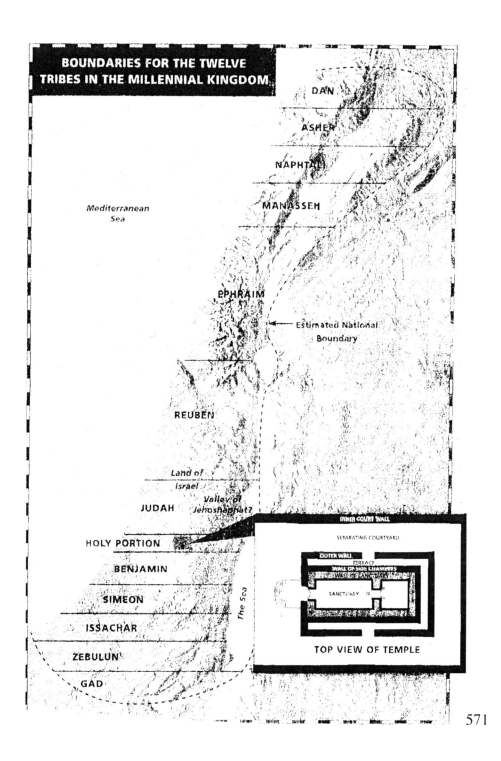

BOUNDARIES FOR THE TWELVE TRIBES IN THE MILLENNIAL KINGDOM

DAN

ASHER

NAPHTALI

MANASSEH

Mediterranean Sea

EPHRAIM

Estimated National Boundary

REUBEN

Land of Israel

Valley of Jehoshaphat?

JUDAH

HOLY PORTION

BENJAMIN

SIMEON

ISSACHAR

ZEBULUN

GAD

The Sea

INNER COURT WALL

SEPARATING COURTYARD

OUTER WALL

TERRACE

WALL OF SIDE CHAMBERS

SANCTUARY

TOP VIEW OF TEMPLE

571

571 LaHaye, Tim, and Jerry B. Jenkins. Kingdom Come. Carol Stream: Tyndale House, 2007. Page 21.

Appendix D.

PLACES OF WORSHIP

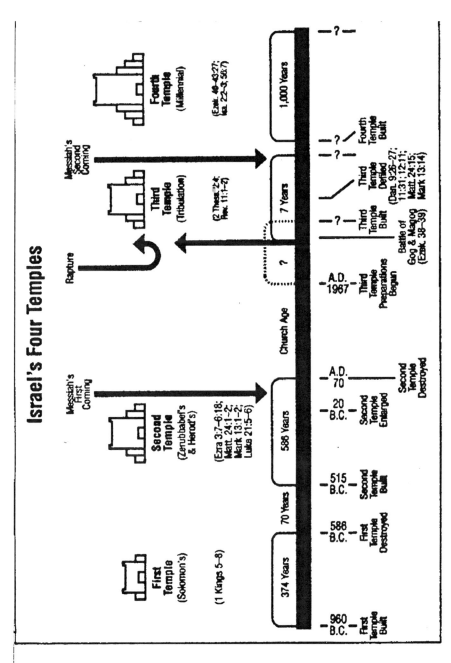

Figure 2: Israel's Four Temples

572

572 Ice, Thomas and Randall Price. *Ready to Rebuild.* Eugene: Harvest House Publishers, 1992.

The tabernacle erected, and the tents of Israel around it.573

573 McGee, J. Vernon, Thru the Bible with J. Vernon McGee. Vol. 1 (Gen-Deu.). Pasadena: Thru the Bible Radio, c 1981. Page 310.

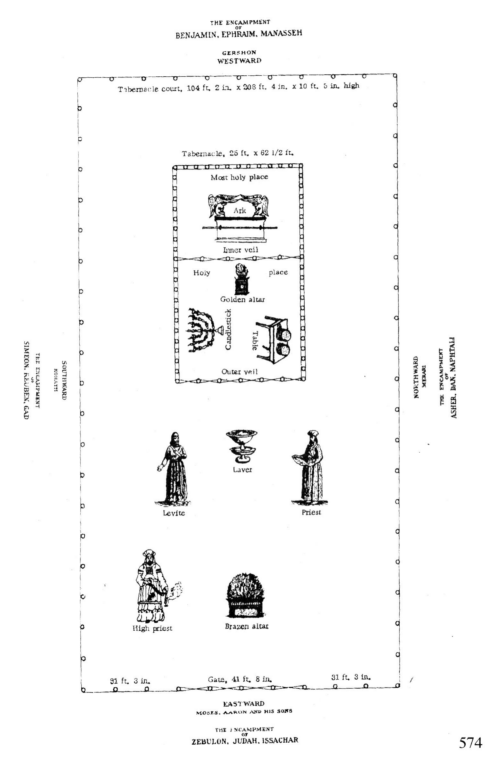

THE ENCAMPMENT
OF
BENJAMIN, EPHRAIM, MANASSEH

GERSHON
WESTWARD

Tabernacle court, 104 ft. 2 in. x 208 ft. 4 in. x 10 ft. 5 in. high

Tabernacle, 25 ft. x 62 1/2 ft.

Most holy place

Ark

Inner veil

Holy   place

Golden altar

Candlestick   Table

Outer veil

Laver

Levite   Priest

High priest   Brazen altar

31 ft. 3 in.   Gate, 41 ft. 8 in.   31 ft. 3 in.

EASTWARD
MOSES, AARON AND HIS SONS

THE ENCAMPMENT
OF
ZEBULON, JUDAH, ISSACHAR

SOUTHWARD
KOHATH

THE ENCAMPMENT
OF
SIMEON, REUBEN, GAD

NORTHWARD
MERARI

THE ENCAMPMENT
OF
ASHER, DAN, NAPHTALI

574

574 Dake, Fenis Jennings. Dake's Annotated Reference Bible. Lawrenceville: Dake Bible Sales, Inc. 196 Charts and Map Section.

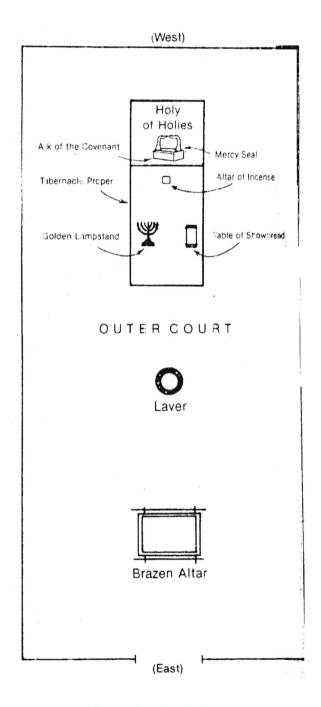

Tabernacle Floor Plan575

575 McGee, J. Vernon, Thru the Bible with J. Vernon McGee. Vol. 1 (Gen-Deu.). Pasadena: Thru the Bible Radio, c 1981. Page 304.

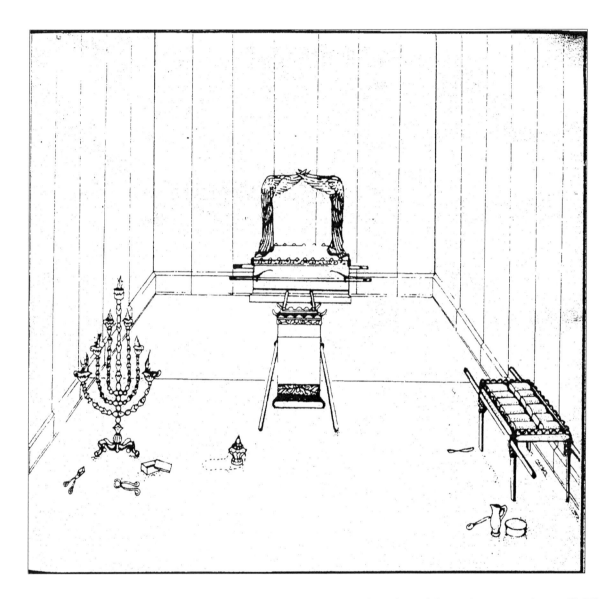

The artist, George Howell, has sketched the tabernacle interior without the separating veil. The rear compartment shows the holy of holies which housed the ark of the covenant. The front compartment pictures the holy place in which were the lampstand, the altar of incense, and the table of showbread.576

576 McGee, J. Vernon, Thru the Bible with J. Vernon McGee. Vol. 1 (Gen-Deu.). Pasadena: Thru the Bible Radio, c 1981. Page 313.

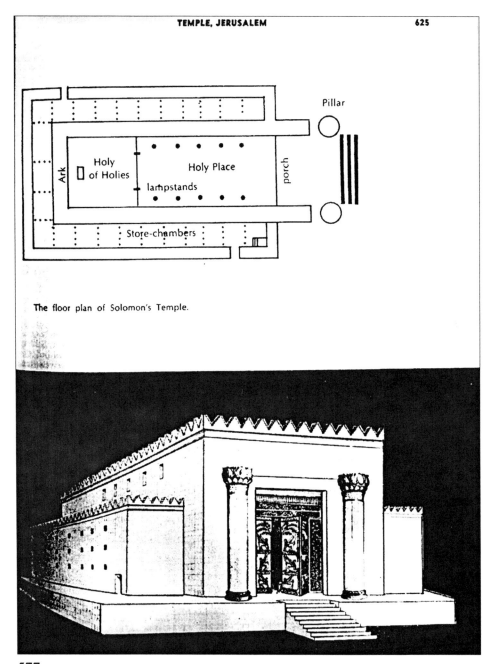

The floor plan of Solomon's Temple.

577

---

577 The Zondervan Pi ctorial Encyclopedia of the Bible. Ed Menill C. Tenney. Volume 5, Q-Z, Zondervan Publishing, Grand Rapids, 1975. Page 625.

An illustration depicting a variety of temple vessels and objects used in worship in the first and second temples. (Illustration c. 1890, from Blackie and Son publishers, Glasgow, Scotland)578

578 Jeffrey, Grant R. The New Temple and the Second Coming. Colorado Springs: Waterbrook Press, 2007. Page 133.

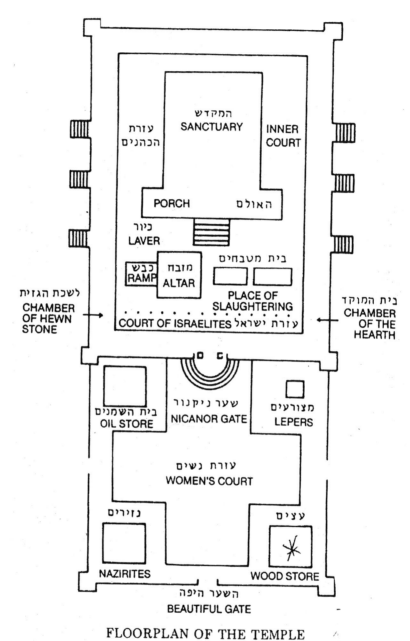

FLOORPLAN OF THE TEMPLE

579

[579] McGee, J. Vernon, Thru the Bible with J. Vernon McGee. Vol. II (Josh-Ps.). Pasadena: Thru the Bible Radio, c 1981, 1982. Page 422.

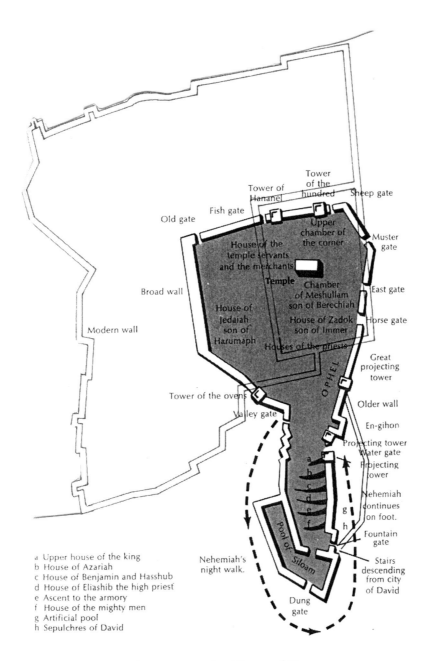

a Upper house of the king
b House of Azariah
c House of Benjamin and Hasshub
d House of Eliashib the high priest
e Ascent to the armory
f House of the mighty men
g Artificial pool
h Sepulchres of David

Temple Area at the Time of Ezra

580

[580] The Zondervan Pictorial Encyclopedia of the Bible. Ed. Merrill C. Tenney. Vol. 10, D-G. Grand Rapids: The Zondervan Corporation. ©1975, 1976. Page 473.

HEROD'S TEMPLE

The construction of Herod's Temple was begun in 19 BC and essentially completed in 64 AD, a mere six years before it was destroyed by the Romans. When he was eight days old, Jesus was brought to this temple by His parents, who were required by the Law to present Him to the Lord and to make a sacrifice of two pigeons or turtledoves for him because He was their firstborn (Luke 2:21-24). During this first visit to the temple, Anna and Simeon prophesied and gave thanks to God at the sight of Him (Luke 2:25-38). At the age of twelve, after Passover, He sat in the midst of the teachers in the temple to listen to them, ask questions and answer the questions they put to Him (Luke 2:46, 47). During His temptation in the wilderness at the beginning of Christ's ministry, Satan set Him on a pinnacle of the temple (Luke 4:9). On one visit to the temple during a feast day, He met the man he had healed by the pool of Bethesda and warned him not to sin anymore (John 5:14). One morning, early, Jesus entered the temple to teach and was confronted by the Pharisees with the woman caught in adultery (John 8:1-59). During one Feast of Dedication Jesus entered the temple and, as He walked in Solomon's Porch, asserted His deity (John 10:22-39). After His triumphal entry into Jerusalem, the Lord entered the temple (Mark 11:11). Then He returned another day to cast out the merchants doing business there, and following that, came daily to teach the people, announce the future destruction of the temple and the resurrection of the temple of His Body (Matthew 21:12-16; 21:23-24:1; Mark 11:15-19;11:25-33;12:1-44; Luke 19:45-47; John 2:13-25). During those teaching sessions He was questioned and His authority was challenged by the chief priests and scribes (Matthew 21:23-27; Mark 11:27-33; Luke 20:1, 2). In the following chapter of this Gospel, Jesus observed the widow who cast in the two mites (Luke 21:1, 2).

In The Acts of the Apostles there are numerous references to this temple: the first apostolic miracle - a lame man healed on Solomon's Porch - and Peter's second sermon, his arrest, and at the same time, 5000 believed on the Lord (3:1-26; 4:1-4). Further miracles were performed there later (5:12-16) and the apostles once again were arrested (5:17, 18). The next morning, having been brought out of prison by an angel, they went back to the temple to teach (5:19-26). After they were beaten by the council and commanded not to speak of Jesus, they went daily to the temple to teach and preach (5:40-42). Paul entered the temple, with a number of other men, to perform a vow and was seized (21:26-40).

The preceding is not intended to be a comprehensive list of biblical references to Herod's Temple, but may help you to better appreciate the prominence of Herod's Temple in the New Testament.

MODEL OF HEROD'S TEMPLE

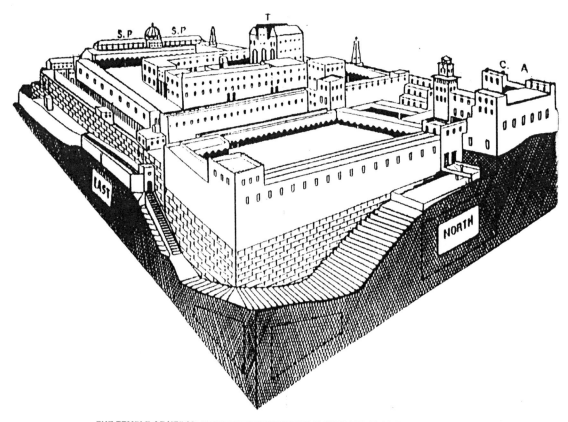

THE TEMPLE OF HEROD, SHOWING THE DIFFERENT ELEVATIONS OF THE VARIOUS COURTS

T. — The Temple proper, containing the Holy Place and the Holy of Holies.

C. A. — The Castle of Antonia, the barracks of the Roman soldiers.

S. P. — Solomon's Porch, a beautiful colonnade extending along the front of the Temple area.

THE PLAN OF THE INTERIOR ARRANGEMENT
OF THE TEMPLE AT JERUSALEM

The building, including the foyer, was divided into six separate areas or courts, rising one above another.

The Court of the Gentiles, the only part to which foreigners were admitted, was situated on the lowest level outside the sacred precincts.

The Sacred Enclosure, three feet above the latter, through which all Gentiles were forbidden to pass under the penalty of death.

The Court of the Women (sometimes called the Treasury), three feet higher, into which Jewish women were permitted to come and beyond which they could not advance.

The Court of Israel, ten feet higher, into which male Jews had entrance.

The Court of the Priests, three feet above the Court of Israel, which was reserved for priests only.

The House of God, eight feet above the Court of the Priests, which was divided into two compartments, the holy place and the holy of holies, or the most holy place. Into the former the priests entered to perform certain duties at stated times, but into the latter only the high priest might enter, and he only once a year on the Day of Atonement, to make atonement for the sins of the people.

The inaccessibility of the holy of holies to all except the high priest on one day in the year, and the various barriers which prevented the common people ever to approach near the supposed dwelling place of the divine presence, was a continual object lesson of the holiness of God and His separation from sinners.

The Christian dispensation ushered in a new era. The redemption through Jesus swept away all barriers between God and penitent men. When Jesus died the veil of the temple was rent in twain, Matthew 27:51, signifying that the way was now opened for immediate access to God through Christ, Hebrews 10:19, 10. In Jesus all class distinctions are obliterated: those that formerly existed between Jews and Gentiles, Romans 10, 12; between men and women, Galatians 3:28; and between priests and laymen, Revelation 1:6.

Thru the Bible Radio newsletter received February 19, 2003. Four Pages.

581

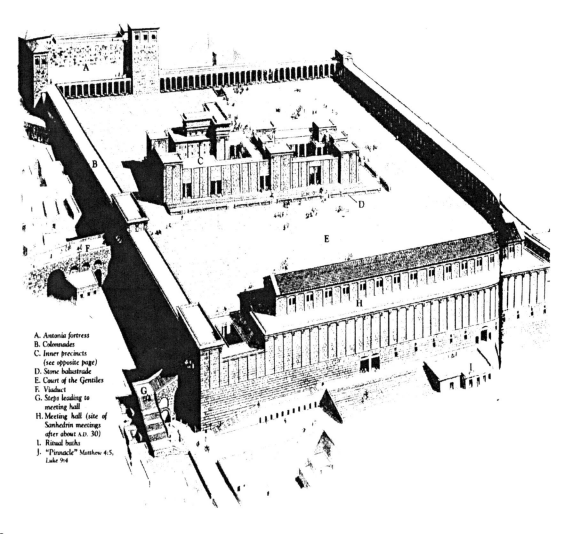

A. Antonia fortress
B. Colonnades
C. Inner precincts
   (see opposite page)
D. Stone balustrade
E. Court of the Gentiles
F. Viaduct
G. Steps leading to
   meeting hall
H. Meeting hall (site of
   Sanhedrin meetings
   after about A.D. 30)
I. Ritual baths
J. "Pinnacle" Matthew 4:5,
   Luke 9:4

582

581 Thru the Bible Radio Newsletter: February 19, 2003. (4 pages)

582 "Jesus and His Times." The Reader's Digest. Pleasantville: The Readers Digest Association Inc., 1987. Page 130.

Photograph of the Second Temple from the model at the Holy Land Hotel in Jerusalem.

583

---

583 The Messianic Times. Vol. 8, No. 3. Oct/Nov 1997. Page 11.

584

584 Israel My Glory. Westville: The Friends ofIsrael Gospel Ministry, Inc., Dec/Jan 1997/1998.

This close-up view of a model of the second temple reflects what the third temple will look like when plans for rebuilding move forward.585

---

585 Jeffrey, Grant R. The New Temple and the Second Coming. Colorado Springs: Waterbrook Press, 2007. Pages 19.

Model of Third Temple

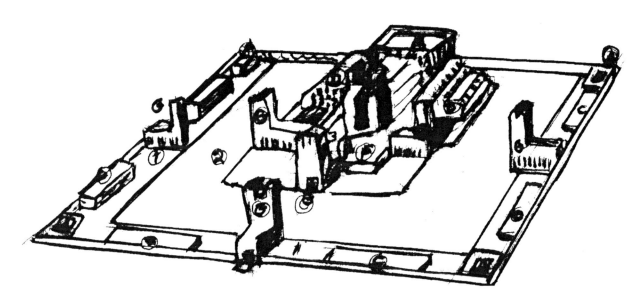

Temple Area Plan Site Identification

A. Corner Kitchen
B. Separate Place
C. Chambers of the Lower Pavement
D. Priests' Chambers
E. Temple Building
F. Altar
G. Gate Buildings

1. Lower Pavement
2. Outer Court
3. Inner Court586

586 Schmitt, John W. and J. Carl Laney. " Temple Area Plan Site Identification." Messiah's Coming Temple. Grand Rapids: Kregel Publications, ©1997. Figure 6.1.

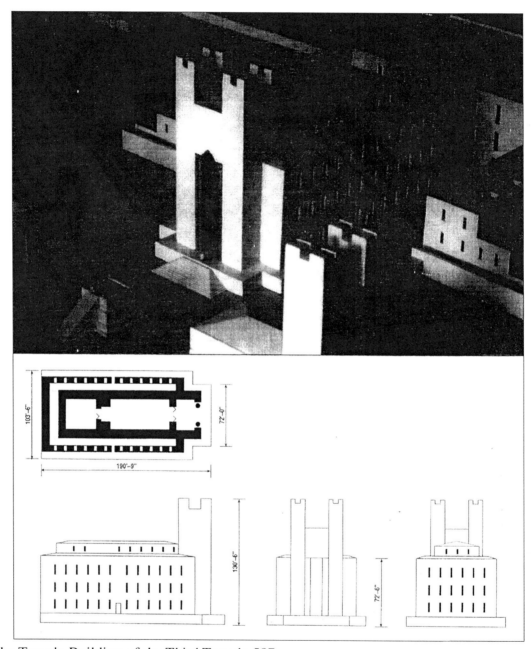

The Temple Building of the Third Temple.587

---

587 Schmitt, John W. and J. Carl Laney. Messiah's Coming Temple. Grand Rapids: Kregel Publication, ©1997. Page 94.

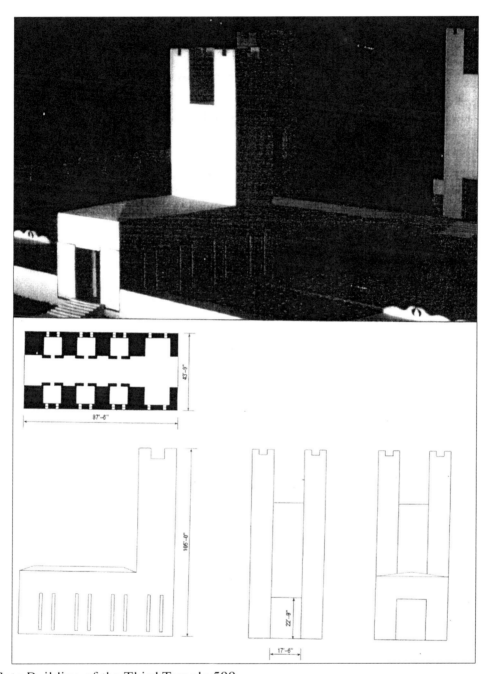

The Gate Building of the Third Temple.588

588 Schmitt, John W. and J. Carl Laney. *Messiah's Coming Temple*. Grand Rapids: Kregel Publication, ©1997. Page 84.

The Dome of the Rock is located beyond the Eastern Gate and to the south of the site of the first and second temples.589

---

589 Jeffrey, Grant R. The New Temple and the Second Coming. Colorado Springs: Waterbrook Press, 2007. Page 24.

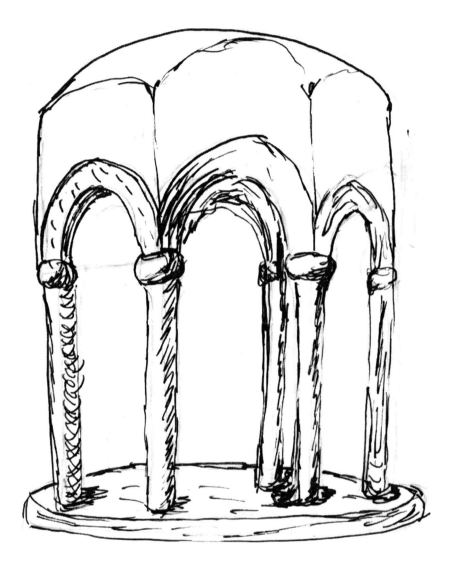

    This Muslim shrine, known as the Dome of the Spirits, is thought to incorporate the foundation stone that supported the ark of the covenant in the ancient holy of holies.590

---

590 Jeffrey, Grant R. The New Temple and the Second Coming. Colorado Springs: Waterbrook Press, 2007. Page 27.

A portion of the network of tunnels that run underneath the Temple Mount.591

591 Jeffrey, Grant R. The New Temple and the Second Coming. Colorado Springs: Waterbrook Press, 2007. Page 67.

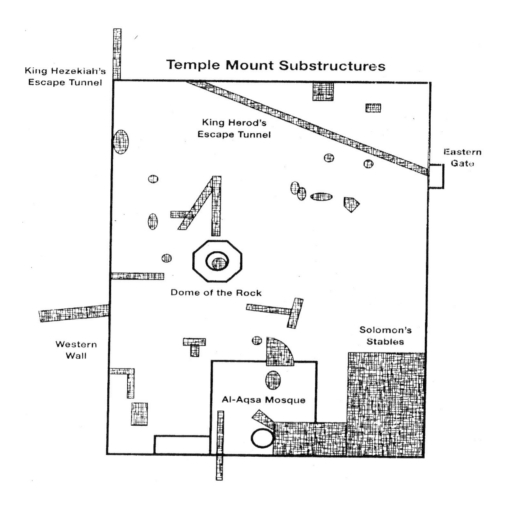

Temple Mount Substructures

King Hezekiah's
Escape Tunnel

King Herod's
Escape Tunnel

Eastern
Gate

Dome of the Rock

Western
Wall

Solomon's
Stables

Al-Aqsa Mosque

This diagram shows the location of two· ancient tunnels that run beneath. the Temple Mount—esctipe tunnels put in place by King Hezekiah and King Herod.

592

[592] Jeffrey, Grant R. The New Temple and the Second Coming. Colorado Springs: Waterbrook Press, 2007.

593

The bulge on wall on the Temple Mount.

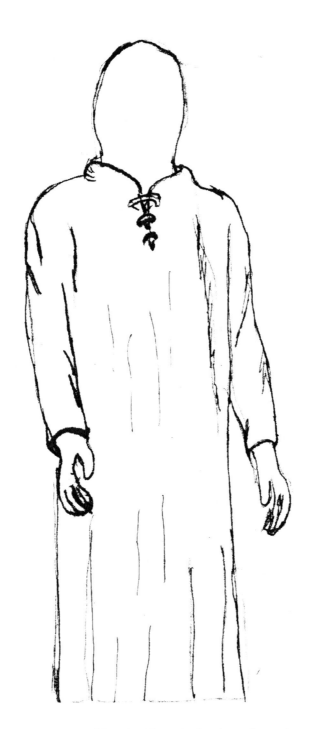

A linen garment, created by the Temple Institute for priests serving
in the third temple.594

---

594 Jeffrey, Grant R. The New Temple and the Second Coming. Colorado Springs: Waterbrook Press, 2007. Page 128

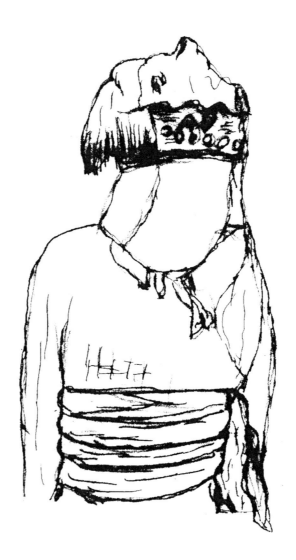

Freshly woven priestly vestments595

595 Lindsted, Robert. The Sound of the Trumpet. Oklahoma City: Southwest Radio Church. Page 10.

Red Heifer 596

596 Prophetic Observer. August 1997. Page 1.

Golden Mizrak 597

597 The Messianic Times. Vol. 8 No.3, Oct/Nov 1997. Page 11.

A golden crown, created for the high priest serving in the future third temple.598

598 Jeffrey, Grant R. The New Temple and the Second Coming. Colorado Springs: Waterbrook Press, 2007. Page 126.

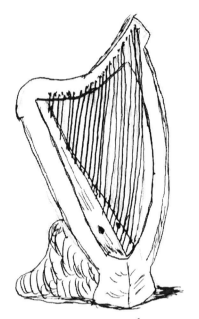

Harp built to Biblical
Specifications

Vessel for Ceremonial
Incense

599

599 Lindsted, Robert. The Sound of the Trumpet. Oklahoma City: Southwest Radio Church. Page 10.

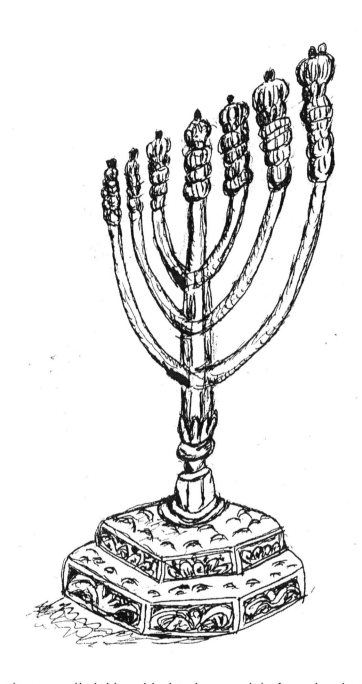

The Temple Institute unveiled this gold-plated menorah in Jerusalem last December.600

600 Price, Dr. Randall. "Groups Collecting Temple Tools." The Messianic Times. Vol. 10 No. 2. Jerusalem: Gospel Truth, Summer 2000. Page 20.

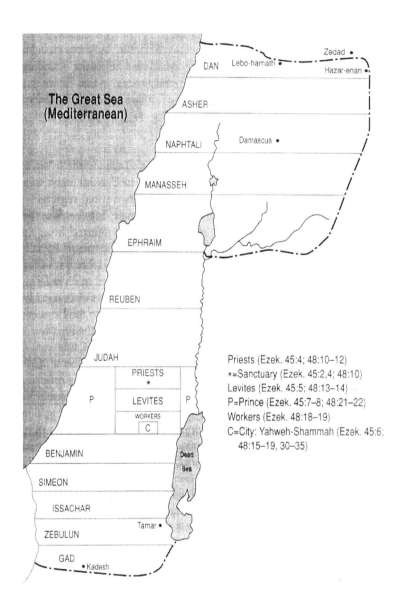

Map of Israel in the Millennium.

The allotments and placement of designated territories are based on Ezekiel 47:13-48:35. Since major topographical changes are expected in preparation for the kingdom (Ezek. 47:1- 12), the land area of the allotments can only be estimated.601

---

[601] Schmitt, John W. and J. Carl Laney. Messiah's Coming Temple. Grand Rapids: Kregel Publications © 1997. Page 125.

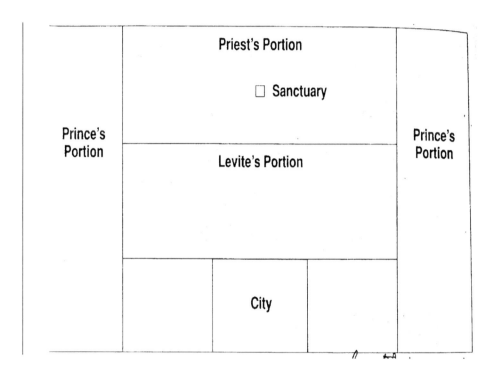

The Sacred Allotment for the Priests and Prince 602

---

602 Schmitt, John W. and J. Carl Laney. Messiah's Coming Temple. Grand Rapids: Kregel Publications. © 1997. Page 128.

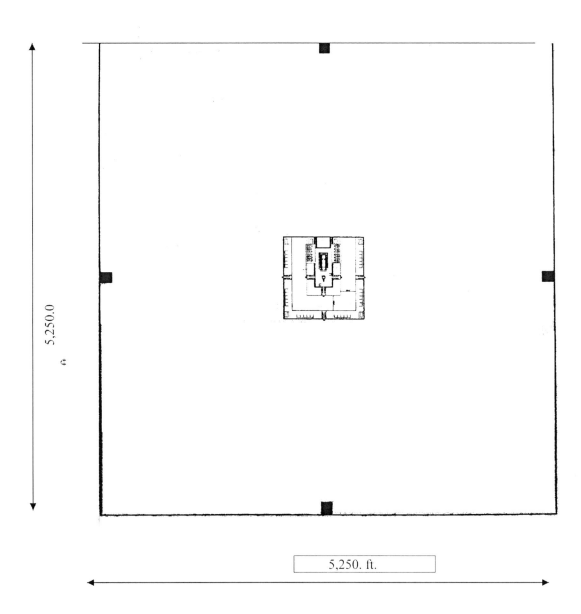

5,250.0

5,250. ft.

The Sanctuary of the Third Temple.603

---

603 Schmitt, John W. and J. Carl Laney. Messiah's Coming Temple. Grand Rapids: Kregel Publications. © 1997. Page 127.

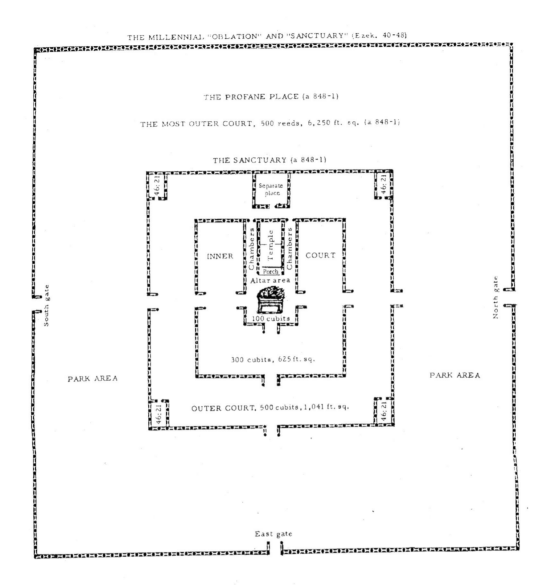

THE MILLENNIAL "OBLATION" AND "SANCTUARY" (Ezek. 40-48)

THE PROFANE PLACE (a 848-1)

THE MOST OUTER COURT, 500 reeds, 6,250 ft. sq. (a 848-1)

THE SANCTUARY (a 848-1)

The above is a representation of the Sanctuary and its great enclosure, called "the profane place" (p. 848). The whole series of courts and buildings are located in the midst of the priests' portion of the 60 x 60 square miles, called "the holy oblation" (see map 5-a). The temple is only one of the buildings located in the Sanctuary, so we cannot speak of the whole series as the temple

From the south side of the altar and out from the temple itself a river will flow eastward through the whole series of walls. Its course will be southward through the city of Jerusalem, after which it will part into two. From there one river will flow southeast into the Dead Sea and the other southwest into the Mediterranean Sea (Ezek. 47)

The walls of the squares will be 12 1/2 ft. thick and 12 1/2 ft. high
The altar of sacrifice will be located in the very center of the fourth square
A highway will run from the south gate to the city of Jerusalem, about 12 miles away (see map 5-a)

FIVE SQUARES OF THE OBLATION AND SANCTUARY:

1 The most outer court: 500 reeds, 6,250 ft. square (a 848-1)
2 The outer court: 500 cubits, 1,041 ft. square (a 848-1)
3 The inner court: 300 cubits, 625 ft. square (a 848-1)
4 The altar court: 100 cubits, 208 ft. 4 in. square (a 848-1)
5 The temple area: 100 cubits, 208 ft. 4 in. square (a 848-1)

The temple and altar areas take 100 x 200 cubits, 208 ft. 4 in. x 415 ft. 8 in.
The temple will be the capital building of Christ - where He will reign over Israel forever (Ezek. 43:7)

604

[604] Duke, Finis Jennings. Duke's Annotated Reference Bible. (KJV). Lawrenceville: Duke Bible Sales Inc. 1963. Charts and Maps Third Temple.

Bibliography

1. "2,574-Year_old Sin Bars Priest From Temple Service. Keeping Time On God's Prophetic Clock." <u>Prophetic Observer</u>. Oklahoma City: Southwest Radio Church, Jan. 1995, c. 1994. Page 4.

2. "Jerusalem's Tunnel and the Temple Mount: Rioting, Bloodshed, and World Condemnation." <u>Zion's Fire, Middle East News & World Views</u>. Vol. 7, number 6. Orlando: Zion's Hope Inc., Nov/Dec 1996. Page 22.

3. "Jesus and His Times." <u>Reader's Digest</u>. Pleasantville: The Reader's Digest Association, Inc., 1987. Page 129-144.

4. "Jewish Year 5768." <u>Messianic Times</u>. Vol. 17 #2, (May/June 2007).

5. "Satan's Lie." <u>The Bible Standard</u>. #101. Chester Springs: The Bible Standard Ministries. Page 8-12.

6. "Tabernacle." <u>The Zondervan Pictorial Encyclopedia of the Bible</u>. Tenney, Merrill C. General editor. Vol. V (Q-Z). Grand Rapids: Zondervan Publishing House, 1975. Page 577.

7. "The Red Heifer." <u>Koinonia House</u>. Coeur d'Alene: Koinonia House. Page 9, 11.

8. "Was Jesus Christ Crucified on Good Friday? Does it Make Any Difference?" <u>The Gospel Truth</u>. Page 20.

9. Barton Gellman. "Israelis, in Nighttime Move, Open Temple Mount Tunnel." <u>Washington Post</u>. Rpt. in <u>End-Time Handmaidens & Servants</u>. Jasper: End-Time Handmaidens, Inc., October 1996.

10. <u>Bible in the News</u>. N-199. Southwest Radio Ministries, Sept. 2007.

11. Brickner, David. "Day of Calamity, Day of Celebration." <u>Jews for Jesus -Newsletter</u>. Vol. 12:5760. San Francisco: Jews for Jesus International, August 2000.

12. "Building the Third Temple." <u>This week in Bible Prophecy</u>. St Catharines: This Week in Bible Prophecy Inc. Vol. 3. Issue 4. April 1995 page 15-16.

13. Cohen, Dr. Gary G. "Zion's Fire. Ezekiel's City — A Millennial Vision." <u>Middle East News & World Views</u>. Orlando: Zion's Hope Inc., July/August 1998. Page 21-23.

14. Confraternity of Christian Doctrine. Board of Trustees. <u>The New American Bible: Translated from the original languages with critical use of all the ancient sources and the revised New Testament.</u> Confraternity of Christian Doctrine, 1996, c1986.

15. Conner, Kevin J. <u>The Tabernacle of Moses</u>. Portland: Bible Temple Publishing, 1975. Page 104.

16. <u>End-Time Handmaidens & Servants (Newsletter)</u>. Jasper, End-Time Handmaidens, Inc., Oct/Nov 2001. Page 3-4

17. End-Time Handmaidens & Servants (Newsletter). Jasper: End-Time Handmaidens, Inc., December 17, 1999. Pages 7-8.

18. End-Time Handmaidens & Servants (Newsletter). Jasper: End-Time Handmaidens, Inc., March 26, 1998. Page 5.

19. End-Time Handmaidens & Servants (Newsletter). Jasper: End-Time Handmaidens, Inc., February 1997.

20. End-Time Handmaidens & Servants (Newsletter). Jasper: End-Time Handmaidens, Inc., August 9, 1996. Page 3-4.

21. Evans, Michael D. "The Temple Mount for Sale." Save Jerusalem Newsletter. Michael D. Evans, Editor, June 14, 2008.

22. Goodwin, Dan (Evangelist), and Pastor Bill Waughn. "A Seven-fold Promise of His Soon Coming." Faith Baptist Church Publications. Goodwin Publishers, Copyright 2008. Pages 56-66

23. "Have You Ever Heard of the Five Jewish Laws?" The Messianic Jewish Movement International Inc. Bethesda: The Messianic Jewish Movement International Inc. 1974. Page 15-17.

24. Holy Bible: New Living Translation. Wheaton: Tyndale House, 1997.

25. Holy Bible: New Living Translation. Wheaton: Tyndale House, 1997.* Referring to Exodus 1:5 says the Dead Sea Scrolls and Greek versions read seventy-five. This is according to the NLT, Second Edition. Carrol Stream: Tyndale House©1996.

26. Hutchings, Noah. "Days of Noah Signs of Times of Later Times before Christ Returns." Prophetic Observer. Oklahoma City: Southwest Radio Church, Dec.1997, c. 1997. Page 3-4.

27. Hutchings, Noah. "The Ashes of the Red Heifer." Prophetic Observer. Vol. 4 #8-L-820. Oklahoma City: Southwest Radio Church, Aug. 1997, c. 1997. Page 1-4.

28. Ice, Thomas and Randall Price. "Tribulation and Beyond." Ready to Rebuild. Harvest House Publishers. Pages 202, 203, 206-207.

29. Ingraham, David A. and Schlomo Goren. "Keeping Time on God's Prophetic Clock." Prophetic Observer. Oklahoma City: Southwest Radio Church, Jan. 1995, c. 1994. Page 4.

30. "Israel at War at Peace." The Bible Standard. Vol. Extra 101. Chester Springs: Bible Standard Ministries. Page 6-7, 15.

31. Jack Van Impe. Troy: Jack Van Impe Ministries, Inc. Newsletter dated April 5, 2008.

32. Jeffrey, Grant R. Heaven the Last Frontier. New York: Bantam Books, 1990. Pages 101, 102, 105, 132, 179-180, 191, 192-193, 204-205.

33. — The New Temple and Second Coming. Colorado Springs: Waterbrook Press. Pages 3-9, 49-58, 91, 105-107, 110-111, 113, 127, 143, 159-161, 170-183, 189-190.

34. — Prophecies of Heaven the Last Frontier. New York: Bantam Books. Pages 82 and 83.

35. Jensen, Irving L. Jensen's' Survey of the New Testament. Chicago: Moody Press, Copyright 1981. Page 236-237.

36. Johnian, Mona. "Epilogue: A Glimpse of Eternity." Life in the Millennium. Pages 200-203.

37. — Life in the Millennium. Pages 83-87, 174-175-182, 185-188, 194-197.

38. — "Kingdom Come." Life in the Millennium. Pages 455-458.

39. — "The Millennial Throne." Life in the Millennium. Page 101-108.

40. Josephus Complete Works. Translated by William Whiston. Grand Rapids: Kregel Publications. Page 581-582.

41. Juster, Dan and Keith Intrater. "Israel, the Church and the Last Days. (Rebuilding the Temple)." The Orthodox Messiah. Page 230, 235-236, 240..

42. Kolber, Rebekah. "Bulging Temple Mount Wall Threatens to Buckle." <u>The Messianic Times</u>. November 2002. Page 8-9.

43. Kremers, Mari F. "Review of Dates." <u>God Intervenes in the Middle East</u>. Page 274-292.

44. LaHaye, Tim and Jerry B. Jenkins. <u>Kingdom Come</u>. (last book in Left Behind Series) Carol Stream: Tyndale House Publishers, Inc. Pages xi-xlvi, 1-66, 343-356.

45. Levy, David. "The New Jerusalem." <u>Israel My Glory</u>. Westville: The Friends of Israel, Gospel Ministry, Inc., Apr/May 1999. Page 24-26.

46. Lewan, Todd "Human Tracking Devices Debated." <u>The Fresno Bee</u>. Associated Press, Sunday, July 22, 2007.

47. Liberman, Paul. <u>Israel Archeology</u>. Number 136. Rancho Mirage: International Messianic Jewish Alliance. Pages 1-2.

48. McGee, J. Vernon. <u>Thru the Bible with J. Vernon McGee</u>. Vol. 1 (Gen-Deut.). Pasadena: Thru the Bible Radio, c 1981. Page 128-129, 318.

49. — <u>Thru the Bible with J. Vernon McGee</u>. Vol. III (Prov. — Mal.). Pasadena: Thru the Bible Radio, c 1981. Pages 586-589, 894.

50. Meredith, J.L. <u>Meredith Book of Bible Lists</u>. Minneapolis: Bethany House Publishers, 1980. Pages 188-189.

51. <u>Messianic Jewish Alliance</u>. Number 136. Rancho Mirage: Messianic Jewish Alliance. Page 2-3.

52. Patti Lalonde. "Building the Third Temple." <u>This Week in Bible Prophecy Inc</u>. Vol. 3/Issue 4. St. Catharines: This Week in Bible Prophecy Inc., April 1995. Page 224.

53. Price, Dr. L. Randall. "Will There be a Third Temple." Phoenix: <u>Jewish Voice Today</u>. January/February 2004. Page 4.

54. Price, Dr. Randall. "Groups collecting Temple 'tools'", <u>The Messianic Times</u>, Vol. 10, number 2, Summer 2000, page 20.

55. — "Time for a Temple? Jewish Plans to Rebuild the Temple." <u>Israel My Glory</u>. Westville: The Friends of Israel, Gospel Ministry, Inc. December/January 1997/1998. Page 15-19.

56. — "'Samuels' Sought for the Third Temple Priesthood." <u>The Messianic Times</u>, Vol. 9, number 1, spring 1998. Page 13.

57. <u>Prophetic Observer</u>. Oklahoma City: Southwest Rodeo Church, December 1995.

58. Sanders, Tobie. "Link to the High Priest." <u>Bible in the News</u>. Vol. 2. Oklahoma City: Southwest Radio Church, February 1997. Page 14.

59. Schneerson, Lubavitcher and Rebbe Rabbi Menachem M. "The Uniqueness of the Altar's Site." <u>Analytical Studies. Seek out the Welfare of Jerusalem</u>. Adapted from Likkutei Sichos Vol. XIX, Parshas Re'eh. Brooklyn: 1994. Pages 49-50.

60. Sorko-kam, Shera. "A Hanukkah Story." 1937. <u>Israel Report</u>. Dec. 2007. Page 3-4.

61. Sorko-Ram, Shira. "Israel at 60: Blinded in Part, Sees in Part." <u>Maoz Israel Report</u>. May 2008. Pages 1-3, 6-9.

62. <u>The Apocrypha, The King James Version</u>. Edited by Manuel Komroff. New York: Tudor Publishing Company, 1937.

63. <u>The Holy Bible : New Revised Standard Version</u>. Nashville: Thomas Nelson, 1996, c1989.

64. <u>The Holy Bible: The Revised Standard Version</u>. Oak Harbor: Logos Research Systems, Inc., 1971.

65. <u>The Holy Bible: King James Version</u>. Oak Harbor: Logos Research Systems, Inc., 1995.

66. The Holy Bible: New Century Version, Containing the Old and New Testaments. Dallas: Word Bibles, 1991.

67. The Holy Bible: The New King James Version. Nashville: Thomas Nelson, 1996, c1982.

68. The Messianic Prophecy Bible Project. Tulsa. May 2008. Page 2-5.

69. The Reese Chronological Bible. The authorized edition of the original work by Edward Reese. Minneapolis: Bethany House Publishers, 1980. Pages 23, 1250.

70. The Zondervan Pictorial Encyclopedia of the Bible. Tenney, Merrill C. General editor. Vol. V (Q-Z). Grand Rapids: Zondervan Publishing House, 1975. Page 626-627.

71. Van Impe, Dr. Jack. Intelligence Briefing. Troy: Jack Van Impe Ministries, Inc., May 2008. Pages 5.

72. — "Get Revived—He's Coming!" Lighting New Fires Inner Circle Report. Troy: Jack Van Impe Ministries. April 2008

73. —. "Information and World Control." Perhaps Today. Troy: Jack Van Impe Ministries, Inc. Newsletter dated May/June, 2008. Pages 3-5.

74. Van Impe, Drs. Jack and Rexella. History's Final Day? DVD. Troy: Jack Van Impe Ministries International. ©2008.

75. Van Impe, Jack Presents (TV Program) (Performer/writer/moderator) Jack Van Impe Ministries (Producer). Trinity Broadcasting Network. (2008, April 10).

76. Vander Hoeven, William. "When will Messiah Come." Jewish Voice Today. Page 6.

77. Wilkerson, David. "The Most Important Issue of This Hour." World Challenge Pulpit Series. Lindale: © 2008 World Challenge, Inc. May 12, 2008. Page 1.

Charts/Tables

1. Jensen, Irving L. <u>Jensen's Survey of the Old Testament</u>. Chicago: Moody Press. 1978. Pages 188-189, 220-221.

2. Jensen, Irving L. <u>Jensen's Survey of the New Testament</u>. Chicago: Moody Press. 1981. Pages 23, 47, 60-62, 104, 208, 495, Appendix A.

3. McGee, J. Vernon, <u>Thru the Bible with J. Vernon McGee</u>. Vol. 1 (Gen-Deut.). Pasadena: Thru the Bible Radio, c 1981. Page 2.

4. Reese, Edward and Frank R. Klossen. <u>The Reese Chronological Bible</u>. Minneapolis: Bethany House Publishers 1975 ©, 1980. Page 118, 588, 672.

5. Reese, Edward. <u>The Reese Chronological Bible</u>. ©1977. Minneapolis: Bethany House publishers 1980. Page 140.

6. <u>The Reese Chronological Bible</u>. The authorized edition of the original work by Edward Reese. Minneapolis: Bethany House Publishers, 1980. Pages 843-844.

7. <u>The Zondervan Pictorial Encyclopedia of the Bible</u>. Ed. Merrill C. Tenney. Vol. 2 (D-G). Grand Rapids: The Zondervan Corporation. ©1975, 1976. Page 357.

8. <u>The Zondervan Pictorial Encyclopedia of the Bible</u>. Ed. Merrill C. Tenney. Vol. 10, D-G. Grand Rapids: The Zondervan Corporation. ©1975, 1976. Page 427.

9. Turner, Pastor Benjamin of Boise Five Mile Church of the Nazarene, Boise, Idaho.

Maps

1. Dake, Fenis Jennings. <u>Dake's Annotated Reference Bible</u>. Lawrenceville: Dake Bible Sales, Inc. ©1963-1991 Charts and Map Section.

2. LaHaye, Tim, and Jerry B. <u>Jenkins. Kingdom Come</u>. Carol Stream: Tyndale House, 2007. Page 21.

Places of Worship

1. "Jesus and His Times." The Reader's Digest, Pleasantville: The Readers Digest Association Inc., 1987. Page 130.

2. Dake, Fenis Jennings. Dake's Annotated Reference Bible. (KJV). Lawrenceville: Dake Bible Sales, Inc. ©1963-1991 Charts and Map Section.

3. Ice, Thomas and Randall Price. Ready to Rebuild. Eugene: Harvest House Publishers, 1992.

4. Israel My Glory. Westville: The Friends of Israel Gospel Ministry, Inc., Dec/Jan 1997/1998

5. Jeffrey, Grant R. The New Temple and the Second Coming. Colorado Springs: Waterbrook Press, 2007. Pages 19, 24, 27, 67, 126, 128, 133.

6. Lindsted, Robert. The Sound of the Trumpet. Oklahoma City: Southwest Radio Church. Page 10.

7. McGee, J. Vernon, Thru the Bible with J. Vernon McGee. Vol. 1 (Gen-Deut.). Pasadena: Thru the Bible Radio, c 1981. Page 304, 310, 313.

8. McGee, J. Vernon, Thru the Bible with J. Vernon McGee. Vol. II (Josh-Ps.). Pasadena: Thru the Bible Radio, c 1981, 1982. Page 422.

9. Price, Dr. Randall. "Groups Collecting Temple Tools." The Messianic Times. Vol. 10 #2. Jerusalem: Gospel Truth, Summer 2000. Page 20.

10. Prophetic Observer. August 1997. page 1

11. Schmitt, John W. and J. Carl Laney. Messiah's Coming Temple. Grand Rapids: Kregel Publications. Figure 6.1 Temple Area Plan Site Identification. ©1997. Pages 84, 94, 125, 127, 128

12. The Messianic Times. Vol. 12 #4, Jerusalem Gospel Truth, Nov 2002. Page 1.

13. The Messianic Times. Vol. 8 #3, Jerusalem Gospel Truth, Oct/Nov 1997. Page 11.

14. The Zondervan Pictorial Encyclopedia of the Bible. Ed. Merrill C. Tenney. Volume 5, Q-Z, Zondervan Publishing, Grand Rapids, 1975. Page 625.

15. The Zondervan Pictorial Encyclopedia of the Bible. Ed. Merrill C. Tenney. Vol. 10, D-G. Grand Rapids: The Zondervan Corporation. ©1975, 1976. Page 473.

16. Thru the Bible Radio Newsletter: February 19, 2003. (5 pages)

'2

03B/1/P

9 781622 302567